Friedrich Nietzsche was born near Leipzig in 1844, the son of a Lutheran clergyman. He attended the famous Pforta School, then went to university at Bonn and at Leipzig, where he studied philology and read Schopenhauer. When he was only 24 he was appointed to the chair of classical philology at Basle University; he stayed there until his health forced him into retirement in 1897. While at Basle he made and broke his friendship with Wagner, participated as an ambulance orderly in the Franco-Prussian War, and published *The Birth of Tragedy* (1872), *Untimely Meditations* (1873–6), and the first two parts of *Human, All Too Human* (1878–9). From 1880 until his final collapse in 1889, except for brief interludes, he divorced himself from everyday life and, supported by his university pension, he lived mainly in France, Italy, and Switzerland. The third part of *Human, All Too Human* appeared in 1880, followed by *The Dawn* in 1881. *Thus Spoke Zarathustra* was written between 1883 and 1885, and his last completed books were *Ecce Homo,* an autobiography, and *Nietzsche contra Wagner.* He became insane in 1889 and remained in a condition of mental and physical paralysis until his death in 1900.

Walter Kaufmann was Professor of Philosophy at Princeton University, where he taught after receiving his Ph.D. from Harvard in 1947 until his death in 1980. He held visiting appointments at many American and foreign universities, including Columbia, Cornell, Heidelberg, Jerusalem, and the Australian National University; and his books have been translated into Dutch, German, Italian, Japanese, and Spanish.

Each volume in The Viking Portable Library either presents a representative selection from the works of a single outstanding writer or offers a comprehensive anthology on a special subject. Averaging 700 pages in length and designed for compactness and readability, these books fill a need not met by other compilations. All are edited by distinguished authorities, who have written introductory essays and included much other helpful material.

The Portable

Nietzsche

*Selected and Translated with an Introduction,
Prefaces, and Notes by*

WALTER KAUFMANN

PENGUIN   BOOKS

PENGUIN BOOKS
Published by the Penguin Group
Penguin Group (USA) Inc., 375 Hudson Street, New York, New York 10014, U.S.A.
Penguin Group (Canada), 90 Eglinton Avenue East, Suite 700, Toronto,
Ontario, Canada M4P 2Y3 (a division of Pearson Penguin Canada Inc.)
Penguin Books Ltd, 80 Strand, London WC2R oRL, England
Penguin Ireland, 25 St Stephen's Green, Dublin 2, Ireland
(a division of Penguin Books Ltd)
Penguin Group (Australia), 250 Camberwell Road, Camberwell,
Victoria 3124, Australia (a division of Pearson Australia Group Pty Ltd)
Penguin Books India Pvt Ltd, 11 Community Centre, Panchsheel Park,
New Delhi – 110 017, India
Penguin Group (NZ), 67 Apollo Drive, Mairangi Bay,
Auckland 1311, New Zealand (a division of Pearson New Zealand Ltd)
Penguin Books (South Africa) (Pty) Ltd, 24 Sturdee Avenue,
Rosebank, Johannesburg 2196, South Africa

Penguin Books Ltd, Registered Offices: 80 Strand, London WC2R oRL, England

First published in the United States of America
by Viking Penguin Inc. 1954
Paperbound edition published 1959
Reprinted 1959 (twice), 1960 (twice), 1961 (three times),
1962 (twice), 1963 (twice), 1964 (twice), 1965 (twice),
1966 (twice), 1967 (twice), 1968 (three times), 1969 (three times),
1970 (three times), 1971 (three times), 1972 (three times),
1973, 1974 (twice), 1975, 1976
Published in Penguin Books 1976

76th Printing

LIBRARY OF CONGRESS CATALOGING IN PUBLICATION DATA
Nietzsche, Friedrich Wilhelm, 1844-1900.
The portable Nietzsche.
Reprint of the 1954 ed. published by The Viking Press, New York,
which was issued as no. 62 of Viking portable library.
Bibliography: p. 688.
1. Philosophy—Collected works. I. Title.
[B3312.E52K3 1976]   193   76-47577
ISBN 978-0-14-0150629

Printed in Canada
Set in Linotype Caledonia

To Edith Kaufmann

Wenn's etwas gibt, gewalt'ger als das Schicksal,
So ist's der Mut, der's unerschüttert trägt.
                                                    —GEIBEL

Acknowledgments

All the translations in this volume are new, except for some passages that have previously appeared in my *Nietzsche: Philosopher, Psychologist, Antichrist*. Princeton University Press has generously given permission for their use here. But even these passages have been revised, and, wherever feasible, I have made available other aphorisms and letters instead of reproducing material already available in that book.

In the Introduction and editorial matter too, Princeton University Press has kindly permitted reliance on my *Nietzsche*. But whereas that book sought to explode the legends woven around Nietzsche and to analyze the break with Wagner, the relation to Lou Salomé and to his sister, the final madness, and, above all, his philosophy, psychology, and critique of Christianity, the editorial matter in the present volume has been wholly subordinated to the translations. Nietzsche himself is to speak, and no lengthy editorial reflections seemed worth a corresponding cut in the space allotted to him.

I am greatly indebted to Princeton University for a year's leave of absence, which enabled me, among other things, to complete this volume; to Jean Yolton, for generous help with proofs; and to Hazel and Felix Kaufmann, my wife and my brother, for many helpful criticisms, particularly of my translation of *Zarathustra*.

W. K.

Contents

INTRODUCTION

There are philosophers who can write and philosophers who cannot. Most of the great philosophers belong to the first group. There are also, much more rarely, philosophers who can write too well for their own good—as philosophers. Plato wrote so dramatically that we shall never know for sure what precisely he himself thought about any number of questions. And Nietzsche furnishes a more recent and no less striking example. His philosophy *can* be determined, but his brilliant epigrams and metaphors, his sparkling polemics and ceaseless stylistic experiments, make it rather difficult to do so; and to read him solely to reconstruct the world of his ideas would be obtuse pedantry. At least two things should come first: sheer enjoyment of his writing, and then the more harrowing experience of exposing oneself to his many passionate perspectives. We should not rashly take a well-phrased point for Nietzsche's ultimate position, but we often stand to gain if we ask ourselves *why* it should not be *ours*. Add to this that few writers in any age were so full of ideas—fruitful, if not acceptable—and it is clear why he has steadily exerted a unique fascination on the most diverse minds and why he is still so eminently worth reading.

An anthologist can easily re-create Nietzsche in his own image, even as writers of lives of Jesus present us, perhaps as often as not, with wishful self-portraits.

1

Doubtless Nietzsche has attracted crackpots and villains, but perhaps the percentage is no higher than in the case of Jesus. As Maritain has said: "If books were judged by the bad uses man can put them to, what book has been more misused than the Bible?"

The present volume is not an anthology. It contains the complete and unabridged texts of four of Nietzsche's works; and the additional selections from his other books, notes, and letters aim to round out the picture of his development, his versatility, his inexhaustibility. There is much here that is surely admirable: formulations, epigrams, insights, suggestions. And there is much that is shocking: bathos, sentences that invite quotation out of context in support of hideous causes, silly arguments—and many will recoil from his abundant blasphemies. For this is no "reader's digest" of Nietzsche, no "essential Nietzsche," no distillation and no whitewash, but an attempt to present as much as possible of him in one small volume. The book can of course be read like Bartlett's *Familiar Quotations,* but what one gets out of Nietzsche may be vaguely proportionate to the sustained attention one accords him.

The arrangement is chronological, and an effort has been made to give some idea of the development of Nietzsche's thought and style, from his artless early notes to his occasionally brilliant aphorisms; then to the gross unevenness of *Zarathustra;* the incisive prose of his last works; and the alternation of diabolical polemic and furious rhetoric in *The Antichrist.* In *Nietzsche contra Wagner,* calm returns as Nietzsche takes time for once to edit some of his earlier prose and in places achieves perfection. His last letters, written right after his breakdown, reflect the disintegration of his mind, but they are still meaningful. The rest is silence.

II

The new translations were made because the older ones are unacceptable. As a single, and admittedly extreme, example, the hitherto standard version of *Zarathustra* is discussed briefly in the editor's preface to that work. Great writers are far more difficult to transpose into another language than is usually supposed, and Nietzsche poses many additional difficulties. While any detailed discussion of principles of translation would lead too far, a few remarks may prove helpful.

Rather than flatten out Nietzsche's highly unusual German into stereotyped idioms, an effort has been made to preserve as much as possible of his cadences, even where they are awkwardly groping or overstrained. What is thus lost in smoothness is gained for the understanding of the development of his style and personality.

A few of his terms create special difficulties; for example, *Geist*. To be perfectly idiomatic, one would have to render it now as spirit, now as mind, now as intellect, now as wit. But generally the connotation of *Geist* is much more inclusive than that of any one of these words, and Nietzsche's meaning depends on this. If we select "spirit" in one sentence and "wit" in another, something essential is lost: we get smooth propositions, not Nietzsche. Hence it seemed important to stick to one English word; and "spirit" was chosen. The religious overtones are entirely in order and altogether indispensable for an understanding of many paradoxical passages, particularly in *The Antichrist;* but it is well to keep in mind that the meaning is sometimes closer to *esprit*.

Mitleid has almost invariably been rendered by "pity," although "compassion" would have the advantage that it too means literally "suffering with." The two English terms, however, do not have entirely the same meaning, and it is no accident that Aristotle, Spinoza, and La Rochefoucauld, of whose precedent Nietzsche makes much, have all been translated in the past as criticizing *"pity."* And "pity" alone suggests the strong possibility of obtrusiveness and condescension apart from which Nietzsche's repugnance cannot be understood. Again, it would not do to alternate the terms: pity, as Zarathustra's "final sin," is one of the central themes of Part Four, in which many statements about pity in Part Two are quoted or alluded to; and such later works as *Twilight of the Idols* and *The Antichrist* explicate the symbolism of *Zarathustra.* Nietzsche, in short, is not only a brilliant writer but also a philosopher who employs certain key terms, which must be rendered consistently. But the problem is even more deeply rooted than has been suggested so far.

After publication, many writers cut the umbilical cord and are ready for another conception. Nietzsche's works, however, are not independent creations. In the first place, Nietzsche wrote, to use his own phrase, with his blood: each book is part of the man, and the resulting existential unity makes all of them part of a single work. Each aphorism looks as if it could be understood by itself—and up to a point, of course, it can be—but in fact not even the books can be understood in isolation from one another. Nietzsche himself insisted on this point and underlined it by frequent quotations from, and allusions to, his earlier works. These internal echoes add essential overtones and are important clues to Nietzsche's meaning. This is another reason for consistency in translating certain words and phrases.

That Nietzsche did not dissociate himself from his published works but kept living with them is surely due in part to the fact that publication was in no case a major experience: for all the response he got, or rather did not get, the books might just as well never have been published at all. They did not become public property but remained his own—as children who fail to find a place in the world continue to be of special concern to their parents. The self-quotations are sometimes, at least in part, attempts to advertise himself. But it is far more fruitful to look at them, and at the far more numerous allusions, as leitmotifs.

Taking their cue from Wagner's leitmotifs, Martin Buber and Franz Rosenzweig have pointed out, in connection with their remarkable German translation of the Hebrew Scriptures, that the style of the Old Testament often depends on *Leitworte,* words which are central and particularly emphasized in one passage and then picked up again elsewhere, thus establishing an unobtrusive cross reference—an association which, even if only dimly felt, adds dimension to the meaning. Perhaps no major writer is as biblical in this respect as Nietzsche.

A professor of philosophy who favored my *Nietzsche* with a most flattering review regretted one lapse "in linguistic usage"—"the most unkindest cut of all." Shakespeare, of course, is generally better known than this, but some apparent lapses in this volume might well be due to the fact that Nietzsche knew the Bible so much better than many people today. Certainly he knew it better than one of his chief translators, who converted publicans into "toll-gatherers," the Last Supper into "The Supper," "unknown god" into "unfamiliar god," and so on. When Zarathustra speaks of trying the reins, the archaism is surely preferable to having him test kidneys.

Nietzsche's style is not Teutonic but European, and more than that: he alludes freely to the books that constitute our Western heritage, from Homer to Dostoevski, and he sprinkles his prose with French and Latin phrases. There is something very modern in this: in his own phrase, Nietzsche was indeed a good European. But he never comes as close to patchwork as Eliot in *The Waste Land*, and he holds a reasonable mean between the cryptograms of the later Joyce and the obtrusive erudition of Toynbee, who underlines every allusion to the Bible with a footnote. Moreover, Nietzsche, unlike Joyce, almost invariably supplies a surface meaning too, and recognition of his allusions reveals a multi-dimensional style of writing and thinking, unlike Toynbee's.

It is not only his attitude toward religion that ranges Nietzsche far closer to Joyce than to Toynbee: there is also his addiction to plays on words, which probably poses the greatest single problem for the translator, especially in *Zarathustra*. But more of that in the editor's preface to that work. Suffice it to say here that it is impossible to be faithful to the content while sacrificing the form: meaning and mood are inseparable. If the translator makes things easy for himself and omits a play on words, he unwittingly makes a lighthearted pun or rhyme look serious, if he does not reduce the whole passage to nonsense. And he abets the common misconception of the austere Nietzsche, when, in fact, no other philosopher knew better how to laugh at himself.

Those who browse in this volume will find a conglomeration where anyone reading it straight through will likely find one of the most fascinating men of all time: a man as multi-dimensional as his style, profound and then again piteous, as tragic as he is widely supposed to have been, but no less comic—almost as different from his popular caricatures as a character in Shakespeare, or more likely in Dostoevski, is from the comic strip version of Superman. In his own formula: *Ecce homo!*

III

Nietzsche was born in 1844; lost his father, a Lutheran minister, in 1849; spent his childhood surrounded by his mother, sister, grandmother, and two maiden aunts; was sent to a first-rate boarding school, Schulpforta; and proceeded to the universities of Bonn and Leipzig to study classical philology. Our knowledge of his youth rests largely on his sister's later hagiographies, but the twenty-four-year-old comes to life for us in the recommendation that earned him a professorship at Basel. The writer was Friedrich Ritschl, a generally conservative professor at Leipzig.

"However many young talents I have seen develop under my eyes for thirty-nine years now, *never yet* have I known a young man, or tried to help one along in my field as best I could, who was so mature as early and as young as this Nietzsche. His *Museum* articles he wrote in the second and third year of his *triennium*. He is the first from whom I have ever accepted any contribution at all while he was still a student. If— God grant—he lives long enough, I prophesy that he will one day stand in the front rank of German philology. He is now twenty-four years old: strong, vigorous, healthy, courageous physically and morally, so constituted as to impress those of a similar nature. On top of that, he possesses the enviable gift of presenting ideas, talking freely, as calmly as he speaks skillfully and clearly. He is the idol and, without wishing it, the leader of the whole younger generation of philologists here in Leipzig who—and they are rather numerous—cannot wait to hear him as a lecturer. You will say, I describe a phenomenon. Well, that is just what he is—and at the same time pleasant and modest. Also a gifted musician, which is irrelevant here."

But Nietzsche had not yet fulfilled his residence requirement and hence had no doctorate. So Ritschl expected the case to be hopeless, "although in the present instance," he wrote, "I should stake my whole philological and academic reputation that the matter would work out happily." It is hardly surprising that Basel decided to ignore the "formal insufficiency." Ritschl was delighted: "In *Germany*, that sort of thing happens absolutely never." And he felt he should further describe his protégé.

"Nietzsche is not at all a specifically political nature. He may have in general, on the whole, some sympathy for the growing greatness of Germany, but, like myself, no special *tendre* for Prussianism; yet he has vivid feeling for free civic and spiritual development, and thus certainly a heart for your Swiss institutions and way of living. What more am I to say? His studies so far have been weighted toward the history of Greek literature (of course, including critical and exegetical treatment of the authors), with special emphasis, it seems to me, on the history of Greek philosophy. But I have not the least doubt that, if confronted by a practical demand, with his great gifts he will work in other fields with the best of success. He will simply be able to do anything he wants to do."

Nietzsche was quite ready to work in other fields.

He had read Schopenhauer as well as Greek philosophy; he was deeply moved by Wagner's music, especially the "shivery and sweet infinity" of *Tristan;* and
no doctor's degree, conferred hurriedly without examination, and no professorship could for a moment give
him the idea that he had "arrived." He was very conscientious when it came to his varied teaching duties
and carried an exceedingly heavy load without demur,
but his mind soared beyond the academic pale, and his
first book was not designed to place him in the front
rank of German philology.

His years at Basel, where Nietzsche was the younger
colleague of Jacob Burckhardt and of Franz Overbeck,
who remained his lifelong friend, were soon interrupted by the Franco-Prussian War. Nietzsche, by now
a Swiss subject, volunteered as a medical orderly and
served briefly before returning in shattered health.
Without waiting for complete recovery he plunged into
an even heavier schedule than before and divided his
remaining time between visits to Richard Wagner in
Tribschen, near Lucerne, and his first book, published
in 1872: *The Birth of Tragedy*. The topic was the sudden birth and no less sudden death of tragedy among
the Greeks. The thesis: born of music, it died of that
rationalism which found its outstanding incarnation in
Socrates and which is evident in the works of Euripides. The significance: an iconoclastic conception of the
Greeks, far removed from the "noble simplicity and
calm grandeur" of Winckelmann and Goethe, then still
popular. The style: an essay, now brilliant, now florid
—without any scholarly apparatus. The greatest weakness: to the fifteen sections on Greek tragedy, Nietzsche added another ten on Wagner and his new music
dramas, thus giving the whole work the appearance of
mere special pleading for his idol. Forty years later the

great British classicist F. M. Cornford was to hail the book as "a work of profound imaginative insight, which left the scholarship of a generation toiling in the rear." But most of the philologists of Nietzsche's own generation considered the book preposterous. What it is best known for today is its contrast between the Apollinian (the serene sense of proportion which Winckelmann had so admired and which found its crowning expression in Greek sculpture) and the Dionysian (that flood which breaks through all restraints in the Dionysian festivals and which finds artistic expression in music). In Nietzsche's later works the Dionysian no longer signifies the flood of passion, but passion controlled as opposed to passion extirpated, the latter being associated with Christianity.

In the following pages no attempt has been made to carve excerpts out of this essay. Instead the almost complete text of *Homer's Contest* has been offered—a fragment of 1872 that should be of greater help for an understanding both of Nietzsche's early conception of ancient Greece and of his subsequent intellectual development.

His later works made not the least pretense of any connection, however slight, with his academic field. While carrying on with his academic duties as before, he followed his first book with four *Untimely Meditations*. In 1873 he vivisected David Strauss's highly successful *The Old and the New Faith*. The following year he published reflections *On the Use and Disadvantage of History for Life*, as well as a meditation on *Schopenhauer as Educator;* and in 1876, shortly before his break with Wagner, an essay on the composer. This was Nietzsche's formative period, represented here by a few notes and another particularly striking fragment.

All of the later books are represented in this volume,

each prefaced by a brief editorial note—a little longer in the case of works offered unabridged.

There are, first, the aphoristic works, beginning with *Human, All-Too-Human* and ending with *The Gay Science*. The two great events in this period of Nietzsche's life were his break with Wagner and his departure from the university. When the composer, no longer the lonely genius of Tribschen, became the center of a cult at Bayreuth, and his influence was widely felt not only *in musicis*, Nietzsche left him. The jingoism and anti-Semitism, which had seemed relatively unimportant personal idiosyncrasies, now called for a clear stand. Moreover Wagner, fond of Nietzsche as a brilliant and likable professorial ally, had no interest in him as a writer and thinker in his own right and stood in the way of Nietzsche's development. These factors, rather than Nietzsche's growing reservations about Wagner's music, precipitated the breach. *Parsifal* merely sealed it —and not because it was Christian but because Nietzsche considered it an essentially insincere obeisance. Wagner, the disciple of Feuerbach and Schopenhauer, the two great atheists, used medieval Christianity for theatrical effect; the self-styled modern Aeschylus glorified the antithesis of all Greek ideals, the "pure fool"; a composer whose personal worldly ambition knew no bounds wrote *Parsifal*. If the friendship had given Nietzsche some of the happiest days of his life, the break was one of his most painful experiences; and if the personal contact had done its share to raise his horizon beyond philology and classical antiquity, the breach spurred his ambition to rival and excel the composer and dramatist as a writer and philosopher.

When Nietzsche resigned from the university in 1879 he claimed ill health, which was true enough, and he obtained a pension. Clearly, however, he also felt that his further development called for a break with his academic career as a professor of philology.

Instead of returning to Germany, he spent most of the rest of his active life in Switzerland and Italy— lonely, pain-racked writing. In 1882 he thought for a short while that he had perhaps found a companion and intellectual heir—a Plato who might fashion his many stimulating suggestions into a great philosophy: a young woman, born in St. Petersburg in 1861, un- questionably of extraordinary intellectual and artistic endowment. But Lou Salomé, who was later to become Rilke's beloved, and still later a close friend of Freud, was then, at twenty-one, much more interested in another young philosopher, Paul Rée. Her walks and talks with Nietzsche meant less to her; but he never found another human being to whom he could ex- pound his inmost ideas as in those few weeks.

After Lou left he made his first attempt to put down his philosophy—not merely sundry observations—in one major work: *Zarathustra*. He still did not proceed systematically, and though the style reveals a decided change from the essays of his first period and the aphorisms of the second, it is less philosophic than ever. Rhapsody, satire, and epigram predominate; but Nietzsche's mature thought is clouded and shrouded by an excess of adolescent emotion. Nevertheless, de- spite the all-too-human self-pity and occasional bathos, the book is full of fascinating ideas; and probably it owes its unique success with the broad mass of readers not least to its worst qualities.

The book consists of four parts, originally published separately, and more were planned. But Nietzsche came to realize that this style was not adequate for his purposes, and he returned to his earlier aphoristic style, though with a difference. *Beyond Good and Evil*, his next book, is much more continuous than appears at first glance; and the *Genealogy of Morals* is composed of three inquiries which might well be called essays.

All the while, Nietzsche assembled notes for a more comprehensive work which he thought of calling *The Will to Power*. But he never got beyond those notes; and the work later published by his sister under that title is nothing but an utterly uncritical collection of some of Nietzsche's notes, including many he had already used, often with significant changes, in his later works. This fabrication, though it certainly contains some highly interesting material, must by no means be considered his last or his main work.

In 1888 Nietzsche dashed off a brilliantly sarcastic polemic, *The Wagner Case*, which was followed by a hundred-page epitome of his thought, *Twilight of the Idols*. Then he gave up his intention of writing *The Will to Power*, decided to write a much shorter *chef-d'oeuvre* instead, under the title *Revaluation of All Values*, and completed the first of four projected parts: *The Antichrist*. No sooner was this finished on a high pitch of rhetoric than he turned around and, on the same day, wrote the relatively calm preface for *Twilight of the Idols;* and, still in the same year, one of the world's strangest autobiographical works, *Ecce Homo*. On Christmas Day, 1888, he completed *Nietzsche contra Wagner*—and less than two weeks later he broke down, insane.

His madness was in all probability an atypical general paresis. If so, he must have had syphilis; and since he is known to have lived a highly ascetic life, it is supposed that, as a student, he had visited a brothel once or twice. This has never been substantiated, and any detailed accounts of such experiences are either poetry or pornography—not biography. Nor has the suggestion ever been disproved that he may have been infected while nursing wounded soldiers in 1870.

IV

It was only after his active life was over that Nietzsche's real career began. When he died in 1900 he was world-famous and the center of a growing literature, of controversies in periodicals and newspapers—an "influence." He has been discussed and written. about ever since, in connection with Darwin, Schopenhauer, psychoanalysis, modern German poetry, World War I, Spengler, Christianity, Tolstoi, the Nazis, World War II, existentialism—and whatever else was needed to fill hundreds upon hundreds of volumes about him.

Nietzsche's impact is as manifold as his prose, and most interpreters select a single strain or style, whether for praise or blame, quite unaware that there are more. It might be best not even to think in terms of "influence"—a word that simplifies the multifarious complexities of history after the manner of Procrustes. In any case, no other German writer of equal stature has been so thoroughly opposed to all proto-nazism—which Nietzsche encountered in Wagner's ideological tracts, in his sister's husband, Bernhard Förster, and in various publications of his time. If some Nazi writers cited him nevertheless, it was at the price of incredible misquotation and exegetical acrobatics, which defy comparison with all the similar devices that Nietzsche himself castigated in the name of the philological conscience. His works were rejected as a series of poses; parenthetical statements were quoted as meaning the opposite of what they plainly mean in context; and views he explicitly rejected were brazenly attributed to him.

This process was greatly aided by Nietzsche's sister (of my *Nietzsche*)—but also by his love of language. He could not resist a *bon mot* or a striking coinage, and he took delight in inventing better slogans and epigrams for hostile positions than his opponents could devise—and in breathing a new and unexpectedly different spirit into such phrases. Witness "the will to power," "the overman," "beyond good and evil," and dozens more.

Or consider a *bon mot*: when Nietzsche said, "Man does *not* strive for pleasure; only the Englishman does," he was of course thinking of the ethics of Hume, Bentham, and Mill, not of English cooking, coal fires, or Cromwell. Yet the remark may conceivably have contributed, however indirectly, to Hitler's happy misconception of the English as essentially effete and hedonistic, which so fortunately aided his defeat. Speaking of influence here is sheer naïveté.

Nietzsche's orientation, as he himself insisted once more in *Ecce Homo*, was fundamentally anti-political. His concern was primarily with the individual who is not satisfied with accepted formulas—ranging all the way from patriotism to Protestantism, and including everything that is in any sense, to use his own phrase, "party." Any attempt to pigeonhole him is purblind. He celebrated reason, like some of the thinkers of the Enlightenment, and passion, like some of the Romantics; he is in many ways close to modern positivism, but the Existentialists recognize their own pathos in him; atheists claim him, and many Christians feel they understand him best.

V

The following reflections, far from classifying him, may help to define his unique achievement. He tried to strengthen the heritage of the Enlightenment with a more profound understanding of the irrational—something Hegel had attempted three-quarters of a century earlier, but metaphysically and rather esoterically. Nietzsche was determined to be empirical, and he approached his subject—as it surely should be —with psychology. Of this Hegel had not yet had more than an inkling, and the lack of any sustained psychological observation is one of the major shortcomings of his magnificently conceived *Phenomenology of the Spirit*. But Hegel's contemporaries had done little better: as psychologists, Bentham, Comte, and Mill were naïve too. One could almost ask with Nietzsche himself (in *Ecce Homo*, in the chapter "Why I Am a Destiny"): "Who among philosophers before me has been a psychologist at all?"

If Nietzsche tried to deepen the Enlightenment with a psychology, he also attempted to harness romanticism: by substituting an understanding of the passions for a blind cult and by extolling the individual whose reason is a match for his passions. He ridiculed license as much—though not as often—as "castratism," and he upheld sublimation and creativity against both. All his heroes were men of superior reason: passionate men who were the masters of their passion. The legend that Cesare Borgia was his idol is easily refuted by an examination of the few references to him in Nietzsche's works. Nietzsche preferred the Borgia (or, as he said, *even* Cesare Borgia) to Parsifal, which is scarcely high praise from Nietzsche. Nor is his declaration in *The*

Antichrist that he wished Cesare had become pope. After all, the context leaves no doubt that this would have delighted the author only because it might have meant the end of the papacy!

This takes us to the third point: Nietzsche's uncompromising attitude toward religion. If one considers the history of modern philosophy from Descartes, it is surely, for good or ill, the story of an emancipation from religion. Or conversely: each philosopher goes just so far, and then bows to Christianity and accepts what becomes unacceptable to his successors. Descartes resolves to doubt everything, but soon offers proofs of God's existence that have long been shown to be fallacious. A similar pattern recurs in Hobbes and Spinoza, though they stray much farther from all orthodoxies, and, a little later, in Berkeley and Leibniz. Locke is an "empiricist" who cites Scripture to his purpose; Voltaire, an anti-Christian who accepts the teleological argument for God's existence. Kant sets out to smash not only the proofs of God but the very foundations of Christian metaphysics, then turns around and "postulates" God and the immortality of the soul, preparing the way for Fichte and idealism. Schopenhauer, finally, breaks with Christianity but accepts the metaphysics of the Upanishads from Hinduism. Nietzsche is one of the first thinkers with a comprehensive philosophy to complete the break with religion. Other equally secular philosophers of the nineteenth century who preceded him do not match the range of his interests and the scope of his vision. Before his time there were really but two modern philosophers who were equally, or almost equally, unchristian: Bacon (whose aphoristic experimentalism Nietzsche admired; but for all his programmatic pathos, Bacon had no comparable philosophy) and Hume (whose skepticism is an exercise in lack of pathos and intensity). Though Hume and Nietzsche are antipodes in temperament, they are in many ways close to each other in their thinking—and this leads us to the final point.

Nietzsche is close not only to the man who was the grandfather of so much in modern English and American philosophy, David Hume, but also to this modern philosophy itself. Occasionally he anticipated it by several decades, and it might still profit from his stimulation. Above all, however, Nietzsche is the last best bridge between positivism and existentialism, if we take both labels in the widest possible sense. Today German and Romance philosophy and Anglo-American "analysis" are completely out of touch with each other. Thus Nietzsche, once stupidly denounced as the mind that caused the First World War, might well become a major aid to international understanding: reminding Continental European and South American thinkers of the benefits of rigorous analysis, while at the same time summoning English-speaking philosophers to consider the "existential" implications of their thinking. In his irreverent exposés of metaphysical foibles and fables he yields to none. But he is inspired not by Hume's comfortable smugness, nor by Comte's conceit that he might revolutionize society, nor by the cliquish delight in sheer proficiency and skill that occasionally besets contemporary efforts. Instead he is motivated by an intense concern with the meaning of his thought for the individual. And thus he not only anticipates both modern "analysis" and existentialism, but he has much to offer each: above all, an approach to the other major strain of modern secular philosophy.

In sum: Nietzsche's challenge is twofold. He might conceivably come into his own by re-establishing some bond between what are now two completely divergent branches of modern thought, thus benefiting both. Meanwhile it is the individual reader whom he addresses. And he does not want to be read as an arsenal of arguments for or against something, nor even for a point of view. He challenges the reader not so much to agree or disagree as to grow.

W.K.

Strobl, Austria
February 1953

Chronology

This includes the original titles and dates of publication of all of Nietzsche's books. The discrepancies between the figures here given and those found in most reference works are due to the fact that it has become customary to copy at least some of the dates from the bindings of various German collected editions. The dates on the bindings, however, refer to the approximate periods of composition. Most of Nietzsche's books were written during the year preceding publication; the outstanding exceptions to this rule are noted.

1844   Nietzsche is born in Röcken, Germany, on October 15.

1849   Death of his father, a Lutheran pastor, on July 30.

1850   The family moves to Naumburg.

1858-64   Nietzsche attends the boarding school Schulpforta.

1864   Studies classical philology at Bonn University.

1865   Continues his studies at Leipzig and accidentally discovers Schopenhauer's main work in a second-hand bookstore.

1868   First meeting with Richard Wagner.

1869   Professor extraordinarius of classical philology at the University of Basel, Switzerland.

1870   Promoted to full professor. A Swiss subject now, he volunteers as a medical orderly in the Franco-Prussian war and serves briefly with the Prussian forces. Returns to Basel in October, his health shattered.

1872   Publication of *Die Geburt der Tragödie aus dem Geiste der Musik* (*The Birth of Tragedy out of the Spirit of Music*), his first book.

1873   Publication of the first two *Unzeitgemässe Betrachtungen* (*Untimely Meditations*): *David Strauss, der Bekenner und Schriftsteller* (*David Strauss, the Confessor and Writer*), and *Vom Nutzen und Nachteil der Historie für das Leben* (*On the Use and Disadvantage of History for Life*).

1874   *Schopenhauer als Erzieher* (*Schopenhauer as Educator*) is published as the third *Untimely Meditation*.

1876   After many delays, Nietzsche completes and publishes *Richard Wagner in Bayreuth* as the last of the *Untimely Meditations*, although more had been planned originally. Poor health. Leave from the university. Sorrento.

1878   *Menschliches, Allzumenschliches* (*Human, All-Too-Human*) appears. For the next ten years a new book is printed every year.

1879   Resignation from the university with pension. *Vermischte Meinungen und Sprüche* (*Mixed Opinions and Maxims*) published as *Anhang* (appendix) of *Human, All-Too-Human*. Summer in St. Moritz in the Engadin.

1880   *Der Wanderer und sein Schatten* (*The Wanderer and His Shadow*) appears as *Zweiter und letzter Nachtrag* (second and final sequel) of *Human, All-Too-Human*.

1881   Publication of *Die Morgenröte* (*The Dawn*). Winter and spring in Genoa, summer in Sils Maria (Engadin), fall in Genoa.

1882   Publication of *Die Fröhliche Wissenschaft* (*The Gay Science*). Winter in Genoa, spring in Messina, summer in Tautenburg with Lou Salomé and his sister Elisabeth, fall in Leipzig. Goes to Rapallo in November.

1883   Writes the First Part of *Also Sprach Zarathustra* in Rapallo during the winter; spends March and April in Genoa, May in Rome, and the summer in Sils Maria, where he completes Part Two. Both parts are published separately in 1883. From now until 1888, Nietzsche spends every summer in Sils Maria, every winter in Nizza.

1884   Writes the Third Part in Nizza in January. It is published later the same year.

1885   The Fourth and Last Part of *Zarathustra* is written during the winter in Nizza and Mentone. Forty copies are printed privately, but only seven distributed among friends.

1886   Publication of *Jenseits von Gut und Böse* (*Beyond Good and Evil*). A new preface is added to the remaining copies of both previous editions of *The Birth of Tragedy* (1872 and 1878, textually different); the last part of the title is now omitted in favor of a new subtitle: *Griechentum und Pessimismus* (*The Greek Spirit and Pessimism*). Second edition of *Human, All-Too-Human* with a new preface and with the two sequels printed as volume two.

1887   Publication of *Zur Genealogie der Moral* (*Toward a Genealogy of Morals*). Second edition of *The Dawn*, with a new preface, and of *The Gay Science*, with a newly added fifth book (aphorisms 343-383) and an appendix of poems.

1888   Winter in Nizza, spring in Turin, summer in Sils Maria, fall in Turin. Publication of *Der Fall Wagner* (*The Wagner Case*). The beginning of fame: Georg Brandes lectures on Nietzsche at the University of Copenhagen.

1889   Nietzsche becomes insane early in January in Turin. Overbeck, a friend and former colleague, brings him back to Basel. He is committed to the asylum in Jena, but soon released in care of his mother, who takes him to Naumburg. *Die Götzen-Dämmerung* (*Twilight of the Idols*), written in 1888, appears in January.

1891   The first public edition of the Fourth Part of *Zarathustra* is held up at the last minute lest it be confiscated. It is published in 1892.

1895   *Der Antichrist* and *Nietzsche contra Wagner*, both written in 1888, are finally published in volume eight of Nietzsche's collected works—the former, mistakenly, as Book One of *Der Wille zur Macht* (*The Will to Power*).

1897   Nietzsche's mother dies. His sister moves him to Weimar.

1900   Nietzsche dies in Weimar on August 25.

1901   His sister publishes some 400 of his notes, many already fully utilized by him, in Volume XV of the collected works under the title *Der Wille zur Macht.*

1904   His sister integrates 200 pages of further material "from *The Will to Power*" in the last volume of her biography, *Das Leben Friedrich Nietzsches.* A completely remodeled version of *The Will to Power,* consisting of 1067 notes, appears in a subsequent edition of the works in Volumes XV (1910) and XVI (1911).

1908   First edition of *Ecce Homo,* written in 1888.

Bibliography

Some studies of Nietzsche are listed here; editions of Nietzsche's writings, both in the original and in English, are listed at the end of this volume, beginning on page 688.

The comprehensive but incomplete *International Nietzsche Bibliography*, ed. Herbert W. Reichert and Karl Schlechta (Chapel Hill: University of North Carolina Press, 1960) lists close to 4000 items in 27 languages. The bibliography in the 3rd rev. ed. (1968) of Kaufmann's *Nietzsche* (see below) includes well over a hundred studies, as well as a detailed account of the various collected editions of his works.

Binion, Rudolph. *Frau Lou*. Princeton: Princeton University Press, 1968. Supersedes all previous studies of Lou Andreas-Salomé and of her relationship to Nietzsche.

Brandes, Georg. *Friedrich Nietzsche*. Tr. from the Danish by A. G. Chater. London: Heinemann, 1914. Four essays by the critic who "discovered" Nietzsche, dated 1889, 1899, 1900, and 1909.

Brinton, Crane. *Nietzsche*. Cambridge, Mass.: Harvard University Press, 1941; New York: Harper & Row, Torchbook ed. with new preface, epilogue, and bibliography, 1965. In the new edition, the numerous errors of the original edition remain uncorrected, but in a short preface Brinton disowns the chapter "Nietzsche in Western Thought." The rev. bibliography adds serious new errors.

Camus, Albert. "Nietzsche et le nihilisme" in *L'homme révolté*. Paris: Gallimard, 1951, pp. 88–105. "Nietzsche and Nihilism" in *The Rebel*, Engl. tr. by Anthony Bower. New York, Vintage Books, 1956, pp. 65–80. This essay throws more light on Camus than on Nietzsche.

Danto, Arthur C. *Nietzsche as Philosopher*. New York: Macmillan, 1965. A hasty study, full of old misconceptions, new mistranslations, and unacknowledged omissions in quotations. The context of the snippets cited is systematically ignored, and no effort is made to consider even most of what Nietzsche wrote on any given subject.

Drimmer, Melvin. *Nietzsche in American Thought: 1895–1925*. Ph.D. thesis, The University of Rochester (N.Y.), 1965. Ann Arbor, Mich.: University Microfilms, Inc., 727 pp., includes Bibliography, 634–727.

Heidegger, Martin. "Nietzsches Wort 'Gott ist tot'" in *Holzwege*. Frankfurt am Main: Klostermann, 1950.

———. "Wer ist Nietzsches Zarathustra?" in *Vorträge und Aufsätze*. Pfullingen: Neske, 1954. English translation by Bernd Magnus in *Lectures and Addresses*. New York: Harper & Row, 1967.

———. *Nietzsche*. 2 vols. Pfullingen: Neske, 1961. One of the major efforts—certainly the bulkiest one—of the later Heidegger: important for those who would understand *him*.

Hollingdale, R. J. *Nietzsche: The Man and His Philosophy*. Baton Rouge: Louisiana State University Press, 1965. Sympathetic, informed, and well written; the best biography in English, but the account of Nietzsche's relationships to Salomé and Rée is dated by Binion's book. Nietzsche's philosophy is discussed in the context of his life.

Jaspers, Karl. *Nietzsche: Einführung in das Verständnis seines Philosophierens*. Berlin and Leipzig: De Gruyter, 1936 (2nd ed., 1947, "unchanged," but with a new preface). Engl. tr. by Charles F. Wallraff and Frederick J. Schmitz, *Nietzsche: An Introduction to the Understanding of His Philosophical Activity*. Tucson: University of Arizona Press, 1965.

———. *Nietzsche und das Christentum*. Hameln: Verlag der Bücherstube Fritz Seifert, n.d. ("This essay was written as the basis for a lecture which was delivered . . . May 12, 1938. It is here printed without any changes or additions. . . .") Engl. tr. by E. B. Ashton, *Nietzsche and Christianity*. Chicago: Henry Regnery, Gateway Editions, 1961. A miniature version of the approach encountered in Jaspers' big *Nietzsche*.

———. "Kierkegaard und Nietzsche" in *Vernunft und Existenz*. Groningen: J. W. Wolters, 1935. Engl. tr. by William Earle in *Reason and Existenz*. New York: Noonday Press, 1955. Reprinted in Walter Kaufmann, *Existentialism from Dostoevsky to Sartre*. New York: Meridian Books, 1956, pp. 158–84.

Kaufmann, Walter. *Nietzsche: Philosopher, Psychologist, Antichrist*. Princeton: Princeton University Press, 1950. 2nd rev. ed., New York: Meridian Books, 1956. 3rd rev. ed. (with substantial additions, including a comprehensive bibliography, a long appendix dealing with recent German editions of Nietzsche, and a detailed discussion of

Nietzsche's relationship to Paul Rée and Lou Salomé), Princeton: Princeton University Press, and New York: Random House, Vintage Books, 1968.

——. Five chapters on Nietzsche in *From Shakespeare to Existentialism*. Boston: Beacon Press, 1959; rev. ed., Garden City, N.Y.: Doubleday Anchor Books, 1960.

——. Articles on Nietzsche in *Encyclopedia Americana; Encyclopaedia Britannica; Collier's Encyclopedia; Grolier Encyclopedia; The Encyclopedia of Philosophy*.

——. *Tragedy and Philosophy*. Garden City, N.Y.: Doubleday, 1968.

——. Exposés of *My Sister and I* as a forgery, falsely attributed to Nietzsche, in *Milwaukee Journal*, February 24, 1952; in *Partisan Review*, vol. XIX no. 3 (May/June 1952), 372–76; and of the rev. ed. in *The Philosophical Review*, vol. LXIV no. 1 (January 1955), 152f.

Klages, Ludwig. *Die Psychologischen Errungenschaften Nietzsches*. Leipzig: Barth, 1926.

Löwith, Karl. *Von Hegel bis Nietzsche*. Zürich and New York: Europa, 1941. Engl. tr. by David E. Green, *From Hegel to Nietzsche*. New York: Holt, 1964; Garden City, N.Y.: Doubleday Anchor Books, 1967. Includes eight sections on Nietzsche.

Love, Frederick R. *Young Nietzsche and the Wagnerian Experience*. Chapel Hill: University of North Carolina Press, 1963. A good monograph that takes into account Nietzsche's compositions, including unpublished items in the archives in Weimar. It is full of pertinent, but untranslated, German quotations. The break with Wagner is not included. Love shows how Nietzsche never was "a passionate devotee of Wagnerian music."

Morgan, George A., Jr. *What Nietzsche Means*. Cambridge, Mass.: Harvard University Press, 1941. Reprinted, unrev., New York: Harper & Row, Torchbooks, 1965. An exceptionally careful study very useful as a reference work.

Vaihinger, Hans. *Die Philosophie des Als-Ob*. Leipzig: Meiner, 1911. Eng. tr. by C. K. Ogden, *The Philosophy of 'As If.'* New York: Harcourt Brace, 1924. The chapter "Nietzsche and His Doctrine of Conscious Illusion (The Will to Illusion)," pp. 341–62, remains one of the most interesting studies in any language of Nietzsche's theory of knowledge.

THE PORTABLE

NIETZSCHE

THE PORTABLE
NIETZSCHE

LETTER TO HIS SISTER

(Bonn, 1865)

. . . As for your principle that truth is always on the side of the more difficult, I admit this in part. However, it is difficult to believe that 2 times 2 is *not* 4; does that make it true? On the other hand, is it really so difficult simply to accept everything that one has been brought up on and that has gradually struck deep roots—what is considered truth in the circle of one's relatives and of many good men, and what, moreover, really comforts and elevates man? Is that more difficult than to strike new paths, fighting the habitual, experiencing the insecurity of independence and the frequent wavering of one's feelings and even one's conscience, proceeding often without any consolation, but ever with the eternal goal of the true, the beautiful, and the good? Is it decisive after all that we arrive at *that* view of God, world, and reconciliation which makes us feel most comfortable? Rather, is not the result of his inquiries something wholly indifferent to the true inquirer? Do we after all seek rest, peace, and pleasure in our inquiries? No, only truth—even if it be the most abhorrent and ugly. Still one last question: if we had believed from childhood that all salvation issued from someone other than Jesus—say, from Mohammed—is it not certain that we should have experienced the same blessings? . . . Faith does not offer the least support for a proof of objective truth. Here the ways of men part: if you wish to strive for peace of soul and pleasure, then believe; if you wish to be a devotee of truth, then inquire. . . .

FRAGMENT OF A CRITIQUE OF SCHOPENHAUER

(1867)

. . . The errors of great men are venerable because they are more fruitful than the truths of little men. . . .   (I, 393)[1]

ON ETHICS

(1868)

Schopenhauer's ethics is often criticized for not having the form of an imperative.

What the philosophers call character is an incurable disease. An imperative ethics is one that deals with the symptoms of the disease, having the faith, while it fights them, that it is getting rid of the real origin, the basic evil. Anyone who would base practical ethics on aesthetics would be like a physician who would fight only those symptoms which are ugly and offend good taste.

Philosophically viewed, it makes no difference whether a character expresses itself or whether its

---

[1] These numbers refer to the Musarion edition.

expressions are kept back: not only the thought but the disposition already makes the murderer; he is guilty without any deed. On the other hand, there is an ethical aristocracy just as there is a spiritual one: one cannot enter it by receiving a title or by marriage.

In what way, then, are education, popular instruction, catechism, justified and even necessary?

The unchangeable character is influenced *in its expressions* by its environment and education—not in its essence. A popular ethics therefore wants to suppress bad expressions as far as possible, for the sake of the general welfare—an undertaking that is strikingly similar to the police. The means for this is a religion with rewards and punishments: for the expressions alone matter. Therefore the catechism can say: Thou shalt not kill! Thou shalt not curse! etc. Nonsensical, however, is an imperative: "Be good!" as well as, "Be wise!" or, "Be talented!"

The "general welfare" is not the sphere of truth; for truth demands to be declared even if it is ugly and unethical.

If we admit, for example, the truth of the doctrine of Schopenhauer (but also of Christianity) concerning the redemptive power of suffering, then it becomes regard for the "general welfare" not only not to lessen suffering, but perhaps even to increase it—not only for oneself but also for others. Pushed to this limit, practical ethics becomes ugly—even consistent cruelty to human beings. Similarly, the effect of Christianity is unnerving when it commands respect for every kind of magistrate, etc., as well as acceptance of all suffering without any attempt at resistance.   (1, 404 f.)

Note (1870-71)

A state that cannot attain its ultimate goal usually swells to an unnaturally large size. The world-wide empire of the Romans is nothing sublime compared to Athens. The strength that really should go into the flower here remains in the leaves and stem, which flourish.   (III, 384)

FROM

Homer's Contest[1]

(1872)

When one speaks of *humanity*, the idea is fundamental that this is something which separates and distinguishes man from nature. In reality, however, there is no such separation: "natural" qualities and those called truly "human" are inseparably grown together. Man, in his highest and noblest capacities, is wholly nature and embodies its uncanny dual character. Those of his abilities which are terrifying and considered inhuman may even be the fertile soil out of which alone all humanity can grow in impulse, deed, and work.

Thus the Greeks, the most humane men of ancient times, have a trait of cruelty, a tigerish lust to annihilate—a trait that is also very distinct in that grotesquely enlarged mirror image of the Hellenes, in Alexander the Great, but that really must strike fear into our hearts throughout their whole history and

[1] A fragment published posthumously.

mythology, if we approach them with the flabby concept of modern "humanity." When Alexander has the feet of Batis, the brave defender of Gaza, pierced, and ties him, alive, to his carriage, to drag him about while his soldiers mock, that is a revolting caricature of Achilles, who maltreats Hector's corpse in a similar fashion at night; and even this trait is offensive to us and makes us shudder. Here we look into the abyss of hatred. With the same feeling we may also observe the mutual laceration, bloody and insatiable, of two Greek parties, for example, in the Corcyrean revolution. When the victor in a fight among the cities executes the entire male citizenry in accordance with the laws of war, and sells all the women and children into slavery, we see in the sanction of such a law that the Greeks considered it an earnest necessity to let their hatred flow forth fully; in such moments crowded and swollen feeling relieved itself: the tiger leaped out, voluptuous cruelty in his terrible eyes. Why must the Greek sculptor give form again and again to war and combat in innumerable repetitions: distended human bodies, their sinews tense with hatred or with the arrogance of triumph; writhing bodies, wounded; dying bodies, expiring? Why did the whole Greek world exult over the combat scenes of the *Iliad?* I fear that we do not understand these in a sufficiently "Greek" manner; indeed, that we should shudder if we were ever to understand them "in Greek."

But what lies *behind* the Homeric world, as the womb of everything Hellenic? For *in* that world the extraordinary artistic precision, calm, and purity of the lines raise us above the mere contents: through an artistic deception the colors seem lighter, milder, warmer; and in this colorful warm light the men appear better and more sympathetic. But what do we behold when, no longer led and protected by the hand of Homer, we stride back into the pre-Homeric world? Only night and terror and an imagination accustomed to the horrible. What kind of earthly existence do these revolting, terrible theogonic myths reflect? A life ruled only by the children of Night: strife, lust, deceit, old age, and death. Let us imagine the atmosphere of Hesiod's poem, already hard to breathe, made still denser and darker, and without all the mollifications and purifications that streamed over Hellas from Delphi and from numerous abodes of the gods; let us mix this thickened Boeotian atmosphere with the gloomy voluptuousness of the Etruscans; then such a reality would wring from us a world of myth in which Uranos, Cronos, Zeus, and the wars with the Titans would seem like a relief: in this brooding atmosphere, combat is salvation; the cruelty of victory is the pinnacle of life's jubilation.

Further, it was in truth from murder and the expiation of murder that the conception of Greek law developed; so, too, the nobler culture takes its first wreath of victory from the altar of the expiation of murder. After the wave of that bloody age comes a trough that cuts deep into Hellenic history. The names of Orpheus, Musaeus, and their cults reveal the consequences to which the uninterrupted spectacle of a world of struggle and cruelty was pressing: toward a disgust with existence, toward the conception of this existence as a punishment and penance, toward the belief in the identity of existence and guilt. But it is precisely these consequences that are not specifically Hellenic: in this respect, Greece is at one with India and the Orient in general. The Hellenic genius was ready with yet another answer to the question, "What is a life of struggle and victory for?" and it gave that answer through the whole breadth of Greek history.

To understand it, we must start with the point that the Greek genius tolerated the terrible presence of this urge and considered it *justified;* while the Orphic movement contained the idea that a life with such an urge as its root was not worth living. Struggle and the joy of victory were recognized—and nothing distinguishes the Greek world from ours as much as the coloring, so derived, of individual ethical concepts, for example, *Eris*[1] and envy. . . .

And not only Aristotle but the whole of Greek antiquity thinks differently from us about hatred and envy, and judges with Hesiod, who in one place calls one Eris evil—namely, the one that leads men into hostile fights of annihilation against one another—while praising another Eris as good—the one that, as jealousy, hatred, and envy, spurs men to activity: not to the activity of fights of annihilation but to the activity of fights which are *contests*. The Greek is envious, and he does not consider this quality a blemish but the gift of a *beneficent* godhead. What a gulf of ethical judgment lies between us and him! . . .

The greater and more sublime a Greek is, the brighter the flame of ambition that flares out of him, consuming everybody who runs on the same course. Aristotle once made a list of such hostile contests in the grand manner; the most striking of the examples is that even a dead man can still spur a live one to consuming jealousy. That is how Aristotle describes the relationship of Xenophanes of Colophon to Homer. We do not understand the full strength of Xenophanes'

[1] "Discord."

attack on the national hero of poetry, unless—as again later with Plato—we see that at its root lay an overwhelming craving to assume the place of the overthrown poet and to inherit his fame. Every great Hellene hands on the torch of the contest; every great virtue kindles a new greatness. When the young Themistocles could not sleep because he was thinking of the laurels of Miltiades, his urge, awakened so early, was finally set free in the long contest with Aristides, to become that remarkably unique, purely instinctive genius of his political activity, which Thucydides describes for us. How characteristic are question and answer when a noted opponent of Pericles is asked whether he or Pericles is the best wrestler in the city, and answers: "Even when I throw him down, he denies that he fell and attains his purpose, persuading even those who saw him fall."

If one wants to observe this conviction—wholly undisguised in its most naïve expression—that the contest is necessary to preserve the health of the state, then one should reflect on the original meaning of *ostracism*, for example, as it is pronounced by the Ephesians when they banish Hermodorus: "Among us, no one shall be the best; but if someone is, then let him be elsewhere and among others." Why should no one be the best? Because then the contest would come to an end and the eternal source of life for the Hellenic state would be endangered. . . . Originally this curious institution is not a safety valve but a means of stimulation: the individual who towers above the rest is eliminated so that the contest of forces may reawaken—an idea that is hostile to the "exclusiveness" of genius in the modern sense and presupposes that in the natural order of things there are always *several* geniuses who spur each other to action, even as they hold each other within the limits of measure. That is the core of the Hellenic notion of the contest: it abominates the rule of one and fears its dangers; it desires, as a *protection* against the genius, another genius.

Every talent must unfold itself in fighting: that is the command of Hellenic popular pedagogy, whereas modern educators dread nothing more than the unleashing of so-called ambition. . . . And just as the youths were educated through contests, their educators were also engaged in contests with each other. The great musical masters, Pindar and Simonides, stood side by side, mistrustful and jealous; in the spirit of contest, the sophist, the advanced teacher of antiquity, meets another sophist; even the most universal type of instruction, through the drama, was meted out to the people only in the form of a tremendous wrestling among the great musical and dramatic artists. How wonderful! "Even the artist hates the artist." Whereas modern man fears nothing in an artist more than the emotion of any personal fight, the Greek knows the artist *only as engaged in a personal fight*. Precisely where modern man senses the weakness of a work of art, the Hellene seeks the source of its greatest strength. What, for example, is of special artistic significance in Plato's dialogues is for the most part the result of a contest with the art of the orators, the sophists, and the dramatists of his time, invented for the purpose of enabling him to say in the end: "Look, I too can do what my great rivals can do; indeed, I can do it better than they. No Protagoras has invented myths as beautiful as mine; no dramatist such a vivid and captivating whole as my *Symposion;* no orator has written orations like those in my *Gorgias*—and now I repudiate all this entirely and condemn all imitative art. Only the contest made me a poet, a sophist, an orator." What a problem opens up before us when we inquire into the relationship of the contest to the conception of the work of art!

However, when we remove the contest from Greek life we immediately look into that pre-Homeric abyss of a terrifying savagery of hatred and the lust to annihilate. This phenomenon unfortunately appears quite frequently when a great personality is suddenly removed from the contest by an extraordinarily brilliant deed and becomes *hors de concours* in his own judgment, as in that of his fellow citizens. The effect is almost without exception a terrifying one; and if one usually infers from this that the Greek was incapable of enduring fame and happiness, one should say more precisely that he was unable to endure fame without any further contest, or the happiness at the end of the contest. There is no clearer example than the last experiences of Miltiades. Placed on a solitary peak and elevated far above every fellow fighter by his incomparable success at Marathon, he feels a base, vengeful craving awaken in him against a Parian citizen with whom he has long had a feud. To satisfy this craving he misuses fame, state property, civic honor—and dishonors himself. . . . An ignominious death sets its seal on his brilliant heroic career and darkens it for all posterity. After the battle of Marathon the envy of the heavenly powers seized him. And this divine envy is inflamed when it beholds a human being without a rival, unopposed, on a solitary peak of fame. Only the gods are beside him now—and therefore they are against him. They seduce him to a deed of *hybris*,[1] and under it he collapses.

[1] "Overbearing."

Let us note well that, just as Miltiades perishes, the noblest Greek cities perish too, when through merit and good fortune they arrive at the temple of Nike from the racecourse. Athens, who had destroyed the independence of her allies and then severely punished the rebellions of her subjects; Sparta, who expressed her domination over Hellas after the battle of Aegospotamoi, in yet much harsher and crueler ways, have also, after the example of Miltiades, brought about their own destruction through deeds of *hybris,* as proof that without envy, jealousy, and ambition in the contest, the Hellenic city, like the Hellenic man, degenerates. He becomes evil and cruel; he becomes vengeful and godless; in short, he became "pre-Homeric." . . .

Notes (1873)

Deification of success is truly commensurate with human meanness. Whoever has closely studied even a single success knows what factors (stupidity, wickedness, laziness, etc.) have always helped—and not as the weakest factors either. It is mad that success is supposed to be worth more than the beautiful possibility which was still there immediately before. But to find in history the realization of the good and the just, that is blasphemy against the good and the just. This beautiful world history is, in Heraclitean terms, "a chaotic pile of rubbish." What is *strong* wins: that is the universal law. If only it were not so often precisely what is stupid and evil!   (VI, 334 *f.*)

❊❊❊

Hegel says: "That at the bottom of history, and particularly of world history, there is a final aim, and that this has actually been realized in it and is being realized—the plan of Providence—that there is *reason* in history: that is to be shown philosophically and thus as altogether necessary." And: "A history without such an aim and without such a point of view would be merely a feeble-minded pastime of the imagination, not even a children's fairy tale, for even children demand some interest in stories, i.e., some aim one can at least feel, and the relation of the occurrences and actions to it." Conclusion: Every story must have an aim, hence also the history of a people and the history of the world. That means: because there is "world history" there must also be some aim in the world process. That means: we demand stories only with aims. But we do not at all *demand* stories about the world process, for we consider it a swindle to talk about it. That my life has no aim is evident even from the accidental nature of its origin; that *I can posit an aim for myself* is another matter. But a state has no aim; we alone give it this aim or that.   (VI, 336)

✾✾✾

On the mythology of the historical. Hegel: "What happens to a people and occurs within it has its essential significance in its relation to the state; the mere particularities of the individuals are most remote from this subject matter of history." But the state is always only the means for the preservation of many individuals: how could it be the aim? The hope is that with the preservation of so many blanks one may also protect a few in whom humanity culminates. Otherwise it makes no sense at all to preserve so many wretched human beings. The history of the state is the history of the egoism of the masses and of the blind desire to exist; this striving is justified to some extent only in the geniuses, inasmuch as they can thus exist. Individual and collective egoisms struggling against each other —an atomic whirl of egoisms—who would look for aims here?

Through the genius something does result from this atomic whirl after all, and now one forms a milder opinion concerning the senselessness of this procedure —as if a blind hunter fired hundreds of times in vain and finally, by sheer accident, hit a bird. A result at last, he says to himself, and goes on firing. (vi, 336 f.)

❊❊❊

The damned *folk* soul! When we speak of the *German spirit* we mean Luther, Goethe, Schiller, and a few others. It would be better even to speak of Luther-like people, etc. We want to be careful about calling something German: in the first place, it is the language; but to understand this as an expression of the folk character is a mere phrase, and so far it has not been possible to do so with any people without fatal vagueness and figures of speech. Greek language and Greek "folk"! Let somebody bring them together! Moreover, it is the same as with writing: the most important basis of the language is not *Greek* but, as one now says, Indo-Germanic. It is somewhat better with style or the human being. To ascribe predicates to a people is always dangerous; in the end, everything is so mixed that a unity develops only late, through the language— or an illusion of unity. Germans, German *Reich*—that is something. Those speaking German—that is something too. But those of German race! What is German as a quality of artistic style—that is yet to be *found,* just as among the Greeks the Greek style was found only late: an earlier unity did not exist, only a terrible mixture. (vi, 338 f.)

FROM

On Truth and Lie in an Extra-Moral Sense[1]

(1873)

In some remote corner of the universe, poured out and glittering in innumerable solar systems, there once was a star on which clever animals invented knowledge. That was the haughtiest and most mendacious minute of "world history"—yet only a minute. After nature had drawn a few breaths the star grew cold, and the clever animals had to die.

One might invent such a fable and still not have illustrated sufficiently how wretched, how shadowy and flighty, how aimless and arbitrary, the human intellect appears in nature. There have been eternities when it did not exist; and when it is done for again, nothing will have happened. For this intellect has no further mission that would lead beyond human life. It is human, rather, and only its owner and producer gives it such importance, as if the world pivoted around it. But if we could communicate with the mosquito, then we would learn that it floats through the air with the same self-importance, feeling within itself the flying center of the world. There is nothing in nature so despicable or insignificant that it cannot immediately be blown up like a bag by a slight breath of this power of knowledge; and just as every porter wants an admirer, the proudest human being, the philosopher, thinks that he sees the eyes of the universe tele-

---

[1] A fragment published posthumously.

scopically focused from all sides on his actions and thoughts.

It is strange that this should be the effect of the intellect, for after all it was given only as an aid to the most unfortunate, most delicate, most evanescent beings in order to hold them for a minute in existence, from which otherwise, without this gift, they would have every reason to flee as quickly as Lessing's son. That haughtiness which goes with knowledge and feeling, which shrouds the eyes and senses of man in a blinding fog, therefore deceives him about the value of existence by carrying in itself the most flattering evaluation of knowledge itself. Its most universal effect is deception; but even its most particular effects have something of the same character.

The intellect, as a means for the preservation of the individual, unfolds its chief powers in simulation; for this is the means by which the weaker, less robust individuals preserve themselves, since they are denied the chance of waging the struggle for existence with horns or the fangs of beasts of prey. In man this art of simulation reaches its peak: here deception, flattery, lying and cheating, talking behind the back, posing, living in borrowed splendor, being masked, the disguise of convention, acting a role before others and before oneself—in short, the constant fluttering around the single flame of vanity is so much the rule and the law that almost nothing is more incomprehensible than how an honest and pure urge for truth could make its appearance among men. They are deeply immersed in illusions and dream images; their eye glides only over the surface of things and sees "forms"; their feeling nowhere leads into truth, but contents itself with the reception of stimuli, playing, as it were, a game of blindman's buff on the backs of things. Moreover, man permits himself to be lied to at night, his life long, when he dreams, and his moral sense never even tries to prevent this—although men have been said to have overcome snoring by sheer will power.

What, indeed, does man know of himself! Can he even once perceive himself completely, laid out as if in an illuminated glass case? Does not nature keep much the most from him, even about his body, to spellbind and confine him in a proud, deceptive consciousness, far from the coils of the intestines, the quick current of the blood stream, and the involved tremors of the fibers? She threw away the key; and woe to the calamitous curiosity which might peer just once through a crack in the chamber of consciousness and look down, and sense that man rests upon the merciless, the greedy, the insatiable, the murderous, in the indifference of his ignorance—hanging in dreams, as it were, upon the back of a tiger. In view of this, whence in all the world comes the urge for truth?

Insofar as the individual wants to preserve himself against other individuals, in a natural state of affairs he employs the intellect mostly for simulation alone. But because man, out of need and boredom, wants to exist socially, herd-fashion, he requires a peace pact and he endeavors to banish at least the very crudest *bellum omnium contra omnes*[1] from his world. This peace pact brings with it something that looks like the first step toward the attainment of this enigmatic urge for truth. For now that is fixed which henceforth shall be "truth"; that is, a regularly valid and obligatory designation of things is invented, and this linguistic legislation also furnishes the first laws of truth: for it is here that the contrast between truth and lie first originates. The liar uses the valid designations, the words, to make the unreal

[1] "War of all against all."

appear as real; he says, for example, "I am rich," when the word "poor" would be the correct designation of his situation. He abuses the fixed conventions by arbitrary changes or even by reversals of the names. When he does this in a self-serving way damaging to others, then society will no longer trust him but exclude him. Thereby men do not flee from being deceived as much as from being damaged by deception: what they hate at this stage is basically not the deception but the bad, hostile consequences of certain kinds of deceptions. In a similarly limited way man wants the truth: he desires the agreeable life-preserving consequences of truth, but he is indifferent to pure knowledge, which has no consequences; he is even hostile to possibly damaging and destructive truths. And, moreover, what about these conventions of language? Are they really the products of knowledge, of the sense of truth? Do the designations and the things coincide? Is language the adequate expression of all realities?

Only through forgetfulness can man ever achieve the illusion of possessing a "truth" in the sense just designated. If he does not wish to be satisfied with truth in the form of a tautology—that is, with empty shells— then he will forever buy illusions for truths. What is a word? The image of a nerve stimulus in sounds. But to infer from the nerve stimulus, a cause outside us, that is already the result of a false and unjustified application of the principle of reason. . . . The different languages, set side by side, show that what matters with words is never the truth, never an adequate expression; else there would not be so many languages. The "thing in itself" (for that is what pure truth, without consequences, would be) is quite incomprehensible to the creators of language and not at all worth aiming for. One designates only the relations of things to man, and to express them one calls on the boldest metaphors. A nerve stimulus, first transposed into an image—first metaphor. The image, in turn, imitated by a sound—second metaphor. . . .

Let us still give special consideration to the formation of concepts. Every word immediately becomes a concept, inasmuch as it is not intended to serve as a reminder of the unique and wholly individualized original experience to which it owes its birth, but must at the same time fit innumerable, more or less similar cases—which means, strictly speaking, never equal—in other words, a lot of unequal cases. Every concept originates through our equating what is unequal. No leaf ever wholly equals another, and the concept "leaf" is formed through an arbitrary abstraction from these individual differences, through forgetting the distinctions; and now it gives rise to the idea that in nature there might be something besides the leaves which would be "leaf"—some kind of original form after which all leaves have been woven, marked, copied, colored, curled, and painted, but by unskilled hands, so that no copy turned out to be a correct, reliable, and faithful image of the original form. We call a person "honest." Why did he act so honestly today? we ask. Our answer usually sounds like this: because of his honesty. Honesty! That is to say again: the leaf is the cause of the leaves. After all, we know nothing of an essence-like quality named "honesty"; we know only numerous individualized, and thus unequal actions, which we equate by omitting the unequal and by then calling them honest actions. In the end, we distill from them a *qualitas occulta* with the name of "honesty". . . .

What, then, is truth? A mobile army of metaphors, metonyms, and anthropomorphisms—in short, a sum of human relations, which have been enhanced, transposed, and embellished poetically and rhetorically, and which after long use seem firm, canonical, and obligatory to a people: truths are illusions about which one has forgotten that this is what they are; metaphors which are worn out and without sensuous power; coins which have lost their pictures and now matter only as metal, no longer as coins.

We still do not know where the urge for truth comes from; for as yet we have heard only of the obligation imposed by society that it should exist: to be truthful means using the customary metaphors—in moral terms: the obligation to lie according to a fixed convention, to lie herd-like in a style obligatory for all. . . .

NOTES ABOUT WAGNER

(January 1874)

If Goethe is a transposed painter and Schiller a transposed orator, then Wagner is a transposed actor.

(VII, 341)

❊❊❊

As a pamphleteer he is an orator without the power to convince. (VII, 353)

❊❊❊

It was a special form of Wagner's ambition to relate himself to high points of the past: Schiller-Goethe, Beethoven, Luther, Greek tragedy, Shakespeare, Bismarck. Only to the Renaissance could he establish no relationship; but he invented the German spirit as opposed to the Romance. (VII, 353)

Notes (1874)

German Culture. . . . Political superiority without any
real human superiority is most harmful. One must seek
to make amends for political superiority. To be
ashamed of one's power. To use it in the most salutary
way. Everybody thinks that the Germans may now rest
on their moral and intellectual superiority. One seems
to think that now it is time for something else, for the
state. Till now, for "art," etc. This is an ignominious
misunderstanding; there are seeds for the most glorious
development of man. And these must perish for the
sake of the state? What, after all, is a state? The time
of the scholars is past. Their place must be taken by
philalethes.[1] Tremendous power. The only way to use
the present kind of German power correctly is to comprehend the tremendous *obligation* which lies in it.
Any slackening of cultural tasks would turn this power
into the most revolting tyranny.   (VII, 145 f.)

�֍

A great value of antiquity lies in the fact that its
writings are the only ones that modern men still *read
with exactness.*   (VII, 156)

Notes (1875)

The political defeat of Greece was the greatest failure of culture: for it has brought with it the revolting
theory that one can foster culture only when one is

[1] "Friends of truth."

armed to the teeth and wears boxing gloves. The rise
of Christianity was the second great failure: raw power
there and the dull intellect here became victors over
the aristocratic genius among the nations. Being a
Hellenophile means: being an enemy of raw power
and dull intellects. In this way Sparta was the ruin of
Hellas, for she forced Athens to become active in a
federation and to throw herself entirely into politics.
(VII, 192)

There remains a grave doubt whether one may argue
from languages to nationalities and relatedness to other
nations. A victorious language is nothing but a frequent
(not even a regular) sign of successful conquest.
Where have there ever been autochthonous peoples?
It is a very imprecise concept to speak of Greeks who
did not yet live in Greece. What is characteristically
Greek is much less the result of any disposition than of
adapted institutions and of the language that has been
accepted. (VII, 193)

For the highest images in every religion there is an
analogue in a state of the soul. The God of Mohammed—the solitude of the desert, the distant roar of a
lion, the vision of a terrible fighter. The God of the
Christians—everything that men and women associate
with the word "love." The God of the Greeks—a beautiful dream image. (VII, 195)

For once I want to enumerate everything that I no
longer believe; also what I believe.

In the great whirlpool of forces man stands with the conceit that this whirlpool is rational and has a rational aim: an error! The only rational thing we know is what little reason man has: he must exert it a lot, and it is always ruinous for him when he abandons himself, say, to "Providence."

The only happiness lies in reason; all the rest of the world is dismal. The highest reason, however, I see in the work of the artist, and he may experience it as such; there may also be something that, if only it could be produced consciously, would result in a still greater feeling of reason and happiness: for example, the course of the solar system, begetting and educating a human being.

Happiness lies in the swiftness of feeling and thinking: all the rest of the world is slow, gradual, and stupid. Whoever could feel the course of a light ray would be very happy, for it is very swift.

Thinking of oneself gives little happiness. If, however, one feels much happiness in this, it is because at bottom one is not thinking of oneself but of one's ideal. This is far, and only the swift reach it and are delighted.　　　　　　　　　　　　　　　(VII, 211 f.)

❊❊❊

To educate educators! But the first ones must educate themselves! And for these I write.　　　(VII, 215)

❊❊❊

The better the state is established, the fainter is humanity.

To make the individual *uncomfortable,* that is my task.　　　　　　　　　　　　　　　　　(VII, 216)

FROM
Human, All-Too-Human

EDITOR'S NOTE

Nietzsche's first five books, *The Birth of Tragedy* and the four *Untimely Meditations*, were essays. All of them dealt, in one way or another, with questions of value: the value of art and life itself, the value of history and the problem whether there are supra-historical values, and the value of self-perfection. This last point was central in the third *Meditation*, in which Nietzsche proposed that a new picture of man was needed to counter the true but deadly Darwinian doctrine of the essential continuity of man and animal. Being determined, however, to build on an empirical foundation, instead of falling back on dogma or intuition, Nietzsche found himself unable to do what he wanted. Then, roughly at the same time he decided to break with Wagner, he gave up his previous style and method and turned to writing books composed of aphorisms—largely concerned with human psychology or, in Nietzsche's phrase, with the "human, all-too-human."

[2]

Original error of the philosopher. All philosophers share this common error: they proceed from contemporary man and think they can reach their goal through an analysis of this man. Automatically they think of "man" as an eternal verity, as something abiding in the whirlpool, as a sure measure of things. Everything that the philosopher says about man, however, is at bottom no more than a testimony about the man of a very limited period. Lack of a historical sense is the original error of all philosophers. . . .

[5]

Misunderstanding of the dream. In the ages of crude primeval culture man believed that in dreams he got to know *another real world;* here is the origin of all metaphysics. Without the dream one would have found no occasion for a division of the world. The separation of body and soul, too, is related to the most ancient conception of the dream; also the assumption of a quasibody of the soul, which is the origin of all belief in spirits and probably also of the belief in gods. "The dead live on; for they appear to the living in dreams"; this inference went unchallenged for many thousands of years.

[83]

The sleep of virtue. When virtue has slept, she will get up more refreshed.

[113]

Christianity as antiquity. When we hear the ancient bells growling on a Sunday morning we ask ourselves: Is it really possible! this, for a Jew, crucified two thousand years ago, who said he was God's son. The proof of such a claim is lacking. Certainly the Christian religion is an antiquity projected into our times from remote prehistory; and the fact that the claim is believed —whereas one is otherwise so strict in examining pretensions—is perhaps the most ancient piece of this heritage. A god who begets children with a mortal woman; a sage who bids men work no more, have no more courts, but look for the signs of the impending end of the world; a justice that accepts the innocent as a vicarious sacrifice; someone who orders his disciples to drink his blood; prayers for miraculous interventions; sins perpetrated against a god, atoned for by a god; fear of a beyond to which death is the portal; the form of the cross as a symbol in a time that no longer knows the function and the ignominy of the cross—how ghoulishly all this touches us, as if from the tomb of a primeval past! Can one believe that such things are still believed?

[146]

The artist's sense of truth. Regarding truths, the artist has a weaker morality than the thinker. He definitely does not want to be deprived of the splendid and profound interpretations of life, and he resists sober, simple methods and results. Apparently he fights for the higher dignity and significance of man; in truth, he does not want to give up the most effective presuppositions of his art: the fantastic, mythical, uncertain, extreme, the sense for the symbolic, the overestimation of the person, the faith in some miraculous element in the genius. Thus he considers the continued existence of his kind of creation more important than scientific devotion to the truth in every form, however plain.

[170]

Artists' ambition. The Greek artists, for example, the tragedians, wrote in order to triumph. Their whole art is unthinkable without the contest: Hesiod's good Eris, ambition, gave wings to their genius. Now this ambition demanded above all that their work attain the highest excellence in their own eyes, as they understood excellence, without consideration for any prevailing taste or public opinion concerning excellence in a work of art. Thus Aeschylus and Euripides remained unsuccessful for a long time, until they had finally educated judges of art who appraised their work by the standards they themselves applied. Thus they strove for a triumph over their rivals in their own estimation, before their own seat of judgment; they really wanted to *be* more excellent; and then they demanded outside agreement with their own estimation, a confirmation of their own judgment. Striving for honor here means "making oneself superior and also wishing to appear so publicly." If the first is lacking and the second is desired nevertheless, then one speaks of *vanity*. If the second is lacking and is not missed, then one speaks of *pride*.

[184]

Untranslatable. It is neither the best nor the worst in a book that is untranslatable.

[189]

Thoughts in a poem. The poet presents his thoughts festively, on the carriage of rhythm: usually because they could not walk.

[224]

Ennoblement through degeneration. History teaches that the best-preserved tribe among a people is the one in which most men have a living communal sense as a consequence of sharing their customary and indisputable principles—in other words, in consequence of a common faith. Here the good, robust *mores* thrive; here the subordination of the individual is learned and the character receives firmness, first as a gift and then is further cultivated. The danger to these strong communities founded on homogeneous individuals who have character is growing stupidity, which is gradually increased by heredity, and which, in any case, follows all stability like a shadow. It is the individuals who have fewer ties and are much more uncertain and morally weaker upon whom *spiritual progress* depends in such communities; they are the men who make new and manifold experiments. Innumerable men of this sort perish because of their weakness without any very visible effect; but in general, especially if they have descendants, they loosen up and from time to time inflict a wound on the stable element of a community. Precisely in this wounded and weakened spot the whole structure is *inoculated,* as it were, with something new; but its over-all strength must be sufficient to accept this new element into its blood and assimilate it. Those who degenerate are of the highest importance wherever progress is to take place; every great progress must be preceded by a partial weakening. The strongest natures *hold fast* to the type; the weaker ones help to *develop it further.*

It is somewhat the same with the individual: rarely is degeneration, a crippling, even a vice or any physical or moral damage, unaccompanied by some gain on the other side. The sicker man in a warlike and restless tribe, for example, may have more occasion to be by himself and may thus become calmer and wiser; the one-eyed will have one stronger eye; the blind will see more deeply within, and in any case have a keener sense of hearing. So the famous *struggle for existence* does not seem to me to be the only point of view from which to explain the progress or the strengthening of a human being or a race. Rather, two things must come together: first, the increase of stable power through close spiritual ties such as faith and communal feeling; then, the possibility of reaching higher goals through the appearance of degenerate types and, as a consequence, a partial weakening and wounding of the stable power: it is precisely the weaker natures who, being more delicate and freer, make progress possible.

A people who crumble somewhere and become weak, but remain strong and healthy on the whole, are able to accept the infection of the new and absorb it to their advantage. In the case of the individual the task of education is this: to put him on his path so firmly and surely that, as a whole, he can never again be diverted. Then, however, the educator must wound him, or utilize the wounds destiny inflicts upon him; and when pain and need have thus developed, something new and noble can then be inoculated in the wounded spots. His whole nature will absorb this, and later, in its fruits, show the ennoblement.

Concerning the state, Machiavelli says that "the form of government is of very little importance, although the half-educated think otherwise. The great goal of statesmanship should be *duration*, which outweighs everything else because it is far more valuable than freedom." Only where the greatest duration is securely established and guaranteed is continual development and ennobling inoculation at all possible. Of course, authority, the dangerous companion of all duration, will usually try to resist this process.

[265]

Reason in the schools. The schools have no more important task than to teach rigorous thinking, cautious judgment, and consistent inference; therefore they should leave alone whatever is not suitable for these operations: religion, for example. After all, they can be sure that later on man's fogginess, habit, and need will slacken the bow of an all-too-taut thinking. But as far as the influence of the schools reaches, they should enforce what is essential and distinctive in man: "reason and science, man's *very highest* power"—so Goethe, at least, judges.

The great scientist von Baer sees the superiority of Europeans over Asiatics in their trained ability to give reasons for what they believe—something of which the latter are wholly incapable. Europe has gone through the school of consistent, critical thinking; Asia still does not know how to distinguish between truth and poetry, and is not conscious of whether its convictions are derived from personal observation and methodical thinking or from fantasies.

Europe was made Europe by reason in the schools; in the Middle Ages Europe was on the way to becoming a piece and an appendix of Asia again—by losing the scientific sense that it owed to the Greeks.

[271]

The art of drawing inferences. The greatest progress men have made lies in their learning how to draw correct inferences. That is by no means something natural, as Schopenhauer assumes when he says: "Of inference, all are capable; of judgment, only a few." It has been learned only late, and it still has not gained dominance. False inferences are the rule in earlier times; and the mythology of all peoples, their magic and their superstition, their religious cults, their laws, are inexhaustible mines of proof for this proposition.

[281]

Higher culture is necessarily misunderstood. He who has but two strings on his instrument—like the scholars who, in addition to the urge for knowledge, have only the religious urge, instilled by education—does not understand those who can play on more strings. It is of the essence of the higher, multi-stringed culture that it is always misinterpreted by the lower culture—as happens, for example, when art is considered a disguised form of religion. Indeed, people who are only religious understand even science as a search of the religious feeling, just as deaf-mutes do not know what music is, if it is not visible movement.

[298]

The most dangerous party member. In every party there is one member who, by his all-too-devout pronouncement of the party principles, provokes the others to apostasy.

[303]

Why one contradicts. One often contradicts an opinion when it is really only the tone in which it has been presented that is unsympathetic.

[361]

The experience of Socrates. When one has become a master in some field one has usually, for that very reason, remained a complete amateur in most other things; but one judges just the other way around, as Socrates had already found out. This is what makes association with masters disagreeable.[1]

[380]

From the mother. Everyone carries in himself an image of woman derived from the mother; by this he is determined to revere women generally, or to hold them in low esteem, or to be generally indifferent to them.

---

[1] Wagner liked to be called "master."

[390]

Friendship with women. Women can form a friendship with a man very well; but to preserve it—to that end a slight physical antipathy must probably help.

[406]

Marriage as a long conversation. When marrying, one should ask oneself this question: Do you believe that you will be able to converse well with this woman into your old age? Everything .else in marriage is transitory, but the most time during the association belongs to conversation.

[407]

Girls' dreams. Inexperienced girls flatter themselves with the notion that it is within their power to make a man happy; later they learn that it means holding a man in low esteem to assume that only a girl is needed to make him happy. The vanity of women demands that a man be more than a happy husband.

[408]

Faust and Gretchen dying out. According to the very good insight of a scholar, the educated men of contemporary Germany resemble a mixture of Mephistopheles and Wagner, but certainly not Faust, whom our grandfathers, at least in their youth, still felt stirring within. Thus there are two reasons—to continue this proposition—why the Gretchens are not suitable for them. And since they are no longer desired, they apparently die out.

[424]

Something about the future of marriage. Those noble free-spirited women who have made the education and

elevation of the female sex their task should not overlook one consideration: marriage, according to its
highest conception as a friendship between the souls
of two human beings of different sex, in other words,
as it is hoped for in the future, concluded for the purpose of begetting and educating a new generation—
such a marriage, which uses the sensual, as it were,
only as a rare means to a greater end, probably requires, I fear, a natural aid: *concubinage*. If, for reasons of the husband's health, the wife should also serve
for the sole satisfaction of the sexual need, then the
choice of a wife will be decisively influenced by a false
consideration that is contrary to the aims suggested;
the production of offspring becomes accidental, and a
good education highly improbable. A good wife—who
is supposed to be friend, helper, bearer of children,
mother, head of the family, manager, and who may
even have to stand at the head of her own business or
office, quite apart from her husband—cannot at the
same time be a concubine: generally, this would be
asking too much of her. Thus the future might see a
contrary development to what occurred in Periclean
Athens: the men, who at that time found little more
than concubines in their wives, turned to the Aspasias
because they desired the attractions of a companion-
ship that would liberate head and heart, as only the
grace and spiritual suppleness of women can provide.
All human institutions, like marriage, permit only a
limited degree of practical idealization; failing that,
crude remedies become immediately necessary.

[444]

War. Against war one can say: It makes the victor
stupid, the vanquished malignant. In favor of war:

Through both of these effects it barbarizes and thereby makes more natural; it is a sleep or a winter for culture, and man emerges from it stronger for good and evil.

[462]

My utopia. In a better arrangement of society hard labor and the troubles of life will be meted out to those who suffer least from them; hence, to the most obtuse, and then, step by step, up to those who are most sensitive to the highest and most sublimated kinds of suffering and who thus still suffer when life is made easiest.

[465]

Resurrection of the spirit. On the political sickbed a people is usually rejuvenated and rediscovers its spirit, after having gradually lost it in seeking and preserving power. Culture owes its peaks to politically weak ages.

[475]

The European man and the abolition of nations. Trade and industry, books and letters, the way in which all higher culture is shared, the rapid change of house and scenery, the present nomadic life of everyone who is not a landowner—these circumstances necessarily produce a weakening, and finally the abolition, of nations, at least in Europe; and as a consequence of continual intermarriage there must develop a mixed race, that of the European man. . . . It is not the interest of the many (of peoples), as is often claimed, but above all the interest of certain royal dynasties and also of certain classes in commerce and society, that drives to nationalism. Once one has recognized this, one should declare oneself without embarrassment as a *good European* and work actively for the amalgamation of nations. In this process the Germans could be helpful by virtue of their long proven skill as interpreters and mediators among peoples.

Incidentally, the whole problem of the *Jews* exists only in nation states, for here their energy and higher intelligence, their accumulated capital of spirit and will, gathered from generation to generation through a long schooling in suffering, must become so preponderant as to arouse mass envy and hatred. In almost all contemporary nations, therefore—in direct proportion to the degree to which they act up nationalistically— the literary obscenity is spreading of leading the Jews to slaughter as scapegoats of every conceivable public and internal misfortune. As soon as it is no longer a matter of preserving nations, but of producing the strongest possible European mixed race, the Jew is just as useful and desirable an ingredient as any other national remnant. Unpleasant, even dangerous, qualities can be found in every nation and every individual: it is cruel to demand that the Jew be an exception. In him, these qualities may even be dangerous and revolting to an unusual degree; and perhaps the young stock-exchange Jew is altogether the most disgusting invention of mankind. In spite of that, I should like to know how much one must forgive a people in a total accounting when they have had the most painful history of all peoples, not without the fault of all of us, and when one owes to them the noblest man (Christ), the purest sage (Spinoza), the most powerful book, and the most effective moral law in the world. Moreover, in the darkest times of the Middle Ages, when the Asiatic cloud masses had gathered heavily over Europe, it was Jewish free-thinkers, scholars, and physicians who clung to the banner of enlightenment and spiritual independence in the face of the harshest personal pressures and defended Europe against Asia. We owe it to their exertions, not least of all, that a more natural, more rational, and certainly unmythical explanation of the world was eventually able to triumph again, and that the bond of culture which now links us with the enlightenment of Greco-Roman antiquity remained unbroken. If Christianity has done everything to orientalize the Occident, Judaism has helped significantly to occidentalize it again and again: in a certain sense this means as much as making Europe's task and history a continuation of the Greek.

[482]

And to say it once more. Public opinions—private lazinesses.

[483]

Enemies of truth. Convictions are more dangerous enemies of truth than lies.

[536]

The value of insipid opponents. At times one remains faithful to a cause only because its opponents do not cease to be insipid.

[579]

Not suitable as a party member. Whoever thinks much is not suitable as a party member: he soon thinks himself right through the party.

[635]

On the whole, scientific methods are at least as important as any other result of research: for it is upon the insight into method that the scientific spirit depends: and if these methods were lost, then all the

results of science could not prevent a renewed triumph
of superstition and nonsense. Clever people may learn
as much as they wish of the results of science—still
one will always notice in their conversation, and especially in their hypotheses, that they lack the scientific spirit; they do not have that instinctive mistrust of
the aberrations of thought which through long training
are deeply rooted in the soul of every scientific person.
They are content to find any hypothesis at all concerning some matter; then they are all fire and flame for it
and think that is enough. To have an opinion means
for them to fanaticize for it and thenceforth to press it
to their hearts as a conviction. If something is unex-
plained, they grow hot over the first notion that comes
into their heads and looks like an explanation—which
results progressively in the worst consequences, especially in the sphere of politics. For that reason everyone should now study at least one science from the
bottom up: then he will know what method means and
how important is the utmost circumspection. . . .

FROM
Mixed Opinions and Maxims

EDITOR'S NOTE

In 1879 Nietzsche brought out another collection of
aphorisms under this title, as a sequel to *Human, All-Too-
Human,* published the year before.

[77]

Dissipation. The mother of dissipation is not joy but
joylessness.

[95]

"Love." The most subtle artifice that distinguishes Christianity from other religions is a word: it speaks of *love.* Thus it became the lyrical religion (whereas in both their other creations the Semites presented the world with heroic-epic religions). There is something so ambiguous and suggestive about the word love, something that speaks to memory and to hope, that even the lowest intelligence and the coldest heart still feel something of the glimmer of this word. The cleverest woman and the most vulgar man recall the relatively least selfish moments of their whole life, even if Eros has taken only a low flight with them; and for those countless ones who *miss* love, whether from their parents or their children or their beloved, and especially for people with sublimated sexuality, Christianity has always been a find.

[129]

Readers of aphorisms. The worst readers of aphorisms are the author's friends if they are intent on guessing back from the general to the particular instance to which the aphorism owes its origin; for with such pot-peeking they reduce the author's whole effort to nothing; so that they deservedly gain, not a philosophic outlook or instruction, but—at best, or at worst—nothing more than the satisfaction of vulgar curiosity.

[141]

Sign of rank. All poets and writers who are in love with the superlative want more than they are capable of.

[202]

Jokes. A joke is the epigram on the death of a feeling.

[231]

Humaneness in friendship and mastership. "If thou wilt go toward morning, then I will go toward evening": to feel this way is a high sign of humaneness in a closer association: without this feeling, every friendship, every discipleship and pupilship, becomes at one time or another hypocrisy.

[248]

Way to a Christian virtue. Learning from one's enemies is the best way toward loving them; for it makes us grateful to them.

[271]

Every philosophy is the philosophy of some stage of life. The stage of life at which a philosopher found his doctrine reverberates through it; he cannot prevent this, however far above time and hour he may feel. Thus Schopenhauer's philosophy remains the reflection of ardent and melancholy *youth*—it is no way of thinking for older people. And Plato's philosophy recalls the middle thirties, when a cold and a hot torrent often roar toward each other, so that a mist and tender little clouds form—and under favorable circumstances and the rays of the sun, an enchanting rainbow.

[301]

The party man. The true party man learns no longer —he only experiences and judges; while Solon, who was never a party man but pursued his goal alongside and above the parties, or against them, is characteristically the father of that plain maxim in which the health and inexhaustibility of Athens is contained: "I grow old and always continue to learn."

[357]

Unfaithfulness, a condition of mastership. Nothing avails: every master has but one disciple, and that one becomes unfaithful to him, for he too is destined for mastership.

[408]

The journey to Hades. I too have been in the underworld, like Odysseus, and I shall yet return there often; and not only sheep have I sacrificed to be able to talk with a few of the dead, but I have not spared my own blood. Four pairs did not deny themselves to me as I sacrificed: Epicurus and Montaigne, Goethe and Spinoza, Plato and Rousseau, Pascal and Schopenhauer. With these I must come to terms when I have long wandered by myself; they shall tell me whether I am right or wrong; to them I want to listen when, in the process, they tell each other whether they are right or wrong. . . .

FROM

The Wanderer and His Shadow

EDITOR'S NOTE

This collection of aphorisms was first published in 1880, as the final sequel to *Human, All-Too-Human*.

[38]

The bite of conscience. The bite of conscience, like the bite of a dog into a stone, is a stupidity.

[48]

Prohibitions without reasons. A prohibition, the reason for which we do not understand or admit, is almost a command not only for the stubborn but also for those who thirst for knowledge: one risks an experiment to find out *why* the prohibition was pronounced. Moral prohibitions, like those of the Decalogue, are suitable only for an age of subjugated reason: now, such a prohibition as "Thou shalt not kill" or "Thou shalt not commit adultery," presented without reasons, would have a harmful rather than a useful effect.

[85]

The persecutor of God. Paul thought up the idea, and Calvin re-thought it, that for innumerable people damnation has been decreed from eternity, and that this beautiful world plan was instituted to reveal the glory of God: heaven and hell and humanity are thus supposed to exist—to satisfy the vanity of God! What cruel and insatiable vanity must have flared in the soul of the man who thought this up first, or second. Paul has remained Saul after all—the persecutor of God.

[86]

Socrates. If all goes well, the time will come when, to develop oneself morally-rationally, one will take up the memorabilia of Socrates rather than the Bible, and when Montaigne and Horace will be employed as precursors and guides to the understanding of the simplest and most imperishable mediator-sage, Socrates. The roads of the most divergent philosophic ways of life lead back to him; at bottom they are the ways of life of the different temperaments, determined by reason and habit, and in all cases pointing with their peaks to joy in life and in one's own self—from which one might well infer that the most characteristic feature of Socrates was that he shared in all temperaments. Above the founder of Christianity, Socrates is distinguished by the gay kind of seriousness and that *wisdom full of pranks* which constitute the best state of the soul of man. Moreover, he had the greater intelligence.

[124]

The Faust idea. A little seamstress is seduced and made unhappy; a great scholar in all four branches of learning is the evildoer. Surely that could not have happened without supernatural interference? No, of course not! Without the aid of the incarnate devil the great scholar could never have accomplished this.

Should this really be the greatest German "tragic idea," as is said among Germans? But for Goethe even this idea was still too terrible. His mild heart could not help putting the little seamstress, "the good soul who forgot herself but once," close to the saints after her involuntary death; indeed, by a trick played on the devil at the decisive moment, he even brought the great scholar to heaven at just the right time—"the good man" with the "darkling aspiration"! And there, in heaven, the lovers find each other again.

Goethe once said that his nature was too conciliatory for the truly tragic.

[217]

Classical and romantic. The classically disposed spirits no less than those romantically inclined—as these two species always exist—carry a vision of the future: but the former out of a strength of their time; the latter, out of its weakness.

[239]

Why beggars still live. If all alms were given only from pity, all beggars would have starved long ago.

[240]

Why beggars still live. The greatest giver of alms is cowardice.

[261]

Letter. A letter is an unannounced visit; the mailman, the mediator of impolite incursions. One ought to have one hour in every eight days for receiving letters, and then take a bath.

[267]

There are no educators. As a thinker, one should speak only of self-education. The education of youth by others is either an experiment, conducted on one as yet unknown and unknowable, or a leveling on principle, to make the new character, whatever it may be, conform to the habits and customs that prevail: in both cases, therefore, something unworthy of the thinker— the work of parents and teachers, whom an audaciously honest person has called *nos ennemis naturels.*

One day, when in the opinion of the world one has long been educated, one discovers oneself: that is where the task of the thinker begins; now the time has come to invoke his aid—not as an educator but as one who has educated himself and thus has experience.

[282]

The teacher a necessary evil. As few people as possible between the productive spirits and the hungering, receiving spirits! For the intermediaries falsify the nourishment almost automatically when they mediate it: then, as a reward for their mediation, they want too much for themselves, which is thus taken away from the original productive spirits; namely, interest, admiration, time, money, and other things. Hence one should consider the teacher, no less than the shopkeeper, a necessary evil, an evil to be kept as small as possible. If the trouble in the German situation today has perhaps its main reason in the fact that too many people live by trade and want to live well (and thus seek to cut the producer's prices as much as possible while at the same time raising the prices to the consumer, in order to derive an advantage from the greatest possible damage to both), then one can certainly find a main reason for the spiritual troubles in the surplus of teachers: on their account, one learns so little and so badly.

[284]

The means to real peace. No government admits any more that it keeps an army to satisfy occasionally the desire for conquest. Rather the army is supposed to serve for defense, and one invokes the morality that approves of self-defense. But this implies one's own morality and the neighbor's immorality; for the neighbor must be thought of as eager to attack and conquer if our state must think of means of self-defense. More-over, the reasons we give for requiring an army imply that our neighbor, who denies the desire for conquest just as much as does our own state, and who, for his part, also keeps an army only for reasons of self-defense, is a hypocrite and a cunning criminal who would like nothing better than to overpower a harmless and awkward victim without any fight. Thus all states are now ranged against each other: they presuppose their neighbor's bad disposition and their own good disposition. This presupposition, however, is *inhumane*, as bad as war and worse. At bottom, indeed, it is itself the challenge and the cause of wars, because, as I have said, it attributes immorality to the neighbor and thus provokes a hostile disposition and act. We must abjure the doctrine of the army as a means of self-defense just as completely as the desire for conquests.

And perhaps the great day will come when a people, distinguished by wars and victories and by the highest development of a military order and intelligence, and accustomed to make the heaviest sacrifices for these things, will exclaim of its own free will, "We break the sword," and will smash its entire military establishment down to its lowest foundations. *Rendering oneself unarmed when one had been the best-armed,* out of a height of feeling—that is the means to real peace, which must always rest on a peace of mind; whereas the so-called armed peace, as it now exists in all countries, is the absence of peace of mind. One trusts neither oneself nor one's neighbor and, half from hatred, half from fear, does not lay down arms. Rather perish than hate and fear, and *twice rather perish than make oneself hated and feared*—this must someday become the highest maxim for every single commonwealth too.

Our liberal representatives, as is well known, lack the time for reflecting on the nature of man: else they would know that they work in vain when they work for a "gradual decrease of the military burden." Rather, only when this kind of need has become greatest will the kind of god be nearest who alone can help here. The tree of war-glory can only be destroyed all at once, by a stroke of lightning: but lightning, as indeed you know, comes from a cloud—and from up high.

LETTER TO OVERBECK

(Naumburg, November 14, 1879)

... My mother read to me: Gogol, Lermontov, Bret Harte, M. Twain, E. A. Poe. If you do not yet know the latest book by Twain, *The Adventures of Tom Sawyer*, it would be a pleasure for me to make you a little present of it. ...

NOTES (1880-81)

A girl who surrenders her virginity to a man who has not first sworn solemnly before witnesses that he will not leave her again for the rest of her life not only is considered imprudent but is also called immoral. She did not follow the *mores;* she was not only imprudent but also disobedient, for she knew what the mores commanded. Where the mores command differently, the conduct of the girl in such a case would not be called immoral either; in fact, there are regions where it is considered moral to lose one's virginity before marriage. Thus the reproach is really directed against disobedience: it is this that is immoral. Is this sufficient? Such a girl is considered contemptible—but what kind of disobedience is it that one despises? (Imprudence is not despised.) One says of her: she could not control herself, that is why she was disobedient against the mores; thus it is the blindness of the desire that one despises, the animal in the girl. With this in mind, one also says: she is unchaste; by this one could not mean that she is doing what the lawfully wedded wife does, too, without being called unchaste. The mores are then seen to demand that one bear the displeasure of unsatisfied desire, that the desire be able to *wait*. To be immoral means therefore, in this case, not to be able to bear a displeasure despite the thought of the power that makes the rules. *A feeling is supposed to be subdued by a thought*—more precisely, by the thought of fear (whether it be fear of the sacred mores or of the punishment and shame threatened by the mores). In itself, it is not at all shameful, but natural and fair, that a desire be satisfied immediately. Therefore what is really contemptible in this girl is the *weakness of her fear*. Being moral means being highly accessible to fear. Fear is the power by which the community is preserved.

If one considers, on the other hand, that every original community requires a high degree of fearlessness in its members in other respects, then it becomes clear that what is to be feared in the case of morality must inspire fear in the very highest degree. Therefore mores have been introduced everywhere as functions of a divine will, hiding under the fearfulness of gods and demonic means of punishment—and being immoral would then mean: not fearing the infinitely fearful.

Of anyone who denied the gods one expected anything: he was automatically the most fearsome human being, whom no community could suffer because he tore out the roots of fear on which the community had grown. It was supposed that in such a person desire raged unlimited: one considered every human being without such fear infinitely evil. . . .

The more peaceful a community has become, the more cowardly the citizens become; the less accustomed they are to standing pain, the more will worldly punishments suffice as deterrents, the faster will religious threats become superfluous. . . . In highly civilized peoples, finally, even punishments should become highly superfluous deterrents; the mere fear of shame, the trembling of vanity, is so continually effective that immoral actions are left undone. The refinement of morality increases together with the refinement of fear. Today the fear of disagreeable feelings in other people is almost the strongest of our own disagreeable feelings. One would like ever so much to live in such a way as to do nothing except what causes others *agreeable* feelings, and even to take pleasure in nothing any more that does not also fulfill this condition.   (x, 372-75)

※※

One hardly dares speak any more of the will to power: it was different in Athens.   (x, 414)

※※

The reabsorption of semen by the blood is the strongest nourishment and, perhaps more than any other factor, it prompts the stimulus of power, the unrest of all forces toward the overcoming of resistances, the thirst for contradiction and resistance. The feeling of power has so far mounted highest in abstinent priests and hermits (for example, among the Brahmins).   (x, 414 *f.*)

FROM
The Dawn

EDITOR'S NOTE

Another collection of aphorisms, first published in 1881.

[16]

First principle of civilization. Among crude peoples there is a species of customs, the intent of which appears to be custom as such: fastidious and at bottom useless ordinances (as, for example, on Kamchatka, never to scrape the snow off the shoes with a knife, never to spear a coal with a knife, never to put any iron into a fire—and death to him who transgresses in such matters!) which, however, keep in the consciousness the perpetual nearness of custom, the relentless compulsion to live up to custom. To confirm the great principle with which civilization begins: any custom is better than no custom.

[68]

The first Christian. All the world still believes in the authorship of the "Holy Spirit" or is at least still affected by this belief: when one opens the Bible one does so for "edification." . . . That it also tells the story of one of the most ambitious and obtrusive of souls, of a head as superstitious as it was crafty, the story of the apostle Paul—who knows this, except a few scholars? Without this strange story, however, without the confusions and storms of such a head, such a soul, there would be no Christianity; we should scarcely have heard of a small Jewish sect whose master died on the cross. Of course, if this story had been understood in time; if Paul's writings had been read not as revelations of the "Holy Spirit" but with an honest and free spirit of one's own, and without at the same time thinking of all our personal troubles, if they had *really been read*—and for a millennium and a half there were no such readers—then Christianity would have been done for long ago: so much do these pages of the Jewish Pascal expose the origin of Christianity, just as the pages of the French Pascal expose its destiny and that of which it will perish.

That the ship of Christianity threw overboard a good deal of its Jewish ballast, that it went, and was able to go, among the pagans—that was due to this one man, a very tortured, very pitiful, very unpleasant man, unpleasant even to himself. He suffered from a fixed idea—or more precisely, from a fixed, ever-present, never resting question: what about the Jewish law? and particularly the fulfillment of this law? In his youth he had himself wanted to satisfy it, with a ravenous hunger for this highest distinction which the Jews could conceive—this people who were propelled higher than any other people by the imagination of the ethically sublime, and who alone succeeded in creating a holy god together with the idea of sin as a transgression against this holiness. Paul became the fanatical defender of this god and his law and guardian of his honor; at the same time, in the struggle against the transgressors and doubters, lying in wait for them, he became increasingly harsh and evilly disposed to them, and inclined toward the most extreme punishments. And now he found that—hot-headed, sensual, melancholy, malignant in his hatred as he was—he was himself unable to fulfill the law; indeed, and this seemed strangest to him, his extravagant lust to domineer pro-

voked him continually to transgress the law, and he
had to yield to this thorn.

Is it really his "carnal nature" that makes him transgress again and again? And not rather, as he himself
suspected later, behind it the law itself, which must
constantly prove itself unfulfillable and which lures him
to transgression with irresistible charm? But at that
time he did not yet have this way out. He had much
on his conscience—he hints at hostility, murder, magic,
idolatry, lewdness, drunkenness, and pleasure in dissolute carousing—and . . . moments came when he said
to himself: "It is all in vain; the torture of the unfulfilled law cannot be overcome." Luther may have had
similar feelings when, in his monastery, he wanted to
become the perfect man of the spiritual ideal: and just
as Luther one day began to hate the spiritual ideal and
the Pope and the saints and the whole clerisy with
a true, deadly hatred—all the more the less he could
own it to himself—so it was with Paul. The law was
the cross to which he felt himself nailed: how he hated
it! how he resented it! how he searched for some means
to annihilate it—not to fulfill it any more himself!

And finally the saving thought struck him, together
with a vision—it could scarcely have happened otherwise to this epileptic. . . . Paul heard the words: "Why
dost thou persecute me?" The essential occurrence,
however, was this: his *head* had suddenly seen a light:
"It is *unreasonable*," he had said to himself, "to persecute this Jesus! Here after all is the way out; here is
the perfect revenge; here and nowhere else I have
and hold *the annihilator of the law!*". . . Until then
the ignominious death had seemed to him the chief
argument against the Messianic claim of which the
adherents of the new doctrine spoke: but what if
it were necessary to get rid of the law?

The tremendous consequences of this idea, of this solution of the riddle, spin before his eyes; at one stroke he becomes the happiest man; the destiny of the Jews —no, of all men—seems to him to be tied to this idea, to this second of its sudden illumination; he has the thought of thoughts, the key of keys, the light of lights; it is around him that all history must revolve henceforth. For he is from now on the teacher of the *annihilation of the law*. . . .

This is the first Christian, the inventor of Christianity. Until then there were only a few Jewish sectarians.

[76]

Thinking evil means making evil. The passions become evil and insidious when they are considered evil and insidious. Thus Christianity has succeeded in turning Eros and Aphrodite—great powers, capable of idealization—into hellish goblins. . . . In themselves the sexual feelings, like those of pity and adoration, are such that one human being thereby gives pleasure to another human being through his delight; one does not encounter such beneficent arrangements too frequently in nature. And to slander just such a one and to corrupt it through bad conscience! To associate the procreation of man with bad conscience!

In the end this transformation of Eros into a devil wound up as a comedy: gradually the "devil" Eros became more interesting to men than all the angels and saints, thanks to the whispering and the secret-mongering of the Church in all erotic matters: this has had the effect, right into our own time, of making the *love story* the only real interest shared by *all* circles—in an exaggeration which would have been incomprehensible in antiquity and which will yet be laughed at someday. . . .

[84]

The philology of Christianity. How little Christianity educates the sense of honesty and justice can be seen pretty well from the writings of its scholars: they advance their conjectures as blandly as dogmas and are hardly ever honestly perplexed by the exegesis of a Biblical verse. Again and again they say, "I am right, for it is written," and the interpretation that follows is of such impudent arbitrariness that a philologist is stopped in his tracks, torn between anger and laughter, and keeps asking himself: Is it possible? Is this honest? Is it even decent?

What dishonesties of this sort are still perpetrated from Protestant pulpits today, how crudely the preachers exploit the advantage that nobody can interrupt them, how the Bible is pricked and pulled and *the art of reading badly* formally inculcated upon the people— all this will be underestimated only by those who go to church either never or always.

In the end, however, what are we to expect of the aftereffects of a religion that enacted during the centuries of its foundation that unheard-of philological farce about the Old Testament? I refer to the attempt to pull away the Old Testament from under the feet of the Jews—with the claim that it contains nothing but Christian doctrines and *belongs* to the Christians as the *true* Israel, while the Jews had merely usurped it. And now the Christians yielded to a rage of interpretation and interpolation, which could not possibly have been accompanied by a good conscience. However much the Jewish scholars protested, everywhere in the Old Testament there were supposed to be references to Christ and only to Christ, and particularly to his cross. Wherever any piece of wood, a switch, a ladder, a twig, a tree, a willow, or a staff is mentioned, this was supposed to indicate a prophecy of the wood of the cross. . . .

Has anybody who claimed this ever *believed* it? . . .

[97]

One becomes moral—not because one is moral. Submission to morality can be slavish or vain or selfish or resigned or obtusely enthusiastic or thoughtless or an act of desperation, like submission to a prince: in itself it is nothing moral.

[101]

Doubtful. To accept a faith just because it is customary, means to be dishonest, to be cowardly, to be lazy. And do dishonesty, cowardice, and laziness then appear as the presupposition of morality?

[123]

Reason. How did reason come into the world? As is fitting, in an irrational manner, by accident. One will have to guess at it as at a riddle.

[164]

Perhaps premature. . . . There is no morality that alone makes moral, and every ethic that affirms itself exclusively kills too much good strength and costs humanity too dearly. The deviants, who are so frequently the inventive and fruitful ones, shall no longer be sacrificed; it shall not even be considered infamous to deviate from morality, in thought and deed; numerous new experiments of life and society shall be made; a tremendous burden of bad conscience shall be removed from the world—these most general aims should be recognized and promoted by all who are honest and seek truth.

[173]

The eulogists of work. Behind the glorification of
"work" and the tireless talk of the "blessings of work"
I find the same thought as behind the praise of impersonal activity for the public benefit: the fear of everything
individual. At bottom, one now feels when confronted
with work—and what is invariably meant is relentless
industry from early till late—that such work is the best
police, that it keeps everybody in harness and power-
fully obstructs the development of reason, of covetousness, of the desire for independence. For it uses up a
tremendous amount of nervous energy and takes it
away from reflection, brooding, dreaming, worry, love,
and hatred; it always sets a small goal before one's eyes
and permits easy and regular satisfactions. In that way
a society in which the members continually work hard
will have more security: and security is now adored as
the supreme goddess. And now—horrors!—it is precisely the "worker" who has become dangerous. "Dangerous individuals are swarming all around. And behind
them, the danger of dangers: the individual.

[179]

As little state as possible. All political and economic
arrangements are not worth it, that precisely the most
gifted spirits should be permitted, or even obliged, to
manage them: such a waste of spirit is really worse
than an extremity. These are and remain fields of work
for the lesser heads, and other than lesser heads should
not be at the service of this workshop: it were better
to let the machine go to pieces again. . . . At such a
price, one pays far too dearly for the "general security";
and what is most insane, one also produces the very
opposite of the general security, as our dear century is

undertaking to prove—as if it had never been proved
before. To make society secure against thieves and fire-
proof and infinitely comfortable for every trade and
activity, and to transform the state into Providence in
the good and bad sense—these are low, mediocre, and
not at all indispensable goals, for which one should not
strive with the highest means and instruments anywhere in existence, the means one ought to reserve for
the highest and rarest ends. Our time, however much
it talks of economy, is a squanderer: it squanders what
is most precious, the spirit.

[193]

Esprit and morality. The Germans, who know the
secret of being boring with spirit, knowledge, and feeling, and who have accustomed themselves to feel boredom as moral, fear the French *esprit* lest it prick out the
eyes of morality—fear and yet are charmed, like the
little bird before the rattlesnake. Of the famous Germans, perhaps none had more *esprit* than Hegel; but
for all that, he too feared it with a great German fear,
which created his peculiar bad style. The essence of this
style is that a core is wrapped around, and wrapped
around again and again, until it scarcely peeks out,
bashful and curious—as "young women look through
their veils," to quote the old woman-hater, Aeschylus;
that core, however, is a witty, often pert perception
about the most spiritual things, a delicate and daring
connection of words, such as belongs in the company
of thinkers, as a side dish of science—but in those
wrappings it presents itself as abstruse science itself,
and by all means as the most highly moral boredom.
Thus the Germans had their permissible form of *esprit*,
and they enjoyed it with such extravagant delight that
Schopenhauer's good, very good, intelligence froze at

the mere sight: all his life he stormed against the spectacle offered him by the Germans, but never could explain it to himself.

[197]

The hostility of the Germans to the Enlightenment. Let us reconsider the contribution to culture in general made by the Germans of the first half of this century with their spiritual labor, and let us first take the German philosophers. They have reverted to the first and most ancient stage of speculation, for they have been satisfied with concepts instead of explanations, like the thinkers of dreamy ages; they revived a prescientific kind of philosophy. Second, there are the German historians and romantics: their general effort was directed toward gaining a place of honor for more ancient, primitive feelings, and especially Christianity, the folk soul, folk sagas, folk language, medievalism, Oriental aesthetics, Indianism. Third, there are the natural scientists: they fought against the spirit of Newton and Voltaire and sought, like Goethe and Schopenhauer, to restore the idea of a divine or devilish nature and its entirely ethical and symbolical significance.

The whole great tendency of the Germans ran counter to the Enlightenment, and to the revolution of society which, by a crude misunderstanding, was considered its consequence: piety toward everything still in existence sought to transform itself into piety toward everything that has ever existed, only to make heart and spirit full once again and to leave no room for future goals and innovations. The cult of feeling was erected in place of the cult of reason; and the German musicians, as the artists of the invisible, the enthusiastic, the fabulous, and the pining, helped to build the new temple with more success than all the artists of words and thoughts. Even if we admit that a vast amount of good was spoken and investigated in detail and that many things are now judged more fairly than ever before, we must still say of this development as a whole: it was no slight universal danger, under the semblance of full and final knowledge of the past, to subordinate knowledge to feeling altogether and—to speak with Kant, who thus determined his own task—"to open the way again for faith by showing knowledge its limits."

Let us breathe free air again: the hour of this danger has passed. And strangely, those very spirits which were so eloquently conjured up by the Germans have in the long run become most harmful to the intentions of the conjurers. History, the understanding of origin and development, sympathy with the past, the renewed passion of feeling and knowledge, after they all seemed for a time helpful apprentices of this obscurantist, enthusiastic, and atavistic spirit, changed their nature one fine day and now soar with the broadest wings past their old conjurers and upward, as new and stronger geniuses of that very Enlightenment against which they were conjured up. This Enlightenment we must now advance further—unconcerned with the fact that there has been a "great revolution" against it, and then a "great reaction" again; indeed that both still exist: all this is mere play of the waves compared to that truly great tide in which *we* drift and want to drift.

[202]

Promoting health. We have scarcely begun to reflect on the physiology of the criminal, and yet we are already confronted with the indisputable realization that there is no essential difference between criminals and the insane—presupposing that one believes that the customary way of moral thinking is the way of thinking of spiritual health. No faith, however, is still as firmly believed as this, and so we should not shrink from drawing its consequences by treating the criminal as an insane person: above all, not with haughty mercy but with the physician's good sense and good will. A change of air, different company, temporary disappearance, perhaps being alone and having a new occupation, are what he needs. Good! Perhaps he himself considers it to his advantage to live in custody for a while to find protection against himself and a burdensome tyrannical urge. Good! One should present him quite clearly with the possibility and the means of a cure (the extirpation, reshaping, and sublimation of that drive); also, in a bad case, with the improbability of a cure; and one should offer the incurable criminal, who has become a horror to himself, the opportunity to commit suicide. Reserving this as the most extreme means of relief, one should not neglect anything to give back to the criminal, above all, confidence and a free mind; one should wipe pangs of conscience from his soul as some uncleanliness and give him pointers as to how he might balance and outbid the harm he may have done to one person by a good turn to another, or perhaps to society as a whole. All this with the utmost consideration. And above all, anonymity or a new name and frequent change of place, so that the irreproachability of his reputation and his future life be endangered as little as possible.

Today, to be sure, he who has been harmed always wants his revenge, quite apart from the question of how this harm might be undone again, and he turns to the courts for its sake; for the present this maintains our abominable penal codes, with their shopkeeper's scales and the desire to balance guilt and punishment. But shouldn't we be able to get beyond this? How relieved the general feeling of life would be if, together with the belief in guilt, we could also get rid of the ancient instinct of revenge, and if we even considered it a fine cleverness in a happy person to pronounce a blessing over his enemies, with Christianity, and if we benefited those who had offended us. Let us remove the concept of sin from the world—and let us soon send the concept of punishment after it. May these banished monsters live somewhere else henceforth, not among men, if they insist on living at all and do not perish of their own disgust.

Meanwhile let us consider that the loss which society and individuals suffer from the criminal is just like the loss they suffer from the sick: the sick spread worry and discontent; they do not produce but consume the earnings of others; they require wardens, physicians, and amusement; and they live on the time and energy of the healthy. Nevertheless one would now designate as inhuman anyone who for these reasons would want to avenge himself against the sick. Formerly, to be sure, this was done; in crude stages of civilization, and even now among some savage peoples, the sick are, in fact, treated as criminals, as a danger to the community, and as the dwelling of some demonic being which has entered them in consequence of some guilt: every sick person is a guilty person. And we—shouldn't we be mature enough for the opposite view? Shouldn't we be able to say: every "guilty" person is a sick person?

No, the hour for that has not yet come. The physicians are still lacking, above all, for whom what we have hitherto called practical morality must be transformed into a piece of their art and science of therapy; as yet, that hungry interest in these things is lacking, but some day it may appear in a manner not unlike the storm and stress of those old religious agitations;

as yet, the churches are not in the hands of the promoters of health; as yet, to teach about the body and the diet is not one of the obligations of all lower and higher schools; as yet, there are no quiet organizations of those who have accepted the common obligation to renounce the help of courts and punishment and revenge against their evildoers; as yet, no thinker has had the courage to measure the health of a society and of individuals by the number of parasites they can stand. . . .

[205]

Of the people of Israel. Among the spectacles to which the next century invites us is the decision on the fate of the European Jews. . . . Every Jew has in the history of his fathers and grandfathers a mine of examples of the coldest composure and steadfastness in terrible situations. . . .

There has been an effort to make them contemptible by treating them contemptibly for two thousand years and by barring them from access to all honors and everything honorable, thus pushing them that much deeper into the dirtier trades; and under this procedure they have certainly not become cleaner. But contemptible? They themselves have never ceased to believe in their calling to the highest things, and the virtues of all who suffer have never ceased to adorn them. The way in which they honor their fathers and their children and the rationality of their marriages and marital customs distinguish them above all Europeans. In addition, they knew how to create for themselves a feeling of power and eternal revenge out of those very trades which were abandoned to them (or to which they were abandoned); one must say, in excuse even of their usury, that without this occasional, agreeable, and useful torture of their despisers they could scarcely have persevered so long in respecting themselves. For our self-respect depends on our ability to repay the good as well as the bad. Moreover, their revenge does not easily push them too far; for they all have that free-mindedness, of the soul too, to which frequent change of location, of climate, and of the customs of neighbors and oppressors educates man. . . .

And where shall this wealth of accumulated great impressions, which Jewish history constitutes for every Jewish family, this wealth of passions, virtues, decisions, renunciations, fights, and victories of all kinds— where shall it flow, if not eventually into great spiritual men and works? Then, when the Jews can point to such gems and golden vessels as their work, such as the European peoples with their shorter and less deep experience cannot produce and never could; when Israel will have transformed its eternal revenge into an eternal blessing for Europe; then that seventh day will come once again on which the ancient Jewish god may rejoice in himself, his creation, and his chosen people— and all of us, all of us want to rejoice with him!

[206]

The impossible class. Poor, gay, and independent— that is possible together. Poor, gay, and a slave—that is possible too. And I would not know what better to say to the workers in factory slavery—provided they do not consider it altogether shameful to be used up as they are, like the gears of a machine, and in a sense as stopgaps of human inventiveness.

Phew! to believe that higher pay could abolish the *essence* of their misery—I mean their impersonal serfdom! Phew! to be talked into thinking that an increase in this impersonality, within the machinelike workings of a new society, could transform the shame of slavery into a virtue! Phew! to have a price for which one remains a person no longer but becomes a gear!

Are you co-conspirators in the current folly of nations, who want above all to produce as much as possible and to be as rich as possible? It would be your affair to present them with the counter-calculation: what vast sums of *inner* worth are thrown away for such an external goal. But where is your inner worth when you no longer know what it means to breathe freely? when you no longer have the slightest control over yourselves? when you all too frequently become sick of yourselves, as of a stale drink? when you listen to the newspapers and leer at your rich neighbor, made lustful by the rapid rise and fall of power, money, and opinions? when you no longer have any faith in philosophy, which wears rags, and in the candor of those who have no wants? when the voluntary idyllic life of poverty, without occupation or marriage, which might well suit the more spiritual among you, has become a laughingstock to you? Do your ears ring from the pipes of the socialistic pied pipers, who want to make you wanton with mad hopes? who bid you be *prepared* and nothing else, prepared from today to tomorrow so that you wait and wait for something from the outside, and live in every other respect as you have lived before—until this waiting turns into hunger and thirst and fever and madness, and finally the day of the *bestia triumphans* rises in all its glory?

Against all this, everyone should think in his heart: Sooner emigrate and in savage fresh regions seek to become *master* of the world, and above all master of myself; keep changing location as long as a single sign of slavery still beckons to me; not avoid adventure and war and be prepared for death if the worst accidents befall—but no more of this indecent serfdom, no more of this becoming sour and poisonous and conspiratorial! This would be the right state of mind: the workers in Europe should declare that henceforth *as a class* they are a human impossibility, and not only, as is customary, a harsh and purposeless establishment. They should introduce an era of a vast swarming out from the European beehive, the like of which has never been experienced, and with this act of emigration in the grand manner protest against the machine, against capital, and against the choice with which they are now threatened, of becoming *of necessity* either slaves of the state or slaves of a revolutionary party. Let Europe relieve itself of the fourth part of its inhabitants! . . . What at home began to degenerate into dangerous discontent and criminal tendencies will, once outside, gain a wild and beautiful naturalness and be called heroism. . . .

[297]

Corruption. The surest way to corrupt a youth is to instruct him to hold in higher esteem those who think alike than those who think differently.

[556]

The good four. Honest with ourselves and with whatever is friend to us; *courageous* toward the enemy; *generous* toward the vanquished; *polite*—always: that is how the four cardinal virtues want us.

[557]

Against an enemy. How good bad music and bad reasons sound when one marches against an enemy!

[573]

Shedding one's skin. The snake that cannot shed its skin perishes. So do the spirits who are prevented from changing their opinons; they cease to be spirit.

POSTCARD TO OVERBECK

(Sils Maria, July 30, 1881)

I am utterly amazed, utterly enchanted. I have a *precursor,* and what a precursor! I hardly knew Spinoza: that I should have turned to him just *now,* was inspired by "instinct." Not only is his over-all tendency like mine—making knowledge the *most powerful* affect —but in five main points of his doctrine I recognize myself; this most unusual and loneliest thinker is closest to me precisely in these matters: he denies the freedom of the will, teleology, the moral world order, the unegoistic, and evil. Even though the divergencies are admittedly tremendous, they are due more to the difference in time, culture, and science. *In summa:* my lonesomeness, which, as on very high mountains, often made it hard for me to breathe and made my blood rush out, is now at least a twosomeness. Strange.

Incidentally, I am not at all as well as I had hoped. Exceptional weather here too. Eternal change of atmospheric conditions—that will yet drive me out of Europe. I must have *clear* skies *for months,* else I get nowhere. Already six severe attacks of two or three days each. With affectionate love, your friend.

FROM
The Gay Science

EDITOR'S NOTE

Nietzsche's last really aphoristic work, first published in
1882. The title in the English collected edition, *Joyful
Wisdom*, is a mistranslation. Aphorisms 285 and 341 are
among the first statements of the "eternal recurrence."

[4]

What preserves the species. The strongest and most
evil spirits have so far advanced humanity the most:
they have always rekindled the drowsing passions—all
ordered society puts the passions to sleep; they have
always reawakened the sense of comparison, of contradiction, of joy in the new, the daring, and the untried;
they force men to meet opinion with opinion, model with
model. For the most part by arms, by the overthrow of
boundary stones, and by offense to the pieties, but also
by new religions and moralities. The same "malice" is
to be found in every teacher and preacher of the
new. . . . The new is always *the evil*, as that which
wants to conquer, to overthrow the old boundary stones
and the old pieties; and only the old is the good. The
good men of every age are those who dig the old ideas
deep down and bear fruit with them, the husbandmen
of the spirit. But all land is finally exhausted, and the
plow of evil must always return.

There is a fundamentally erroneous doctrine in contemporary morality, celebrated particularly in England:

according to this, the judgments "good" and "evil" are condensations of the experiences concerning "expedient" and "inexpedient"; what is called good preserves the species, while what is called evil is harmful to the species. In truth, however, the evil urges are expedient and indispensable and preserve the species to as high a degree as the good ones—only their function is different.

[7]

Something for the industrious. . . . So far, everything that has given color to existence still lacks a history: or, where could one find a history of love, of avarice, of envy, of conscience, of piety, or of cruelty? Even a comparative history of law, or merely of punishment, is completely lacking so far. Has anyone yet conducted research into the different ways of dividing the day and the consequences of a regular arrangement of work, holiday, and rest? Does one know the moral effects of food? Is there a philosophy of nourishment? (The ever-renewed clamor for and against vegetarianism is sufficient proof that there is no such philosophy as yet.) Have the experiences of living together been assembled; for example, the experiences in the monasteries? Has the dialectic of marriage and friendship been presented as yet? . . .

[34]

Historia abscondita. Every great human being has a retroactive force: all history is again placed in the scales for his sake, and a thousand secrets of the past crawl out of their hideouts—into *his* sun. There is no way of telling what may yet become history some day. Perhaps the past is still essentially undiscovered! So many retroactive forces are still required!

[125]

The Madman. Have you not heard of that madman
who lit a lantern in the bright morning hours, ran to
the market place, and cried incessantly, "I seek God!
I seek God!" As many of those who do not believe in
God were standing around just then, he provoked much
laughter. Why, did he get lost? said one. Did he lose
his way like a child? said another. Or is he hiding? Is
he afraid of us? Has he gone on a voyage? or emigrated?
Thus they yelled and laughed. The madman jumped
into their midst and pierced them with his glances.

"Whither is God" he cried. "I shall tell you. *We have
killed him*—you and I. All of us are his murderers.
But how have we done this? How were we able to
drink up the sea? Who gave us the sponge to wipe
away the entire horizon? What did we do when we
unchained this earth from its sun? Whither is it moving
now? Whither are we moving now? Away from all
suns? Are we not plunging continually? Backward, side-
ward, forward, in all directions? Is there any up or
down left? Are we not straying as through an infinite
nothing? Do we not feel the breath of empty space?
Has it not become colder? Is not night and more night
coming on all the while? Must not lanterns be lit in the
morning? Do we not hear anything yet of the noise
of the gravediggers who are burying God? Do we not
smell anything yet of God's decomposition? Gods too
decompose. God is dead. God remains dead. And we
have killed him. How shall we, the murderers of all
murderers, comfort ourselves? What was holiest and
most powerful of all that the world has yet owned has
bled to death under our knives. Who will wipe this
blood off us? What water is there for us to clean

ourselves? What festivals of atonement, what sacred games shall we have to invent? Is not the greatness of this deed too great for us? Must not we ourselves become gods simply to seem worthy of it? There has never been a greater deed; and whoever will be born after us—for the sake of this deed he will be part of a higher history than all history hitherto."

Here the madman fell silent and looked again at his listeners; and they too were silent and stared at him in astonishment. At last he threw his lantern on the ground, and it broke and went out. "I come too early," he said then; "my time has not come yet. This tremendous event is still on its way, still wandering—it has not yet reached the ears of man. Lightning and thunder require time, the light of the stars requires time, deeds require time even after they are done, before they can be seen and heard. This deed is still more distant from them than the most distant stars— *and yet they have done it themselves.*"

It has been related further that on that same day the madman entered divers churches and there sang his *requiem aeternam deo.* Led out and called to account, he is said to have replied each time, "What are these churches now if they are not the tombs and sepulchers of God?"

[193]

Kant's joke. Kant wanted to prove in a way that would dumfound the common man that the common man was right: that was the secret joke of this soul. He wrote against the scholars in favor of the popular prejudice, but for scholars and not popularly.

[250]

Guilt. Although the most acute judges of the witches, and even the witches themselves, were convinced of the guilt of witchery, the guilt nevertheless was nonexistent. It is thus with all guilt.

[283]

Preparatory men. I welcome all signs that a more manly, a warlike, age is about to begin, an age which, above all, will give honor to valor once again. For this age shall prepare the way for one yet higher, and it shall gather the strength which this higher age will need one day—this age which is to carry heroism into the pursuit of knowledge and *wage wars* for the sake of thoughts and their consequences. To this end we now need many preparatory valorous men who cannot leap into being out of nothing—any more than out of the sand and slime of our present civilization and metropolitanism: men who are bent on seeking for that aspect in all things which must be *overcome;* men characterized by cheerfulness, patience, unpretentiousness, and contempt for all great vanities, as well as by magnanimity in victory and forbearance regarding the small vanities of the vanquished; men possessed of keen and free judgment concerning all victors and the share of chance in every victory and every fame; men who have their own festivals, their own weekdays, their own periods of mourning, who are accustomed to command with assurance and are no less ready to obey when necessary, in both cases equally proud and serving their own cause; men who are in greater danger, more fruitful, and happier! For, believe me, the secret of the greatest fruitfulness and the greatest enjoyment of existence is: to *live dangerously!* Build your cities under Vesuvius! Send your ships into uncharted seas! Live at war with your peers and yourselves! Be robbers and conquerors, as long as you cannot be rulers and owners, you lovers of knowledge! Soon the age will be past when you could be satisfied to live like shy deer, hidden in the woods! At long last the pursuit of knowledge will reach out for its due: it will want to *rule* and *own*, and you with it!

[285]

Excelsior! "You will never pray again, never adore again, never again rest in endless trust; you deny yourself any stopping before ultimate wisdom, ultimate goodness, ultimate power, while unharnessing your thoughts; you have no perpetual guardian and friend for your seven solitudes; you live without a view of mountains with snow on their peaks and fire in their hearts; there is no avenger for you, no eventual improver; there is no reason any more in what happens, no love in what will happen to you; no resting place is any longer open to your heart, where it has only to find and no longer to seek; you resist any ultimate peace, you want the eternal recurrence of war and peace. Man of renunciation, do you want to renounce all this? Who will give you the necessary strength? Nobody yet has had this strength." There is a lake which one day refused to flow off and erected a dam where it had hitherto flowed off: ever since, this lake has been rising higher and higher. Perhaps that very renunciation will also lend us the strength to bear the renunciation itself; perhaps man will rise ever higher when he once ceases to *flow out* into a god.

[290]

One thing is needful. "Giving style" to one's character—a great and rare art! It is exercised by those who see all the strengths and weaknesses of their own natures and then comprehend them in an artistic plan

until everything appears as art and reason and even
weakness delights the eye. Here a large mass of second
nature has been added; there a piece of original nature
has been removed: both by long practice and daily labor. Here the ugly which could not be removed is
hidden; there it has been reinterpreted and made sublime. . . . It will be the strong and domineering natures who enjoy their finest gaiety in such compulsion,
in such constraint and perfection under a law of their
own; the passion of their tremendous will relents when
confronted with stylized, conquered, and serving nature; even when they have to build palaces and lay
out gardens, they demur at giving nature a free hand.
Conversely, it is the weak characters without power
over themselves who *hate* the constraint of style. . . .
They become slaves as soon as they serve; they hate to
serve. Such spirits—and they may be of the first rank
—are always out to interpret themselves and their environment as *free* nature—wild, arbitrary, fantastic,
disorderly, astonishing; and they do well because only
in this way do they please themselves. For one thing
is needful: that a human being attain his satisfaction
with himself—whether it be by this or by that poetry
and art; only then is a human being at all tolerable to
behold. Whoever is dissatisfied with himself is always
ready to revenge himself therefor; we others will be his
victims, if only by always having to stand his ugly
sight. For the sight of the ugly makes men bad and
gloomy.

[310]

Will and wave. How greedily this wave approaches,
as if there were some objective to be reached! How,
with awe-inspiring haste, it crawls into the inmost

nooks of the rocky cliff! It seems that it wants to antici-
pate somebody; it seems that something is hidden
there, something of value, high value.

And now it comes back, a little more slowly, still
quite white with excitement—is it disappointed? But
already another wave is approaching, still greedier and
wilder than the first, and its soul too seems to be full of
secrets and the lust to dig up treasures. Thus live the
waves—thus live we who will—more I shall not say.

So? You mistrust me? You are angry with me, you
beautiful monsters? Are you afraid that I might betray
your secret entirely? Well, then be angry with me!
Raise your dangerous green bodies as high as you can!
Make a wall between me and the sun—as you do now!
Verily, even now nothing is left of the world but green
dusk and green lightning flashes. Carry on as you please,
you pranksters; roar with delight and malice—or dive
again, pouring your emeralds into the deepest depths,
and cast your endless white manes of foam and spray
over them—everything suits me, for everything suits
you so well, and I am so well disposed toward you for
everything: how could I think of betraying *you!* For—
heed it well!—I know you and your secret, I know
your kind! You and I—are we not of one kind? You
and I—do we not have *one* secret?

[319]

As interpreters of our experiences. A kind of honesty
has been alien to all founders of religions and others
like them: they have never made their experiences a
matter of conscience for knowledge. "What did I really
experience? What happened in me then, and around
me? Was my reason bright enough? Was my will
turned against all deceptions of the senses and was it
courageous in its resistance to the fantastic?"—none of

them has raised such questions; all the dear religious
people still do not raise such questions even now:
rather, they have a thirst for things that are *against
reason,* and they do not want to make it too hard for
themselves to satisfy it. And so they experience "mira-
cles" and "rebirths" and hear the voices of the little
angels! We, however, we others, who thirst for reason,
want to look our experiences as straight in the eye as
if they represented a scientific experiment, hour after
hour, day after day. We ourselves want to be our experiments and guinea pigs.

[340]

The dying Socrates. I admire the courage and wisdom of Socrates in everything he did, said—and did
not say. This mocking and enamored monster and pied
piper of Athens, who made the most arrogant youths
tremble and sob, was not only the wisest talker who
ever lived: he was just as great in his silence. . . .

[341]

The greatest stress. How, if some day or night a
demon were to sneak after you into your loneliest
loneliness and say to you, "This life as you now live it
and have lived it, you will have to live once more and
innumerable times more; and there will be nothing new
in it, but every pain and every joy and every thought
and sigh and everything immeasurably small or great
in your life must return to you—all in the same succession and sequence—even this spider and this moonlight between the trees, and even this moment and I
myself. The eternal hourglass of existence is turned
over and over, and you with it, a dust grain of dust."
Would you not throw yourself down and gnash your
teeth and curse the demon who spoke thus? Or did you

once experience a tremendous moment when you would have answered him, "You are a god, and never have I heard anything more godly." If this thought were to gain possession of you, it would change you, as you are, or perhaps crush you. The question in each and every thing, "Do you want this once more and innumerable times more?" would weigh upon your actions as the greatest stress. Or how well disposed would you have to become to yourself and to life to *crave nothing more fervently* than this ultimate eternal confirmation and seal?

DRAFT OF A LETTER TO PAUL RÉE

(1882)

. . . She told me herself that she had no morality—and I thought she had, like myself, a more severe morality than anybody. . . .

THUS SPOKE ZARATHUSTRA
A BOOK FOR ALL AND NONE

EDITOR'S PREFACE

Zarathustra is by far Nietzsche's most popular book, but
Nietzsche himself never witnessed its success. The first
three parts, each composed in about ten days, were at first
published separately, and scarcely sold at all. Of Part Four,
Nietzsche had only a few copies printed privately; and the
first public edition was held up at the last moment in 1891
when his family feared that it would be confiscated on a
charge of blasphemy. By then Nietzsche was insane and
unaware of what was happening. Part Four appeared in
1892, and it was not confiscated. The first edition of the
whole work followed not long after.

Zarathustra is as different from its reputation as its author
is different from the widely reproduced busts and pictures
commissioned by his sister. Her grandiose conception of
the heroic strikes us as childish and has provoked the reaction, understandably enough, that Nietzsche was really a
mere *petit rentier*. But perhaps there are more kinds of
valor than are dreamed of by most of Nietzsche's admirers
and detractors. And the most important single clue to
Zarathustra is that it is the work of an utterly lonely man.

He is shy, about five-foot-eight, but a little stooped, almost blind, reserved, unaffected, and especially polite; he
lives in modest boarding houses in Sils Maria, Nizza, Mentone, Rome, Turin. This is how Stefan Zweig brings him to

life for us: "Carefully the myopic man sits down to a table; carefully, the man with the sensitive stomach considers every item on the menu: whether the tea is not too strong, the food not spiced too much, for every mistake in his diet upsets his sensitive digestion, and every transgression in his nourishment wreaks havoc with his quivering nerves for days. No glass of wine, no glass of beer, no alcohol, no coffee at his place, no cigar and no cigarette after his meal, nothing that stimulates, refreshes, or rests him: only the short meager meal and a little urbane, unprofound conversation in a soft voice with an occasional neighbor (as a man speaks who for years has been unused to talking and is afraid of being asked too much).

"And up again into the small, narrow, modest, coldly furnished *chambre garnie,* where innumerable notes, pages, writings, and proofs are piled up on the table, but no flower, no decoration, scarcely a book and rarely a letter. Back in a corner, a heavy and graceless wooden trunk, his only possession, with the two shirts and the other worn suit. Otherwise only books and manuscripts, and on a tray innumerable bottles and jars and potions: against the migraines, which often render him all but senseless for hours, against his stomach cramps, against spasmodic vomiting, against the slothful intestines, and above all the dreadful sedatives against his insomnia, chloral hydrate and Veronal. A frightful arsenal of poisons and drugs, yet the only helpers in the empty silence of this strange room in which he never rests except in brief and artificially conquered sleep. Wrapped in his overcoat and a woolen scarf (for the wretched stove smokes only and does not give warmth), his fingers freezing, his double glasses pressed close to the paper, his hurried hand writes for hours— words the dim eyes can hardly decipher. For hours he sits like this and writes until his eyes burn."

That is the framework, which changes little wherever he is. But his letters seem to reveal another dimension, for at times they are shrill and strange and remind us of his vitriolic remark about Jesus: it is regrettable that no Dostoevski lived near him. Who else could do justice to this weird, paradoxical personality? Yet the clue to these letters, as also to *Zarathustra* and some of the last books, is that they are the work of a thoroughly lonely man. Sometimes they are really less letters than fantastic fragments out of the soul's dialogue with itself. Now pleasant and polite, now such that arrogance is far too mild a word—and yet his feeling of his own importance, painfully pronounced even in some very early letters, was of course not as insane as it must have appeared at times to those to whom he wrote. Resigned that those surrounding him had no idea who he was, and invariably kind to his social and intellectual inferiors, he sometimes felt doubly hurt that those who ought to have understood him really had less respect for him than his most casual acquaintances. Book after book—and either no response, or some kind words, which were far more unkind than any serious criticism, or even good advice, or pity, worst of all. Is it surprising that on rare occasions, when he was sufficiently provoked, we find appeals to his old-fashioned sense of honor, even his brief military service, and at one point the idea that he must challenge a man to a duel with pistols? For that matter, he once wrote a close friend: "The barrel of a pistol is for me at the moment a source of relatively agreeable thoughts."

Then there are his several hasty proposals of marriage, apparently followed by a real sense of relief when the suggestion was refused politely. The proposals may seem quite fantastic, the more so because, except in the case of Lou Salomé, no really deep feelings were involved. But a few times he was desperate enough to grasp at any possibility at all of rescue from the sea of his solitude.

In his letters these dramatic outbursts are relatively exceptional. But the histrionics of *Zarathustra* should be seen in the same light. For impulses that others vent upon their wives or friends, or at a party, perhaps over drinks, Nietzsche had no other outlet. In Nizza, where he wrote Part Three of *Zarathustra*, he met a young man, Dr. Paneth, who had read the published portion and was eager to talk with the author. On December 26, 1883, Paneth wrote home: "There is not a trace of false pathos or the prophet's pose in him, as I had rather feared after his last work. Instead his manner is completely inoffensive and natural. We began a very banal conversation about the climate, living accommodations, and the like. Then he told me, but without the least affectation or conceit, that he always felt himself to have a task and that now, as far as his eyes would permit it, he wanted to get out of himself and work up whatever might be in him."

We might wish that he had taken out his histrionics on Paneth and spared us some of the melodrama in *Zarathustra*. In places, of course, the writing is superb and only a pedant could prefer a drabber style. But often painfully adolescent emotions distract our attention from ideas that we cannot dismiss as immature at all. For that matter, adolescence is not simply immaturity; it also marks a breakdown of communication, a failure in human relations, and generally the first deep taste of solitude. And what we find again and again in *Zarathustra* are the typical emotions with which a boy tries to compensate himself.

Nietzsche's apparent blindness to these faults and his extravagant praise of the book in some of his last works are understandable. His condition had become even more unbearable as time went on; and we should also keep in mind not only the complete failure of the book to elicit any adequate response or understanding, but also the frantic sense of inspiration which had marked the rapid writing of the first three parts. Moreover, others find far lesser obstacles sufficient excuse for creating nothing. Nietzsche had every reason for not writing anything—the doctors, for example, told him not to use his eyes for any length of time, and he often wrote for ten hours at a time—and fashioned work on work, making his suffering and his torments the occasion for new insights.

After all has been said, *Zarathustra* still cries out to be blue-penciled; and if it were more compact, it would be more lucid too. Even so, there are few works to match its wealth of ideas, the abundance of profound suggestions, the epigrams, the wit. What distinguishes *Zarathustra* is the profusion of "sapphires in the mud." But what the book loses artistically and philosophically by never having been critically edited by its author, it gains as a uniquely personal record.

In a passage that is quoted again as the motto of Part Three, Zarathustra asks: "Who among you can laugh and be elevated at the same time?" The fusion of seriousness and satire, pathos and pun, is as characteristic of the message as it is of the style of the book. This modern blend of the sublime and the ridiculous places the work somewhere between the Second Part of *Faust* and Joyce's *Ulysses*— both of which, after all, might also have profited from further editing—and it helps to account for Nietzsche's admiration for Heine.

This overflowing sense of humor, which prefers even a poor joke to no joke at all, runs counter to the popular images of Nietzsche—not only to the grim creation of his sister, but also to the piteous portrait of Stefan Zweig, who was, in this respect, still too much under the influence of Bertram's *Nietzsche: Attempt at a Mythology*. Nietzsche had the sense of humor which Stefan George and his minions, very much including Bertram, lacked; and if Zarathustra occasionally excels George's austere prophetic affectation, he soon laughs at his own failings and punctures his pathos, like Heine, whom George hated. The puncture, however, does not give the impression of diffident self-consciousness and a morbid fear of self-betrayal, but rather of that Dionysian exuberance which *Zarathustra* celebrates.

Nietzsche's fate in the English-speaking world has been rather unkind, in spite of, or perhaps even in some measure because of, the ebullient enthusiasm of some of the early English and American Nietzscheans. He has rarely been accorded that perceptive understanding which is relatively common among the French. And when we look back today, one of the main reasons must be sought in the inadequacies of some of the early translations, particularly of *Zarathustra*. For one thing, they completely misrepresent the mood of the original—beginning, but unfortunately not ending, with their many unjustified archaisms, their "thou" and "ye" with the clumsy attendant verb forms, and their whole misguided effort to approximate the King James Bible. As if Zarathustra's attacks on the spirit of gravity and his praise of "light feet" were not among the leitmotifs of the book! In fact, this alone makes the work bearable.

To be sure, *Zarathustra* abounds in allusions to the Bible, most of them highly irreverent, but just these have been missed for the most part by Thomas Common. His version, nevertheless, was considered a sufficient improvement over Alexander Tille's earlier attempt to merit inclusion in the "Authorized English Translation of the Complete Works"; and while some of Common's other efforts were supplanted by slightly better translations, his *Zarathustra* survived, *faute de mieux*. For that matter, the book comes close to being untranslatable.

What is one to do with Nietzsche's constant plays on words? Say, *in der rechten Wissen-Gewissenschaft gibt es nichts grosses und nichts kleines*. This can probably be salvaged only for the eye, not for the ear, with "the conscience of science." But then almost anything would be better than Common's "true knowing-knowledge." Such passages, and there are many, make us wonder whether he had little German and less English. More often than not, he either overlooks a play on words or misunderstands it, and in both cases makes nonsense of Nietzsche. What is the point, to give a final example, of Nietzsche's derision of German writing, once "plain language" is substituted for "German"? One can sympathize with the translator, but one cannot understand or discuss Nietzsche on the basis of the versions hitherto available.

The problems encountered in translating *Zarathustra* are tremendous. Where Nietzsche does not deliberately bypass idioms in favor of coinages, he makes fun of them—now by taking them literally, then again by varying them slightly. Here too he is a dedicated enemy of all convention, intent on exposing the stupidity and arbitrariness of custom. This linguistic iconoclasm greatly impressed Christian Morgenstern and helped to inspire his celebrated *Galgenlieder*, in which similar aims are pursued more systematically.

Nietzsche, like Morgenstern a generation later, even creates a new animal when he speaks of *Pöbel-Schwind-hunde*. *Windhund* means greyhound but, more to the point, is often used to designate a person without brains or character. Yet *Wind*, the wind, is celebrated in this passage, and so the first part of the animal's name had to be varied to underline the opprobrium. What kind of animal should the translator create? A weathercock is the same sort of person as a *Windhund* (he turns with the wind) and permits the coinage of blether-cock. Hardly a major triumph, but few works of world literature can rival *Zarathustra* in its abundance of coinages, some of them clearly prompted by the feeling that the worst coinage is still better than the best cliché. And this lightheartedness is an essential aspect of Nietzsche.

Many of Nietzsche's plays on words are, of course, extremely suggestive. To give one example among scores, there is his play on *Eheschliessen, Ehebrechen, Ehe-biegen, Ehe-lügen*, in section 24 of "Old and New Tablets." Here the old translations did not even try, and it is surely scant compensation when Common gratuitously introduces, elsewhere in the book, "sumpter asses and assesses" or coins "baddest" in a passage in which Nietzsche says "most evil." In fact, Nietzsche devoted one-third of his *Genealogy of Morals* to his distinction between "bad" and "evil."

The poems in *Zarathustra* present a weird blend of passion and whimsy, but the difference between "Oh, everything human is strange" and "O human hubbub, thou wonderful thing!" in the hitherto standard translation is still considerable. Or consider the fate of two perfectly straightforward lines at the end of "The Song of Melancholy": "That I should banned be/From all the trueness!" And two chapters later Common gives us these lines:

How it, to a dance-girl, like,
Doth bow and bend and on its haunches bob,
—One doth it too, when one view'th it long!—

In fact, Common still doth it in the next chapter: "How it

bobbeth, the blessed one, the home-returning one, in its purple saddles!"

It may be ungracious, though hardly un-Nietzschean, to ridicule such faults. But in the English-speaking world, *Zarathustra* has been read, written about, and discussed for decades on the basis of such travesties, and most criticisms of the style have no relevance whatever to the original. A few thrusts at those who exposed Nietzsche to so many thrusts may therefore be defensible—in defense of Nietzsche.

For that matter, the new translation here offered certainly does not do justice to him either. Probably no translation could; and perhaps the faults of his predecessors are really a comfort to the translator who can ask to have his work compared with theirs as well as with the original. Or is the spirit of *Zarathustra* with its celebration of laughter contagious? After all, most of the plays on words have no ulterior motive whatever. Must we have a justification for laughing?

Much of what is most untranslatable is an expression of that *Übermut* which Nietzsche associates with the *Übermensch:* a lightness of mind, a prankish exuberance—though the term can also designate that overbearing which the Greeks called *hybris*. In any case, such plays on words must be kept in translation: how else is the reader to know which remarks are inspired primarily by the possibility of a pun or a daring rhyme? And robbed of its rapidly shifting style, clothed in archaic solemnity, *Zarathustra* would become a different work—like Faulkner done into the King's English. Nietzsche's writing, too, is occasionally downright bad, but at its best—superb.

The often elusive ideas of the book cannot be explained briefly, apart from the text. The editor's notes, however, which introduce each of the four parts, may facilitate a preliminary orientation, aid the reader in finding passages for which he may be looking, and provide a miniature commentary.

Only one of Zarathustra's notions shall be mentioned here: the eternal recurrence of the same events. In the plot this thought becomes more and more central as the work progresses, yet it is not an afterthought. Nietzsche himself, in *Ecce Homo,* called it "the basic conception of the work" which had struck him in August 1881; and, as a matter of fact, he first formulated it in *The Gay Science,* the book immediately preceding *Zarathustra.* As long as Nietzsche was misunderstood as a Darwinist who expected the improvement of the human race in the course of evolution, this conception was considered a stumbling block, and Nietzsche was gratuitously charged with gross self-contradiction. But Nietzsche himself rejected the evolutionary misinterpretation as the fabrication of "scholarly oxen." And while he was mistaken in believing that the eternal recurrence must be accepted as an ineluctable implication of impartial science, its personal meaning for him is expressed very well in *Ecce Homo,* in the sentence already cited, where he calls it the "highest formula of affirmation which is at all attainable." The eternal recurrence of his solitude and despair and of all the agonies of his tormented body! And yet it was not his own recurrence that he found hardest to accept, but that of the small man too. For the existence of paltriness and pettiness seemed meaningless even after he had succeeded in giving meaning to his own inherently meaningless suffering. Were not his work and his love of his work and his joy in it inseparable from his tortures? And man is capable of standing superhuman suffering if only he feels sure that there is some point and purpose to it, while much less pain will seem intolerable if devoid of meaning.

Zarathustra is not only a mine of ideas but also a major work of literature and a personal triumph.

Contents

Thus Spoke Zarathustra: First Part

EDITOR'S NOTE

Prologue: Zarathustra speaks of the death of God and proclaims the overman. Faith in God is dead as a matter of cultural fact, and any "meaning" of life in the sense of a supernatural purpose is gone. Now it is up to man to give his life meaning by raising himself above the animals and the all-too-human. What else is human nature but a euphemism for inertia, cultural conditioning, and what we are before we make something of ourselves? Our so-called human nature is precisely what we should do well to overcome; and the man who has overcome it Zarathustra calls the overman.

Shaw has popularized the ironic word "superman," which has since become associated with Nietzsche and the comics without ever losing its sarcastic tinge. In the present translation the older term, "overman," has been reinstated: it may help to bring out the close relation between Nietzsche's conceptions of the overman and self-overcoming, and to recapture something of his rhapsodical play on the words "over" and "under," particularly marked throughout the Prologue. Of the many "under" words, the German *untergehen* poses the greatest problem of translation: it is the ordinary word for the setting of the sun, and it also means "to perish"; but Nietzsche almost always uses it with the accent on "under"—either by way of echoing another "under" in the same sentence or, more often, by way of contrast with an "over" word, usually overman. Again and again, a smooth idiomatic translation would make nonsense of such passages, and "go under" seemed the least evil. After all, Zarathustra has no compunctions about worse linguistic sins.

"Over" words, some of them coinages, are common in this work, and *Übermensch* has to be understood in its context. *Mensch* means human being as opposed to animal, and what is called for is not a super-brute but a human being who has created for himself that unique

115

position in the cosmos which the Bible considered his divine birthright. The meaning of life is thus found on earth, in *this* life, not as the inevitable outcome of evolution, which might well give us the "last man" instead, but in the few human beings who raise themselves above the all-too-human mass. In the first edition the Prologue had the title "On the Overman and the Last Man." The latter invites comparison with Huxley's *Brave New World* and with Heidegger's famous discussion of *Das Man* in *Sein und Zeit*.

1. *On the Three Metamorphoses:* To become more than an all-too-human animal man must become a creator. But this involves a break with previous norms. Beethoven, for example, creates new norms with his works. Yet this break is constructive only when accomplished not by one who wants to make things easy for himself, but by one who has previously subjected himself to the discipline of tradition. First comes the beast of burden, then the defiant lion, then creation. "Parting from our cause when it triumphs"—as Nietzsche did when Wagner triumphed in Bayreuth.

2. *On the Teachers of Virtue:* Sunny sarcasm. Our traditional virtues consecrate stereotyped mediocrity and make for sound sleep. But where sleep is the goal, life lacks meaning. To bring out the full meaning of the blasphemous final sentence, it may be well to quote from Stefan Zweig's essay, "Friedrich Nietzsche," which is unsurpassed in its brief sketch of Nietzsche's way of life: "No devilish torture is lacking in this dreadful pandemonium of sickness: headaches, deafening, hammering headaches, which knock out the reeling Nietzsche for days and prostrate him on sofa and bed, stomach cramps with bloody vomiting, migraines, fevers, lack of appetite, weariness, hemorrhoids, constipation, chills, night sweat—a gruesome circle. In addition, there are his 'three-quarters blind eyes,' which, at the least exertion, begin immediately to swell and fill with tears and grant the intellectual worker only 'an hour and a half of vision a day.' But Nietzsche despises this hygiene

of his body and works at his desk for ten hours, and for this excess his overheated brain takes revenge with raging headaches and a nervous overcharge; at night, when the body has long become weary, it does not permit itself to be turned off suddenly, but continues to burrow in visions and ideas until it is forcibly knocked out by opiates. But ever greater quantities are needed (in two months Nietzsche uses up fifty grams of chloral hydrate to purchase this handful of sleep); then the stomach refuses to pay so high a price and rebels. And now—vicious circle—spasmodic vomiting, new headaches which require new medicines, an inexorable, insatiable, passionate conflict of the infuriated organs, which throw the thorny ball of suffering to each other as in a mad game. Never a point of rest in this up and down, never an even stretch of contentment or a short month full of comfort and self-forgetfulness." For Nietzsche, sleep was clearly not the end of life. Yet he could well say, "Blessed are the sleepy ones: for they shall soon drop off."

3. *On the Afterworldly:* A literal translation of "metaphysicians"; but Zarathustra takes issue with all who deprecate this world for the greater glory of another world. The passage about the "leap" may seem to be aimed at Kierkegaard—of whom Nietzsche, however, heard only in 1888, too late to acquaint himself with the ideas of the Dane.

4. *On the Despisers of the Body:* The psychological analysis begun in the previous chapter is here carried further. The use of the term "ego" influenced Freud, via Georg Groddeck.

5. *On Enjoying and Suffering the Passions (Von den Freuden- und Leidenschaften):* The passions, called evil because they are potentially destructive, can also be creatively employed and enjoyed. Unlike Kant, who had taught that "a collision of duties is unthinkable," Nietzsche knows that a passion for justice or honesty may frequently conflict with other virtues. But even if Rembrandt was torn between his dedication to his art and his devotion to his

family, who would wish that he had been less passionate
a painter or poorer in compassion?

6. *On the Pale Criminal:* Too abstract to make sense to
Nietzsche's first readers, including even his once close
friend Rohde, much of this chapter now seems like reflections on Dostoevski's Raskolnikov. But Nietzsche had not
yet discovered Dostoevski. And some of the psychological
insights offered here go beyond Dostoevski.

7. *On Reading and Writing:* Compulsory education for all
has lowered cultural standards; thinkers and writers have
come to think and write for the masses. References to
novelists and artists who end up in Hollywood are lacking
because Nietzsche died in 1900. The dance is to Nietzsche a
symbol of joy and levity, and the antithesis of gravity. He
associates it with Dionysus; but the Hindus too have a
dancing god, Shiva Nataraja—no less a contrast to the
three great monotheistic religions.

8. *On the Tree on the Mountainside:* Advice for adolescents.

9. *On the Preachers of Death:* An encounter with a sick
man, an old man, and a corpse is said to have prompted
the Buddha's departure from his father's palace. But
relentless work, too, can be sought as a narcotic and a
living death.

10. *On War and Warriors:* The "saints of knowledge" are
above "hatred and envy"; but those still seeking knowledge
must fight, must wage war, for their thoughts. Vanquished
in this contest, they may yet find cause for triumph in
the victory of truth. They must be like warriors: brave and
without consideration for the feelings of others. In this
context, "You should love peace as a means to new wars—
and the short peace more than the long," is surely far
from fascism; but the epigram invites quotation out of
context. The same applies to "the good war that hallows
any cause"; we revere Plato's *Republic* not for its cause
(which many of us believe to have been, at least in part,
totalitarianism), but because few men, if any, have ever
waged a more brilliant war for any cause.

Being able to coin better slogans for positions he detested than the men believing in them—and then using such phrases in an entirely different sense—seems to have given Nietzsche uncommon satisfaction. He felt that he was hitting right and left, and he was horrified when he found that the rightist parties began brazenly to use him. (For a more detailed discussion of this chapter, see my *Nietzsche,* Chapter 12, section VII.)

11. *On the New Idol:* A vehement denunciation of the state and of war in the literal sense. Straight anti-fascism, but not in the name of any rival political creed. In Nietzsche's own phrase: anti-political.

12. *On the Flies of the Market Place:* Against the mass and its idols. Inspired by the contrast of Bayreuth and Sils Maria, Wagner and Nietzsche. But today we are more apt to think of Hitler than of Wagner.

13. *On Chastity:* One man's virtue is another man's poison.

14. *On the Friend:* Nietzsche's extreme individualism is tempered by his development of the Greek conception of friendship.

15. *On the Thousand and One Goals:* Except for private notes, published much later, this chapter contains the first mention of the will to power. What is meant in this context is clearly power over self, and the phrase is taken up again in the chapter "On Self-Overcoming" in Part Two. The four historical examples are: Greeks, Persians, Jews, Germans. (For an analysis, see my *Nietzsche,* 6, III; for a discussion of "The Discovery of the Will to Power," the whole of Chapter 6.)

16. *On Love of the Neighbor:* Jesus said: "Ye have heard that it hath been said, Thou shalt love thy neighbor; and hate thine enemy. But I say unto you: Love your enemies." He took issue not with the old Mosaic commandment to love thy neighbor—that had never been coupled with any commandment to hate the enemy but had even been pointedly extended to include him—but with that comfortable state of mind which makes things easy for itself while

niding behind a façade of virtue. In this respect Nietzsche's polemic is profoundly similar to Jesus'. But, in the words of Zarathustra, he remains "faithful to the earth" and deprecates the shortcomings of mutual indulgence, while celebrating friendship between those who spur each other on toward man's perfection. (See my *Nietzsche*, 12, IV.)

17. *On the Way of the Creator:* Zarathustra does not preach universal anarchy: only the creator must break with ancient norms.

18. *On Little Old and Young Women:* The affectionate diminutive in the title (*Weiblein*) suggests at once what is the main difference between this chapter and its vitriolic prototype, Schopenhauer's essay *Von den Weibern:* a touch of humor. In Part Three, moreover, in "The Other Dancing Song," Nietzsche makes fun of the little old woman's dictum that concludes the present chapter. A photograph taken less than a year before he wrote Part One also supplies an amusing perspective. It shows Nietzsche and his friend Paul Rée (author of *Der Ursprung der moralischen Empfindungen*) pretending to pull a little cart on which Lou Salomé, then their mutual friend, is enthroned with a tiny whip. We have it on her authority that the picture was posed under Nietzsche's direction, and that he decorated the whip with flowers. But although Nietzsche should be defended against witless admirers and detractors, his remarks about women are surely, more often than not, second-hand and third-rate.

19. *On the Adder's Bite:* One might wish that the following lines were better known than the preceding chapter: "But if you have an enemy, do not requite him evil with good, for that would put him to shame. Rather prove that he did you some good. And rather be angry than put to shame. And if you are cursed, I do not like it that you want to bless. Rather join a little in the cursing." This should be compared with Paul's Epistle to the Romans, *12:14 ff.:* "Bless them which persecute you: bless, and curse not. . . . Avenge not yourselves, but give place unto wrath: for it is written, Vengeance is mine: I will repay,

saith the Lord. Therefore, if thine enemy hunger, feed him; if he thirst, give him drink: for in so doing thou shalt heap coals of fire on his head." Nietzsche's whole chapter is an attack on what he later called *ressentiment*. (See my *Nietzsche*, 12, V.)

20. *On Child and Marriage:* It may require careful reading to see that Nietzsche repudiates only certain kinds of pity and love of the neighbor, but in this chapter he makes a clear distinction indeed between the kind of marriage he opposes and the kind he would applaud.

21. *On Free Death:* A celebration of Socrates' way of dying as opposed to Jesus'. Nietzsche's own creeping death was to take eleven years to destroy his body after it had destroyed his mind.

22. *On the Gift-Giving Virtue:* The egoism of the powerful, whose happiness consists in giving, is contrasted with that of the weak. The core of the last section is quoted again in the Preface to *Ecce Homo*, late in 1888: Nietzsche wants no believers but, like Socrates, aims to help others to find themselves and surpass him.

Zarathustra's Prologue

1

When Zarathustra was thirty years old he left his home and the lake of his home and went into the mountains. Here he enjoyed his spirit and his solitude, and for ten years did not tire of it. But at last a change came over his heart, and one morning he rose with the dawn, stepped before the sun, and spoke to it thus:

"You great star, what would your happiness be had you not those for whom you shine?

"For ten years you have climbed to my cave: you would have tired of your light and of the journey had it not been for me and my eagle and my serpent.

"But we waited for you every morning, took your overflow from you, and blessed you for it.

"Behold, I am weary of my wisdom, like a bee that has gathered too much honey; I need hands outstretched to receive it.

"I would give away and distribute, until the wise among men find joy once again in their folly, and the poor in their riches.

"For that I must descend to the depths, as you do in the evening when you go behind the sea and still bring light to the underworld, you overrich star.

"Like you, I must *go under*—go down, as is said by man, to whom I want to descend.

"So bless me then, you quiet eye that can look even upon an all-too-great happiness without envy!

"Bless the cup that wants to overflow, that the water may flow from it golden and carry everywhere the reflection of your delight.

"Behold, this cup wants to become empty again, and Zarathustra wants to become man again."

Thus Zarathustra began to go under.

2

Zarathustra descended alone from the mountains, encountering no one. But when he came into the forest, all at once there stood before him an old man who had left his holy cottage to look for roots in the woods. And thus spoke the old man to Zarathustra:

"No stranger to me is this wanderer: many years ago he passed this way. Zarathustra he was called, but he has changed. At that time you carried your ashes to the mountains; would you now carry your fire into the valleys? Do you not fear to be punished as an arsonist?

"Yes, I recognize Zarathustra. His eyes are pure, and

around his mouth there hides no disgust. Does he not walk like a dancer?

"Zarathustra has changed, Zarathustra has become a child, Zarathustra is an awakened one; what do you now want among the sleepers? You lived in your solitude as in the sea, and the sea carried you. Alas, would you now climb ashore? Alas, would you again drag your own body?"

Zarathustra answered: "I love man."

"Why," asked the saint, "did I go into the forest and the desert? Was it not because I loved man all-too-much? Now I love God; man I love not. Man is for me too imperfect a thing. Love of man would kill me."

Zarathustra answered: "Did I speak of love? I bring men a gift."

"Give them nothing!" said the saint. "Rather, take part of their load and help them to bear it—that will be best for them, if only it does you good! And if you want to give them something, give no more than alms, and let them beg for that!"

"No," answered Zarathustra. "I give no alms. For that I am not poor enough."

The saint laughed at Zarathustra and spoke thus: "Then see to it that they accept your treasures. They are suspicious of hermits and do not believe that we come with gifts. Our steps sound too lonely through the streets. And what if at night, in their beds, they hear a man walk by long before the sun has risen— they probably ask themselves, Where is the thief going?

"Do not go to man. Stay in the forest! Go rather even to the animals! Why do you not want to be as I am—a bear among bears, a bird among birds?"

"And what is the saint doing in the forest?" asked Zarathustra.

The saint answered: "I make songs and sing them; and when I make songs, I laugh, cry, and hum: thus I praise God. With singing, crying, laughing, and humming, I praise the god who is my god. But what do you bring us as a gift?"

When Zarathustra had heard these words he bade the saint farewell and said: "What could I have to give you? But let me go quickly lest I take something from you!" And thus they separated, the old one and the man, laughing as two boys laugh.

But when Zarathustra was alone he spoke thus to his heart: "Could it be possible? This old saint in the forest has not yet heard anything of this, that *God is dead!*"

3

When Zarathustra came into the next town, which lies on the edge of the forest, he found many people gathered together in the market place; for it had been promised that there would be a tightrope walker. And Zarathustra spoke thus to the people:

"*I teach you the overman.* Man is something that shall be overcome. What have you done to overcome him?

"All beings so far have created something beyond themselves; and do you want to be the ebb of this great flood and even go back to the beasts rather than overcome man? What is the ape to man? A laughingstock or a painful embarrassment. And man shall be just that for the overman: a laughingstock or a painful embarrassment. You have made your way from worm to man, and much in you is still worm. Once you were apes, and even now, too, man is more ape than any ape.

"Whoever is the wisest among you is also a mere

conflict and cross between plant and ghost. But do I bid you become ghosts or plants?

"Behold, I teach you the overman. The overman is the meaning of the earth. Let your will say: the overman *shall be* the meaning of the earth! I beseech you, my brothers, *remain faithful to the earth*, and do not believe those who speak to you of otherworldly hopes! Poison-mixers are they, whether they know it or not. Despisers of life are they, decaying and poisoned themselves, of whom the earth is weary: so let them go.

"Once the sin against God was the greatest sin; but God died, and these sinners died with him. To sin against the earth is now the most dreadful thing, and to esteem the entrails of the unknowable higher than the meaning of the earth.

"Once the soul looked contemptuously upon the body, and then this contempt was the highest: she wanted the body meager, ghastly, and starved. Thus she hoped to escape it and the earth. Oh, this soul herself was still meager, ghastly, and starved: and cruelty was the lust of this soul. But you, too, my brothers, tell me: what does your body proclaim of your soul? Is not your soul poverty and filth and wretched contentment?

"Verily, a polluted stream is man. One must be a sea to be able to receive a polluted stream without becoming unclean. Behold, I teach you the overman: he is this sea; in him your great contempt can go under.

"What is the greatest experience you can have? It is the hour of the great contempt. The hour in which your happiness, too, arouses your disgust, and even your reason and your virtue.

"The hour when you say, 'What matters my happiness? It is poverty and filth and wretched contentment. But my happiness ought to justify existence itself.'

"The hour when you say, 'What matters my reason?

Does it crave knowledge as the lion his food? It is poverty and filth and wretched contentment.'

"The hour when you say, 'What matters my virtue? As yet it has not made me rage. How weary I am of my good and my evil! All that is poverty and filth and wretched contentment.'

"The hour when you say, 'What matters my justice? I do not see that I am flames and fuel. But the just are flames and fuel.'

"The hour when you say, 'What matters my pity? Is not pity the cross on which he is nailed who loves man? But my pity is no crucifixion.'

"Have you yet spoken thus? Have you yet cried thus? Oh, that I might have heard you cry thus!

"Not your sin but your thrift cries to heaven; your meanness even in your sin cries to heaven.

"Where is the lightning to lick you with its tongue? Where is the frenzy with which you should be inoculated?

"Behold, I teach you the overman: he is this lightning, he is this frenzy."

When Zarathustra had spoken thus, one of the people cried: "Now we have heard enough about the tightrope walker; now let us see him too!" And all the people laughed at Zarathustra. But the tightrope walker, believing that the word concerned him, began his performance.

4

Zarathustra, however, beheld the people and was amazed. Then he spoke thus:

"Man is a rope, tied between beast and overman—a rope over an abyss. A dangerous across, a dangerous on-the-way, a dangerous looking-back, a dangerous shuddering and stopping.

"What is great in man is that he is a bridge and not an end: what can be loved in man is that he is an *overture* and a *going under.*

"I love those who do not know how to live, except by going under, for they are those who cross over.

"I love the great despisers because they are the great reverers and arrows of longing for the other shore.

"I love those who do not first seek behind the stars for a reason to go under and be a sacrifice, but who sacrifice themselves for the earth, that the earth may some day become the overman's.

"I love him who lives to know, and who wants to know so that the overman may live some day. And thus he wants to go under.

"I love him who works and invents to build a house for the overman and to prepare earth, animal, and plant for him: for thus he wants to go under.

"I love him who loves his virtue, for virtue is the will to go under and an arrow of longing.

"I love him who does not hold back one drop of spirit for himself, but wants to be entirely the spirit of his virtue: thus he strides over the bridge as spirit.

"I love him who makes his virtue his addiction and his catastrophe: for his virtue's sake he wants to live on and to live no longer.

"I love him who does not want to have too many virtues. One virtue is more virtue than two, because it is more of a noose on which his catastrophe may hang.

"I love him whose soul squanders itself, who wants no thanks and returns none: for he always gives away and does not want to preserve himself.

"I love him who is abashed when the dice fall to make his fortune, and asks, 'Am I then a crooked gambler?' For he wants to perish.

"I love him who casts golden words before his deeds

and always does even more than he promises: for he wants to go under.

"I love him who justifies future and redeems past generations: for he wants to perish of the present.

"I love him who chastens his god because he loves his god: for he must perish of the wrath of his god.

"I love him whose soul is deep, even in being wounded, and who can perish of a small experience: thus he goes gladly over the bridge.

"I love him whose soul is overfull so that he forgets himself, and all things are in him: thus all things spell his going under.

"I love him who has a free spirit and a free heart: thus his head is only the entrails of his heart, but his heart drives him to go under.

"I love all those who are as heavy drops, falling one by one out of the dark cloud that hangs over men: they herald the advent of lightning, and, as heralds, they perish.

"Behold, I am a herald of the lightning and a heavy drop from the cloud; but this lightning is called *overman*."

5

When Zarathustra had spoken these words he beheld the people again and was silent. "There they stand," he said to his heart; "there they laugh. They do not understand me; I am not the mouth for these ears. Must one smash their ears before they learn to listen with their eyes? Must one clatter like kettledrums and preachers of repentance? Or do they believe only the stammerer?

"They have something of which they are proud. What do they call that which makes them proud? Education they call it; it distinguishes them from goatherds.

That is why they do not like to hear the word 'contempt' applied to them. Let me then address their pride. Let me speak to them of what is most contemptible: but that is the *last man*."

And thus spoke Zarathustra to the people: "The time has come for man to set himself a goal. The time has come for man to plant the seed of his highest hope. His soil is still rich enough. But one day this soil will be poor and domesticated, and no tall tree will be able to grow in it. Alas, the time is coming when man will no longer shoot the arrow of his longing beyond man, and the string of his bow will have forgotten how to whir!

"I say unto you: one must still have chaos in oneself to be able to give birth to a dancing star. I say unto you: you still have chaos in yourselves.

"Alas, the time is coming when man will no longer give birth to a star. Alas, the time of the most despicable man is coming, he that is no longer able to despise himself. Behold, I show you the *last man*.

" 'What is love? What is creation? What is longing? What is a star?' thus asks the last man, and he blinks.

"The earth has become small, and on it hops the last man, who makes everything small. His race is as ineradicable as the flea-beetle; the last man lives longest.

" 'We have invented happiness,' say the last men, and they blink. They have left the regions where it was hard to live, for one needs warmth. One still loves one's neighbor and rubs against him, for one needs warmth.

"Becoming sick and harboring suspicion are sinful to them: one proceeds carefully. A fool, whoever still stumbles over stones or human beings! A little poison now and then: that makes for agreeable dreams. And much poison in the end, for an agreeable death.

"One still works, for work is a form of entertainment. But one is careful lest the entertainment be too harrowing. One no longer becomes poor or rich: both require too much exertion. Who still wants to rule? Who obey? Both require too much exertion.

"No shepherd and one herd! Everybody wants the same, everybody is the same: whoever feels different goes voluntarily into a madhouse.

" 'Formerly, all the world was mad,' say the most refined, and they blink.

"One is clever and knows everything that has ever happened: so there is no end of derision. One still quarrels, but one is soon reconciled—else it might spoil the digestion.

"One has one's little pleasure for the day and one's little pleasure for the night: but one has a regard for health.

" 'We have invented happiness,' say the last men, and they blink."

And here ended Zarathustra's first speech, which is also called "the Prologue"; for at this point he was interrupted by the clamor and delight of the crowd. "Give us this last man, O Zarathustra," they shouted. "Turn us into these last men! Then we shall make you a gift of the overman!" And all the people jubilated and clucked with their tongues.

But Zarathustra became sad and said to his heart: "They do not understand me: I am not the mouth for these ears. I seem to have lived too long in the mountains; I listened too much to brooks and trees: now I talk to them as to goatherds. My soul is unmoved and bright as the mountains in the morning. But they think I am cold and I jeer and make dreadful jests. And now

they look at me and laugh: and as they laugh they
even hate me. There is ice in their laughter."

6

Then something happened that made every mouth
dumb and every eye rigid. For meanwhile the tightrope walker had begun his performance: he had
stepped out of a small door and was walking over the
rope, stretched between two towers and suspended
over the market place and the people. When he had
reached the exact middle of his course the small door
opened once more and a fellow in motley clothes, looking like a jester, jumped out and followed the first one
with quick steps.

"Forward, lamefoot!" he shouted in an awe-inspiring
voice. "Forward, lazybones, smuggler, pale-face, or I
shall tickle you with my heel! What are you doing here
between towers? The tower is where you belong. You
ought to be locked up; you block the way for one better than yourself." And with every word he came
closer and closer; but when he was but one step behind, the dreadful thing happened which made every
mouth dumb and every eye rigid: he uttered a devilish
cry and jumped over the man who stood in his way.
This man, however, seeing his rival win, lost his head
and the rope, tossed away his pole, and plunged into
the depth even faster, a whirlpool of arms and legs.
The market place became as the sea when a tempest
pierces it: the people rushed apart and over one another, especially at the place where the body must hit
the ground.

Zarathustra, however, did not move; and it was right
next to him that the body fell, badly maimed and disfigured, but not yet dead. After a while the shattered
man recovered consciousness and saw Zarathustra

kneeling beside him. "What are you doing here?" he asked at last. "I have long known that the devil would trip me. Now he will drag me to hell. Would you prevent him?"

"By my honor, friend," answered Zarathustra, "all that of which you speak does not exist: there is no devil and no hell. Your soul will be dead even before your body: fear nothing further."

The man looked up suspiciously. "If you speak the truth," he said, "I lose nothing when I lose my life. I am not much more than a beast that has been taught to dance by blows and a few meager morsels."

"By no means," said Zarathustra. "You have made danger your vocation; there is nothing contemptible in that. Now you perish of your vocation: for that I will bury you with my own hands."

When Zarathustra had said this, the dying man answered no more; but he moved his hand as if he sought Zarathustra's hand in thanks.

7

Meanwhile the evening came, and the market place hid in darkness. Then the people scattered, for even curiosity and terror grow weary. But Zarathustra sat on the ground near the dead man, and he was lost in thought, forgetting the time. At last night came, and a cold wind blew over the lonely one.

Then Zarathustra rose and said to his heart: "Verily, it is a beautiful catch of fish that Zarathustra has brought in today! Not a man has he caught but a corpse. Human existence is uncanny and still without meaning: a jester can become man's fatality. I will teach men the meaning of their existence—the overman, the lightning out of the dark cloud of man. But I am still far from them, and my sense does not speak to their senses. To men I am still the mean between a fool and a corpse.

"Dark is the night, dark are Zarathustra's ways. Come, cold, stiff companion! I shall carry you where I may bury you with my own hands."

8

When Zarathustra had said this to his heart he hoisted the corpse on his back and started on his way. And he had not taken a hundred steps when a man sneaked up to him and whispered in his ear—and behold, it was the jester from the tower. "Go away from this town, Zarathustra," said he; "there are too many here who hate you. You are hated by the good and the just, and they call you their enemy and despiser; you are hated by the believers in the true faith, and they call you the danger of the multitude. It was your good fortune that you were laughed at; and verily, you talked like a jester. It was your good fortune that you stooped to the dead dog; when you lowered yourself so far, you saved your own life for today. But go away from this town, or tomorrow I shall leap over you, one living over one dead." And when he had said this the man vanished; but Zarathustra went on through the dark lanes.

At the gate of the town he met the gravediggers; they shone their torches in his face, recognized Zarathustra, and mocked him. "Zarathustra carries off the dead dog: how nice that Zarathustra has become a gravedigger! For our hands are too clean for this roast. Would Zarathustra steal this bite from the devil? Well then, we wish you a good meal. If only the devil were not a better thief than Zarathustra: he will steal them both, he will gobble up both." And they laughed and put their heads together.

Zarathustra never said a word and went his way. When he had walked two hours, past forests and swamps, he heard so much of the hungry howling of the wolves that he himself felt hungry. So he stopped at a lonely house in which a light was burning.

"Like a robber, hunger overtakes me," said Zarathustra. "In forests and swamps my hunger overtakes me, and in the deep of night. My hunger is certainly capricious: often it comes to me only after a meal, and today it did not come all day; where could it have been?"

And at that Zarathustra knocked at the door of the house. An old man appeared, carrying the light, and asked: "Who is it that comes to me and to my bad sleep?"

"A living and a dead man," said Zarathustra. "Give me something to eat and to drink; I forgot about it during the day. He who feeds the hungry refreshes his own soul: thus speaks wisdom."

The old man went away, but returned shortly and offered Zarathustra bread and wine. "This is an evil region for the hungry," he said; "that is why I live here. Beast and man come to me, the hermit. But bid your companion, too, eat and drink; he is wearier than you are."

Zarathustra replied: "My companion is dead; I should hardly be able to persuade him."

"I don't care," said the old man peevishly. "Whoever knocks at my door must also take what I offer. Eat and be off!"

Thereupon Zarathustra walked another two hours, trusting the path and the light of the stars; for he was used to walking at night and he liked to look in the face of all that slept. But when the dawn came Zarathustra found himself in a deep forest, and he did not see a path anywhere. So he laid the dead man into a hollow tree—for he wanted to protect him from the wolves—and he himself lay down on the ground and the moss, his head under the tree. And soon he fell asleep, his body weary but his soul unmoved.

9

For a long time Zarathustra slept, and not only dawn passed over his face but the morning too. At last, however, his eyes opened: amazed, Zarathustra looked into the woods and the silence; amazed, he looked into himself. Then he rose quickly, like a seafarer who suddenly sees land, and jubilated, for he saw a new truth. And thus he spoke to his heart:

"An insight has come to me: companions I need, living ones—not dead companions and corpses whom I carry with myself wherever I want to. Living companions I need, who follow me because they want to follow themselves—wherever I want.

"An insight has come to me: let Zarathustra speak not to the people but to companions. Zarathustra shall not become the shepherd and dog of a herd.

"To lure many away from the herd, for that I have come. The people and the herd shall be angry with me: Zarathustra wants to be called a robber by the shepherds.

"Shepherds, I say; but they call themselves the good and the just. Shepherds, I say; but they call themselves believers in the true faith.

"Behold the good and the just! Whom do they hate most? The man who breaks their tables of values, the breaker, the lawbreaker; yet he is the creator.

"Behold the believers of all faiths! Whom do they

hate most? The man who breaks their tables of values, the breaker, the lawbreaker; yet he is the creator.

"Companions, the creator seeks, not corpses, not herds and believers. Fellow creators, the creator seeks —those who write new values on new tablets. Companions, the creator seeks, and fellow harvesters; for everything about him is ripe for the harvest. But he lacks a hundred sickles: so he plucks ears and is annoyed. Companions, the creator seeks, and such as know how to whet their sickles. Destroyers they will be called, and despisers of good and evil. But they are the harvesters and those who celebrate. Fellow creators, Zarathustra seeks, fellow harvesters and fellow celebrants: what are herds and shepherds and corpses to him?

"And you, my first companion, farewell! I buried you well in your hollow tree; I have hidden you well from the wolves. But I part from you; the time is up. Between dawn and dawn a new truth has come to me. No shepherd shall I be, nor gravedigger. Never again shall I speak to the people: for the last time have I spoken to the dead.

"I shall join the creators, the harvesters, the celebrants: I shall show them the rainbow and all the steps to the overman. To the hermits I shall sing my song, to the lonesome and the twosome; and whoever still has ears for the unheard-of—his heart shall become heavy with my happiness.

"To my goal I will go—on my own way; over those who hesitate and lag behind I shall leap. Thus let my going be their going under."

10

This is what Zarathustra had told his heart when the sun stood high at noon; then he looked into the air, questioning, for overhead he heard the sharp call of a bird. And behold! An eagle soared through the sky in wide circles, and on him there hung a serpent, not like prey but like a friend: for she kept herself wound around his neck.

"These are my animals," said Zarathustra and was happy in his heart. "The proudest animal under the sun and the wisest animal under the sun—they have gone out on a search. They want to determine whether Zarathustra is still alive. Verily, do I still live? I found life more dangerous among men than among animals; on dangerous paths walks Zarathustra. May my animals lead me!"

When Zarathustra had said this he recalled the words of the saint in the forest, sighed, and spoke thus to his heart: "That I might be wiser! That I might be wise through and through like my serpent! But there I ask the impossible: so I ask my pride that it always go along with my wisdom. And when my wisdom leaves me one day—alas, it loves to fly away—let my pride then fly with my folly."

Thus Zarathustra began to go under.

Zarathustra's Speeches

ON THE THREE METAMORPHOSES

Of three metamorphoses of the spirit I tell you: how the spirit becomes a camel; and the camel, a lion; and the lion, finally, a child.

There is much that is difficult for the spirit, the strong reverent spirit that would bear much: but the difficult and the most difficult are what its strength demands.

What is difficult? asks the spirit that would bear much, and kneels down like a camel wanting to be well loaded. What is most difficult, O heroes, asks the spirit that would bear much, that I may take it upon myself and exult in my strength? Is it not humbling oneself to wound one's haughtiness? Letting one's folly shine to mock one's wisdom?

Or is it this: parting from our cause when it triumphs? Climbing high mountains to tempt the tempter?

Or is it this: feeding on the acorns and grass of knowledge and, for the sake of the truth, suffering hunger in one's soul?

Or is it this: being sick and sending home the comforters and making friends with the deaf, who never hear what you want?

Or is it this: stepping into filthy waters when they are the waters of truth, and not repulsing cold frogs and hot toads?

Or is it this: loving those who despise us and offering a hand to the ghost that would frighten us?

All these most difficult things the spirit that would bear much takes upon itself: like the camel that, burdened, speeds into the desert, thus the spirit speeds into its desert.

In the loneliest desert, however, the second metamorphosis occurs: here the spirit becomes a lion who would conquer his freedom and be master in his own desert. Here he seeks out his last master: he wants to fight him and his last god; for ultimate victory he wants to fight with the great dragon.

Who is the great dragon whom the spirit will no longer call lord and god? "Thou shalt" is the name of the great dragon. But the spirit of the lion says, "I will." "Thou shalt" lies in his way, sparkling like gold, an animal covered with scales; and on every scale shines a golden "thou shalt."

Values, thousands of years old, shine on these scales; and thus speaks the mightiest of all dragons: "All value of all things shines on me. All value has long been created, and I am all created value. Verily, there shall be no more 'I will.'" Thus speaks the dragon.

My brothers, why is there a need in the spirit for the lion? Why is not the beast of burden, which renounces and is reverent, enough?

To create new values—that even the lion cannot do; but the creation of freedom for oneself for new creation—that is within the power of the lion. The creation of freedom for oneself and a sacred "No" even to duty—for that, my brothers, the lion is needed. To assume the right to new values—that is the most terrifying assumption for a reverent spirit that would bear much. Verily, to him it is preying, and a matter for a beast of prey. He once loved "thou shalt" as most sacred: now he must find illusion and caprice even in the most sacred, that freedom from his love may become his prey: the lion is needed for such prey.

But say, my brothers, what can the child do that even the lion could not do? Why must the preying lion still become a child? The child is innocence and forgetting, a new beginning, a game, a self-propelled wheel, a first movement, a sacred "Yes." For the game of creation, my brothers, a sacred "Yes" is needed: the spirit now wills his own will, and he who had been lost to the world now conquers his own world.

Of three metamorphoses of the spirit I have told you: how the spirit became a camel; and the camel, a lion; and the lion, finally, a child.

Thus spoke Zarathustra. And at that time he sojourned in the town that is called The Motley Cow.

ON THE TEACHERS OF VIRTUE

A sage was praised to Zarathustra for knowing how to speak well of sleep and of virtue: he was said to be honored and rewarded highly for this, and all the youths were said to be sitting at his feet. To him Zarathustra went, and he sat at his feet with all the youths. And thus spoke the sage:

"Honor sleep and be bashful before it—that first of all. And avoid all who sleep badly and stay awake at night. Even the thief is bashful before sleep: he always steals silently through the night. Shameless, however, is the watchman of the night; shamelessly he carries his horn.

"Sleeping is no mean art: for its sake one must stay awake all day. Ten times a day you must overcome yourself: that makes you good and tired and is opium for the soul. Ten times you must reconcile yourself again with yourself; for, overcoming is bitterness, and the unreconciled sleep badly. Ten truths a day you must find; else you will still be seeking truth by night, and your soul will remain hungry. Ten times a day you must laugh and be cheerful; else you will be disturbed at night by your stomach, this father of gloom.

"Few know it, but one must have all the virtues to sleep well. Shall I bear false witness? Shall I commit adultery? Shall I covet my neighbor's maid? All that would go ill with good sleep.

"And even if one has all the virtues, there is one further thing one must know: to send even the virtues to sleep at the right time. Lest they quarrel with each other, the fair little women, about you, child of misfortune. Peace with God and the neighbor: that is what good sleep demands. And peace even with the neighbor's devil—else he will haunt you at night.

"Honor the magistrates and obey them—even the crooked magistrates. Good sleep demands it. Is it my fault that power likes to walk on crooked legs?

"I shall call him the best shepherd who leads his sheep to the greenest pasture: that goes well with good sleep.

"I do not want many honors, or great jewels: that inflames the spleen. But one sleeps badly without a good name and a little jewel.

"A little company is more welcome to me than evil company: but they must go and come at the right time. That goes well with good sleep.

"Much, too, do I like the poor in spirit: they promote sleep. Blessed are they, especially if one always tells them that they are right.

"Thus passes the day of the virtuous. And when night comes I guard well against calling sleep. For sleep, who is the master of the virtues, does not want to be called. Instead, I think about what I have done and thought during the day. Chewing the cud, I ask myself, patient as a cow, Well, what were your ten overcomings? and what were your ten reconciliations and the ten truths and the ten laughters with which your heart edified itself? Weighing such matters and rocked by forty thoughts, I am suddenly overcome by sleep, the uncalled, the master of the virtues. Sleep knocks at my eyes: they become heavy. Sleep touches my mouth: it stays open. Verily, on soft soles he comes to me, the dearest of thieves, and steals my thoughts: stupid I stand, like this chair here. But not for long do I stand like this: soon I lie."

When Zarathustra heard the sage speak thus he

laughed in his heart, for an insight had come to him. And thus he spoke to his heart:

"This sage with his forty thoughts is a fool; but I believe that he knows well how to sleep. Happy is he that even lives near this sage! Such sleep is contagious—contagious even through a thick wall. There is magic even in his chair; and it is not in vain that the youths sit before this preacher of virtue. His wisdom is: to wake in order to sleep well. And verily, if life had no sense and I had to choose nonsense, then I too should consider this the most sensible nonsense.

"Now I understand clearly what was once sought above all when teachers of virtue were sought. Good sleep was sought, and opiate virtues for it. For all these much praised sages who were teachers of virtue, wisdom was the sleep without dreams: they knew no better meaning of life.

"Today too there may still be a few like this preacher of virtue, and not all so honest; but their time is up. And not for long will they stand like this: soon they will lie.

"Blessed are the sleepy ones: for they shall soon drop off."

Thus spoke Zarathustra.

ON THE AFTERWORLDLY

At one time Zarathustra too cast his delusion beyond man, like all the afterworldly. The work of a suffering and tortured god, the world then seemed to me. A dream the world then seemed to me, and the fiction of a god: colored smoke before the eyes of a dissatisfied deity. Good and evil and joy and pain and I and you—colored smoke this seemed to me before creative eyes. The creator wanted to look away from himself; so he created the world.

Drunken joy it is for the sufferer to look away from his suffering and to lose himself. Drunken joy and loss of self the world once seemed to me. This world, eternally imperfect, the image of an eternal contradiction, an imperfect image—a drunken joy for its imperfect creator: thus the world once appeared to me.

Thus I too once cast my delusion beyond man, like all the afterworldly. Beyond man indeed?

Alas, my brothers, this god whom I created was man-made and madness, like all gods! Man he was, and only a poor specimen of man and ego: out of my own ashes and fire this ghost came to me, and, verily, it did not come to me from beyond. What happened, my brothers? I overcame myself, the sufferer; I carried my own ashes to the mountains; I invented a brighter flame for myself. And behold, then this ghost *fled* from me. Now it would be suffering for me and agony for the recovered to believe in such ghosts: now it would be suffering for me and humiliation. Thus I speak to the afterworldly.

It was suffering and incapacity that created all afterworlds—this and that brief madness of bliss which is experienced only by those who suffer most deeply.

Weariness that wants to reach the ultimate with one leap, with one fatal leap, a poor ignorant weariness that does not want to want any more: this created all gods and afterworlds.

Believe me, my brothers: it was the body that despaired of the body and touched the ultimate walls with the fingers of a deluded spirit. Believe me, my brothers: it was the body that despaired of the earth and heard the belly of being speak to it. It wanted to crash through these ultimate walls with its head, and not only with its head—over there to "that world." But "that world" is well concealed from humans—that dehumanized inhuman world which is a heavenly nothing; and the belly of being does not speak to humans at all, except as a human.

Verily, all being is hard to prove and hard to induce to speak. Tell me, my brothers, is not the strangest of all things proved most nearly?

Indeed, this ego and the ego's contradiction and confusion still speak most honestly of its being—this creating, willing, valuing ego, which is the measure and value of things. And this most honest being, the ego, speaks of the body and still wants the body, even when it poetizes and raves and flutters with broken wings. It learns to speak ever more honestly, this ego: and the more it learns, the more words and honors it finds for body and earth.

A new pride my ego taught me, and this I teach men: no longer to bury one's head in the sand of heavenly things, but to bear it freely, an earthly head, which creates a meaning for the earth.

A new will I teach men: to *will* this way which man has walked blindly, and to affirm it, and no longer to sneak away from it like the sick and decaying.

It was the sick and decaying who despised body and earth and invented the heavenly realm and the redemptive drops of blood: but they took even these sweet and gloomy poisons from body and earth. They wanted to escape their own misery, and the stars were too far for them. So they sighed: "Would that there were heavenly ways to sneak into another state of being and happiness!" Thus they invented their sneaky ruses and bloody potions. Ungrateful, these people deemed themselves transported from their bodies and this earth. But to whom did they owe the convulsions and raptures of their transport? To their bodies and this earth.

Zarathustra is gentle with the sick. Verily, he is not angry with their kinds of comfort and ingratitude. May they become convalescents, men of overcoming, and create a higher body for themselves! Nor is Zarathustra angry with the convalescent who eyes his delusion tenderly and, at midnight, sneaks around the grave of his god: but even so his tears still betray sickness and a sick body to me.

Many sick people have always been among the poetizers and God-cravers; furiously they hate the lover of knowledge and that youngest among the virtues, which is called "honesty." They always look backward toward dark ages; then, indeed, delusion and faith were another matter: the rage of reason was godlikeness, and doubt was sin.

I know these godlike men all too well: they want one to have faith in them, and doubt to be sin. All too well I also know what it is in which they have most faith. Verily, it is not in afterworlds and redemptive drops of blood, but in the body, that they too have most faith; and their body is to them their thing-in-itself. But a sick thing it is to them, and gladly would they shed their skins. Therefore they listen to the preachers of death and themselves preach afterworlds.

Listen rather, my brothers, to the voice of the healthy body: that is a more honest and purer voice. More honestly and purely speaks the healthy body that is perfect and perpendicular: and it speaks of the meaning of the earth.

Thus spoke Zarathustra.

ON THE DESPISERS OF THE BODY

I want to speak to the despisers of the body. I would not have them learn and teach differently, but merely say farewell to their own bodies—and thus become silent.

"Body am I, and soul"—thus speaks the child. And why should one not speak like children?

But the awakened and knowing say: body am I entirely, and nothing else; and soul is only a word for something about the body.

The body is a great reason, a plurality with one sense, a war and a peace, a herd and a shepherd. An instrument of your body is also your little reason, my brother, which you call "spirit"—a little instrument and toy of your great reason.

"I," you say, and are proud of the word. But greater is that in which you do not wish to have faith—your body and its great reason: that does not say "I," but does "I."

What the sense feels, what the spirit knows, never has its end in itself. But sense and spirit would persuade you that they are the end of all things: that is how vain they are. Instruments and toys are sense and spirit: behind them still lies the self. The self also seeks with the eyes of the senses; it also listens with the ears of the spirit. Always the self listens and seeks: it compares, overpowers, conquers, destroys. It controls, and it is in control of the ego too.

Behind your thoughts and feelings, my brother, there stands a mighty ruler, an unknown sage—whose name is self. In your body he dwells; he is your body.

There is more reason in your body than in your best

wisdom. And who knows why your body needs precisely your best wisdom?

Your self laughs at your ego and at its bold leaps. "What are these leaps and flights of thought to me?" it says to itself. "A detour to my end. I am the leading strings of the ego and the prompter of its concepts."

The self says to the ego, "Feel pain here!" Then the ego suffers and thinks how it might suffer no more—and that is why it is *made* to think.

The self says to the ego, "Feel pleasure here!" Then the ego is pleased and thinks how it might often be pleased again—and that is why it is *made* to think.

I want to speak to the despisers of the body. It is their respect that begets their contempt. What is it that created respect and contempt and worth and will? The creative self created respect and contempt; it created pleasure and pain. The creative body created the spirit as a hand for its will.

Even in your folly and contempt, you despisers of the body, you serve your self. I say unto you: your self itself wants to die and turns away from life. It is no longer capable of what it would do above all else: to create beyond itself. That is what it would do above all else, that is its fervent wish.

But now it is too late for it to do this: so your self wants to go under, O despisers of the body. Your self wants to go under, and that is why you have become despisers of the body! For you are no longer able to create beyond yourselves.

And that is why you are angry with life and the earth. An unconscious envy speaks out of the squint-eyed glance of your contempt.

I shall not go your way, O despisers of the body! You are no bridge to the overman!

Thus spoke Zarathustra.

ON ENJOYING AND SUFFERING THE PASSIONS

My brother, if you have a virtue and she is your virtue, then you have her in common with nobody. To be sure, you want to call her by name and pet her; you want to pull her ear and have fun with her. And behold, now you have her name in common with the people and have become one of the people and herd with your virtue.

You would do better to say, "Inexpressible and nameless is that which gives my soul agony and sweetness and is even the hunger of my entrails."

May your virtue be too exalted for the familiarity of names: and if you must speak of her, then do not be ashamed to stammer of her. Then speak and stammer, "This is *my* good; this I love; it pleases me wholly; thus alone do *I* want the good. I do not want it as divine law; I do not want it as human statute and need: it shall not be a signpost for me to overearths and paradises. It is an earthly virtue that I love: there is little prudence in it, and least of all the reason of all men. But this bird built its nest with me: therefore I love and caress it; now it dwells with me, siting on its golden eggs." Thus you shall stammer and praise your virtue.

Once you suffered passions and called them evil. But now you have only your virtues left: they grew out of your passions. You commended your highest goal to the heart of these passions: then they become your virtues and passions you enjoyed.

And whether you came from the tribe of the choleric or of the voluptuous or of the fanatic or of the vengeful, in the end all your passions became virtues and all your devils, angels. Once you had wild dogs in your cellar, but in the end they turned into birds and lovely singers. Out of your poisons you brewed your balsam. You milked your cow, melancholy; now you drink the sweet milk of her udder.

And nothing evil grows out of you henceforth, unless it be the evil that grows out of the fight among your virtues. My brother, if you are fortunate you have only one virtue and no more: then you will pass over the bridge more easily. It is a distinction to have many virtues, but a hard lot; and many have gone into the desert and taken their lives because they had wearied of being the battle and battlefield of virtues.

My brother, are war and battle evil? But this evil is necessary; necessary are the envy and mistrust and calumny among your virtues. Behold how each of your virtues covets what is highest: each wants your whole spirit that it might become *her* herald; each wants your whole strength in wrath, hatred, and love. Each virtue is jealous of the others, and jealousy is a terrible thing. Virtues too can perish of jealousy. Surrounded by the flame of jealousy, one will in the end, like the scorpion, turn one's poisonous sting against oneself. Alas, my brother, have you never yet seen a virtue deny and stab herself?

Man is something that must be overcome; and therefore you shall love your virtues, for you will perish of them.

Thus spoke Zarathustra.

ON THE PALE CRIMINAL

You do not want to kill, O judges and sacrificers, until the animal has nodded? Behold, the pale criminal has nodded: out of his eyes speaks the great contempt.

"My ego is something that shall be overcome: my

ego is to me the great contempt of man," that is what his eyes say.

That he judged himself, that was his highest moment; do not let the sublime return to his baseness! There is no redemption for one who suffers so of himself, except a quick death.

Your killing, O judges, shall be pity and not revenge. And as you kill, be sure that you yourselves justify life! It is not enough to make your peace with the man you kill. Your sadness shall be love of the overman: thus you shall justify your living on.

"Enemy" you shall say, but not "villain"; "sick" you shall say, but not "scoundrel"; "fool" you shall say, but not "sinner."

And you, red judge, if you were to tell out loud all that you have already done in thought, everyone would cry, "Away with this filth and this poisonous worm!"

But thought is one thing, the deed is another, and the image of the deed still another: the wheel of causality does not roll between them.

An image made this pale man pale. He was equal to his deed when he did it; but he could not bear its image after it was done. Now he always saw himself as the doer of one deed. Madness I call this: the exception now became the essence for him. A chalk streak stops a hen; the stroke that he himself struck stopped his poor reason: madness *after* the deed I call this.

Listen, O judges: there is yet another madness, and that comes *before* the deed. Alas, you have not yet crept deep enough into this soul.

Thus speaks the red judge, "Why did this criminal murder? He wanted to rob." But I say unto you: his soul wanted blood, not robbery; he thirsted after the bliss of the knife. His poor reason, however, did not comprehend this madness and persuaded him: "What matters blood?" it asked; "don't you want at least to commit a robbery with it? To take revenge?" And he listened to his poor reason: its speech lay upon him like lead; so he robbed when he murdered. He did not want to be ashamed of his madness.

And now the lead of his guilt lies upon him, and again his poor reason is so stiff, so paralyzed, so heavy. If only he could shake his head, then his burden would roll off: but who could shake this head?

What is this man? A heap of diseases, which, through his spirit, reach out into the world: there they want to catch their prey.

What is this man? A ball of wild snakes, which rarely enjoy rest from each other: so they go forth singly and seek prey in the world.

Behold this poor body! What it suffered and coveted this poor soul interpreted for itself: it interpreted it as murderous lust and greed for the bliss of the knife.

Those who become sick today are overcome by that evil which is evil today: they want to hurt with that which hurts them. But there have been other ages and another evil and good. Once doubt was evil and the will to self. Then the sick became heretics or witches: as heretics or witches they suffered and wanted to inflict suffering.

But your ears do not want to accept this: it harms your good people, you say to me. But what matter your good people to me? Much about your good people nauseates me; and verily, it is not their evil. Indeed, I wish they had a madness of which they might perish like this pale criminal.

Verily, I wish their madness were called truth or

loyalty or justice: but they have their virtue in order to live long and in wretched contentment.

I am a railing by the torrent: let those who can, grasp me! Your crutch, however, I am not.

Thus spoke Zarathustra.

ON READING AND WRITING

Of all that is written I love only what a man has written with his blood. Write with blood, and you will experience that blood is spirit.

It is not easily possible to understand the blood of another: I hate reading idlers. Whoever knows the reader will henceforth do nothing for the reader. Another century of readers—and the spirit itself will stink.

That everyone may learn to read, in the long run corrupts not only writing but also thinking. Once the spirit was God, then he became man, and now he even becomes rabble.

Whoever writes in blood and aphorisms does not want to be read but to be learned by heart. In the mountains the shortest way is from peak to peak: but for that one must have long legs. Aphorisms should be peaks—and those who are addressed, tall and lofty. The air thin and pure, danger near, and the spirit full of gay sarcasm: these go well together. I want to have goblins around me, for I am courageous. Courage that puts ghosts to flight creates goblins for itself: courage wants to laugh.

I no longer feel as you do: this cloud which I see beneath me, this blackness and gravity at which I laugh—this is your thundercloud.

You look up when you feel the need for elevation. And I look down because I am elevated. Who among you can laugh and be elevated at the same time? Whoever climbs the highest mountains laughs at all tragic plays and tragic seriousness.

Brave, unconcerned, mocking, violent—thus wisdom wants us: she is a woman and always loves only a warrior.

You say to me, "Life is hard to bear." But why would you have your pride in the morning and your resignation in the evening? Life is hard to bear; but do not act so tenderly! We are all of us fair beasts of burden, male and female asses. What do we have in common with the rosebud, which trembles because a drop of dew lies on it?

True, we love life, not because we are used to living but because we are used to loving. There is always some madness in love. But there is also always some reason in madness.

And to me too, as I am well disposed toward life, butterflies and soap bubbles and whatever among men is of their kind seem to know most about happiness. Seeing these light, foolish, delicate, mobile little souls flutter—that seduces Zarathustra to tears and songs.

I would believe only in a god who could dance. And when I saw my devil I found him serious, thorough, profound, and solemn: it was the spirit of gravity—through him all things fall.

Not by wrath does one kill but by laughter. Come, let us kill the spirit of gravity!

I have learned to walk: ever since, I let myself run. I have learned to fly: ever since, I do not want to be pushed before moving along.

Now I am light, now I fly, now I see myself beneath myself, now a god dances through me.

Thus spoke Zarathustra.

ON THE TREE ON THE MOUNTAINSIDE

Zarathustra's eye had noted that a youth avoided him. And one evening as he walked alone through the mountains surrounding the town which is called The Motley Cow—behold, on his walk he found this youth as he sat leaning against a tree, looking wearily into the valley. Zarathustra gripped the tree under which the youth was sitting and spoke thus:

"If I wanted to shake this tree with my hands I should not be able to do it. But the wind, which we do not see, tortures and bends it in whatever direction it pleases. It is by invisible hands that we are bent and tortured worst."

Then the youth got up in consternation and said: "I hear Zarathustra, and just now I was thinking of him."

Zarathustra replied: "Why should that frighten you? But it is with man as it is with the tree. The more he aspires to the height and light, the more strongly do his roots strive earthward, downward, into the dark, the deep—into evil."

"Yes, into evil!" cried the youth. "How is it possible that you discovered my soul?"

Zarathustra smiled and said: "Some souls one will never discover, unless one invents them first."

"Yes, into evil!" the youth cried once more. "You have spoken the truth, Zarathustra. I no longer trust myself since I aspire to the height, and nobody trusts me any more; how did this happen? I change too fast: my today refutes my yesterday. I often skip steps when I climb: no step forgives me that. When I am at the top I always find myself alone. Nobody speaks to me; the frost of loneliness makes me shiver. What do I

want up high? My contempt and my longing grow at
the same time; the higher I climb, the more I despise
the climber. What does he want up high? How ashamed
I am of my climbing and stumbling! How I mock at
my violent panting! How I hate the flier! How weary
I am up high!"

Here the youth stopped. And Zarathustra contemplated the tree beside which they stood and spoke thus:
"This tree stands lonely here in the mountains; it grew
high above man and beast. And if it wanted to speak
it would have nobody who could understand it, so
high has it grown. Now it waits and waits—for what
is it waiting? It dwells too near the seat of the clouds:
surely, it waits for the first lightning."

When Zarathustra had said this the youth cried with
violent gestures: "Yes, Zarathustra, you are speaking
the truth. I longed to go under when I aspired to the
height, and you are the lightning for which I waited.
Behold, what am I, now that you have appeared
among us? It is the *envy* of you that has destroyed me."
Thus spoke the youth, and he wept bitterly. But Zarathustra put his arm around him and led him away.

And when they had walked together for a while,
Zarathustra began to speak thus: "It tears my heart.
Better than your words tell it, your eyes tell me of
all your dangers. You are not yet free, you still *search*
for freedom. You are worn from your search and overawake. You aspire to the free heights, your soul thirsts
for the stars. But your wicked instincts, too, thirst for
freedom. Your wild dogs want freedom; they bark with
joy in their cellar when your spirit plans to open all
prisons. To me you are still a prisoner who is plotting
his freedom: alas, in such prisoners the soul becomes
clever, but also deceitful and bad. And even the liber-

ated spirit must still purify himself. Much prison and mustiness still remain in him: his eyes must still become pure.

"Indeed, I know your danger. But by my love and hope I beseech you: do not throw away your love and hope.

"You still feel noble, and the others too feel your nobility, though they bear you a grudge and send you evil glances. Know that the noble man stands in everybody's way. The noble man stands in the way of the good too: and even if they call him one of the good, they thus want to do away with him. The noble man wants to create something new and a new virtue. The good want the old, and that the old be preserved. But this is not the danger of the noble man, that he might become one of the good, but a churl, a mocker, a destroyer.

"Alas, I knew noble men who lost their highest hope. Then they slandered all high hopes. Then they lived impudently in brief pleasures and barely cast their goals beyond the day. Spirit too is lust, so they said. Then the wings of their spirit broke: and now their spirit crawls about and soils what it gnaws. Once they thought of becoming heroes: now they are voluptuaries. The hero is for them an offense and a fright.

"But by my love and hope I beseech you: do not throw away the hero in your soul! Hold holy your highest hope!"

Thus spoke Zarathustra.

ON THE PREACHERS OF DEATH

There are preachers of death; and the earth is full of those to whom one must preach renunciation of life. The earth is full of the superfluous; life is spoiled by the all-too-many. May they be lured from this life with the "eternal life"! Yellow the preachers of death wear, or black. But I want to show them to you in still other colors.

There are the terrible ones who carry around within themselves the beast of prey and have no choice but lust or self-laceration. And even their lust is still self-laceration. They have not even become human beings yet, these terrible ones: let them preach renunciation of life and pass away themselves!

There are those with consumption of the soul: hardly are they born when they begin to die and to long for doctrines of weariness and renunciation. They would like to be dead, and we should welcome their wish. Let us beware of waking the dead and disturbing these living coffins!

They encounter a sick man or an old man or a corpse, and immediately they say, "Life is refuted." But only they themselves are refuted, and their eyes, which see only this one face of existence. Shrouded in thick melancholy and eager for the little accidents that bring death, thus they wait with clenched teeth. Or they reach for sweets while mocking their own childishness; they clutch the straw of their life and mock that they still clutch a straw. Their wisdom says, "A fool who stays alive—but such fools are we. And this is surely the most foolish thing about life."

"Life is only suffering," others say, and do not lie: see to it, then, that *you* cease! See to it, then, that the life which is only suffering ceases!

And let this be the doctrine of your virtue: "Thou shalt kill thyself! Thou shalt steal away!"

"Lust is sin," says one group that preaches death; "let us step aside and beget no children."

"Giving birth is troublesome," says another group; "why go on giving birth? One bears only unfortunates!"

And they too are preachers of death.

"Pity is needed," says the third group. "Take from me what I have! Take from me what I am! Life will bind me that much less!"

If they were full of pity through and through, they would make life insufferable for their neighbors. To be evil, that would be their real goodness. But they want to get out of life: what do they care that with their chains and presents they bind others still more tightly?

And you, too, for whom life is furious work and unrest—are you not very weary of life? Are you not very ripe for the preaching of death? All of you to whom furious work is dear, and whatever is fast, new, and strange—you find it hard to bear yourselves; your industry is escape and the will to forget yourselves. If you believed more in life you would fling yourselves less to the moment. But you do not have contents enough in yourselves for waiting—and not even for idleness.

Everywhere the voice of those who preach death is heard; and the earth is full of those to whom one must preach death. Or "eternal life"—that is the same to me, if only they pass away quickly.

Thus spoke Zarathustra.

ON WAR AND WARRIORS

We do not want to be spared by our best enemies, nor by those whom we love thoroughly. So let me tell you the truth!

My brothers in war, I love you thoroughly; I am and I was of your kind. And I am also your best enemy. So let me tell you the truth!

I know of the hatred and envy of your hearts. You

are not great enough not to know hatred and envy. Be great enough, then, not to be ashamed of them.

And if you cannot be saints of knowledge, at least be its warriors. They are the companions and forerunners of such sainthood.

I see many soldiers: would that I saw many warriors! "Uniform" one calls what they wear: would that what it conceals were not uniform!

You should have eyes that always seek an enemy—your enemy. And some of you hate at first sight. Your enemy you shall seek, your war you shall wage—for your thoughts. And if your thought be vanquished, then your honesty should still find cause for triumph in that. You should love peace as a means to new wars—and the short peace more than the long. To you I do not recommend work but struggle. To you I do not recommend peace but victory. Let your work be a struggle. Let your peace be a victory! One can be silent and sit still only when one has bow and arrow: else one chatters and quarrels. Let your peace be a victory!

You say it is the good cause that hallows even war? I say unto you: it is the good war that hallows any cause. War and courage have accomplished more great things than love of the neighbor. Not your pity but your courage has so far saved the unfortunate.

"What is good?" you ask. To be brave is good. Let the little girls say, "To be good is what is at the same time pretty and touching."

They call you heartless: but you have a heart, and I love you for being ashamed to show it. You are ashamed of your flood, while others are ashamed of their ebb.

You are ugly? Well then, my brothers, wrap the sublime around you, the cloak of the ugly. And when your soul becomes great, then it becomes prankish; and in your sublimity there is sarcasm. I know you.

In sarcasm the prankster and the weakling meet. But they misunderstand each other. I know you.

You may have only enemies whom you can hate, not enemies you despise. You must be proud of your enemy: then the successes of your enemy are your successes too.

Recalcitrance—that is the nobility of slaves. Your nobility should be obedience. Your very commanding should be an obeying. To a good warrior "thou shalt" sounds more agreeable than "I will." And everything you like you should first let yourself be commanded to do.

Your love of life shall be love of your highest hope; and your highest hope shall be the highest thought of life. Your highest thought, however, you should receive as a command from me—and it is: man is something that shall be overcome.

Thus live your life of obedience and war. What matters long life? What warrior wants to be spared?

I do not spare you; I love you thoroughly, my brothers in war!

Thus spoke Zarathustra.

ON THE NEW IDOL

Somewhere there are still peoples and herds, but not where we live, my brothers: here there are states. State? What is that? Well then, open your ears to me, for now I shall speak to you about the death of peoples.

State is the name of the coldest of all cold monsters. Coldly it tells lies too; and this lie crawls out of its mouth: "I, the state, am the people." That is a lie! It was creators who created peoples and hung a faith and a love over them: thus they served life.

It is annihilators who set traps for the many and call them "state": they hang a sword and a hundred appetites over them.

Where there is still a people, it does not understand the state and hates it as the evil eye and the sin against customs and rights.

This sign I give you: every people speaks its tongue of good and evil, which the neighbor does not understand. It has invented its own language of customs and rights. But the state tells lies in all the tongues of good and evil; and whatever it says it lies—and whatever it has it has stolen. Everything about it is false; it bites with stolen teeth, and bites easily. Even its entrails are false. Confusion of tongues of good and evil: this sign I give you as the sign of the state. Verily, this sign signifies the will to death. Verily, it beckons to the preachers of death.

All-too-many are born: for the superfluous the state was invented.

Behold, how it lures them, the all-too-many—and how it devours them, chews them, and ruminates!

"On earth there is nothing greater than I: the ordering finger of God am I"—thus roars the monster. And it is not only the long-eared and shortsighted who sink to their knees. Alas, to you too, you great souls, it whispers its dark lies. Alas, it detects the rich hearts which like to squander themselves. Indeed, it detects you too, you vanquishers of the old god. You have grown weary with fighting, and now your weariness still serves the new idol. With heroes and honorable men it would surround itself, the new idol! It likes to bask in the sunshine of good consciences—the cold monster!

It will give you everything if you will adore it, this

new idol: thus it buys the splendor of your virtues and the look of your proud eyes. It would use you as bait for the all-too-many.

Indeed, a hellish artifice was invented there, a horse of death, clattering in the finery of divine honors. Indeed, a dying for many was invented there, which praises itself as life: verily, a great service to all preachers of death!

State I call it where all drink poison, the good and the wicked; state, where all lose themselves, the good and the wicked; state, where the slow suicide of all is called "life."

Behold the superfluous! They steal the works of the inventors and the treasures of the sages for themselves; "education" they call their theft—and everything turns to sickness and misfortune for them.

Behold the superfluous! They are always sick; they vomit their gall and call it a newspaper. They devour each other and cannot even digest themselves.

Behold the superfluous! They gather riches and become poorer with them. They want power and first the lever of power, much money—the impotent paupers!

Watch them clamber, these swift monkeys! They clamber over one another and thus drag one another into the mud and the depth. They all want to get to the throne: that is their madness—as if happiness sat on the throne. Often mud sits on the throne—and often also the throne on mud. Mad they all appear to me, clambering monkeys and overardent. Foul smells their idol, the cold monster: foul they smell to me altogether, these idolators.

My brothers, do you want to suffocate in the fumes of their snouts and appetites? Rather break the windows and leap to freedom.

Escape from the bad smell! Escape from the idolatry of the superfluous!

Escape from the bad smell! Escape from the steam of these human sacrifices!

The earth is free even now for great souls. There are still many empty seats for the lonesome and the twosome, fanned by the fragrance of silent seas.

A free life is still free for great souls. Verily, whoever possesses little is possessed that much less: praised be a little poverty!

Only where the state ends, there begins the human being who is not superfluous: there begins the song of necessity, the unique and inimitable tune.

Where the state *ends*—look there, my brothers! Do you not see it, the rainbow and the bridges of the overman?

Thus spoke Zarathustra.

ON THE FLIES OF THE MARKET PLACE

Flee, my friend, into your solitude! I see you dazed by the noise of the great men and stung all over by the stings of the little men. Woods and crags know how to keep a dignified silence with you. Be like the tree that you love with its wide branches: silently listening, it hangs over the sea.

Where solitude ceases the market place begins; and where the market place begins the noise of the great actors and the buzzing of the poisonous flies begins too.

In the world even the best things amount to nothing without someone to make a show of them: great men the people call these showmen.

Little do the people comprehend the great—that is, the creating. But they have a mind for all showmen and actors of great things.

Around the inventors of new values the world revolves: invisibly it revolves. But around the actors
revolve the people and fame: that is "the way of the
world."

The actor has spirit but little conscience of the
spirit. Always he has faith in that with which he inspires the most faith—faith in himself. Tomorrow he
has a new faith, and the day after tomorrow a newer
one. He has quick senses, like the people, and capricious moods. To overthrow—that means to him: to
prove. To drive to frenzy—that means to him: to persuade. And blood is to him the best of all reasons. A
truth that slips into delicate ears alone he calls a lie
and nothing. Verily, he believes only in gods who make
a big noise in the world!

Full of solemn jesters is the market place—and the
people pride themselves on their great men, their masters of the hour. But the hour presses them; so they
press you. And from you too they want a Yes or No.
Alas, do you want to place your chair between pro and
con?

Do not be jealous of these unconditional, pressing
men, you lover of truth! Never yet has truth hung on
the arm of the unconditional. On account of these
sudden men, go back to your security: it is only in
the market place that one is assaulted with Yes? or No?
Slow is the experience of all deep wells: long must
they wait before they know *what* fell into their depth.

Far from the market place and from fame happens
all that is great: far from the market place and from
fame the inventors of new values have always dwelt.

Flee, my friend, into your solitude: I see you stung
all over by poisonous flies. Flee where the air is raw
and strong.

Flee into your solitude! You have lived too close to

the small and the miserable. Flee their invisible revenge! Against you they are nothing but revenge.

No longer raise up your arm against them. Numberless are they, and it is not your lot to shoo flies. Numberless are these small and miserable creatures; and many a proud building has perished of raindrops and weeds. You are no stone, but you have already become hollow from many drops. You will yet burst from many drops. I see you wearied by poisonous flies, bloody in a hundred places; and your pride refuses even to be angry. Blood is what they want from you in all innocence. Their bloodless souls crave blood, and so they sting in all innocence. But you, you deep one, suffer too deeply even from small wounds; and even before you have healed, the same poisonous worm crawls over your hand. You are too proud to kill these greedy creatures. But beware lest it become your downfall that you suffer all their poisonous injustice.

They hum around you with their praise too: obtrusiveness is their praise. They want the proximity of your skin and your blood. They flatter you as a god or devil; they whine before you as before a god or devil. What does it matter? They are flatterers and whiners and nothing more.

Often they affect charm. But that has always been the cleverness of cowards. Indeed, cowards are clever! They think a lot about you with their petty souls—you always seem problematic to them. Everything that one thinks about a lot becomes problematic.

They punish you for all your virtues. They forgive you entirely—your mistakes.

Because you are gentle and just in disposition you say, "They are guiltless in their small existence." But their petty souls think, "Guilt is every great existence."

Even when you are gentle to them they still feel

despised by you: and they return your benefaction with hidden malefactions. Your silent pride always runs counter to their taste; they are jubilant if for once you are modest enough to be vain. That which we recognize in a person we also inflame in him: therefore, beware of the small creatures. Before you they feel small, and their baseness glimmers and glows in invisible revenge. Have you not noticed how often they became mute when you stepped among them, and how their strength went from them like smoke from a dying fire?

Indeed, my friend, you are the bad conscience of your neighbors: for they are unworthy of you. They hate you, therefore, and would like to suck your blood. Your neighbors will always be poisonous flies; that which is great in you, just that must make them more poisonous and more like flies.

Flee, my friend, into your solitude and where the air is raw and strong! It is not your lot to shoo flies.

Thus spoke Zarathustra.

ON CHASTITY

I love the forest. It is bad to live in cities: there too many are in heat. Is it not better to fall into the hands of a murderer than into the dreams of a woman in heat? And behold these men: their eyes say it—they know of nothing better on earth than to lie with a woman. Mud is at the bottom of their souls; and woe if their mud also has spirit!

Would that you were as perfect as animals at least! But animals have innocence.

Do I counsel you to slay your senses? I counsel the innocence of the senses.

Do I counsel you to chastity? Chastity is a virtue in some, but almost a vice in many. They abstain, but the bitch, sensuality, leers enviously out of everything they do. Even to the heights of their virtue and to the cold regions of the spirit this beast follows them with her lack of peace. And how nicely the bitch, sensuality, knows how to beg for a piece of spirit when denied a piece of meat.

Do you love tragedies and everything that breaks the heart? But I mistrust your bitch. Your eyes are too cruel and you search lustfully for sufferers. Is it not merely your lust that has disguised itself and now calls itself pity?

And this parable too I offer you: not a few who wanted to drive out their devil have themselves entered into swine.

Those for whom chastity is difficult should be counseled against it, lest it become their road to hell—the mud and heat of their souls.

Do I speak of dirty things? That is not the worst that could happen. It is not when truth is dirty, but when it is shallow, that the lover of knowledge is reluctant to step into its waters. Verily, some are chaste through and through: they are gentler of heart, fonder of laughter, and laugh more than you. They laugh at chastity too and ask, "What is chastity? Is chastity not folly? Yet this folly came to us, not we to it. We offered this guest hostel and heart: now it dwells with us—may it stay as long as it will!"

Thus spoke Zarathustra.

ON THE FRIEND

"There is always one too many around me"—thus thinks the hermit. "Always one times one—eventually that makes two."

I and me are always too deep in conversation: how

could one stand that if there were no friend? For the hermit the friend is always the third person: the third is the cork that prevents the conversation of the two from sinking into the depths. Alas, there are too many depths for all hermits; therefore they long so for a friend and his height.

Our faith in others betrays in what respect we would like to have faith in ourselves. Our longing for a friend is our betrayer. And often love is only a device to overcome envy. And often one attacks and makes an enemy in order to conceal that one is open to attack. "At least be my enemy!"—thus speaks true reverence, which does not dare ask for friendship.

If one wants to have a friend one must also want to wage war for him: and to wage war, one must be *capable* of being an enemy.

In a friend one should still honor the enemy. Can you go close to your friend without going over to him?

In a friend one should have one's best enemy. You should be closest to him with your heart when you resist him.

You do not want to put on anything for your friend? Should it be an honor for your friend that you give yourself to him as you are? But he sends you to the devil for that. He who makes no secret of himself, enrages: so much reason have you for fearing nakedness. Indeed, if you were gods, then you might be ashamed of your clothes. You cannot groom yourself too beautifully for your friend: for you shall be to him an arrow and a longing for the overman.

Have you ever seen your friend asleep—and found out how he looks? What is the face of your friend anyway? It is your own face in a rough and imperfect mirror.

Have you ever seen your friend asleep? Were you not shocked that you friend looks like that? O my friend, man is something that must be overcome.

A friend should be a master at guessing and keeping still: you must not want to see everything. Your dream should betray to you what your friend does while awake.

Your compassion should be a guess—to know first whether your friend wants compassion. Perhaps what he loves in you is the unbroken eye and the glance of eternity. Compassion for the friend should conceal itself under a hard shell, and you should break a tooth on it. That way it will have delicacy and sweetness.

Are you pure air and solitude and bread and medicine for your friend? Some cannot loosen their own chains and can nevertheless redeem their friends.

Are you a slave? Then you cannot be a friend. Are you a tyrant? Then you cannot have friends. All-too-long have a slave and a tyrant been concealed in woman. Therefore woman is not yet capable of friendship: she knows only love.

Woman's love involves injustice and blindness against everything that she does not love. And even in the knowing love of a woman there are still assault and lightning and night alongside light.

Woman is not yet capable of friendship: women are still cats and birds. Or at best, cows.

Woman is not yet capable of friendship. But tell me, you men, who among you is capable of friendship?

Alas, behold your poverty, you men, and the meanness of your souls! As much as you give the friend, I will give even my enemy, and I shall not be any the poorer for it. There is comradeship: let there be friendship!

Thus spoke Zarathustra.

ON THE THOUSAND AND ONE GOALS

Zarathustra saw many lands and many peoples: thus he discovered the good and evil of many peoples. And Zarathustra found no greater power on earth than good and evil.

No people could live without first esteeming; but if they want to preserve themselves, then they must not esteem as the neighbor esteems. Much that was good to one people was scorn and infamy to another: thus I found it. Much I found called evil here, and decked out with purple honors there. Never did one neighbor understand the other: ever was his soul amazed at the neighbor's delusion and wickedness.

A tablet of the good hangs over every people. Behold, it is the tablet of their overcomings; behold, it is the voice of their will to power.

Praiseworthy is whatever seems difficult to a people; whatever seems indispensable and difficult is called good; and whatever liberates even out of the deepest need, the rarest, the most difficult—that they call holy.

Whatever makes them rule and triumph and shine, to the awe and envy of their neighbors, that is to them the high, the first, the measure, the meaning of all things.

Verily, my brother, once you have recognized the need and land and sky and neighbor of a people, you may also guess the law of their overcomings, and why they climb to their hope on this ladder.

"You shall always be the first and excel all others: your jealous soul shall love no one, unless it be the friend"—that made the soul of the Greek quiver: thus he walked the path of his greatness.

"To speak the truth and to handle bow and arrow well"—that seemed both dear and difficult to the people who gave me my name—the name which is both dear and difficult to me.

"To honor father and mother and to follow their will to the root of one's soul"— this was the tablet of overcoming that another people hung up over themselves and became powerful and eternal thereby.

"To practice loyalty and, for the sake of loyalty, to risk honor and blood even for evil and dangerous things"—with this teaching another people conquered themselves; and through this self-conquest they became pregnant and heavy with great hopes.

Verily, men gave themselves all their good and evil. Verily, they did not take it, they did not find it, nor did it come to them as a voice from heaven. Only man placed values in things to preserve himself—he alone created a meaning for things, a human meaning. Therefore he calls himself "man," which means: the esteemer.

To esteem is to create: hear this, you creators! Esteeming itself is of all esteemed things the most estimable treasure. Through esteeming alone is there value: and without esteeming, the nut of existence would be hollow. Hear this, you creators!

Change of values—that is a change of creators. Whoever must be a creator always annihilates.

First, peoples were creators; and only in later times, individuals. Verily, the individual himself is still the most recent creation.

Once peoples hung a tablet of the good over themselves. Love which would rule and love which would obey have together created such tablets.

The delight in the herd is more ancient than the

delight in the ego; and as long as the good conscience is identified with the herd, only the bad conscience says: I.

Verily, the clever ego, the loveless ego that desires its own profit in the profit of the many—that is not the origin of the herd, but its going under.

Good and evil have always been created by lovers and creators. The fire of love glows in the names of all the virtues, and the fire of wrath.

Zarathustra saw many lands and many peoples. No greater power did Zarathustra find on earth than the works of the lovers: "good" and "evil" are their names.

Verily, a monster is the power of this praising and censuring. Tell me, who will conquer it, O brothers? Tell me, who will throw a yoke over the thousand necks of this beast?

A thousand goals have there been so far, for there have been a thousand peoples. Only the yoke for the thousand necks is still lacking: the one goal is lacking. Humanity still has no goal.

But tell me, my brothers, if humanity still lacks a goal—is humanity itself not still lacking too?

Thus spoke Zarathustra.

ON LOVE OF THE NEIGHBOR

You crowd around your neighbor and have fine words for it. But I say unto you: your love of the neighbor is your bad love of yourselves. You flee to your neighbor from yourselves and would like to make a virtue out of that: but I see through your "selflessness."

The *you* is older than the *I*; the *you* has been pronounced holy, but not yet the *I*: so man crowds toward his neighbor.

Do I recommend love of the neighbor to you? Sooner I should even recommend flight from the neighbor and love of the farthest. Higher than love of the neighbor is love of the farthest and the future; higher yet than the love of human beings I esteem the love of things and ghosts. This ghost that runs after you, my brother, is more beautiful than you; why do you not give him your flesh and your bones? But you are afraid and run to your neighbor.

You cannot endure yourselves and do not love yourselves enough: now you want to seduce your neighbor to love, and then gild yourselves with his error. Would that you could not endure all sorts of neighbors and their neighbors; then you would have to create your friend and his overflowing heart out of yourselves.

You invite a witness when you want to speak well of yourselves; and when you have seduced him to think well of you, then you think well of yourselves.

Not only are they liars who speak when they know better, but even more those who speak when they know nothing. And thus you speak of yourselves to others and deceive the neighbor with yourselves.

Thus speaks the fool: "Association with other people corrupts one's character—especially if one has none."

One man goes to his neighbor because he seeks himself; another because he would lose himself. Your bad love of yourselves turns your solitude into a prison. It is those farther away who must pay for your love of your neighbor; and even if five of you are together, there is always a sixth who must die.

I do not love your festivals either: I found too many actors there, and the spectators, too, often behaved like actors.

I teach you not the neighbor, but the friend. The friend should be the festival of the earth to you and

an anticipation of the overman. I teach you the friend
and his overflowing heart. But one must learn to be a
sponge if one wants to be loved by hearts that overflow. I teach you the friend in whom the world stands
completed, a bowl of goodness—the creating friend
who always has a completed world to give away.
And as the world rolled apart for him, it rolls together
again in circles for him, as the becoming of the good
through evil, as the becoming of purpose out of accident.

Let the future and the farthest be for you the cause
of your today: in your friend you shall love the overman as your cause.

My brothers, love of the neighbor I do not recommend to you: I recommend to you love of the farthest.

Thus spoke Zarathustra.

ON THE WAY OF THE CREATOR

Is it your wish, my brother, to go into solitude? Is
it your wish to seek the way to yourself? Then linger
a moment, and listen to me.

"He who seeks, easily gets lost. All loneliness is
guilt"—thus speaks the herd. And you have long belonged to the herd. The voice of the herd will still be
audible in you. And when you will say, "I no longer
have a common conscience with you," it will be a
lament and an agony. Behold, this agony itself was
born of the common conscience, and the last glimmer
of that conscience still glows on your affliction.

But do you want to go the way of your affliction,
which is the way to yourself? Then show me your right
and your strength to do so. Are you a new strength
and a new right? A first movement? A self-propelled

wheel? Can you compel the very stars to revolve around you?

Alas, there is so much lusting for the heights! There are so many convulsions of the ambitious. Show me that you are not one of the lustful and ambitious.

Alas, there are so many great thoughts which do no more than a bellows: they puff up and make emptier.

You call yourself free? Your dominant thought I want to hear, and not that you have escaped from a yoke. Are you one of those who had the *right* to escape from a yoke? There are some who threw away their last value when they threw away their servitude.

Free *from* what? As if that mattered to Zarathustra! But your eyes should tell me brightly: free *for* what?

Can you give yourself your own evil and your own good and hang your own will over yourself as a law? Can you be your own judge and avenger of your law? Terrible it is to be alone with the judge and avenger of one's own law. Thus is a star thrown out into the void and into the icy breath of solitude. Today you are still suffering from the many, being one: today your courage and your hopes are still whole. But the time will come when solitude will make you weary, when your pride will double up and your courage gnash its teeth. And you will cry, "I am alone!" The time will come when that which seems high to you will no longer be in sight, and that which seems low will be all-too-near; even what seems sublime to you will frighten you like a ghost. And you will cry, "All is false!"

There are feelings which want to kill the lonely; and if they do not succeed, well, then they themselves must die. But are you capable of this—to be a murderer?

My brother, do you know the word "contempt" yet? And the agony of your justice—being just to those who despise you? You force many to relearn about you; they charge it bitterly against you. You came close to them and yet passed by: that they will never forgive. You pass over and beyond them: but the higher you ascend, the smaller you appear to the eye of envy. But most of all they hate those who fly.

"How would you be just to me?" you must say. "I choose your injustice as my proper lot." Injustice and filth they throw after the lonely one: but, my brother, if you would be a star, you must not shine less for them because of that.

And beware of the good and the just! They like to crucify those who invent their own virtue for themselves—they hate the lonely one. Beware also of holy simplicity! Everything that is not simple it considers unholy; it also likes to play with fire—the stake. And beware also of the attacks of your love! The lonely one offers his hand too quickly to whomever he encounters. To some people you may not give your hand, only a paw: and I desire that your paw should also have claws.

But the worst enemy you can encounter will always be you, yourself; you lie in wait for yourself in caves and woods.

Lonely one, you are going the way to yourself. And your way leads past yourself and your seven devils. You will be a heretic to yourself and a witch and soothsayer and fool and doubter and unholy one and a villain. You must wish to consume yourself in your own flame: how could you wish to become new unless you had first become ashes!

Lonely one, you are going the way of the creator:

you would create a god for yourself out of your seven devils.

Lonely one, you are going the way of the lover: yourself you love, and therefore you despise yourself, as only lovers despise. The lover would create because he despises. What does he know of love who did not have to despise precisely what he loved!

Go into your loneliness with your love and with your creation, my brother; and only much later will justice limp after you.

With my tears go into your loneliness, my brother. I love him who wants to create over and beyond himself and thus perishes.

Thus spoke Zarathustra.

ON LITTLE OLD AND YOUNG WOMEN

"Why do you steal so cautiously through the twilight, Zarathustra? And what do you conceal so carefully under your coat? Is it a treasure you have been given? or a child born to you? Or do you yourself now follow the ways of thieves, you friend of those who are evil?"

"Verily, my brother," said Zarathustra, "it is a treasure I have been given: it is a little truth that I carry. But it is troublesome like a young child, and if I don't hold my hand over its mouth, it will cry overloudly.

"When I went on my way today, alone, at the hour when the sun goes down, I met a little old woman who spoke thus to my soul: 'Much has Zarathustra spoken to us women too; but never did he speak to us about woman.' And I answered her: 'About woman one should speak only to men.' Then she said: 'Speak to me too of woman; I am old enough to forget it immediately.' And I obliged the little old woman and I spoke to her thus:

"Everything about woman is a riddle, and everything about woman has one solution: that is pregnancy. Man is for woman a means: the end is always the child. But what is woman for man?

"A real man wants two things: danger and play. Therefore he wants woman as the most dangerous plaything. Man should be educated for war, and woman for the recreation of the warrior; all else is folly. The warrior does not like all-too-sweet fruit; therefore he likes woman: even the sweetest woman is bitter. Woman understands children better than man does, but man is more childlike than woman.

"In a real man a child is hidden—and wants to play. Go to it, women, discover the child in man! Let woman be a plaything, pure and fine, like a gem, irradiated by the virtues of a world that has not yet arrived. Let the radiance of a star shine through your love! Let your hope be: May I give birth to the overman!

"Let there be courage in your love! With your love you should proceed toward him who arouses fear in you. Let your honor be in your love! Little does woman understand of honor otherwise. But let this be your honor: always to love more than you are loved, and never to be second.

"Let man fear woman when she loves: then she makes any sacrifice, and everything else seems without value to her. Let man fear woman when she hates: for deep down in his soul man is merely evil, while woman is bad. Whom does woman hate most? Thus spoke the iron to the magnet: 'I hate you most because you attract, but are not strong enough to pull me to you.'

"The happiness of man is: I will. The happiness of woman is: he wills. 'Behold, just now the world became perfect!'—thus thinks every woman when she obeys out of entire love. And woman must obey and find a depth for her surface. Surface is the disposition of woman: a mobile, stormy film over shallow water. Man's disposition, however, is deep; his river roars in subterranean caves: woman feels his strength but does not comprehend it.

"Then the little old woman answered me: 'Many fine things has Zarathustra said, especially for those who are young enough for them. It is strange: Zarathustra knows women little, and yet he is right about them. Is this because nothing is impossible with woman? And now, as a token of gratitude, accept a little truth. After all, I am old enough for it. Wrap it up and hold your hand over its mouth: else it will cry overloudly, this little truth.'

"Then I said: 'Woman, give me your little truth.' And thus spoke the little old woman:

"'You are going to women? Do not forget the whip!'"

Thus spoke Zarathustra.

ON THE ADDER'S BITE

One day Zarathustra had fallen asleep under a fig tree, for it was hot, and had put his arms over his face. And an adder came and bit him in the neck, so that Zarathustra cried out in pain. When he had taken his arm from his face, he looked at the snake, and it recognized the eyes of Zarathustra, writhed awkwardly, and wanted to get away. "Oh no," said Zarathustra, "as yet you have not accepted my thanks. You waked me in time, my way is still long." "Your way is short," the adder said sadly; "my poison kills." Zarathustra smiled. "When has a dragon ever died of the poison of a snake?" he said. "But take back your poison. You are not rich enough to give it to me." Then the adder fell around his neck a second time and licked his wound.

When Zarathustra once related this to his disciples they asked: "And what, O Zarathustra, is the moral of your story?" Then Zarathustra answered thus:

The annihilator of morals, the good and just call me: my story is immoral.

But if you have an enemy, do not requite him evil with good, for that would put him to shame. Rather prove that he did you some good.

And rather be angry than put to shame. And if you are cursed, I do not like it that you want to bless. Rather join a little in the cursing.

And if you have been done a great wrong, then quickly add five little ones: a gruesome sight is a person single-mindedly obsessed by a wrong.

Did you already know this? A wrong shared is half right. And he who is able to bear it should take the wrong upon himself.

A little revenge is more human than no revenge. And if punishment is not also a right and an honor for the transgressor, then I do not like your punishments either.

It is nobler to declare oneself wrong than to insist on being right—especially when one is right. Only one must be rich enough for that.

I do not like your cold justice; and out of the eyes of your judges there always looks the executioner and his cold steel. Tell me, where is that justice which is love with open eyes? Would that you might invent for me the love that bears not only all punishment but also all guilt! Would that you might invent for me the justice that acquits everyone, except him that judges!

Do you still want to hear this too? In him who would be just through and through even lies become kindness to others. But how could I think of being just through and through? How can I give each his own? Let this be sufficient for me: I give each my own.

Finally, my brothers, beware of doing wrong to any hermit. How could a hermit forget? How could he repay? Like a deep well is a hermit. It is easy to throw in a stone; but if the stone sank to the bottom, tell me, who would get it out again? Beware of insulting the hermit. But if you have done so—well, then kill him too.

Thus spoke Zarathustra.

ON CHILD AND MARRIAGE

I have a question for you alone, my brother: like a sounding lead, I cast this question into your soul that I might know how deep it is.

You are young and wish for a child and marriage. But I ask you: Are you a man *entitled* to wish for a child? Are you the victorious one, the self-conqueror, the commander of your senses, the master of your virtues? This I ask you. Or is it the animal and need that speak out of your wish? Or loneliness? Or lack of peace with yourself?

Let your victory and your freedom long for a child. You shall build living monuments to your victory and your liberation. You shall build over and beyond yourself, but first you must be built yourself, perpendicular in body and soul. You shall not only reproduce yourself, but produce something higher. May the garden of marriage help you in that!

You shall create a higher body, a first movement, a self-propelled wheel—you shall create a creator.

Marriage: thus I name the will of two to create the one that is more than those who created it. Reverence for each other, as for those willing with such a will, is what I name marriage. Let this be the meaning and truth of your marriage. But that which the all-too-many, the superfluous, call marriage—alas, what shall I name that? Alas, this poverty of the soul in pair! Alas, this filth of the soul in pair! Alas, this wretched contentment in pair! Marriage they call this; and they say that their marriages are made in heaven. Well, I do not like it, this heaven of the superfluous. No, I do not like them—these animals entangled in the heavenly net. And let the god who limps near to bless what he never joined keep his distance from me! Do not laugh at such marriages! What child would not have cause to weep over its parents?

Worthy I deemed this man, and ripe for the sense of the earth; but when I saw his wife, the earth seemed to me a house for the senseless. Indeed, I wished that the earth might tremble in convulsions when a saint mates with a goose.

This one went out like a hero in quest of truths, and eventually he conquered a little dressed-up lie. His marriage he calls it.

That one was reserved and chose choosily. But all at once he spoiled his company forever: his marriage he calls it.

That one sought a maid with the virtues of an angel. But all at once he became the maid of a woman; and now he must turn himself into an angel.

Careful I have found all buyers now, and all of them have cunning eyes. But even the most cunning still buys his wife in a poke.

Many brief follies—that is what you call love. And your marriage concludes many brief follies, as a long stupidity. Your love of woman, and woman's love of man—oh, that it were compassion for suffering and shrouded gods! But, for the most part, two beasts find each other.

But even your best love is merely an ecstatic parable and a painful ardor. It is a torch that should light up higher paths for you. Over and beyond yourselves you shall love one day. Thus *learn* first to love. And for that you had to drain the bitter cup of your love. Bitterness lies in the cup of even the best love: thus it arouses longing for the overman; thus it arouses your thirst, creator. Thirst for the creator, an arrow and longing for the overman: tell me, my brother, is this your will to marriage? Holy I call such a will and such a marriage.

Thus spoke Zarathustra.

ON FREE DEATH

Many die too late, and a few die too early. The doctrine still sounds strange: "Die at the right time!"

Die at the right time—thus teaches Zarathustra. Of course, how could those who never live at the right time die at the right time? Would that they had never been born! Thus I counsel the superfluous. But even the superfluous still make a fuss about their dying; and even the hollowest nut still wants to be cracked. Everybody considers dying important; but as yet death is no festival. As yet men have not learned how one hallows the most beautiful festivals.

I show you the death that consummates—a spur and a promise to the survivors. He that consummates his life dies his death victoriously, surrounded by those who hope and promise. Thus should one learn to die; and there should be no festival where one dying thus does not hallow the oaths of the living.

To die thus is best; second to this, however, is to die fighting and to squander a great soul. But equally hateful to the fighter and the victor is your grinning death, which creeps up like a thief—and yet comes as the master.

My death I praise to you, the free death which comes to me because *I* want it. And when shall I want it? He who has a goal and an heir will want death at the right time for his goal and heir. And from reverence for his goal and heir he will hang no more dry wreaths in the sanctuary of life. Verily, I do not want to be like the ropemakers: they drag out their threads and always walk backwards.

Some become too old even for their truths and victories: a toothless mouth no longer has the right to every truth. And everybody who wants fame must take leave of honor betimes and practice the difficult art of leaving at the right time.

One must cease letting oneself be eaten when one tastes best: that is known to those who want to be loved long. There are sour apples, to be sure, whose lot requires that they wait till the last day of autumn: and they become ripe, yellow, and wrinkled all at once. In some, the heart grows old first; in others, the spirit. And some are old in their youth: but late youth preserves long youth.

For some, life turns out badly: a poisonous worm eats its way to their heart. Let them see to it that their dying turns out that much better. Some never become sweet; they rot already in the summer. It is cowardice that keeps them on their branch.

All-too-many live, and all-too-long they hang on their

branches. Would that a storm came to shake all this worm-eaten rot from the tree!

Would that there came preachers of *quick* death! I would like them as the true storms and shakers of the trees of life. But I hear only slow death preached, and patience with everything "earthly."

Alas, do you preach patience with the earthly? It is the earthly that has too much patience with you, blasphemers!

Verily, that Hebrew died too early whom the preachers of slow death honor; and for many it has become a calamity that he died too early. As yet he knew only tears and the melancholy of the Hebrew, and hatred of the good and the just—the Hebrew Jesus: then the longing for death overcame him. Would that he had remained in the wilderness and far from the good and the just! Perhaps he would have learned to live and to love the earth—and laughter too.

Believe me, my brothers! He died too early; he himself would have recanted his teaching, had he reached my age. Noble enough was he to recant. But he was not yet mature. Immature is the love of the youth, and immature his hatred of man and earth. His mind and the wings of his spirit are still tied down and heavy.

But in the man there is more of the child than in the youth, and less melancholy: he knows better how to die and to live. Free to die and free in death, able to say a holy No when the time for Yes has passed: thus he knows how to die and to live.

That your dying be no blasphemy against man and earth, my friends, that I ask of the honey of your soul. In your dying, your spirit and virtue should still glow like a sunset around the earth: else your dying has turned out badly.

Thus I want to die myself that you, my friends, may

love the earth more for my sake; and to earth I want to return that I may find rest in her who gave birth to me.

Verily, Zarathustra had a goal; he threw his ball: now you, my friends, are the heirs of my goal; to you I throw my golden ball. More than anything, I like to see you, my friends, throwing the golden ball. And so I still linger a little on the earth: forgive me for that.

Thus spoke Zarathustra.

ON THE GIFT-GIVING VIRTUE

1

When Zarathustra had said farewell to the town to which his heart was attached, and which was named The Motley Cow, many who called themselves his disciples followed him and escorted him. Thus they came to a crossroads; then Zarathustra told them that he now wanted to walk alone, for he liked to walk alone. His disciples gave him as a farewell present a staff with a golden handle on which a serpent coiled around the sun. Zarathustra was delighted with the staff and leaned on it; then he spoke thus to his disciples:

Tell me: how did gold attain the highest value? Because it is uncommon and useless and gleaming and gentle in its splendor; it always gives itself. Only as the image of the highest virtue did gold attain the highest value. Goldlike gleam the eyes of the giver. Golden splendor makes peace between moon and sun. Uncommon is the highest virtue and useless; it is gleaming and gentle in its splendor: a gift-giving virtue is the highest virtue.

Verily, I have found you out, my disciples: you strive, as I do, for the gift-giving virtue. What would you have in common with cats and wolves? This is your thirst: to become sacrifices and gifts yourselves; and that is why you thirst to pile up all the riches in your soul. Insatiably your soul strives for treasures and gems, because your virtue is insatiable in wanting to give. You force all things to and into yourself that they may flow back out of your well as the gifts of your love. Verily, such a gift-giving love must approach all values as a robber; but whole and holy I call this selfishness.

There is also another selfishness, an all-too-poor and hungry one that always wants to steal—the selfishness of the sick: sick selfishness. With the eyes of a thief it looks at everything splendid; with the greed of hunger it sizes up those who have much to eat; and always it sneaks around the table of those who give. Sickness speaks out of such craving and invisible degeneration; the thievish greed of this selfishness speaks of a diseased body.

Tell me, my brothers: what do we consider bad and worst of all? Is it not *degeneration*? And it is degeneration that we always infer where the gift-giving soul is lacking. Upward goes our way, from genus to overgenus. But we shudder at the degenerate sense which says, "Everything for me." Upward flies our sense: thus it is a parable of our body, a parable of elevation. Parables of such elevations are the names of the virtues.

Thus the body goes through history, becoming and fighting. And the spirit—what is that to the body? The herald of its fights and victories, companion and echo.

All names of good and evil are parables: they do not define, they merely hint. A fool is he who wants knowledge of them!

Watch for every hour, my brothers, in which your spirit wants to speak in parables: there lies the origin of your virtue. There your body is elevated and resurrected; with its rapture it delights the spirit so that it turns creator and esteemer and lover and benefactor of all things.

When your heart flows broad and full like a river, a blessing and a danger to those living near: there is the origin of your virtue.

When you are above praise and blame, and your will wants to command all things, like a lover's will: there is the origin of your virtue.

When you despise the agreeable and the soft bed and cannot bed yourself far enough from the soft: there is the origin of your virtue.

When you will with a single will and you call this cessation of all need "necessity": there is the origin of your virtue.

Verily, a new good and evil is she. Verily, a new deep murmur and the voice of a new well!

Power is she, this new virtue; a dominant thought is she, and around her a wise soul: a golden sun, and around it the serpent of knowledge.

2

Here Zarathustra fell silent for a while and looked lovingly at his disciples. Then he continued to speak thus, and the tone of his voice had changed:

Remain faithful to the earth, my brothers, with the power of your virtue. Let your gift-giving love and your knowledge serve the meaning of the earth. Thus I beg and beseech you. Do not let them fly away from earthly things and beat with their wings against eternal walls. Alas, there has always been so much virtue that has flown away. Lead back to the earth the virtue that flew away, as I do—back to the body, back to life, that it may give the earth a meaning, a human meaning.

In a hundred ways, thus far, have spirit as well as virtue flown away and made mistakes. Alas, all this delusion and all these mistakes still dwell in our body: they have there become body and will.

In a hundred ways, thus far, spirit as well as virtue has tried and erred. Indeed, an experiment was man. Alas, much ignorance and error have become body within us.

Not only the reason of millennia, but their madness too, breaks out in us. It is dangerous to be an heir. Still we fight step by step with the giant, accident; and over the whole of humanity there has ruled so far only nonsense—no sense.

Let your spirit and your virtue serve the sense of the earth, my brothers; and let the value of all things be posited newly by you. For that shall you be fighters! For that shall you be creators!

With knowledge, the body purifies itself; making experiments with knowledge, it elevates itself; in the lover of knowledge all instincts become holy; in the elevated, the soul becomes gay.

Physician, help yourself: thus you help your patient too. Let this be his best help that he may behold with his eyes the man who heals himself.

There are a thousand paths that have never yet been trodden—a thousand healths and hidden isles of life. Even now, man and man's earth are unexhausted and undiscovered.

Wake and listen, you that are lonely! From the future come winds with secret wing-beats; and good tidings are proclaimed to delicate ears. You that are lonely today, you that are withdrawing, you shall one day be the people: out of you, who have chosen yourselves, there shall grow a chosen people—and out of them, the overman. Verily, the earth shall yet become a site of recovery. And even now a new fragrance surrounds it, bringing salvation—and a new hope.

3

When Zarathustra had said these words he became silent, like one who has not yet said his last word; long he weighed his staff in his hand, doubtfully. At last he spoke thus, and the tone of his voice had changed.

Now I go alone, my disciples. You too go now, alone. Thus I want it. Verily, I counsel you: go away from me and resist Zarathustra! And even better: be ashamed of him! Perhaps he deceived you.

The man of knowledge must not only love his enemies, he must also be able to hate his friends.

One repays a teacher badly if one always remains nothing but a pupil. And why do you not want to pluck at my wreath?

You revere me; but what if your reverence tumbles one day? Beware lest a statue slay you.

You say you believe in Zarathustra? But what matters Zarathustra? You are my believers—but what matter all believers? You had not yet sought yourselves: and you found me. Thus do all believers; therefore all faith amounts to so little.

Now I bid you lose me and find yourselves; and only when you have all denied me will I return to you.

Verily, my brothers, with different eyes shall I then seek my lost ones; with a different love shall I then love you.

And once again you shall become my friends and the children of a single hope—and then shall I be with you the third time, that I may celebrate the great noon with you.

And that is the great noon when man stands in the middle of his way between beast and overman and celebrates his way to the evening as his highest hope: for it is the way to a new morning.

Then will he who goes under bless himself for being one who goes over and beyond; and the sun of his knowledge will stand at high noon for him.

"*Dead are all gods: now we want the overman to live*"—on that great noon, let this be our last will.

Thus spoke Zarathustra.

Thus Spoke Zarathustra: Second Part

. . . and only when you have all denied me will I return to you.

Verily, my brothers, with different eyes shall I then seek my lost ones; with a different love shall I then love you. (Zarathustra, *"On the Gift-Giving Virtue." I, p. 190*)

EDITOR'S NOTES

1. *The Child with the Mirror:* Transition to Part Two with its partly new style: "A new speech comes to me. . . . My spirit no longer wants to walk on worn soles."

2. *Upon the Blessed Isles:* The creative life versus belief in God: "God is a conjecture." The polemic against the opening lines of the final chorus in Goethe's *Faust* is taken up again in the chapter "On Poets" (see comments, p. 193). But the lines immediately following in praise of impermanence and creation are thoroughly in the spirit of Goethe.

3. *On the Pitying:* A return to the style of Part One and a major statement of Nietzsche's ideas on pity, *ressentiment,* and repression.

4. *On Priests:* Relatively mild, compared to the portrait of the priest in *The Antichrist* five years later.

5. *On the Virtuous:* A typology of different conceptions of virtue, with vivisectional intent. Nietzsche denounces "the filth of the words: revenge, punishment, reward, retribution," which he associates with Christianity; but also

that rigorism for which "virtue is the spasm under the scourge" and those who "call it virtue when their vices grow lazy." The pun on "I am just" is, in German: *wenn sie sagen: "ich bin gerecht," so klingt es immer gleich wie: "ich bin gerächt!"*

6. *On the Rabble:* The theme of Zarathustra's nausea is developed *ad nauseam* in later chapters. *La Nausée*—to speak in Sartre's terms—is one of his chief trials, and its eventual conquest is his greatest triumph. "I often grew weary of the spirit when I found that even the rabble had *esprit*" may help to account for some of Nietzsche's remarks elsewhere. Generally he celebrates the spirit—not in opposition to the body but as *mens sana in corpore sano.*

7. *On the Tarantulas:* One of the central motifs of Nietzsche's philosophy is stated in italics: "that man be delivered from revenge." In this chapter, the claim of human equality is criticized as an expression of the *ressentiment* of the sub-equal.

8. *On the Famous Wise Men:* One cannot serve two masters: the people and the truth. The philosophers of the past have too often rationalized popular prejudices. But the service of truth is a passion and martyrdom, for "spirit is the life that itself cuts into life: with its agony it increases its own knowledge." The song of songs on the spirit in this chapter may seem to contradict Nietzsche's insistence, in the chapter "On the Despisers of the Body," that the spirit is a mere instrument. Both themes are central in Nietzsche's thought, and their apparent contradiction is partly due to the fact that both are stated metaphorically. For, in truth, Nietzsche denies any crude dualism of body and spirit as a popular prejudice. The life of the spirit and the life of the body are aspects of a single life. But up to a point the contradiction can also be resolved metaphorically: life uses the spirit against its present form to attain a higher perfection. Man's enhancement is inseparable from the spirit; but Nietzsche denounces the occasional efforts of the spirit to destroy life instead of pruning it.

9. *The Night Song:* "Light am I; ah, that I were night!"

10. *The Dancing Song:* Life and wisdom as jealous women.

11. *The Tomb Song:* "Invulnerable am I only in the heel."

12. *On Self-Overcoming:* The first long discussion of the will to power marks, together with the chapters "On the Pitying" and "On the Tarantulas," one of the high points of Part Two. Philosophically, however, it raises many difficulties. (See my *Nietzsche,* 6, III.)

13. *On Those Who Are Sublime:* The doctrine of self-overcoming is here guarded against misunderstandings: far from favoring austere heroics, Nietzsche praises humor (and practices it: witness the whole of *Zarathustra,* especially Part Four) and, no less, gracefulness and graciousness. The three sentences near the end, beginning "And there is nobody . . . ," represent a wonderfully concise statement of much of his philosophy.

14. *On the Land of Education:* Against modern eclecticism and lack of style. "Rather would I be a day laborer in Hades . . .": in the *Odyssey,* the shade of Achilles would rather be a day laborer on the smallest field than king of all the dead in Hades. *Zarathustra* abounds in similar allusions. "Everything deserves to perish," for example, is an abbreviation of a dictum of Goethe's Mephistopheles.

15. *On Immaculate Perception:* Labored sexual imagery, already notable in "The Dancing Song," keeps this critique of detachment from becoming incisive. Not arid but, judged by high standards, a mismatch of message and metaphor. Or put positively: something of a personal document. Therefore the German references to the sun as feminine have been retained in translation. "Loving and perishing (*Lieben und Untergehn*)" do not rhyme in German either.

16. *On Scholars:* Nietzsche's, not Zarathustra's, autobiography.

17. *On Poets:* This chapter is full of allusions to the final chorus in Goethe's *Faust,* which might be translated thus:

What is destructible
Is but a parable;

What fails ineluctably
The undeclarable,
Here it was seen,
Here it was action;
The Eternal-Feminine
Lures to perfection.

18. *On Great Events:* How successful Nietzsche's attempts at narrative are is at least debatable. Here the story distracts from his statement of his anti-political attitude. But the curious mixture of the solemn and frivolous, myth, epigram, and "bow-wow," is of course entirely intentional. Even the similarity between the ghost's cry and the words of the white rabbit in *Alice in Wonderland* probably would not have dismayed Nietzsche in the least.

19. *The Soothsayer:* In the chapter "On the Adder's Bite" a brief parable introduces some of Zarathustra's finest sayings; but here the parable is offered for its own sake, and we feel closer to Rimbaud than to Proverbs. The soothsayer reappears in Part Four.

20. *On Redemption:* In the conception of inverse cripples and the remarks on revenge and punishment Zarathustra's moral pathos reappears to some extent; but the mood of the preceding chapter figures in his subsequent reflections, which lead up to, but stop short of, Nietzsche's notion of the eternal recurrence of the same events.

21. *On Human Prudence:* First: better to be deceived occasionally than always to watch out for deceivers. Second: vanity versus pride. Third: men today (1883) are too concerned about petty evil, but great things are possible only where great evil is harnessed.

22. *The Stillest Hour:* Zarathustra cannot yet get himself to proclaim the eternal recurrence and hence he must leave in order to "ripen."

THE CHILD WITH THE MIRROR

Then Zarathustra returned again to the mountains and to the solitude of his cave and withdrew from men, waiting like a sower who has scattered his seed. But his soul grew full of impatience and desire for those whom he loved, because he still had much to give them. For this is what is hardest: to close the open hand because one loves, and to keep a sense of shame as a giver.

Thus months and years passed for the solitary; but his wisdom grew and caused him pain with its fullness. One morning, however, he woke even before the dawn, reflected long, lying on his bed, and at last spoke to his heart:

Why was I so startled in my dream that I awoke? Did not a child step up to me, carrying a mirror? "O Zarathustra," the child said to me, "look at yourself in the mirror." But when I looked into the mirror I cried out, and my heart was shaken: for it was not myself I saw, but a devil's grimace and scornful laughter. Verily, all-too-well do I understand the sign and admonition of the dream: my *teaching* is in danger; weeds pose as wheat. My enemies have grown powerful and have distorted my teaching till those dearest to me must be ashamed of the gifts I gave them. I have lost my friends; the hour has come to seek my lost ones."

With these words Zarathustra leaped up, not like a frightened man seeking air but rather as a seer and singer who is moved by the spirit. Amazed, his eagle and his serpent looked at him: for, like dawn, a coming happiness lay reflected in his face.

What has happened to me, my animals? said Zarathustra. Have I not changed? Has not bliss come to me as a storm? My happiness is foolish and will say foolish things: it is still young, so be patient with it. I am wounded by my happiness: let all who suffer be my physicians. I may go down again to my friends, and to my enemies too. Zarathustra may speak again and give and do what is dearest to those dear to him. My impatient love overflows in rivers, downward, toward sunrise and sunset. From silent mountains and thunderstorms of suffering my soul rushes into the valleys.

Too long have I longed and looked into the distance. Too long have I belonged to loneliness; thus I have forgotten how to be silent. Mouth have I become through and through, and the roaring of a stream from towering cliffs: I want to plunge my speech down into the valleys. Let the river of my love plunge where there is no way! How could a river fail to find its way to the sea? Indeed, a lake is within me, solitary and self-sufficient; but the river of my love carries it along, down to the sea.

New ways I go, a new speech comes to me; weary I grow, like all creators, of the old tongues. My spirit no longer wants to walk on worn soles.

Too slowly runs all speech for me: into your chariot I leap, storm! And even you I want to whip with my sarcasm. Like a cry and a shout of joy I want to sweep over wide seas, till I find the blessed isles where my friends are dwelling. And my enemies among them! How I now love all to whom I may speak! My enemies too are part of my bliss.

And when I want to mount my wildest horse, it is always my spear that helps me up best, as the ever-ready servant of my foot: the spear that I hurl against my enemies. How grateful I am to my enemies that I may finally hurl it!

The tension of my cloud was too great: between the laughter of lightning bolts I want to throw showers of hail into the depths. Violently my chest will expand, violently will it blow its storm over the mountains and thus find relief. Verily, like a storm come my happiness and my freedom. But let my enemies believe that *the evil one* rages over their heads.

Indeed, you too will be frightened, my friends, by my wild wisdom; and perhaps you will flee from it, together with my enemies. Would that I knew how to lure you back with shepherds' flutes! Would that my lioness, wisdom, might learn how to roar tenderly! And many things have we already learned together.

My wild wisdom became pregnant on lonely mountains; on rough stones she gave birth to her young, her youngest. Now she runs foolishly through the harsh desert and seeks and seeks gentle turf—my old wild wisdom. Upon your hearts' gentle turf, my friends, upon your love she would bed her most dearly beloved.

Thus spoke Zarathustra.

UPON THE BLESSED ISLES

The figs are falling from the trees; they are good and sweet; and, as they fall, their red skin bursts. I am a north wind to ripe figs.

Thus, like figs, these teachings fall to you, my friends; now consume their juice and their sweet meat. It is autumn about us, and pure sky and afternoon. Behold what fullness there is about us! And out of such overflow it is beautiful to look out upon distant seas. Once one said God when one looked upon distant seas; but now I have taught you to say: overman.

God is a conjecture; but I desire that your conjectures should not reach beyond your creative will. Could you *create* a god? Then do not speak to me of any gods. But you could well create the overman. Perhaps not you yourselves, my brothers. But into fathers and forefathers of the overman you could re-create yourselves: and let this be your best creation.

God is a conjecture; but I desire that your conjectures should be limited by what is thinkable. Could you *think* a god? But this is what the will to truth should mean to you: that everything be changed into what is thinkable for man, visible for man, feelable by man. You should think through your own senses to their consequences.

And what you have called world, that shall be created only by you: your reason, your image, your will, your love shall thus be realized. And verily, for your own bliss, you lovers of knowledge.

And how would you bear life without this hope, you lovers of knowledge? You could not have been born either into the incomprehensible or into the irrational.

But let me reveal my heart to you entirely, my friends: *if* there were gods, how could I endure not to be a god! *Hence* there are no gods. Though I drew this conclusion, now it draws me.

God is a conjecture; but who could drain all the agony of this conjecture without dying? Shall his faith be taken away from the creator, and from the eagle, his soaring to eagle heights?

God is a thought that makes crooked all that is straight, and makes turn whatever stands. How? Should time be gone, and all that is impermanent a mere lie? To think this is a dizzy whirl for human bones, and a vomit for the stomach; verily, I call it the turning sickness to conjecture thus. Evil I call it, and misanthropic —all this teaching of the One and the Plenum and the Unmoved and the Sated and the Permanent. All the permanent—that is only a parable. And the poets lie too much.

It is of time and becoming that the best parables

should speak: let them be a praise and a justification of all impermanence.

Creation—that is the great redemption from suffering, and life's growing light. But that the creator may be, suffering is needed and much change. Indeed, there must be much bitter dying in your life, you creators. Thus are you advocates and justifiers of all impermanence. To be the child who is newly born, the creator must also want to be the mother who gives birth and the pangs of the birth-giver.

Verily, through a hundred souls I have already passed on my way, and through a hundred cradles and birth pangs. Many a farewell have I taken; I know the heart-rending last hours. But thus my creative will, my destiny, wills it. Or, to say it more honestly: this very destiny—my will wills.

Whatever in me has feeling, suffers and is in prison; but my will always comes to me as my liberator and joy-bringer. Willing liberates: that is the true teaching of will and liberty—thus Zarathustra teaches it. Willing no more and esteeming no more and creating no more—oh, that this great weariness might always remain far from me! In knowledge too I feel only my will's joy in begetting and becoming; and if there is innocence in my knowledge, it is because the will to beget is in it. Away from God and gods this will has lured me; what could one create if gods existed?

But my fervent will to create impels me ever again toward man; thus is the hammer impelled toward the stone. O men, in the stone there sleeps an image, the image of my images. Alas, that it must sleep in the hardest, the ugliest stone! Now my hammer rages cruelly against its prison. Pieces of rock rain from the stone: what is that to me? I want to perfect it; for a shadow came to me—the stillest and lightest of all things once came to me. The beauty of the overman came to me as a shadow. O my brothers, what are the gods to me now?

Thus spoke Zarathustra.

ON THE PITYING

My friends, a gibe was related to your friend: "Look at Zarathustra! Does he not walk among us as if we were animals?"

But it were better said: "He who has knowledge walks among men *as* among animals."

To him who has knowledge, man himself is "the animal with red cheeks." How did this come about? Is it not because man has had to be ashamed too often? O my friends! Thus speaks he who has knowledge: shame, shame, shame—that is the history of man. And that is why he who is noble bids himself not to shame: shame he imposes on himself before all who suffer.

Verily, I do not like them, the merciful who feel blessed in their pity: they are lacking too much in shame. If I must pity, at least I do not want it known; and if I do pity, it is preferably from a distance.

I should also like to shroud my face and flee before I am recognized; and thus I bid you do, my friends. Would that my destiny led those like you, who do not suffer, across my way, and those with whom I *may* share hope and meal and honey. Verily, I may have done this and that for sufferers; but always I seemed to have done better when I learned to feel better joys. As long as there have been men, man has felt too little joy: that alone, my brothers, is our original sin. And learning better to feel joy, we learn best not to hurt others or to plan hurts for them.

Therefore I wash my hand when it has helped the

sufferer; therefore I wipe even my soul. Having seen the sufferer suffer, I was ashamed for the sake of his shame; and when I helped him, I transgressed grievously against his pride.

Great indebtedness does not make men grateful, but vengeful; and if a little charity is not forgotten, it turns into a gnawing worm.

"Be reserved in accepting! Distinguish by accepting!" Thus I advise those who have nothing to give.

But I am a giver of gifts: I like to give, as a friend to friends. Strangers, however, and the poor may themselves pluck the fruit from my tree: that will cause them less shame.

But beggars should be abolished entirely! Verily, it is annoying to give to them and it is annoying not to give to them.

And also sinners and bad consciences! Believe me, my friends: the bite of conscience teaches men to bite.

Worst of all, however, are petty thoughts. Verily, even evil deeds are better than petty thoughts.

To be sure, you say: "The pleasure in a lot of petty nastiness saves us from many a big evil deed." But here one should not wish to save.

An evil deed is like a boil: it itches and irritates and breaks open—it speaks honestly. "Behold, I am disease" —thus speaks the evil deed; that is its honesty.

But a petty thought is like a fungus: it creeps and stoops and does not want to be anywhere—until the whole body is rotten and withered with little fungi.

But to him who is possessed by the devil I whisper this word: "Better for you to rear up your devil! Even for you there is still a way to greatness!"

My brothers, one knows a little too much about everybody. And we can even see through some men and yet we can by no means *pass* through them.

It is difficult to live with people because it is so difficult to be silent. And not against him who is repugnant to us are we most unfair, but against him who is no concern of ours.

But if you have a suffering friend, be a resting place for his suffering, but a hard bed as it were, a field cot: thus will you profit him best.

And if a friend does you evil, then say: "I forgive you what you did to me; but that you have done it to *yourself*—how could I forgive that?" Thus speaks all great love: it overcomes even forgiveness and pity.

One ought to hold on to one's heart; for if one lets it go, one soon loses control of the head too. Alas, where in the world has there been more folly than among the pitying? And what in the world has caused more suffering than the folly of the pitying? Woe to all who love without having a height that is above their pity!

Thus spoke the devil to me once: "God too has his hell: that is his love of man." And most recently I heard him say this: "God is dead; God died of his pity for man."

Thus be warned of pity: from there a heavy cloud will yet come to man. Verily, I understand weather signs. But mark this too: all great love is even above all its pity; for it still wants to create the beloved.

"Myself I sacrifice to my love, *and my neighbor as myself*"—thus runs the speech of all creators. But all creators are hard.

Thus spoke Zarathustra.

ON PRIESTS

Once Zarathustra gave his disciples a sign and spoke these words to them:

"Here are priests; and though they are my enemies,

pass by them silently and with sleeping swords. Among them too there are heroes; many of them have suffered too much: therefore they want to make others suffer.

"They are evil enemies: nothing is more vengeful than their humility. And whoever attacks them, soils himself easily. Yet my blood is related to theirs, and I want to know that my blood is honored even in theirs."

And when they had passed, pain seized Zarathustra; and he had not wrestled long with his pain when he began to speak thus:

I am moved by compassion for these priests. I also find them repulsive; but that matters least of all to me since I have been among men. But I suffer and have suffered with them: prisoners they are to me, and marked men. He whom they call Redeemer has put them in fetters: in fetters of false values and delusive words. Would that someone would yet redeem them from their Redeemer!

Once when the sea cast them about, they thought they were landing on an island; but behold, it was a sleeping monster. False values and delusive words: these are the worst monsters for mortals; long does calamity sleep and wait in them. But eventually it comes and wakes and eats and devours what built huts upon it. Behold these huts which these priests built! Churches they call their sweet-smelling caves. Oh, that falsified light! That musty air! Here the soul is not allowed to soar to its height. For thus their faith commands: "Crawl up the stairs on your knees, ye sinners!"

Verily, rather would I see even the shameless than the contorted eyes of their shame and devotion! Who created for themselves such caves and stairways of repentance? Was it not such as wanted to hide themselves and were ashamed before the pure sky?

And only when the pure sky again looks through

broken ceilings and down upon grass and red poppies near broken walls, will I again turn my heart to the abodes of this god.

They have called "God" what was contrary to them and gave them pain; and verily, there was much of the heroic in their adoration. And they did not know how to love their god except by crucifying man.

As corpses they meant to live; in black they decked out their corpses; out of their speech, too, I still smell the bad odor of death chambers. And whoever lives near them lives near black ponds out of which an ominous frog sings its song with sweet melancholy. They would have to sing better songs for me to learn to have faith in their Redeemer: and his disciples would have to look more redeemed!

Naked would I see them: for only beauty should preach repentance. But who would be persuaded by this muffled melancholy? Verily, their redeemers themselves did not come out of freedom and the seventh heaven of freedom. Verily, they themselves have never walked on the carpets of knowledge. Of gaps was the spirit of these redeemers made up; but into every gap they put their delusion, their stopgap, which they called God.

Their spirit was drowned in their pity; and when they were swollen and overswollen with pity, it was always a great folly that swam on top. Eagerly and with much shouting they drove their herd over their path; as if there were but a single path to the future. Verily, these shepherds themselves belonged among the sheep. Small spirits and spacious souls these shepherds had; but my brothers, what small domains have even the most spacious souls proved to be so far!

They wrote signs of blood on the way they walked, and their folly taught that with blood one proved truth.

But blood is the worst witness of truth; blood poisons even the purest doctrine and turns it into delusion and hatred of the heart. And if a man goes through fire for his doctrine—what does that prove? Verily, it is more if your own doctrine comes out of your own fire.

A sultry heart and a cold head: where these two meet there arises the roaring wind, the "Redeemer." There have been greater ones, verily, and more highborn than those whom the people call redeemers, those roaring winds which carry away. And you, my brothers, must be redeemed from still greater ones than all the redeemers if you would find the way to freedom.

Never yet has there been an overman. Naked I saw both the greatest and the smallest man: they are still all-too-similar to each other. Verily, even the greatest I found all-too-human.

Thus spoke Zarathustra.

ON THE VIRTUOUS

Slack and sleeping senses must be addressed with thunder and heavenly fireworks. But the voice of beauty speaks gently: it creeps only into the most awakened souls. Gently trembled and laughed my shield today; that is the holy laughter and tremor of beauty. About you, the virtuous, my beauty laughed today. And thus its voice came to me: "They still want to be paid."

You who are virtuous still want to be paid! Do you want rewards for virtue, and heaven for earth, and the eternal for your today?

And now are you angry with me because I teach that there is no reward and paymaster? And verily, I do not even teach that virtue is its own reward.

Alas, that is my sorrow: they have lied reward and punishment into the foundation of things, and now also into the foundation of your souls, you who are virtuous. But like the boar's snout, my words shall tear open the foundation of your souls: a plowshare will I be to you. All the secrets of your foundation shall come to light; and when you lie uprooted and broken in the sun, then will your lies also be separated from your truths.

For this is your truth: you are too *pure* for the filth of the words: revenge, punishment, reward, retribution. You love your virtue as a mother her child; but when has a mother ever wished to be paid for her love? Your virtue is what is dearest to you. The thirst of the ring lives in you: every ring strives and turns to reach itself again. And like a dying star is every work of your virtue: its light is always still on its way and it wanders— and when will it no longer be on its way? Thus the light of your virtue is still on its way even when the work has been done. Though it be forgotten and dead, the ray of its light still lives and wanders. That your virtue is your self and not something foreign, a skin, a cloak, that is the truth from the foundation of your souls, you who are virtuous.

Yet there are those for whom virtue is the spasm under the scourge, and you have listened to their clamor too much.

And there are others who call it virtue when their vices grow lazy; and when their hatred and jealousy stretch their limbs for once, then their "justice" comes to life and rubs its sleepy eyes.

And there are others who are drawn downward: their devils draw them. But the more they sink, the more fervently glow their eyes and their lust for their god. Alas, their clamor too has reached your ears, you who are virtuous: "What I am not, that, that to me are God and virtue!"

And there are others who come along, heavy and

creaking like carts carrying stones downhill: they talk much of dignity and virtue—they call their brake virtue.

And there are others who are like cheap clocks that must be wound: they tick and they want the tick-tock to be called virtue. Verily, I have my pleasure in these: wherever I find such clocks, I shall wind and wound them with my mockery, and they shall whir for me.

And others are proud of their handful of justice and commit outrages against all things for its sake, till the world is drowned in their injustice. Oh, how ill the word virtue comes out of their mouths! And when they say, "I am just," it always sounds like "I am just—revenged." With their virtue they want to scratch out the eyes of their enemies, and they exalt themselves only to humble others.

And then again there are such as sit in their swamp and speak thus out of the reeds: "Virtue—that is sitting still in a swamp. We bite no one and avoid those who want to bite; and in all things we hold the opinion that is given to us."

And then again there are such as love gestures and think that virtue is some kind of gesture. Their knees always adore, and their hands are hymns to virtue, but their heart knows nothing about it.

And then again there are such as consider it virtue to say, "Virtue is necessary"; but at bottom they believe only that the police is necessary.

And some who cannot see what is high in man call it virtue that they see all-too-closely what is low in man: thus they call their evil eye virtue.

And some want to be edified and elevated, and they call that virtue, while others want to be bowled over, and they call that virtue too.

And thus almost all believe that they have a share in

virtue; and at the very least everyone wants to be an expert on good and evil.

Yet Zarathustra did not come to say to all these liars and fools: "What do *you* know of virtue? What *could* you know of virtue?"

Rather, that you, my friends, might grow weary of the old words you have learned from the fools and liars.

Weary of the words: reward, retribution, punishment, and revenge in justice.

Weary of saying: what makes an act good is that it is unselfish.

Oh, my friends, that your self be in your deed as the mother is in her child—let that be *your* word concerning virtue!

Verily, I may have taken a hundred words from you and the dearest toys of your virtue, and now you are angry with me, as children are angry. They played by the sea, and a wave came and carried off their toy to the depths: now they are crying. But the same wave shall bring them new toys and shower new colorful shells before them. Thus they will be comforted; and like them, you too, my friends, shall have your comfortings—and new colorful shells.

Thus spoke Zarathustra.

ON THE RABBLE

Life is a well of joy; but where the rabble drinks too, all wells are poisoned. I am fond of all that is clean, but I have no wish to see the grinning snouts and the thirst of the unclean. They cast their eye into the well: now their revolting smile shines up out of the well. They have poisoned the holy water with their lustfulness; and when they called their dirty dreams "pleasure," they poisoned the language too. The flame is vexed when their moist hearts come near the fire; the spirit itself seethes and smokes where the rabble steps near the fire. In their hands all fruit grows sweetish and overmellow; their glance makes the fruit tree a prey of the wind and withers its crown.

And some who turned away from life only turned away from the rabble: they did not want to share well and flame and fruit with the rabble.

And some who went into the wilderness and suffered thirst with the beasts of prey merely did not want to sit around the cistern with filthy camel drivers.

And some who came along like annihilators and like a hailstorm to all orchards merely wanted to put a foot into the gaping jaws of the rabble to plug up its throat.

The bite on which I gagged the most is not the knowledge that life itself requires hostility and death and torture-crosses—but once I asked, and I was almost choked by my question: What? does life require even the rabble? Are poisoned wells required, and stinking fires and soiled dreams and maggots in the bread of life?

Not my hatred but my nausea gnawed hungrily at my life. Alas, I often grew weary of the spirit when I found that even the rabble had *esprit*. And I turned my back on those who rule when I saw what they now call ruling: higgling and haggling for power—with the rabble. I have lived with closed ears among people with foreign tongues: would that the tongue of their higgling and their haggling for power might remain foreign to me. And, holding my nose, I walked disgruntled through all of yesterday and today: verily, all of yesterday and today smells foul of the writing rabble.

Like a cripple who has become deaf and blind and dumb: thus have I lived for many years lest I live with the power-, writing- and pleasure-rabble. Laboriously and cautiously my spirit climbed steps; alms of pleasure

were its refreshment; and life crept along for the blind
as on a cane.

What was it that happened to me? How did I redeem
myself from nausea? Who rejuvenated my sight? How
did I fly to the height where no more rabble sits by the
well? Was it my nausea itself which created wings for
me and water-divining powers? Verily, I had to fly to
the highest spheres that I might find the fount of pleasure again.

Oh, I found it, my brothers! Here, in the highest
spheres, the fount of pleasure wells up for me! And here
is a life of which the rabble does not drink.

You flow for me almost too violently, fountain of
pleasure. And often you empty the cup again by wanting to fill it. And I must still learn to approach you more
modestly: all-too-violently my heart still flows toward
you—my heart, upon which my summer burns, short,
hot, melancholy, overblissful: how my summer-heart
craves your coolness!

Gone is the hesitant gloom of my spring! Gone the
malice of my snowflakes in June! Summer have I become entirely, and summer noon! A summer in the
highest spheres with cold wells and blissful silence: oh,
come, my friends, that the silence may become still
more blissful!

For this is *our* height and our home: we live here too
high and steep for all the unclean and their thirst. Cast
your pure eyes into the well of my pleasure, friends!
How should that make it muddy? It shall laugh back at
you in its own purity.

On the tree, Future, we build our nest; and in our
solitude eagles shall bring us nourishment in their beaks.
Verily, no nourishment which the unclean might share:
they would think they were devouring fire and they
would burn their mouths. Verily, we keep no homes

here for the unclean: our pleasure would be an ice cave to their bodies and their spirits.

And we want to live over them like strong winds, neighbors of the eagles, neighbors of the snow, neighbors of the sun: thus live strong winds. And like a wind I yet want to blow among them one day, and with my spirit take the breath of their spirit: thus my future wills it.

Verily, a strong wind is Zarathustra for all who are low; and this counsel he gives to all his enemies and all who spit and spew: "Beware of spitting *against* the wind!"

Thus spoke Zarathustra.

ON THE TARANTULAS

Behold, this is the hole of the tarantula. Do you want to see the tarantula itself? Here hangs its web; touch it, that it tremble!

There it comes willingly: welcome, tarantula! Your triangle and symbol sits black on your back; and I also know what sits in your soul. Revenge sits in your soul: wherever you bite, black scabs grow; your poison makes the soul whirl with revenge.

Thus I speak to you in a parable—you who make souls whirl, you preachers of *equality*. To me you are tarantulas, and secretly vengeful. But I shall bring your secrets to light; therefore I laugh in your faces with my laughter of the heights. Therefore I tear at your webs, that your rage may lure you out of your lie-holes and your revenge may leap out from behind your word justice. For *that man be delivered from revenge, that is* for me the bridge to the highest hope, and a rainbow after long storms.

The tarantulas, of course, would have it otherwise.

"What justice means to us is precisely that the world be filled with the storms of our revenge"—thus they speak to each other. "We shall wreak vengeance and abuse on all whose equals we are not"—thus do the tarantula-hearts vow. "And 'will to equality' shall henceforth be the name for virtue; and against all that has power we want to raise our clamor!"

You preachers of equality, the tyrannomania of impotence clamors thus out of you for equality: your most secret ambitions to be tyrants thus shroud themselves in words of virtue. Aggrieved conceit, repressed envy —perhaps the conceit and envy of your fathers—erupt from you as a flame and as the frenzy of revenge.

What was silent in the father speaks in the son; and often I found the son the unveiled secret of the father.

They are like enthusiasts, yet it is not the heart that fires them—but revenge. And when they become elegant and cold, it is not the spirit but envy that makes them elegant and cold. Their jealousy leads them even on the paths of thinkers; and this is the sign of their jealousy: they always go too far, till their weariness must in the end lie down to sleep in the snow. Out of every one of their complaints sounds revenge; in their praise there is always a sting, and to be a judge seems bliss to them.

But thus I counsel you, my friends: Mistrust all in whom the impulse to punish is powerful. They are people of a low sort and stock; the hangman and the blood-hound look out of their faces. Mistrust all who talk much of their justice! Verily, their souls lack more than honey. And when they call themselves the good and the just, do not forget that they would be pharisees, if only they had—power.

My friends, I do not want to be mixed up and confused with others. Some preach my doctrine of life and

are at the same time preachers of equality and tarantulas. Although they are sitting in their holes, these
poisonous spiders, with their backs turned on life, they
speak in favor of life, but only because they wish to
hurt. They wish to hurt those who now have power, for
among these the preaching of death is still most at
home. If it were otherwise, the tarantulas would teach
otherwise; they themselves were once the foremost slan-
derers of the world and burners of heretics.

I do not wish to be mixed up and confused with
these preachers of equality. For, to *me* justice speaks
thus: "Men are not equal." Nor shall they become
equal! What would my love of the overman be if I
spoke otherwise?

On a thousand bridges and paths they shall throng
to the future, and ever more war and inequality shall
divide them: thus does my great love make me speak.
In their hostilities they shall become inventors of images
and ghosts, and with their images and ghosts they shall
yet fight the highest fight against one another. Good
and evil, and rich and poor, and high and low, and all
the names of values—arms shall they be and clattering
signs that life must overcome itself again and again.

Life wants to build itself up into the heights with
pillars and steps; it wants to look into vast distances
and out toward stirring beauties: therefore it requires
height. And because it requires height, it requires steps
and contradiction among the steps and the climbers.
Life wants to climb and to overcome itself climbing.

And behold, my friends: here where the tarantula
has its hole, the ruins of an ancient temple rise; behold
it with enlightened eyes! Verily, the man who once
piled his thoughts to the sky in these stones—he, like
the wisest, knew the secret of all life. That struggle and
inequality are present even in beauty, and also war for

power and more power: that is what he teaches us here in the plainest parable. How divinely vault and arches break through each other in a wrestling match; how they strive against each other with light and shade, the godlike strivers—with such assurance and beauty let us be enemies too, my friends! Let us strive against one another like gods.

Alas, then the tarantula, my old enemy, bit me. With godlike assurance and beauty it bit my finger. "Punishment there must be and justice," it thinks; "and here he shall not sing songs in honor of enmity in vain."

Indeed, it has avenged itself. And alas, now it will make my soul, too, whirl with revenge. But to keep me from whirling, my friends, tie me tight to this column. Rather would I be a stylite even, than a whirl of revenge.

Verily, Zarathustra is no cyclone or whirlwind; and if he is a dancer, he will never dance the tarantella.

Thus spoke Zarathustra.

ON THE FAMOUS WISE MEN

You have served the people and the superstition of the people, all you famous wise men—and *not* truth. And that is precisely why you were accorded respect. And that is also why your lack of faith was tolerated: it was a joke and a circuitous route to the people. Thus the master lets his slaves have their way and is even amused by their pranks.

But the free spirit, the enemy of fetters, the non-adorer who dwells in the woods, is as hateful to the people as a wolf to dogs. To hound him out of his lair —that is what the people have ever called "a sense of

decency"; and against him the people still set their
fiercest dogs.

"Truth is there: after all, the people are there! Let
those who seek beware!"—these words have echoed
through the ages. You wanted to prove your people
right in their reverence: that is what you called "will
to truth," you famous wise men. And your hearts ever
said to themselves: "From among the people I came,
and from there too the voice of God came to me. As
the people's advocates you have always been stiff-necked
and clever like asses.

And many who were powerful and wanted to get
along smoothly with the people harnessed in front of
their horses a little ass, a famous wise man.

And now I should wish, you famous wise men, that
you would at long last throw off the lion's skin completely. The skin of the beast of prey, mottled, and the
mane of those who search, seek, and conquer.

Oh, to make me believe in your "truthfulness" you
would first have to break your revering will.

Truthful I call him who goes into godless deserts,
having broken his revering heart. In the yellow sands,
burned by the sun, he squints thirstily at the islands
abounding in wells, where living things rest under dark
trees. Yet his thirst does not persuade him to become
like these, dwelling in comfort; for where there are
oases there are also idols.

Hungry, violent, lonely, godless: thus the lion-will
wants itself. Free from the happiness of slaves, redeemed from gods and adorations, fearless and fear-
inspiring, great and lonely: such is the will of the truthful.

It was ever in the desert that the truthful have dwelt,
the free spirits, as masters of the desert; but in the

cities dwell the well-fed, famous wise men—the beasts
of burden. For, as asses, they always pull the people's
cart. Not that I am angry with them for that: but for
me they remain such as serve and work in a harness,
even when they shine in harnesses of gold. And often
they have been good servants, worthy of praise. For thus
speaks virtue: "If you must be a servant, seek him who
profits most from your service. The spirit and virtue of
your master shall grow by your being his servant: then
you yourself will grow with his spirit and his virtue."
And verily, you famous wise men, you servants of the
people, you yourselves have grown with the spirit and
virtue of the people—and the people through you. In
your honor I say this. But even in your virtues you remain for me part of the people, the dumb-eyed people
—the people, who do not know what spirit is.

Spirit is the life that itself cuts into life: with its own
agony it increases its own knowledge. Did you know
that?

And the happiness of the spirit is this: to be anointed
and through tears to be consecrated as a sacrificial
animal. Did you know that?

And the blindness of the blind and their seeking and
groping shall yet bear witness to the power of the sun,
into which they have looked. Did you know that?

And the lover of knowledge shall learn to *build* with
mountains. It means little that the spirit moves mountains. Did you know that?

You know only the spark of the spirit, but you do not
see the anvil it is, nor the cruelty of its hammer.

Verily, you do not know the pride of the spirit! But
even less would you endure the modesty of the spirit,
if ever it would speak.

And you have never yet been able to cast your spirit

into a pit of snow: you are not hot enough for that. Hence you also do not know the ecstasies of its coldness.

In all things, however, you act too familiarly with the spirit, and you have often made wisdom into a poorhouse and a hospital for bad poets.

You are no eagles: hence you have never experienced the happiness that is in the terror of the spirit. And he who is not a bird should not build his nest over abysses.

You are lukewarm to me, but all profound knowledge flows cold. Ice cold are the inmost wells of the spirit: refreshing for hot hands and men of action. You stand there honorable and stiff and with straight backs, you famous wise men: no strong wind and will drives you.

Have you never seen a sail go over the sea, rounded and taut and trembling with the violence of the wind? Like the sail, trembling with the violence of the spirit, my wisdom goes over the sea—my wild wisdom.

But you servants of the people, you famous wise men—how could you go with me?

Thus spoke Zarathustra.

THE NIGHT SONG

Night has come; now all fountains speak more loudly. And my soul too is a fountain.

Night has come; only now all the songs of lovers awaken. And my soul too is the song of a lover.

Something unstilled, unstillable is within me; it wants to be voiced. A craving for love is within me; it speaks the language of love.

Light am I; ah, that I were night! But this is my loneliness that I am girt with light. Ah, that I were dark and nocturnal! How I would suck at the breasts of light!

And even you would I bless, you little sparkling stars and glowworms up there, and be overjoyed with your gifts of light.

But I live in my own light; I drink back into myself the flames that break out of me. I do not know the happiness of those who receive; and I have often dreamed that even stealing must be more blessed than receiving. This is my poverty, that my hand never rests from giving; this is my envy, that I see waiting eyes and the lit-up nights of longing. Oh, wretchedness of all givers! Oh, darkening of my sun! Oh, craving to crave! Oh, ravenous hunger in satiation!

They receive from me, but do I touch their souls? There is a cleft between giving and receiving; and the narrowest cleft is the last to be bridged. A hunger grows out of my beauty: I should like to hurt those for whom I shine; I should like to rob those to whom I give; thus do I hunger for malice. To withdraw my hand when the other hand already reaches out to it; to linger like the waterfall, which lingers even while it plunges: thus do I hunger for malice. Such revenge my fullness plots: such spite wells up out of my loneliness. My happiness in giving died in giving; my virtue tired of itself in its overflow.

The danger of those who always give is that they lose their sense of shame; and the heart and hand of those who always mete out become callous from always meting out. My eye no longer wells over at the shame of those who beg; my hand has grown too hard for the trembling of filled hands. Where have the tears of my eyes gone and the down of my heart? Oh, the loneliness of all givers! Oh, the taciturnity of all who shine!

Many suns revolve in the void: to all that is dark they speak with their light—to me they are silent. Oh, this is the enmity of the light against what shines:

merciless it moves in its orbit. Unjust in its heart against all that shines, cold against suns—thus moves every sun.

The suns fly like a storm in their orbits: that is their motion. They follow their inexorable will: that is their coldness.

Oh, it is only you, you dark ones, you nocturnal ones, who create warmth out of that which shines. It is only you who drink milk and refreshment out of the udders of light.

Alas, ice is all around me, my hand is burned by the icy. Alas, thirst is within me that languishes after your thirst.

Night has come: alas, that I must be light! And thirst for the nocturnal! And loneliness!

Night has come: now my craving breaks out of me like a well; to speak I crave.

Night has come; now all fountains speak more loudly. And my soul too is a fountain.

Night has come; now all the songs of lovers awaken. And my soul too is the song of a lover.

Thus sang Zarathustra.

THE DANCING SONG

One evening Zarathustra walked through a forest with his disciples; and as he sought a well, behold, he came upon a green meadow, silently surrounded by trees and shrubs, and upon it girls were dancing with each other. As soon as the girls recognized Zarathustra they ceased dancing. But Zarathustra walked up to them with a friendly gesture and spoke these words:

"Do not cease dancing, you lovely girls! No killjoy has come to you with evil eyes, no enemy of girls. God's advocate am I before the devil: but the devil is the spirit of gravity. How could I, you lightfooted ones, be an enemy of godlike dances? Or of girls' feet with pretty ankles?

"Indeed, I am a forest and a night of dark trees: but he who is not afraid of my darkness will also find rose slopes under my cypresses. And he will also find the little god whom girls like best: beside the well he lies, still, with his eyes shut. Verily, in bright daylight he fell asleep, the sluggard! Did he chase after butterflies too much? Do not be angry with me, you beautiful dancers, if I chastise the little god a bit. He may cry and weep—but he is laughable even when he weeps. And with tears in his eyes he shall ask you for a dance, and I myself will sing a song for his dance: a dancing and mocking song on the spirit of gravity, my supreme and most powerful devil, of whom they say that he is 'the master of the world.'"

And this is the song that Zarathustra sang while Cupid and the girls danced together:

Into your eyes I looked recently, O life! And into the unfathomable I then seemed to be sinking. But you pulled me out with a golden fishing rod; and you laughed mockingly when I called you unfathomable.

"Thus runs the speech of all fish," you said; "what *they* do not fathom is unfathomable. But I am merely changeable and wild and a woman in every way, and not virtuous—even if you men call me profound, faithful, eternal, and mysterious. But you men always present us with your own virtues, O you virtuous men!"

Thus she laughed, the incredible one; but I never believe her and her laughter when she speaks ill of herself.

And when I talked in confidence with my wild wisdom she said to me in anger, "You will, you want, you love—that is the only reason why you *praise* life." Then

I almost answered wickedly and told the angry woman the truth; and there is no more wicked answer than telling one's wisdom the truth.

For thus matters stand among the three of us: Deeply I love only life—and verily, most of all when I hate life. But that I am well disposed toward wisdom, and often too well, that is because she reminds me so much of life. She has her eyes, her laugh, and even her little golden fishing rod: is it my fault that the two look so similar?

And when life once asked me, "Who is this wisdom?" I answered fervently, "Oh yes, wisdom! One thirsts after her and is never satisfied; one looks through veils, one grabs through nets. Is she beautiful? How should I know? But even the oldest carps are baited with her. She is changeable and stubborn; often I have seen her bite her lip and comb her hair against the grain. Perhaps she is evil and false and a female in every way; but just when she speaks ill of herself she is most seductive."

When I said this to life she laughed sarcastically and closed her eyes. "Of whom are you speaking?" she asked; "no doubt, of me. And even if you are right —should *that* be said to my face? But now speak of your wisdom too."

Ah, and then you opened your eyes again, O beloved life. And again I seemed to myself to be sinking into the unfathomable.

Thus sang Zarathustra. But when the dance was over and the girls had gone away, he grew sad.

"The sun has set long ago," he said at last; "the meadow is moist, a chill comes from the woods. Something unknown is around me and looks thoughtful. What? Are you still alive, Zarathustra?

"Why? What for? By what? Whither? Where? How? Is it not folly still to be alive?

"Alas, my friends, it is the evening that asks thus through me. Forgive me my sadness. Evening has come; forgive me that evening has come."

Thus spoke Zarathustra.

THE TOMB SONG

"There is the isle of tombs, the silent isle; there too are the tombs of my youth. There I wish to carry an evergreen wreath of life." Resolving this in my heart, I crossed the sea.

O you visions and apparitions of my youth! O all you glances of love, you divine moments! How quickly you died. Today I recall you like dead friends. From you, my dearest friends among the dead, a sweet scent comes to me, loosening heart and tears. Verily, it perturbs and loosens the heart of the lonely seafarer. I am still the richest and most enviable—I, the loneliest! For once I possessed you, and you still possess me: say, to whom fell, as to me, such rose apples from the bough? I am still the heir of your love and its soil, flowering in remembrance of you with motley wild virtues, O you most loved ones.

Alas, we were fashioned to remain close to each other, you fair and strange wonders; and you came to me and my craving, not like shy birds, but like trusting ones to him who trusts. Indeed, fashioned for loyalty, like myself, and for tender eternities—I must now call you after your disloyalty, you divine glances and moments: I have not yet learned any other name. Verily, you have died too soon for me, you fugitives. Yet you did not flee from me, nor did I flee from you: we are equally innocent in our disloyalty.

To kill *me*, they strangled you, songbirds of my hopes. Indeed, after you, my dearest friends, malice has ever shot its arrows—to hit *my* heart. And it hit! For you have always been closest to my heart, my possession and what possessed me: that is why you had to die young and all-too-early. The arrow was shot at my most vulnerable possession—at you, whose skin is like down and even more like a smile that dies of a glance.

But this word I want to speak to my enemies: What is all murder of human beings compared to that which you have done to me? What you have done to me is more evil than any murder of human beings; you have taken from me the irretrievable: thus I speak to you, my enemies. For you murdered the visions and dearest wonders of my youth. My playmates you took from me, the blessed spirits. In their memory I lay down this wreath and this curse. This curse against you, my enemies! For you have cut short my eternal bliss, as a tone that breaks off in a cold night. Scarcely as the gleam of divine eyes it came to me—passing swiftly as a glance.

Thus spoke my purity once in a fair hour: "All beings shall be divine to me." Then you assaulted me with filthy ghosts; alas, where has this fair hour fled now?

"All days shall be holy to me"—thus said the wisdom of my youth once; verily, it was the saying of a gay wisdom. But then you, my enemies, stole my nights from me and sold them into sleepless agony; alas, where has this gay wisdom fled now?

Once I craved happy omens from the birds; then you led a monster of an owl across my way, a revolting one. Alas, where did my tender desire flee then?

All nausea I once vowed to renounce: then you changed those near and nearest me into putrid boils. Alas, where did my noblest vow flee then?

I once walked as a blind man along blessed paths; then you threw filth in the path of the blind man, and now his old footpath nauseates him.

And when I did what was hardest for me and celebrated the triumph of my overcomings, then you made those who loved me scream that I was hurting them most.

Verily, this was always your practice: you galled my best honey and the industry of my best bees. To my charity you always dispatched the most impudent beggars; around my pity you always pushed the incurably shameless. Thus you wounded my virtue in its faith. And whenever I laid down for a sacrifice even what was holiest to me, your "piety" immediately placed its fatter gifts alongside, and in the fumes of your fat what was holiest to me suffocated.

And once I wanted to dance as I had never danced before: over all the heavens I wanted to dance. Then you persuaded my dearest singer. And he struck up a horrible dismal tune; alas, he tooted in my ears like a gloomy horn. Murderous singer, tool of malice, most innocent yourself! I stood ready for the best dance, when you murdered my ecstasy with your sounds. Only in the dance do I know how to tell the parable of the highest things: and now my highest parable remained unspoken in my limbs. My highest hope remained unspoken and unredeemed. And all the visions and consolations of my youth died! How did I endure it? How did I get over and overcome such wounds? How did my soul rise again out of such tombs?

Indeed, in me there is something invulnerable and unburiable, something that explodes rock: that is *my will*. Silent and unchanged it strides through the years. It would walk its way on my feet, my old will, and its mind is hard of heart and invulnerable.

Invulnerable am I only in the heel. You are still alive and your old self, most patient one. You have still broken out of every tomb. What in my youth was unredeemed lives on in you; and as life and youth you sit there, full of hope, on yellow ruins of tombs.

Indeed, for me, you are still the shatterer of all tombs. Hail to thee, my will! And only where there are tombs are there resurrections.

Thus sang Zarathustra.

ON SELF-OVERCOMING

"Will to truth," you who are wisest call that which impels you and fills you with lust?

A will to the thinkability of all beings: this *I* call your will. You want to *make* all being thinkable, for you doubt with well-founded suspicion that it is already thinkable. But it shall yield and bend for you. Thus your will wants it. It shall become smooth and serve the spirit as its mirror and reflection. That is your whole will, you who are wisest: a will to power—when you speak of good and evil too, and of valuations. You still want to create the world before which you can kneel: that is your ultimate hope and intoxication.

The unwise, of course, the people—they are like a river on which a bark drifts; and in the bark sit the valuations, solemn and muffled up. Your will and your valuations you have placed on the river of becoming; and what the people believe to be good and evil, that betrays to me an ancient will to power.

It was you who are wisest who placed such guests in this bark and gave them pomp and proud names—you and your dominant will. Now the river carries your bark farther; it *has* to carry it. It avails nothing that the broken wave foams and angrily opposes the keel. Not the river is your danger and the end of your good and evil, you who are wisest, but that will itself, the will to power—the unexhausted procreative will of life.

But to make you understand my word concerning good and evil, I shall now say to you my word concerning life and the nature of all the living.

I pursued the living; I walked the widest and the narrowest paths that I might know its nature. With a hundredfold mirror I still caught its glance when its mouth was closed, so that its eyes might speak to me. And its eyes spoke to me.

But wherever I found the living, there I heard also the speech on obedience. Whatever lives, obeys.

And this is the second point: he who cannot obey himself is commanded. That is the nature of the living.

This, however, is the third point that I heard: that commanding is harder than obeying; and not only because he who commands must carry the burden of all who obey, and because this burden may easily crush him. An experiment and hazard appeared to me to be in all commanding; and whenever the living commands, it hazards itself. Indeed, even when it commands *itself*, it must still pay for its commanding. It must become the judge, the avenger, and the victim of its own law. How does this happen? I asked myself. What persuades the living to obey and command, and to practice obedience even when it commands?

Hear, then, my word, you who are wisest. Test in all seriousness whether I have crawled into the very heart of life and into the very roots of its heart.

Where I found the living, there I found will to power; and even in the will of those who serve I found the will to be master.

That the weaker should serve the stronger, to that it is persuaded by its own will, which would be master over what is weaker still: this is the one pleasure it does not want to renounce. And as the smaller yields to the greater that it may have pleasure and power over the smallest, thus even the greatest still yields, and for the sake of power risks life. That is the yielding of the greatest: it is hazard and danger and casting dice for death.

And where men make sacrifices and serve and cast amorous glances, there too is the will to be master. Along stealthy paths the weaker steals into the castle and into the very heart of the more powerful—and there steals power.

And life itself confided this secret to me: "Behold," it said, "I am *that which must always overcome itself*. Indeed, you call it a will to procreate or a drive to an end, to something higher, farther, more manifold: but all this is one, and one secret.

"Rather would I perish than forswear this; and verily, where there is perishing and a falling of leaves, behold, there life sacrifices itself—for power. That I must be struggle and a becoming and an end and an opposition to ends—alas, whoever guesses what is my will should also guess on what *crooked* paths it must proceed.

"Whatever I create and however much I love it— soon I must oppose it and my love; thus my will wills it. And you too, lover of knowledge, are only a path and footprint of my will; verily, my will to power walks also on the heels of your will to truth.

"Indeed, the truth was not hit by him who shot at it with the word of the 'will to existence': that will does not exist. For, what does not exist cannot will; but what is in existence, how could that still want existence? Only where there is life is there also will: not will to life but—thus I teach you—will to power.

"There is much that life esteems more highly than

life itself; but out of the esteeming itself speaks the will to power."

Thus life once taught me; and with this I shall yet solve the riddle of your heart, you who are wisest.

Verily, I say unto you: good and evil that are not transitory, do not exist. Driven on by themselves, they must overcome themselves again and again. With your values and words of good and evil you do violence when you value; and this is your hidden love and the splendor and trembling and overflowing of your soul. But a more violent force and a new overcoming grow out of your values and break egg and eggshell.

And whoever must be a creator in good and evil, verily, he must first be an annihilator and break values. Thus the highest evil belongs to the highest goodness: but this is creative.

Let us speak of this, you who are wisest, even if it be bad. Silence is worse; all truths that are kept silent become poisonous.

And may everything be broken that cannot brook our truths! There are yet many houses to be built!

Thus spoke Zarathustra.

ON THOSE WHO ARE SUBLIME

Still is the bottom of my sea: who would guess that it harbors sportive monsters? Imperturbable is my depth, but it sparkles with swimming riddles and laughters.

One who was sublime I saw today, one who was solemn, an ascetic of the spirit; oh, how my soul laughed at his ugliness! With a swelled chest and like one who holds in his breath, he stood there, the sublime one, silent, decked out with ugly truths, the spoil of his hunting, and rich in torn garments; many thorns too adorned him—yet I saw no rose.

As yet he has not learned laughter or beauty. Gloomy this hunter returned from the woods of knowledge. He came home from a fight with savage beasts; but out of his seriousness there also peers a savage beast—one not overcome. He still stands there like a tiger who wants to leap; but I do not like these tense souls, and my taste does not favor all these who withdraw.

And you tell me, friends, that there is no disputing of taste and tasting? But all of life is a dispute over taste and tasting. Taste—that is at the same time weight and scales and weigher; and woe unto all the living that would live without disputes over weight and scales and weighers!

If he grew tired of his sublimity, this sublime one, only then would his beauty commence; and only then will I taste him and find him tasteful. And only when he turns away from himself, will he jump over his shadow—and verily, into *his* sun. All-too-long has he been sitting in the shadow, and the cheeks of this ascetic of the spirit have grown pale; he almost starved to death on his expectations. Contempt is still in his eyes, and nausea hides around his mouth. Though he is resting now, his rest has not yet lain in the sun. He should act like a bull, and his happiness should smell of the earth, and not of contempt for the earth. I would like to see him as a white bull, walking before the plowshare, snorting and bellowing; and his bellowing should be in praise of everything earthly.

His face is still dark; the shadow of the hand plays upon him. His sense of sight is still in shadows. His deed itself still lies on him as a shadow: the hand still darkens the doer. As yet he has not overcome his deed.

Though I love the bull's neck on him, I also want to see the eyes of the angel. He must still discard his heroic will; he shall be elevated, not merely sublime: the ether itself should elevate him, the will-less one.

He subdued monsters, he solved riddles: but he must still redeem his own monsters and riddles, changing them into heavenly children. As yet his knowledge has not learned to smile and to be without jealousy; as yet his torrential passion has not become still in beauty.

Verily, it is not in satiety that his desire shall grow silent and be submerged, but in beauty. Gracefulness is part of the graciousness of the great-souled.

His arm placed over his head: thus should the hero rest; thus should he overcome even his rest. But just for the hero the *beautiful* is the most difficult thing. No violent will can attain the beautiful by exertion. A little more, a little less: precisely this counts for much here, this matters most here.

To stand with relaxed muscles and unharnessed will: that is most difficult for all of you who are sublime.

When power becomes gracious and descends into the visible—such descent I call beauty.

And there is nobody from whom I want beauty as much as from you who are powerful: let your kindness be your final self-conquest.

Of all evil I deem you capable: therefore I want the good from you.

Verily, I have often laughed at the weaklings who thought themselves good because they had no claws.

You shall strive after the virtue of the column: it grows more and more beautiful and gentle, but internally harder and more enduring, as it ascends.

Indeed, you that are sublime shall yet become beautiful one day and hold up a mirror to your own beauty.

Then your soul will shudder with godlike desires, and there will be adoration even in your vanity.

For this is the soul's secret: only when the hero has abandoned her, she is approached in a dream by the overhero.

Thus spoke Zarathustra.

ON THE LAND OF EDUCATION

I flew too far into the future: dread overcame me. and when I looked around, behold, time was my sole contemporary. Then I flew back toward home, faster and faster; and thus I came to you, O men of today, and into the land of education. For the first time I really had eyes for you, and a genuine desire; verily, it was with longing in my heart that I came.

But what happened to me? For all my anxiety I had to laugh. Never had my eyes beheld anything so dappled and motley. I laughed and laughed while my foot was still trembling, and my heart no less. "This is clearly the home of all paint pots," I said.

With fifty blotches painted on your faces and limbs you were sitting there, and I was amazed, you men of today. And with fifty mirrors around you to flatter and echo your color display! Verily, you could wear no better masks, you men of today, than your own faces! Who could possibly find you out?

With the characters of the past written all over you, and these characters in turn painted over with new characters: thus have you concealed yourselves perfectly from all interpreters of characters. And even if one could try the reins, who would be fool enough to believe that you have reins? You seem baked out of colors and pasted notes. Motley, all ages and peoples peek out of your veils; motley, all customs and faiths speak out of your gestures.

If one took the veils and wraps and colors and gestures away from you, just enough would be left to scare away the crows. Verily, I myself am the scared crow who once saw you naked and without color; and I flew away when the skeleton beckoned to me lovingly. Rather would I be a day laborer in Hades among the shades of the past! Even the underworldly are plumper and fuller than you.

This, indeed this, is bitterness for my bowels, that I can endure you neither naked nor clothed, you men of today. All that is uncanny in the future and all that has ever made fugitive birds shudder is surely more comfortable and cozy than your "reality." For thus you speak: "Real are we entirely, and without belief or superstition." Thus you stick out your chests—but alas, they are hollow! Indeed, how should you be *capable* of any belief, being so dappled and motley—you who are paintings of all that men have ever believed? You are walking refutations of all belief, and you break the limbs of all thought. Unbelievable: thus I call you, for all your pride in being real!

All ages prate against each other in your spirits; and the dreams and pratings of all ages were yet more real than your waking. You are sterile: that is why you lack faith. But whoever had to create also had his prophetic dreams and astral signs—and had faith in faith. You are half-open gates at which the gravediggers wait. And this is *your* reality: "Everything deserves to perish."

How you stand there, you who are sterile, how thin around the ribs! And some among you probably realized this and said, "Probably some god secretly took something from me while I slept. Verily, enough to make himself a little female! Strange is the poverty of my ribs." Thus have some men of today already spoken.

Indeed, you make me laugh, you men of today, and particularly when you are amazed at yourselves. And I should be in a sorry plight if I could not laugh at your amazement and had to drink down everything disgusting out of your bowls. But I shall take you more lightly, for I have a heavy burden; and what does it matter to me if bugs and winged worms still light on my bundle? Verily, that will not make it heavier. And not from you, you men of today, shall the great weariness come over me.

Alas, where shall I climb now with my longing? From all mountains I look out for fatherlands and motherlands. But home I found nowhere; a fugitive am I in all cities and a departure at all gates. Strange and a mockery to me are the men of today to whom my heart recently drew me; and I am driven out of fatherlands and motherlands. Thus I now love only my *children's land*, yet undiscovered, in the farthest sea: for this I bid my sails search and search.

In my children I want to make up for being the child of my fathers—and to all the future, for *this* today.

Thus spoke Zarathustra.

ON IMMACULATE PERCEPTION

When the moon rose yesterday I fancied that she wanted to give birth to a sun: so broad and pregnant she lay on the horizon. But she lied to me with her pregnancy; and I should sooner believe in the man in the moon than in the woman.

Indeed, he is not much of a man either, this shy nocturnal enthusiast. Verily, with a bad conscience he passes over the roofs. For he is lecherous and jealous, the monk in the moon, lecherous after the earth and all the joys of lovers.

No, I do not like him, this tomcat on the roofs! I loathe all that crawl about half-closed windows! Piously and silently he passes over carpets of stars; but I do not like softly treading men's feet, on which no spur jingles. The step of everything honest speaks; but the cat steals over the ground. Behold, like a cat the moon comes along, dishonestly.

This parable I offer you, sentimental hypocrites, you who are "pure perceivers." *I* call you—lechers.

You too love the earth and the earthly: I have seen through you; but there is shame in your love and bad conscience—you are like the moon. Your spirit has been persuaded to despise the earthly; but your entrails have not been persuaded, and they are what is strongest in you. And now your spirit is ashamed at having given in to your entrails, and, to hide from its shame, it sneaks on furtive and lying paths.

"This would be the highest to my mind"—thus says your lying spirit to itself—"to look at life without desire and not, like a dog, with my tongue hanging out. To be happy in looking, with a will that has died and without the grasping and greed of selfishness, the whole body cold and ashen, but with drunken moon eyes. This *I* should like best"—thus the seduced seduces himself—"to love the earth as the moon loves her, and to touch her beauty only with my eyes. And this is what the immaculate perception of all things shall mean to me: that I want nothing from them, except to be allowed to lie prostrate before them like a mirror with a hundred eyes."

O you sentimental hypocrites, you lechers! You lack innocence in your desire and therefore you slander all desire. Verily, it is not as creators, procreators, and those who have joy in becoming that you love the earth. Where is innocence? Where there is a will to procreate. And he who wants to create beyond himself has the purest will.

Where is beauty? Where I must will with all my will; where I want to love and perish that an image may not remain a mere image. Loving and perishing: that has rhymed for eternities. The will to love, that is to be willing also to die. Thus I speak to you cowards!

But now your emasculated leers wish to be called "contemplation." And that which permits itself to be touched by cowardly glances you would baptize "beautiful." How you soil noble names!

But this shall be your curse, you who are immaculate, you pure perceivers, that you shall never give birth, even if you lie broad and pregnant on the horizon. Verily, you fill your mouth with noble words; and are we to believe that your heart is overflowing, you liars? But *my* words are small, despised, crooked words: gladly I pick up what falls under the table at your meals. I can still use it to tell hypocrites the truth. Indeed, my fishbones, clamshells, and thorny leaves shall tickle the noses of hypocrites. Bad air always surrounds you and your meals: for your lecherous thoughts, your lies and secrets, are in the air. Would that you dared to believe yourselves—yourselves and your entrails. Whoever does not believe himself always lies.

Behind a god's mask you hide from yourselves, in your "purity"; your revolting worm has crawled into a god's mask. Verily, you deceive with your "contemplation." Zarathustra too was once fooled by your godlike skins and did not realize that they were stuffed with snakes' coils. I once fancied that I saw a god's soul at play in your play, you pure perceivers. No better art I once fancied than your arts. Snakes' filth and bad odors were concealed from me by the distance, and that the cunning of a lizard was crawling around lecherously.

But I came close to you, and the day dawned on me, and now it dawns on you too; the moon's love has come to an end. Look there! Caught and pale he stands there, confronted by the dawn. For already she approaches, glowing; her love for the earth approaches. All solar love is innocence and creative longing.

Look there: how she approaches impatiently over the sea. Do you not feel the thirst and the hot breath of her love? She would suck at the sea and drink its depth into her heights; and the sea's desire rises toward her with a thousand breasts. It wants to be kissed and sucked by the thirst of the sun; it wants to become air and height and a footpath of light, and itself light.

Verily, like the sun I love life and all deep seas. And this is what perceptive knowledge means to me: all that is deep shall rise up to my heights.

Thus spoke Zarathustra.

ON SCHOLARS

As I lay asleep, a sheep ate of the ivy wreath on my brow—ate and said, "Zarathustra is no longer a scholar." Said it and strutted away proudly. A child told it to me.

I like to lie here where the children play, beside the broken wall, among thistles and red poppies. I am still a scholar to the children, and also to the thistles and red poppies. They are innocent even in their malice. But to the sheep I am no longer a scholar; thus my lot decrees it—bless it!

For this is the truth: I have moved from the house of the scholars and I even banged the door behind me. My soul sat hungry at their table too long; I am not, like them, trained to pursue knowledge as if it were nut-cracking. I love freedom and the air over the fresh earth; rather would I sleep on ox hides than on their decorums and respectabilities.

I am too hot and burned by my own thoughts; often it nearly takes my breath away. Then I must go out into the open and away from all dusty rooms. But they sit cool in the cool shade: in everything they want to be mere spectators, and they beware of sitting where the sun burns on the steps. Like those who stand in the street and gape at the people who pass by, they too wait and gape at thoughts that others have thought.

If you seize them with your hands they raise a cloud of dust like flour bags, involuntarily; but who could guess that their dust comes from grain and from the yellow delight of summer fields? When they pose as wise, their little epigrams and truths chill me: their wisdom often has an odor as if it came from the swamps; and verily, I have also heard frogs croak out of it. They are skillful and have clever fingers: why would my simplicity want to be near their multiplicity? All threading and knotting and weaving their fingers understand: thus they knit the socks of the spirit.

They are good clockworks; but take care to wind them correctly! Then they indicate the hour without fail and make a modest noise. They work like mills and like stamps: throw down your seed-corn to them and they will know how to grind it small and reduce it to white dust.

They watch each other closely and mistrustfully. Inventive in petty cleverness, they wait for those whose knowledge walks on lame feet: like spiders they wait. I have always seen them carefully preparing poison; and they always put on gloves of glass to do it. They also know how to play with loaded dice; and I have seen them play so eagerly that they sweated.

We are alien to each other, and their virtues are even more distasteful to me than their falseness and their loaded dice. And when I lived with them, I lived above them. That is why they developed a grudge against me. They did not want to hear how someone was living over their heads; and so they put wood and earth and filth between me and their heads. Thus they muffled the sound of my steps: and so far I have been heard least well by the most scholarly. Between themselves and me they laid all human faults and weaknesses: "false ceilings" they call them in their houses. And yet I live *over* their heads with my thoughts; and even if I wanted to walk upon my own mistakes, I would still be over their heads.

For men are *not* equal: thus speaks justice. And what I want, they would have no right to want!

Thus spoke Zarathustra.

ON POETS

"Since I have come to know the body better," Zarathustra said to one of his disciples, "the spirit is to me only quasi-spirit; and all that is 'permanent' is also a mere parable."

"I have heard you say that once before," the disciple replied; "and at that time you added, 'But the poets lie too much.' Why did you say that the poets lie too much?"

"Why?" said Zarathustra. "You ask, why? I am not one of those whom one may ask about their why. Is my experience but of yesterday? It was long ago that I experienced the reasons for my opinions. Would I not have to be a barrel of memory if I wanted to carry my reasons around with me? It is already too much for me to remember my own opinions; and many a bird flies away. And now and then I also find a stray in my dove-cot that is strange to me and trembles when I place my hand on it. But what was it that Zarathustra once said to you? That the poets lie too much? But Zarathustra too is a poet. Do you now believe that he spoke the truth here? Why do you believe that?"

The disciple answered, "I believe in Zarathustra." But Zarathustra shook his head and smiled.

"Faith does not make me blessed," he said, "especially not faith in me. But suppose somebody said in all seriousness, the poets lie too much: he would be right; *we* do lie too much. We also know too little and we are bad learners; so we simply have to lie. And who among us poets has not adulterated his wine? Many a poisonous hodgepodge has been contrived in our cellars; much that is indescribable was accomplished there. And because we know so little, the poor in spirit please us heartily, particularly when they are young females. And we are covetous even of those things which the old females tell each other in the evening. That is what we ourselves call the Eternal-Feminine in us. And, as if there were a special secret access to knowledge, *buried* for those who learn something, we believe in the people and their 'wisdom.'

"This, however, all poets believe: that whoever pricks up his ears as he lies in the grass or on lonely slopes will find out something about those things that are between heaven and earth. And when they feel tender sentiments stirring, the poets always fancy that nature herself is in love with them; and that she is creeping to their ears to tell them secrets and amorous flatteries; and of this they brag and boast before all mortals.

"Alas, there are so many things between heaven and earth of which only the poets have dreamed.

"And especially *above* the heavens: for all gods are poets' parables, poets' prevarications. Verily, it always lifts us higher—specifically, to the realm of the clouds: upon these we place our motley bastards and call them gods and overmen. For they are just light enough for these chairs—all these gods and overmen. Ah, how weary I am of all the imperfection which must at all costs become event! Ah, how weary I am of poets!"

When Zarathustra spoke thus, his disciple was angry with him, but he remained silent. And Zarathustra too remained silent; and his eye had turned inward as if he were gazing into vast distances. At last he sighed and drew a deep breath.

"I am of today and before," he said then, "but there is something in me that is of tomorrow and the day after tomorrow and time to come. I have grown weary of the poets, the old and the new: superficial they all seem to me, and shallow seas. Their thoughts have not penetrated deeply enough; therefore their feelings did not touch bottom.

"Some lust and some boredom: that has so far been their best reflection. All their harp jingling is to me the breathing and flitting of ghosts; what have they ever known of the fervor of tones?

"Nor are they clean enough for me: they all muddy their waters to make them appear deep. And they like to pose as reconcilers: but mediators and mixers they remain for me, and half-and-half and unclean.

"Alas, I cast my net into their seas and wanted to catch good fish; but I always pulled up the head of some old god. Thus the sea gave him who was hungry a stone. And they themselves may well have come from the sea. Certainly, pearls are found in them: they are that much more similar to hard shellfish. And instead of a soul I often found salted slime in them.

"From the sea they learned even its vanity: is not the sea the peacock of peacocks? Even before the ugliest buffalo it still spreads out its tail, and never wearies of its lace fan of silver and silk. Sulky, the buffalo stares back, close to the sand in his soul, closer still to the thicket, closest of all to the swamp. What are beauty and sea and peacock's finery to him? This parable I offer the poets. Verily, their spirit itself is the peacock of peacocks and a sea of vanity! The spirit of the poet craves spectators—even if only buffaloes.

"But I have grown weary of this spirit; and I foresee that it will grow weary of itself. I have already seen the poets changed, with their glances turned back on themselves. I saw ascetics of the spirit approach; they grew out of the poets."

Thus spoke Zarathustra.

ON GREAT EVENTS

There is an island in the sea—not far from Zarathustra's blessed isles—on which a fire-spewing mountain smokes continually; and the people say of it, and especially the old women among the people say, that it has been placed like a huge rock before the gate to the underworld, and that the narrow path that leads to this gate to the underworld goes through the fire-spewing mountain.

Now it was during the time when Zarathustra was staying on the blessed isles that a ship anchored at the island with the smoking mountain and the crew went ashore to shoot rabbits. Around noon, however, when the captain and his men were together again, they suddenly saw a man approach through the air, and a voice said distinctly, "It is time! It is high time!" And when the shape had come closest to them—and it flew by swiftly as a shadow in the direction of the fire-spewing mountain—they realized with a great sense of shock that it was Zarathustra; for all of them had seen him before, except the captain, and they loved him as the people love—with a love that is mixed with an equal amount of awe. "Look there!" said the old helmsman. "There is Zarathustra descending to hell!"

At the time these seamen landed at the isle of fire there was a rumor abroad that Zarathustra had disappeared; and when his friends were asked, they said that he had embarked by night without saying where he intended to go. Thus uneasiness arose; and after three days the story of the seamen was added to this uneasiness; and now all the people said that the devil had taken Zarathustra. His disciples laughed at such talk to be sure, and one of them even said, "Sooner would I believe that Zarathustra has taken the devil." But deep in their souls they were all of them full of worry and longing; thus their joy was great when on the fifth day Zarathustra appeared among them.

And this is the story of Zarathustra's conversation with the fire hound:

"The earth," he said, "has a skin, and this skin has diseases. One of these diseases, for example, is called 'man.' And another one of these diseases is called 'fire hound': about *him* men have told each other, and believed, many lies. To get to the bottom of this mystery I went over the sea, and I have seen truth naked—verily, barefoot up to the throat. Now I am informed concerning the fire hound, and also concerning all scum-

and overthrow devils, of whom not only old women are afraid.

" 'Out with you, fire hound! Out from your depth!' I cried. 'And confess how deep this depth is! Whence comes what you are snorting up here? You drink copiously from the sea: your salty eloquence shows that. Indeed, for a hound of the depth you take your nourishment too much from the surface. At most, I take you for the earth's ventriloquist; and whenever I have heard overthrow- and scum-devils talking, I found them like you: salty, mendacious, and superficial. You know how to bellow and to darken with ashes. You are the best braggarts and great experts in the art of making mud seethe. Wherever you are, mud must always be nearby, and much that is spongy, cavernous, compressed—and wants freedom. Freedom is what all of you like best to bellow; but I have outgrown the belief in "great events" wherever there is much bellowing and smoke.

" 'Believe me, friend Hellishnoise: the greatest events —they are not our loudest but our stillest hours. Not around the inventors of new noise, but around the inventors of new values does the world revolve; it revolves *inaudibly*.

" 'Admit it! Whenever your noise and smoke were gone, very little had happened. What does it matter if a town became a mummy and a statue lies in the mud? And this word I shall add for those who overthrow statues: nothing is more foolish than casting salt into the sea and statues into the mud. The statue lay in the mud of your contempt; but precisely this is its law, that out of contempt life and living beauty come back to it. It rises again with more godlike features, seductive through suffering; and verily, it will yet thank you for having overthrown it, O you overthrowers. This counsel, however, I give to kings and churches and everything that is weak with age and weak in virtue: let yourselves be overthrown—so that you may return to life, and virtue return to you.'

"Thus I spoke before the fire hound; then he interrupted me crossly and asked, 'Church? What is that?'

" 'Church?' I answered. 'That is a kind of state—the most mendacious kind. But be still, you hypocritical hound! You know your own kind best! Like you, the state is a hypocritical hound; like you, it likes to talk with smoke and bellowing—to make himself believe, like you, that he is talking out of the belly of reality. For he wants to be by all means the most important beast on earth, the state; and they believe him too.'

"When I had said that, the fire hound carried on as if crazy with envy. 'What?' he cried, 'the most important beast on earth? And they believe him too?' And so much steam and so many revolting voices came out of his throat that I thought he would suffocate with anger and envy.

"At last, he grew calmer and his gasping eased; and as soon as he was calm I said, laughing, 'You are angry, fire hound; so I am right about you! And that I may continue to be right, let me tell you about another fire hound. He really speaks out of the heart of the earth. He exhales gold and golden rain; thus his heart wants it. What are ashes and smoke and hot slime to him? Laughter flutters out of him like colorful clouds; nor is he well disposed toward your gurgling and spewing and intestinal rumblings. This gold, however, and this laughter he takes from the heart of the earth; for— know this—*the heart of the earth is of gold.*'

"When the fire hound heard this he could no longer bear listening to me. Shamed, he drew in his tail, in a cowed manner said 'bow-wow,' and crawled down into his cave."

Thus related Zarathustra. But his disciples barely listened, so great was their desire to tell him of the seamen, the rabbits, and the flying man.

"What shall I think of that?" said Zarathustra; "am I a ghost then? But it must have been my shadow. I suppose you have heard of the wanderer and his shadow? This, however, is clear: I must watch it more closely—else it may yet spoil my reputation."

And once more Zarathustra shook his head and wondered. "What shall I think of that?" he said once more. "Why did the ghost cry, 'It is time! It is high time!' High time for *what?*"

Thus spoke Zarathustra.

THE SOOTHSAYER

"—And I saw a great sadness descend upon mankind. The best grew weary of their works. A doctrine appeared, accompanied by a faith: 'All is empty, all is the same, all has been!' And from all the hills it echoed: 'All is empty, all is the same, all has been!' Indeed we have harvested: but why did all our fruit turn rotten and brown? What fell down from the evil moon last night? In vain was all our work; our wine has turned to poison; an evil eye has seared our fields and hearts. We have all become dry; and if fire should descend on us, we should turn to ashes; indeed, we have wearied the fire itself. All our wells have dried up; even the sea has withdrawn. All the soil would crack, but the depth refuses to devour. 'Alas, where is there still a sea in which one might drown?' thus are we wailing across shallow swamps. Verily, we have become too weary even to die. We are still waking and living on—in tombs."

Thus Zarathustra heard a soothsayer speak, and the

prophecy touched his heart and changed him. He walked about sad and weary; and he became like those of whom the soothsayer had spoken.

"Verily," he said to his disciples, "little is lacking and this long twilight will come. Alas, how shall I save my light through it? It must not suffocate in this sadness. For it shall be a light for distant worlds and even more distant nights."

Thus grieved in his heart, Zarathustra walked about; and for three days he took neither food nor drink, had no rest, and lost his speech. At last he fell into a deep sleep. But his disciples sat around him in long night watches and waited with great concern for him to wake and speak again and recover from his melancholy.

And this is the speech of Zarathustra when he awoke; but his voice came to his disciples as if from a great distance:

"Listen to the dream which I dreamed, my friends, and help me guess its meaning. This dream is still a riddle to me; its meaning is concealed in it and imprisoned and does not yet soar above it with unfettered wings.

"I had turned my back on all life, thus I dreamed. I had become a night watchman and a guardian of tombs upon the lonely mountain castle of death. Up there I guarded his coffins: the musty vaults were full of such marks of triumph. Life that had been overcome, looked at me out of glass coffins. I breathed the odor of dusty eternities: sultry and dusty lay my soul. And who could have aired his soul there?

"The brightness of midnight was always about me; loneliness crouched next to it; and as a third, death-rattle silence, the worst of my friends. I had keys, the rustiest of all keys; and I knew how to use them to open the most creaking of all gates. Like a wickedly angry croaking, the sound ran through the long corridors when the gate's wings moved: fiendishly cried this bird, ferocious at being awakened. Yet still more terrible and heart-constricting was the moment when silence returned and it grew quiet about me, and I sat alone in this treacherous silence.

"Thus time passed and crawled, if time still existed—how should I know? But eventually that happened which awakened me. Thrice, strokes struck at the gate like thunder; the vaults echoed and howled thrice; then I went to the gate. 'Alpa,' I cried, 'who is carrying his ashes up the mountain? Alpa! Alpa! Who is carrying his ashes up the mountain?' And I pressed the key and tried to lift the gate and exerted myself; but still it did not give an inch. Then a roaring wind tore its wings apart; whistling, shrilling, and piercing, it cast up a black coffin before me.

"And amid the roaring and whistling and shrilling the coffin burst and spewed out a thousandfold laughter. And from a thousand grimaces of children, angels, owls, fools, and butterflies as big as children, it laughed and mocked and roared at me. Then I was terribly frightened; it threw me to the ground. And I cried in horror as I have never cried. And my own cry awakened me—and I came to my senses."

Thus Zarathustra told his dream and then became silent; for as yet he did not know the interpretation of his dream. But the disciple whom he loved most rose quickly, took Zarathustra's hand, and said:

"Your life itself interprets this dream for us, O Zarathustra. Are you not yourself the wind with the shrill whistling that tears open the gates of the castles of death? Are you not yourself the coffin full of colorful sarcasms and the angelic grimaces of life? Verily, like a thousandfold children's laughter Zarathustra enters all death chambers, laughing at all the night watchmen and guardians of tombs and at whoever else is rattling with gloomy keys. You will frighten and prostrate them with your laughter; and your power over them will make them faint and wake them. And even when the long twilight and the weariness of death come, you will not set in our sky, you advocate of life. New stars you have let us see, and new wonders of the night; verily, laughter itself you have spread over us like a colorful tent. Henceforth children's laughter will well forth from all coffins; henceforth a strong wind will come triumphantly to all weariness of death: of this you yourself are our surety and soothsayer. Verily, *this is what you dreamed of:* your enemies. That was your hardest dream. But as you woke from them and came to your senses, thus they shall awaken from themselves—and come to you."

Thus spoke the disciple; and all the others crowded around Zarathustra and took hold of his hands and wanted to persuade him to leave his bed and his sadness and to return to them. But Zarathustra sat erect on his resting place with a strange look in his eyes. Like one coming home from a long sojourn in strange lands, he looked at his disciples and examined their faces; and as yet he did not recognize them. But when they lifted him up and put him on his feet, behold, his eyes suddenly changed; he comprehended all that had happened, stroked his beard, and said in a strong voice:

"Now then, there is a time for this too. But see to it, my disciples, that we shall have a good meal, and soon. Thus I plan to atone for bad dreams. The soothsayer, however, shall eat and drink by my side; and verily, I shall show him a sea in which he can drown."

Thus spoke Zarathustra. But then he looked a long

time into the face of the disciple who had played the dream interpreter and he shook his head.

ON REDEMPTION

When Zarathustra crossed over the great bridge one day the cripples and beggars surrounded him, and a hunchback spoke to him thus: "Behold, Zarathustra. The people too learn from you and come to believe in your doctrine; but before they will believe you entirely one thing is still needed: you must first persuade us cripples. Now here you have a fine selection and, verily, an opportunity with more than one handle. You can heal the blind and make the lame walk; and from him who has too much behind him you could perhaps take away a little. That, I think, would be the right way to make the cripples believe in Zarathustra."

But Zarathustra replied thus to the man who had spoken: "When one takes away the hump from the hunchback one takes away his spirit—thus teach the people. And when one restores his eyes to the blind man he sees too many wicked things on earth, and he will curse whoever healed him. But whoever makes the lame walk does him the greatest harm: for when he can walk his vices run away with him—thus teach the people about cripples. And why should Zarathustra not learn from the people when the people learn from Zarathustra?

"But this is what matters least to me since I have been among men: to see that this one lacks an eye and that one an ear and a third a leg, while there are others who have lost their tongues or their noses or their heads. I see, and have seen, what is worse, and many things so vile that I do not want to speak of everything; and concerning some things I do not even like to be silent: for there are human beings who lack everything, except one thing of which they have too much—human beings who are nothing but a big eye or a big mouth or a big belly or anything at all that is big. Inverse cripples I call them.

"And when I came out of my solitude and crossed over this bridge for the first time I did not trust my eyes and looked and looked again, and said at last, 'An ear! An ear as big as a man!' I looked still more closely—and indeed, underneath the ear something was moving, something pitifully small and wretched and slender. And, no doubt of it, the tremendous ear was attached to a small, thin stalk—but this stalk was a human being! If one used a magnifying glass one could even recognize a tiny envious face; also, that a bloated little soul was dangling from the stalk. The people, however, told me that this great ear was not only a human being, but a great one, a genius. But I never believed the people when they spoke of great men; and I maintained my belief that it was an inverse cripple who had too little of everything and too much of one thing."

When Zarathustra had spoken thus to the hunchback and to those whose mouthpiece and advocate the hunchback was, he turned to his disciples in profound dismay and said: "Verily, my friends, I walk among men as among the fragments and limbs of men. This is what is terrible for my eyes, that I find man in ruins and scattered as over a battlefield or a butcher-field. And when my eyes flee from the now to the past, they always find the same: fragments and limbs and dreadful accidents—but no human beings.

"The now and the past on earth—alas, my friends, that is what I find most unendurable; and I should not know how to live if I were not also a seer of that which must come. A seer, a willer, a creator, a future himself and a bridge to the future—and alas, also, as it were, a cripple at this bridge: all this is Zarathustra.

"And you too have often asked yourselves, 'Who is Zarathustra to us? What shall be call him?' And, like myself, you replied to yourselves with questions. Is he a promiser? or a fulfiller? A conqueror? or an inheritor? An autumn? or a plowshare? A physician? or one who has recovered? Is he a poet? or truthful? A liberator? or a tamer? good? or evil?

"I walk among men as among the fragments of the future—that future which I envisage. And this is all my creating and striving, that I create and carry together into One what is fragment and riddle and dreadful accident. And how could I bear to be a man if man were not also a creator and guesser of riddles and redeemer of accidents?

"To redeem those who lived in the past and to re-create all 'it was' into a 'thus I willed it'—that alone should I call redemption. Will—that is the name of the liberator and joy-bringer; thus I taught you, my friends. But now learn this too: the will itself is still a prisoner. Willing liberates; but what is it that puts even the liberator himself in fetters? 'It was'—that is the name of the will's gnashing of teeth and most secret melancholy. Powerless against what has been done, he is an angry spectator of all that is past. The will cannot will backwards; and that he cannot break time and time's covetousness, that is the will's loneliest melancholy.

"Willing liberates; what means does the will devise for himself to get rid of his melancholy and to mock his dungeon? Alas, every prisoner becomes a fool; and the imprisoned will redeems himself foolishly. That time does not run backwards, that is his wrath; 'that which was' is the name of the stone he cannot move. And so he moves stones out of wrath and displeasure, and he wreaks revenge on whatever does not feel wrath and displeasure as he does. Thus the will, the liberator, took to hurting; and on all who can suffer he wreaks revenge for his inability to go backwards. This, indeed this alone, is what *revenge* is: the will's ill will against time and its 'it was.'

"Verily, a great folly dwells in our will; and it has become a curse for everything human that this folly has acquired spirit.

"*The spirit of revenge*, my friends, has so far been the subject of man's best reflection; and where there was suffering, one always wanted punishment too.

"For 'punishment' is what revenge calls itself; with a hypocritical lie it creates a good conscience for itself.

"Because there is suffering in those who will, inasmuch as they cannot will backwards, willing itself and all life were supposed to be—a punishment. And now cloud upon cloud rolled over the spirit, until eventually madness preached, 'Everything passes away; therefore everything deserves to pass away. And this too is justice, this law of time that it must devour its children.' Thus preached madness.

" 'Things are ordered morally according to justice and punishment. Alas, where is redemption from the flux of things and from the punishment called existence?' Thus preached madness.

" 'Can there be redemption if there is eternal justice? Alas, the stone *It was* cannot be moved: all punishments must be eternal too.' Thus preached madness.

" 'No deed can be annihilated: how could it be undone by punishment? This, this is what is eternal in the punishment called existence, that existence must eternally become deed and guilt again. Unless the will should at last redeem himself, and willing should become not willing.' But, my brothers, you know this fable of madness.

"I led you away from these fables when I taught you, 'The will is a creator.' All 'it was' is a fragment, a riddle, a dreadful accident—until the creative will says to it, 'But thus I willed it.' Until the creative will says to it, 'But thus I will it; thus shall I will it.'

"But has the will yet spoken thus? And when will that happen? Has the will been unharnessed yet from his own folly? Has the will yet become his own redeemer and joy-bringer? Has he unlearned the spirit of revenge and all gnashing of teeth? And who taught him reconciliation with time and something higher than any reconciliation? For that will which is the will to power must will something higher than any reconciliation; but how shall this be brought about? Who could teach him also to will backwards?"

At this point in his speech it happened that Zarathustra suddenly stopped and looked altogether like one who has received a severe shock. Appalled, he looked at his disciples; his eyes pierced their thoughts and the thoughts behind their thoughts as with arrows. But after a little while he laughed again and, pacified, he said: "It is difficult to live with people because silence is so difficult. Especially for one who is garrulous."

Thus spoke Zarathustra.

The hunchback, however, had listened to this discourse and covered his face the while; but when he heard Zarathustra laugh he looked up curiously and said slowly: "But why does Zarathustra speak otherwise to us than to his disciples?"

Zarathustra answered: "What is surprising in that? With hunchbacks one may well speak in a hunchbacked way."

"All right," said the hunchback; "and one may well tell pupils tales out of school. But why does Zarathustra speak otherwise to his pupils than to himself?"

ON HUMAN PRUDENCE

Not the height but the precipice is terrible. That precipice where the glance plunges *down* and the hand reaches *up*. There the heart becomes giddy confronted with its double will. Alas, friends, can you guess what is my heart's double will?

This, this is *my* precipice and my danger, that my glance plunges into the height and that my hand would grasp and hold on to the depth. My will clings to man; with fetters I bind myself to man because I am swept up toward the overman; for that way my other will wants to go. And therefore I live blind among men as if I did not know them, that my hand might not wholly lose its faith in what is firm.

I do not know you men: this darkness and consolation are often spread around me. I sit at the gateway, exposed to every rogue, and I ask: who wants to deceive me? That is the first instance of my human prudence, that I let myself be deceived in order not to be on guard against deceivers. Alas, if I were on guard against men, how could man then be an anchor for my ball? I should be swept up and away too easily. This providence lies over my destiny, that I must be without caution.

And whoever does not want to die of thirst among men must learn to drink out of all cups; and whoever would stay clean among men must know how to wash even with dirty water. And thus I often comforted myself, "Well then, old heart! One misfortune failed you; enjoy this as your good fortune."

This, however, is the second instance of my human prudence: I spare the *vain* more than the proud. Is not hurt vanity the mother of all tragedies? But where pride is hurt, there something better than pride is likely to grow.

That life may be good to look at, its play must be well acted; but for that good actors are needed. All the vain are good actors: they act and they want people to enjoy looking at them; all their spirit is behind this will. They enact themselves, they invent themselves; near them I love to look at life: that cures my melancholy. Therefore I spare the vain, for they are the physicians of my melancholy and keep me attached to life as to a play.

And then: who could fathom the full depth of the modesty of the vain man? I am well disposed to him and I pity his modesty. It is from you that he wants to acquire his faith in himself; he nourishes himself on your glances, he eats your praise out of your hands. He even believes your lies if you lie well about him; for, at bottom, his heart sighs: what am I? And if the true virtue is the one that is unaware of itself—well, the vain man is unaware of his modesty.

This, however, is the third instance of my human prudence: that I do not permit the sight of the *evil* to be spoiled for me by your timidity. I am delighted to see the wonders hatched by a hot sun: tigers and palms and rattlesnakes. Among men too a hot sun hatches a beautiful breed. And there are many wonderful things in those who are evil.

To be sure, even as your wisest men did not strike me as so very wise, I found men's evil too smaller than its reputation. And often I asked myself, shaking my head: why go on rattling, you rattlesnakes?

Verily, there is yet a future for evil too. And the hottest south has not yet been discovered for man. How many things are now called grossest wickedness and are yet only twelve shoes wide and three months long! One day, however, bigger dragons will come into this world. For in order that the overman should not lack his dragon, the overdragon that is worthy of him, much hot sunshine must yet glow upon damp jungles. Your wildcats must first turn into tigers, and your poisonous toads into crocodiles; for the good hunter shall have good hunting.

Verily, you who are good and just, there is much about you that is laughable, and especially your fear of that which has hitherto been called devil. What is great is so alien to your souls that the overman would be awesome to you in his kindness. And you who are wise and knowing, you would flee from the burning sun of that wisdom in which the overman joyously bathes his nakedness. You highest men whom my eyes have seen, this is my doubt concerning you and my secret laughter: I guess that you would call my overman—devil.

Alas, I have wearied of these highest and best men: from their "height" I longed to get up, out, and away to the overman. A shudder came over me when I saw these best ones naked; then I grew wings to soar off into distant futures. Into more distant futures, into more southern souths than any artist ever dreamed of—where gods are ashamed of all clothes. But I want to see *you* disguised, my neighbors and fellow men, and well decked out, and vain, and dignified, as "the good and the just." And I myself want to sit among you disguised—*misjudging* you and myself: for that is the final instance of my human prudence.

Thus spoke Zarathustra.

THE STILLEST HOUR

What happened to me, my friends? You see me distracted, driven away, unwillingly obedient, prepared to go—alas, to go away from you. Indeed, Zarathustra must return once more to his solitude; but this time the bear goes back to his cave without joy. What happened to me? Who ordered this? Alas, my angry mistress wants it, she spoke to me; have I ever yet mentioned her name to you? Yesterday, toward evening, there spoke to me *my stillest hour:* that is the name of my awesome mistress. And thus it happened; for I must tell you everything lest your hearts harden against me for departing suddenly.

Do you know the fright of him who falls asleep? He is frightened down to his very toes because the ground gives under him and the dream begins. This I say to you as a parable. Yesterday, in the stillest hour, the ground gave under me, the dream began. The hand moved, the clock of my life drew a breath; never had I heard such stillness around me: my heart took fright.

Then it spoke to me without voice: "You know it, Zarathustra?" And I cried with fright at this whispering, and the blood left my face; but I remained silent.

Then it spoke to me again without voice: "You know it, Zarathustra, but you do not say it!" And at last I answered defiantly: "Yes, I know it, but I do not want to say it!"

Then it spoke to me again without voice: "You do not *want* to, Zarathustra? Is this really true? Do not hide in your defiance." And I cried and trembled like a child and spoke: "Alas, I would like to, but how can I? Let me off from this! It is beyond my strength!"

Then it spoke to me again without voice: "What do

you matter, Zarathustra? Speak your word and break!"

And I answered: "Alas, is it *my* word? Who am *I*? I await the worthier one; I am not worthy even of being broken by it."

Then it spoke to me again without voice: "What do you matter? You are not yet humble enough for me. Humility has the toughest hide." And I answered: "What has the hide of my humility not borne? I dwell at the foot of my height. How high are my peaks? No one has told me yet. But my valleys I know well."

Then it spoke to me again without voice: "O Zarathustra, he who has to move mountains also moves valleys and hollows." And I answered: "As yet my words have not moved mountains, and what I said did not reach men. Indeed, I have gone to men, but as yet I have not arrived."

Then it spoke to me again without voice: "What do you know of *that*? The dew falls on the grass when the night is most silent." And I answered: "They mocked me when I found and went my own way; and in truth my feet were trembling then. And thus they spoke to me: 'You have forgotten the way, now you have also forgotten how to walk.'"

Then it spoke to me again without voice: "What matters their mockery? You are one who has forgotten how to obey: now you shall command. Do you not know who is most needed by all? He that commands great things. To do great things is difficult; but to command great things is more difficult. This is what is most unforgivable in you: you have the power, and you do not want to rule." And I answered: "I lack the lion's voice for commanding."

Then it spoke to me again as a whisper: "It is the stillest words that bring on the storm. Thoughts that come on doves' feet guide the world. O Zarathustra, you shall go as a shadow of that which must come: thus you will command and, commanding, lead the way." And I answered: "I am ashamed."

Then it spoke to me again without voice: "You must yet become as a child and without shame. The pride of youth is still upon you; you have become young late; but whoever would become as a child must overcome his youth too." And I reflected for a long time and trembled. But at last I said what I had said at first: "I do not want to."

Then laughter surrounded me. Alas, how this laughter tore my entrails and slit open my heart! And it spoke to me for the last time: "O Zarathustra, your fruit is ripe, but you are not ripe for your fruit. Thus you must return to your solitude again; for you must yet become mellow." And again it laughed and fled; then it became still around me as with a double stillness. But I lay on the ground and sweat poured from my limbs.

Now you have heard all, and why I must return to my solitude. Nothing have I kept from you, my friends. But this too you have heard from me, who is still the most taciturn of all men—and wants to be. Alas, my friends, I still could tell you something, I still could give you something. Why do I not give it? Am I stingy?

But when Zarathustra had spoken these words he was overcome by the force of his pain and the nearness of his parting from his friends, and he wept loudly; and no one knew how to comfort him. At night, however, he went away alone and left his friends.

Thus Spoke Zarathustra: Third Part

You look up when you feel the need for elevation. And I look down because I am elevated. Who among you can laugh and be elevated at the same time? Whoever climbs the highest mountains laughs at all tragic plays and tragic seriousness. (Zarathustra, "On Reading and Writing," I, p. 152)

EDITOR'S NOTES

1. *The Wanderer:* The contrast between Zarathustra's sentimentality and his praise of hardness remains characteristic of the rest of the book.

2. *On the Vision and the Riddle:* Zarathustra's first account of the eternal recurrence (see my *Nietzsche*, 11, II) is followed by a proto-surrealistic vision of a triumph over nausea.

3. *On Involuntary Bliss:* Zarathustra still cannot face the thought of the eternal recurrence.

4. *Before Sunrise:* An ode to the sky. Another quotation from Zweig's essay on Nietzsche seems pertinent: "His nerves immediately register every meter of height and every pressure of the weather as a pain in his organs, and they react rebelliously to every revolt in nature. Rain or gloomy skies lower his vitality ('overcast skies depress me deeply'), the weight of low clouds he feels down into his very intestines, rain 'lowers the potential,' humidity debilitates, dryness vivifies, sunshine is salvation, winter is a kind of paralysis and death. The quivering barometer needle of his April-like, changeable nerves never stands still—most nearly perhaps in cloudless landscapes, on the windless tablelands of the Engadine." In this chapter the phrase "beyond good and evil" is introduced; also one line, slightly varied, of the "Drunken Song" (see below). Another important

theme in Nietzsche's thought: the praise of chance and "a *little* reason" as opposed to any divine purpose.

5. *On Virtue That Makes Small:* "Do whatever you will, but . . .": What Nietzsche is concerned with is not casuistry but character, not a code of morals but a kind of man, not a syllabus of behavior but a state of being.

6. *Upon the Mount of Olives:* " 'The ice of knowledge will yet freeze him to *death!*' they moan." Compare Stefan George's poem on the occasion of Nietzsche's death (my *Nietzsche,* Prologue, II): "He came too late who said to thee imploring: There is no way left over icy cliffs."

7. *On Passing By:* Zarathustra's ape, or "grunting swine," unintentionally parodies Zarathustra's attitude and style. His denunciations are born of wounded vanity and vengefulness, while Zarathustra's contempt is begotten by love; and "where one can no longer love, there one should *pass by.*"

8. *On Apostates:* Stylistically, Zarathustra is now often little better than his ape. But occasional epigrams show his old power: the third paragraph in section 2, for instance.

9. *The Return Home:* "Among men you will always seem wild and strange," his solitude says to Zarathustra. But "here all things come caressingly to your discourse and flatter you, for they want to ride on your back. On every parable you ride to every truth." The discipline of communication might have served the philosopher better than the indiscriminate flattery of his solitude. But in this respect too, it was not given to Nietzsche to live in blissful ignorance: compare, for example, "The Song of Melancholy" in Part Four.

10. *On the Three Evils:* The praise of so-called evil as an ingredient of greatness is central in Nietzsche's thought, from his early fragment, *Homer's Contest,* to his *Antichrist.* There are few problems the self-styled immoralist pursued so persistently. Whether he calls attention to the element of cruelty in the Greek *agon* or denounces Christianity for vilifying sex, whether he contrasts sublimation and extirpation or the egoism of the creative and the vengeful: all

these are variations of one theme. In German, the three evils in this chapter are *Wollust, Herrschsucht, Selbstsucht*. For the first there is no exact equivalent in English. In this chapter, "lust" might do in some sentences, "voluptuousness" in others, but each would be quite inaccurate half the time, and the context makes it imperative that the same word be used throughout. There is only one word in English that renders Nietzsche's meaning perfectly in every single sentence: sex. Its only disadvantage: it is, to put it mildly, a far less poetic word than *Wollust*, and hence modifies the tone though not Nietzsche's meaning. But if we reflect on the three things which, according to Nietzsche, had been maligned most, under the influence of Christianity, and which he sought to rehabilitate or revaluate—were they not selfishness, the will to power, and sex? Nietzsche's early impact was in some ways comparable to that of Freud or Havelock Ellis. But prudery was for him at most one of three great evils, one kind of hypocrisy, one aspect of man's betrayal of the earth and of himself.

11. *On the Spirit of Gravity:* It is not only the metaphor of the camel that points back to the first chapter of Part One: the dead weight of convention is a prime instance of what is meant by the spirit of gravity; and the bird that outsoars tradition is, like the child and the self-propelled wheel at the beginning of the book, a symbol of creativity. The creator, however, is neither an "evil beast" nor an "evil tamer of beasts"—neither a profligate nor an ascetic: he integrates what is in him, perfects and lavishes himself, and says, "This is *my* way; where is yours?" Michelangelo and Mozart do not offer us "*the* way" but a challenge and a promise of what is possible.

12. *On Old and New Tablets:* Attempt at a grand summary, full of allusions to, and quotations from, previous chapters. Its unevenness is nowhere more striking than in section 12, with its puns on "crusades." Such sections as 5, 7, and 8, on the other hand, certainly deserve attention. The despot in section 11, who has all history rewritten, seems to point forward in time to Hitler, of whose racial legislation it

could indeed be said: "with the grandfather, however, time ends." Section 15 points back to Luther. Section 20 exposes in advance Stefan George's misconception when he ended his second poem on Nietzsche (my *Nietzsche*, p. 11): "The warner went—the wheel that downward rolls / To emptiness no arm now tackles in the spokes." The penultimate paragraph of this section is more "playful" in the original: *Ein Vorspiel bin ich besserer Spieler, oh meine Brüder! Ein Beispiel!* In section 25 the key word is *Versuch*, one of Nietzsche's favorite words, which means experiment, attempt, trial. Sometimes he associates it with *suchen*, searching. (In Chapter 2, "On the Vision and the Riddle," *Sucher, Versucher* has been rendered "searchers, researchers.") Section 29, finally, is used again, with minute changes, to conclude *Twilight of the Idols*.

13. *The Convalescent:* Zarathustra still cannot face the thought of the eternal recurrence but speaks about human speech and cruelty. In the end, his animals expound the eternal recurrence.

14. *On the Great Longing:* Hymn to his soul: Zarathustra and his soul wonder which of them should be grateful to the other.

15. *The Other Dancing Song:* Life and wisdom as women again; but in *this* dancing song, life is in complete control, and when Zarathustra's imagination runs away with him he gets his face slapped. What he whispers into the ear of life at the end of section 2 is, no doubt, that after his death he will yet recur eternally. The song at the end, punctuated by the twelve strokes of the bell, is interpreted in "The Drunken Song" in Part Four.

16. *The Seven Seals:* The eternal recurrence of the small man no longer nauseates Zarathustra. His affirmation now is boundless and without reservation: "For I love you, O eternity."

THE WANDERER

It was about midnight when Zarathustra started across the ridge of the island so that he might reach the other coast by early morning; for there he wanted to embark. There he would find a good roadstead where foreign ships too liked to anchor, and they often took along people who wanted to cross the sea from the blessed isles.

Now as Zarathustra was climbing the mountain he thought how often since his youth he had wandered alone and how many mountains and ridges and peaks he had already climbed.

I am a wanderer and a mountain climber, he said to his heart; I do not like the plains, and it seems I cannot sit still for long. And whatever may yet come to me as destiny and experience will include some wandering and mountain climbing: in the end, one experiences only oneself. The time is gone when mere accidents could still happen to me; and what could still come to me now that was not mine already? What returns, what finally comes home to me, is my own self and what of myself has long been in strange lands and scattered among all things and accidents. And one further thing I know: I stand before my final peak now and before that which has been saved up for me the longest. Alas, now I must face my hardest path! Alas, I have begun my loneliest walk! But whoever is of my kind cannot escape such an hour—the hour which says to him:

"Only now are you going your way to greatness! Peak and abyss—they are now joined together.

"You are going your way to greatness: now that which has hitherto been your ultimate danger has become your ultimate refuge.

"You are going your way to greatness: now this must give you the greatest courage that there is no longer any path behind you.

"You are going your way to greatness: here nobody shall sneak after you. Your own foot has effaced the path behind you, and over it there is written: impossibility.

"And if you now lack all ladders, then you must know how to climb on your own head: how else would you want to climb upward? On your own head and away over your own heart! Now what was gentlest in you must still become the hardest. He who has always spared himself much will in the end become sickly of so much consideration. Praised be what hardens! I do not praise the land where butter and honey flow.

"One must learn to *look away* from oneself in order to see *much*: this hardness is necessary to every climber of mountains.

"But the lover of knowledge who is obtrusive with his eyes—how could he see more of all things than their foregrounds? But you, O Zarathustra, wanted to see the ground and background of all things; hence you must climb over yourself—upward, up until even your stars are *under* you!"

Indeed, to look down upon myself and even upon my stars, that alone I should call my *peak*; that has remained for me as my *ultimate* peak.

Thus spoke Zarathustra to himself as he was climbing, comforting his heart with hard maxims; for his heart was sore as never before. And when he reached the height of the ridge, behold, the other sea lay spread out before him; and he stood still and remained silent a long time. But the night was cold at this height, and clear and starry bright.

I recognize my lot, he finally said sorrowfully. Well, I am ready. Now my ultimate loneliness has begun.

Alas, this black sorrowful sea below me! Alas, this pregnant nocturnal dismay! Alas, destiny and sea! To you I must now go *down!* Before my highest mountain I stand and before my longest wandering; to that end I must first go down deeper than ever I descended— deeper into pain than ever I descended, down into its blackest flood. Thus my destiny wants it. Well, I am ready.

Whence come the highest mountains? I once asked. Then I learned that they came out of the sea. The evidence is written in their rocks and in the walls of their peaks. It is out of the deepest depth that the highest must come to its height.

Thus spoke Zarathustra on the peak of the mountain, where it was cold; but when he came close to the sea and at last stood alone among the cliffs, he had become weary from walking and even more full of longing than before.

Everything is still asleep now, he said; even the sea is asleep. Drunk with sleep and strange it looks at me. But its breath is warm, that I feel. And I also feel that it is dreaming. In its dreams it tosses on hard pillows. Listen! Listen! How it groans with evil memories! Or evil forebodings? Alas, I am sad with you, you dark monster, and even annoyed with myself for your sake. Alas, that my hand does not have strength enough! Verily, I should like to deliver you from evil dreams.

And as Zarathustra was speaking thus he laughed at himself in melancholy and bitterness. What, Zarathustra, he said, would you sing comfort even to the sea? O you loving fool, Zarathustra, you are trust-overfull. But thus have you always been: you have always approached everything terrible trustfully. You have wanted to pet every monster. A whiff of warm breath, a little soft tuft on the paw—and at once you were ready to love and to lure it.

Love is the danger of the loneliest; love of everything if only it is alive. Laughable, verily, are my folly and my modesty in love.

Thus spoke Zarathustra and laughed for the second time. But then he recalled his friends whom he had left; and, as if he had wronged them with his thoughts, he was angry with himself for his thoughts. And soon it happened that he who had laughed wept: from wrath and longing Zarathustra wept bitterly.

ON THE VISION AND THE RIDDLE

1

When it got abroad among the sailors that Zarathustra was on board—for another man from the blessed isles had embarked with him—there was much curiosity and anticipation. But Zarathustra remained silent for two days and was cold and deaf from sadness and answered neither glances nor questions. But on the evening of the second day he opened his ears again, although he still remained silent, for there was much that was strange and dangerous to be heard on this ship, which came from far away and wanted to sail even farther. But Zarathustra was a friend of all who travel far and do not like to live without danger. And behold, eventually his own tongue was loosened as he listened, and the ice of his heart broke. Then he began to speak thus:

To you, the bold searchers, researchers, and whoever

embarks with cunning sails on terrible seas—to you, drunk with riddles, glad of the twilight, whose soul flutes lure astray to every whirlpool, because you do not want to grope along a thread with cowardly hand; and where you can *guess*, you hate to *deduce*—to you alone I tell the riddle that I *saw*, the vision of the loneliest.

Not long ago I walked gloomily through the deadly pallor of dusk—gloomy and hard, with lips pressed together. Not only one sun had set for me. A path that ascended defiantly through stones, malicious, lonely, not cheered by herb or shrub—a mountain path crunched under the defiance of my foot. Striding silently over the mocking clatter of pebbles, crushing the rock that made it slip, my foot forced its way upward. Upward—defying the spirit that drew it downward toward the abyss, the spirit of gravity, my devil and archenemy. Upward—although he sat on me, half dwarf, half mole, lame, making lame, dripping lead into my ear, leaden thoughts into my brain.

"O Zarathustra," he whispered mockingly, syllable by syllable; "you philosopher's stone! You threw yourself up high, but every stone that is thrown must fall. O Zarathustra, you philosopher's stone, you slingstone, you star-crusher! You threw yourself up so high; but every stone that is thrown must fall. Sentenced to yourself and to your own stoning—O Zarathustra, far indeed have you thrown the stone, but it will fall back on yourself."

Then the dwarf fell silent, and that lasted a long time. His silence, however, oppressed me; and such twosomeness is surely more lonesome than being alone. I climbed, I climbed, I dreamed, I thought; but everything oppressed me. I was like one sick whom his wicked torture makes weary, and who as he falls asleep is awakened by a still more wicked dream. But there is something in me that I call courage; that has so far slain my every discouragement. This courage finally bade me stand still and speak: "Dwarf! It is you or I!"

For courage is the best slayer, courage which *attacks;* for in every attack there is playing and brass.

Man, however, is the most courageous animal: hence he overcame every animal. With playing and brass he has so far overcome every pain; but human pain is the deepest pain.

Courage also slays dizziness at the edge of abysses: and where does man not stand at the edge of abysses? Is not seeing always—seeing abysses?

Courage is the best slayer: courage slays even pity. But pity is the deepest abyss: as deeply as man sees into life, he also sees into suffering.

Courage, however, is the best slayer—courage which attacks: which slays even death itself, for it says, "Was *that* life? Well then! Once more!"

In such words, however, there is much playing and brass. He that has ears to hear, let him hear!

2

"Stop, dwarf!" I said. "It is I or you! But I am the stronger of us two: you do not know my abysmal thought. *That* you could not bear!"

Then something happened that made me lighter, for the dwarf jumped from my shoulder, being curious; and he crouched on a stone before me. But there was a gateway just where we had stopped.

"Behold this gateway, dwarf!" I continued. "It has two faces. Two paths meet here; no one has yet followed either to its end. This long lane stretches back for an eternity. And the long lane out there, that is another eternity. They contradict each other, these paths; they offend each other face to face; and it is here at this gateway that they come together. The name of the gateway is inscribed above: 'Moment.' But whoever would follow one of them, on and on, farther and farther—do you believe, dwarf, that these paths contradict each other eternally?"

"All that is straight lies," the dwarf murmured contemptuously. "All truth is crooked; time itself is a circle."

"You spirit of gravity," I said angrily, "do not make things too easy for yourself! Or I shall let you crouch where you are crouching, lamefoot; and it was I that carried you to this *height*.

"Behold," I continued, "this moment! From this gateway, Moment, a long, eternal lane leads *backward:* behind us lies an eternity. Must not whatever *can* walk have walked on this lane before? Must not whatever *can* happen have happened, have been done, have passed by before? And if everything has been there before—what do you think, dwarf, of this moment? Must not this gateway too have been there before? And are not all things knotted together so firmly that this moment draws after it *all* that is to come? Therefore—itself too? For whatever *can* walk—in this long lane out *there* too, it *must* walk once more.

"And this slow spider, which crawls in the moonlight, and this moonlight itself, and I and you in the gateway, whispering together, whispering of eternal things—must not all of us have been there before? And return and walk in that other lane, out there, before us, in this long dreadful lane—must we not eternally return?"

Thus I spoke, more and more softly; for I was afraid of my own thoughts and the thoughts behind my thoughts. Then suddenly I heard a dog howl nearby. Had I ever heard a dog howl like this? My thoughts raced back. Yes, when I was a child, in the most distant childhood: then I heard a dog howl like this. And I saw him too, bristling, his head up, trembling, in the stillest midnight when even dogs believe in ghosts—and I took pity: for just then the full moon, silent as death, passed over the house; just then it stood still, a round glow—still on the flat roof, as if on another's property —that was why the dog was terrified, for dogs believe in thieves and ghosts. And when I heard such howling again I took pity again.

Where was the dwarf gone now? And the gateway? And the spider? And all the whispering? Was I dreaming, then? Was I waking up?

Among wild cliffs I stood suddenly alone, bleak, in the bleakest moonlight. *But there lay a man.* And there —the dog, jumping, bristling, whining—now he saw me coming; then he howled again, he *cried.* Had I ever heard a dog cry like this for help? And verily, what I saw—I had never seen the like. A young shepherd I saw, writhing, gagging, in spasms, his face distorted, and a heavy black snake hung out of his mouth. Had I ever seen so much nausea and pale dread on one face? He seemed to have been asleep when the snake crawled into his throat, and there bit itself fast. My hand tore at the snake and tore in vain; it did not tear the snake out of his throat. Then it cried out of me: "Bite! Bite its head off! Bite!" Thus it cried out of me— my dread, my hatred, my nausea, my pity, all that is good and wicked in me cried out of me with a single cry.

You bold ones who surround me! You searchers, researchers, and whoever among you has embarked with cunning sails on unexplored seas. You who are glad of riddles! Guess me this riddle that I saw then, interpret me the vision of the loneliest. For it was a vision

and a foreseeing. *What* did I see then in a parable?
And *who* is it who must yet come one day? *Who* is the
shepherd into whose throat the snake crawled thus?
Who is the man into whose throat all that is heaviest
and blackest will crawl thus?

The shepherd, however, bit as my cry counseled him;
he bit with a good bite. Far away he spewed the head
of the snake—and he jumped up. No longer shepherd,
no longer human—one changed, radiant, *laughing!*
Never yet on earth has a human being laughed as he
laughed! O my brothers, I heard a laughter that was no
human laughter; and now a thirst gnaws at me, a longing that never grows still. My longing for this laughter
gnaws at me; oh, how do I bear to go on living! And
how could I bear to die now!

Thus spoke Zarathustra.

ON INVOLUNTARY BLISS

With such riddles and bitternesses in his heart Zarathustra crossed the sea. But when he was four days
away from the blessed isles and from his friends, he
had overcome all his pain; triumphant and with firm
feet he stood on his destiny again. And then Zarathustra spoke thus to his jubilant conscience:

I am alone again and I want to be so; alone with
the pure sky and open sea; again it is afternoon around
me. It was in the afternoon that I once found my
friends for the first time; it was afternoon the second
time too, at the hour when all light grows quieter. For
whatever of happiness is still on its way between heaven
and earth now seeks a shelter in a bright soul; it is from
happiness that all light has grown quieter.

O afternoon of my life! Once my happiness too descended to the valley to seek shelter; and found those open, hospitable souls. O afternoon of my life! What have I not given up to have one single thing: this living plantation of my thoughts and this morning light of my highest hope!

Companions the creator once sought, and children of his hope; and behold, it turned out that he could not find them, unless he first created them himself. Thus I am in the middle of my work, going to my children and returning from them: for his children's sake, Zarathustra must perfect himself. For from the depths one loves only one's child and work; and where there is great love of oneself it is the sign of pregnancy: thus I found it to be. My children are still verdant in their first spring, standing close together and shaken by the same winds—the trees of my garden and my best soil. And verily, where such trees stand together there are blessed isles. But one day I want to dig them up and place each by itself, so it may learn solitude and defiance and caution. Gnarled and bent and with supple hardness it shall then stand by the sea, a living lighthouse of invincible life.

Where the storms plunge down into the sea and the mountain stretches out its trunk for water, there every one shall once have his day and night watches for his testing and knowledge. He shall be known and tested, whether he is of my kind and kin, whether he is the master of a long will, taciturn even when he speaks, and yielding so that in giving he receives—so that he may one day become my companion and a fellow creator and fellow celebrant of Zarathustra—one who writes my will on my tablets to contribute to the greater perfection of all things. And for his sake and the sake of those like him I must perfect myself; therefore I now evade my happiness and offer myself to all unhappiness, for my final testing and knowledge.

And verily, it was time for me to leave; and the wanderer's shadow and the longest boredom and the stillest hour—they all urged me: "It is high time." The wind blew through my keyhole and said, "Come!" Cunningly, the door flew open and said to me, "Go!" But I lay there chained to the love for my children: desire set this snare for me—the desire for love that I might become my children's prey and lose myself to them. Desire—this means to me to have lost myself. *I have you, my children!* In this experience everything shall be security and nothing desire.

But, brooding, the sun of my love lay on me; Zarathustra was cooking in his own juice—then shadows and doubts flew over me. I yearned for frost and winter: "Oh, that frost and winter might make me crack and crunch again!" I sighed; then icy mists rose from me. My past burst its tombs; many a pain that had been buried alive awoke, having merely slept, hidden in burial shrouds.

Thus everything called out to me in signs: "It is time!" But I did not hear, until at last my abyss stirred and my thought bit me. Alas, abysmal thought that is *my* thought, when shall I find the strength to hear you burrowing, without trembling any more? My heart pounds to my very throat whenever I hear you burrowing. Even your silence wants to choke me, you who are so abysmally silent. As yet I have never dared to summon you; it was enough that I carried you with me. As yet I have not been strong enough for the final overbearing, prankish bearing of the lion. Your gravity was always terrible enough for me; but one day I shall yet find the strength and the lion's voice to summon you.

And once I have overcome myself that far, then I also want to overcome myself in what is still greater; and a victory shall seal my perfection.

Meanwhile I still drift on uncertain seas; smooth-tongued accident flatters me; forward and backward I look, and still see no end. As yet the hour of my final struggle has not come to me—or is it coming just now? Verily, with treacherous beauty sea and life look at me.

O afternoon of my life! O happiness before evening! O haven on the high seas! O peace in uncertainty! How I mistrust all of you! Verily, I am mistrustful of your treacherous beauty. I am like the lover who mistrusts the all-too-velvet smile. As he pushes his most beloved before him, tender even in his hardness, and jealous, thus I push this blessed hour before me.

Away with you, blessed hour: with you bliss came to me against my will. Willing to suffer my deepest pain, I stand here: you came at the wrong time.

Away with you, blessed hour: rather seek shelter there—with my children. Hurry and bless them before evening with *my* happiness.

There evening approaches even now: the sun sinks. Gone—my happiness!

Thus spoke Zarathustra. And he waited for his unhappiness the entire night, but he waited in vain. The night remained bright and still, and happiness itself came closer and closer to him. Toward morning, however, Zarathustra laughed in his heart and said mockingly, "Happiness runs after me. That is because I do not run after women. For happiness is a woman."

BEFORE SUNRISE

O heaven above me, pure and deep! You abyss of light! Seeing you, I tremble with godlike desires. To throw myself into your height, that is *my* depth. To hide in your purity, that is *my* innocence.

Gods are shrouded by their beauty; thus you conceal your stars. You do not speak; thus you proclaim your wisdom to me. Today you rose for me silently over the roaring sea; your love and your shyness are a revelation to my roaring soul. That you came to me, beautiful, shrouded in your beauty, that you speak to me silently, revealing your wisdom—oh, how should I not guess all that is shy in your soul! *Before* the sun you came to me, the loneliest of all.

We are friends from the beginning: we share grief and ground and gray dread; we even share the sun. We do not speak to each other, because we know too much; we are silent to each other, we smile our knowledge at each other. Are you not the light for my fire? Have you not the sister soul to my insight? Together we have learned everything; together we have learned to ascend over ourselves to ourselves and to smile cloudlessly—to smile down cloudlessly from bright eyes and from a vast distance when constraint and contrivance and guilt steam beneath us like rain.

And when I wandered alone, for *whom* did my soul hunger at night, on false paths? And when I climbed mountains, *whom* did I always seek on the mountains, if not you? And all my wandering and mountain climbing were sheer necessity and a help in my helplessness: what I want with all my will is to *fly*, to fly up into *you*.

And whom did I hate more than drifting clouds and

all that stains you? And I hated even my own hatred because it stained you. I loathe the drifting clouds, those stealthy great cats which prey on what you and I have in common—the uncanny, unbounded Yes and Amen. We loathe these mediators and mixers, the drifting clouds that are half-and-half and have learned neither to bless nor to curse from the heart.

Rather would I sit in a barrel under closed heavens, rather sit in the abyss without a heaven, than see you, bright heaven, stained by drifting clouds.

And often I had the desire to tie them fast with the jagged golden wires of the lightning, that, like thunder, I might beat the big drums on their kettle-belly—an angry kettle-drummer—because they rob me of your Yes and Amen, O heaven over me, pure and light! You abyss of light! Because they rob you of *my* Yes and Amen. For I prefer even noise and thunder and storm-curses to this deliberate, doubting cats' calm; and among men too I hate most of all the soft-treaders and those who are half-and-half and doubting, tottering drift clouds.

And "whoever cannot bless should *learn* to curse"—this bright doctrine fell to me from a bright heaven; this star stands in my heaven even in black nights.

But I am one who can bless and say Yes, if only you are about me, pure and light, you abyss of light; then I carry the blessings of my Yes into all abysses. I have become one who blesses and says Yes; and I fought long for that and was a fighter that I might one day get my hands free to bless. But this is my blessing: to stand over every single thing as its own heaven, as its round roof, its azure bell, and eternal security; and blessed is he who blesses thus.

For all things have been baptized in the well of

eternity and are beyond good and evil; and good and evil themselves are but intervening shadows and damp depressions and drifting clouds.

Verily, it is a blessing and not a blasphemy when I teach: "Over all things stand the heaven Accident, the heaven Innocence, the heaven Chance, the heaven Prankishness."

"By Chance"—that is the most ancient nobility of the world, and this I restored to all things: I delivered them from their bondage under Purpose. This freedom and heavenly cheer I have placed over all things like an azure bell when I taught that over them and through them no "eternal will" wills. This prankish folly I have put in the place of that will when I taught: "In everything one thing is impossible: rationality."

A *little* reason, to be sure, a seed of wisdom scattered from star to star—this leaven is mixed in with all things: for folly's sake, wisdom is mixed in with all things. A little wisdom is possible indeed; but this blessed certainty I found in all things: that they would rather *dance* on the feet of Chance.

O heaven over me, pure and high! That is what your purity is to me now, that there is no eternal spider or spider web of reason; that you are to me a dance floor for divine accidents, that you are to me a divine table for divine dice and dice players. But you blush? Did I speak the unspeakable? Did I blaspheme, wishing to bless you? Or is it the shame of twosomeness that makes you blush? Do you bid me go and be silent because the *day* is coming now?

The world is deep—and deeper than day had ever been aware. Not everything may be put into words in the presence of the day. But the day is coming, so let us part.

O heaven over me, bashful and glowing! O you, my happiness before sunrise! The day is coming, so let us part!

Thus spoke Zarathustra.

ON VIRTUE THAT MAKES SMALL

1

When Zarathustra was on land again he did not proceed straight to his mountain and his cave, but he undertook many ways and questions and found out this and that; so that he said of himself, joking: "Behold a river that flows, winding and twisting, back to its source!" For he wanted to determine what had happened to man meanwhile: whether he had become greater or smaller. And once he saw a row of new houses; then he was amazed and said:

"What do these houses mean? Verily, no great soul put them up as its likeness. Might an idiotic child have taken them out of his toy box? Would that another child might put them back into his box! And these rooms and chambers—can *men* go in and out of them? They look to me as if made for silken dolls, or for stealthy nibblers who probably also let themselves be nibbled stealthily."

And Zarathustra stood still and reflected. At last he said sadly: "Everything has become smaller! Everywhere I see lower gates: those who are of my kind probably still go through, but they must stoop. Oh, when shall I get back to my homeland, where I need no longer stoop—no longer stoop before *those who are small?*" And Zarathustra sighed and looked into the distance. On that same day, however, he made his speech on virtue that makes small.

2

I walk among this people and I keep my eyes open: they do not forgive me that I do not envy their virtues. They bite at me because I say to them: small people need small virtues—and because I find it hard to accept that small people are needed.

I am still like the rooster in a strange yard, where the hens also bite at him; but I am not angry with the hens on that account. I am polite to them as to all small annoyances; to be prickly to what is small strikes me as wisdom for hedgehogs.

They all speak of me when they sit around the fire in the evening; they speak of me, but no one thinks of me. This is the new stillness I have learned: their noise concerning me spreads a cloak over my thoughts.

They noise among themselves: "What would this gloomy cloud bring us? Let us see to it that it does not bring us a plague." And recently a woman tore back her child when it wanted to come to me. "Take the children away!" she cried; "such eyes scorch children's souls." They cough when I speak: they think that a cough is an argument against strong winds; they guess nothing of the roaring of my happiness. "We have no time yet for Zarathustra," they argue; but what matters a time that "has no time" for Zarathustra?

And when they praise me, how could I go to sleep on *their* praise? Their praise is a belt of thorns to me: it scratches me even as I shake it off. And this too I have learned among them: he who gives praise poses as if he were giving back; in truth, however, he wants more gifts.

Ask my foot whether it likes their way of lauding and luring! Verily, after such a beat and ticktock it has no wish either to dance or to stand still. They would laud and lure me into a small virtue; they would persuade my foot to the ticktock of a small happiness.

I walk among this people and I keep my eyes open: they have become smaller, and they are becoming smaller and smaller; *but this is due to their doctrine of happiness and virtue.* For they are modest in virtue, too—because they want contentment. But only a modest virtue gets along with contentment.

To be sure, even they learn in their way to stride and to stride forward: I call it their hobbling. Thus they become a stumbling block for everyone who is in a hurry. And many among them walk forward while looking backward with their necks stiff: I like running into them. Foot and eye should not lie nor give the lie to each other. But there is much lying among the small people. Some of them will, but most of them are only willed. Some of them are genuine, but most of them are bad actors. There are unconscious actors among them and involuntary actors; the genuine are always rare, especially genuine actors.

There is little of man here; therefore their women strive to be mannish. For only he who is man enough will release the woman in woman.

And this hypocrisy I found to be the worst among them, that even those who command, hypocritically feign the virtues of those who serve. "I serve, you serve, we serve"—thus prays even the hypocrisy of the rulers; and woe, if the first lord is *merely* the first servant!

Alas, into their hypocrisies too the curiosity of my eyes flew astray; and well I guessed their fly-happiness and their humming around sunny windowpanes. So much kindness, so much weakness do I see; so much justice and pity, so much weakness.

Round, righteous, and kind they are to each other,

round like grains of sand, righteous and kind with grains of sand. Modestly to embrace a small happiness—that they call "resignation"—and modestly they squint the while for another small happiness. At bottom, these simpletons want a single thing most of all: that nobody should hurt them. Thus they try to please and gratify everybody. This, however, is cowardice, even if it be called virtue.

And if they once speak roughly, these small people, I hear only their hoarseness, for every draft makes them hoarse. They are clever, their virtues have clever fingers. But they lack fists, their fingers do not know how to hide behind fists. Virtue to them is that which makes modest and tame: with that they have turned the wolf into a dog and man himself into man's best domestic animal.

"We have placed our chair in the middle," your smirking says to me; "and exactly as far from dying fighters as from amused sows." That, however, is mediocrity, though it be called moderation.

3

I walk among this people and I let many a word drop; but they know neither how to accept nor how to retain.

They are amazed that I did not come to revile venery and vice; and verily, I did not come to warn against pickpockets either.

They are amazed that I am not prepared to teach wit to their cleverness and to whet it—as if they did not have enough clever boys, whose voices screech like slate pencils!

And when I shout, "Curse all cowardly devils in you who like to whine and fold their hands and pray," they shout, "Zarathustra is godless." And their teachers of resignation shout it especially; but it is precisely into their ears that I like to shout, "Yes, I *am* Zarathustra the godless!" These teachers of resignation! Whatever is small and sick and scabby, they crawl to like lice; and only my nausea prevents me from squashing them.

Well then, this is my preaching for *their* ears: I am Zarathustra the godless, who speaks: "Who is more godless than I, that I may delight in his instruction?"

I am Zarathustra the godless: where shall I find my equal? And all those are my equals who give themselves their own will and reject all resignation.

I am Zarathustra the godless: I still cook every chance in my pot. And only when it has been cooked through there do I welcome it as my food. And verily, many a chance came to me domineeringly; but my will spoke to it still more domineeringly—and immediately it lay imploringly on its knees, imploring that it might find a hearth and heart in me, and urging with flattery, "Look, Zarathustra, how only a friend comes to his friend!"

But why do I speak where nobody has *my* ears? And so let me shout it into all the winds: You are becoming smaller and smaller, you small people! You are crumbling, you comfortable ones. You will yet perish of your many small virtues, of your many small abstentions, of your many small resignations. Too considerate, too yielding is your soil. But that a tree may become *great*, it must strike hard roots around hard rocks.

What you abstain from too weaves at the web of all human future; your nothing too is a spider web and a spider, which lives on the blood of the future. And when you receive it is like stealing, you small men of virtue; but even among rogues, *honor* says, "One should steal only where one cannot rob."

"It will give eventually"—that is another teaching of

resignation. But I tell you who are comfortable: *it will take* and will take more and more from you! Oh, that you would reject all *halfhearted* willing and would become resolute in sloth and deed!

Alas, that you would understand my word: "Do whatever you will, but first be such as are *able to will.*

"Do love your neighbor as yourself, but first be such as *love themselves*—loving with a great love, loving with a great contempt." Thus speaks Zarathustra the godless.

But why do I speak where nobody has *my* ears? It is still an hour too early for me here. I am my own precursor among this people, my own cock's crow through dark lanes. But *their* hour will come! And mine will come too! Hourly, they are becoming smaller, poorer, more sterile—poor herbs! poor soil! and *soon* they shall stand there like dry grass and prairie—and verily, weary of themselves and languishing even more than for water—for *fire.*

O blessed hour of lightning! O secret before noon! I yet hope to turn them into galloping fires and heralds with fiery tongues—they shall yet proclaim with fiery tongues: It is coming, it is near—*the great noon!*

Thus spoke Zarathustra.

UPON THE MOUNT OF OLIVES

Winter, a wicked guest, is sitting at home with me; my hands are blue from the handshake of his friendship. I honor this wicked guest, but I like to let him sit alone. I like to run away from him; and if one runs *well,* one escapes him. With warm feet and warm thoughts I run where the wind stands still, to the sunny nook of my mount of olives. There I laugh at my severe guest and am still well disposed toward him for catching the flies at home and for silencing much small noise. For he does not suffer it when a mosquito would sing, or even two; he even makes the lane lonely till the moonlight in it is afraid at night.

He is a hard guest, but I honor him, and I do not pray, like the pampered, to the potbellied fire idol. Even a little chattering of the teeth rather than adoring idols —thus my nature dictates. And I have a special grudge against all fire idols that are in heat, steaming and musty.

Whomever I love, I love better in winter than in summer; I mock my enemies better and more heartily since winter dwells in my home. Heartily, in truth, even when I crawl into bed; even then my hidden happiness still laughs and is full of pranks; even the dream that lies to me still laughs. I—a crawler? Never in my life have I crawled before the mighty; and if ever I lied, I lied out of love. Therefore I am glad in the wintry bed too. A simple bed warms me more than a rich one, for I am jealous of my poverty, and in winter it is most faithful to me.

I begin every day with a bit of malice: I mock the winter with a cold bath; that makes my severe house guest grumble. Besides, I like to tickle him with a little wax candle to make him let the sky come out of the ashen gray twilight at last. For I am especially malicious in the morning, in that early hour when the pail rattles at the well and the horses whinny warmly through gray lanes. Then I wait impatiently for the bright sky to rise before me at last, the snow-bearded winter sky, the old man with his white hair—the winter sky, so taciturn that it often tacitly hides even its sun.

Was it from him that I learned the long bright silence? Or did he learn it from me? Or did each of us invent it independently? The origin of all good things is thousandfold; all good prankish things leap into existence from sheer joy: how could one expect them to do that only once? Long silence too is a good prankish thing—and to look out of a bright round-eyed face, like the winter sky, and tacitly to hide one's sun and one's indomitable solar will: verily, this art and this winter prank I have learned well.

It is my favorite malice and art that my silence has learned not to betray itself through silence. Rattling with discourse and dice, I outwit those who wait solemnly: my will and purpose shall elude all these severe inspectors. That no one may discern my ground and ultimate will, for that I have invented my long bright silence. Many I found who were clever: they veiled their faces and muddied their waters that nobody might see through them, deep down. But precisely to them came the cleverer mistrusters and nutcrackers: precisely their most hidden fish were fished out. It is the bright, the bold, the transparent who are cleverest among those who are silent: their ground is down so deep that even the brightest water does not betray it.

You snow-bearded silent winter sky, you round-eyed white-head above me! O you heavenly parable of my soul and its pranks!

And *must* I not conceal myself like one who has swallowed gold, lest they slit open my soul? *Must* I not walk on stilts that they overlook my long legs—all these grudge-joys and drudge-boys who surround me? These smoky, room-temperature, used-up, wilted, fretful souls —how *could* their grudge endure my happiness? Hence I show them only the ice and the winter of my peaks— and not that my mountain still winds all the belts of the sun round itself. They hear only my winter winds whistling—and not that I also cross warm seas, like longing, heavy, hot south winds. They still have pity on my accidents; but *my* word says, "Let accidents come to me, they are innocent as little children."

How could they endure my happiness if I did not wrap my happiness in accidents and winter distress and polar-bear caps and covers of snowy heavens—if I myself did not have mercy on their *pity,* which is the pity of grudge-joys and drudge-boys, if I myself did not sigh before them and chatter with cold and patiently *suffer* them to wrap me in their pity. This is the wise frolicsomeness and friendliness of my soul, that it does not conceal its winter and its icy winds; nor does it conceal its chilblains.

Loneliness can be the escape of the sick; loneliness can also be escape *from* the sick.

Let them *hear* me chatter and sigh with the winter cold, all these poor jealous jokers around me! With such sighing and chattering I still escape their heated rooms.

Let them suffer and sigh over my chilblains. "The ice of knowledge will yet freeze him to death!" they moan.

Meanwhile I run crisscross on my mount of olives with warm feet; in the sunny nook of my mount of olives I sing and I mock all pity.

Thus sang Zarathustra.

ON PASSING BY

Thus, walking slowly among many peoples and through numerous towns, Zarathustra returned on roundabout paths to his mountains and his cave. And on the way he also came unexpectedly to the gate of the great city; but here a foaming fool jumped toward him with outspread hands and barred his way. This, however, was the same fool whom the people called "Zarathustra's ape": for he had gathered something of his phrasing and cadences and also liked to borrow from the treasures of his wisdom. But the fool spoke thus to Zarathustra:

"O Zarathustra, here is the great city; here you could find nothing and lose everything. Why do you want to wade through this mire? Have pity on your foot! Rather spit on the city gate and turn back. Here is hell for a hermit's thoughts: here great thoughts are boiled alive and cooked till they are small. Here all great feelings decay: only the smallest rattleboned feelings may rattle here. Don't you smell the slaughterhouses and ovens of the spirit even now? Does not this town steam with the fumes of slaughtered spirit?

"Don't you see the soul hanging like a limp, dirty rag? And they still make newspapers of these rags!

"Don't you hear how the spirit has here been reduced to plays on words? It vomits revolting verbal swill. And they still make newspapers of this swill!

"They hound each other and know not where. They overheat each other and know not why. They tinkle with their tin, they jingle with their gold. They are cold and seek warmth from brandy; they are heated and seek coolness from frozen spirits; they are all diseased and sick with public opinions.

"All lusts and vices are at home here; but there are also some here who are virtuous: there is much service-able, serving virtue—much serviceable virtue with pen fingers and hard sitting- and waiting-flesh, blessed with little stars on the chest and with padded, rumpless daughters. There is also much piety, and there are many devout lickspittles, batteries of fakers and flattery-bakers before the God of Hosts. For it is 'from above' that the stars and the gracious spittle trickle; every starless chest longs above.

"The moon has her courtyard, and the courtyard has its mooncalves; to everything, however, that comes from the court, the beggarly mob and all serviceable beggar-virtue pray. 'I serve, you serve, we serve'—thus all serviceable virtue prays to the prince, that the deserved star may finally be pinned on the narrow chest.

"The moon, however, still revolves around all that is earthly: So too the prince still revolves around that which is earthliest—but that is the gold of the shop-keeper. The God of Hosts is no god of gold bars; the prince proposes, but the shopkeeper disposes.

"By everything in you that is bright and strong and good, O Zarathustra, spit on this city of shopkeepers and turn back! Here all blood flows putrid and luke-warm and spumy through all the veins; spit on the great city which is the great swill room where all the swill spumes together. Spit on the city of compressed souls and narrow chests, of popeyes and sticky fingers—on the city of the obtrusive, the impudent, the scribble-and scream-throats, the overheated ambitious-conceited—where everything infirm, infamous, lustful, dusky, overmusty, pussy, and plotting putrefies together: spit on the great city and turn back!"

Here, however, Zarathustra interrupted the foaming fool and put his hand over the fool's mouth. "Stop at last!" cried Zarathustra; "your speech and your manner have long nauseated me. Why did you live near the swamps so long, until you yourself have become a frog and a toad? Does not putrid, spumy swamp-blood flow through your own veins now that you have learned to croak and revile thus? Why have you not gone into the woods? Or to plow the soil? Does not the sea abound in green islands? I despise your despising; and if you warned me, why did you not warn yourself?

"Out of love alone shall my despising and my warn-ing bird fly up, not out of the swamp.

"They call you my ape, you foaming fool; but I call you my grunting swine: with your grunting you spoil for me my praise of folly. What was it that first made you grunt? That nobody flattered you sufficiently; you sat down to this filth so as to have reason to grunt much —to have reason for much *revenge*. For all your foaming is revenge, you vain fool; I guessed it well.

"But your fool's words injure me, even where you are right. And even if Zarathustra's words *were* a thousand times right, still *you* would always *do* wrong with my words."

Thus spoke Zarathustra; and he looked at the great city, sighed, and long remained silent. At last he spoke thus: "I am nauseated by this great city too, and not only by this fool. Here as there, there is nothing to better, nothing to worsen. Woe unto this great city! And I wish I already saw the pillar of fire in which it will be burned. For such pillars of fire must precede the great noon. But this has its own time and its own destiny.

"This doctrine, however, I give you, fool, as a parting present: where one can no longer love, there one should *pass by*."

Thus spoke Zarathustra, and he passed by the fool and the great city.

ON APOSTATES

1

Alas, all lies withered and gray that but recently stood green and colorful on this meadow. And how much honey of hope I carried from here to my beehives! These young hearts have all become old already—and not even old; only weary, ordinary, and comfortable. They put it, "We have become pious again."

Only recently I saw them run out in the morning on bold feet: but the feet of their thirst for knowledge have grown weary, and now they even slander the courage they had in the morning. Verily, many among them once lifted their legs like dancers, cheered by the laughter in my wisdom; then they thought better of it. Just now I saw one groveling—crawling back to the cross. Around light and freedom they once fluttered like mosquitoes and young poets. A little older, a little colder—and already they are musty mystifiers and hearth-squatters.

Did their hearts perhaps grow faint because solitude swallowed me like a whale? Did their ears perhaps listen longingly long, *in vain*, for me and my trumpet and herald's calls? Alas, there are always only a few whose hearts long retain their courageous bearing and overbearing prankishness, and whose spirits also remain patient. The rest, however, are cowards. The rest—those are always by far the most, the commonplace, the superfluous, the all-too-many: all these are cowards.

Whoever is of my kind will also encounter the experiences of my kind: so his first companions will have to be corpses and jesters. His second companions, however, will call themselves his *believers*: a living swarm, much love, much folly, much beardless veneration. To these believers, whoever is of my kind among men should not tie his heart; those who know the changeful, cowardly nature of mankind should not believe in these springtimes and colorful meadows.

Were their ability different, their will would be different too. Those who are half-and-half spoil all that is whole. That leaves wilt—what is there to wail about? Let them fly and fall, O Zarathustra, and do not wail! It is better to blow among them with rustling winds—

blow among these leaves, O Zarathustra, that everything wilted may run away from you even faster!

2

"We have become pious again"—so these apostates confess; and some among them are even too cowardly to confess it.

Those I look in the eye, and then I say it to their faces and to their blushing cheeks: you are such as pray again.

But it is a disgrace to pray! Not for everybody, but for you and me and whoever else has a conscience in his head too. For *you* it is a disgrace to pray!

You know it well: your cowardly devil within you, who would like to fold his hands and rest his hands in his lap and be more comfortable—this cowardly devil urges you, "There *is* a God." With this, however, you belong to the light-shunning kind who cannot rest where there is light; now you must daily bury your head deeper in night and haze.

And verily, you chose the hour well, for just now the nocturnal birds are flying again. The hour has come for all light-shunning folk, the hour of evening and rest, when they do not rest. I hear and smell it: their hour for chase and procession has come—not indeed for a wild chase, but for a tame, lame, snooping, pussyfooting, prayer-muttering chase—for a chase after soulful sneaks: all the heart's mousetraps have now been set again. And wherever I lift a curtain a little night moth rushes out. Did it perhaps squat there together with another little night moth? For everywhere I smell little hidden communities; and wherever there are closets, there are new canters praying inside and the fog of canters.

They sit together long evenings and say, "Let us become as little children again and say 'dear God!' "—their mouths and stomachs upset by pious confectioners.

Or they spend long evenings watching a cunning, ambushing, cross-marked spider, which preaches cleverness to the other spiders and teaches thus: "Under crosses one can spin well."

Or they spend the day sitting at swamps with fishing rods, thinking themselves profound; but whoever fishes where there are no fish, I would not even call superficial.

Or they learn to play the harp with pious pleasure—from a composer of songs who would like to harp himself right into the hearts of young females; for he has grown weary of old females and their praise.

Or they learn to shudder from a scholarly half-madman who waits in dark rooms for the spirits to come to him—so his spirit will flee completely.

Or they listen to an old traveling, caviling zany who has learned the sadness of tones from sad winds; now he whistles after the wind and preaches sadness in sad tones.

And some of them have even become night watchmen: now they know how to blow horns and to walk about at night and to awaken old things that had long gone to sleep. I heard five sayings about old things last night at the garden wall: they came from such old, saddened, dried-up night watchmen.

"For a father, he does not care enough about his children: human fathers do this better."

"He is too old. He does not care about his children at all any more"—thus the other night watchman replied.

"But does he *have* any children? Nobody can prove it, if he does not prove it himself. I have long wished he would for once prove it thoroughly."

"Prove? As if *he* had ever proved anything! Proof is difficult for him; he considers it terribly important that one should have *faith* in him."

"Sure! Sure! Faith makes him blessed, faith in him. That is the way of old people. We are no different ourselves."

Thus the two old night watchmen and scarelights spoke to each other and then tooted sadly on their horns: so it happened last night at the garden wall. In me, however, my heart twisted with laughter and wanted to break and did not know whither, and sank into my diaphragm. Verily, this will yet be my death, that I shall suffocate with laughter when I see asses drunk and hear night watchmen thus doubting God. Is not the time long past for all such doubts too? Who may still awaken such old sleeping, light-shunning things?

For the old gods, after all, things came to an end long ago; and verily, they had a good gay godlike end. They did not end in a "twilight," though this lie is told. Instead: one day they *laughed* themselves to death. That happened when the most godless word issued from one of the gods themselves—the word: "There is one god. Thou shalt have no other god before me!" An old grimbeard of a god, a jealous one, thus forgot himself. And then all the gods laughed and rocked on their chairs and cried, "Is not just this godlike that there are gods but no God?"

He that has ears to hear, let him hear!

Thus Zarathustra discoursed in the town which he loved and which is also called The Motley Cow. For from here he had only two more days to go to reach his cave and his animals again; but his soul jubilated continually because of the nearness of his return home.

THE RETURN HOME

O solitude! O my *home,* solitude! Too long have I
lived wildly in wild strange places not to return home
to you in tears. Now you may threaten me with your
finger, as mothers threaten; now you may smile at me,
as mothers smile; now you may say to me:

"And who was it that, like a storm, once stormed
away from me? Who shouted in parting, 'Too long I
have sat with solitude; I have forgotten how to be
silent!' That, I suppose, you have learned again now? O
Zarathustra, I know everything. Also that you were
more forsaken among the many, being one, than ever
with me. To be forsaken is one thing, to be lonely, another: that you have learned now. And that among men
you will always seem wild and strange—wild and
strange even when they love you; for above all things
they want *consideration.*

"Here, however, you are in your own home and
house; here you can talk freely about everything and
pour out all the reasons; nothing here is ashamed of
obscure, obdurate feelings. Here all things come caressingly to your discourse and flatter you, for they want to
ride on your back. On every parable you ride to every
truth. Here you may talk fairly and frankly to all things:
and verily, it rings in their ears like praise when somebody talks straight to all things.

"To be forsaken, however, is another matter. For—
do you still remember, Zarathustra? When your bird
cried high above you, when you stood in the forest, un-
decided where to turn, ignorant, near a corpse—when
you said, 'May my animals lead me! I found it more
dangerous to be among men than among animals'—

then you were forsaken! And do you still remember, Zarathustra? When you sat on your island, a well of wine among empty pails, spending and expending, bestowing and flowing among the thirsty, until finally you sat thirsty among drunks and complained by night, 'Is it not more blessed to receive than to give, and to steal still more blessed than to receive?'—then you were forsaken! And do you still remember, Zarathustra? When your stillest hour came and drove you away from yourself, speaking in an evil whisper, 'Speak and break!'—when it made you repent all your waiting and silence and discouraged your humble courage—then you were forsaken."

O solitude! O my home, solitude! How happily and tenderly your voice speaks to me! We do not question each other, we do not complain to each other, we often walk together through open doors. For where you are, things are open and bright; and the hours too walk on lighter feet here. For in darkness, time weighs more heavily on us than in the light. Here the words and word-shrines of all being open up before me: here all being wishes to become word, all becoming wishes to learn from me how to speak.

Down there, however, all speech is in vain. There, forgetting and passing by are the best wisdom: *that* I have learned now. He who would grasp everything human would have to grapple with everything. But for that my hands are too clean. I do not even want to inhale their breath; alas, that I lived so long among their noises and vile breath!

O happy silence around me! O clean smells around me! Oh, how this silence draws deep breaths of clean air! Oh, how it listens, this happy silence!

But down there everyone talks and no one listens.

You could ring in your wisdom with bells: the shop-keepers in the market place would outjingle it with pennies.

Everyone among them talks; no one knows how to understand any more. Everything falls into the water, nothing falls into deep wells any longer.

Everyone among them talks; nothing turns out well any more and is finished. Everyone cackles; but who still wants to sit quietly in the nest and hatch eggs?

Everyone among them talks; everything is talked to pieces. And what even yesterday was still too hard for time itself and its tooth, today hangs, spoiled by scraping and gnawing, out of the mouths of the men of today.

Everyone among them talks; everything is betrayed. And what was once called the secret and the secrecy of deep souls today belongs to the street trumpeters and other butterflies.

Oh, everything human is strange, a noise on dark streets! But now it lies behind me again: my greatest danger lies behind me!

Consideration and pity have ever been my greatest dangers, and everything human wants consideration and pity. With concealed truths, with a fool's hands and a fond, foolish heart and a wealth of the little lies of pity: thus I always lived among men. Disguised I sat among them, ready to mistake *myself* that I might endure *them*, and willingly urging myself, "You fool, you do not know men."

One forgets about men when one lives among men; there is too much foreground in all men: what good are far-sighted, far-seeking eyes *there*? And whenever they mistook me, I, fool that I am, showed them more consideration than myself, being used to hardness against myself, and often I even took revenge on myself for being too considerate. Covered with the bites of poisonous flies and hollowed out like a stone by many drops of malice, thus I sat among them, and I still reminded myself, "Everything small is innocent of its smallness."

Especially those who call themselves "the good" I found to be the most poisonous flies: they bite in all innocence, they lie in all innocence; how could they possibly be just to me? Pity teaches all who live among the good to lie. Pity surrounds all free souls with musty air. For the stupidity of the good is unfathomable.

To conceal myself and my wealth, that I learned down there; for I have found everyone poor in spirit. The lie of my pity was this, that I knew I could see and smell in everyone what was spirit enough for him and what was too much spirit for him. Their stiff sages—I called them sagacious, not stiff; thus I learned to swallow words. Their gravediggers—I called them researchers and testers; thus I learned to change words. The gravediggers dig themselves sick; under old rubbish lie noxious odors. One should not stir up the morass. One should live on mountains.

With happy nostrils I again breathe mountain freedom. At last my nose is delivered from the smell of everything human. Tickled by the sharp air as by sparkling wines, my soul sneezes—sneezes and jubilates to itself: *Gesundheit!*

Thus spoke Zarathustra.

ON THE THREE EVILS

1

In a dream, in the last dream of the morning, I stood in the foothills today—beyond the world, held scales, and weighed the world. Alas, the jealous dawn came too early and glowed me awake! She is always jealous of my glowing morning dreams.

Measurable by him who has time, weighable by a good weigher, reachable by strong wings, guessable by divine nutcrackers: thus my dream found the world— my dream, a bold sailor, half ship, half hurricane, taciturn as butterflies, impatient as falcons: how did it have the patience or the time to weigh the world? Did my wisdom secretly urge it, my laughing, wide-awake day-wisdom which mocks all "infinite worlds"? For it speaks: "Wherever there is force, *number* will become mistress: she has more force."

How surely my dream looked upon this finite world, not inquisitively, not acquisitively, not afraid, not begging, as if a full apple offered itself to my hand, a ripe golden apple with cool, soft, velvet skin, thus the world offered itself to me; as if a tree waved to me, broad-branched, strong-willed, bent as a support, even as a footstool for one weary of his way, thus the world stood on my foothills; as if delicate hands carried a shrine toward me, a shrine open for the delight of bashful, adoring eyes, thus the world offered itself to me today; not riddle enough to frighten away human love, not solution enough to put to sleep human wisdom: a humanly good thing the world was to me today, though one speaks so much evil of it.

How shall I thank my morning dream that I thus weighed the world this morning? As a humanly good thing it came to me, this dream and heart-comforter. And to imitate it by day and to learn from it what was best in it, I shall now place the three most evil things on the scales and weigh them humanly well. He that taught to bless also taught to curse; what are the three best cursed things in the world? I shall put them on the scales.

Sex, the lust to rule, selfishness: these three have so far been best cursed and worst reputed and lied about; these three I will weigh humanly well.

Well then, here are my foothills and there the sea: *that* rolls toward me, shaggy, flattering, the faithful old hundred-headed canine monster that I love. Well then, here I will hold the scales over the rolling sea; and a witness I choose too, to look on—you, solitary tree, fragrant and broad-vaulted, that I love.

On what bridge does the present pass to the future? By what compulsion does the higher compel itself to the lower? And what bids even the highest grow still higher?

Now the scales are balanced and still: three weighty questions I threw on it; three weighty answers balance the other scale.

2

Sex: to all hair-shirted despisers of the body, their thorn and stake, and cursed as "world" among all the afterworldly because it mocks and fools all teachers of error and confusion.

Sex: for the rabble, the slow fire on which they are burned; for all worm-eaten wood and all stinking rags, the ever-ready rut and oven.

Sex: for free hearts, innocent and free, the garden happiness of the earth, the future's exuberant gratitude to the present.

Sex: only for the wilted, a sweet poison; for the lion-willed, however, the great invigoration of the heart and the reverently reserved wine of wines.

Sex: the happiness that is great parable of a higher happiness and the highest hope. For to many is marriage promised, and more than marriage—to many who are stranger to each other than man and woman. And who can wholly comprehend *how* strange man and woman are to each other?

Sex—but I want to have fences around my thoughts and even around my words, lest swine and swooners break into my garden!

The lust to rule: the scalding scourge of the hardest among the hardhearted; the hideous torture that is saved up for the cruelest; the dark flame of living pyres.

The lust to rule: the malicious gadfly imposed on the vainest peoples; the mocker of all uncertain virtues; the rider on every horse and every pride.

The lust to rule: the earthquake that breaks and breaks open everything worm-eaten and hollow; the rumbling, grumbling punisher that breaks open whited sepulchers; the lightning-like question mark beside premature answers.

The lust to rule: before whose glances man crawls and ducks and slaves and becomes lower than snake and swine, until finally the great contempt cries out of him.

The lust to rule: the terrible teacher of the great contempt, who preaches "away with you" to the very faces of cities and empires, until it finally cries out of them themselves, "Away with *me!*"

The lust to rule: which, however, also ascends luringly to the pure and lonely and up to self-sufficient heights, glowing like a love that luringly paints crimson fulfillments on earthly skies.

The lust to rule—but who would call it *lust* when what is high longs downward for power? Verily, there is nothing diseased or lustful in such longing and condescending. That the lonely heights should not remain lonely and self-sufficient eternally; that the mountain should descend to the valley and the winds of the height to the low plains—oh, who were to find the right name for such longing? "Gift-giving virtue"—thus Zarathustra once named the unnamable.

And at that time it also happened—and verily, it happened for the first time—that his word pronounced *selfishness* blessed, the wholesome, healthy selfishness that wells from a powerful soul—from a powerful soul to which belongs the high body, beautiful, triumphant, refreshing, around which everything becomes a mirror —the supple, persuasive body, the dancer whose parable and epitome is the self-enjoying soul. The self-enjoyment of such bodies and souls calls itself "virtue."

With its words about good and bad, such self-enjoyment screens itself as with sacred groves; with the names of its happiness it banishes from its presence whatever is contemptible. From its presence it banishes whatever is cowardly; it says: bad—*that is* cowardly! Contemptible to its mind is anyone who always worries, sighs, is miserable, and also anyone who picks up even the smallest advantages. It also despises all wisdom that wallows in grief; for verily, there is also wisdom that blooms in the dark, a nightshade wisdom, which always sighs: all is vain.

Shy mistrust it holds in low esteem, also anyone who wants oaths instead of eyes and hands; also all wisdom that is all-too-mistrustful, for that is the manner of cowardly souls. In still lower esteem it holds the subservient, the doglike, who immediately lie on their backs, the humble; and there is wisdom too that is humble and doglike and pious and subservient. Altogether hateful and nauseating it finds those who never offer resistance, who swallow poisonous spittle and evil glances, the all-too-patient, all-suffering, always satisfied; for that is servile.

Whether one be servile before gods and gods' kicks or before men and stupid men's opinions—whatever is servile it spits on, this blessed selfishness. Bad: that is what it calls everything that is sorely stooped and sordidly servile, unfree blink-eyes, oppressed hearts, and that false yielding manner that kisses with wide cowardly lips.

And sham wisdom: that is what it calls the would-be wit of the servile and old and weary, and especially the whole wicked, nitwitted, witless foolishness of priests. The sham-wise, however—all the priests, the world-weary, and all those whose souls are womanish and servile—oh, what wicked tricks has their trickery always played on selfishness! And what was considered virtue and called virtue *was* playing wicked tricks on selfishness! And "selfless"—that is how all these world-weary cowards and cross-marked spiders wanted themselves, for good reasons.

But for all these the day is now at hand, the change, the sword of judgment, *the great noon:* much shall be revealed there.

And whoever proclaims the ego wholesome and holy, and selfishness blessed, verily, he will also tell what he knows, foretelling: "Verily, it is at hand, it is near, the great noon!"

Thus spoke Zarathustra.

ON THE SPIRIT OF GRAVITY

1

My tongue is of the people: I speak too crudely and heartily for Angora rabbits. And my speech sounds even stranger to all ink-fish and pen-hacks.

My hand is a fool's hand: beware, all tables and walls and whatever else still offer room for foolish frill or scribbling skill.

My foot is a cloven foot; with it I trample and trot over sticks and stones, crisscross, and I am happy as the devil while running so fast.

My stomach—is it an eagle's stomach? For it likes lamb best of all. Certainly it is the stomach of some bird. Nourished on innocent things and on little, ready and impatient to fly, to fly off—that happens to be my way: how could there not be something of the bird's way in that? And above all, I am an enemy of the spirit of gravity, that is the bird's way—and verily, a sworn enemy, archenemy, primordial enemy. Oh, where has not my enmity flown and misflown in the past?

Of that I could well sing a song—and *will* sing it, although I am alone in an empty house and must sing it to my own ears. There are other singers, of course, whose throats are made mellow, whose hands are made talkative, whose eyes are made expressive, whose hearts are awakened, only by a packed house. But I am not like those.

2

He who will one day teach men to fly will have moved all boundary stones; the boundary stones themselves will fly up into the air before him, and he will rebaptize the earth—"the light one."

The ostrich runs faster than the fastest horse, but even he buries his head gravely in the grave earth; even so, the man who has not yet learned to fly. Earth and life seem grave to him; and thus the spirit of gravity wants it. But whoever would become light and a bird must love himself: thus *I* teach.

Not, to be sure, with the love of the wilting and

wasting: for among those even self-love stinks. One must learn to love oneself—thus I teach—with a wholesome and healthy love, so that one can bear to be with oneself and need not roam. Such roaming baptizes itself "love of the neighbor": with this phrase the best lies and hypocrisies have been perpetrated so far, and especially by such as were a grave burden for all the world.

And verily, this is no command for today and tomorrow, to *learn* to love oneself. Rather, it is of all arts the subtlest, the most cunning, the ultimate, and the most patient. For whatever is his own is well concealed from the owner; and of all treasures, it is our own that we dig up last: thus the spirit of gravity orders it.

We are presented with grave words and values almost from the cradle: "good" and "evil" this gift is called. For its sake we are forgiven for living.

And therefore one suffers little children to come unto one—in order to forbid them betimes to love themselves: thus the spirit of gravity orders it.

And we—we carry faithfully what one gives us to bear, on hard shoulders and over rough mountains. And should we sweat, we are told: "Yes, life is a grave burden." But only man is a grave burden for himself! That is because he carries on his shoulders too much that is alien to him. Like a camel, he kneels down and lets himself be well loaded. Especially the strong, reverent spirit that would bear much: he loads too many *alien* grave words and values on himself, and then life seems a desert to him.

And verily, much that is our *own* is also a grave burden! And much that is inside man is like an oyster: nauseating and slippery and hard to grasp, so that a noble shell with a noble embellishment must plead for it. But this art too one must learn: to *have* a shell and shiny sheen and shrewd blindness. Moreover, one is deceived about many things in man because many a shell is shabby and sad and altogether too much shell. Much hidden graciousness and strength is never guessed; the most exquisite delicacies find no tasters. Women know this—the most exquisite do: a little fatter, a little slimmer—oh, how much destiny lies in so little!

Man is hard to discover—hardest of all for himself: often the spirit lies about the soul. Thus the spirit of gravity orders it. He, however, has discovered himself who says, "This is *my* good and evil"; with that he has reduced to silence the mole and dwarf who say, "Good for all, evil for all."

Verily, I also do not like those who consider everything good and this world the best. Such men I call the omni-satisfied. Omni-satisfaction, which knows how to taste everything, that is not the best taste. I honor the recalcitrant choosy tongues and stomachs, which have learned to say "I" and "yes" and "no." But to chew and digest everything—that is truly the swine's manner. Always to bray Yea-Yuh—that only the ass has learned, and whoever is of his spirit.

Deep yellow and hot red: thus *my* taste wants it; it mixes blood into all colors. But whoever whitewashes his house betrays a whitewashed soul to me. Some in love with mummies, the others with ghosts, and both alike enemies of all flesh and blood—oh, how both offend my taste. For I love blood.

And I do not want to reside and abide where everybody spits and spews: that happens to be *my* taste; rather I would live even among thieves and perjurers. Nobody has gold in his mouth. Still more revolting, however, I find all lickspittles; and the most revolting human animal that I found I baptized "parasite": it did not want to love and yet it wanted to live on love.

Cursed I call all who have only one choice: to become evil beasts or evil tamers of beasts; among such men I would not build my home.

Cursed I call those too who must always *wait;* they offend my taste: all the publicans and shopkeepers and kings and other land- and storekeepers. Verily, I too have learned to wait—thoroughly—but only to wait for *myself.* And above all I learned to stand and walk and run and jump and climb and dance. This, however, is my doctrine: he who would learn to fly one day must first learn to stand and walk and run and climb and dance: one cannot fly into flying. With rope ladders I have learned to climb to many a window; with swift legs I climbed high masts; and to sit on high masts of knowledge seemed to me no small happiness: to flicker like small flames on high masts—a small light only and yet a great comfort for shipwrecked sailors and castaways.

By many ways, in many ways, I reached my truth: it was not on one ladder that I climbed to the height where my eye roams over my distance. And it was only reluctantly that I ever inquired about the way: that always offended my taste. I preferred to question and try out the ways themselves.

A trying and questioning was my every move; and verily, one must also learn to answer such questioning. That, however, is my taste—not good, not bad, but *my* taste of which I am no longer ashamed and which I have no wish to hide.

"This is *my* way; where is yours?"—thus I answered those who asked me "the way." For *the* way—that does not exist.

Thus spoke Zarathustra.

ON OLD AND NEW TABLETS

1

Here I sit and wait, surrounded by broken old tablets and new tablets half covered with writing. When will my hour come? The hour of my going down and going under; for I want to go among men once more. For that I am waiting now, for first the signs must come to me that *my* hour has come: the laughing lion with the flock of doves. Meanwhile I talk to myself as one who has time. Nobody tells me anything new: so I tell myself—myself.

2

When I came to men I found them sitting on an old conceit: the conceit that they have long known what is good and evil for man. All talk of virtue seemed an old and weary matter to man; and whoever wanted to sleep well still talked of good and evil before going to sleep.

I disturbed this sleepiness when I taught: what is good and evil *no one knows yet*, unless it be he who creates. He, however, creates man's goal and gives the earth its meaning and its future. That anything at all is good and evil—that is his creation.

And I bade them overthrow their old academic chairs and wherever that old conceit had sat; I bade them laugh at their great masters of virtue and saints and poets and world-redeemers. I bade them laugh at their gloomy sages and at whoever had at any time sat on the tree of life like a black scarecrow. I sat down by their great tomb road among cadavers and vultures, and I laughed at all their past and its rotting, decaying glory.

Verily, like preachers of repentance and fools, I raised a hue and cry of wrath over what among them is great and small, and that their best is still so small. And that their greatest evil too is still so small—at that I laughed.

My wise longing cried and laughed thus out of me —born in the mountains, verily, a wild wisdom—my great broad-winged longing! And often it swept me away and up and far, in the middle of my laughter; and I flew, quivering, an arrow, through sun-drunken delight, away into distant futures which no dream had yet seen, into hotter souths than artists ever dreamed of, where gods in their dances are ashamed of all clothes— to speak in parables and to limp and stammer like poets; and verily, I am ashamed that I must still be a poet.

Where all becoming seemed to me the dance of gods and the prankishness of gods, and the world seemed free and frolicsome and as if fleeing back to itself—as an eternal fleeing and seeking each other again of many gods, as the happy controverting of each other, conversing again with each other, and converging again of many gods.

Where all time seemed to me a happy mockery of moments, where necessity was freedom itself playing happily with the sting of freedom.

Where I also found again my old devil and archenemy, the spirit of gravity, and all that he created: constraint, statute, necessity and consequence and purpose and will and good and evil.

For must there not be that *over* which one dances and dances away? For the sake of the light and the lightest, must there not be moles and grave dwarfs?

3

There it was too that I picked up the word "over-man" by the way, and that man is something that must be overcome—that man is a bridge and no end: proclaiming himself blessed in view of his noon and evening, as the way to new dawns—Zarathustra's word of the great noon, and whatever else I hung up over man like the last crimson light of evening.

Verily, I also let them see new stars along with new nights; and over clouds and day and night I still spread out laughter as a colorful tent.

I taught them all *my* creating and striving, to create and carry together into One what in man is fragment and riddle and dreadful accident; as creator, guesser of riddles, and redeemer of accidents, I taught them to work on the future and to redeem with their creation all that *has been*. To redeem what is past in man and to re-create all "it was" until the will says, "Thus I willed it! Thus I shall will it"—this I called redemption and this alone I taught them to call redemption.

Now I wait for my own redemption—that I may go to them for the last time. For I want to go to men once more; under their eyes I want to go under; dying, I want to give them my richest gift. From the sun I learned this: when he goes down, overrich; he pours gold into the sea out of inexhaustible riches, so that even the poorest fisherman still rows with golden oars. For this I once saw and I did not tire of my tears as I watched it.

Like the sun, Zarathustra too wants to go under; now he sits here and waits, surrounded by broken old tablets and new tablets half covered with writing.

4

Behold, here is a new tablet; but where are my brothers to carry it down with me to the valley and into hearts of flesh?

Thus my great love of the farthest demands it: *do not spare your neighbor!* Man is something that must be overcome.

There are many ways of overcoming: see to that *yourself!* But only a jester thinks: "Man can also be *skipped over.*"

Overcome yourself even in your neighbor: and a right that you can rob you should not accept as a gift.

What you do, nobody can do to you in turn. Behold, there is no retribution.

He who cannot command himself should obey. And many *can* command themselves, but much is still lacking before they also obey themselves.

5

This is the manner of noble souls: they do not want to have anything for nothing; least of all, life. Whoever is of the mob wants to live for nothing; we others, however, to whom life gave itself, we always think about what we might best give in return. And verily, that is a noble speech which says, "What life promises us, we ourselves want to keep to life."

One shall not wish to enjoy where one does not give joy. And one shall not *wish* to enjoy! For enjoyment and innocence are the most bashful things: both do not want to be sought. One shall *possess* them—but rather *seek* even guilt and suffering.

6

My brothers, the firstling is always sacrificed. We, however, are firstlings. All of us bleed at secret sacrificial altars; all of us burn and roast in honor of old idols. What is best in us is still young: that attracts old palates. Our flesh is tender, our hide is a mere lambskin: how could we fail to attract old idol-priests? *Even in ourselves* the old idol-priest still lives who roasts what is best in us for his feast. Alas, my brothers, how could firstlings fail to be sacrifices?

But thus our kind wants it; and I love those who do not want to preserve themselves. Those who are going under I love with my whole love: for they cross over.

7

To be true—only a few are *able!* And those who are still lack the will. But the good have this ability least of all. Oh, these good men! *Good men never speak the truth;* for the spirit, to be good in this way is a disease. They give in, these good men; they give themselves up; their heart repeats and their ground obeys: but whoever heeds commands does not heed *himself.*

Everything that the good call evil must come together so that one truth may be born. O my brothers, are you evil enough for this truth? The audacious daring, the long mistrust, the cruel No, the disgust, the cutting into the living—how rarely does all this come together. But from such seed is truth begotten.

Alongside the bad conscience, all science has grown so far. Break, break, you lovers of knowledge, the old tablets!

8

When the water is spanned by planks, when bridges and railings leap over the river, verily, those are not believed who say, "Everything is in flux." Even the blockheads contradict them. "How now?" say the blockheads. "Everything should be in flux? After all, planks and railings are *over* the river. Whatever is *over* the river is firm; all the values of things, the bridges, the concepts, all 'good' and 'evil'—all that is *firm*."

But when the hard winter comes, the river-animal tamer, then even the most quick-witted learn mistrust; and verily, not only the blockheads then say, "Does not everything *stand still?*"

"At bottom everything stands still"—that is truly a winter doctrine, a good thing for sterile times, a fine comfort for hibernators and hearth-squatters.

"At bottom everything stands still"—*against* this the thawing wind preaches. The thawing wind, a bull that is no plowing bull, a raging bull, a destroyer who breaks the ice with wrathful horns. Ice, however, *breaks bridges!*

O my brothers, is not everything in flux *now?* Have not all railings and bridges fallen into the water? Who could still cling to "good" and "evil"?

"Woe to us! Hail to us! The thawing wind blows!"— thus preach in every street, my brothers.

9

There is an old illusion, which is called good and evil. So far the wheel of this illusion has revolved around soothsayers and stargazers. Once man believed in soothsayers and stargazers, and therefore believed: "All is destiny: you ought to, for you must."

Then man again mistrusted all soothsayers and stargazers, and therefore believed: "All is freedom: you can, for you will."

O my brothers, so far there have been only illusions about stars and the future, not knowledge; and therefore there have been only illusions so far, not knowledge, about good and evil.

10

"Thou shalt not rob! Thou shalt not kill!" Such words were once called holy; one bent the knee and head and took off one's shoes before them. But I ask you: where have there ever been better robbers and killers in this world than such holy words?

Is there not in all life itself robbing and killing? And that such words were called holy—was not truth itself killed thereby? Or was it the preaching of death that was called holy, which contradicted and contravened all life? O my brothers, break, break the old tablets!

11

This is my pity for all that is past: I see how all of it is abandoned—abandoned to the pleasure, the spirit, the madness of every generation, which comes along and reinterprets all that has been as a bridge to itself.

A great despot might come along, a shrewd monster who, according to his pleasure and displeasure, might constrain and strain all that is past till it becomes a bridge to him, a harbinger and herald and cockcrow.

This, however, is the other danger and what prompts my further pity: whoever is of the rabble, thinks back as far as the grandfather; with the grandfather, however, time ends.

Thus all that is past is abandoned: for one day the rabble might become master and drown all time in shallow waters.

Therefore, my brothers, a *new nobility* is needed to be the adversary of all rabble and of all that is despotic and to write anew upon new tablets the word "noble."

For many who are noble are needed, and noble men of many kinds, that there may be a nobility. Or as I once said in a parable: "Precisely this is godlike that there are gods, but no God."

12

O my brothers, I dedicate and direct you to a new nobility: you shall become procreators and cultivators and sowers of the future—verily, not to a nobility that you might buy like shopkeepers and with shopkeepers' gold: for whatever has its price has little value.

Not whence you come shall henceforth constitute your honor, but whither you are going! Your will and your foot which has a will to go over and beyond yourselves—that shall constitute your new honor.

Verily, not that you have served a prince—what do princes matter now?—or that you became a bulwark for what stands that it might stand more firmly.

Not that your tribe has become courtly at court and that you have learned, like a flamingo, to stand for long hours in a colorful costume in shallow ponds—for the ability to stand is meritorious among courtiers; and all courtiers believe that blessedness after death must comprise permission to sit.

Nor that a spirit which they call holy led your ancestors into promised lands, which I do not praise—for where the worst of all trees grew, the cross, that land deserves no praise. And verily, wherever this "Holy Spirit" led his knights, on all such crusades goose aids goat in leading the way, and the contrary and crude sailed foremost.

O my brothers, your nobility should not look backward but ahead! Exiles shall you be from all father- and forefather-lands! Your *children's land* shall you love: this love shall be your new nobility—the undiscovered land in the most distant sea. For that I bid your sails search and search.

In your children you shall make up for being the children of your fathers: thus shall you redeem all that is past. This new tablet I place over you.

13

"Why live? All is vanity! Living—that is threshing straw; living—that is consuming oneself in flames without becoming warm." Such antiquarian babbling is still considered "wisdom"; it is honored all the more for being old and musty. Mustiness too ennobles.

Children might speak thus: they fear the fire because it burned them. There is much childishness in the old books of wisdom. And why should those who always "thresh *straw*" be allowed to blaspheme threshing? Such oxen should be muzzled after all.

Such men sit down to the table and bring nothing along, not even a good appetite; and then they blaspheme: "All is vanity." But eating and drinking well, O my brothers, is verily no vain art. Break, break the old tablets of the never gay!

14

"To the clean all is clean," the people say. But I say unto you, "To the mean all becomes mean."

Therefore the swooners and head-hangers, whose hearts also hang limply, preach, "The world itself is a filthy monster." For all these have an unclean spirit—but especially those who have neither rest nor repose except when they see the world from *abaft*, the after-worldly. To these I say to their faces, even though it may not sound nice: the world is like man in having a backside abaft; that much is true. There is much filth in the world; that much is true. But that does not make the world itself a filthy monster.

There is wisdom in this, that there is much in the world that smells foul: nausea itself creates wings and water-divining powers. Even in the best there is still something that nauseates; and even the best is something that must be overcome. O my brothers, there is much wisdom in this, that there is much filth in the world.

15

Such maxims I heard pious afterworldly people speak to their conscience—verily, without treachery or falseness, although there is nothing falser in the whole world, nothing more treacherous:

"Let the world go its way! Do not raise one finger against it!"

"Let him who wants to, strangle and stab and fleece and flay the people. Do not raise one finger against it! Thus will they learn to renounce the world."

"And your own reason—you yourself should stifle and strangle it; for it is a reason of this world; thus will you yourself learn to renounce the world."

Break, break, O my brothers, these old tablets of the pious. Break the maxims of those who slander the world.

16

"Whoever learns much will unlearn all violent desire" —that is whispered today in all the dark lanes.

"Wisdom makes weary; worth while is—nothing; thou shalt not desire!"—this new tablet I found hanging even in the open market places.

Break, O my brothers, break this *new* tablet too. The world-weary hung it up, and the preachers of death, and also the jailers; for behold, it is also an exhortation to bondage. Because they learned badly, and the best things not at all, and everything too early and everything too hastily; because they *ate* badly, therefore they got upset stomachs; for their spirit is an upset stomach which counsels death. For verily, my brothers, the spirit *is* a stomach. Life is a well of joy; but for those out of whom an upset stomach speaks, which is the father of melancholy, all wells are poisoned.

To gain knowledge is a *joy* for the lion-willed! But those who have become weary are themselves merely being "willed," and all the billows play with them. And this is always the manner of the weak: they get lost on the way. And in the end their weariness still asks, "Why did we ever pursue any way at all? It is all the same." *Their* ears appreciate the preaching, "Nothing is worth while! You shall not will!" Yet this is an exhortation to bondage.

O my brothers, like a fresh roaring wind Zarathustra comes to all who are weary of the way; many noses he will yet make sneeze. Through walls too, my free breath blows, and into prisons and imprisoned spirits. To will liberates, for to will is to create: thus I teach. And you shall learn solely in order to create.

And you shall first *learn* from me how to learn—how to learn well. He that has ears to hear, let him hear!

17

There stands the bark; over there perhaps the great nothing lies. But who would embark on this "perhaps"? No one of you wants to embark on the bark of death. Why then do you want to be world-weary? World-weary! And you are not even removed from the earth.

Lusting after the earth I have always found you, in love even with your own earth-weariness. Not for nothing is your lip hanging; a little earthly wish still sits on it. And in your eyes—does not a little cloud of unforgotten earthly joy float there?

There are many good inventions on earth, some useful, some pleasing: for their sake, the earth is to be loved. And there is such a variety of well-invented things that the earth is like the breasts of a woman: useful as well as pleasing.

But you who are world-weary, you who are earth-lazy, you should be lashed with switches: with lashes one should make your legs sprightly again. For when you are not invalids and decrepit wretches of whom the earth is weary, you are shrewd sloths or sweet-toothed, sneaky pleasure-cats. And if you do not want to *run* again with pleasure, then you should pass away. To the incurable, one should not try to be a physician—thus Zarathustra teaches—so you shall pass away!

But it takes more *courage* to make an end than to make a new verse: all physicians and poets know that.

18

O my brothers, there are tablets created by weariness and tablets created by rotten, rotting sloth; but though they speak alike, they must be understood differently.

Behold this man languishing here! He is but one span from his goal, but out of weariness he has defiantly lain down in the dust—this courageous man! Out of weariness he yawns at the way and the earth and the goal and himself: not one step farther will he go—this courageous man! Now the sun glows on him and the dogs lick his sweat; but he lies there in his defiance and would sooner die of thirst—die of thirst one span away from his goal! Verily, you will yet have to drag him by the hair into his heaven—this hero! Better yet, let him lie where he lay down, and let sleep, the comforter, come to him with cooling, rushing rain. Let him lie till he awakes by himself, till he renounces by himself all weariness and whatever weariness taught through him. Only, my brothers, drive the dogs away from him, the lazy creepers, and all the ravenous vermin—all the raving vermin of the "educated," who feast on every hero's sweat.

19

I draw circles around me and sacred boundaries; fewer and fewer men climb with me on ever higher mountains: I am building a mountain range out of ever more sacred mountains. But wherever you may climb with me, O my brothers, see to it that no *parasite* climbs with you. Parasites: creeping, cringing worms which would batten on your secret sores. And this is their art, that they find where climbing souls are weary; in your grief and discouragement, in your tender parts, they build their nauseating nests. Where the strong are weak and the noble all-too-soft—there they build their nauseating nests: the parasites live where the great have little secret sores.

What is the highest species of all being and what is the lowest? The parasite is the lowest species; but whoever is of the highest species will nourish the most parasites. For the soul that has the longest ladder and reaches down deepest—how should the most parasites not sit on that? The most comprehensive soul, which can run and stray and roam farthest within itself; the most necessary soul, which out of sheer joy plunges itself into chance; the soul which, having being, dives into becoming; the soul which *has*, but *wants* to want and will; the soul which flees itself and catches up with itself in the widest circle; the wisest soul, which folly exhorts most sweetly; the soul which loves itself most, in which all things have their sweep and countersweep and ebb and flood—oh, how should the highest soul not have the worst parasites?

20

O my brothers, am I cruel? But I say: what is falling, we should still push. Everything today falls and decays: who would check it? But I—I even want to push it.

Do you know the voluptuous delight which rolls stones into steep depths? These human beings of today—look at them, how they roll into my depth!

I am a prelude of better players, O my brothers! A precedent! Follow my precedent!

And he whom you cannot teach to fly, teach to fall faster!

21

I love the valiant; but it is not enough to wield a broadsword, one must also know against whom. And often there is more valor when one refrains and passes by, in order to save oneself for the worthier enemy.

You shall have only enemies who are to be hated, but not enemies to be despised: you must be proud of your enemy; thus I taught once before. For the worthier enemy, O my friends, you shall save yourselves; therefore you must pass by much—especially much rabble who raise a din in your ears about the people and about peoples. Keep your eyes undefiled by their pro and con! There is much justice, much injustice; and whoever looks on becomes angry. Sighting and smiting here become one; therefore go away into the woods and lay your sword to sleep.

Go your *own* ways! And let the people and peoples

go theirs—dark ways, verily, on which not a single hope flashes any more. Let the shopkeeper rule where all that still glitters is—shopkeepers' gold. The time of kings is past: what calls itself a people today deserves no kings. Look how these peoples are now like shopkeepers: they pick up the smallest advantages from any rubbish. They lie around lurking and spy around smirking—and call that "being good neighbors." O blessed remote time when a people would say to itself, "I want to be *master* —over peoples." For, my brothers, the best should rule, the best also want to rule. And where the doctrine is different, there the best is *lacking*.

22

If *those* got free bread, alas! For what would they clamor? Their sustenance—that is what sustains their attention; and it should be hard for them. They are beasts of prey: in their "work" there is still an element of preying, in their "earning" still an element of over-reaching. Therefore it should be hard for them. Thus they should become better beasts of prey, subtler, more prudent, more *human;* for man is the best beast of prey. Man has already robbed all the beasts of their virtues, for of all beasts man has had the hardest time. Only the birds are still over and above him. And if man were to learn to fly—woe, to what heights would his rapaciousness fly?

23

Thus I want man and woman: the one fit for war, the other fit to give birth, but both fit to dance with head and limbs. And we should consider every day lost on which we have not danced at least once. And we should call every truth false which was not accompanied by at least one laugh.

24

Your wedlock: see to it that it not be a bad lock. If you lock it too quickly, there follows wedlock-breaking: adultery. And better even such wedlock-breaking than wedlock-picking, wedlock-tricking. Thus said a woman to me: "Indeed I committed adultery and broke my wedlock, but first my wedlock broke me!"

The worst among the vengeful I always found to be the ill-matched: they would make all the world pay for it that they no longer live singly.

Therefore I would have those who are honest say to each other, "We love each other; let us see to it that we remain in love. Or shall our promise be a mistake?"

"Give us a probation and a little marriage, so that we may see whether we are fit for a big marriage. It is a big thing always to be two."

Thus I counsel all who are honest; and what would my love for the overman and for all who shall yet come amount to if I counseled and spoke differently? Not merely to reproduce, but to produce something *higher* —toward that, my brothers, the garden of marriage should help you.

25

Whoever has gained wisdom concerning ancient origins will eventually look for wells of the future and for new origins. O my brothers, it will not be overlong before *new peoples* originate and new wells roar down into new depths. For earthquakes bury many wells and leave many languishing, but they also bring to light inner powers and secrets. Earthquakes reveal new wells. In earthquakes that strike ancient peoples, new wells break open.

And whoever shouts, "Behold, a well for many who

are thirsty, a heart for many who are longing, a will for many instruments"—around that man there will gather a *people;* that is: many triers.

Who can command, who must obey—*that is tried out there.* Alas, with what long trials and surmises and unpleasant surprises and learning and retrials!

Human society is a trial: thus I teach it—a long trial; and what it tries to find is the commander. A trial, O my brothers, and *not* a "contract." Break, break this word of the softhearted and half-and-half!

26

O my brothers, who represents the greatest danger for all of man's future? Is it not the good and the just? Inasmuch as they say and feel in their hearts, "We already know what is good and just, and we have it too; woe unto those who still seek here!" And whatever harm the evil may do, the harm done by the good is the most harmful harm. And whatever harm those do who slander the world, the harm done by the good is the most harmful harm.

O my brothers, one man once saw into the hearts of the good and the just and said, "They are the pharisees." But he was not understood. The good and the just themselves were not permitted to understand him: their spirit is imprisoned in their good conscience. The stupidity of the good is unfathomably shrewd. This, however, is the truth: the good *must* be pharisees—they have no choice. The good *must* crucify him who invents his own virtue. That is the truth!

The second one, however, who discovered their land —the land, heart, and soil of the good and the just— was he who asked, "Whom do they hate most?" The *creator* they hate most: he breaks tablets and old values. He is a breaker, they call him lawbreaker. For the good

are *unable* to create; they are always the beginning of
the end: they crucify him who writes new values on
new tablets; they sacrifice the future to *themselves*—
they crucify all man's future.

The good have always been the beginning of the end.

27

O my brothers, have you really understood this word?
And what I once said concerning the "last man"? Who
represents the greatest danger for all of man's future?
Is it not the good and the just? *Break, break the good
and the just!* O my brothers, have you really understood
this word?

28

You flee from me? You are frightened? You tremble
at this word?

O my brothers, when I bade you break the good and
the tablets of the good, only then did I embark man on
his high sea. And only now does there come to him the
great fright, the great looking-around, the great sickness, the great nausea, the great seasickness.

False coasts and false assurances the good have
taught you; in the lies of the good you were hatched
and huddled. Everything has been made fraudulent and
has been twisted through and through by the good.

But he who discovered the land "man," also discovered the land "man's future." Now you shall be sea-
farers, valiant and patient. Walk upright betimes, O my
brothers; learn to walk upright. The sea is raging; many
want to right themselves again with your help. The sea
is raging; everything is in the sea. Well then, old sea
dogs! What of fatherland? Our helm steers us toward
our *children's land!* Out there, stormier than the sea,
storms our great longing!

29

"Why so hard?" the kitchen coal once said to the diamond. "After all, are we not close kin?"

Why so soft? O my brothers, thus I ask you: are you not after all my brothers?

Why so soft, so pliant and yielding? Why is there so much denial, self-denial, in your hearts? So little destiny in your eyes?

And if you do not want to be destinies and inexorable ones, how can you triumph with me?

And if your hardness does not wish to flash and cut and cut through, how can you one day create with me?

For creators are hard. And it must seem blessedness to you to impress your hand on millennia as on wax,

Blessedness to write on the will of millennia as on bronze—harder than bronze, nobler than bronze. Only the noblest is altogether hard.

This new tablet, O my brothers, I place over you: *become hard!*

30

O thou my will! Thou cessation of all need, my *own* necessity! Keep me from all small victories! Thou destination of my soul, which I call destiny! Thou in-me! Over-me! Keep me and save me for a great destiny!

And thy last greatness, my will, save up for thy last feat that thou mayest be inexorable in thy victory. Alas, who was not vanquished in his victory? Alas, whose eye would not darken in this drunken twilight? Alas, whose foot would not reel in victory and forget how to stand?

That I may one day be ready and ripe in the great noon: as ready and ripe as glowing bronze, clouds pregnant with lightning, and swelling milk udders—

ready for myself and my most hidden will: a bow lusting for its arrow, an arrow lusting for its star—a star ready and ripe in its noon, glowing, pierced, enraptured by annihilating sun arrows—a sun itself and an inexorable solar will, ready to annihilate in victory!

O will, cessation of all need, my *own* necessity! Save me for a great victory!

Thus spoke Zarathustra.

THE CONVALESCENT

1

One morning, not long after his return to the cave, Zarathustra jumped up from his resting place like a madman, roared in a terrible voice, and acted as if somebody else were still lying on his resting place who refused to get up. And Zarathustra's voice resounded so that his animals approached in a fright, while out of all the caves and nooks that were near Zarathustra's cave all animals fled—flying, fluttering, crawling, jumping, according to the kind of feet or wings that were given to them. Zarathustra, however, spoke these words:

Up, abysmal thought, out of my depth! I am your cock and dawn, sleepy worm. Up! Up! My voice shall yet crow you awake! Unfasten the fetters of your ears: listen! For I want to hear you. Up! Up! Here is thunder enough to make even tombs learn to listen. And wipe sleep and all that is purblind and blind out of your eyes! Listen to me even with your eyes: my voice cures even those born blind. And once you are awake, you shall remain awake eternally. It is not my way to awaken great-grandmothers from their sleep to bid them sleep on!

You are stirring, stretching, wheezing? Up! Up! You shall not wheeze but speak to me. Zarathustra, the god-

less, summons you! I, Zarathustra, the advocate of life,
the advocate of suffering, the advocate of the circle; I
summon you, my most abysmal thought!

Hail to me! You are coming, I hear you. My abyss
speaks, I have turned my ultimate depth inside out into
the light. Hail to me! Come here! Give me your hand!
Huh! Let go! Huhhuh! Nausea, nausea, nausea—woe
unto me!

2

No sooner had Zarathustra spoken these words than
he fell down as one dead and long remained as one
dead. But when he regained his senses he was pale, and
he trembled and remained lying there, and for a long
time he wanted neither food nor drink. This behavior
lasted seven days; but his animals did not leave him by
day or night, except that the eagle flew off to get food.
And whatever prey he got together, he laid on Zarathustra's resting place; and eventually Zarathustra lay
among yellow and red berries, grapes, rose apples,
fragrant herbs, and pine cones. But at his feet two
lambs lay spread out, which the eagle had with difficulty robbed from their shepherds.

At last, after seven days, Zarathustra raised himself
on his resting place, took a rose apple into his hand,
smelled it, and found its fragrance lovely. Then his
animals thought that the time had come to speak to him.

"O Zarathustra," they said, "it is now seven days that
you have been lying like this with heavy eyes; won't
you at last get up on your feet again? Step out of your
cave: the world awaits you like a garden. The wind is
playing with heavy fragrances that want to get to you,
and all the brooks would run after you. All things have
been longing for you, while you have remained alone for

seven days. Step out of your cave! All things would be your physicians. Has perhaps some new knowledge come to you, bitter and hard? Like leavened dough you have been lying; your soul rose and swelled over all its rims."

"O my animals," replied Zarathustra, "chatter on like this and let me listen. It is so refreshing for me to hear you chattering: where there is chattering, there the world lies before me like a garden. How lovely it is that there are words and sounds! Are not words and sounds rainbows and illusive bridges between things which are eternally apart?

"To every soul there belongs another world; for every soul, every other soul is an afterworld. Precisely between what is most similar, illusion lies most beautifully; for the smallest cleft is the hardest to bridge.

"For me—how should there be any outside-myself? There is no outside. But all sounds make us forget this; how lovely it is that we forget. Have not names and sounds been given to things that man might find things refreshing? Speaking is a beautiful folly: with that man dances over all things. How lovely is all talking, and all the deception of sounds! With sounds our love dances on many-hued rainbows."

"O Zarathustra," the animals said, "to those who think as we do, all things themselves are dancing: they come and offer their hands and laugh and flee—and come back. Everything goes, everything comes back; eternally rolls the wheel of being. Everything dies, everything blossoms again; eternally runs the year of being. Everything breaks, everything is joined anew; eternally the same house of being is built. Everything parts, everything greets every other thing again; eternally the ring of being remains faithful to itself. In every Now, being begins; round every Here rolls the sphere There. The center is everywhere. Bent is the path of eternity."

"O you buffoons and barrel organs!" Zarathustra replied and smiled again. "How well you know what had to be fulfilled in seven days, and how that monster crawled down my throat and suffocated me. But I bit off its head and spewed it out. And you, have you already made a hurdy-gurdy song of this? But now I lie here, still weary of this biting and spewing, still sick from my own redemption. *And you watched all this?* O my animals, are even you cruel? Did you want to watch my great pain as men do? For man is the cruelest animal.

"At tragedies, bullfights, and crucifixions he has so far felt best on earth; and when he invented hell for himself, behold, that was his heaven on earth.

"When the great man screams, the small man comes running with his tongue hanging from lasciviousness. But he calls it his 'pity.'

"The small man, especially the poet—how eagerly he accuses life with words! Hear him, but do not fail to hear the delight that is in all accusation. Such accusers of life—life overcomes with a wink. 'Do you love me?' she says impudently. 'Wait a little while, just yet I have no time for you.'

"Man is the cruelest animal against himself; and whenever he calls himself 'sinner' and 'cross-bearer' and 'penitent,' do not fail to hear the voluptuous delight that is in all such lamentation and accusation.

"And I myself—do I thus want to be man's accuser? Alas, my animals, only this have I learned so far, that man needs what is most evil in him for what is best in him—that whatever is most evil is his best power and the hardest stone for the highest creator; and that man must become better and more evil.

"My torture was not the knowledge that man is evil—but I cried as no one has yet cried: 'Alas, that his greatest evil is so very small! Alas, that his best is so very small!'

"The great disgust with man—*this* choked me and had crawled into my throat; and what the soothsayer said: 'All is the same, nothing is worth while, knowledge chokes.' A long twilight limped before me, a sadness, weary to death, drunken with death, speaking with a yawning mouth. 'Eternally recurs the man of whom you are weary, the small man'—thus yawned my sadness and dragged its feet and could not go to sleep. Man's earth turned into a cave for me, its chest sunken; all that is living became human mold and bones and musty past to me. My sighing sat on all human tombs and could no longer get up; my sighing and questioning croaked and gagged and gnawed and wailed by day and night: 'Alas, man recurs eternally! The small man recurs eternally!'

"Naked I had once seen both, the greatest man and the smallest man: all-too-similar to each other, even the greatest all-too-human. All-too-small, the greatest!—that was my disgust with man. And the eternal recurrence even of the smallest—that was my disgust with all existence. Alas! Nausea! Nausea! Nausea!"

Thus spoke Zarathustra and sighed and shuddered, for he remembered his sickness. But then his animals would not let him go on.

"Do not speak on, O convalescent!" thus his animals answered him; "but go out where the world awaits you like a garden. Go out to the roses and bees and dovecots. But especially to the songbirds, that you may learn from them how to sing! For singing is for the convalescent; the healthy can speak. And when the healthy man also wants songs, he wants different songs from the convalescent."

"O you buffoons and barrel organs, be silent!" Zarathustra replied and smiled at his animals. "How well you know what comfort I invented for myself in seven days! That I must sing again, this comfort and convalescence I invented for myself. Must you immediately turn this too into a hurdy-gurdy song?"

"Do not speak on!" his animals answered him again; "rather even, O convalescent, fashion yourself a lyre first, a new lyre! For behold, Zarathustra, new lyres are needed for your new songs. Sing and overflow, O Zarathustra; cure your soul with new songs that you may bear your great destiny, which has never yet been any man's destiny. For your animals know well, O Zarathustra, who you are and must become: behold, *you are the teacher of the eternal recurrence*—that is your destiny! That you as the first must teach this doctrine— how could this great destiny not be your greatest danger and sickness too?

"Behold, we know what you teach: that all things recur eternally, and we ourselves too; and that we have already existed an eternal number of times, and all things with us. You teach that there is a great year of becoming, a monster of a great year, which must, like an hourglass, turn over again and again so that it may run down and run out again; and all these years are alike in what is greatest as in what is smallest; and we ourselves are alike in every great year, in what is greatest as in what is smallest.

"And if you wanted to die now, O Zarathustra, behold, we also know how you would then speak to yourself. But your animals beg you not to die yet. You would speak, without trembling but breathing deeply with happiness, for a great weight and sultriness would be taken from you who are most patient.

" 'Now I die and vanish,' you would say, 'and all at once I am nothing. The soul is as mortal as the body. But the knot of causes in which I am entangled recurs and will create me again. I myself belong to the causes of the eternal recurrence. I come again, with this sun, with this earth, with this eagle, with this serpent—*not* to a new life or a better life or a similar life: I come back eternally to this same, selfsame life, in what is greatest as in what is smallest, to teach again the eternal recurrence of all things, to speak again the word of the great noon of earth and man, to proclaim the overman again to men. I spoke my word, I break of my word: thus my eternal lot wants it; as a proclaimer I perish. The hour has now come when he who goes under should bless himself. Thus *ends* Zarathustra's going under.' "

When the animals had spoken these words they were silent and waited for Zarathustra to say something to them; but Zarathustra did not hear that they were silent. Rather he lay still with his eyes closed, like one sleeping, although he was not asleep; for he was conversing with his soul. The serpent, however, and the eagle, when they found him thus silent, honored the great stillness around him and cautiously stole away.

ON THE GREAT LONGING

O my soul, I taught you to say "today" and "one day" and "formerly" and to dance away over all Here and There and Yonder.

O my soul, I delivered you from all nooks; I brushed dust, spiders, and twilight off you.

O my soul, I washed the little bashfulness and the

nook-virtue off you and persuaded you to stand naked before the eyes of the sun. With the storm that is called "spirit" I blew over your wavy sea; I blew all clouds away; I even strangled the strangler that is called "sin."

O my soul, I gave you the right to say No like the storm, and to say Yes as the clear sky says Yes: now you are still as light whether you stand or walk through storms of negation.

O my soul, I gave you back the freedom over the created and uncreated; and who knows, as you know, the voluptuous delight of what is yet to come?

O my soul, I taught you the contempt that does not come like the worm's gnawing, the great, the loving contempt that loves most where it despises most.

O my soul, I taught you to persuade so well that you persuade the very ground—like the sun who persuades even the sea to his own height.

O my soul, I took from you all obeying, knee-bending, and "Lord"-saying; I myself gave you the name "cessation of need" and "destiny."

O my soul, I gave you new names and colorful toys; I called you "destiny" and "circumference of circumferences" and "umbilical cord of time" and "azure bell."

O my soul, I gave your soil all wisdom to drink, all the new wines and also all the immemorially old strong wines of wisdom.

O my soul, I poured every sun out on you, and every night and every silence and every longing: then you grew up like a vine.

O my soul, overrich and heavy you now stand there, like a vine with swelling udders and crowded brown gold-grapes—crowded and pressed by your happiness, waiting in your superabundance and still bashful about waiting.

O my soul, now there is not a soul anywhere that

would be more loving and comprehending and comprehensive. Where would future and past dwell closer together than in you?

O my soul, I gave you all, and I have emptied all my hands to you; and now—now you say to me, smiling and full of melancholy, "Which of us has to be thankful? Should not the giver be thankful that the receiver received? Is not giving a need? Is not receiving mercy?"

O my soul, I understand the smile of your melancholy: now your own overrichness stretches out longing hands. Your fullness gazes over roaring seas and seeks and waits; the longing of overfullness gazes out of the smiling skies of your eyes. And verily, O my soul, who could see your smile and not be melted by tears? The angels themselves are melted by tears because of the overgraciousness of your smile. Your graciousness and overgraciousness do not want to lament and weep; and yet, O my soul, your smile longs for tears and your trembling mouth for sobs. "Is not all weeping a lamentation? And all lamentation an accusation?" Thus you speak to yourself, and therefore, my soul, you would sooner smile than pour out your suffering—pour out into plunging tears all your suffering over your fullness and over the vine's urge for the vintager and his knife.

But if you will not weep, not weep out your crimson melancholy, then you will have to *sing*, O my soul. Behold, I myself smile as I say this before you: sing with a roaring song till all seas are silenced, that they may listen to your longing—till over silent, longing seas the bark floats, the golden wonder around whose gold all good, bad, wondrous things leap—also many great and small animals and whatever has light, wondrous feet for running on paths blue as violets—toward the golden wonder, the voluntary bark and its master; but that is the vintager who is waiting with his diamond knife—

your great deliverer, O my soul, the nameless one for whom only future songs will find names. And verily, even now your breath is fragrant with future songs; even now you are glowing and dreaming and drinking thirstily from all deep and resounding wells of comfort; even now your melancholy is resting in the happiness of future songs.

O my soul, now I have given you all, and even the last I had, and I have emptied all my hands to you: *that I bade you sing*, behold, that was the last I had. That I bade you sing—speak now, speak: which of us has to be thankful now? Better yet, however: sing to me, sing, O my soul! And let me be thankful.

Thus spoke Zarathustra.

THE OTHER DANCING SONG

1

Into your eyes I looked recently, O life: I saw gold blinking in your night-eye; my heart stopped in delight: a golden boat I saw blinking on nocturnal waters, a golden rocking-boat, sinking, drinking, and winking again. At my foot, frantic to dance, you cast a glance, a laughing, questioning, melting rocking-glance: twice only you stirred your rattle with your small hands, and my foot was already rocking with dancing frenzy.

My heels twitched, then my toes hearkened to understand you, and rose: for the dancer has his ear in his toes.

I leaped toward you, but you fled back from my leap, and the tongue of your fleeing, flying hair licked me in its sweep.

Away from you I leaped, and from your serpents' ire; and already you stood there, half turned, your eyes full of desire.

With crooked glances you teach me—crooked ways; on crooked ways my foot learns treachery.

I fear you near, I love you far; your flight lures me, your seeking cures me: I suffer, but what would I not gladly suffer for you?

You, whose coldness fires, whose hatred seduces, whose flight binds, whose scorn inspires:

Who would not hate you, you great binder, entwiner, temptress, seeker, and finder? Who would not love you, you innocent, impatient, wind-swift, child-eyed sinner?

Whereto are you luring me now, you never-tame extreme? And now you are fleeing from me again, you sweet wildcat and ingrate!

I dance after you, I follow wherever your traces linger. Where are you? Give me your hand! Or only one finger!

Here are caves and thickets; we shall get lost. Stop! Stand still! Don't you see owls and bats whirring past?

You owl! You bat! Intent to confound! Where are we? Such howling and yelping you have learned from a hound.

Your lovely little white teeth are gnashing at me; out of a curly little mane your evil eyes are flashing at me.

That is a dance up high and down low: I am the hunter; would you be my dog or my doe?

Alongside me now! And swift, you malicious leaping belle! Now up and over there! Alas, as I leaped I fell.

Oh, see me lying there, you prankster, suing for grace. I should like to walk with you in a lovelier place.

Love's paths through silent bushes, past many-hued plants. Or there along that lake: there goldfish swim and dance.

You are weary now? Over there are sunsets and sheep: when shepherds play on their flutes—is it not lovely to sleep?

You are so terribly weary? I'll carry you there; just let your arms sink. And if you are thirsty—I have got something, but your mouth does not want it to drink.

Oh, this damned nimble, supple snake and slippery witch! Where are you? In my face two red blotches from your hand itch.

I am verily weary of always being your sheepish shepherd. You witch, if *I* have so far sung to you, now you shall cry.

Keeping time with my whip, you shall dance and cry! Or have I forgotten the whip? Not I!

2

Then life answered me thus, covering up her delicate ears: "O Zarathustra, don't crack your whip so frightfully! After all, you know that noise murders thought— and just now such tender thoughts are coming to me. We are both two real good-for-nothings and evil-for-nothings. Beyond good and evil we found our island and our green meadow—we two alone. Therefore we had better like each other. And even if we do not love each other from the heart—need we bear each other a grudge if we do not love each other from the heart? And that I like you, often too well, that you know; and the reason is that I am jealous of your wisdom. Oh, this mad old fool of a wisdom! If your wisdom ever ran away from you, then my love would quickly run away from you too."

Then life looked back and around thoughtfully and said softly: "O Zarathustra, you are not faithful enough to me. You do not love me nearly as much as you say; I know you are thinking of leaving me soon. There is an old heavy, heavy growl-bell that growls at night all the way up to your cave; when you hear this bell strike the hour at midnight, then you think between one and twelve—you think, O Zarathustra, I know it, of how you want to leave me soon."

"Yes," I answered hesitantly, "but you also know—" and I whispered something into her ear, right through her tangled yellow foolish tresses.

"You *know* that, O Zarathustra? Nobody knows that."

And we looked at each other and gazed on the green meadow over which the cool evening was running just then, and we wept together. But then life was dearer to me than all my wisdom ever was.

Thus spoke Zarathustra.

3

One!

O man, take care!

Two!

What does the deep midnight declare?

Three!

"I was asleep—

Four!

"From a deep dream I woke and swear:

Five!

"The world is deep,

Six!

"Deeper than day had been aware.

Seven!

"Deep is its woe;

Eight!

"Joy—deeper yet than agony:

Nine!

"Woe implores: Go!

Ten!

"But all joy wants eternity—

Eleven!
"Wants deep, wants deep eternity."
Twelve!

THE SEVEN SEALS
(OR: THE YES AND AMEN SONG)

1

If I am a soothsayer and full of that soothsaying spirit which wanders on a high ridge between two seas, wandering like a heavy cloud between past and future, an enemy of all sultry plains and all that is weary and can neither die nor live—in its dark bosom prepared for lightning and the redemptive flash, pregnant with lightning bolts that say Yes and laugh Yes, soothsaying lightning bolts—blessed is he who is thus pregnant! And verily, long must he hang on the mountains like a dark cloud who shall one day kindle the light of the future: Oh, how should I not lust after eternity and after the nuptial ring of rings, the ring of recurrence?

Never yet have I found the woman from whom I wanted children, unless it be this woman whom I love: for I love you, O eternity.

For I love you, O eternity!

2

If ever my wrath burst tombs, moved boundary stones, and rolled old tablets, broken, into steep depths; if ever my mockery blew moldy words into the wind, and I came as a broom to the cross-marked spiders and as a sweeping gust to old musty tomb chambers; if ever I sat jubilating where old gods lie buried, world-blessing, world-loving, beside the monuments of old world-slanders—for I love even churches and tombs of gods, once the sky gazes through their broken roofs with its pure eyes, and like grass and red poppies, I love to sit on broken churches: Oh, how should I not lust after eternity and after the nuptial ring of rings, the ring of recurrence?

Never yet have I found the woman from whom I wanted children, unless it be this woman whom I love: for I love you, O eternity.

For I love you, O eternity!

3

If ever one breath came to me of the creative breath and of that heavenly need that constrains even accidents to dance star-dances; if I ever laughed the laughter of creative lightning which is followed obediently but grumblingly by the long thunder of the deed; if I ever played dice with gods at the gods' table, the earth, till the earth quaked and burst and snorted up floods of fire—for the earth is a table for gods and trembles with creative new words and gods' throws: Oh, how should I not lust after eternity and after the nuptial ring of rings, the ring of recurrence?

Never yet have I found the woman from whom I wanted children, unless it be this woman whom I love: for I love you, O eternity.

For I love you, O eternity!

4

If ever I drank full drafts from that foaming spice- and blend-mug in which all things are well blended; if my hand ever poured the farthest to the nearest, and fire to spirit, and joy to pain, and the most wicked to the most gracious; if I myself am a grain of that re- deeming salt which makes all things blend well in the blend-mug—for there is a salt that unites good with evil; and even the greatest evil is worthy of being used

as spice for the last foaming over: Oh, how should I
not lust after eternity and after the nuptial ring of rings,
the ring or recurrence?

Never yet have I found the woman from whom I
wanted children, unless it be this woman whom I love:
for I love you, O eternity.

For I love you, O eternity!

5

If I am fond of the sea and of all that is of the sea's
kind, and fondest when it angrily contradicts me; if that
delight in searching which drives the sails toward the
undiscovered is in me, if a seafarer's delight is in my
delight; if ever my jubilation cried, "The coast has
vanished, now the last chain has fallen from me; the
boundless roars around me, far out glisten space and
time; be of good cheer, old heart!" Oh, how should I
not lust after eternity and after the nuptial ring of rings,
the ring of recurrence?

Never yet have I found the woman from whom I
wanted children, unless it be this woman whom I love:
for I love you, O eternity.

For I love you, O eternity!

6

If my virtue is a dancer's virtue and I have often
jumped with both feet into golden-emerald delight; if
my sarcasm is a laughing sarcasm, at home under rose
slopes and hedges of lilies—for in laughter all that is
evil comes together, but is pronounced holy and ab-
solved by its own bliss; and if this is my alpha and
omega, that all that is heavy and grave should become
light; all that is body, dancer; all that is spirit, bird—
and verily, that is my alpha and omega: Oh, how should

I not lust after eternity and after the nuptial ring of rings, the ring of recurrence?

Never yet have I found the woman from whom I wanted children, unless it be this woman whom I love: for I love you, O eternity.

For I love you, O eternity!

7

If ever I spread tranquil skies over myself and soared on my own wings into my own skies; if I swam playfully in the deep light-distances, and the bird-wisdom of my freedom came—but bird-wisdom speaks thus: "Behold, there is no above, no below! Throw yourself around, out, back, you who are light! Sing! Speak no more! Are not all words made for the grave and heavy? Are not all words lies to those who are light? Sing! Speak no more!" Oh, how should I not lust after eternity and after the nuptial ring of rings, the ring of recurrence?

Never yet have I found the woman from whom I wanted children, unless it be this woman whom I love: for I love you, O eternity.

For I love you, O eternity!

Thus Spoke Zarathustra:
Fourth and Last Part

Alas, where in the world has there been more folly than among the pitying? And what in the world has caused more suffering than the folly of the pitying? Woe to all who love without having a height that is above their pity!

> *Thus spoke the devil to me once: "God too has*
> *his hell: that is his love of man." And most re-*
> *cently I heard him say this: "God is dead; God*
> *died of his pity for man."* (Zarathustra, II, p. 202)

EDITOR'S NOTES

Part Four was originally intended as an intermezzo, not as the end of the book. The very appearance of a collection of sayings is abandoned: Part Four forms a whole, and as such represents a new stylistic experiment—as well as a number of widely different stylistic experiments, held together by a unity of plot and a pervasive sense of humor.

1. *The Honey Sacrifice:* Prologue. The "queer fish" are not long in coming: the first of them appears in the next chapter.

2. *The Cry of Distress:* Beginning of the story that continues to the end of the book. The soothsayer of Part Two reappears, and Zarathustra leaves in search of the higher man. Now that he has overcome his nausea, his final trial is: pity.

3. *Conversation with the Kings:* The first of seven encounters in each of which Zarathustra meets men who have accepted some part of his teaching without, however, embodying the type he envisages. Their revolting and tiresome flatteries might be charged to their general inadequacy. But Zarathustra's own personality, as it emerges in chapter after chapter, poses a more serious problem. At least in part, this is clearly due to the author's deliberate malice: he does not want to be a "new idol": "I do not want to be a saint, rather even a buffoon. Perhaps I am a buffoon. And nevertheless, or rather *not* nevertheless—for there has never been anybody more mendacious than saints—truth speaks out of me" (*Ecce Homo*). Earlier in the same work he says of Shakespeare: "What must a man have suffered to have found it that necessary to be a buffoon!" In these pages Nietzsche would resemble the

dramatist rather than the hagiographer, and a Shakespearean fool rather than the founder of a new cult.

4. *The Leech:* Encounter with "the conscientious in spirit."

5. *The Magician:* In the magician some of Nietzsche's own features blend with some of Wagner's as conceived by Nietzsche. The poem appears again in a manuscript of 1888, which bears the title "Dionysus Dithyrambs" and the motto: "These are the songs of Zarathustra which he sang to himself to endure his ultimate loneliness." In this later context, the poem is entitled "Ariadne's Lament," and a new conclusion has been added by Nietzsche:

(*Lightning. Dionysus becomes visible in emerald beauty.*)

> DIONYSUS: Be clever, Ariadne!
> You have small ears, you have my ears:
> Put a clever word into them!
> Must one not first hate each other
>   if one is to love each other?
> I am your labyrinth.

The song is not reducible to a single level of meaning. The outcry is (1) Nietzsche's own; and the unnamable, terrible thought near the beginning is surely that of the eternal recurrence; it is (2) projected onto Wagner, who is here imagined as feeling desperately forsaken after Nietzsche left him (note especially the penultimate stanza); it is (3) wishfully projected onto Cosima Wagner—Nietzsche's Ariadne (see my *Nietzsche*, 1, II)—who is here imagined as desiring and possessed by Nietzsche-Dionysus. Part Four is all but made up of similar projections. *All* the characters are caricatures of Nietzsche. And like the magician, he too would lie if he said: " 'I did all this *only* as a game.' There was *seriousness* in it too."

6. *Retired:* Encounter with the last pope. Reflections on the death and inadequacies of God.

7. *The Ugliest Man:* The murderer of God. The sentence beginning "Has not all success . . ." reads in German:

*War nicht aller Erfolg bisher bei den Gut-Verfolgten? Und
wer gut verfolgt, lernt leicht folgen:—ist er doch einmal—
hinterher!*

8. *The Voluntary Beggar:* A sermon on a mount—about
cows.

9. *The Shadow:* An allusion to Nietzsche's earlier work,
The Wanderer and His Shadow (1880).

10. *At Noon:* A charming intermezzo.

11. *The Welcome:* Zarathustra rejects his guests, though
together they form a kind of higher man compared to their
contemporaries. He repudiates these men of great longing
and nausea as well as all those who enjoy his diatribes and
denunciations and desire recognition and consideration
for being out of tune with their time. What Nietzsche
envisages is the creator for whom all negation is merely
incidental to his great affirmation: joyous spirits, "laughing
lions."

12. *The Last Supper:* One of the persistent themes of Part
Four reaches its culmination in this chapter: Nietzsche not
only satirizes the Gospels, and all hagiography generally,
but he also makes fun of and laughs at himself.

13. *On the Higher Man:* A summary comparable to "On
Old and New Tablets" in Part Three. Section 5 epitomizes
Nietzsche's praise of "evil"—too briefly to be clear apart
from the rest of his work—and the conclusion should be
noted. The opening paragraph of section 7 takes up the
same theme: Nietzsche opposes sublimation to both license
and what he elsewhere calls "castratism." A fine epigram
is mounted in the center of section 9. The mellow moderation of the last lines of section 15 is not usually associated
with Nietzsche. And the chapter ends with a praise of
laughter.

14. *The Song of Melancholy:* In the 1888 manuscript of
the "Dionysus Dithyrambs" this is the first poem and it
bears the title "Only Fool! Only Poet!" The two introductory sections of this chapter help to dissociate Nietzsche
from the poem, while the subsquent references to this song
show that he considered it far more depressing than it

appears in its context. Though his solitude sometimes flattered him, "On every parable you ride to every truth" ("The Return Home"), he also knew moments when he said to himself, "I am ashamed that I must still be a poet" ("On Old and New Tablets"). Although Zarathustra's buffooneries are certainly intended as such by the author, the thought that he might be *"only"* a fool, *"only"* a poet "climbing around on mendacious word bridges," made Nietzsche feel more than despondent. Soon it led him to abandon further attempts to ride on parables in favor of some of the most supple prose in German literature.

15. *On Science:* Only the origin of science is considered. The attempt to account for it in terms of fear goes back to the period of *The Dawn* (1881), in which Nietzsche tried to see how far he could reduce different phenomena to fear and power. Zarathustra suggests that courage is crucial —that is, the will to power over fear.

16. *Among Daughters of the Wilderness:* Zarathustra, about to slip out of his cave for the second time because he cannot stand the bad smell of the "higher men," is called back by his shadow, who has nowhere among men smelled better air—except once. In the following song Nietzsche's buffoonery reaches its climax. But though it can and should be read as thoroughly delightful nonsense, it is not entirely void of personal significance. *Wüste* means "desert" or "wilderness," and *wüst* can also mean wild and dissolute; and the "flimsy little fan-, flutter-, and tinsel-skirts" seem to have been suggested by the brothel to which a porter in Cologne once took the young Nietzsche, who had asked to be shown to a hotel. (He ran away, shocked; cf. my *Nietzsche*, 1, I.) Certainly the poem is full of sexual fantasies. But the double meaning of "date" is not present in the original.

17. *The Awakening:* The titles of this and the following chapter might well be reversed; for it is this chapter that culminates in the ass festival, Nietzsche's version of the Black Mass. But "the awakening" here does not refer to the moment when an angry Moses holds his people accountable

for their worship of the golden calf, but to the moment when "they have learned to laugh at themselves." In this art, incidentally, none of the great philosophers excelled the author of Part Four of *Zarathustra*.

8. *The Ass Festival:* Five of the participants try to justify themselves. The pope satirizes Catholicism (Luther was last made fun of at the end of the song in Chapter 16), while the conscientious in spirit develops a new theology —and suggests that Zarathustra himself is pretty close to being an ass.

19. *The Drunken Song:* Nietzsche's great hymn to joy invites comparison with Schiller's—minus Beethoven's music. That they use different German words is the smallest difference. Schiller writes:

> Suffer bravely, myriads!
> Suffer for the better world!
> Up above the firmament
> A great God will give rewards.

Nietzsche wants the eternity of *this* life with all its agonies —and seeing that it flees, its eternal recurrence. As it is expressed in sections 9, 10, and 11, the conception of the eternal recurrence is certainly meaningful; but its formulation as a doctrine depended on Nietzsche's mistaken belief that science compels us to accept the hypothesis of the eternal recurrence of the same events at gigantic intervals. (See "On the Vision and the Riddle" and "The Convalescent," both in Part Three, and, for a detailed discussion, my *Nietzsche*, 11, II.)

20. *The Sign:* In "The Welcome," Zarathustra repudiated the "higher men" in favor of "laughing lions." Now a lion turns up and laughs, literally. And in place of the single dove in the New Testament, traditionally understood as a symbol of the Holy Ghost, we are presented with a whole flock. Both the lion and the doves were mentioned before ("On Old and New Tablets," section 1) as the signs for which Zarathustra must wait, and now afford Nietzsche an

opportunity to preserve his curious blend of myth, irony, and hymn to the very end.

THE HONEY SACRIFICE

And again months and years passed over Zarathustra's soul, and he did not heed them; but his hair turned white. One day when he sat on a stone before his cave and looked out—and one looks on the sea from there, across winding abysses—his animals walked about him thoughtfully and at last stood still before him.

"O Zarathustra," they said, "are you perhaps looking out for your happiness?"

"What matters happiness?" he replied; "I have long ceased to be concerned with happiness; I am concerned with my work."

"O Zarathustra," the animals spoke again, "you say that as one having overmuch of the good. Do you not lie in a sky-blue lake of happiness?"

"You buffoons," Zarathustra replied and smiled; "how well you chose your metaphor. But you also know that my happiness is heavy and not like a flowing wave of water: it presses me and will not leave me and acts like melted tar."

Again the animals walked about him thoughtfully and then stood still before him. "O Zarathustra," they said, "is that why you yourself are becoming ever yellower and darker, although your hair wants to look white and flaxen? You are in a dreadful mess!"

"What are you saying there, my animals?" Zarathustra said and laughed; "verily, I was abusive when I spoke of tar. What is happening to me, happens to every fruit when it grows ripe. It is the *honey* in my veins that makes my blood thicker and my soul calmer."

"That is what it will be, Zarathustra," the animals answered and nestled against him; "but do you not want to climb a high mountain today? The air is clear and one sees more of the world today than ever before."

"Yes, my animals," he replied, "your advice is excellent and quite after my own heart: I want to climb a high mountain today. But see to it that honey will be at hand there: yellow, white, good, ice-fresh, golden comb honey. For you should know that up there I want to offer the honey sacrifice."

But when Zarathustra had reached the height he sent back the animals who had accompanied him, and he found himself alone. Then he laughed heartily, looked around, and spoke thus:

That I spoke of sacrifices and honey sacrifices was mere cunning and, verily, a useful folly. Up here I may speak more freely than before hermits' caves and hermits' domestic animals.

Why sacrifice? I squander what is given to me, I—a squanderer with a thousand hands; how could I call that sacrificing? And when I desired honey, I merely desired bait and sweet mucus and mucilage, which make even growling bears and queer, sullen, evil birds put out their tongues—the best bait, needed by hunters and fishermen. For if the world is like a dark jungle and a garden of delight for all wild hunters, it strikes me even more, and so I prefer to think of it, as an abysmal, rich sea—a sea full of colorful fish and crabs, which even gods might covet, that for their sakes they would wish to become fishermen and net-throwers: so rich is the world in queer things, great and small. Especially the human world, the human sea: *that* is where I now cast my golden fishing rod and say: Open up, you human abyss!

Open up and cast up to me your fish and glittering crabs! With my best bait I shall today bait the queerest human fish. My happiness itself I cast out far and wide, between sunrise, noon, and sunset, to see if many human fish might not learn to wriggle and wiggle from my happiness until, biting at my sharp hidden hooks, they must come up to *my* height—the most colorful abysmal groundlings, to the most sarcastic of all who fish for men. For *that* is what I am through and through: reeling, reeling in, raising up, raising, a raiser, cultivator, and disciplinarian, who once counseled himself, not for nothing: Become who you are!

Thus men may now come *up* to me; for I am still waiting for the sign that the time has come for my descent; I still do not myself go under, as I must do, under the eyes of men. That is why I wait here, cunning and mocking on high mountains, neither impatient nor patient, rather as one who has forgotten patience too, because his "passion" is over. For my destiny leaves me time; perhaps it has forgotten me. Or does it sit in the shade behind a big stone, catching flies? And verily, I like it for this, my eternal destiny: it does not hurry and press me, and it leaves me time for jests and sarcasm, so that I could climb this high mountain today to catch fish.

Has a man ever caught fish on high mountains? And even though what I want and do up here be folly, it is still better than if I became solemn down there from waiting, and green and yellow—a swaggering wrath-snorter from waiting, a holy, howling storm out of the mountains, an impatient one who shouts down into the valleys, "Listen or I shall whip you with the scourge of God!"

Not that I bear such angry men a grudge! They are good enough for my laughter. They must surely be im-

patient—these big noisy drums, which find their chance
to speak today or never. I, however, and my destiny—
we do not speak to the Today, nor do we speak to the
Never; we have patience and time and overmuch time
in which to speak. For one day it must yet come and
may not pass. What must come one day and may not
pass? Our great *Hazar:* that is, our great distant human
kingdom, the Zarathustra kingdom of a thousand years.
How distant may this "distant" be? What is that to me?
But for all that, this is no less certain: with both feet I
stand firmly on this ground, on eternal ground, on hard
primeval rock, on this highest, hardest, primeval mountain range to which all winds come as to the "weather-
shed" and ask: where? and whence? and whither?

Laugh, laugh, my bright, wholesome sarcasm! From
high mountains cast down your glittering mocking
laughter! With your glitter bait me the most beautiful
human fish! And whatever in all the seas belongs to *me,*
my in-and-for-me in all things—*that* fish out for me,
that bring up to me: for that I, the most sarcastic of all
fishermen, am waiting.

Out, out, my fishing rod! Down, down, bait of my
happiness! Drip your sweetest dew, honey of my heart!
Bite, my fishing rod, into the belly of all black melancholy!

Out there, out there, my eye! Oh, how many seas surround me, what dawning human futures! And over me
—what rose-red stillness! What unclouded silence!

THE CRY OF DISTRESS

The next day Zarathustra again sat on his stone before his cave, while the animals were roaming through
the outside world to find new nourishment—also new

honey, for Zarathustra had spent and squandered the old honey down to the last drop. But as he was sitting there, a stick in his hand, tracing his shadow on the ground, thinking—and verily, not about himself and his shadow—he was suddenly frightened, and he started: for beside his own shadow he saw another shadow. And as he looked around quickly and got up, behold, the soothsayer stood beside him—the same he had once feted at his table, the proclaimer of the great weariness who taught, "All is the same, nothing is worth while, the world is without meaning, knowledge strangles." But his face had changed meanwhile; and when Zarathustra looked into his eyes, his heart was frightened again: so many ill tidings and ashen lightning bolts ran over this face.

The soothsayer, who had noticed what went on in Zarathustra's soul, wiped his hand over his face as if he wanted to wipe it away; and Zarathustra did likewise. And when both had thus silently composed and strengthened themselves, they shook hands as a sign that they wanted to recognize each other.

"Welcome," said Zarathustra, "you soothsayer of the great weariness; not for nothing were you once my guest. Eat and drink with me again today, and forgive a cheerful old man for sitting at the table with you."

"A cheerful old man?" the soothsayer replied, shaking his head; "but whatever you may be or want to be, Zarathustra, you shall not be up here much longer: soon your bark shall not be stranded any more."

"But am I stranded?" Zarathustra asked, laughing.

"The waves around your mountain," replied the soothsayer, "are climbing and climbing, the waves of great distress and melancholy; soon they will lift up your bark too, and carry you off."

Zarathustra fell silent at that and was surprised.

"Do you not hear anything yet?" continued the sooth-sayer. "Does it not rush and roar up from the depth?"

Zarathustra remained silent and listened, and he heard a long, long cry, which the abysses threw to each other and handed on, for none wanted to keep it: so evil did it sound.

"You proclaimer of ill tidings," Zarathustra said finally, "this is a cry of distress and the cry of a man; it might well come out of a black sea. But what is human distress to me? My final sin, which has been saved up for me—do you know what it is?"

"*Pity!*" answered the soothsayer from an overflowing heart, and he raised both hands. "O Zarathustra, I have come to seduce you to your final sin."

And no sooner had these words been spoken than the cry resounded again, and longer and more anxious than before; also much closer now.

"Do you hear? Do you hear, O Zarathustra?" the soothsayer shouted. "The cry is for you. It calls you: Come, come, come! It is time! It is high time!"

Then Zarathustra remained silent, confused and shaken. At last he asked, as one hesitant in his own mind, "And who is it that calls me?"

"But you know that," replied the soothsayer violently; "why do you conceal yourself? It is *the higher man* that cries for you!"

"The higher man?" cried Zarathustra, seized with horror. "What does he want? What does he want? The higher man! What does he want here?" And his skin was covered with perspiration.

The soothsayer, however, made no reply to Zara-thustra's dread, but listened and listened toward the depth. But when there was silence for a long time, he turned his glance back and saw Zarathustra standing there trembling. "O Zarathustra," he began in a sad tone of voice, "you are not standing there as one made giddy by his happiness: you had better dance lest you fall. But even if you would dance before me, leaping all your side-leaps, no one could say to me, 'Behold, here dances the last gay man!' Anybody coming to this height, looking for *that* man, would come in vain: caves he would find, and caves behind caves, hiding-places for those addicted to hiding, but no mines of happiness or treasure rooms or new gold veins of happiness. Happiness—how should one find happiness among hermits and those buried like this? Must I still seek the last happiness on blessed isles and far away between forgotten seas? But all is the same, nothing is worth while, no seeking avails, nor are there any blessed isles any more."

Thus sighed the soothsayer. At his last sigh, however, Zarathustra grew bright and sure again, like one emerging into the light out of a deep gorge. "No! No! Three times no!" he shouted with a strong voice and stroked his beard. "*That* I know better: there still are blessed isles. Be quiet about *that*, you sighing bag of sadness! Stop splashing about *that*, you raincloud in the morning! Do I not stand here even now, wet from your melancholy and drenched like a dog? Now I shake myself and run away from you to dry again; you must not be surprised at that. Do I strike you as discourteous? But this is *my* court. As for your higher man—well then, I shall look for him at once in those woods: *thence* came his cry. Perhaps an evil beast troubles him there. He is in *my* realm: there he shall not come to grief. And verily, there are many evil beasts around me."

With these words Zarathustra turned to leave. Then the soothsayer said, "O Zarathustra, you are a rogue! I know it: you want to get rid of me. You would sooner run into the woods and look for evil beasts. But what will it avail you? In the evening you will have me back anyway; in your own cave I shall be sitting, patient and heavy as a block—waiting for you."

"So be it!" Zarathustra shouted back as he was walking away. "And whatever is mine in my cave belongs to you too, my guest. And if you should find honey in there—well, then, lick it up, you growling bear, and sweeten your soul. For in the evening we should both be cheerful—cheerful and gay that this day has come to an end. And you yourself shall dance to my songs as my dancing bear. You do not believe it? You shake your head? Well then, old bear! But I too am a soothsayer."

Thus spoke Zarathustra.

CONVERSATION WITH THE KINGS

1

Zarathustra had not yet walked an hour in his mountains and woods when he suddenly saw a strange procession. On the very path he wanted to follow down, two kings were approaching, adorned with crowns and crimson belts and colorful as flamingos; and they were driving a laden ass before them. "What do these kings want in my realm?" Zarathustra said in his heart, surprised, and quickly he hid behind a bush. But when the kings came close he said half aloud, as if talking to himself, "Strange! Strange! How does this fit together? Two kings I see—and only one ass!"

The two kings stopped, smiled, looked in the direction from which the voice had come, and then looked at each other. "Something of the sort may have occurred to one of us too," said the king at the right; "but one does not say it." The king at the left, however, shrugged his shoulders and replied, "It may well be a goatherd.

Or a hermit who has lived too long among rocks and trees. For no society at all also spoils good manners."

"Good manners?" the other king retorted angrily and bitterly; "then what is it that we are trying to get away from? Is it not 'good manners'? Our 'good society'? It is indeed better to live among hermits and goatherds than among our gilded, false, painted mob—even if they call themselves 'good society,' even if they call themselves 'nobility.' They are false and foul through and through, beginning with the blood, thanks to bad old diseases and worse quacks. Best and dearest to me today is a healthy peasant, coarse, cunning, stubborn, enduring: that is the noblest species today. The peasant is the best type today, and the peasant type should be master. But it is the realm of the mob; I shall not be deceived any more. Mob, however, means hodgepodge. Mob-hodgepodge: there everything is mixed up in every way, saint and scamp and Junker and Jew and every kind of beast out of Noah's ark. Good manners! Everything among us is false and foul. Nobody knows how to revere any longer: we are trying to get away from precisely that. They are saccharine, obtrusive curs; they gild palm leaves.

"This nausea suffocates me: we kings ourselves have become false, overhung and disguised with ancient yellowed grandfathers' pomp, showpieces for the most stupid and clever and anyone who haggles for power today. We are not the first and yet must represent them: it is this deception that has come to disgust and nauseate us. We have tried to get away from the rabble, all these scream-throats and scribbling bluebottles, the shopkeepers' stench, the ambitious wriggling, the foul breath—phew for living among the rabble! Phew for representing the first among the rabble! Nausea! Nausea! Nausea! What do we kings matter now?"

"Your old illness is upon you," the king at the left said at this point; "nausea is seizing you, my poor brother. But you know that somebody is listening to us."

Immediately Zarathustra, who had opened his ears and eyes wide at this talk, rose from his hiding-place, walked toward the kings, and began, "He who is listening to you, he who likes to listen to you, O kings, is called Zarathustra. I am Zarathustra, who once said, 'What do kings matter now?' Forgive me, I was delighted when you said to each other, 'What do we kings matter now?' Here, however, is *my* realm and my dominion: what might you be seeking in my realm? But perhaps you found on your way what I am looking for: the higher man."

When the kings heard this, they beat their breasts and said as with one voice, "We have been found out. With the sword of this word you cut through our hearts' thickest darkness. You have discovered our distress, for behold, we are on our way to find the higher man—the man who is higher than we, though we are kings. To him we are leading this ass. For the highest man shall also be the highest lord on earth. Man's fate knows no harsher misfortune than when those who have power on earth are not also the first men. That makes everything false and crooked and monstrous. And when they are even the last, and more beast than man, then the price of the mob rises and rises, and eventually the virtue of the mob even says, 'Behold, I alone am virtue!' "

"What did I just hear?" replied Zarathustra. "What wisdom in kings! I am delighted and, verily, even feel the desire to make a rhyme on this—even if it should be a rhyme which is not fit for everybody's ears. I have long become unaccustomed to any consideration for long ears. Well then!" (But at this point it happened that the ass too got in a word; but he said clearly and with evil intent, Yea-Yuh.)

"Once—in the year of grace number one, I think—
The Sibyl said, drunken without any drink,
'Now everything goes wrong! Oh, woe!
Decay! The world has never sunk so low!
Rome sank to whoredom and became a stew,
The Caesars became beasts, and God—a Jew!' "

2

These rhymes of Zarathustra delighted the kings; but the king at the right said, "O Zarathustra, how well we did to go forth to see you! For your enemies showed us your image in their mirror: there you had the mocking grimace of a devil, so that we were afraid of you. But what could we do? Again and again you pierced our ears and hearts with your maxims. So we said at last: what difference does it make how he looks? We must *hear* him who teaches: 'You shall love peace as a means to new wars, and the short peace more than the long!' Nobody ever spoke such warlike words: 'What is good? To be brave is good. It is the good war that hallows any cause.' Zarathustra, the blood of our fathers stirred in our bodies at such words: it was like the speech of spring to old wine barrels. When the swords ran wild like snakes with red spots, our fathers grew fond of life; the sun of all peace struck them as languid and lukewarm, and any long peace caused shame. How our fathers sighed when they saw flashing dried-up swords on the wall! Like them, they thirsted for war. For a sword wants to drink blood and glistens with desire."

When the kings talked thus and chatted eagerly of the happiness of their fathers, Zarathustra was overcome with no small temptation to mock their eagerness: for obviously they were very peaceful kings with old and fine faces. But he restrained himself. "Well!" he said, "that is where the path leads; there lies Zarathustra's cave; and this day shall yet have a long evening. Now, however, a cry of distress calls me away from you urgently. My cave is honored if kings want to sit in it and wait: only, you will have to wait long. But what does it matter? Where does one now learn better how to wait than at court? And all the virtue left to kings today—is it not called: being able to wait?"

Thus spoke Zarathustra.

THE LEECH

And thoughtfully Zarathustra went farther and deeper, through woods and past swampy valleys; but as happens to everybody who reflects on grave matters, he stepped on a man unwittingly. And behold, all at once a cry of pain and two curses and twenty bad insults splashed into his face and startled him so that he raised his stick and beat the man on whom he had stepped. A moment later, however, he recovered his senses, and his heart laughed at the folly he had just committed.

"Forgive me," he said to the man he had stepped on, who had angrily risen and sat down; "forgive me and, above all, listen to a parable first. As a wanderer who dreams of distant matters will unwittingly stumble over a sleeping dog on a lonely road—a dog lying in the sun—and both start and let fly at each other like mortal enemies, because both are mortally frightened: thus it happened to us. And yet—and yet, how little was lacking, and they might have caressed each other, this dog and this lonely man. For after all they were both lonely."

"Whoever you may be," said the man he had stepped on, still angry, "your parable too offends me, and not only your foot. After all, am I a dog?" And at that the seated man got up and pulled his bare arm out of the swamp. For at first he had been lying stretched out on the ground, concealed and unrecognizable, as one lying in wait for some swamp animal.

"But what are you doing?" cried Zarathustra, startled, for he saw that much blood was flowing down the bare arm. "What has happened to you? Did a bad animal bite you, you poor wretch?"

The bleeding man laughed, still angry. "What is that to you?" he said and wanted to go on. "Here I am at home and in my realm. Let whoever wants to, ask me; but I certainly won't answer a bumpkin."

"You are wrong," said Zarathustra, full of pity, and he held him back. "You are wrong. This is not your realm but mine, and here nobody shall come to grief. Call me whatever you like; I am who I must be. I call myself Zarathustra. Well! Up there runs the path to Zarathustra's cave, which is not far. Do you not want to look after your wounds in my place? Things have gone badly for you in this life, you poor wretch; first the beast bit you and then man stepped on you."

When the man who had been stepped on heard Zarathustra's name he changed completely. "What is happening to me?" he cried out. "*Who* else matters to me any more in this life but this one man, Zarathustra, and that one beast which lives on blood, the leech? For the leech's sake I lay here beside this swamp like a fisherman, and my arm, which I had cast, had already been bitten ten times when a still more beautiful leech bit, seeking my blood, Zarathustra himself. O happiness! O miracle! Praised be this day that lured me into this swamp! Praised be the best, the most alive cupper living today, praised be the great leech of the conscience, Zarathustra!"

Thus spoke the man who had been stepped on; and Zarathustra enjoyed his words and their fine, respectful manner. "Who are you?" he asked and offered him his hand. "There is much between us that remains to be cleared up and cheered up; but even now, it seems to me, the day dawns pure and bright."

"I am *the conscientious in spirit*," replied the man; "and in matters of the spirit there may well be none stricter, narrower, and harder than I, except he from whom I have learned it, Zarathustra himself.

"Rather know nothing than half-know much! Rather be a fool on one's own than a sage according to the opinion of others! I go to the ground—what does it matter whether it be great or small? whether it be called swamp or sky? A hand's breadth of ground suffices me, provided it is really ground and foundation. A hand's breadth of ground—on that one can stand. In the conscience of science there is nothing great and nothing small."

"Then perhaps you are the man who knows the leech?" Zarathustra asked. "And do you pursue the leech to its ultimate grounds, my conscientious friend?"

"O Zarathustra," replied the man who had been stepped on, "that would be an inmensity; how could I presume so much! That of which I am the master and expert is the *brain* of the leech: that is *my* world. And it really is a world too. Forgive me that here my pride speaks up, for I have no equal here. That is why I said, 'Here is my home.' How long have I been pursuing this one thing, the brain of the leech, lest the slippery truth slip away from me here again! Here is *my* realm. For its sake I have thrown away everything else; for its sake everything else has become indifferent to me; and close to my knowledge lies my black ignorance.

"The conscience of my spirit demands of me that I know one thing and nothing else: I loathe all the half in spirit, all the vaporous that hover and rave.

"Where my honesty ceases, I am blind and I also want to be blind. But where I want to know, I also want to be honest—that is, hard, strict, narrow, cruel, and inexorable.

"That *you*, O Zarathustra, once said, 'Spirit is the life that itself cuts into life,' that introduced and seduced me to your doctrine. And verily, with my own blood I increased my own knowledge."

"As is quite apparent," Zarathustra interrupted, for the blood still flowed down the bare arm of the conscientious man, ten leeches having bitten deep into it. "O you strange fellow, how much I learn from what is apparent here, namely from you. And perhaps I had better not pour all of it into your strict ears. Well! Here we part. But I should like to find you again. Up there goes the path to my cave: tonight you shall be my dear guest there. To your body too, I should like to make up for Zarathustra's having stepped on you with his feet: I shall reflect on that. Now, however, a cry of distress urgently calls me away from you."

Thus spoke Zarathustra.

THE MAGICIAN

1

But when Zarathustra came around a rock he beheld, not far below on the same path, a man who threw his limbs around like a maniac and finally flopped down on his belly. "Wait!" Zarathustra said to his heart; "that must indeed be the higher man; from him came that terrible cry of distress; let me see if he can still be helped." But when he ran to the spot where the man lay on the ground he found a trembling old man with vacant eyes; and however Zarathustra exerted himself to help the man to get up on his feet again, it was all in vain. Nor did the unfortunate man seem to notice that anybody was with him; rather he kept looking around with piteous gestures, like one abandoned and forsaken by all the world. At last, however, after many shudders, convulsions, and contortions, he began to moan thus:

"Who warms me, who loves me still?
Give hot hands!
Give a heart as glowing coals!
Stretched out, shuddering,
Like something half dead whose feet one warms—
Shaken, alas, by unknown fevers,
Shivering with piercing icy frost-arrows,
Hunted by thee, O thought!
Unnamable, shrouded, terrible one!
Thou hunter behind clouds!
Struck down by thy lightning bolt,
Thou mocking eye that stares at me from the dark:
Thus I lie
Writhing, twisting, tormented
With all eternal tortures,
Hit
By thee, cruelest hunter,
Thou unknown *god!*

Hit deeper!
Hit once more yet!
Drive a stake through and break this heart!

Why this torture
With blunt-toothed arrows?
Why dost thou stare again,
Not yet weary of human agony,
With gods' lightning eyes that delight in suffering?
Thou wouldst not kill,
Only torture, torture?
Why torture *me*,
Delighted by suffering, thou unknown god?

Hah! hah! Thou art crawling close?
In such midnight—
What dost thou want? Speak!
Thou art crowding, pressing me—
Hah! Far too close!
Away! Away!
Thou art listening to me breathe,
Thou art listening to my heart,
Thou jealous one—
Jealous of what?
Away! Away! Why the ladder?
Wouldst thou *enter*
The heart,
Climb in, deep into my
Most secret thoughts?
Shameless one! Unknown thief!
What wouldst thou steal?
What wouldst thou gain by listening?
What wouldst thou gain by torture,
Thou torturer!
Thou hangman-god!
Or should I, doglike,
Roll before thee?
Devotedly, frantic, beside myself,
Wag love to thee?

In vain! Pierce on,
Cruelest thorn! No,
No dog—only thy game am I,
Cruelest hunter!
Thy proudest prisoner,
Thou robber behind clouds!
Speak at last!
What wouldst thou, waylayer, from *me?*
Thou lightning-shrouded one! Unknown one! Speak,
What wilt thou, unknown—god?

What? Ransom?
Why wilt thou ransom?
Demand much! Thus my pride advises.
And make thy speech short! That my other pride
    advises.

Hah, hah!
Me thou wilt have? Me?
Me—entirely?

Hah, hah!
And art torturing me, fool that thou art,
Torturing my pride?
Give love to me—who warms me still?
Who loves me still?—Give hot hands,
Give a heart as glowing coals,
Give me, the loneliest
Whom ice, alas, sevenfold ice
Teaches to languish for enemies,
Even for enemies,
Give, yes, give wholly,
Cruelest enemy,
Give me—*thyself!*

Away!
He himself fled,
My last, only companion,
My great enemy,
My unknown,
My hangman-god.

No! Do come back
With all thy tortures!
To the last of all that are lonely,
Oh, come back!
All my tear-streams run
Their course to thee;
And my heart's final flame—
Flares up for *thee!*
Oh, come back,
My unknown god! My *pain!* My last—happiness!"

2

At this point, however, Zarathustra could not restrain himself any longer, raised his stick, and started to beat the moaning man with all his might. "Stop it!" he shouted at him furiously. "Stop it, you actor! You counterfeiter! You liar from the bottom! I recognize you well! I'll warm your legs for you, you wicked magician. I know well how to make things hot for such as you."

"Leave off!" the old man said and leaped up from the ground. "Don't strike any more, Zarathustra! I did all this only as a game. Such things belong to my art; it was you that I wanted to try when I treated you to this tryout. And verily, you have seen through me very well. But you too have given me no small sample of yourself to try out: you are hard, wise Zarathustra. Hard do you hit with your 'truths'; your stick forces this truth out of me."

"Don't flatter!" replied Zarathustra, still excited and angry, "you actor from the bottom! You are false; why do you talk of truth? You peacock of peacocks, you sea of vanity, *what* were you playing before me, you wicked magician? In *whom* was I to believe when you were moaning in this way?"

"*The ascetic of the spirit*," said the old man, "I played *him*—you yourself once coined this word—the poet and magician who at last turns his spirit against himself, the changed man who freezes to death from his evil science and conscience. And you may as well confess it: it took a long time, O Zarathustra, before you saw through my art and lie. You *believed* in my distress when you held my head with both your hands; I heard you moan, 'He has been loved too little, loved too little.' That I deceived you to that extent made my malice jubilate inside me."

"You may have deceived people subtler than I," Zarathustra said harshly. "I do not guard against deceivers; I have to be without caution; thus my lot wants it. You, however, have to deceive: that far I know you. You always have to be equivocal—tri-, quadri-, quinquevocal. And what you have now confessed, that too was not nearly true enough or false enough to suit me. You wicked counterfeiter, how could you do otherwise? You would rouge even your disease when you show yourself naked to your doctor. In the same way you have just now rouged your lie when you said to me, 'I did all this *only* as a game.' There was *seriousness* in it too: you *are* something of an ascetic of the spirit. I solve your riddle: your magic has enchanted everybody, but no lie or cunning is left to you to use against yourself: you are disenchanted for yourself. You have harvested nausea as your one truth. Not a word of yours is genuine any more, except your mouth—namely, the nausea that sticks to your mouth."

"Who are you?" cried the old magician at this point, his voice defiant. "Who may speak thus to *me*, the greatest man alive today?" And a green lightning bolt flashed from his eye toward Zarathustra. But immediately afterward he changed and said sadly, "O Zarathustra, I am weary of it; my art nauseates me; I am not *great*—why do I dissemble? But you know it too: I sought greatness. I wanted to represent a great human being and I persuaded many; but this lie went beyond my strength. It is breaking me. O Zarathustra, everything about me is a lie; but that I am breaking—this, my breaking, is genuine."

"It does you credit," said Zarathustra gloomily, looking aside to the ground, "it does you credit that you sought greatness, but it also betrays you. You are not great. You wicked old magician, this is what is best and most honest about you, and this I honor: that you wearied of yourself and said it outright: 'I am not great.' In this I honor you as an ascetic of the spirit; and even if it was only a wink and a twinkling, in this one moment you were genuine.

"But speak, what are you seeking here in *my* woods and rocks? And lying down on *my* path, how did you want to try me? In what way were you seeking to test *me*?" Thus spoke Zarathustra, and his eyes flashed.

The old magician remained silent for a while, then said, "Did I seek to test you? I—merely seek. O Zarathustra, I seek one who is genuine, right, simple, unequivocal, a man of all honesty, a vessel of wisdom, a saint of knowledge, a great human being. Do you not know it, Zarathustra? *I seek Zarathustra.*"

And at this point there began a long silence between the two. But Zarathustra became deeply absorbed and closed his eyes. Then, however, returning to his partner in the conversation, he seized the hand of the magician and said, full of kindness and cunning, "Well! Up there goes the path; there lies Zarathustra's cave. There you may seek him whom you would find. And ask my animals for advice, my eagle and my serpent: they shall help you seek. But my cave is large. I myself, to be sure—I have not yet seen a great human being. For what is great, even the eyes of the subtlest today are too coarse. It is the realm of the mob. Many have I seen, swollen and straining, and the people cried, 'Behold a great man!' But what good are all bellows? In the end, the wind comes out. In the end, a frog which has puffed itself up too long will burst: the wind comes out. To stab a swollen man in the belly, I call that a fine pastime. Hear it well, little boys!

"Today belongs to the mob: who could still know what is great and what small? Who could still successfully seek greatness? Only a fool: fools succeed. You seek great human beings, you queer fool? Who *taught* you that? Is today the time for that? O you wicked seeker, why did you seek to test me?"

Thus spoke Zarathustra, his heart comforted, and he continued on his way, laughing.

RETIRED

Not long, however, after Zarathustra had got away from the magician, he again saw somebody sitting by the side of his path: a tall man in black, with a gaunt pale face; and *this* man displeased him exceedingly. "Alas!" he said to his heart, "there sits muffled-up melancholy, looking like the tribe of priests: what do *they* want in my realm? How now? I have scarcely escaped that magician; must another black artist cross my way so soon—some wizard with laying-on of hands, some dark miracle worker by the grace of God, some anointed world-slanderer whom the devil should fetch? But the devil is never where he should be: he always comes too late, this damned dwarf and clubfoot!"

Thus cursed Zarathustra, impatient in his heart, and he wondered how he might sneak past the black man, looking the other way. But behold, it happened otherwise. For at the same moment the seated man had already spotted him; and not unlike one on whom unexpected good fortune has been thrust, he jumped up and walked toward Zarathustra.

"Whoever you may be, you wanderer," he said, "help one who has lost his way, a seeker, an old man who might easily come to grief here. This region is remote and strange to me, and I have heard wild animals howling; and he who might have offered me protection no longer exists himself. I sought the last pious man, a saint and hermit who, alone in his forest, had not yet heard what all the world knows today."

"What does all the world know today?" asked Zarathustra. "Perhaps this, that the old god in whom all the world once believed no longer lives?"

"As you say," replied the old man sadly. "And I served that old god until his last hour. But now I am retired, without a master, and yet not free, nor ever cheerful except in my memories. That is why I climbed these mountains, that I might again have a festival at last, as is fitting for an old pope and church father—for behold, I am the last pope—a festival of pious memories and divine services. But now he himself is dead, the most pious man, that saint in the forest who constantly praised his god with singing and humming. I did not find him when I found his cave; but there were two wolves inside, howling over his death, for all animals loved him. So I ran away. Had I then come to these woods and mountains in vain? Then my heart decided that I should seek another man, the most pious of all those who do not believe in God—that I should seek Zarathustra!"

Thus spoke the old man, and he looked with sharp eyes at the man standing before him; but Zarathustra seized the hand of the old pope and long contemplated it with admiration. "Behold, venerable one!" he said then; "what a beautiful long hand! That is the hand of one who has always dispensed blessings. But now it holds him whom you seek, me, Zarathustra. It is I, the godless Zarathustra, who speaks: who is more godless than I, that I may enjoy his instruction?"

Thus spoke Zarathustra, and with his glances he pierced the thoughts and the thoughts behind the thoughts of the old pope. At last the pope began, "He who loved and possessed him most has also lost him most now; behold, now I myself am probably the more godless of the two of us. But who could rejoice in that?"

"You served him to the last?" Zarathustra asked thoughtfully after a long silence. "You know *how* he died? Is it true what they say, that pity strangled him, that he saw how *man* hung on the cross and that he could not bear it, that love of man became his hell, and in the end his death?"

The old pope, however, did not answer but looked aside, shy, with a pained and gloomy expression. "Let him go!" Zarathustra said after prolonged reflection, still looking the old man straight in the eye. "Let him go! He is gone. And although it does you credit that you say only good things about him who is now dead, you know as well as I *who* he was, and that his ways were queer."

"Speaking in the confidence of three eyes," the old

pope said cheerfully (for he was blind in one eye), "in what pertains to God, I am—and have the right to be —more enlightened than Zarathustra himself. My love served him many years, my will followed his will in everything. A good servant, however, knows everything, including even things that his master conceals from himself. He was a concealed god, addicted to secrecy. Verily, even a son he got himself in a sneaky way. At the door of his faith stands adultery.

"Whoever praises him as a god of love does not have a high enough opinion of love itself. Did this god not want to be a judge too? But the lover loves beyond reward and retribution.

"When he was young, this god out of the Orient, he was harsh and vengeful and he built himself a hell to amuse his favorites. Eventually, however, he became old and soft and mellow and pitying, more like a grandfather than a father, but most like a shaky old grandmother. Then he sat in his nook by the hearth, wilted, grieving over his weak legs, weary of the world, weary of willing, and one day he choked on his all-too-great pity."

"You old pope," Zarathustra interrupted at this point, "did you see that with your own eyes? Surely it might have happened that way—that way, and also in some other way. When gods die, they always die several kinds of death. But—well then! This way or that, this way and that—he is gone! He offended the taste of my ears and eyes; I do not want to say anything worse about him now that he is dead.

"I love all that looks bright and speaks honestly. But he—you know it, you old priest, there was something of your manner about him, of the priest's manner: he was equivocal. He was also indistinct. How angry he got with us, this wrath-snorter, because we understood him badly! But why did he not speak more cleanly? And if it was the fault of our ears, why did he give us ears that heard him badly? If there was mud in our ears—well, who put it there? He bungled too much, this potter who had never finished his apprenticeship. But that he wreaked revenge on his pots and creations for having bungled them himself, that was a sin against *good taste*. There is good taste in piety too; and it was this that said in the end, 'Away with *such* a god! Rather no god, rather make destiny on one's own, rather be a fool, rather be a god oneself!' "

"What is this I hear?" said the old pope at this point, pricking up his ears. "O Zarathustra, with such disbelief you are more pious than you believe. Some god in you must have converted you to your godlessness. Is it not your piety itself that no longer lets you believe in a god? And your overgreat honesty will yet lead you beyond good and evil too. Behold, what remains to you? You have eyes and hands and mouth, predestined for blessing from all eternity. One does not bless with the hand alone. Near you, although you want to be the most godless, I scent a secret, sacred, pleasant scent of long blessings: it gives me gladness and grief. Let me be your guest, O Zarathustra, for one single night! Nowhere on earth shall I now feel better than with you."

"Amen! So be it!" said Zarathustra in great astonishment. "Up there goes the way, there lies Zarathustra's cave. I should indeed like to accompany you there myself, you venerable one, for I love all who are pious. But now a cry of distress urgently calls me away from you. In my realm no one shall come to grief; my cave is a good haven. And I wish that I could put everyone who is sad back on firm land and firm legs.

"But who could take *your* melancholy off your shoulders? For that I am too weak. Verily, we might wait long before someone awakens your god again. For this old god lives no more: he is thoroughly dead."

Thus spoke Zarathustra.

THE UGLIEST MAN

And again Zarathustra's feet ran over mountains and through woods, and his eyes kept seeking, but he whom they wanted to see was nowhere to be seen: the great distressed one who had cried out. All along the way, however, Zarathustra jubilated in his heart and was grateful. "What good things," he said, "has this day given me to make up for its bad beginning! What strange people have I found to talk with! Now I shall long chew their words like good grains; my teeth shall grind them and crush them small till they flow like milk into my soul."

But when the path turned around a rock again the scenery changed all at once, and Zarathustra entered a realm of death. Black and red cliffs rose rigidly: no grass, no tree, no bird's voice. For it was a valley that all animals avoided, even the beasts of prey; only a species of ugly fat green snakes came here to die when they grew old. Therefore the shepherds called this valley Snakes' Death.

Zarathustra, however, sank into a black reminiscence, for he felt as if he had stood in this valley once before. And much that was grave weighed on his mind; he walked slowly, and still more slowly, and finally stood still. But when he opened his eyes he saw something sitting by the way, shaped like a human being, yet scarcely like a human being—something inexpressible. And all at once a profound sense of shame overcame Zarathustra for having laid eyes on such a thing: blushing right up to his white hair, he averted his eyes and raised his feet to leave this dreadful place. But at that moment the dead waste land was filled with a noise, for something welled up from the ground, gurgling and rattling, as water gurgles and rattles by night in clogged waterpipes; and at last it became a human voice and human speech—thus:

"Zarathustra! Zarathustra! Guess my riddle! Speak, speak! What is *the revenge against the witness?* I lure you back, here is slippery ice. Take care, take care that your pride does not break its legs here! You think yourself wise, proud Zarathustra. Then guess the riddle, you cracker of hard nuts—the riddle that I am. Speak then: who am I?"

But when Zarathustra had heard these words—what do you suppose happened to his soul? *Pity seized him;* and he sank down all at once, like an oak tree that has long resisted many woodcutters—heavily, suddenly, terrifying even those who had wanted to fell it. But immediately he rose from the ground again, and his face became hard.

"I recognize you well," he said in a voice of bronze; *"you are the murderer of God!* Let me go. You could not *bear* him who saw *you*—who always saw you through and through, you ugliest man! You took revenge on this witness!"

Thus spoke Zarathustra, and he wanted to leave; but the inexpressible one seized a corner of his garment and began again to gurgle and seek for words. "Stay!" he said finally. "Stay! Do not pass by! I have guessed what ax struck you to the ground: hail to you, O Zarathustra, that you stand again! You have guessed, I know it well, how he who killed him feels—the murderer of God. Stay! Sit down here with me! It is not for nothing. Whom did I want to reach, if not you? Stay! Sit down! But do not look at me! In that way honor my ugliness!

They persecute me; now *you* are my last refuge. *Not* with their hatred, *not* with their catchpoles: I would mock such persecution and be proud and glad of it!

"Has not all success hitherto been with the well-persecuted? And whoever persecutes well, learns readily how to *follow;* for he is used to going after somebody else. But it is their *pity*—it is their pity that I flee, fleeing to you. O Zarathustra, protect me, you my last refuge, the only one who has solved my riddle: you guessed how he who killed him feels. Stay! And if you would go, you impatient one, do not go the way I came. *That* way is bad. Are you angry with me that I have even now stammered too long—and even advise you? But know, it is I, the ugliest man, who also has the largest and heaviest feet. Where *I* have gone, the way is bad. I tread all ways till they are dead and ruined.

"But that you passed me by, silent; that you blushed, I saw it well: that is how I recognized you as Zarathustra. Everyone else would have thrown his alms to me, his pity, with his eyes and words. But for that I am not beggar enough, as you guessed; for that I am too rich, rich in what is great, in what is terrible, in what is ugliest, in what is most inexpressible. Your shame, Zarathustra, honored me! With difficulty I escaped the throng of the pitying, to find the only one today who teaches, 'Pity is obtrusive'—you, O Zarathustra. Whether it be a god's pity or man's—pity offends the sense of shame. And to be unwilling to help can be nobler than that virtue which jumps to help.

"But today that is called virtue itself among all the little people—pity. They have no respect for great misfortune, for great ugliness, for great failure. Over this multitude I look away as a dog looks away over the backs of teeming flocks of sheep. They are little gray people, full of good wool and good will. As a heron looks away contemptuously over shallow ponds, its head leaning back, thus I look away over the teeming mass of gray little waves and wills and souls. Too long have we conceded to them that they are right, these little people; so that in the end we have also conceded them might. Now they teach: 'Good is only what little people call good.'

"And today 'truth' is what the preacher said, who himself came from among them, that queer saint and advocate of the little people who bore witness about himself: 'I am the truth.' This immodest fellow has long given the little people swelled heads—he who taught no small error when he taught, 'I am the truth.' Has an immodest fellow ever been answered more politely? You, however, O Zarathustra, passed him by and said, 'No! No! Three times no!' You warned against his error, you, as the first, warned against pity—not all, not none, but you and your kind.

"You are ashamed of the shame of the great sufferer; and verily, when you say, 'From pity, a great cloud approaches; beware, O men!'; when you teach, 'All creators are hard, all great love is over and above its pity'—O Zarathustra, how well you seem to me to understand storm signs. But you—warn yourself also against *your* pity. For many are on their way to you, many who are suffering, doubting, despairing, drowning, freezing. And I also warn you against myself. You guessed my best, my worst riddle: myself and what I did. I know the ax that fells you.

"But he *had to* die: he saw with eyes that saw everything; he saw man's depths and ultimate grounds, all his concealed disgrace and ugliness. His pity knew no shame: he crawled into my dirtiest nooks. This most curious, overobtrusive, overpitying one had to die. He always saw me: on such a witness I wanted to have revenge or not live myself. The god who saw everything, *even man*—this god had to die! Man cannot bear it that such a witness should live."

Thus spoke the ugliest man. But Zarathustra rose and was about to leave, for he felt frozen down to his very entrails. "You inexpressible one," he said, "you have warned me against *your* way. In thanks I shall praise mine to you. Behold, up there lies Zarathustra's cave. My cave is large and deep and has many nooks; even the most hidden can find a hiding-place there. And close by there are a hundred dens and lodges for crawling, fluttering, and jumping beasts. You self-exiled exile, would you not live among men and men's pity? Well then! Do as I do. Thus you also learn from me; only the doer learns. And speak first of all to my animals. The proudest animal and the wisest animal—they should be the right counselors for the two of us."

Thus spoke Zarathustra, and he went his way, still more reflectively and slowly than before; for he asked himself much, and he did not know how to answer himself readily. "How poor man is after all," he thought in his heart; "how ugly, how wheezing, how full of hidden shame! I have been told that man loves himself: ah, how great must this self-love be! How much contempt stands against it! This fellow too loved himself, even as he despised himself: a great lover he seems to me, and a great despiser. None have I found yet who despised himself more deeply: that too is a kind of height. Alas, was *he* perhaps the higher man whose cry I heard? I love the great despisers. Man, however, is something that must be overcome."

THE VOLUNTARY BEGGAR

When Zarathustra had left the ugliest man, he felt frozen and lonely: for much that was cold and lonely passed through his mind and made his limbs too feel colder. But as he climbed on and on, up and down, now past green pastures, then again over wild stony places where an impatient brook might once have made its bed, all at once he felt warmer and more cheerful again.

"What happened to me?" he asked himself. "Something warm and alive refreshes me, something that must be near me. Even now I am less alone; unknown companions and brothers roam about me; their warm breath touches my soul."

But when he looked around to find those who had comforted his loneliness, behold, they were cows, standing together on a knoll; their proximity and smell had warmed his heart. These cows, however, seemed to be listening eagerly to a speaker and did not heed him that was approaching. But when Zarathustra had come quite close to them, he heard distinctly that a human voice was speaking in the middle of the herd; and they had evidently all turned their heads toward the speaker.

Thereupon Zarathustra jumped up eagerly and pushed the animals apart, for he was afraid that somebody had suffered some harm here, which the pity of cows could scarcely cure. But he was wrong, for behold, there sat a man on the ground, and he seemed to be urging the animals to have no fear of him, a peaceful man and sermonizer on the mount out of whose eyes goodness itself was preaching. "What do you seek here?" shouted Zarathustra, amazed.

"What do I seek here?" he replied. "The same thing

you are seeking, you disturber of the peace: happiness on earth. But I want to learn that from these cows. For, you know, I have already been urging them half the morning, and just now they wanted to tell me. Why do you disturb them?

"Except we turn back and become as cows, we shall not enter the kingdom of heaven. For we ought to learn one thing from them: chewing the cud. And verily, what would it profit a man if he gained the whole world and did not learn this one thing: chewing the cud! He would not get rid of his melancholy—his great melancholy; but today that is called *nausea*. Who today does not have his heart, mouth, and eyes full of nausea? You too! You too! But behold these cows!"

Thus spoke the sermonizer on the mount, and then he turned his own eyes toward Zarathustra, for until then they had dwelt lovingly on the cows. But then his eyes changed. "Who is this to whom I am talking?" he cried, startled, and jumped up from the ground. "This is the man without nausea, this is Zarathustra himself, the man who overcame the great nausea; this is the eye, this is the mouth, this is the heart of Zarathustra himself." And as he spoke thus, he kissed the hands of the man to whom he was talking, and his eyes welled over, and he behaved exactly as one to whom a precious gift and treasure falls unexpectedly from the sky. But the cows watched all this with amazement.

"Do not speak of me, you who are so strange, so lovely!" Zarathustra said and restrained his tender affection. "First speak to me of yourself. Are you not the voluntary beggar who once threw away great riches? Who was ashamed of his riches and of the rich, and fled to the poorest to give them his fullness and his heart? But they did not accept him."

"But they did not accept me," said the voluntary beggar; "you know it. So I finally went to the animals and to these cows."

"There you have learned," Zarathustra interrupted the speaker, "how right giving is harder than right receiving, and that to give presents well is an *art* and the ultimate and most cunning master-art of graciousness."

"Especially today," answered the voluntary beggar; "today, I mean, when everything base has become rebellious and shy and, in its own way, arrogant—I mean, in the way of the mob. For the hour has come, you know it, for the great, bad, long, slow revolt of the mob and slaves: it grows and grows. Now the base are outraged by any charity and any little giving away; and the overrich should beware. Whoever drips today, like bulging bottles out of all-too-narrow necks—such bottles they like to seize today to break their necks. Lascivious greed, galled envy, aggrieved vengefulness, mob pride: all that leaped into my face. It is no longer true that the poor are blessed. But the kingdom of heaven is among the cows."

"And why is it not among the rich?" asked Zarathustra temptingly as he warded off the cows, which were breathing trustingly on the peaceful man.

"Why do you tempt me?" he replied. "You yourself know it even better than I. What was it after all that drove me to the poorest, O Zarathustra? Was it not that I was nauseated by our richest men? By the convicts of riches, who pick up their advantage out of any rubbish, with cold eyes, lewd thoughts; by this rabble that stinks to high heaven; by this gilded, false mob whose fathers have been pickpockets or carrion birds or ragpickers—with women, obliging, lascivious, and for-

getful: for none of them is too far from the whores—
mob above and mob below! What do 'poor' and 'rich'
matter today? This difference I have forgotten. I·fled,
farther, ever farther, till I came to these cows."

Thus spoke the peaceful man, and he himself
breathed hard and sweated as he spoke, so that the
cows were amazed again. But Zarathustra kept looking
into his face, smiling as he spoke so harshly, and
silently he shook his head. "You do yourself violence,
you sermonizer on the mount, when you use such harsh
words. Your mouth was not formed for such harshness,
nor your eyes. Nor, it seems to me, your stomach either:
it is offended by all such wrath and hatred and frothing.
Your stomach wants gentler things: you are no butcher.
You seem much more like a plant-and-root man to me.
Perhaps you gnash grain. Certainly, however, you are
averse to the joys of the flesh and you love honey."

"You have unriddled me well," answered the voluntary beggar, his heart relieved. "I love honey; I also
gnash grain, for I sought what tastes lovely and gives
a pure breath; also what takes a long time, a day's and
a mouth's work for gentle idlers and loafers. Nobody,
to be sure, has achieved more than these cows: they
invented for themselves chewing the cud and lying in
the sun. And they abstain from all grave thoughts,
which bloat the heart."

"Well then!" said Zarathustra. "You should also see
my animals, my eagle and my serpent: their like is not
to be found on earth today. Behold, there goes the way
to my cave: be its guest tonight. And talk with my animals of the happiness of animals—till I myself return
home. For now a cry of distress urgently calls me away
from you. You will also find new honey in my cave, ice-
fresh golden comb honey: eat that! But now quickly

take leave from your cows, you who are so strange, so lovely!—though it may be hard for you. For they are your warmest friends and teachers."

"Excepting one whom I love still more," answered the voluntary beggar. "You yourself are good, and even better than a cow, O Zarathustra."

"Away, away with you, you wicked flatterer!" Zarathustra cried with malice. "Why do you corrupt me with such praise and honeyed flattery? Away, away from me!" he cried once more and brandished his stick at the affectionate beggar, who ran away quickly.

THE SHADOW

But as soon as the voluntary beggar had run away and Zarathustra was alone again, he heard a new voice behind him, shouting, "Stop, Zarathustra! Wait! It is I, O Zarathustra, I, your shadow!" But Zarathustra did not wait, for a sudden annoyance came over him at the many intruders and obtruders in his mountains. "Where has my solitude gone?" he said. "Verily, it is becoming too much for me; this mountain range is teeming, my kingdom is no longer of *this* world, I need new mountains. My shadow calls me? What does my shadow matter? Let him run after me! I shall run away from him."

Thus spoke Zarathustra to his heart, and he ran away. But he who was behind him followed him, so that soon there were three runners, one behind the other, first the voluntary beggar, then Zarathustra, and third and last his shadow. It was not long that they ran this way before Zarathustra realized his folly and with a single shrug shook off all discontent and disgust. "Well!" he said; "have not the most ridiculous things always happened among us old hermits and saints? Verily, my folly has grown tall in the mountains. Now I hear six old fools' legs clattering along in a row. But may Zarathustra be afraid of a shadow? Moreover, it seems to me that he has longer legs than I."

Thus spoke Zarathustra, laughing with his eyes and entrails; he stopped quickly and turned around—and behold, he almost threw his follower and shadow to the ground: so close was the shadow by then, and so weak too. And when Zarathustra examined him with his eyes, he was startled as by a sudden ghost: so thin, swarthy, hollow, and outlived did this follower look. "Who are you?" Zarathustra asked violently. "What are you doing here? And why do you call yourself my shadow? I do not like you."

"Forgive me," answered the shadow, "that it is I; and if you do not like me, well then, O Zarathustra, for that I praise you and your good taste. I am a wanderer who has already walked a great deal at your heels—always on my way, but without any goal, also without any home; so that I really lack little toward being the Eternal Jew, unless it be that I am not eternal, and not a Jew. How? Must I always be on my way? Whirled by every wind, restless, driven on? O earth, thou hast become too round for me!

"I have already sat on every surface; like weary dust, I have gone to sleep on mirrors and windowpanes: everything takes away from me, nothing gives, I become thin—I am almost like a shadow. But after you, O Zarathustra, I flew and blew the longest; and even when I hid from you I was still your best shadow: wherever you sat, I sat too.

"With you I haunted the remotest, coldest worlds like a ghost that runs voluntarily over wintery roofs and snow. With you I strove to penetrate everything that is forbidden, worst, remotest; and if there is anything in me that is virtue, it is that I had no fear of any forbiddance. With you I broke whatever my heart revered; I overthrew all boundary stones and images; I pursued the most dangerous wishes: verily, over every crime I have passed once. With you I unlearned faith in words and values and great names. When the devil sheds his skin, does not his name fall off too? For that too is skin. The devil himself is perhaps—skin.

" 'Nothing is true, all is permitted': thus I spoke to myself. Into the coldest waters I plunged, with head and heart. Alas, how often have I stood there afterward, naked as a red crab! Alas, where has all that is good gone from me—and all shame, and all faith in those who are good? Alas, where is that mendacious innocence that I once possessed, the innocence of the good and their noble lies?

"Too often, verily, did I follow close on the heels of truth: so she kicked me in the face. Sometimes I thought I was lying, and behold, only then did I hit the truth. Too much has become clear to me: now it no longer concerns me. Nothing is alive any more that I love; how should I still love myself? 'To live as it pleases me, or not to live at all': that is what I want, that is what the saintliest want too. But alas, how could anything please me any more? Do I have a goal any more? A haven toward which my sail is set? A good wind? Alas, only he who knows where he is sailing also knows which wind is good and the right wind for him. What is left to me now? A heart, weary and impudent, a restless will, flutter-wings, a broken backbone. Trying thus to find *my* home—O Zarathustra, do you know it?—trying this was *my* trial; it consumes me. 'Where is—my home?' I ask and search and have searched for it, but I have not found it. O eternal everywhere, O eternal nowhere, O eternal—in vain!"

Thus spoke the shadow, and Zarathustra's face grew long as he listened. "You are my shadow," he finally said sadly. "Your danger is no small one, you free spirit and wanderer. You have had a bad day; see to it that you do not have a still worse evening. To those who are as restless as you, even a jail will at last seem bliss. Have you ever seen how imprisoned criminals sleep? They sleep calmly, enjoying their new security. Beware lest a narrow faith imprison you in the end—some harsh and severe illusion. For whatever is narrow and solid seduces and tempts you now.

"You have lost your goal; alas, how will you digest and jest over this loss? With this you have also lost your way. You poor roaming enthusiast, you weary butterfly! Would you have a rest and home this evening? Then go up to my cave. Up there goes the path to my cave.

"And now let me quickly run away from you again. Even now a shadow seems to lie over me. I want to run alone so that it may become bright around me again. For that, I shall still have to stay merrily on my legs a long time. In the evening, however, there will be dancing in my cave."

Thus spoke Zarathustra.

AT NOON

And Zarathustra ran and ran and did not find anybody any more, and he was alone and found himself again and again, and he enjoyed and quaffed his solitude and thought of good things for hours. But around the hour of noon, when the sun stood straight over Zarathustra's head, he came to an old crooked and knotty tree that was embraced, and hidden from itself, by the rich love of a grapevine; and yellow grapes hung from it in abundance, inviting the wanderer. Then he felt the desire to quench a slight thirst and to break off a grape; but even as he was stretching out his arm to do so, he felt a still greater desire for something else: namely, to lie down beside the tree at the perfect noon hour, and to sleep.

This Zarathustra did; and as soon as he lay on the ground in the stillness and secrecy of the many-hued grass, he forgot his slight thirst and fell asleep. For, as Zarathustra's proverb says, one thing is more necessary than another. Only his eyes remained open: for they did not tire of seeing and praising the tree and the love of the grapevine. Falling asleep, however, Zarathustra spoke thus to his heart:

Still! Still! Did not the world become perfect just now? What is happening to me? As a delicate wind dances unseen on an inlaid sea, light, feather-light, thus sleep dances on me. My eyes he does not close, my soul he leaves awake. Light he is, verily, feather-light. He persuades me, I know not how. He touches me inwardly with caressing hands, he conquers me. Yes, he conquers me and makes my soul stretch out: how she is becoming long and tired, my strange soul! Did the eve of a seventh day come to her at noon? Has she already roamed happily among good and ripe things too long? She stretches out long, long—longer. She lies still, my strange soul. Too much that is good has she tasted; this golden sadness oppresses her, she makes a wry mouth.

Like a ship that has sailed into its stillest cove—now it leans against the earth, tired of the long voyages and the uncertain seas. Is not the earth more faithful? The way such a ship lies close to, and nestles to, the land—it is enough if a spider spins its thread to it from the land: no stronger ropes are needed now. Like such a tired ship in the stillest cove, I too rest now near the earth, faithful, trusting, waiting, tied to it with the softest threads.

O happiness! O happiness! Would you sing, O my soul? You are lying in the grass. But this is the secret solemn hour when no shepherd plays his pipe. Refrain! Hot noon sleeps on the meadows. Do not sing! Still! The world is perfect. Do not sing, you winged one in the grass, O my soul—do not even whisper! Behold—still!—the old noon sleeps, his mouth moves: is he not just now drinking a drop of happiness, an old brown drop of golden happiness, golden wine? It slips over him, his happiness laughs. Thus laughs a god. Still!

"O happiness, how little is sufficient for happiness!" Thus I spoke once and seemed clever to myself. But it was a blasphemy: *that* I have learned now. Clever fools speak better. Precisely the least, the softest, lightest, a lizard's rustling, a breath, a breeze, a moment's glance—it is *little* that makes the *best* happiness. Still!

What happened to me? Listen! Did time perhaps fly away? Do I not fall? Did I not fall—listen!—into the well of eternity? What is happening to me? Still! I have been stung, alas—in the heart? In the heart! Oh break, break, heart, after such happiness, after such a sting. How? Did not the world become perfect just now? Round and ripe? Oh, the golden round ring—where may it fly? Shall I run after it? Quick! Still! (And here Zarathustra stretched and felt that he was asleep.)

"Up!" he said to himself; "you sleeper! You noon napper! Well, get up, old legs! It is time and overtime; many a good stretch of road still lies ahead of you. Now you have slept out—how long? Half an eternity! Well! Up with you now, my old heart! After such a sleep, how long will it take you to—wake it off?" (But then he fell asleep again, and his soul spoke against him and resisted and lay down again.) "Leave me alone! Still! Did not the world become perfect just now? Oh, the golden round ball!"

"Get up!" said Zarathustra, "you little thief, you lazy little thief of time! What? Still stretching, yawning, sighing, falling into deep wells? Who are you? O my soul!" (At this point he was startled, for a sunbeam fell from the sky onto his face.) "O heaven over me!" he said, sighing, and sat up. "You are looking on? You are listening to my strange soul? When will you drink this drop of dew which has fallen upon all earthly things? When will you drink this strange soul? When, well of eternity? Cheerful, dreadful abyss of noon! When will you drink my soul back into yourself?"

Thus spoke Zarathustra, and he got up from his resting place at the tree as from a strange drunkenness; and behold, the sun still stood straight over his head. But from this one might justly conclude that Zarathustra had not slept long.

THE WELCOME

It was only late in the afternoon that Zarathustra, after much vain searching and roaming, returned to his cave again. But when he was opposite it, not twenty paces away, that which he now least expected came about: again he heard the great *cry of distress*. And— amazing!—this time it came from his own cave. But it was a long-drawn-out, manifold, strange cry, and Zarathustra could clearly discern that it was composed of many voices, though if heard from a distance it might sound like a cry from a single mouth.

Then Zarathustra leaped toward his cave, and be- hold, what a sight awaited him after this sound! For all the men whom he had passed by during the day were sitting there together: the king at the right and the king at the left, the old magician, the pope, the voluntary beggar, the shadow, the conscientious in spirit, the sad soothsayer, and the ass; and the ugliest man had put on a crown and adorned himself with two crimson belts, for like all who are ugly he loved to disguise himself and pretend that he was beautiful. But in the middle of this melancholy party stood Zarathustra's eagle, bristling and restless, for he had been asked too many questions for which his pride had no answer; and the wise serpent hung around his neck.

Zarathustra beheld all this with great amazement; then he examined every one of his guests with friendly curiosity, read their souls, and was amazed again. Meanwhile all those gathered had risen from their seats and were waiting respectfully for Zarathustra to speak. But Zarathustra spoke thus:

"You who despair! You who are strange! So it was *your* cry of distress that I heard? And now I also know where to find him whom I sought in vain today: *the higher man.* He sits in my own cave, the higher man. But why should I be amazed? Have I not lured him to myself with honey sacrifices and the cunning siren calls of my happiness?

"Yet it seems to me that you are poor company; you who utter cries of distress upset each other's hearts as you sit here together. First someone must come—someone to make you laugh again, a good gay clown, a dancer and wind and wildcat, some old fool. What do you think?

"Forgive me, you who despair, that I speak to you with such little words, unworthy, verily, of such guests. But you do not guess *what* makes me so prankish: it is you yourselves who do it, and the sight of you; forgive me! For everyone becomes brave when he observes one who despairs. To encourage one who despairs—for that everyone feels strong enough. Even to me you gave this strength: a good gift, my honored guests! A proper present to ensure hospitality! Well then, do not be angry if I also offer you something of what is mine.

"This is my realm and my dominion; but whatever is mine shall be yours for this evening and this night. My animals shall serve you, my cave shall be your place of rest. In my home and house nobody shall despair; in my region I protect everybody from his wild animals. And this is the first thing I offer you: security. The second thing, however, is my little finger. And once you have *that*, by all means take the whole hand; well, and my heart too! Be welcome here, welcome, my guests!"

Thus spoke Zarathustra, and he laughed from love and malice. After this welcome his guests bowed again and were respectfully silent; but the king at the right hand answered him in their name: "From the manner, O Zarathustra, in which you offered us hand and welcome, we recognize you as Zarathustra. You humbled yourself before us; you almost wounded our reverence. But who would know as you do, how to humble himself with such pride? *That* in itself uplifts us; it is refreshing for our eyes and hearts. Merely to see this one thing, we would gladly climb mountains higher than this one. For we came, eager to see; we wanted to behold what makes dim eyes bright. And behold, even now we are done with all our cries of distress. Even now our minds and hearts are opened up and delighted. Little is lacking, and our spirits will become sportive.

"Nothing more delightful grows on earth, O Zarathustra, than a lofty, strong will: that is the earth's most beautiful plant. A whole landscape is refreshed by one such tree. Whoever grows up high like you, O Zarathustra, I compare to the pine: long, silent, hard, alone, of the best and most resilient wood, magnificent—and in the end reaching out with strong green branches for his *own* dominion, questioning wind and weather and whatever else is at home on the heights with forceful questions, and answering yet more forcefully, a commander, triumphant: oh, who would not climb high mountains to see such plants? Your tree here, O Zarathustra, refreshes even the gloomy ones, the failures; your sight reassures and heals the heart even of the restless. And verily, toward your mountain and tree many eyes are directed today; a great longing has arisen, and many have learned to ask, 'Who is Zarathustra?'

"And those into whose ears you have once dripped your song and your honey, all the hidden, the lonesome, the twosome, have all at once said to their hearts, 'Does Zarathustra still live? Life is no longer worth while, all is the same, all is in vain, or—we must live with Zarathustra.'

" 'Why does he not come who has so long announced himself?' ask many. 'Has solitude swallowed him up? Or are we perhaps supposed to come to him?'

"Now it happens that solitude itself grows weary and breaks, like a tomb that breaks and can no longer hold its dead. Everywhere one sees the resurrected. Now the waves are climbing and climbing around your mountain, O Zarathustra. And however high your height may be, many must come up to you: your bark shall not be stranded much longer. And that we who were despairing have now come to your cave and no longer despair—that is but a sign and symbol that those better than we are on their way to you; for this is what is on its way to you: the last remnant of God among men— that is, all the men of great longing, of great nausea, of great disgust, all who do not want to live unless they learn to *hope* again, unless they learn from you, O Zarathustra, the *great* hope."

Thus spoke the king at the right, and he seized Zarathustra's hand to kiss it; but Zarathustra resisted his veneration and stepped back, startled, silent, and as if he were suddenly fleeing into remote distances. But after a little while he was back with his guests again, looking at them with bright, examining eyes, and he said: "My guests, you higher men, let me speak to you in plain and clear German. It was not for *you* that I waited in these mountains."

("Plain and clear German? Good God!" the king at the left said at this point, in an aside. "One can see that he does not know our dear Germans, this wise man from the East! But what he means is 'coarse German'; well, these days that is not the worst of tastes.")

"You may indeed all be higher men," continued Zarathustra, "but for me you are not high and strong enough. For me—that means, for the inexorable in me that is silent but will not always remain silent. And if you do belong to me, it is not as my right arm. For whoever stands on sick and weak legs himself, as you do, wants *consideration* above all, whether he knows it or hides it from himself. To my arms and my legs, however, I show no consideration; *I show my warriors no consideration:* how then could you be fit for *my* war? With you I should spoil my every victory. And some among you would collapse as soon as they heard the loud roll of my drums.

"Nor are you beautiful and wellborn enough for me. I need clean, smooth mirrors for my doctrines; on your surface even my own image is distorted. Many a burden, many a reminiscence press on your shoulders; many a wicked dwarf crouches in your nooks. There is hidden mob in you too. And even though you may be high and of a higher kind, much in you is crooked and misshapen. There is no smith in the world who could hammer you right and straight for me.

"You are mere bridges: may men higher than you stride over you. You signify steps: therefore do not be angry with him who climbs over you to *his* height. A genuine son and perfect heir may yet grow from your seed, even for me: but that is distant. You yourselves are not those to whom my heritage and name belong.

"It is not for you that I wait in these mountains; it is not with you that I am to go down for the last time. Only as signs have you come to me, that those higher than you are even now on their way to me: *not* the men of great longing, of great nausea, of great disgust, and that which you called the remnant of God; no, no, three times no! It is for others that I wait here in these mountains, and I will not lift my feet from here without them; it is for those who are higher, stronger, more triumphant, and more cheerful, such as are built perpendicular in body and soul: *laughing lions* must come!

"O my strange guests! Have you not yet heard anything of my children? And that they are on their way to me? Speak to me of my gardens, of my blessed isles, of my new beauty—why do you not speak to me of that? This present I beseech from your love, that you speak to me of my children. For this I am rich, for this I grew poor; what did I not give, what would I not give to have one thing: these children, this living plantation, these life-trees of my will and my highest hope!"

Thus spoke Zarathustra, and suddenly he stopped in his speech, for a longing came over him, and he closed his eyes and mouth as his heart was moved. And all his guests too fell silent and stood still in dismay; only the old soothsayer made signs and gestures with his hands.

THE LAST SUPPER

For it was at this point that the soothsayer interrupted the welcome, pushed forward like one who has no time to lose, seized Zarathustra's hand, and shouted: "But Zarathustra! One thing is more necessary than another: thus you say yourself. Well then, one thing is more necessary to *me* now than anything else. A word at the right time: did you not invite me to *supper?* And here are many who have come a long way. Surely, you would not feed us speeches alone? Also, all of you have thought far too much, for my taste, of freezing, drowning, suffocating, and other physical distress; but nobody has thought of *my* distress, namely, starving—"

(Thus spoke the soothsayer; but when Zarathustra's animals heard these words they ran away in fright. For they saw that whatever they had brought home during the day would not be enough to fill this one soothsayer.)

"Including dying of thirst," continued the soothsayer. "And although I hear water splashing nearby like speeches of wisdom—that is, abundantly and tirelessly —I want *wine*. Not everybody is a born water drinker like Zarathustra. Nor is water fit for the weary and wilted: *we* deserve wine. *That* alone gives sudden convalescence and immediate health."

On this occasion, as the soothsayer asked for wine, it happened that the king at the left, the taciturn one, got a word in too, for once. "For wine," he said, "*we* have taken care—I together with my brother, the king at the right; we have wine enough—a whole ass-load. So nothing is lacking but bread."

"Bread?" countered Zarathustra, and he laughed. "Bread is the one thing hermits do not have. But man does not live by bread alone, but also of the meat of good lambs, of which I have two. *These* should be slaughtered quickly and prepared tastily with sage: I love it that way. Nor is there a lack of roots and fruit, good enough even for gourmets and gourmands, nor of nuts and other riddles to be cracked. Thus we shall have a good meal in a short while. But whoever would join in the eating must also help in the preparation, even the kings. For at Zarathustra's even a king may be cook."

This suggestion appealed to the hearts of all; only the voluntary beggar objected to meat and wine and spices. "Now listen to this glutton Zarathustra!" he said jokingly; "is that why one goes into caves and high mountain ranges, to prepare such meals? Now indeed I understand what he once taught us: 'Praised be a little poverty!' And why he wants to abolish beggars."

"Be of good cheer," Zarathustra answered him, "as I am. Stick to your custom, my excellent friend, crush your grains, drink your water, praise your fare; as long as it makes you gay!

"I am a law only for my kind, I am no law for all. But whoever belongs with me must have strong bones and light feet, be eager for war and festivals, not gloomy, no dreamer, as ready for what is most difficult as for his festival, healthy and wholesome. The best belongs to my kind and to me; and when one does not give it to us, we take it: the best food, the purest sky, the strongest thoughts, the most beautiful women."

Thus spoke Zarathustra; but the king at the right retorted: "Strange! Has one ever heard such clever things out of the mouth of a sage? And verily, he is the strangest sage who is also clever and no ass."

Thus spoke the king at the right, and he was amazed; but the ass commented on his speech with evil intent:

Yeah-Yuh. But this was the beginning of that long-drawn-out meal which the chronicles call "the last supper." And in the course of it, nothing else was discussed but *the higher man*.

ON THE HIGHER MAN

1

The first time I came to men I committed the folly of hermits, the great folly: I stood in the market place. And as I spoke to all, I spoke to none. But in the evening, tightrope walkers and corpses were my companions; and I myself was almost a corpse. But with the new morning a new truth came to me: I learned to say, "Of what concern to me are market and mob and mob noise and long mob ears?"

You higher men, learn this from me: in the market place nobody believes in higher men. And if you want to speak there, very well! But the mob blinks: "We are all equal."

"You higher men"—thus blinks the mob—"there are no higher men, we are all equal, man is man; before God we are all equal."

Before God! But now this god has died. And before the mob we do not want to be equal. You higher men, go away from the market place!

2

Before God! But now this god has died. You higher men, this god was your greatest danger. It is only since he lies in his tomb that you have been resurrected. Only now the great noon comes; only now the higher man becomes—lord.

Have you understood this word, O my brothers? You are startled? Do your hearts become giddy? Does the abyss yawn before you? Does the hellhound howl at you? Well then, you higher men! Only now is the mountain of man's future in labor. God died: now *we* want the overman to live.

3

The most concerned ask today: "How is man to be preserved?" But Zarathustra is the first and only one to ask: "How is man to be overcome?"

I have the overman at heart, *that* is my first and only concern—and *not* man: not the neighbor, not the poorest, not the most ailing, not the best.

O my brothers, what I can love in man is that he is an overture and a going under. And in you too there is much that lets me love and hope. That you despise, you higher men, that lets me hope. For the great despisers are the great reverers. That you have despaired, in that there is much to revere. For you did not learn how to surrender, you did not learn petty prudences. For today the little people lord it: they all preach surrender and resignation and prudence and industry and consideration and the long etcetera of the small virtues.

What is womanish, what derives from the servile, and especially the mob hodgepodge: *that* would now become master of all human destiny. O nausea! Nausea! Nausea! *That* asks and asks and never grows weary: "How is man to be preserved best, longest, most agreeably?" With that—they are the masters of today.

Overcome these masters of today, O my brothers—these small people, *they* are the overman's greatest danger.

You higher men, overcome the small virtues, the small prudences, the grain-of-sand consideration, the ants' riffraff, the wretched contentment, the "happiness of the greatest number"! And rather despair than surrender. And verily, I love you for not knowing how to live today, you higher men! For thus *you* live best.

4

Do you have courage, O my brothers? Are you brave? *Not* courage before witnesses but the courage of hermits and eagles, which is no longer watched even by a god.

Cold souls, mules, the blind, and the drunken I do not call brave. Brave is he who knows fear but *conquers* fear, who sees the abyss, but with *pride*.

Who sees the abyss but with the eyes of an eagle; who grasps the abyss with the talons of an eagle—that man has courage.

5

"Man is evil"—thus said all the wisest to comfort me. Alas, if only it were still true today! For evil is man's best strength.

"Man must become better and more evil"—thus *I* teach. The greatest evil is necessary for the overman's best. It may have been good for that preacher of the little people that he suffered and tried to bear man's sin. But I rejoice over great sin as my great consolation.

But this is not said for long ears. Not every word belongs in every mouth. These are delicate distant matters: they should not be reached for by sheeps' hoofs.

6

You higher men, do you suppose I have come to set right what you have set wrong? Or that I have come to you that suffer to bed you more comfortably? Or to you that are restless, have gone astray or climbed astray, to show you new and easier paths?

No! No! Three times no! Ever more, ever better ones

of your kind shall perish—for it shall be ever worse and harder for you. Thus alone—thus alone, man grows to the height where lightning strikes and breaks him: lofty enough for lightning.

My mind and my longing are directed toward the few, the long, the distant; what are your many small short miseries to me? You do not yet suffer enough to suit me! For you suffer from yourselves, you have not yet suffered *from man*. You would lie if you claimed otherwise! You all do not suffer from what *I* have suffered.

7

It is not enough for me that lightning no longer does any harm. I do not wish to conduct it away: it shall learn to work for me.

My wisdom has long gathered like a cloud; it is becoming stiller and darker. Thus does every wisdom that is yet to give birth to lightning bolts.

For these men of today I do not wish to be *light*, or to be called light. *These* I wish to blind. Lightning of my wisdom! put out their eyes!

8

Will nothing beyond your capacity: there is a wicked falseness among those who will beyond their capacity. Especially if they will great things! For they arouse mistrust against great things, these subtle counterfeiters and actors—until finally they are false before themselves, squinters, whited worm-eaten decay, cloaked with strong words, with display-virtues, with splendid false deeds.

Take good care there, you higher men! For nothing today is more precious to me and rarer than honesty.

Is this today not the mob's? But the mob does not

know what is great, what is small, what is straight and honest: it is innocently crooked, it always lies.

9

Have a good mistrust today, you higher men, you stouthearted ones, you openhearted ones! And keep your reasons secret! For this today is the mob's.

What the mob once learned to believe without reasons —who could overthrow that with reasons?

And in the market place one convinces with gestures. But reasons make the mob mistrustful.

And if truth was victorious for once, then ask yourself with good mistrust: "What strong error fought for it?"

Beware of the scholars! They hate you, for they are sterile. They have cold, dried-up eyes; before them every bird lies unplumed.

Such men boast that they do not lie: but the inability to lie is far from the love of truth. Beware!

Freedom from fever is not yet knowledge by any means! I do not believe chilled spirits. Whoever is unable to lie does not know what truth is.

10

If you would go high, use your own legs. Do not let yourselves be *carried* up; do not sit on the backs and heads of others. But you mounted a horse? You are now riding quickly up to your goal? All right, my friend! But your lame foot is sitting on the horse too. When you reach your goal, when you jump off your horse—on your very *height*, you higher man, you will stumble.

11

You creators, you higher men! One is pregnant only with one's own child. Do not let yourselves be gulled and beguiled! Who, after all, is *your* neighbor? And even if you act "for the neighbor"—you still do not create for him.

Unlearn this "for," you creators! Your very virtue wants that you do nothing "for" and "in order" and "because." You shall plug up your ears against these false little words. "For the neighbor" is only the virtue of the little people: there one says "birds of a feather" and "one hand washes the other." They have neither the right nor the strength for *your* egoism. In your egoism, you creators, is the caution and providence of the pregnant. What no one has yet laid eyes on, the fruit: that your whole love shelters and saves and nourishes. Where your whole love is, with your child, there is also your whole virtue. Your work, your will, that is *your* "neighbor": do not let yourselves be gulled with false values!

12

You creators, you higher men! Whoever has to give birth is sick; but whoever has given birth is unclean. Ask women: one does not give birth because it is fun. Pain makes hens and poets cackle.

You creators, there is much that is unclean in you. That is because you had to be mothers.

A new child: oh, how much new filth has also come into the world! Go aside! And whoever has given birth should wash his soul clean.

13

Do not be virtuous beyond your strength! And do not desire anything of yourselves against probability.

Walk in the footprints where your fathers' virtue walked before you. How would you climb high if your fathers' will does not climb with you?

But whoever would be a firstling should beware lest

he also become a lastling. And wherever the vices of your fathers are, there you should not want to represent saints. If your fathers consorted with women, strong wines, and wild boars, what would it be if you wanted chastity of yourself? It would be folly! Verily, it seems much to me if such a man is the husband of one or two or three women. And if he founded monasteries and wrote over the door, "The way to sainthood," I should yet say, What for? It is another folly. He founded a reformatory and refuge for himself: may it do him good! But I do not believe in it.

In solitude, whatever one has brought into it grows—also the inner beast. Therefore solitude is inadvisable for many. Has there been anything filthier on earth so far than desert saints? Around them not only was the devil loose, but also the swine.

14

Shy, ashamed, awkward, like a tiger whose leap has failed: thus I have often seen you slink aside, you higher men. A throw had failed you. But, you dice-throwers, what does it matter? You have not learned to gamble and jest as one must gamble and jest. Do we not always sit at a big jesting-and-gaming table? And if something great has failed you, does it follow that you yourselves are failures? And if you yourselves are failures, does it follow that *man* is a failure? But if man is a failure—well then!

15

The higher its type, the more rarely a thing succeeds. You higher men here, have you not all failed?

Be of good cheer, what does it matter? How much is still possible! Learn to laugh at yourselves as one must laugh!

Is it any wonder that you failed and only half succeeded, being half broken? Is not something thronging and pushing in you—man's *future?* Man's greatest distance and depth and what in him is lofty to the stars, his tremendous strength—are not all these frothing against each other in your pot? Is it any wonder that many a pot breaks? Learn to laugh at yourselves as one must laugh! You higher men, how much is still possible!

And verily, how much has already succeeded! How rich is the earth in little good perfect things, in what has turned out well!

Place little good perfect things around you, O higher men! Their golden ripeness heals the heart. What is perfect teaches hope.

16

What has so far been the greatest sin here on earth? Was it not the word of him who said, "Woe unto those who laugh here"? Did he himself find no reasons on earth for laughing? Then he searched very badly. Even a child could find reasons here. He did not love enough: else he would also have loved us who laugh. But he hated and mocked us: howling and gnashing of teeth he promised us.

Does one have to curse right away, where one does not love? That seems bad taste to me. But thus he acted, being unconditional. He came from the mob. And he himself simply did not love enough: else he would not have been so wroth that one did not love him. All great love does not *want* love: it wants more.

Avoid all such unconditional people! They are a poor sick sort, a sort of mob: they look sourly at this life, they have the evil eye for this earth. Avoid all such unconditional people! They have heavy feet and sultry hearts: they do not know how to dance. How should the earth be light for them?

17

All good things approach their goal crookedly. Like cats, they arch their backs, they purr inwardly over their approaching happiness: all good things laugh.

A man's stride betrays whether he has found his own way: behold me walking! But whoever approaches his goal dances. And verily, I have not become a statue: I do not yet stand there, stiff, stupid, stony, a column; I love to run swiftly. And though there are swamps and thick melancholy on earth, whoever has light feet runs even over mud and dances as on swept ice.

Lift up your hearts, my brothers, high, higher! And do not forget your legs either. Lift up your legs too, you good dancers; and better yet, stand on your heads!

18

This crown of him who laughs, this rose-wreath crown: I myself have put on this crown, I myself have pronounced my laughter holy. Nobody else have I found strong enough for this today.

Zarathustra the dancer, Zarathustra the light, waves with his wings, ready for flight, waving at all birds, ready and heady, happily lightheaded; Zarathustra the soothsayer, Zarathustra the sooth-laugher, not impatient, not unconditional, one who loves leaps and side-leaps: I myself have put on this crown!

19

Lift up your hearts, my brothers, high, higher! And do not forget your legs either. Lift up your legs too, you good dancers; and better yet, stand on your heads!

In happiness too there are heavy animals; there are

pondrous-pedes through and through. Curiously they labor, like an elephant laboring to stand on its head. But it is still better to be foolish from happiness than foolish from unhappiness; better to dance ponderously than to walk lamely. That you would learn my wisdom from me: even the worst thing has two good reverse sides—even the worst thing has good dancing legs; that you would learn, you higher men, to put yourselves on your right legs! That you would unlearn nursing melancholy and all mob-sadness! Oh, how sad even the mob's clowns seem to me today! But this today is the mob's.

20

Be like the wind rushing out of his mountain caves: he wishes to dance to his own pipe; the seas tremble and leap under his feet.

What gives asses wings, what milks lionesses— praised be this good intractable spirit that comes like a cyclone to all today and to all the mob. What is averse to thistle-heads and casuists' heads and to all wilted leaves and weeds—praised be this wild, good, free storm spirit that dances on swamps and on melancholy as on meadows. What hates the mob's blethercocks and all the bungled gloomy brood—praised be this spirit of all free spirits, the laughing gale that blows dust into the eyes of all the black-sighted, soreblighted.

You higher men, the worst about you is that all of you have not learned to dance as one must dance—dancing away over yourselves! What does it matter that you are failures? How much is still possible! So *learn* to laugh away over yourselves! Lift up your hearts, you good dancers, high, higher! And do not forget good laughter. This crown of him who laughs, this rose-wreath crown: to you, my brothers, I throw this crown. Laughter I have pronounced holy; you higher men, *learn* to laugh!

THE SONG OF MELANCHOLY

1

While Zarathustra delivered these discourses he stood near the entrance of his cave; but with the last words he slipped away from his guests and fled into the open for a short while.

"O pure smells about me!" he cried out. "O happy silence about me! But where are my animals? Come here, come here, my eagle and my serpent! Tell me, my animals: these higher men, all of them—do they perhaps *smell* bad? O pure smells about me! Only now I know and feel how much I love you, my animals."

And Zarathustra spoke once more: "I love you, my animals." But the eagle and the serpent pressed close to him as he spoke these words, and looked up to him. In this way the three of them were together silently, and they sniffed and sipped the good air together. For the air out here was better than among the higher men.

2

But Zarathustra had scarcely left his cave when the old magician got up, looked around cunningly, and said: "He has gone out! And immediately, you higher men— if I may tickle you with this laudatory, flattering name, as he did—immediately my wicked spirit of deception and magic seizes me, my melancholy devil, who is through and through an adversary of this Zarathustra— forgive him! Now he *wants* to show you his magic; he has *his* hour right now; in vain do I wrestle with this evil spirit. Of all of you, whatever honors you may confer on yourselves with words, whether you call your- selves 'free spirits' or 'truthful' or 'ascetics of the spirit' or 'the unbound' or 'the great longers'—of all of you who, like me, are suffering of *the great nausea*, for whom the old god has died and for whom no new god lies as yet in cradles and swaddling clothes—of all of you my evil spirit and magic devil is fond.

"I know you, you higher men; I know him; I also know this monster whom I love against my will, this Zarathustra: he himself sometimes seems to me like a beautiful mask of a saint, like a new strange masquerade in which my evil spirit, the melancholy devil, enjoys himself. I love Zarathustra, it often seems to me, for the sake of my evil spirit.

"But even now he attacks me and forces me, this spirit of melancholy, this devil of the dusk; and verily, you higher men, he has the desire—you may well open your eyes wide!—he has the desire to come *naked;* whether male or female I do not know yet—but he is coming, he is forcing me; alas, open up your senses! The day is fading away, evening is now coming to all things, even to the best things: hear then and see, you higher men, what kind of devil, whether man or woman, this spirit of evening melancholy is!"

Thus spoke the old magician, looked around cunningly, and then reached for his harp.

3

In dim, de-lighted air
When the dew's comfort is beginning
To well down to the earth,
Unseen, unheard—
For tender is the footwear of
The comforter dew, as of all that gently comfort—
Do you remember then, remember, hot heart,
How you thirsted once
For heavenly tears and dripping dew,

Thirsting, scorched and weary,
While on yellow paths in the grass
The glances of the evening sun were running
Maliciously around you through black trees—
Blinding, glowing glances of the sun, mocking your
   pain?

"Suitor of truth?" they mocked me; "you?
No! Only poet!
An animal, cunning, preying, prowling,
That must lie,
That must knowingly, willingly lie:
Lusting for prey,
Colorfully masked,
A mask for itself,
Prey for itself—
This, the suitor of truth?
No! Only fool! Only poet!
Only speaking colorfully,
Only screaming colorfully out of fools' masks,
Climbing around on mendacious word bridges,
On colorful rainbows,
Between false heavens
And false earths,
Roaming, hovering—
Only fool! *Only* poet!

This—the suitor of truth?
Not still, stiff, smooth, cold,
Become a statue,
A pillar of God,
Not placed before temples,
A god's gate guard—
No! an enemy of all such truth statues,
More at home in any desert than before temples,

Full of cats' prankishness,
Leaping through every window—
Swish! into every chance,
Sniffing for every jungle,
Eagerly, longingly sniffing:
That in jungles
Among colorfully speckled beasts of prey
You might roam, sinfully sound and colorful, beautiful
With lusting lips,
Blissfully mocking, blissfully hellish, blissfully blood-
    thirsty—
Preying, prowling, peering—

Or like the eagle that gazes long,
Long with fixed eyes into abysses,
His *own* abysses—
Oh, how they wind downward,
Lower and lower
And into ever deeper depths!—
Then,
Suddenly, straight as sight
In brandished flight,
Pounce on *lambs*,
Abruptly down, hot-hungry,
Lusting for lambs,
Hating all lamb souls,
Grimly hating whatever looks
Sheepish, lamb-eyed, curly-wooled,
Gray, with lambs' and sheeps' goodwill.

Thus
Eagle-like, panther-like,
Are the poet's longings,
Are *your* longings under a thousand masks,
You fool! You poet!

You that have seen man
As god and sheep:
Tearing to pieces the god in man
No less than the sheep in man,
And *laughing* while tearing—

This, this is your bliss!
A panther's and eagle's bliss!
A poet's and fool's bliss!"

In dim, de-lighted air
When the moon's sickle is beginning
To creep, green between crimson
Reds, enviously—
Hating the day,
Secretly step for step
Scything at sloping rose meads
Till they sink and, ashen,
Drown in night—

Thus I myself once sank
Out of my truth-madness,
Out of my day-longings,
Weary of day, sick from the light—
Sank downward, eveningward, shadowward,
Burned by one truth,
And thirsty:
Do you remember still, remember, hot heart,
How you thirsted?
That I be banished
From all truth,
Only fool!
Only poet!

ON SCIENCE

Thus sang the magician; and all who were gathered there went unwittingly as birds into the net of his cunning and melancholy lust. Only the conscientious in spirit was not caught: quickly he took the harp away from the magician and cried: "Air! Let in good air! Let in Zarathustra! You are making this cave sultry and poisonous, you wicked old magician. You are seducing us, you false and subtle one, to unknown desires and wildernesses. And beware when such as you start making speeches and fuss about *truth!* Woe unto all free spirits who do not watch out against such magicians! Then it is over with their freedom: you teach us and lure us back into prisons. You old melancholy devil: out of your lament a bird call lures us; you are like those whose praise of chastity secretly invites to voluptuous delights."

Thus spoke the conscientious man; but the old magician looked around, enjoyed his triumph, and for its sake swallowed the annoyance caused him by the conscientious man. "Be still!" he said in a modest voice; "good songs want to resound well; after good songs one should long keep still. Thus do all these higher men. But perhaps you have understood very little of my song? In you there is little of a magic spirit."

"You praise me by distinguishing me from yourself," retorted the conscientious man. "Well then! But you others, what do I see? You are all still sitting there with lusting eyes: you free souls, where is your freedom gone? You are almost like men, it seems to me, who have long watched wicked, dancing, naked girls: your souls are dancing too. In you, you higher men, there must be more of what the magician calls his evil spirit of magic and deception: we must be different.

"And verily, we talked and thought together enough before Zarathustra returned home to his cave for me to know that we *are* different. We also seek different things up here, you and I. For I seek more *security,* that is why I came to Zarathustra. For he is the firmest tower and will today, when everything is tottering and all the earth is quaking. But you—when I see the eyes you make, it almost seems to me that you are seeking *more insecurity:* more thrills, more danger, more earthquakes. You desire, I should almost presume—forgive my presumption, you higher men—you desire the most wicked, most dangerous life, of which *I* am most afraid: the life of wild animals, woods, caves, steep mountains, and labyrinthian gorges. And it is not the leaders *out* of danger who appeal to you most, but those who induce you to leave all ways, the seducers. But even if such desire in you is real, it still seems impossible to me.

"For fear is the original and basic feeling of man; from fear everything is explicable, original sin and original virtue. From fear my own virture too has grown, and it is called: science. For the fear of wild animals, that was bred in man longest of all—including the animal he harbors inside himself and fears: Zarathustra calls it 'the inner beast.' Such long old fear, finally refined, spiritualized, spiritual—today, it seems to me, this is called *science.*"

Thus spoke the conscientious man; but Zarathustra, who was just coming back into his cave and had heard and guessed this last speech, threw a handful of roses at the conscientious man and laughed at his "truths." "What?" he cried. "What did I hear just now? Verily, it seems to me that you are a fool, or that I am one myself; and your 'truth' I simply reverse. For *fear*—that is our exception. But courage and adventure and pleasure in the uncertain, in the undared—*courage* seems to me man's whole prehistory. He envied the wildest, most courageous animals and robbed all their virtues: only thus did he become man. *This* courage, finally refined, spiritualized, spiritual, this human courage with eagles' wings and serpents' wisdom—*that*, it seems to me, is today called—"

"*Zarathustra!*" all who were sitting together cried as with one mouth, and they raised a great laughter that rose above them like a heavy cloud. The magician too laughed and said cleverly: "Well then, he is gone, my evil spirit. And have I myself not warned you of him when I said that he was a deceiver, a spirit of lies and deceptions? Especially when he appears naked. But am *I* responsible for his wiles? Did *I* create him and the world? Well then, let us make up again and make merry! And although Zarathustra looks angry—look at him, he bears me a grudge—before night falls he will learn again to love me and laud me; he cannot live long without committing such follies. He loves his enemies; this art he understands best of all whom I have ever seen. But he takes revenge for this on his friends."

Thus spoke the old magician, and the higher men applauded him; so Zarathustra walked around and shook his friends' hands with malice and love—like one who has to make up for something and apologize. But when he reached the door of his cave, behold, he again felt a desire for the good air outside and for his animals—and he wanted to slip out.

AMONG DAUGHTERS OF THE WILDERNESS

1

"Do not go away!" said the wanderer who called himself Zarathustra's shadow. "Stay with us. Else our old musty depression might seize us again. Even now that old magician has given us a sample of his worst; and behold, that good pious pope there has tears in his eyes and has again embarked on the sea of melancholy. These kings may still put up a bold front, for of all of us here today they have learned this best. But if they had no witness, I wager that for them too the evil routine would resume—the evil routine of drifting clouds, of moist melancholy, of overcast skies, of stolen suns, of howling autumn winds—the evil routine of our own howling and cries of distress. Stay with us, O Zarathustra! There is much hidden misery here that desires to speak, much evening, much cloud, much musty air. You have nourished us with strong virile food and forceful maxims: do not let the feeble feminine spirits seize us again after dinner! You alone make the air around you strong and clear. Have I ever found such good air anywhere on earth as here in your cave? Many countries have I seen; my nose has learned to test and estimate many kinds of air: but in your cave my nostrils are tasting their greatest pleasure.

"Unless it were—unless it were—oh, forgive an old reminiscence! Forgive me an old afterdinner song that I once composed among daughters of the wilderness: for near them the air was equally good, bright, and oriental; never was I farther away from cloudy, moist, melancholy old Europe. In those days I loved such Oriental girls and other blue skies over which no clouds and thoughts hang. You would not believe how nicely they sat there when they were not dancing, deep but without thoughts, like little secrets, like beribboned riddles, like afterdinner nuts—colorful and strange, to be sure, but without clouds; riddles that let themselves be guessed: for such girls I then thought out an afterdinner psalm."

Thus spoke the wanderer and shadow; and before anyone answered him he had already seized the harp of the old magician, crossed his legs, and looked around, composed and wise. But with his nostrils he drew in the air slowly and questioningly, as one tastes the new foreign air in a new country. Then he began to sing with a kind of roar.

2

Wilderness grows: woe unto him that harbors wildernesses!

Hah! Solemn!
Indeed solemn!
A worthy beginning.
African solemnity.
Worthy of a lion
Or of a moral howling monkey—
But nothing for you,
My most charming friends
At whose feet I,
As the first
European under palm trees,
Am allowed to sit. Selah.

Wonderful surely!
There I sit now,
Near the wilderness and already
So far from the wilderness again,

And in no way wild or wanton—
Merely swallowed
By this smallest oasis:
It just opened, yawning,
Its lovely orifice,
The most fragrant of all little mouths—
And I fell in
And down and through—among you,
My most charming friends. Selah.

Hail, hail to that whale
If he let his guest be that
Well off! You do understand
My scholarly allusion?
Hail to his belly
If it was as
Lovely an oasis belly
As this—which, however, I should certainly doubt;
After all, I come from Europe
Which is more doubt-addicted than all
Elderly married women.
May God improve it!
Amen.

There I sit now,
In this smallest oasis,
Just like a date,
Brown, sweet through, oozing gold, lusting
For the round mouth of a girl,
But even more for girlish,
Ice-cold, snow-white, cutting
Incisors: for after these
Pants the heart of all hot dates. Selah.

Similar, all-too-similar

To the aforementioned fruit,
I lie here, sniffed at
And played about
By little winged bugs—
Also by still smaller,
More foolish, more sinful
Wishes and notions—
Enveloped by you,
Silent and foreboding
Girl-cats,
Dudu and Suleika—
Ensphinxed, to crowd many
Feelings into one word
(May God forgive me
This linguistic sin!)—
I sit here, sniffing the best air,
Verily, paradise air,
Bright, light air, golden-striped,
As good air as ever
Fell down from the moon—
Whether by chance
Or did it happen from prankishness?
As the old poets relate.
I, being a doubter, however, should
Doubt it; after all, I come
From Europe
Which is more doubt-addicted than all
Elderly married women.
May God improve it!
Amen.

Drinking this most beautiful air,
My nostrils distended like cups,
Without future, without reminiscences,
Thus I sit here, O

My most charming friends,
And am watching the palm tree
As, like a dancer, she curves
And swerves and sways above her hips—
One does it too, if one watches long.
Like a dancer who, as it would seem to me,
Has stood too long, dangerously long
Always, always only on one little leg.
She has forgotten, it would seem to me,
The other leg.
In vain, at least,
I looked for the missed
Twin jewel—
Namely, the other leg—
In the holy proximity
Of her most lovely, most delicate
Flimsy little fan-, flutter-, and tinsel-skirt.
Yes, if you would, my beautiful friends,
Believe me wholly:
She has lost it!
It is gone!
Forever gone!
The other leg!
What a shame about that lovely other leg!
Where may it be staying and mourning, forsaken?
The lonely leg?
Perhaps afraid of a
Grim, blond, curly
Lion monster? Or even now
Gnawed away, nibbled away—
Misery, alas! alas! Nibbled away! Selah.

Oh do not weep,
Soft hearts!
Do not weep, you

Date hearts! Milk bosoms!
You little licorice
Heart-sacs!
Weep no more,
Pale Dudu!
Be a man, Suleika! Courage! Courage!
Or should
Something invigorating, heart-invigorating
Be appropriate here?
An unctuous maxim?
A solemn exhortation?

Hah! Come up, dignity!
Virtuous dignity! European dignity!
Blow, blow again,
Bellows of virtue!
Hah!
Once more roar,
Roar morally!
As a moral lion
Roar before the daughters of the wilderness!
For virtuous howling,
My most charming girls,
Is more than anything else
European fervor, European ravenous hunger.
And there I stand even now
As a European;
I cannot do else; God help me!
Amen.

*Wilderness grows: woe unto him that harbors wilder-
nesses!*

THE AWAKENING

1

After the song of the wanderer and shadow, the cave all at once became full of noise and laughter; and since all of the assembled guests talked at the same time and even the ass, thus encouraged, would no longer remain silent, Zarathustra was overcome by a slight aversion and by scorn for his company, although he enjoyed their gaiety. For this seemed to him a sign of convalescence. So he slipped out into the open and talked to his animals.

"Where is their distress now?" he said, and immediately he felt relief from his own little annoyance. "Up here with me, it seems, they have unlearned crying in distress. Although unfortunately not yet crying in general." And Zarathustra covered up his ears, for just then the Yeah-Yuh of the ass was strangely blended with the jubilating noise of these higher men.

"They are merry," he began again, "and, who knows? perhaps at their host's expense. And if they learned to laugh from me, it still is not *my* laughter that they have learned. But what does it matter? They are old people, convalescing in their own way, laughing in their own way; my ears have suffered worse things without becoming grumpy. This day represents a triumph: he is even now retreating, he is fleeing, *the spirit of gravity,* my old archenemy. How happily this day wants to end after beginning so badly and gravely. And it *wants* to end. Even now evening is approaching: he is riding over the sea, this good rider. How the blessed one, returning home, sways in his crimson saddle! The sky looks clear, the world lies deep: O all you strange visitors, living with me is well worth while!"

Thus spoke Zarathustra. And again the clamor and laughter of the higher men came to him from the cave, so he began again: "They are biting, my bait is working: from them too their enemy retreats, the spirit of gravity. Even now they have learned to laugh at themselves: do I hear right? My virile nourishment, the savor and strength of my words, are taking effect; and verily, I did not feed them bloating vegetables, but warriors' nourishment, conquerors' nourishment: I wakened new desires. New hopes throb in their arms and legs; their hearts stretch out. They are finding new words, soon their spirit will breathe prankishness. Such nourishment, to be sure, may not be suitable for children or for nostalgic old and young little females. Their entrails are persuaded in a different way; I am not their physician and teacher.

"Nausea is retreating from these higher men. Well then! That is my triumph. In my realm they feel safe, all stupid shame runs away, they unburden themselves. They unburden their hearts, good hours come back to them, they celebrate and chew the cud: they become grateful. *This* I take to be the best sign: they become grateful. Not much longer, and they will think up festivals and put up monuments to their old friends. They are convalescing!" Thus spoke Zarathustra gaily to his heart, and he looked out; but his animals pressed close to him and respected his happiness and his silence.

2

Suddenly, however, Zarathustra's ears were startled; for the cave which had so far been full of noise and laughter suddenly became deathly still, while his nose perceived a pleasant smoke and incense, as of burning pine cones. "What is going on? What are they doing?"

he asked himself, and he stole to the entrance to watch his guests, unnoticed. But, wonder upon wonder! What did he have to see with his own eyes?

"They have all become pious again, they are praying, they are mad!" he said, and he was amazed beyond measure. And indeed, all these higher men, the two kings, the retired pope, the wicked magician, the voluntary beggar, the wanderer and shadow, the old soothsayer, the conscientious in spirit, and the ugliest man— they were all kneeling like children and devout little old women and adoring the ass. And just then the ugliest man began to gurgle and snort as if something inexpressible wanted to get out of him; but when he really found words, behold, it was a pious, strange litany to glorify the adored and censed ass. And this litany went thus:

Amen! And praise and honor and wisdom and thanks and glory and strength be to our god, from everlasting to everlasting!

But the ass brayed: Yea-Yuh.

He carries our burden, he took upon himself the form of a servant, he is patient of heart and never says No; and whoever loves his God, chastises him.

But the ass brayed: Yea-Yuh.

He does not speak, except he always says Yea to the world he created: thus he praises his world. It is his cleverness that does not speak: thus he is rarely found to be wrong.

But the ass brayed: Yea-Yuh.

Plain-looking, he walks through the world. Gray is the body color in which he shrouds his virtue. If he has spirit, he hides it; but everybody believes in his long ears.

But the ass brayed: Yea-Yuh.

What hidden wisdom it is that he has long ears and only says Yea and never No! Has he not created the world in his own image, namely, as stupid as possible?

But the ass brayed: Yea-Yuh.

You walk on straight and crooked paths; it matters little to you what seems straight or crooked to us men. Beyond good and evil is your kingdom. It is your innocence not to know what innocence is.

But the ass brayed: Yea-Yuh.

Behold how you push none away from you, not the beggars nor the kings. Little children you let come unto you, and when sinners entice you, you simply say Yea-Yuh.

But the ass brayed: Yea-Yuh.

You love she-asses and fresh figs; you do not despise food. A thistle tickles your heart if you happen to be hungry. In this lies the wisdom of a god.

But the ass brayed: Yea-Yuh.

THE ASS FESTIVAL

1

At this point of the litany Zarathustra could no longer control himself and himself shouted Yea-Yuh, even louder than the ass, and he jumped right into the middle of his guests, who had gone mad. "But what are you doing there, children of men?" he cried as he pulled the praying men up from the floor. "Alas, if someone other than Zarathustra had watched you! Everyone would judge that with your new faith you were the worst blasphemers or the most foolish of all little old women.

"And you too, old pope, how do you reconcile this with yourself that you adore an ass in this way as a god?"

"O Zarathustra," replied the pope, "forgive me, but

in what pertains to God I am even more enlightened than you. And that is proper. Better to adore God in this form than in no form at all! Think about this maxim, my noble friend: you will quickly see that there is wisdom in such a maxim.

"He who said, 'God is a spirit,' took the biggest step and leap to disbelief that anybody has yet taken on earth: such a saying can hardly be redressed on earth. My old heart leaps and jumps that there is still something on earth to adore. Forgive, O Zarathustra, an old pious pope's heart!"

"And you," Zarathustra said to the wanderer and shadow, "you call and consider yourself a free spirit? And you go in for such idolatry and popery? You are behaving even more wickedly, verily, than with your wicked brown girls, you wicked new believer."

"Wickedly enough," replied the wanderer and shadow; "you are right: but is it my fault? The old god lives again, Zarathustra, you may say what you will. It is all the fault of the ugliest man: he has awakened him again. And when he says that he once killed him—in the case of gods *death* is always a mere prejudice."

"And you," said Zarathustra, "you wicked old magician, what have you done? Who should henceforth believe in you in this free age, if *you* believe in such theoasininities? It was a stupidity that you committed; how could you, you clever one, commit such a stupidity?"

"O Zarathustra," replied the clever magician, "you are right, it was a stupidity; and it was hard enough for me too."

"And you of all people," said Zarathustra to the conscientious in spirit, "consider with a finger alongside your nose: doesn't anything here go against your conscience? Is your spirit not too clean for such praying and the haze of these canters?"

"There is something in this," replied the conscientious man, placing a finger alongside his nose; "there is something in this spectacle that even pleases my conscience. Perhaps I may not believe in God; but it is certain that God seems relatively most credible to me in this form. God is supposed to be eternal, according to the witness of the most pious: whoever has that much time, takes his time. As slowly and as stupidly as possible: in *this* way, one like that can still get very far.

"And whoever has too much spirit might well grow foolishly fond of stupidity and folly itself. Think about yourself, O Zarathustra! You yourself—verily, overabundance and wisdom could easily turn you too into an ass. Is not the perfect sage fond of walking on the most crooked ways? The evidence shows this, O Zarathustra—and *you* are the evidence."

"And you yourself, finally," said Zarathustra, turning to the ugliest man, who still lay on the ground, and raising his arm toward the ass (for he was offering him wine to drink). "Speak, you inexpressible one, what have you done? You seem changed to me, your eyes are glowing, the cloak of the sublime lies over your ugliness: *what* have you done? Is it true what they say, that you have wakened him again? And why? Had he not been killed and finished for a reason? You yourself seem awakened to me: what have you done? Why did *you* revert? Why did *you* convert yourself? Speak, you inexpressible one!"

"O Zarathustra," replied the ugliest man, "you are a rogue! Whether that one *still* lives or lives again or is thoroughly dead—which of the two of us knows that best? I ask you. But one thing I do know; it was from you yourself that I learned it once, O Zarathustra: whoever would kill most thoroughly, *laughs.*

" 'Not by wrath does one kill, but by laughter'—thus

you once spoke. O Zarathustra, you hidden one, you annihilator without wrath, you dangerous saint—you are a rogue!"

2

But then it happened that Zarathustra, amazed at all these roguish answers, jumped back toward the door of his cave and, turning against all his guests, cried out with a strong voice:

"O you roguish fools, all of you, you jesters! Why do you dissemble and hide before me? How all your hearts wriggled with pleasure and malice that at last you had become again as little children, that is, pious; that at last you did again what children do, namely, prayed, folded your hands, and said, 'Dear God!' But now leave *this* nursery, my own cave, where all childishness is at home today! Cool your hot children's prankishness and the noise of your hearts out there!

"To be sure: except ye become as little children, ye shall not enter into *that* kingdom of heaven. (And Zarathustra pointed upward with his hands.) But we have no wish whatever to enter into the kingdom of heaven: we have become men—*so we want the earth.*"

3

And yet once more Zarathustra began to speak. "O my new friends," he said, "you strange higher men, how well I like you now since you have become gay again. Verily, you have all blossomed; it seems to me such flowers as you are require *new festivals*, a little brave nonsense, some divine service and ass festival, some old gay fool of a Zarathustra, a roaring wind that blows your souls bright.

"Do not forget this night and this ass festival, you higher men. *This* you invented when you were with me and I take that for a good sign: such things are invented only by convalescents.

"And when you celebrate it again, this ass festival, do it for your own sakes, and also do it for my sake. And in remembrance of *me*."

Thus spoke Zarathustra.

THE DRUNKEN SONG

1

Meanwhile one after the other had stepped out into the open and into the cool reflective night; but Zarathustra himself led the ugliest man by the hand to show him his night-world and the big round moon and the silvery waterfalls near his cave. There they stood together at last in silence, old people all of them, but with comforted brave hearts and secretly amazed at feeling so well on this earth; but the secrecy of the night came closer and closer to their hearts. And again Zarathustra thought to himself: "How well I like them now, these higher men!" But he did not say it out loud, for he respected their happiness and their silence.

But then that happened which, on that whole long amazing day, was the most amazing thing of all: the ugliest man began once more and for the last time to gurgle and snort, and when he found words, behold, a question jumped out of his mouth, round and clean, a good, deep, clear question, which moved the hearts of all who were listening to him.

"My friends, all of you," said the ugliest man, "what do you think? For the sake of this day, *I* am for the first time satisfied that I have lived my whole life. And that I attest so much is still not enough for me. Living on earth is worth while: one day, one festival with Zarathustra, taught me to love the earth.

" 'Was *that* life?' I want to say to death. 'Well then! Once more!'

"My friends, what do you think? Do you not want to say to death as I do: Was *that* life? For Zarathustra's sake! Well then! Once more!"

Thus spoke the ugliest man; but it was not long before midnight. And what do you suppose happened then? As soon as the higher men had heard his question they all at once became conscious of how they had changed and convalesced and to whom they owed this: then they jumped toward Zarathustra to thank, revere, caress him, and kiss his hands, each according to his own manner; and some were laughing and some were crying. But the old soothsayer was dancing with joy; and even if, as some of the chroniclers think, he was full of sweet wine, he was certainly still fuller of the sweetness of life and he had renounced all weariness. There are even some who relate that the ass danced too, and that it had not been for nothing that the ugliest man had given him wine to drink before. Now it may have been so or otherwise; and if the ass really did not dance that night, yet greater and stranger wonders occurred than the dancing of an ass would have been. In short, as the proverb of Zarathustra says: "What does it matter?"

2

But when this happened to the ugliest man, Zarathustra stood there like a drunkard: his eyes grew dim, his tongue failed, his feet stumbled. And who could guess what thoughts were then running over Zarathustra's soul? But his spirit fled visibly and flew ahead and was in remote distances and, as it were, "on a high ridge," as it is written, "between two seas, wandering like a heavy cloud between past and future." But as the higher men held him in their arms, he gradually recovered his senses to some extent and with his hands warded off the throng of the revering and worried; yet he did not speak. All at once, however, he turned his head quickly, for he seemed to be hearing something. Then he put one finger to his mouth and said, *"Come!"*

And presently it became quiet and secret around; but from the depth the sound of a bell came up slowly. Zarathustra and the higher men listened for it; but then he put one finger to his mouth another time and said again, *"Come! Come! Midnight approaches."* And his voice had changed. But still he did not stir from his place. Then it grew still more quiet and secret, and everything listened, even the ass and Zarathustra's animals of honor, the eagle and the serpent, as well as Zarathustra's cave and the big cool moon and the night itself. But Zarathustra put his hand to his mouth, for the third time and said, *"Come! Come! Let us wander now! The hour has come: let us wander into the night!"*

3

You higher men, midnight approaches: I want to whisper something to you as that old bell whispers it into my ears—as secretly, as terribly, as cordially as that midnight bell, which has experienced more than any man, says it to me. It has counted the beats even of your fathers' hearts and smarts. Alas! Alas! How it sighs! How it laughs in a dream! Old deep, deep midnight!

Still! Still! Here things are heard that by day may not become loud; but now in the cool air, when all the noise of your hearts too has become still—now it speaks, now it is heard, now it steals into nocturnal, overawake souls. Alas! Alas! How it sighs! How it laughs in a dream!

Do you not hear how it speaks secretly, terribly, cordially to *you*—the old deep, deep midnight?

O man, take care!

4

Woe unto me! Where is time gone? Have I not sunk into deep wells? The world sleeps. Alas! Alas! The dog howls, the moon shines. Sooner would I die, die rather than tell you what my midnight heart thinks now.

Now I have died. It is gone. Spider, what do you spin around me? Do you want blood? Alas! Alas! The dew falls, the hour approaches—the hour when I shiver and freeze, which asks and asks and asks, "Who has heart enough for it? Who shall be the lord of the earth? Who will say: thus shall you run, you big and little rivers!" The hour approaches: O man, you higher man, take care! This speech is for delicate ears, for your ears: *What does the deep midnight declare?*

5

I am carried away, my soul dances. Day's work! Day's work! Who shall be the lord of the earth?

The moon is cool, the wind is silent. Alas! Alas! Have you flown high enough yet? You have danced: but a leg is no wing. You good dancers, now all pleasure is gone: wine has become lees, every cup has become brittle, the tombs stammer. You did not fly high enough: now the tombs stammer, "Redeem the dead! Why does the night last so long? Does not the moon make us drunken?"

You higher men, redeem the tombs, awaken the corpses! Alas, why does the worm still burrow? The hour approaches, approaches; the bell hums, the heart still rattles, the deathwatch, the heart-worm still burrows. Alas! Alas! *The world is deep.*

6

Sweet lyre! Sweet lyre! I love your sound, your drunken ranunculus' croaking. From how long ago, from how far away your sound comes to me, from the distant ponds of love! You old bell, you sweet lyre! Every pain has torn into your heart, father-pain, fathers' pain, fore-fathers' pain; your speech grew ripe—ripe as golden autumn and afternoon, as my hermit's heart; now you say: the world itself has grown ripe, the grape is turning brown, now it would die, die of happiness. You higher men, do you not smell it? A smell is secretly welling up, a fragrance and smell of eternity, a rose-blessed, brown gold-wine fragrance of old happiness, of the drunken happiness of dying at midnight, that sings: the world is deep, *deeper than day had been aware.*

7

Leave me! Leave me! I am too pure for you. Do not touch me! Did not my world become perfect just now? My skin is too pure for your hands. Leave me, you stupid, boorish, dumb day! Is not the midnight brighter? The purest shall be the lords of the earth—the most unknown, the strongest, the midnight souls who are brighter and deeper than any day.

O day, you grope for me? You seek my happiness? I seem rich to you, lonely, a treasure pit, a gold-chamber? O world, you want me? Am I worldly to you? Am I spiritual to you? Am I godlike to you? But day and world, you are too ponderous; have cleverer hands, reach for deeper happiness, for deeper unhappiness, reach for any god, do not reach for me: my unhappiness, my happiness is deep, you strange day, but I am yet no god, no god's hell: *deep is its woe.*

8

God's woe is deeper, you strange world! Reach for God's woe, not for me! What am I? a drunken sweet lyre—a midnight lyre, an ominous bell-frog that nobody understands but that *must* speak, before the deaf, you higher men. For you do not understand me!

Gone! Gone! O youth! O noon! O afternoon! Now evening has come and night and midnight—the dog howls, the wind: is not the wind a dog? It whines, it yelps, it howls. Alas! Alas! How the midnight sighs! How it laughs, how it rattles and wheezes!

How she speaks soberly now, this drunken poetess! Perhaps she overdrank her drunkenness? She became overawake? She ruminates? Her woe she ruminates in a dream, the old deep midnight, and even more her joy. For joy, even if woe is deep, *joy is deeper yet than agony.*

9

You vine! Why do you praise me? Did I not cut you? I am cruel, you bleed; what does your praise of my drunken cruelty mean?

"What has become perfect, all that is ripe—wants to die"—thus you speak. Blessed, blessed be the vintager's knife! But all that is unripe wants to live: woe!

Woe entreats: Go! Away, woe! But all that suffers wants to live, that it may become ripe and joyous and longing—longing for what is farther, higher, brighter. "I want heirs"—thus speaks all that suffers; "I want children, I do not want *myself*."

Joy, however, does not want heirs, or children—joy wants itself, wants eternity, wants recurrence, wants everything eternally the same.

Woe says, "Break, bleed, heart! Wander, leg! Wing,

fly! Get on! Up! Pain!" Well then, old heart: *Woe implores, "Go!"*

10

You higher men, what do you think? Am I a soothsayer? A dreamer? A drunkard? An interpreter of dreams? A midnight bell? A drop of dew? A haze and fragrance of eternity? Do you not hear it? Do you not smell it? Just now my world became perfect; midnight too is noon; pain too is a joy; curses too are a blessing; night too is a sun—go away or you will learn: a sage too is a fool.

Have you ever said Yes to a single joy? O my friends, then you said Yes too to *all* woe. All things are entangled, ensnared, enamored; if ever you wanted one thing twice, if ever you said, "You please me, happiness! Abide, moment!" then you wanted *all* back. All anew, all eternally, all entangled, ensnared, enamored—oh, then you *loved* the world. Eternal ones, love it eternally and evermore; and to woe too, you say: go, but return! *For all joy wants—eternity.*

11

All joy wants the eternity of all things, wants honey, wants lees, wants drunken midnight, wants tombs, wants tomb-tears' comfort, wants gilded evening glow.

What does joy not want? It is thirstier, more cordial, hungrier, more terrible, more secret than all woe; it wants *itself*, it bites into *itself*, the ring's will strives in it; it wants love, it wants hatred, it is overrich, gives, throws away, begs that one might take it, thanks the taker, it would like to be hated; so rich is joy that it thirsts for woe, for hell, for hatred, for disgrace, for the cripple, for *world*—this world, oh, you know it!

You higher men, for you it longs, joy, the intractable

blessed one—for your woe, you failures. All eternal joy longs for failures. For all joy wants itself, hence it also wants agony. O happiness, O pain! Oh, break, heart! You higher men, do learn this, joy wants eternity. Joy wants the eternity of *all* things, *wants deep, wants deep eternity.*

12

Have you now learned my song? Have you guessed its intent? Well then, you higher men, sing me now my round. Now you yourselves sing me the song whose name is "Once More" and whose meaning is "into all eternity"—sing, you higher men, Zarathustra's round!

> O man, take care!
> What does the deep midnight declare?
> "I was asleep—
> From a deep dream I woke and swear:
> The world is deep,
> Deeper than day had been aware.
> Deep is its woe;
> Joy—deeper yet than agony:
> Woe implores: Go!
> But all joy wants eternity—
> Wants deep, wants deep eternity."

THE SIGN

In the morning after this night, Zarathustra jumped up from his resting place, girded his loins, and came out of his cave glowing and strong as a morning sun that comes out of dark mountains.

"You great star," he said as he had said once before, "you deep eye of happiness, what would your happiness be had you not those for whom you shine? And if they stayed in their chambers even after you had awakened and come and given and distributed, how angry would your proud shame be!

"Well then, they still sleep, these higher men, while *I* am awake: *these* are not my proper companions. It is not for them that I wait here in my mountains. I want to go to my work, to my day: but they do not understand the signs of my morning; my stride is for them no summons to awaken. They still sleep in my cave, their dream still drinks of my drunken songs. The ear that listens for *me*, the *heedful* ear is lacking in their limbs."

Thus had Zarathustra spoken to his heart when the sun rose; then he looked questioning into the height, for he heard the sharp cry of his eagle above him. "Well then!" he cried back; "thus it pleases and suits me. My animals are awake, for I am awake. My eagle is awake and honors the sun as I do. With eagle talons he grasps for the new light. You are the right animals for me; I love you. But I still lack the right men."

Thus spoke Zarathustra. But then it happened that he suddenly heard himself surrounded as by innumerable swarming and fluttering birds: but the whirring of so many wings and the thronging about his head were so great that he closed his eyes. And verily, like a cloud it came over him, like a cloud of arrows that empties itself over a new enemy. But behold, here it was a cloud of love, and over a new friend.

"What is happening to me?" thought Zarathustra in his surprised heart, and slowly he sat down on the big stone that lay near the exit of his cave. But as he reached out with his hands around and over and under himself, warding off the affectionate birds, behold, something stranger yet happened to him: for unwittingly he reached into a thick warm mane; and at the same time he heard a roar in front of him—a soft, long lion roar.

"*The sign is at hand,*" said Zarathustra, and a change came over his heart. And indeed, as it became light before him, a mighty yellow animal lay at his feet and pressed its head against his knees and out of love did not want to let go of him, and acted like a dog that finds its old master again. But the doves were no less eager in their love than the lion; and whenever a dove slipped over the lion's nose, the lion shook its head and was amazed and laughed.

About all this Zarathustra spoke but a single sentence: "*My children are near, my children.*" Then he became entirely silent. But his heart was loosed, and tears dropped from his eyes and fell on his hands. And he no longer heeded anything and sat there motionless, without warding off the animals any more. Then the doves flew about and sat on his shoulders and caressed his white hair and did not weary of tenderness and jubilation. But the strong lion kept licking up the tears that fell on Zarathustra's hands and roared and growled bashfully. Thus acted these animals.

All this lasted a long time, or a short time: for properly speaking, there is *no* time on earth for such things. But meanwhile the higher men in Zarathustra's cave had awakened and arranged themselves in a procession to meet Zarathustra and bid him good morning; for they had found when they awakened that he was no longer among them. But when they reached the door of the cave and the sound of their steps ran ahead of them, the lion started violently, turned away from Zarathustra suddenly, and jumped toward the cave, roaring savagely. But when the higher men heard it roar, they all cried out as with a single mouth, and they fled back and disappeared in a flash.

Zarathustra himself, however, dazed and strange, rose from his seat, looked around, stood there amazed, questioned his heart, reflected, and was alone. "What did I hear?" he finally said slowly; "what happened to me just now?" And presently memory came to him and with a single glance he grasped everything that had happened between yesterday and today. "Here is the stone," he said, stroking his beard, "where I sat yesterday morning; and here the soothsayer came to me, and here I first heard the cry which I heard just now, the great cry of distress.

"O you higher men, it was *your* distress that this old soothsayer prophesied to me yesterday morning; to your distress he wanted to seduce and tempt me. O Zarathustra, he said to me, I come to seduce you to your final sin.

"To my final sin?" shouted Zarathustra, and he laughed angrily at his own words; "*what* was it that was saved up for me as my final sin?"

And once more Zarathustra became absorbed in himself, and he sat down again on the big stone and reflected. Suddenly he jumped up. "Pity! Pity for the higher man!" he cried out, and his face changed to bronze. "Well then, *that* has had its time! My suffering and my pity for suffering—what does it matter? Am I concerned with *happiness?* I am concerned with my *work*.

"Well then! The lion came, my children are near, Zarathustra has ripened, my hour has come: this is *my* morning, *my* day is breaking: *rise now, rise, thou great noon!*"

Thus spoke Zarathustra, and he left his cave, glowing and strong as a morning sun that comes out of dark mountains.

Note (1884)[1]

. . . The degeneration of rulers and of the ruling classes has made for the greatest mischief in history. Without the Roman Caesars and Roman society, the insanity of Christianity would never have come to rule.

When the lesser men begin to doubt whether there are higher men, then the danger is great. . . . When Nero and Caracalla sat up there, the paradox originated that "the lowest man is worth more than that man up there." And an image of God was spread which was as far removed as possible from the image of the most powerful—the god on the cross. . . .

Letters

TO OVERBECK

Sils Maria, September 14, 1884

. . . This is the mistake which I seem to make eternally, that I imagine the sufferings of others as far greater than they really are. Ever since my childhood, the proposition "my greatest dangers lie in pity" has been confirmed again and again. . . .

Nizza, December 22, 1884

. . . I am having translated into German for me (in writing) a longish essay by Emerson, which gives some clarity about his development. If you want it, it is at your disposal and your wife's. I do not know how much I would give if only I could bring it about, *ex post facto,*

[1] Published as section 874 of *The Will to Power* by Nietzsche's executors.

that such a glorious, great nature, rich in soul and spirit, might have gone through some *strict* discipline, a really *scientific education.* As it is, in Emerson we have *lost a philosopher.* . . .

TO HIS SISTER

Nizza, March 1885

. . . It seems to me that a human being with the very best of intentions can do immeasurable harm, if he is immodest enough to wish to profit those whose spirit and will are concealed from him. . . .

TO OVERBECK

Sils Maria, July 2, 1885

. . . I hold up before myself the images of Dante and Spinoza, who were better at accepting the lot of solitude. Of course, their way of thinking, compared to mine, was one which made solitude bearable; and in the end, for all those who somehow still had a "God" for company, what *I* experience as "solitude" really did not yet exist. My life now consists in the wish that it might be otherwise with all things than I comprehend, and that somebody might make *my* "truths" appear incredible to me. . . .

NOTES

Rule? Press my type on others? Dreadful. Is not·my happiness precisely the sight of many who are *different?* Problem. (xiv, 126)

※※

The will to a *system:* in a philosopher, morally speaking, a subtle corruption, a disease of the character;

amorally speaking, his will to pose as more stupid than he is—more stupid, that means: stronger, simpler, more commanding, less educated, more masterful, more tyrannical.   (XIV, 313)

∷∷

Being nationalistic in the sense in which it is now demanded by public opinion would, it seems to me, be for us who are more spiritual not mere insipidity but dishonesty, a deliberate deadening of our better will and conscience.   (XIV, 332)

From a Draft for a Preface

Fall of 1885

THE WILL TO POWER

A book for *thinking*, nothing else: it belongs to those to whom thinking is a *delight*, nothing else. That it is written in German is untimely, to say the least: I wish I had written it in French so that it might not appear to be a confirmation of the aspirations of the German *Reich*. The Germans of today are not thinkers any more: something else delights and impresses them. The will to power as a principle might be intelligible to them. Among Germans today the least thinking is done. But who knows? In two generations one will no longer require the sacrifice involved in any nationalistic squandering of power, and in hebetation. (Formerly, I wished I had not written my *Zarathustra* in German.)

FROM
Beyond Good and Evil

EDITOR'S NOTE

First published in 1886, aphoristic in appearance, this book
is more continuous than it seems at first glance.

[52]

In the Jewish "Old Testament," the book of divine
justice, there are men, things, and speeches in so grand
a style that Greek and Indian literature have nothing
to compare with it. One stands in awe and reverence
before these tremendous remnants of what man once
was, and sad thoughts come to one about ancient Asia
and its jutting peninsula, Europe, which wants so definitely to signify, as against Asia, the "progress of man."
Of course, those who are merely wretched tame domestic
animals and know only the wants of domestic animals
(like our cultivated people of today, including the
Christians of "cultivated" Christianity) need neither be
amazed nor even sorry when faced with these ruins: the
taste for the Old Testament is a touchstone of "greatness" and "smallness." Perhaps they will even find the
New Testament, the book of grace, more to their taste (it
is full of the odor of the real, effeminate, stupid canter
and petty soul). To have glued this New Testament, a
kind of rococo of taste in every respect, to the Old
Testament to form one book—the "Bible," *the* book—
that is perhaps the greatest audacity and "sin against
the spirit" which literary Europe has on its conscience.

[75]

The degree and kind of a person's sexuality reach up into the ultimate pinnacle of his spirit.

[126]

A people is nature's detour to arrive at six or seven great men—and then to get around them.

[153]

What is done out of love always occurs beyond good and evil.

[164]

Jesus said to his Jews: "The law was for servants; love God as I love him, as his son. What are morals to us sons of God?"

[212]

It seems to me more and more that the philosopher, as a *necessary* man of tomorrow and the day after tomorrow, has always found himself, and always had to find himself, in opposition to his today: the ideal of the day was always his enemy. Hitherto all these extraordinary promoters of man, who are called philosophers, and who rarely have felt themselves to be friends of wisdom, but rather disagreeable fools and dangerous question marks, have found their task, their hard, unwanted, inescapable task, but finally also the greatness of their task, in being the bad conscience of their time. By applying the knife vivisectionally to the very *virtues of the time* they betrayed their own secret: to know of a *new* greatness of man, of a new untrodden way to his enhancement. Each time they have uncovered how much hypocrisy, comfortableness, letting oneself go and letting oneself drop, how many lies, were concealed under the most honored type of their contemporary morality, how much virtue was *outlived*. Each time they said: "We must proceed there, that way, where today you are least at home."

Confronted with a world of "modern ideas," which would banish everybody into a corner and a "specialty," a philosopher—if there could be any philosophers today—would be forced to define the greatness of man, the concept of "greatness," in terms precisely of man's comprehensiveness and multiplicity, his wholeness in manifoldness: he would even determine worth and rank according to how much and how many things a person could bear and take upon himself, how far a person could extend his responsibility. Today the taste and virtue of the time weaken and thin out the will; nothing is more timely than weakness of the will. Therefore, according to the philosopher's ideal, it is precisely strength of will, hardness, and the capacity for long-range decisions which must form part of the concept of "greatness"—with as much justification as the opposite doctrine, and the ideal of a dumb, renunciatory, humble, selfless humanity, was suitable for an opposite age, one which, like the sixteenth century, suffered from its accumulated will power and the most savage floods and tidal waves of selfishness.

At the time of Socrates, among men of fatigued instincts, among the conservatives of ancient Athens who let themselves go—"for happiness," as they said; for pleasure, as they behaved—and who at the same time still used the old ornate words to which their life had long ceased to entitle them, *irony* was perhaps necessary for greatness of soul—that Socratic sarcastic assurance of the old physician and plebeian who cut ruthlessly into his own flesh, as well as into the flesh and heart of the "nobility," with a glance that said unmistakably: "Don't try to deceive me by dissimulation. Here we are equal."

Today, conversely, when only the herd animal is honored and dispenses honors in Europe, and when "equality of rights" could all too easily be converted into an equality in violating rights—by that I mean, into a common war on all that is rare, strange, or privileged, on the higher man, the higher soul, the higher duty, the higher responsibility, and on the wealth of creative power and mastery—today the concept of "greatness" entails being noble, wanting to be by oneself, being capable of being different, standing alone, and having to live independently; and the philosopher will betray something of his own ideal when he posits: "He shall be the greatest who can be the loneliest, the most hidden, the most deviating, the human being beyond good and evil, the master of his virtues, he that is overrich in will. Precisely this should be called *greatness*: to be capable of being as manifold as whole, as wide as full." And to ask this once more: today—is greatness *possible?*

[230]

. . . The commanding something, which the people call "spirit," wants to be master over itself and its surroundings and to feel its mastery: it has the will from multiplicity to simplicity—a will that would tie together, harness, be master, and that really is masterly. Its needs and capacities are thus the same as those the physiologists find in everything that lives, grows, and reproduces. The power of the spirit to appropriate what is foreign manifests itself in a strong tendency to assimilate the new to the old, to simplify the manifold. . . .

FROM
The Gay Science: Book V

EDITOR'S NOTE

Book V was added to the second edition in 1887.

[343]

The background of our cheerfulness. The greatest
recent event—that "God is dead," that the belief in the
Christian God has ceased to be believable—is even now
beginning to cast its first shadows over Europe. For the
few, at least, whose eyes, whose *suspicion* in their eyes,
is strong and sensitive enough for this spectacle, some
sun seems to have set just now. . . . In the main, however, this may be said: the event itself is much too great,
too distant, too far from the comprehension of the many
even for the tidings of it to be thought of as having
arrived yet, not to speak of the notion that many people
might know what has really happened here, and what
must collapse now that this belief has been undermined
—all that was built upon it, leaned on it, grew into it;
for example, our whole European morality. . . .

Even we born guessers of riddles who are, as it were,
waiting on the mountains, put there between today and
tomorrow and stretched in the contradiction between
today and tomorrow, we firstlings and premature births
of the coming century, to whom the shadows that must
soon envelop Europe really *should* have appeared by now
—why is it that even we look forward to it without any
real compassion for this darkening, and above all without any worry and fear for *ourselves?* Is it perhaps that

we are still too deeply impressed by the first consequences of this event—and these first consequences,
the consequences for *us*, are perhaps the reverse of
what one might expect: not at all sad and dark, but
rather like a new, scarcely describable kind of light,
happiness, relief, exhilaration, encouragement, dawn?
Indeed, we philosophers and "free spirits" feel as if a
new dawn were shining on us when we receive the tidings that "the old god is dead"; our heart overflows
with gratitude, amazement, anticipation, expectation. At
last the horizon appears free again to us, even granted
that it is not bright; at last our ships may venture out
again, venture out to face any danger; all the daring of
the lover of knowledge is permitted again; the sea, *our*
sea, lies open again; perhaps there has never yet been
such an "open sea."

[344]

How far we too are still pious. In science, convictions
have no rights of citizenship, as is said with good reason.
Only when they decide to descend to the modesty of a
hypothesis, of a provisional experimental point of view,
of a·regulative fiction, may they be granted admission
and even a certain value within the realm of knowledge
—though always with the restriction that they remain
under police supervision, under the police of mistrust.
But does this not mean, more precisely considered, that
a conviction may obtain admission to science only when
it *ceases* to be a conviction? Would not the discipline
of the scientific spirit begin with this, no longer to permit oneself any convictions? Probably that is how it is.
But one must still ask whether it is not the case that,
in order that this discipline could begin, a conviction
must have been there already, and even such a commanding and unconditional one that it sacrificed all

other convictions for its own sake. It is clear that science too rests on a faith; there is no science "without presuppositions." The question whether truth is needed must not only have been affirmed in advance, but affirmed to the extent that the principle, the faith, the conviction is expressed: "*nothing* is needed *more* than truth, and in relation to it everything else has only second-rate value."

This unconditional will to truth: what is it? . . . What do you know in advance of the character of existence, to be able to decide whether the greater advantage is on the side of the unconditionally mistrustful or of the unconditionally trusting? Yet if both are required, much trust *and* much mistrust: whence might science then take its unconditional faith, its conviction, on which it rests, that truth is more important than anything else, even than any other conviction? Just this conviction could not have come into being if both truth *and* untruth showed themselves to be continually useful, as is the case. Thus, though there undeniably exists a faith in science, it cannot owe its origin to such a utilitarian calculus but it must rather have originated *in spite* of the fact that the inutility and dangerousness of the "will to truth," of "truth at any price," are proved to it continually. . . .

Consequently, "will to truth" does *not* mean "I will not let myself be deceived" but—there is no choice—"I will not deceive, not even myself": *and with this we are on the ground of morality*. For one should ask oneself carefully: "Why don't you want to deceive?" especially if it should appear—and it certainly does appear—that life depends on appearance; I mean, on error, simulation, deception, self-deception; and when life has, as a matter of fact, always shown itself to be on the side of the most unscrupulous *polytropoi*. Such an intent, charitably interpreted, could perhaps be a quixotism, a little enthusiastic impudence; but it could also be something worse, namely, a destructive principle, hostile to life. "Will to truth"—that might be a concealed will to death.

Thus the question "Why science?" leads back to the moral problem, "For what end any morality at all" if life, nature, and history are "not moral"? . . . But one will have gathered what I am driving at, namely, that it always remains a *metaphysical faith* upon which our faith in science rests—that even we devotees of knowledge today, we godless ones and anti-metaphysicians, still take *our* fire too from the flame which a faith thousands of years old has kindled: that Christian faith, which was also Plato's faith, that God is truth, that truth is divine. . . .

FROM

Toward a Genealogy of Morals

EDITOR'S NOTE

This book of roughly two hundred pages was first published in 1887. It consists of three inquiries. The first, entitled "Good and Evil versus Good and Bad," contrasts "slave morality" and "master morality." The origin of the former is found in *ressentiment*. Nietzsche has reservations about "master morality" too, as he explains in the chapter on "The 'Improvers' of Mankind" in *The Twilight of the Idols*. The second inquiry has the title: "Guilt, Bad Conscience, and Related Matters." The third: "What is the Meaning of Ascetic Ideals?"

The decision to present in this volume, unabridged, Nietzsche's later works rather than his earliest efforts, and to represent his aphoristic books by selections, seemed obvious. The *Genealogy* is a late work and not aphoristic, but its major ideas, and much else too, will be gleaned from *Zarathustra* and the books of 1888 which are offered complete—and from the following selections which represent the core of each of the three inquiries.

GOOD AND EVIL VERSUS GOOD AND BAD

[10]

The slaves' revolt in morals begins with this, that *ressentiment* itself becomes creative and gives birth to values: the *ressentiment* of those who are denied the real reaction, that of the deed, and who compensate with an imaginary revenge. Whereas all noble morality grows out of a triumphant affirmation of oneself, slave morality immediately says No to what comes from outside, to what is different, to what is not oneself: and *this* No is its creative deed. This reversal of the value-positing glance—this *necessary* direction outward instead of back to oneself—is of the nature of *ressentiment:* to come into being, slave morality requires an outside world, a counterworld; physiologically speaking, it requires external stimuli in order to react at all: its action is at bottom always a reaction.

The reverse is true of the noble way of evaluating: it acts and grows spontaneously, it seeks out its opposite only in order to say Yes to itself still more gratefully, still more jubilantly; and its negative concept, "base," "mean," "bad," is only an after-born, pale, contrasting image in relation to the positive basic concept, which is nourished through and through with life and passion: "we who are noble, good, beautiful, happy!"

. . . To be unable to take one's own enemies, accidents, and misdeeds seriously for long—that is the sign of strong and rich natures. . . . Such a man simply shakes off with one shrug much vermin that would have buried itself deep in others; here alone is it also possible —assuming that it is possible at all on earth—that there be real "*love* of one's enemies." How much respect has a noble person for his enemies! And such respect is already a bridge to love. After all, he demands his enemy for himself, as his distinction; he can stand no enemy but one in whom there is nothing to be despised and *much* to be honored. Conversely, imagine "the enemy" as conceived by a man of *ressentiment*—and here precisely is his deed, his creation: he has conceived "the evil enemy," "*the evil one*"—and indeed as the fundamental concept from which he then derives, as an afterimage and counterinstance, a "good one"—himself.

GUILT, BAD CONSCIENCE, AND RELATED MATTERS

[12]

Let us add a word here concerning the origin and aim of punishment—two problems which are, or should be, distinct. Unfortunately, they are usually confounded. . . . For every kind of historiography there is no more important proposition than this, which has been discovered with so much effort, but now also ought to be discovered once and for all: the cause of the origin of a thing and its eventual usefulness, its actual employment and incorporation into a system of aims, lie worlds apart. . . .

[13]

To return to the subject, namely *punishment*, we must distinguish two things: first, the relatively *enduring* aspect, the custom, the act, the "drama," a certain strict succession of procedures; on the other hand, the fluid aspect, the meaning, the aim, the expectation which attends the execution of these procedures. . . . Today it is impossible to say definitely *why* punishment is meted out: all concepts in which a whole process is comprehended semeiotically, escape definition; only what has no history is definable. . . .

WHAT IS THE MEANING OF ASCETIC IDEALS?

[28]

Apart from the ascetic ideal, man—the animal, man —had no meaning hitherto. His existence on earth had no goal. "Why have man at all?" was a question without an answer. . . . Precisely this was the meaning of the ascetic ideal, that something was lacking, that a tremendous gap surrounded man: he did not know how to justify, explain, or affirm himself, he suffered from the problem of his meaning. He suffered in other ways too; he was in the main a *sickly* animal: yet suffering as such was not his problem, but that the answer was lacking to the cry of the question "*Why* suffer?" Man, as the animal that is most courageous, most accustomed to suffering, does not negate suffering as such: he *wants* it, even seeks it out, provided one shows him some *meaning* in it, some *wherefore* of suffering. The meaninglessness of suffering, not suffering itself, was the curse which hitherto lay spread out over mankind—*and the ascetic ideal offered mankind meaning.* So far it has been the only meaning; any meaning at all is better than no meaning at all; the ascetic ideal was in every respect the *faute de mieux* par excellence that we have had so far. Through this, suffering was *interpreted;* the tremendous emptiness seemed filled out; the door was closed to all suicidal nihilism. The interpretation undoubtedly involved new suffering, even more profound, more inward, more poisonous, that gnawed at life more: it

placed all suffering in the perspective of *guilt*. Yet
in spite of that—man was saved: he had a *meaning;*
henceforth he was no longer like a leaf in the wind,
a football of nonsense, of "no-sense"; he could now
want something—and to begin with, it mattered not
what, whereto, or how he wanted: *the will itself was
saved.* In the end, one can hardly conceal what it
was that this will really expressed when it received
its direction from the ascetic ideal: that hatred against
everything human, even more, against everything animal, everything material, this disgust with the senses,
with reason itself, this fear of happiness and beauty,
this desire to get away from all semblance, change,
becoming, death, wish, desire itself—the meaning of
all this, should we dare to comprehend it, is a *will to
nothingness*, a will running counter to life, a revolt
against the most fundamental presuppositions of life;
yet it is and remains a *will!* And, to repeat at the end
what I said in the beginning: rather than want nothing,
man even wants *nothingness*.

LETTER TO OVERBECK

Nizza, February 23, 1887
. . . I did not even know the name of Dostoevski just
a few weeks ago—uneducated person that I am, not
reading any journals. An accidental reach of the arm in
a bookstore brought to my attention *L'esprit souterrain*,
a work just translated into French. (It was a similar
accident with Schopenhauer in my 21st year and with
Stendhal in my 35th.) The instinct of kinship (or how
should I name it?) spoke up immediately; my joy was
extraordinary: I must go back all the way to my first
acquaintance with Stendhal's *Rouge et Noir* to remem-

ber an equal joy. (It is two novellas, the first really a
piece of music, *very* strange, very *un*-German music; the
second, a stroke of genius in psychology, a kind of self-
derision of the γνῶθι σαυτόν.[1]) Incidentally, these
Greeks have a lot on their conscience—falsification was
their true trade; the whole of European psychology is
sick with Greek *superficiality;* and without that little
bit of Judaism—etc., etc., etc. . . .

NOTES (1887)[2]

[484]

"There is thinking; consequently there is that which
thinks"—that is what Descartes' argument comes to.
Yet this means positing our faith in the concept of *substance* as "*a priori* true." When there is thinking, something must be there which thinks—that is merely a
formulation of our grammatical habit, which posits a
doer for what is done. . . .

[522]

. . . Rational thought is interpretation according to
a scheme which we cannot escape.

[776]

Concerning the "Machiavellism" of power. The will
to power manifests itself

(*a*) among the suppressed, among slaves of all kinds,
as a will to "freedom": merely to get away appears as

---

[1] "Know thyself!"
[2] Published as part of *The Will to Power* by Nietzsche's
executors.

the goal (morally and religiously: "responsible only to one's own conscience," "evangelical freedom," etc.);

(*b*) among a stronger type which is growing up to reach for power, as a will to overpower; if unsuccessful at first, it may then limit itself to a will to "justice," that is, to equal rights with the ruling type;

(*c*) among the strongest, richest, most independent, and most courageous as "love of humanity," of the "people," of the Gospel, of truth, of God; as pity, "self-sacrifice," etc. . . .

[893]

Hatred of mediocrity is unworthy of a philosopher: it is almost a question mark against his "*right* to philosophy." Just because he is the exception, he must protect the rule, and he must encourage self-confidence in all the mediocre.

[910]

Type of my disciples. To those human beings in whom I have a stake I wish suffering, being forsaken, sickness, maltreatment, humiliation—I wish that that profound self-contempt, the torture of mistrust of oneself, and the misery of him who is overcome, not remain unknown to them: I have no pity for them because I wish them the only thing which can prove today whether one has worth or not—that one holds out.

LETTER TO HIS SISTER

Christmas 1887

. . . You have committed one of the greatest stupidities—for yourself and for me! Your association with an anti-Semitic chief expresses a foreignness to my whole way of life which fills me again and again with ire or melancholy. . . . It is a matter of honor with me to be absolutely clean and unequivocal in relation to anti-Semitism, namely, *opposed* to it, as I am in my writings. I have recently been persecuted with letters and *Anti-Semitic Correspondence Sheets.* My disgust with this party (which would like the benefit of my name only too well!) is as pronounced as possible, but the relation to Förster,[1] as well as the aftereffects of my former publisher, the anti-Semitic Schmeitzner, always brings the adherents of this disagreeable party back to the idea that I must belong to them after all. . . . It arouses mistrust against my character, as if publicly I condemned something which I favored secretly—and that I am unable to do anything against it, that the name of Zarathustra is used in every *Anti-Semitic Correspondence Sheet,* has almost made me sick several times. . . .

Notes (1888)[2]

[291]

That the value of an act should depend on what preceded it in *consciousness*—how false that is! And yet morality has been measured that way, even criminality.

The value of an act must be measured by its consequences, the utilitarians say: measuring it by its origin implies an impossibility, namely, *knowing* the origin.

But does one know the consequences? Perhaps as far as five steps. Who could say what an act stimulates, excites, provokes against itself? As a stimulus? Perhaps

[1] Nietzsche's sister's husband.
[2] Published as part of *The Will to Power* by Nietzsche's executors.

as the ignition spark for an explosive? The utilitarians are naïve. And in the end we would first have to know what *is* useful: here too their vision extends for only five steps. They have no conception of any great economy which does not know how to dispense with evil. . . .

[481]

Against that positivism which stops before phenomena, saying "there are only *facts*," I should say: no, it is precisely facts that do not exist, only *interpretations*. . . .

[814]

Artists are *not* the men of *great* passion, whatever they may try to tell us and themselves. And that for two reasons: they have no shame before themselves (they observe themselves *while they live;* they lie in wait for themselves, they are too curious), and they also have no shame before great passion (they exploit it artistically). Secondly, their vampire—their talent—generally begrudges them any such squandering of energy as is involved in passion. With a talent, one is also the victim of that talent: one lives under the vampirism of one's talent.

One is not finished with one's passion because one represents it: rather, one is finished with it *when* one represents it. (Goethe teaches it differently; but it seems that here he wished to misunderstand himself—out of *delicatezza*.)

[882]

One recognizes the superiority of the Greek man, of the man of the Renaissance—but one would like to have it without its causes and conditions.

[1052]

. . . Dionysus versus "the Crucified One": there you have the contrast. It is not martyrdom that constitutes the difference—only here it has two different senses. Life itself, its eternal fruitfulness and recurrence, involves agony, destruction, the will to annihilation. In the other case, suffering—"the Crucified One as the Innocent One"—is considered an objection to this life, as the formula of its condemnation. Clearly, the problem is that of the meaning of suffering: whether a Christian meaning or a tragic meaning. In the first case, it is supposed to be the path to a sacred existence; in the second case, *existence is considered sacred enough* to justify even a tremendous amount of suffering. The tragic man affirms even the harshest suffering: he is sufficiently strong, rich, and deifying for this; the Christian negates even the happiest life on earth: he is sufficiently weak, poor, and disinherited to suffer from life in any form. The God on the cross is a curse on life, a pointer to seek redemption from it; Dionysus cut to pieces is a *promise* of life: it is eternally reborn and comes back from destruction.

FROM

The Wagner Case

EDITOR'S NOTE

An often very funny polemic of about fifty pages. The following excerpt is from section 3.

There is nothing on which Wagner has reflected so much as on redemption: his opera is the opera of

redemption. Somebody or other always wants to be redeemed: now a little man, now a little woman—that is
his problem. And how richly he varies his leitmotif!
What rare, what deeply thoughtful modulations! Who,
if not Wagner, would have taught us that innocence
prefers to redeem interesting sinners? (The case in
Tannhäuser.) Or that even the Wandering Jew is redeemed and settles down when he marries? (The case
in *The Flying Dutchman*.) Or that old corrupted
females prefer to be redeemed by chaste young men?
(The case of Kundry.) Or that beautiful girls like best
to be redeemed by a knight, who is a Wagnerian? (The
case in *Die Meistersinger*.) Or that even married women
like being redeemed by a knight? (The case of Isolde.)
Or that "the old god," after having compromised himself morally in every way, is finally redeemed by a free
spirit and immoralist? (The case in *The Ring*.) Admire
this last profundity in particular! Do you understand it?
I—beware of understanding it.

That there are also other teachings to be derived from
the works enumerated I would sooner prove than contest. That a Wagnerian ballet can drive one to despair—
and to virtue! (Again the case in *Tannhäuser*.) That
the worst consequences may ensue if one does not go
to bed at the right time. (Again the case in *Lohengrin*.)
That one should never know too precisely whom one
has really married. (For the third time, the case in
Lohengrin.)

Tristan and Isolde glorifies the perfect spouse who, in
a certain situation, has but one question: "But why
didn't you tell me that before? Nothing simpler than
that!" The answer:

> "That I may not tell you;
> And what you ask,
> That you may never know."

Lohengrin contains a solemn excommunication of inquiry and questioning. Wagner here advocates the Christian concept: "You shall and must have *faith*." It is a crime against the highest, the holiest, to be scientific.

The Flying Dutchman preaches the sublime doctrine that woman settles even the most unsettled man—in Wagnerian terms, she "redeems him." Here we permit ourselves a question: Suppose this were true—does that also make it desirable? What becomes of the eternal "Wandering Jew" whom a wife adores and settles? He merely ceases to be eternal; he gets married and does not concern us any more. . . .

TWILIGHT
OF THE IDOLS

OR,

HOW ONE PHILOSOPHIZES
WITH A HAMMER

EDITOR'S PREFACE

Nietzsche's last productive year, 1888, was also his most productive. He began with *The Wagner Case* and ended with *Nietzsche contra Wagner,* and in between he dashed off *Twilight of the Idols, The Antichrist,* and *Ecce Homo.* These books are sometimes dismissed as mere products of insanity, and they certainly manifest a rapid breakdown of the author's inhibitions. In some passages of *The Antichrist,* Nietzsche's fury breaks all dams; and the madness of his conceit in *Ecce Homo* is harnessed only by his matchless irony, though much of this is lost on readers who do not know Nietzsche's earlier works. Compared to such fireworks, *Twilight of the Idols* is relatively calm and sane, except for its title; and none of his other works contains an equally comprehensive summary of his later philosophy and psychology. With its roughly one hundred pages, the book furnishes a fine epitome of Nietzsche.

The spectacular title was an afterthought. Nietzsche had become interested in Francis Bacon, and his own discussion of "Four Great Errors" probably reminded him of Bacon's "Four Idols." Hence the thought of varying Wagner's title, *Götterdämmerung,* by coining *Götzen-Dämmerung,* "Twilight of the Idols." When he wrote the preface, however, the title was still to be *A Psychologist's Idleness*. But on September 20 his worshipful admirer Peter Gast wrote him a fateful letter. Gast's real name was Heinrich Köselitz. He was a composer, and he assisted Nietzsche by copying manuscripts and reading proofs. Having completed his first reading of this manuscript, he wrote: "The title, *A Psychologist's Idleness*, sounds too unassuming to me when I think how it might impress other people: you have driven your artillery on the highest mountains, you have such guns as have never yet existed, and you need only shoot blindly to inspire terror all around. The stride [*Gang*] of a giant, which makes the mountains shake to their foundations, is no longer idleness [*Müssiggang*]. . . . So I beg you, if an incompetent person may beg: a more sumptuous, more resplendent title!" Such adulatory flattery was surely what Nietzsche needed least just then. He changed the title and added as a subtitle: "How One Philosophizes With a Hammer." It is usually assumed that he means a sledge hammer. The preface, however, from which the image is derived as an afterthought, explains: idols "are here touched with a hammer as with a tuning fork."

This was the last work Nietzsche himself published: when it came out in January 1889, he was insane and no longer aware of any of his works. *The Antichrist* and *Nietzsche contra Wagner* were not published until 1895; *Ecce Homo* only in 1908.

CONTENTS

PREFACE

Maintaining cheerfulness in the midst of a gloomy affair, fraught with immeasurable responsibility, is no small feat; and yet what is needed more than cheerfulness? Nothing succeeds if prankishness has no part in it. Excess of strength alone is the proof of strength.

A *revaluation of all values,* this question mark, so black, so tremendous that it casts shadows upon the man who puts it down—such a destiny of a task compels one to run into the sun every moment to shake off a heavy, all-too-heavy seriousness. Every means is proper for this; every "case" [1] a case of luck. Especially, *war.* War has always been the great wisdom of all spirits who have become too inward, too profound; even in a wound there is the power to heal. A maxim, the origin of which I withhold from scholarly curiosity, has long been my motto:

Increscunt animi, virescit volnere virtus. [2]

Another mode of convalescence—under certain circumstances even more to my liking—is *sounding out idols.* There are more idols than realities in the world: that is *my* "evil eye" for this world; that is also my "evil *ear.*" For once to pose questions here with a *hammer,* and, perhaps, to hear as a reply that famous hollow sound which speaks of bloated entrails—what a delight for one who has ears even behind his ears, for

[1] An allusion to Nietzsche's *The Wagner Case* (1888), a polemic.
[2] "The spirits increase, vigor grows through a wound."

me, an old psychologist and pied piper before whom just that which would remain silent must become outspoken.

This essay too—the title betrays it—is above all a recreation, a spot of sunshine, a leap sideways into the idleness of a psychologist. Perhaps a new war, too? And are new idols sounded out? This little essay is a great declaration of war; and regarding the sounding out of idols, this time they are not just idols of the age, but eternal idols, which are here touched with a hammer as with a tuning fork: there are altogether no older, no more convinced, no more puffed-up idols—and none more hollow. That does not prevent them from being those in which people have the most faith; nor does one ever say "idol," especially not in the most distinguished instance.

Turin, September 30, 1888,
on the day when the first book[1] *of the* Revaluation of All Values *was completed.*

FRIEDRICH NIETZSCHE

MAXIMS AND ARROWS

1

Idleness is the beginning of all psychology. What? Should psychology be a vice?[2]

2

Even the most courageous among us only rarely has the courage for that which he really knows.

[1] That is, *The Antichrist.*
[2] There is a German proverb: "Idleness is the beginning of all vices."

3

To live alone one must be a beast or a god, says Aristotle. Leaving out the third case: one must be both —a philosopher.

4

"All truth is simple." Is that not doubly a lie?

5

I want, once and for all, *not* to know many things. Wisdom sets limits to knowledge too.

6

In our own wild nature we find the best recreation from our un-nature, from our spirituality.

7

What? Is man merely a mistake of God's? Or God merely a mistake of man's?

8

Out of life's school of war: What does not destroy me, makes me stronger.

9

Help yourself, then everyone will help you. Principle of neighbor-love.

10

Not to perpetrate cowardice against one's own acts! Not to leave them in the lurch afterward! The bite of conscience is indecent.

11

Can an *ass* be tragic? To perish under a burden one can neither bear nor throw off? The case of the philosopher.

12

If we have our own *why* of life, we shall get along with almost any *how*. Man does *not* strive for pleasure; only the Englishman does.

13

Man has created woman—out of what? Out of a rib of his god—of his "ideal."

14

What? You search? You would multiply yourself by ten, by a hundred? You seek followers? Seek *zeros!*

15

Posthumous men—I, for example—are understood worse than timely ones, but *heard* better. More precisely: we are never understood—*hence* our authority.

16

Among women: "Truth? Oh, you don't know truth! Is it not an attempt to assassinate all our *pudeurs?*"

17

That is an artist as I love artists, modest in his needs: he really wants only two things, his bread and his art —*panem et Circen.*[1]

[1] *panem et circenses,* "bread and circuses"—here changed by Nietzsche into "bread and Circe," art being compared to the Homeric sorceress.

18

Whoever does not know how to lay his will into things, at least lays some *meaning* into them: that means, he has the faith that they already obey a will. (Principle of "faith.")

19

What? You elected virtue and the swelled bosom and yet you leer enviously at the advantages of those without qualms? But virtue involves *renouncing* "advantages." (Inscription for an anti-Semite's door.)

20

The perfect woman perpetrates literature as she perpetrates a small sin: as an experiment, in passing, looking around to see if anybody notices it—and to make sure that somebody does.

21

To venture into all sorts of situations in which one may not have any sham virtues, where, like the tightrope walker on his rope, one either stands or falls—or gets away.

22

"Evil men have no songs." How is it, then, that the Russians have songs?

23

"German spirit": for the past eighteen years a contradiction in terms.

24

By searching out origins, one becomes a crab. The historian looks backward; eventually he also *believes* backward.

25

Contentment protects even against colds. Has a woman who knew herself to be well dressed ever caught cold? I am assuming that she was barely dressed.

26

I mistrust all systematizers and I avoid them. The will to a system is a lack of integrity.

27

Women are considered profound. Why? Because one never fathoms their depths. Women aren't even shallow.

28

If a woman has manly virtues, one feels like running away; and if she has no manly virtues, she herself runs away.

29

"How much conscience has had to chew on in the past! And what excellent teeth it had! And today—what is lacking?" A dentist's question.

30

One rarely rushes into a single error. Rushing into the first one, one always does too much. So one usually perpetrates another one—and now one does too little.

31

When stepped on, a worm doubles up. That is clever. In that way he lessens the probability of being stepped on again. In the language of morality: *humility.*

32

There is a hatred of lies and simulation, stemming from an easily provoked sense of honor. There is another such hatred, from cowardice, since lies are *forbidden* by a divine commandment. Too cowardly to lie.

33

How little is required for pleasure! The sound of a bagpipe. Without music, life would be an error. The German imagines even God singing songs.

34

On ne peut penser et écrire qu'assis[1] (G. Flaubert). There I have caught you, nihilist! The sedentary life is the very sin against the Holy Spirit. Only thoughts reached by walking have value.

35

There are cases in which we are like horses, we psychologists, and become restless: we see our own shadow wavering up and down before us. A psychologist must turn his eyes from himself to eye anything at all.

36

Whether we immoralists are *harming* virtue? Just as little as anarchists harm princes. Only since the latter

---

[1] "One cannot think and write, except sitting."

are shot at do they again sit securely on their thrones.
Moral: *morality must be shot at*.

37

You run *ahead*? Are you doing it as a shepherd? Or
as an exception? A third case would be the fugitive.
First question of conscience.

38

Are you genuine? Or merely an actor? A representative? Or that which is represented? In the end, perhaps
you are merely a copy of an actor. *Second* question of
conscience.

39

The disappointed one speaks. I searched for great
human beings; I always found only the *apes* of their
ideals.

40

Are you one who looks on? Or one who lends a hand?
Or one who looks away and walks off? *Third* question
of conscience.

41

Do you want to walk along? Or walk ahead? Or walk
by yourself? One must know *what* one wants and *that*
one wants. *Fourth* question of conscience.

42

Those were steps for me, and I have climbed up over
them: to that end I had to pass over them. Yet they
thought that I wanted to retire on them.

43

What does it matter if *I* remain right. I am much too right. And he who laughs best today will also laugh last.

44

The formula of my happiness: a Yes, a No, a straight line, a *goal*.

THE PROBLEM OF SOCRATES

1

Concerning life, the wisest men of all ages have judged alike: *it is no good*. Always and everywhere one has heard the same sound from their mouths—a sound full of doubt, full of melancholy, full of weariness of life, full of resistance to life. Even Socrates said, as he died: "To live—that means to be sick a long time: I owe Asclepius the Savior a rooster." Even Socrates was tired of it. What does that evidence? What does it evince? Formerly one would have said (—oh, it has been said, and loud enough, and especially by our pessimists): "At least something of all this must be true! The consensus of the sages evidences the truth." Shall we still talk like that today? *May* we? "At least something must be *sick* here," *we* retort. These wisest men of all ages— they should first be scrutinized closely. Were they all perhaps shaky on their legs? late? tottery? decadents? Could it be that wisdom appears on earth as a raven, inspired by a little whiff of carrion?

2

This irreverent thought that the great sages are *types of decline* first occurred to me precisely in a case where it is most strongly opposed by both scholarly and un-scholarly prejudice: I recognized Socrates and Plato to be symptoms of degeneration, tools of the Greek disso-lution, pseudo-Greek, anti-Greek (*Birth of Tragedy*, 1872). The consensus of the sages—I comprehended this ever more clearly—proves least of all that they were right in what they agreed on: it shows rather that they themselves, these wisest men, agreed in some *physio-logical* respect, and hence adopted the same negative attitude to life—*had to* adopt it. Judgments, judgments of value, concerning life, for it or against it, can, in the end, never be true: they have value only as symptoms, they are worthy of consideration only as symptoms; in themselves such judgments are stupidities. One must by all means stretch out one's fingers and make the attempt to grasp this amazing finesse, *that the value of life can-not be estimated.* Not by the living, for they are an in-terested party, even a bone of contention, and not judges; not by the dead, for a different reason. For a philosopher to see a problem in the value of life is thus an objection to him, a question mark concerning his wisdom, an un-wisdom. Indeed? All these great wise men—they were not only decadents but not wise at all? But I return to the problem of Socrates.

3

In origin, Socrates belonged to the lowest class: Soc-rates was plebs. We know, we can still see for ourselves, how ugly he was. But ugliness, in itself an objection, is among the Greeks almost a refutation. Was Socrates a Greek at all? Ugliness is often enough the expression of a development that has been crossed, *thwarted* by cross-ing. Or it appears as *declining* development. The anthro-pologists among the criminologists tell us that the typical criminal is ugly: *monstrum in fronte, monstrum in animo*. But the criminal is a decadent. Was Socrates a typical criminal? At least that would not be contradicted by the famous judgment of the physiognomist which sounded so offensive to the friends of Socrates. A foreigner who knew about faces once passed through Athens and told Socrates to his face that he *was* a *monstrum*—that he harbored in himself all the bad vices and appetites. And Socrates merely answered: "You know me, sir!"

4

Socrates' decadence is suggested not only by the admitted wantonness and anarchy of his instincts, but also by the hypertrophy of the logical faculty and that *sarcasm of the rachitic* which distinguishes him. Nor should we forget those auditory hallucinations which, as "the *daimonion* of Socrates," have been interpreted religiously. Everything in him is exaggerated, *buffo*, a caricature; everything is at the same time concealed, ulterior, subterranean. I seek to comprehend what idiosyncrasy begot that Socratic equation of reason, virtue, and happiness: that most bizarre of all equations, which, moreover, is opposed to all the instincts of the earlier Greeks.

5

With Socrates, Greek taste changes in favor of dialectics. What really happened there? Above all, a *noble* taste is thus vanquished; with dialectics the plebs come to the top. Before Socrates, dialectic manners were repudiated in good society: they were considered bad manners, they were compromising. The young were warned against them. Furthermore, all such presentations of one's reasons were distrusted. Honest things, like honest men, do not carry their reasons in their hands like that. It is indecent to show all five fingers. What must first be proved is worth little. Wherever authority still forms part of good bearing, where one does not give reasons but commands, the dialectician is a kind of buffoon: one laughs at him, one does not take him seriously. Socrates was the buffoon who *got himself taken seriously:* what really happened there?

6

One chooses dialectic only when one has no other means. One knows that one arouses mistrust with it, that it is not very persuasive. Nothing is easier to erase than a dialectical effect: the experience of every meeting at which there are speeches proves this. It can only be *self-defense* for those who no longer have other weapons. One must have to *enforce* one's right: until one reaches that point, one makes no use of it. The Jews were dialecticians for that reason; Reynard the Fox was one—and Socrates too?

7

Is the irony of Socrates an expression of revolt? Of plebeian *ressentiment?* Does he, as one oppressed, enjoy his own ferocity in the knife-thrusts of his syllogisms? Does he *avenge* himself on the noble people whom he fascinates? As a dialectician, one holds a merciless tool in one's hand; one can become a tyrant by means of it; one compromises those one conquers. The dialectician leaves it to his opponent to prove that he is no idiot: he makes one furious and helpless at the same time. The dialectician renders the intellect of his opponent powerless. Indeed? Is dialectic only a form of *revenge* in Socrates?

8

I have given to understand how it was that Socrates could repel: it is therefore all the more necessary to explain his fascination. That he discovered a new kind of *agon*,[1] that he became its first fencing master for the noble circles of Athens, is one point. He fascinated by appealing to the agonistic impulse of the Greeks—he introduced a variation into the wrestling match between young men and youths. Socrates was also a great *erotic*.

9

But Socrates guessed even more. He saw *through* his noble Athenians; he comprehended that his own case, his idiosyncrasy, was no longer exceptional. The same kind of degeneration was quietly developing everywhere: old Athens was coming to an end. And Socrates understood that all the world *needed* him—his means, his cure, his personal artifice of self-preservation. Everywhere the instincts were in anarchy; everywhere one was within five paces of excess: *monstrum in animo* was the general danger. "The impulses want to play the tyrant; one must invent a *counter-tyrant* who is stronger." When the physiognomist had revealed to Socrates who he was—a cave of bad appetites—the great master of irony let slip another word which is the key to his character. "This is true," he said, "but I mastered them all." *How* did Socrates become master over *himself*? His case was, at bottom, merely the extreme case, only the most striking instance of what was then beginning to be a universal distress: no one was any longer master over himself, the instincts turned *against* each other. He fascinated, being this extreme case; his awe-inspiring ugliness proclaimed him as such to all who could see:

[1] "Contest."

he fascinated, of course, even more as an answer, a solution, an apparent *cure* of this case.

10

When one finds it necessary to turn *reason* into a tyrant, as Socrates did, the danger cannot be slight that something else will play the tyrant. Rationality was then hit upon as the savior; neither Socrates nor his "patients" had any choice about being rational: it was *de rigeur,* it was their last resort. The fanaticism with which all Greek reflection throws itself upon rationality betrays a desperate situation; there was danger, there was but one choice: either to perish or—to be *absurdly rational.* The moralism of the Greek philosophers from Plato on is pathologically conditioned; so is their esteem of dialectics. Reason-virtue-happiness, that means merely that one must imitate Socrates and counter the dark appetites with a permanent daylight—the daylight of reason. One must be clever, clear, bright at any price: any concession to the instincts, to the unconscious, leads *downward.*

11

I have given to understand how it was that Socrates fascinated: he seemed to be a physician, a savior. Is it necessary to go on to demonstrate the error in his faith in "rationality at any price"? It is a self-deception on the part of philosophers and moralists if they believe that they are extricating themselves from decadence when they merely wage war against it. Extrication lies beyond their strength: what they choose as a means, as salvation, is itself but another expression of decadence; they change its expression, but they do not get rid of decadence itself. Socrates was a misunderstanding; *the whole improvement-morality, including the*

Christian, was a misunderstanding. The most blinding daylight; rationality at any price; life, bright, cold, cautious, conscious, without instinct, in opposition to the instincts—all this too was a mere disease, another disease, and by no means a return to "virtue," to "health," to happiness. To *have* to fight the instincts—that is the formula of decadence: as long as life is *ascending,* happiness equals instinct.

12

Did he himself still comprehend this, this most brilliant of all self-outwitters? Was this what he said to himself in the end, in the *wisdom* of his courage to die? Socrates *wanted* to die: not Athens, but he himself chose the hemlock; he forced Athens to sentence him. "Socrates is no physician," he said softly to himself; "here death alone is the physician. Socrates himself has merely been sick a long time."

"REASON" IN PHILOSOPHY

1

You ask me which of the philosophers' traits are really idiosyncrasies? For example, their lack of historical sense, their hatred of the very idea of becoming, their Egypticism. They think that they show their *respect* for a subject when they de-historicize it, *sub specie aeterni* —when they turn it into a mummy. All that philosophers have handled for thousands of years have been concept-mummies; nothing real escaped their grasp alive. When these honorable idolators of concepts worship something, they kill it and stuff it; they threaten the life of everything they worship. Death, change, old age, as well as procreation and growth, are to their minds objections—even refutations. Whatever has being does not become; whatever becomes does not have being. Now they all believe, desperately even, in what has being. But since they never grasp it, they seek for reasons why it is kept from them. "There must be mere appearance, there must be some deception which prevents us from perceiving that which has being: where is the deceiver?"

"We have found him," they cry ecstatically; "it is the senses! These senses, which are so immoral in other ways too, deceive us concerning the *true* world. Moral: let us free ourselves from the deception of the senses, from becoming, from history, from lies; history is nothing but faith in the senses, faith in lies. Moral: let us say No to all who have faith in the senses, to all the rest of mankind; they are all 'mob.' Let us be philosophers! Let us be mummies! Let us represent monotono-theism by adopting the expression of a gravedigger! And above all, away with the body, this wretched *idée fixe* of the senses, disfigured by all the fallacies of logic, refuted, even impossible, although it is impudent enough to behave as if it were real!"

2

With the highest respect, I except the name of *Heraclitus*. When the rest of the philosophic folk rejected the testimony of the senses because they showed multiplicity and change, he rejected their testimony because they showed things as if they had permanence and unity. Heraclitus too did the senses an injustice. They lie neither in the way the Eleatics believed, nor as he believed—they do not lie at all. What we *make* of their testimony, that alone introduces lies; for example, the lie of unity, the lie of thinghood, of substance, of permanence. "Reason" is the cause of our falsification of the testimony of the senses. Insofar as the senses show becoming, passing away, and change, they do not lie. But Heraclitus will remain eternally right with his assertion that being is an empty fiction. The "apparent" world is the only one: the "true" world is merely added by a lie.

3

And what magnificent instruments of observation we possess in our senses! This nose, for example, of which no philosopher has yet spoken with reverence and gratitude, is actually the most delicate instrument so far at our disposal: it is able to detect minimal differences of motion which even a spectroscope cannot detect. Today we possess science precisely to the extent to which we have decided to *accept* the testimony of the senses—to the extent to which we sharpen them further, arm them, and have learned to think them through. The rest is miscarriage and not-yet-science—in other words, metaphysics, theology, psychology, epistemology—or formal science, a doctrine of signs, such as logic and that applied logic which is called mathematics. In them reality is not encountered at all, not even as a problem—no more than the question of the value of such a sign-convention as logic.

4

The other idiosyncrasy of the philosophers is no less dangerous; it consists in confusing the last and the first. They place that which comes at the end—unfortunately! for it ought not to come at all!—namely, the "highest concepts," which means the most general, the emptiest concepts, the last smoke of evaporating reality, in the beginning, *as* the beginning. This again is nothing but their way of showing reverence: the higher *may* not grow out of the lower, may not have grown at all.

Moral: whatever is of the first rank must be *causa sui*.[1]
Origin out of something else is considered an objection,
a questioning of value. All the highest values are of the
first rank; all the highest concepts, that which has being,
the unconditional, the good, the true, the perfect—all
these cannot have become and must therefore be *causa
sui*. All these, moreover, cannot be unlike each other or
in contradiction to each other. Thus they arrive at their
stupendous concept, "God." That which is last, thinnest,
and emptiest is put first, as *the* cause, as *ens realissimum*.[2] Why did mankind have to take seriously the
brain afflictions of sick web-spinners? They have paid
dearly for it!

5

At long last, let us contrast the very different manner
in which we conceive the problem of error and appearance. (I say "we" for politeness' sake.) Formerly, alter-
ation, change, any becoming at all, were taken as
proof of mere appearance, as an indication that there
must be something which led us astray. Today, conversely, precisely insofar as the prejudice of reason forces
us to posit unity, identity, permanence, substance, cause,
thinghood, being, we see ourselves somehow caught in
error, compelled into error. So certain are we, on the
basis of rigorous examination, that this is where the error
lies.

It is no different in this case than with the movement of the sun: there our eye is the constant advocate
of error, here it is our language. In its origin language
belongs in the age of the most rudimentary form of psychology. We enter a realm of crude fetishism when we
summon before consciousness the basic presuppositions

[1] "Self-caused."
[2] "The most real being."

of the metaphysics of language, in plain talk, the presuppositions of reason. Everywhere it sees a doer and doing; it believes in will as *the* cause; it believes in the ego, in the ego as being, in the ego as substance, and it projects this faith in the ego-substance upon all things—only thereby does it first *create* the concept of "thing." Everywhere "being" is projected by thought, pushed underneath, as the cause; the concept of being follows, and is a derivative of, the concept of ego. In the beginning there is that great calamity of an error that the will is something which is effective, that will is a capacity. Today we know that it is only a word.

Very much later, in a world which was in a thousand ways more enlightened, philosophers, to their great surprise, became aware of the sureness, the subjective certainty, in our handling of the categories of reason: they concluded that these categories could not be derived from anything empirical—for everything empirical plainly contradicted them. Whence, then, were they derived?

And in India, as in Greece, the same mistake was made: "We must once have been at home in a higher world (instead of a very much lower one, which would have been the truth); we must have been divine, *for* we have reason!" Indeed, nothing has yet possessed a more naïve power of persuasion than the error concerning being, as it has been formulated by the Eleatics, for example. After all, every word we say and every sentence speak in its favor. Even the opponents of the Eleatics still succumbed to the seduction of their concept of being: Democritus, among others, when he invented his atom. "Reason" in language—oh, what an old deceptive female she is! I am afraid we are not rid of God because we still have faith in grammar.

6

It will be appreciated if I condense so essential and so new an insight into four theses. In that way I facilitate comprehension; in that way I provoke contradiction.

First proposition. The reasons for which "this" world has been characterized as "apparent" are the very reasons which indicate its reality; any other kind of reality is absolutely indemonstrable.

Second proposition. The criteria which have been bestowed on the "true being" of things are the criteria of not-being, of *naught;* the "true world" has been constructed out of contradiction to the actual world: indeed an apparent world, insofar as it is merely a moral-optical illusion.

Third proposition. To invent fables about a world "other" than this one has no meaning at all, unless an instinct of slander, detraction, and suspicion against life has gained the upper hand in us: in that case, we avenge ourselves against life with a phantasmagoria of "another," a "better" life.

Fourth proposition. Any distinction between a "true" and an "apparent" world—whether in the Christian manner or in the manner of Kant (in the end, an underhanded Christian)—is only a suggestion of decadence, a symptom of the *decline of life.* That the artist esteems appearance higher than reality is no objection to this proposition. For "appearance" in this case means reality *once more,* only by way of selection, reinforcement, and correction. The tragic artist is no pessimist: he is precisely the one who says Yes to everything questionable, even to the terrible—he is *Dionysian.*

HOW THE "TRUE WORLD" FINALLY BECAME
A FABLE

The History of an Error

1. The true world—attainable for the sage, the pious, the virtuous man; he lives in it, *he is it*.

(The oldest form of the idea, relatively sensible, simple, and persuasive. A circumlocution for the sentence, "I, Plato, *am* the truth.")

2. The true world—unattainable for now, but promised for the sage, the pious, the virtuous man ("for the sinner who repents").

(Progress of the idea: it becomes more subtle, insidious, incomprehensible—*it becomes female*, it becomes Christian.)

3. The true world—unattainable, indemonstrable, unpromisable; but the very thought of it—a consolation, an obligation, an imperative.

(At bottom, the old sun, but seen through mist and skepticism. The idea has become elusive, pale, Nordic, Königsbergian.[1])

4. The true world—unattainable? At any rate, unattained. And being unattained, also *unknown*. Consequently, not consoling, redeeming, or obligating: how could something unknown obligate us?

(Gray morning. The first yawn of reason. The cockcrow of positivism.)

5. The "true" world—an idea which is no longer good for anything, not even obligating—an idea which has become useless and superfluous—*consequently*, a refuted idea: let us abolish it!

(Bright day; breakfast; return of *bon sens* and cheer-

[1] That is, Kantian.

fulness; Plato's embarrassed blush; pandemonium of all free spirits.)

6. The true world—we have abolished. What world has remained? The apparent one perhaps? But no! *With the true world we have also abolished the apparent one.*

(Noon; moment of the briefest shadow; end of the longest error; high point of humanity; INCIPIT ZARA-THUSTRA.[1])

MORALITY AS ANTI-NATURE

1

All passions have a phase when they are merely disastrous, when they drag down their victim with the weight of stupidity—and a later, very much later phase when they wed the spirit, when they "spiritualize" themselves. Formerly, in view of the element of stupidity in passion, war was declared on passion itself, its destruction was plotted; all the old moral monsters are agreed on this: *il faut tuer les passions.*[2] The most famous formula for this is to be found in the New Testament, in that Sermon on the Mount, where, incidentally, things are by no means looked at from a height. There it is said, for example, with particular reference to sexuality: "If thy eye offend thee, pluck it out." Fortunately, no Christian acts in accordance with this precept. *Destroying* the passions and cravings, merely as a preventive measure against their stupidity and the unpleasant consequences of this stupidity—today this itself strikes us as

[1] "Zarathustra begins." An echo of the conclusion of *The Gay Science* (1882): Nietzsche had used the first section of the Prologue of *Zarathustra*, his next work, as the final aphorism of Book Four, and given it the title: *Incipit tragoedia.*

[2] "One must kill the passions."

merely another acute form of stupidity. We no longer admire dentists who "pluck out" teeth so that they will not hurt any more.

To be fair, it should be admitted, however, that on the ground out of which Christianity grew, the concept of the "*spiritualization* of passion" could never have been formed. After all the first church, as is well known, fought *against* the "intelligent" in favor of the "poor in spirit." How could one expect from it an intelligent war against passion? The church fights passion with excision in every sense: its practice, its "cure," is *castratism*. It never asks: "How can one spiritualize, beautify, deify a craving?" It has at all times laid the stress of discipline on extirpation (of sensuality, of pride, of the lust to rule, of avarice, of vengefulness). But an attack on the roots of passion means an attack on the roots of life: the practice of the church is *hostile to life*.

2

The same means in the fight against a craving—castration, extirpation—is instinctively chosen by those who are too weak-willed, too degenerate, to be able to impose moderation on themselves; by those who are so constituted that they require *La Trappe*,[1] to use a figure of speech, or (without any figure of speech) some kind of definitive declaration of hostility, a *cleft* between themselves and the passion. Radical means are indispensable only for the degenerate; the weakness of the will—or, to speak more definitely, the inability *not* to respond to a stimulus—is itself merely another form of degeneration. The radical hostility, the deadly hostility against sensuality, is always a symptom to reflect on: it entitles us to suppositions concerning the total state of one who is excessive in this manner.

[1] The Trappist Order.

This hostility, this hatred, by the way, reaches its climax only when such types lack even the firmness for this radical cure, for this renunciation of their "devil." One should survey the whole history of the priests and philosophers, including the artists: the most poisonous things against the senses have been said not by the impotent, nor by ascetics, but by the impossible ascetics, by those who really were in dire need of being ascetics.

3

The spiritualization of sensuality is called *love:* it represents a great triumph over Christianity. Another triumph is our spiritualization of *hostility.* It consists in a profound appreciation of the value of having enemies: in short, it means acting and thinking in the opposite way from that which has been the rule. The church always wanted the destruction of its enemies; we, we immoralists and Antichristians, find our advantage in this, that the church exists. In the political realm too, hostility has now become more spiritual—much more sensible, much more thoughtful, much more *considerate.* Almost every party understands how it is in the interest of its own self-preservation that the opposition should not lose all strength; the same is true of power politics. A new creation in particular—the new *Reich,* for example—needs enemies more than friends: in opposition alone does it *feel* itself necessary, in opposition alone does it *become* necessary.

Our attitude to the "internal enemy" is no different: here too we have spiritualized hostility; here too we have come to appreciate its value. The price of fruitfulness is to be rich in internal opposition; one remains young only as long as the soul does not stretch itself and desire peace. Nothing has become more alien to us than that desideratum of former times, "peace of soul," the *Christian* desideratum; there is nothing we envy less than the moralistic cow and the fat happiness of the good conscience. One has renounced the *great* life when one renounces war.

In many cases, to be sure, "peace of soul" is merely a misunderstanding—something else, which lacks only a more honest name. Without further ado or prejudice, a few examples. "Peace of soul" can be, for one, the gentle radiation of a rich animality into the moral (or religious) sphere. Or the beginning of weariness, the first shadow of evening, of any kind of evening. Or a sign that the air is humid, that south winds are approaching. Or unrecognized gratitude for a good digestion (sometimes called "love of man"). Or the attainment of calm by a convalescent who feels a new relish in all things and waits. Or the state which follows a thorough satisfaction of our dominant passion, the well-being of a rare repletion. Or the senile weakness of our will, our cravings, our vices. Or laziness, persuaded by vanity to give itself moral airs. Or the emergence of certainty, even a dreadful certainty, after long tension and torture by uncertainty. Or the expression of maturity and mastery in the midst of doing, creating, working, and willing—calm breathing, *attained* "freedom of the will." *Twilight of the Idols*—who knows? perhaps also only a kind of "peace of soul."

4

I reduce a principle to a formula. Every naturalism in morality—that is, every healthy morality—is dominated by an instinct of life; some commandment of life is fulfilled by a determinate canon of "shalt" and "shalt not"; some inhibition and hostile element on the path of life is thus removed. *Anti-natural* morality—that is, almost every morality which has so far been taught, revered, and preached—turns, conversely, *against* the instincts of life: it is *condemnation* of these instincts, now secret, now outspoken and impudent. When it says, "God looks at the heart," it says No to both the lowest and the highest desires of life, and posits God as the *enemy of life.* The saint in whom God delights is the ideal eunuch. Life has come to an end where the "kingdom of God" begins.

5

Once one has comprehended the outrage of such a revolt against life as has become almost sacrosanct in Christian morality, one has, fortunately, also comprehended something else: the futility, apparentness, absurdity, and *mendaciousness* of such a revolt. A condemnation of life by the living remains in the end a mere symptom of a certain kind of life: the question whether it is justified or unjustified is not even raised thereby. One would require a position *outside* of life, and yet have to know it as well as one, as many, as all who have lived it, in order to be permitted even to touch the problem of the *value* of life: reasons enough to comprehend that this problem is for us an unapproachable problem. When we speak of values, we speak with the inspiration, with the way of looking at things, which is part of life: life itself forces us to posit values; life itself values through us when we posit values. From this it follows that even that anti-natural morality which conceives of God as the counter-concept and condemnation of life is only a value judgment of life—but of what life? of what kind of life? I have already given the answer: of declining, weakened, weary, condemned life. Morality, as it has so far been understood—as it has in the end been formulated once more by Schopenhauer, as "negation of the will to life"—is the very *instinct of decadence*, which makes an imperative of itself. It says: *"Perish!"* It is a condemnation pronounced by the condemned.

6

Let us finally consider how naïve it is altogether to say: "Man *ought* to be such and such!" Reality shows us an enchanting wealth of types, the abundance of a lavish play and change of forms—and some wretched loafer of a moralist comments: "No! Man ought to be different." He even knows what man should be like, this wretched bigot and prig: he paints himself on the wall and comments, *"Ecce homo!"* But even when the moralist addresses himself only to the single human being and says to him, "You ought to be such and such!" he does not cease to make himself ridiculous. The single human being is a piece of *fatum* from the front and from the rear, one law more, one necessity more for all that is yet to come and to be. To say to him, "Change yourself!" is to demand that everything be changed, even retroactively. And indeed there have been consistent moralists who wanted man to be different, that is, virtuous—they wanted him remade in their own image, as a prig: to that end, they *negated* the world! No small madness! No modest kind of immodesty!

Morality, insofar as it *condemns* for its own sake, and *not* out of regard for the concerns, considerations, and contrivances of life, is a specific error with which one ought to have no pity—an *idiosyncrasy of degenerates* which has caused immeasurable harm.

We others, we immoralists, have, conversely, made room in our hearts for every kind of understanding, comprehending, and *approving*. We do not easily negate; we make it a point of honor to be *affirmers*. More and more, our eyes have opened to that economy which needs and knows how to utilize all that the holy witlessness of the priest, of the *diseased* reason in the priest, rejects—that economy in the law of life which finds an advantage even in the disgusting species of the prigs, the priests, the virtuous. *What* advantage? But we ourselves, we immoralists, are the answer.

THE FOUR GREAT ERRORS

1

The error of confusing cause and effect. There is no more dangerous error than that of mistaking the effect for the cause: I call it the real corruption of reason. Yet this error belongs among the most ancient and recent habits of mankind: it is even hallowed among us and goes by the name of "religion" or "morality." Every single sentence which religion and morality formulate contains it; priests and legislators of moral codes are the originators of this corruption of reason.

I give an example. Everybody knows the book of the famous Cornaro in which he recommends his slender diet as a recipe for a long and happy life—a virtuous one too. Few books have been read so much; even now thousands of copies are sold in England every year. I do not doubt that scarcely any book (except the Bible, as is meet) has done as much harm, has *shortened* as many lives, as this well-intentioned *curiosum*. The reason: the mistaking of the effect for the cause. The worthy Italian thought his diet was the *cause* of his long life, whereas the precondition for a long life, the extraordinary slowness of his metabolism, the consumption of so little, was the cause of his slender diet. He was not free to eat little *or* much; his frugality was not a matter of "free will": he became sick when he ate more. But whoever is no carp not only does well to eat properly,

but needs to. A scholar in our time, with his rapid consumption of nervous energy, would simply destroy himself with Cornaro's diet. *Crede experto.*[1]

2

The most general formula on which every religion
and morality is founded is: "Do this and that, refrain
from this and that—then you will be happy! Otherwise
. . ." Every morality, every religion, *is* this imperative;
I call it the great original sin of reason, the *immortal un-
reason.* In my mouth, this formula is changed into its
opposite—first example of my "revaluation of all values": a ·well-turned-out human being, a "happy one,"
must perform certain actions and shrinks instinctively
from other actions; he carries the order, which he represents physiologically, into his relations with other
human beings and things. In a formula: his virtue is the
effect of his happiness. A long life, many descendants—
this is not the wages of virtue; rather virtue itself is
that slowing down of the metabolism which leads,
among other things, also to a long life, many descendants—in short, to *Cornarism.*

The church and morality say: "A generation, a
people, are destroyed by license and luxury." My *recovered* reason says: when a people approaches destruction, when it degenerates physiologically, then license
and luxury *follow* from this (namely, the craving for
ever stronger and more frequent stimulation, as every
exhausted nature knows it). This young man turns pale
early and wilts; his friends say: that is due to this or
that disease. I say: that he became diseased, that he
did not resist the disease, was already the effect of an
impoverished life or hereditary exhaustion. The newspaper reader says: this party destroys itself by making

[1] "Believe him who has tried!"

such a mistake. My *higher* politics says: a party which makes such mistakes has reached its end; it has lost its sureness of instinct. Every mistake in every sense is the effect of the degeneration of instinct, of the disintegration of the will: one could almost define what is bad in this way. All that is good is instinct—and hence easy, necessary, free. Laboriousness is an objection; the god is typically different from the hero. (In my language: light feet are the first attribute of divinity.)

3

The error of a false causality. People have believed at all times that they knew what a cause is; but whence did we take our knowledge—or more precisely, our faith that we had such knowledge? From the realm of the famous "inner facts," of which not a single one has so far proved to be factual. We believed ourselves to be causal in the act of willing: we thought that here at least we caught causality in the act. Nor did one doubt that all the antecedents of an act, its causes, were to be sought in consciousness and would be found there once sought—as "motives": else one would not have been free and responsible for it. Finally, who would have denied that a thought is caused? that the ego causes the thought?

Of these three "inward facts" which seem to guarantee causality, the first and most persuasive is that of the will as cause. The conception of a consciousness ("spirit") as a cause, and later also that of the ego as cause (the "subject"), are only afterbirths: first the causality of the will was firmly accepted as given, as *empirical.*

Meanwhile we have thought better of it. Today we no longer believe a word of all this. The "inner world" is full of phantoms and will-o'-the-wisps: the will is one of them. The will no longer moves anything, hence does not explain anything either—it merely accompanies events; it can also be absent. The so-called *motive:* another error. Merely a surface phenomenon of consciousness, something alongside the deed that is more likely to cover up the antecedents of the deeds than to represent them. And as for the *ego!* That has become a fable, a fiction, a play on words: it has altogether ceased to think, feel, or will!

What follows from this? There are no mental causes at all. The whole of the allegedly empirical evidence for that has gone to the devil. That is what follows! And what a fine abuse we had perpetrated with this "empirical evidence"; we *created* the world on this basis as a world of causes, a world of will, a world of spirits. The most ancient and enduring psychology was at work here and did not do anything else: all that happened was considered a doing, all doing the effect of a will; the world became to it a multiplicity of doers; a doer (a "subject") was slipped under all that happened. It was out of himself that man projected his three "inner facts"— that in which he believed most firmly, the will, the spirit, the ego. He even took the concept of being from the concept of the ego; he posited "things" as "being," in his image, in accordance with his concept of the ego as a cause. Small wonder that later he always found in things only that *which he had put into them.* The thing itself, to say it once more, the concept of thing is a mere reflex of the faith in the ego as cause. And even your atom, my dear mechanists and physicists—how much error, how much rudimentary psychology is still residual in your atom! Not to mention the "thing-in-itself," the *horrendum pudendum* of the metaphysicians! The error of the spirit as cause mistaken for reality! And made the very measure of reality! And called God!

4

The error of imaginary causes. To begin with dreams: *ex post facto,* a cause is slipped under a particular sensation (for example, one following a far-off cannon shot) —often a whole little novel in which the dreamer turns up as the protagonist. The sensation endures meanwhile in a kind of resonance: it waits, as it were, until the causal instinct permits it to step into the foreground— now no longer as a chance occurrence, but as "meaning." The cannon shot appears in a *causal* mode, in an apparent reversal of time. What is really later, the motivation, is experienced first—often with a hundred details which pass like lightning—and the shot *follows*. What has happened? The representations which were *produced* by a certain state have been misunderstood as its causes.

In fact, we do the same thing when awake. Most of our general feelings—every kind of inhibition, pressure, tension, and explosion in the play and counterplay of our organs, and particularly the state of the *nervus sympathicus*—excite our causal instinct: we want to have a reason for feeling this way or that—for feeling bad or for feeling good. We are never satisfied merely to state the fact that we feel this way or that: we admit this fact only—become conscious of it only—when we have furnished some kind of motivation. Memory, which swings into action in such cases, unknown to us, brings up earlier states of the same kind, together with the causal interpretations associated with them—not their real causes. The faith, to be sure, that such representations, such accompanying conscious processes, are the causes, is also brought forth by memory. Thus originates a habitual acceptance of a particular causal interpretation, which, as a matter of fact, inhibits any investigation into the real cause—even precludes it.

5

The psychological explanation of this. To derive something unknown from something familiar relieves, comforts, and satisfies, besides giving a feeling of power. With the unknown, one is confronted with danger, discomfort, and care; the first instinct is to abolish these painful states. First principle: any explanation is better than none. Since at bottom it is merely a matter of wishing to be rid of oppressive representations, one is not too particular about the means of getting rid of them: the first representation that explains the unknown as familiar feels so good that one "considers it true." The proof of pleasure ("of strength") as a criterion of truth.

The causal instinct is thus conditional upon, and excited by, the feeling of fear. The "why?" shall, if at all possible, not give the cause for its own sake so much as for *a particular kind of cause*—a cause that is comforting, liberating, and relieving. That it is something already familiar, experienced, and inscribed in the memory, which is posited as a cause, that is the first consequence of this need. That which is new and strange and has not been experienced before, is excluded as a cause. Thus one searches not only for some kind of explanation to serve as a cause, but for a particularly selected and preferred kind of explanation—that which has most quickly and most frequently abolished the feeling of the strange, new, and hitherto unexperienced: the *most habitual* explanations. Consequence: one kind of positing of causes predominates more and more, is concentrated into a system, and finally emerges as *dominant,* that is, as simply precluding other causes and explana-

tions. The banker immediately thinks of "business," the
Christian of "sin," and the girl of her love.

6

*The whole realm of morality and religion belongs
under this concept of imaginary causes.* The "explanation" of *disagreeable* general feelings. They are produced by beings that are hostile to us (evil spirits: the
most famous case—the misunderstanding of the hysterical as witches). They are produced by acts which cannot be approved (the feeling of "sin," of "sinfulness," is
slipped under a physiological discomfort; one always
finds reasons for being dissatisfied with oneself). They
are produced as punishments, as payment for something
we should not have done, for what we should not have
been (impudently generalized by Schopenhauer into a
principle in which morality appears as what it really
is—as the very poisoner and slanderer of life: "Every
great pain, whether physical or spiritual, declares what
we deserve; for it could not come to us if we did not
deserve it." *World as Will and Representation* II, 666).
They are produced as effects of ill-considered actions
that turn out badly. (Here the affects, the senses, are
posited as causes, as "guilty"; and physiological calamities are interpreted with the help of other calamities as
"deserved.")

The "explanation" of *agreeable* general feelings. They
are produced by trust in God. They are produced by
the consciousness of good deeds (the so-called "good
conscience"—a physiological state which at times looks
so much like good digestion that it is hard to tell them
apart). They are produced by the successful termination of some enterprise (a naïve fallacy: the successful
termination of some enterprise does not by any means
give a hypochondriac or a Pascal agreeable general

feelings). They are produced by faith, charity, and hope
—the Christian virtues.

In truth, all these supposed explanations are resultant states and, as it were, translations of pleasurable or
unpleasurable feelings into a false dialect: one is in a
state of hope *because* the basic physiological feeling is
once again strong and rich; one trusts in God *because*
the feeling of fullness and strength gives a sense of rest.
Morality and religion belong altogether to the *psychology of error:* in every single case, cause and effect are
confused; or truth is confused with the effects of *believing* something to be true; or a state of consciousness
is confused with its causes.

7

The error of free will. Today we no longer have any
pity for the concept of "free will": we know only too
well what it really is—the foulest of all theologians'
artifices, aimed at making mankind "responsible" in
their sense, that is, *dependent upon them.* Here I simply
supply the psychology of all "making responsible."

Wherever responsibilities are sought, it is usually the
instinct of wanting to judge and punish which is at work.
Becoming has been deprived of its innocence when any
being-such-and-such is traced back to will, to purposes,
to acts of responsibility: the doctrine of the will has
been invented essentially for the purpose of punishment,
that is, because one wanted to impute guilt. The entire
old psychology, the psychology of will, was conditioned
by the fact that its originators, the priests at the head
of ancient communities, wanted to create for themselves
the right to punish—or wanted to create this right for
God. Men were considered "free" so that they might be
judged and punished—so that they might become
guilty: consequently, every act had to be considered as

willed, and the origin of every act had to be considered
as lying within the consciousness (and thus the most
fundamental counterfeit *in psychologicis* was made the
principle of psychology itself).

Today, as we have entered into the reverse movement
and we immoralists are trying with all our strength to
take the concept of guilt and the concept of punishment
out of the world again, and to cleanse psychology, history, nature, and social institutions and sanctions of
them, there is in our eyes no more radical opposition
than that of the theologians, who continue with the
concept of a "moral world-order" to infect the innocence
of becoming by means of "punishment" and "guilt."
Christianity is a metaphysics of the hangman.

8

What alone can be *our* doctrine? That no one *gives*
man his qualities—neither God, nor society, nor his
parents and ancestors, nor he himself. (The nonsense of
the last idea was taught as "intelligible freedom" by
Kant—perhaps by Plato already.) No one is responsible
for man's being there at all, for his being such-and-such,
or for his being in these circumstances or in this environment. The fatality of his essence is not to be dis-
entangled from the fatality of all that has been and
will be. Man is not the effect of some special purpose,
of a will, and end; nor is he the object of an attempt to
attain an "ideal of humanity" or an "ideal of happiness"
or an "ideal of morality." It is absurd to wish to devolve
one's essence on some end or other. We have invented
the concept of "end": in reality there is no end.

One is necessary, one is a piece of fatefulness, one
belongs to the whole, one is in the whole; there is
nothing which could judge, measure, compare, or sentence our being, for that would mean judging, measur-

ing, comparing, or sentencing the whole. But there is nothing besides the whole. That nobody is held responsible any longer, that the mode of being may not be traced back to a *causa prima,* that the world does not form a unity either as a sensorium or as "spirit"— that alone is the great liberation; with this alone is the innocence of becoming restored. The concept of "God" was until now the greatest objection to existence. We deny God, we deny the responsibility in God: only thereby do we redeem the world.

THE "IMPROVERS" OF MANKIND

1

My demand upon the philosopher is known, that he take his stand *beyond* good and evil and leave the illusion of moral judgment *beneath* himself. This demand follows from an insight which I was the first to formulate: that *there are altogether no moral facts.* Moral judgments agree with religious ones in believing in realities which are no realities. Morality is merely an interpretation of certain phenomena—more precisely, a misinterpretation. Moral judgments, like religious ones, belong to a stage of ignorance at which the very concept of the real and the distinction between what is real and imaginary, are still lacking; thus "truth," at this stage, designates all sorts of things which we today call "imaginings." Moral judgments are therefore never to be taken literally: so understood, they always contain mere absurdity. Semeiotically, however, they remain invaluable: they reveal, at least for those who know, the most valuable realities of cultures and inwardnesses which did not know enough to "understand" themselves. Morality is mere sign language, mere symptomatology: one must know what it is all about to be able to profit from it.

2

A first example, quite provisional. At all times they have wanted to "improve" men: this above all was called morality. Under the same word, however, the most divergent tendencies are concealed. Both the *taming* of the beast, man, and the *breeding* of a particular kind of man have been called "improvement." Such zoological terms are required to express the realities— realities, to be sure, of which the typical "improver," the priest, neither knows anything, nor wants to know anything.

To call the taming of an animal its "improvement" sounds almost like a joke to our ears. Whoever knows what goes on in menageries doubts that the beasts are "improved" there. They are weakened, they are made less harmful, and through the depressive effect of fear, through pain, through wounds, and through hunger they become sickly beasts. It is no different with the tamed man whom the priest has "improved." In the early Middle Ages, when the church was indeed, above all, a menagerie, the most beautiful specimens of the "blond beast" were hunted down everywhere; and the noble Teutons, for example, were "improved." But how did such an "improved" Teuton who had been seduced into a monastery look afterward? Like a caricature of man, like a miscarriage: he had become a "sinner," he was stuck in a cage, imprisoned among all sorts of terrible concepts. And there he lay, sick, miserable, malevolent against himself: full of hatred against the springs of life, full of suspicion against all that was still strong and happy. In short, a "Christian."

Physiologically speaking: in the struggle with beasts, to make them sick *may* be the only means for making them weak. This the church understood: it *ruined* man, it weakened him—but it claimed to have "improved" him.

3

Let us consider the other case of so-called morality, the case of *breeding* a particular race and kind. The most magnificent example of this is furnished by Indian morality, sanctioned as religion in the form of "the law of Manu." Here the task set is to breed no less than four races at once: one priestly, one warlike, one for trade and agriculture, and finally a race of servants, the Sudras. Obviously, we are here no longer among animal tamers: a kind of man that is a hundred times milder and more reasonable is the condition for even conceiving such a plan of breeding. One heaves a sigh of relief at leaving the Christian atmosphere of disease and dungeons for this healthier, higher, and *wider* world. How wretched is the New Testament compared to Manu, how foul it smells!

Yet this organization too found it necessary to be *terrible*—this time not in the struggle with beasts, but with their counter-concept, the unbred man, the mishmash man, the chandala. And again it had no other means for keeping him from being dangerous, for making him weak, than to make him *sick*—it was the fight with the "great number." Perhaps there is nothing that contradicts our feeling more than *these* protective measures of Indian morality. The third edict, for example (Avadana-Sastra I), "on impure vegetables," ordains that the only nourishment permitted to the chandala shall be garlic and onions, seeing that the holy scripture prohibits giving them grain or fruit with grains, or water or fire. The same edict orders that the water they need may not be taken from rivers or wells, nor from ponds, but only from the approaches to swamps and from holes made by the footsteps of animals. They are also prohibited from washing their laundry and *from washing themselves,* since the water they are conceded as an act of grace may be used only to quench thirst. Finally, a prohibition that Sudra women may not assist chandala women in childbirth, and a prohibition that the latter may not *assist each other* in this condition.

The success of such sanitary police measures was inevitable: murderous epidemics, ghastly venereal diseases, and thereupon again "the law of the knife," ordaining circumcision for male children and the removal of the internal labia for female children. Manu himself says: "The chandalas are the fruit of adultery, incest, and crime (these, the *necessary* consequences of the concept of breeding). For clothing they shall have only rags from corpses; for dishes, broken pots; for adornment, old iron; for divine services, only evil spirits. They shall wander without rest from place to place. They are prohibited from writing from left to right, and from using the right hand in writing: the use of the right hand and of from-left-to-right is reserved for the virtuous, for the people of *race.*"

4

These regulations are instructive enough: here we encounter for once *Aryan* humanity, quite pure, quite primordial—we learn that the concept of "pure blood" is the opposite of a harmless concept. On the other hand, it becomes clear in which people the hatred, the chandala hatred, against this "humaneness" has eternalized itself, where it has become religion, where it has become *genius.* Seen in this perspective, the Gospels represent a document of prime importance; even more, the Book of Enoch. Christianity, sprung from Jewish roots and comprehensible only as a growth on this soil, rep-

resents the counter-movement to any morality of breeding, of race, of privilege: it is the *anti-Aryan* religion
par excellence. Christianity—the revaluation of all
Aryan values, the victory of chandala values, the gospel
preached to the poor and base, the general revolt of all
the downtrodden, the wretched, the failures, the less
favored, against "race": the undying chandala hatred
as the *religion of love*.

5

The morality of *breeding* and the morality of *taming*
are, in the means they use, entirely worthy of each
other: we may proclaim it as the supreme principle
that, to *make* morality, one must have the unconditional
will to its opposite. This is the great, the uncanny
problem which I have been pursuing the longest: the
psychology of the "improvers" of mankind. A small, and
at bottom modest, fact—that of the so-called *pia fraus*[1]
—offered me the first approach to this problem: the
pia fraus, the heirloom of all philosophers and priests
who "improved" mankind. Neither Manu nor Plato nor
Confucius nor the Jewish and Christian teachers have
ever doubted their *right* to lie. They have not doubted
that they had very different rights too. Expressed in a
formula, one might say: *all* the means by which one
has so far attempted to make mankind moral were
through and through *immoral*.

WHAT THE GERMANS LACK

1

Among Germans today it is not enough to have
spirit: one must arrogate it, one must have the *arrogance*
to have spirit.

[1] "Holy lie."

Perhaps I know the Germans, perhaps I may even tell them some truths. The new Germany represents a large quantum of fitness, both inherited and acquired by training, so that for a time it may expend its accumulated store of strength, even squander it. It is *not* a high culture that has thus become the master, and even less a delicate taste, a noble "beauty" of the instincts; but more *virile* virtues than any other country in Europe can show. Much cheerfulness and self-respect, much assurance in social relations and in the reciprocality of duties, much industriousness, much perseverance—and an inherited moderation which needs the spur rather than the brake. I add that here one still obeys without feeling that obedience humiliates. And nobody despises his opponent.

One will notice that I wish to be just to the Germans: I do not want to break faith with myself here. I must therefore also state my objections to them. One pays heavily for coming to power: power *makes stupid*. The Germans—once they were called the people of thinkers: do they think at all today? The Germans are now bored with the spirit, the Germans now mistrust the spirit; politics swallows up all serious concern for really spiritual matters. *Deutschland, Deutschland über alles*—I fear that was the end of German philosophy.

"Are there any German philosophers? Are there German poets? Are there *good* German books?" they ask me abroad. I blush; but with the courage which I maintain even in desperate situations I reply: "Well, *Bismarck*." Would it be permissible for me to confess what books are read today? Accursed instinct of mediocrity!

2

What the German spirit *might* be—who has not had his melancholy ideas about that! But this people has deliberately made itself stupid, for nearly a millennium: nowhere have the two great European narcotics, alcohol and Christianity, been abused more dissolutely. Recently even a third has been added—one that alone would be sufficient to dispatch all fine and bold flexibility of the spirit—music, our constipated, constipating German music.

How much disgruntled heaviness, lameness, dampness, dressing gown—how much *beer* there is in the German intelligence! How is it at all possible that young men who dedicate their lives to the most spiritual goals do not feel the first instinct of spirituality, *the spirit's instinct of self-preservation*—and drink beer? The alcoholism of the young scholars is perhaps no question mark concerning their scholarliness—without spirit one can still be a great scholar—but in every other respect it remains a problem. Where would one not find the gentle degeneration which beer produces in the spirit? Once, in a case that has almost become famous, I put my finger on such a degeneration—the degeneration of our number-one German free spirit, the *clever* David Strauss, into the author of a beer-bench gospel and "new faith." It was not for nothing that he had made his vow to the "fair brunette" [1] in verse—loyalty unto death.

3

I was speaking of the German spirit: it is becoming cruder, it is becoming shallower. Is that enough? At bottom, it is something quite different that alarms me: how German seriousness, German depth, German *passion* in spiritual matters are declining more and more. The verve has changed, not just the intellectuality. Here and there I come into contact with German universities:

[1] "Beer."

what an atmosphere prevails among their scholars, what desolate spirituality—and how contented and lukewarm it has become! It would be a profound misunderstanding if one wanted to adduce German science against me—it would also be proof that one has not read a word I have written. For seventeen years I have never tired of calling attention to the *despiritualizing* influence of our current science-industry. The hard helotism to which the tremendous range of the sciences condemns every scholar today is a main reason why those with a fuller, richer, *profounder* disposition no longer find a congenial education and congenial *educators*. There is nothing of which our culture suffers more than of the superabundance of pretentious jobbers and fragments of humanity; our universities are, *against* their will, the real hothouses for this kind of withering of the instincts of the spirit. And the whole of Europe already has some idea of this—power politics deceives nobody. Germany is considered more and more as Europe's *flatland*. I am still looking for a German with whom I might be able to be serious in my own way—and how much more for one with whom I might be cheerful! *Twilight of the Idols:* who today would comprehend from what seriousness a philosopher seeks recreation here? Our cheerfulness is what is most incomprehensible about us.

4

Even a rapid estimate shows that it is not only obvious that German culture is declining but that there is sufficient reason for that. In the end, no one can spend more than he has: that is true of the individual, it is true of a people. If one spends oneself for power, for power politics, for economics, world trade, parliamentarianism, and military interests—if one spends in *this* direction the quantum of understanding, seriousness, will, and self-overcoming which one represents, then it will be lacking for the other direction.

Culture and the state—one should not deceive oneself about this—are antagonists: "*Kultur-Staat*" is merely a modern idea. One lives off the other, one thrives at the expense of the other. All great ages of culture are ages of political decline: what is great culturally has always been unpolitical, even *anti-political*. Goethe's heart opened at the phenomenon of Napoleon—it closed at the "Wars of Liberation." At the same moment when Germany comes up as a great power, France gains a new importance as a *cultural power*. Even today much new seriousness, much new *passion* of the spirit, have migrated to Paris; the question of pessimism, for example, the question of Wagner, and almost all psychological and artistic questions are there weighed incomparably more delicately and thoroughly than in Germany—the Germans are altogether incapable of this kind of seriousness. In the history of European culture the rise of the "*Reich*" means one thing above all: a displacement of the center of gravity. It is already known everywhere: in what matters most—and that always remains culture—the Germans are no longer worthy of consideration. One asks: Can you point to even a single spirit who counts from a European point of view, as your Goethe, your Hegel, your Heinrich Heine, your Schopenhauer counted? That there is no longer a single German philosopher—about that there is no end of astonishment.

5

The entire system of higher education in Germany has lost what matters most: the end as well as the means to the end. That education, that *Bildung*, is itself an end—and *not* "the *Reich*"—and that *educators* are needed to that end, and *not* secondary-school teachers and university scholars—that has been forgotten. Educators are needed who have themselves been educated, superior, noble spirits, proved at every moment, proved by words and silence, representing culture which has grown ripe and sweet—not the learned louts whom secondary schools and universities today offer our youth as "higher wet nurses." Educators are lacking, not counting the most exceptional of exceptions, the very first condition of education: hence the decline of German culture. One of this rarest of exceptions is my venerable friend, Jacob Burckhardt in Basel: it is primarily to him that Basel owes its pre-eminence in humaneness.

What the "higher schools" in Germany really achieve is a brutal training, designed to prepare huge numbers of young men, with as little loss of time as possible, to become usable, abusable, in government service. "Higher education" and huge numbers—that is a contradiction to start with. All higher education belongs only to the exception: one must be privileged to have a right to so high a privilege. All great, all beautiful things can never be common property: *pulchrum est paucorum hominum*. What conditions the decline of German culture? That "higher education" is no longer a privilege—the democratism of *Bildung*, which has become "common"—too common. Let it not be forgotten that military privileges really compel an all-too-great attendance in the higher schools, and thus their downfall.

In present-day Germany no one is any longer free to give his children a noble education: our "higher schools" are all set up for the most ambiguous mediocrity, with their teachers, curricula, and teaching aims. And everywhere an indecent haste prevails, as if something would

be lost if the young man of twenty-three were not yet
"finished," or if he did not yet know the answer to the
"main question": *which* calling? A higher kind of human being, if I may say so, does not like "callings,"
precisely because he knows himself to be called. He has
time, he takes time, he does not even think of "finish-
ing": at thirty one is, in the sense of high culture, a
beginner, a child. Our overcrowded secondary schools,
our overworked, stupefied secondary-school teachers,
are a scandal: for one to defend such conditions, as the
professors at Heidelberg did recently, there may perhaps be *causes*—reasons there are none.

6

I put forward at once—lest I break with my style,
which is *affirmative* and deals with contradiction and
criticism only as a means, only involuntarily—the three
tasks for which educators are required. One must learn
to *see*, one must learn to *think*, one must learn to *speak*
and *write:* the goal in all three is a noble culture. Learning to *see*—accustoming the eye to calmness, to patience, to letting things come up to it; postponing
judgment, learning to go around and grasp each individual case from all sides. That is the *first* preliminary
schooling for spirituality: not to react at once to a
stimulus, but to gain control of all the inhibiting, excluding instincts. Learning to *see*, as I understand it, is
almost what, unphilosophically speaking, is called a
strong will: the essential feature is precisely *not* to "will"
—to *be able* to suspend decision. All un-spirituality, all
vulgar commonness, depend on the inability to resist a
stimulus: one *must* react, one follows every impulse. In
many cases, such a compulsion is already pathology,
decline, a symptom of exhaustion—almost everything
that unphilosophical crudity designates with the word

"vice" is merely this physiological inability *not* to react. A practical application of having learned to see: as a learner, one will have become altogether slow, mistrustful, recalcitrant. One will let strange, new things of every kind come up to oneself, inspecting them with hostile calm and withdrawing one's hand. To have all doors standing open, to lie servilely on one's stomach before every little fact, always to be prepared for the leap of putting oneself into the place of, or of *plunging* into, others and other things—in short, the famous modern "objectivity" is bad taste, is *ignoble* par excellence.

7

Learning to *think:* in our schools one no longer has any idea of this. Even in the universities, even among the real scholars of philosophy, logic as a theory, as a practice, as a *craft*, is beginning to die out. One need only read German books: there is no longer the remotest recollection that thinking requires a technique, a teaching curriculum, a will to mastery—that thinking wants to be learned like dancing, *as* a kind of dancing. Who among Germans still knows from experience the delicate shudder which light feet in spiritual matters send into every muscle? The stiff clumsiness of the spiritual gesture, the bungling hand at grasping—that is German to such a degree that abroad one mistakes it for the German character as such. The German has no fingers for nuances.

That the Germans have been able to stand their philosophers at all, especially that most deformed concept-cripple of all time, the *great* Kant, provides not a bad notion of German grace. For one cannot subtract dancing in every form from a noble education—to be able to dance with one's feet, with concepts, with words: need I still add that one must be able to do it with the pen too—that one must learn to *write?* But at this point I should become completely enigmatic for German readers.

SKIRMISHES OF AN UNTIMELY MAN

1

My impossible ones. Seneca: or the toreador of virtue. *Rousseau:* or the return to nature *in impuris naturalibus.* *Schiller:* or the Moral-Trumpeter of Säckingen. *Dante:* or the hyena who *writes poetry* in tombs. *Kant:* or cant as an intelligible character. *Victor Hugo:* or the pharos at the sea of nonsense. *Liszt:* or the school of smoothness—with women. *George Sand:* or *lactea ubertas—* in translation, the milk cow with "a beautiful style." *Michelet:* or the enthusiasm which takes off its coat. *Carlyle:* or pessimism as a poorly digested dinner. *John Stuart Mill:* or insulting clarity. *Les frères de Goncourt:* or the two Ajaxes in battle with Homer—music by Offenbach. *Zola:* or "the delight in stinking."

2

Renan. Theology: or the corruption of reason by "original sin" (Christianity). Witness Renan who, whenever he risks a Yes or No of a more general nature, scores a miss with painful regularity. He wants, for example, to weld together *la science* and *la noblesse:* but *la science* belongs with democracy; what could be plainer? With no little ambition, he wishes to represent an aristocracy of the spirit: yet at the same time he is on his knees before its very counter-doctrine, the *évangile des humbles*—and not only on his knees. To what avail is all free-spiritedness, modernity, mockery, and wry-neck suppleness, if in one's guts one is still a Christian, a Catholic—in fact, a priest! Renan is most inventive, just like a Jesuit and father confessor, when it comes to seduction; his spirituality does not even lack the broad fat popish smile—like all priests, he becomes dangerous only when he loves. Nobody can equal him when it comes to adoring in a manner endangering life itself. This spirit of Renan's, a spirit which is enervated, is one more calamity for poor, sick, will-sick France.

3

Sainte Beuve. Nothing of virility, full of petty wrath against all virile spirits. Wanders around, cowardly, curious, bored, eavesdropping—a female at bottom, with a female's lust for revenge and a female's sensuality. As a psychologist, a genius of *médisance*,[1] inexhaustibly rich in means to that end; no one knows better how to mix praise with poison. Plebeian in the lowest instincts and related to the *ressentiment* of Rousseau: consequently, a romantic—for underneath all *romantisme* lie the grunting and greed of Rousseau's instinct for revenge. A revolutionary, but still pretty well harnessed by fear. Without freedom when confronted with anything strong (public opinion, the Academy, the court, even Port Royal). Embittered against everything great in men and things, against whatever believes in itself. Poet and half-female enough to sense the great as a power; always writhing like the famous worm because he always feels stepped upon. As a critic, without any standard, steadiness, and backbone, with the cosmopolitan libertine's tongue for a medley of things, but without the courage even to confess his *libertinage*. As a historian, without philosophy, without the power of the philosophical eye—hence declining the task of judging in all significant matters, hiding behind the mask of

[1] "Slander."

"objectivity." It is different with his attitude to all things in which a fine, well-worn taste is the highest tribunal: there he really has the courage to stand by himself and delight in himself—there he is a master. In some respects, a preliminary version of Baudelaire.

4

De imitatione Christi is one of those books which I cannot hold in my hand without a physiological reaction: it exudes a perfume of the Eternal-Feminine which is strictly for Frenchmen—or Wagnerians. This saint has a way of talking about love which arouses even Parisian women to curiosity. I am told that that cleverest of Jesuits, A. Comte, who wanted to lead his Frenchmen to Rome via the detour of science, found his inspiration in this book. I believe it: "the religion of the heart."

5

G. Eliot. They are rid of the Christian God and now believe all the more firmly that they must cling to Christian morality. That is an English consistency; we do not wish to hold it against little moralistic females à la Eliot. In England one must rehabilitate oneself after every little emancipation from theology by showing in a veritably awe-inspiring manner what a moral fanatic one is. That is the penance they pay there.

We others hold otherwise. When one gives up the Christian faith, one pulls the right to Christian morality out from under one's feet. This morality is by no means self-evident: this point has to be exhibited again and again, despite the English flatheads. Christianity is a system, a *whole* view of things thought out together. By breaking one main concept out of it, the faith in God, one breaks the whole: nothing necessary remains in one's hands. Christianity presupposes that man does not know, *cannot* know, what is good for him, what evil: he believes in God, who alone knows it. Christian morality is a command; its origin is transcendent; it *is* beyond all criticism, all right to criticism; it has truth only if God is the truth—it stands and falls with faith in God.

When the English actually believe that they know "intuitively" what is good and evil, when they therefore suppose that they no longer require Christianity as the guarantee of morality, we merely witness the *effects* of the dominion of the Christian value judgment and an expression of the strength and depth of this dominion: such that the origin of English morality has been forgotten, such that the very conditional character of its right to existence is no longer felt. For the English, morality is not yet a problem.

6

George Sand. I read the first *Lettres d'un voyageur:* like everything that is descended from Rousseau, false, fabricated, bellows, exaggerated. I cannot stand this motley wallpaper style any more than the mob aspiration for generous feelings. The worst feature, to be sure, is the female's coquetry with male attributes, with the manners of naughty boys. How cold she must have been throughout, this insufferable artist! She wound herself like a clock—and wrote. Cold, like Hugo, like Balzac, like all the romantics as soon as they took up poetic invention. And how self-satisfied she may have lain there all the while, this fertile writing-cow who had in her something German in the bad sense, like Rousseau himself, her master, and who in any case was possible only during the decline of French taste! But Renan reveres her.

7

Moral for psychologists. Not to go in for backstairs psychology. Never to observe in order to observe! That gives a false perspective, leads to squinting and something forced and exaggerated. Experience as the *wish* to experience does not succeed. One *must* not eye oneself while having an experience; else the eye becomes "an evil eye." A born psychologist guards instinctively against seeing in order to see; the same is true of the born painter. He never works "from nature"; he leaves it to his instinct, to his *camera obscura,* to sift through and express the "case," "nature," that which is "experienced." He is conscious only of what is general, of the conclusion, the result: he does not know arbitrary abstractions from an individual case.

What happens when one proceeds differently? For example, if, in the manner of the Parisian novelists, one goes in for backstairs psychology and deals in gossip, wholesale and retail? Then one lies in wait for reality, as it were, and every evening one brings home a handful of curiosities. But note what finally comes of all this: a heap of splotches, a mosaic at best, but in any case something added together, something restless, a mess of screaming colors. The worst in this respect is accomplished by the Goncourts; they do not put three sentences together without really hurting the eye, the psychologist's eye.

Nature, estimated artistically, is no model. It exaggerates, it distorts, it leaves gaps. Nature is *chance.* To study "from nature" seems to me to be a bad sign: it betrays submission, weakness, fatalism; this lying in the dust before *petit faits* is unworthy of a *whole* artist. To see *what is*—that is the mark of another kind of spirit, the anti-artistic, the factual. One must know *who* one is.

8

Toward a psychology of the artist. If there is to be art, if there is to be any aesthetic doing and seeing, one physiological condition is indispensable: frenzy. Frenzy must first have enhanced the excitability of the whole machine; else there is no art. All kinds of frenzy, however diversely conditioned, have the strength to accomplish this: above all, the frenzy of sexual excitement, this most ancient and original form of frenzy. Also the frenzy that follows all great cravings, all strong affects; the frenzy of feasts, contests, feats of daring, victory, all extreme movement; the frenzy of cruelty; the frenzy in destruction; the frenzy under certain meteorological influences, as for example the frenzy of spring; or under the influence of narcotics; and finally the frenzy of will, the frenzy of an overcharged and swollen will. What is essential in such frenzy is the feeling of increased strength and fullness. Out of this feeling one lends to things, one *forces* them to accept from us, one violates them—this process is called *idealizing.* Let us get rid of a prejudice here: idealizing does not consist, as is commonly held, in subtracting or discounting the petty and inconsequential. What is decisive is rather a tremendous drive to bring out the main features so that the others disappear in the process.

9

In this state one enriches everything out of one's own fullness: whatever one sees, whatever one wills, is seen swelled, taut, strong, overloaded with strength. A man in this state transforms things until they mirror his power—until they are reflections of his perfection. This *having to* transform into perfection is—art. Even everything that he is not yet, becomes for him an occasion of joy in himself; in art man enjoys himself as perfection.

It would be permissible to imagine an opposite state, a specific anti-artistry by instinct—a mode of being which would impoverish all things, making them thin and consumptive. And, as a matter of fact, history is rich in such anti-artists, in such people who are starved by life and must of necessity grab things, eat them out, and make them more meager. This is, for example, the case of the genuine Christian—of Pascal, for example: a Christian who would at the same time be an artist simply does not occur. One should not be childish and object by naming Raphael or some homeopathic Christian of the nineteenth century: Raphael said Yes, Raphael *did* Yes; consequently, Raphael was no Christian.

10

What is the meaning of the conceptual opposites which I have introduced into aesthetics, *Apollinian* and *Dionysian*, both conceived as kinds of frenzy? The Apollinian frenzy excites the eye above all, so that it gains the power of vision. The painter, the sculptor, the epic poet are visionaries par excellence. In the Dionysian state, on the other hand, the whole affective sytem is excited and enhanced: so that it discharges all its means of expression at once and drives forth simultaneously the power of representation, imitation, transfiguration, transformation, and every kind of mimicking and acting. The essential feature here remains the ease of metamorphosis, the inability *not* to react (similar to certain hysterical types who also, upon any suggestion, enter into *any* role). It is impossible for the Dionysian type not to understand any suggestion; he does not overlook any sign of an affect; he possesses the instinct of understanding and guessing in the highest degree, just as he commands the art of communication in the highest degree. He enters into any skin, into any affect: he constantly transforms himself.

Music, as we understand it today, is also a total excitement and a total discharge of the affects, but even so only the remnant of a much fuller world of expression of the affects, a mere residue of the Dionysian histrionicism. To make music possible as a separate art, a number of senses, especially the muscle sense, have been immobilized (at least relatively, for to a certain degree all rhythm still appeals to our muscles); so that man no longer bodily imitates and represents everything he feels. Nevertheless, that is really the normal Dionysian state, at least the original state. Music is the specialization of this state attained slowly at the expense of those faculties which are most closely related to it.

11

The actor, the mime, the dancer, the musician, and the lyric poet are basically related in their instincts and, at bottom, one—but gradually they have become specialized and separated from each other, even to the point of mutual opposition. The lyric poet remained united with the musician for the longest time; the actor, with the dancer.

The *architect* represents neither a Dionysian nor an Apollinian state: here it is the great act of will, the will that moves mountains, the frenzy of the great will which aspires to art. The most powerful human beings have always inspired architects; the architect has always been under the spell of power. His buildings are supposed to render pride visible, and the victory over gravity, the will to power. Architecture is a kind of eloquence of power in forms—now persuading, even flattering, now only commanding. The highest feeling of power and sureness finds expression in a *grand style*. The power which no longer needs any proof, which spurns pleasing, which does not answer lightly, which feels no witness near, which lives oblivious of all opposition to it, which reposes within itself, fatalistically, a law among laws—that speaks of itself as a grand style.

12

I have been reading the life of *Thomas Carlyle*, this unconscious and involuntary farce, this heroic-moralistic interpretation of dyspeptic states. Carlyle: a man of strong words and attitudes, a rhetor from *need*, constantly lured by the craving for a strong faith and the feeling of his incapacity for it (in this respect, a typical romantic!). The craving for a strong faith is no proof of a strong faith, but quite the contrary. If one has such a faith, then one can afford the beautiful luxury of skepticism: one is sure enough, firm enough, has ties enough for that. Carlyle drugs something in himself with the fortissimo of his veneration of men of strong faith and with his rage against the less simple-minded: he *requires* noise. A constant passionate dishonesty against himself—that is his *proprium;* in this respect he is and remains interesting. Of course, in England he is admired precisely for his honesty. Well, that is English; and in view of the fact that the English are the people of consummate cant, it is even as it should be, and not only comprehensible. At bottom, Carlyle is an English atheist who makes it a point of honor not to be one.

13

Emerson. Much more enlightened, more roving, more manifold, subtler than Carlyle; above all, happier. One who instinctively nourishes himself only on ambrosia, leaving behind what is indigestible in things. Compared with Carlyle, a man of taste. Carlyle, who loved him very much, nevertheless said of him: "He does not give us enough to chew on"—which may be true, but is no reflection on Emerson. Emerson has that gracious and clever cheerfulness which discourages all seriousness; he simply does not know how old he is already and how young he is still going to be; he could say of himself, quoting Lope de Vega: *"Yo me sucedo a mi mismo."* [1] His spirit always finds reasons for being satisfied and even grateful; and at times he touches on the cheerful transcendency of the worthy gentleman who returned from an amorous rendezvous, *tamquam re bene gesta. "Ut desint vires,"* he said gratefully, *"tamen est laudanda voluptas."* [2]

14

Anti-Darwin. As for the famous "struggle for *existence,*" so far it seems to me to be asserted rather than proved. It occurs, but as an exception; the total appearance of life is not the extremity, not starvation, but rather riches, profusion, even absurd squandering—and where there is struggle, it is a struggle for *power.* One should not mistake Malthus for nature.

Assuming, however, that there is such a struggle for existence—and, indeed, it occurs—its result is un-

[1] "I am my own heir."
[2] "As if he had accomplished his mission. 'Though the power is lacking, the lust is nevertheless praiseworthy.'"

fortunately the opposite of what Darwin's school desires, and of what one *might* perhaps desire with them—namely, in favor of the strong, the privileged, the fortunate exceptions. The species do *not* grow in perfection: the weak prevail over the strong again and again, for they are the great majority—and they are also more *intelligent*. Darwin forgot the spirit (that is English!); *the weak have more spirit*. One must need spirit to acquire spirit; one loses it when one no longer needs it. Whoever has strength dispenses with the spirit ("Let it go!" they think in Germany today; "the *Reich* must still remain to us."[1]). It will be noted that by "spirit" I mean care, patience, cunning, simulation, great self-control, and everything that is mimicry (the latter includes a great deal of so-called virtue).

15

Casuistry of Psychologists. This man knows human nature; why does he really study people? He wants to seize little advantages over them—or big ones, for that matter—he is a politician. That one over there also knows human nature, and you say that he seeks no profit for himself, that he is thoroughly "impersonal." Look more closely! Perhaps he even wants a worse advantage: to feel superior to other human beings, to be able to look down on them, and no longer to mistake himself for one of them. This "impersonal" type is a *despiser* of human beings, while the first type is the more humane species, appearances notwithstanding. At least he places himself on the same plane, he places himself among them.

[1] Quotation from Luther's most famous hymn, *Ein feste Burg*. In its original context, *Reich* refers to the kingdom of God.

16

The *psychological tact* of the Germans seems very questionable to me, in view of quite a number of cases which modesty prevents me from enumerating. In one case I shall not lack a great occasion to substantiate my thesis: I bear the Germans a grudge for having made such a mistake about *Kant* and his "backdoor philosophy," as I call it—for that was not the type of intellectual integrity. The other thing I do not like to hear is a notorious "and": the Germans say "Goethe *and* Schiller"—I am afraid they say "Schiller and Goethe." Don't they *know* this Schiller yet? And there are even worse "ands"; with my own ears I have heard, if only among university professors, "Schopenhauer *and* Hartmann."

17

The most spiritual human beings, if we assume that they are the most courageous, also experience by far the most painful tragedies: but just for that reason they honor life because it pits its greatest opposition against them.

18

On the "intellectual conscience." Nothing seems rarer to me today than genuine hypocrisy. I greatly suspect that the soft air of our culture is insalubrious for this plant. Hypocrisy belongs in the ages of strong faith when, even though *constrained* to display another faith, one did not abandon one's own faith. Today one does abandon it; or, even more commonly, one adds a second faith—and in either case one remains *honest*. Without a doubt, a very much greater number of convictions is possible today than formerly: "possible" means permissible, which means *harmless*. This begets tolerance toward oneself.

Tolerance toward oneself permits several convictions, and they get along with each other: they are careful, like all the rest of the world, not to compromise themselves. How does one compromise oneself today? If one is consistent. If one proceeds in a straight line. If one is not ambiguous enough to permit five conflicting interpretations. If one is genuine.

I fear greatly that modern man is simply too comfortable for some vices, so that they die out by default. All evil that is a function of a strong will—and perhaps there is no evil without strength of will—degenerates into virtue in our tepid air. The few hypocrites whom I have met imitated hypocrisy: like almost every tenth person today, they were actors.

19

Beautiful and ugly. Nothing is more conditional—or, let us say, narrower—than our feeling for beauty. Whoever would think of it apart from man's joy in man would immediately lose any foothold. "Beautiful in itself" is a mere phrase, not even a concept. In the beautiful, man posits himself as the measure of perfection; in special cases he worships himself in it. A species cannot do otherwise but thus affirm itself alone. Its *lowest* instinct, that of self-preservation and self-expansion, still radiates in such sublimities. Man believes the world itself to be overloaded with beauty—and he forgets himself as the cause of this. He alone has presented the world with beauty—alas! only with a very human, all-too-human beauty. At bottom, man mirrors himself in things; he considers everything beautiful that reflects his own image: the judgment "beautiful" is the *vanity of his species*. For a little suspicion may whisper this question into the skeptic's ear: Is the world really beautified by the fact that man thinks it beautiful? He has *humanized* it, that is all. But nothing, absolutely nothing, guarantees that man should be the model of beauty. Who knows what he looks like in the eyes of a higher judge of beauty? Daring perhaps? Perhaps even amusing? Perhaps a little arbitrary?

"O Dionysus, divine one, why do you pull me by my ears?" Ariadne once asked her philosophic lover during one of those famous dialogues on Naxos. "I find a kind of humor in your ears, Ariadne: why are they not even longer?"

20

Nothing is beautiful, except man alone: all aesthetics rests upon this naïveté, which is its *first* truth. Let us immediately add the second: nothing is ugly except the degenerating man—and with this the realm of aesthetic judgment is circumscribed. Physiologically, everything ugly weakens and saddens man. It reminds him of decay, danger, impotence; it actually deprives him of strength. One can measure the effect of the ugly with a dynamometer. Wherever man is depressed at all, he senses the proximity of something "ugly." His feeling of power, his will to power, his courage, his pride—all fall with the ugly and rise with the beautiful. In both cases we draw an inference: the premises for it are piled up in the greatest abundance in instinct. The ugly is understood as a sign and symptom of degeneration: whatever reminds us in the least of degeneration causes in us the judgment of "ugly." Every suggestion of exhaustion, of heaviness, of age, of weariness; every kind of lack of freedom, such as cramps, such as paralysis; and above all, the smell, the color, the form of dissolution, of decomposition—even in the ultimate attenuation into a symbol—all evoke the same reaction, the value judgment, "ugly." A *hatred* is aroused—but whom does man hate then? There is no doubt: the *decline of his type*. Here he hates out of the deepest instinct of the species; in this hatred there is a shudder, caution, depth, farsightedness—it is the deepest hatred there is. It is because of this that art is deep.

21

Schopenhauer. Schopenhauer, the last German worthy of consideration (who represents a *European* event like Goethe, like Hegel, like Heinrich Heine, and not merely a local event, a "national" one), is for a psychologist a first-rate case: namely, as a maliciously ingenious attempt to adduce in favor of a nihilistic total depreciation of life precisely the counter-instances, the great self-affirmations of the "will to life," life's forms of exuberance. He has interpreted *art*, heroism, genius, beauty, great sympathy, knowledge, the will to truth, and tragedy, in turn, as consequences of "negation" or of the "will's" need to negate—the greatest psychological counterfeit in all history, not counting Christianity. On closer inspection, he is at this point merely the heir of the Christian interpretation: only he knew how to approve that which Christianity had repudiated, the great cultural facts of humanity—albeit in a Christian, that is, nihilistic, manner (namely, as ways of "redemption," as anticipations of "redemption," as stimuli of the need for "redemption").

22

I take a single case. Schopenhauer speaks of *beauty* with a melancholy fervor. Why? Because he sees in it a bridge on which one will go farther, or develp a thirst to go farther. Beauty is for him a momentary redemption from the "will"—a lure to eternal redemption. Particularly, he praises beauty as the redeemer from "the focal point of the will," from sexuality—in beauty he sees the negation of the drive toward procreation. Queer saint! Somebody seems to be contradicting you; I fear it is nature. To what end is there any such thing as beauty in tone, color, fragrance, or rhythmic movement in nature? What is it that beauty evokes? Fortunately, a philosopher contradicts him too. No lesser authority than that of the divine Plato (so Schopenhauer himself calls him) maintains a different proposition: that all beauty incites procreation, that just this is the *proprium* of its effect, from the most sensual up to the most spiritual.

23

Plato goes further. He says with an innocence possible only for a Greek, not a "Christian," that there would be no Platonic philosophy at all if there were not such beautiful youths in Athens: it is only their sight that transposes the philosopher's soul into an erotic trance, leaving it no peace until it lowers the seed of all exalted things into such beautiful soil. Another queer saint! One does not trust one's ears, even if one should trust Plato. At least one guesses that they philosophized differently in Athens, especially in public. Nothing is less Greek than the conceptual web-spinning of a hermit—*amor intellectualis dei* [1] after the fashion of Spinoza. Philosophy after the fashion of Plato might rather be defined as an erotic contest, as a further development and turning inward of the ancient agonistic gymnastics and of its *presuppositions*. What ultimately grew out of this philosophic eroticism of Plato? A new art form of the Greek agon: dialectics. Finally, I recall—

[1] "Intellectual love of God."

against Schopenhauer and in honor of Plato—that the whole higher culture and literature of *classical* France too grew on the soil of sexual interest. Everywhere in it one may look for the amatory, the senses, the sexual contest, "the woman"—one will never look in vain.

24

L'art pour l'art. The fight against purpose in art is always a fight against the moralizing tendency in art, against its subordination to morality. *L'art pour l'art* means, "The devil take morality!" But even this hostility still betrays the overpowering force of the prejudice. When the purpose of moral preaching and of improving man has been excluded from art, it still does not follow by any means that art is altogether purposeless, aimless, senseless—in short, *l'art pour l'art*, a worm chewing its own tail. "Rather no purpose at all than a moral purpose!"—that is the talk of mere passion. A psychologist, on the other hand, asks: what does all art do? does it not praise? glorify? choose? prefer? With all this it strengthens or weakens certain valuations. Is this merely a "moreover"? an accident? something in which the artist's instinct had no share? Or is it not the very presupposition of the artist's ability? Does his basic instinct aim at art, or rather at the sense of art, at life? at a desirability of life? Art is the great stimulus to life: how could one understand it as purposeless, as aimless, as *l'art pour l'art?*

One question remains: art also makes apparent much that is ugly, hard, and questionable in life; does it not thereby spoil life for us? And indeed there have been philosophers who attributed this sense to it: "liberation from the will" was what Schopenhauer taught as the over-all end of art; and with admiration he found the great utility of tragedy in its "evoking resignation." But this, as I have already suggested, is the pessimist's perspective and "evil eye." We must appeal to the artists themselves. What does the tragic artist communicate of himself? Is it not precisely the state *without* fear in the face of the fearful and questionable that he is showing? This state itself is a great desideratum; whoever knows it, honors it with the greatest honors. He communicates it—*must* communicate it, provided he is an artist, a genius of communication. Courage and freedom of feeling before a powerful enemy, before a sublime calamity, before a problem that arouses dread—this triumphant state is what the tragic artist chooses, what he glorifies. Before tragedy, what is warlike in our soul celebrates its Saturnalia; whoever is used to suffering, whoever seeks out suffering, the heroic man praises his own being through tragedy—to him alone the tragedian presents this drink of sweetest cruelty.

25

To put up with people, to keep open house with one's heart—that is liberal, but that is merely liberal. One recognizes those hearts which are capable of *noble* hospitality by the many draped windows and closed shutters: they keep their best rooms empty. Why? Because they expect guests with whom one does not "put up."

26

We no longer esteem ourselves sufficiently when we communicate ourselves. Our true experiences are not at all garrulous. They could not communicate themselves even if they tried. That is because they lack the right word. Whatever we have words for, that we have already got beyond. In all talk there is a grain of contempt. Language, it seems, was invented only for what is average, medium, communicable. With language the speaker immediately vulgarizes himself. Out of a morality for deaf-mutes and other philosophers.

27

"This picture is enchantingly beautiful!" [1] The literary female: unsatisfied, excited, her heart and entrails void, ever listening, full of painful curiosity, to the imperative, which whispers from the depths of her organism, *"aut liberi aut libri"* [2]—the literary female: educated enough to understand the voice of nature even when it speaks Latin, and yet vain enough and goose enough to speak secretly with herself in French, *"je me verrai, je me lirai, je m'extasierai et je dirai: Possible, que j'aie eu tant d'esprit?"* [3]

28

The "impersonal" get a word in. "Nothing is easier for us than to be wise, patient, and superior. We drip with the oil of forgiveness and sympathy, we are absurdly just, we pardon everything. For that very reason we ought to be a little more strict with ourselves; for that very reason we ought to breed a little affect in ourselves from time to time, a little vice of an affect. It may be hard on us; and among ourselves we may even laugh at the sight we thus offer. But what can be done about it? No other way of self-overcoming is left to us any more: this is *our* asceticism, *our* penance." Developing personal traits: the virtue of the "impersonal."

---

[1] Quotation from *The Magic Flute.*
[2] "Either children or books."
[3] "I shall see myself, I shall read myself, I shall go into ecstasies, and I shall say: Is it possible that I should have had so much *esprit?*"

29

From a doctoral examination. "What is the task of all higher education?" To turn men into machines. "What are the means?" Man must learn to be bored. "How is that accomplished?" By means of the concept of duty. "Who serves as the model?" The philologist: he teaches grinding. "Who is the perfect man?" The civil servant. "Which philosophy offers the highest formula for the civil servant?" Kant's: the civil servant as a thing-in-itself raised up to be judge over the civil servant as phenomenon.

30

The right to stupidity. The weary laborer who breathes slowly, looks genial, and lets things go as they may—this typical figure, encountered today, in the age of labor (and of the "*Reich*"!), in all classes of society, claims *art,* no less, as his own sphere, including books and, above all, magazines—and even more the beauties of nature, Italy. The man of the evening, with his "savage drives gone to sleep" (as Faust says), needs a summer resort, the seashore, glaciers, Bayreuths. In such ages art has a right to pure foolishness—as a kind of vacation for spirit, wit, and feeling. Wagner understood that. Pure foolishness restores.[1]

31

Another problem of diet. The means by which Julius Caesar defended himself against sickliness and headaches: tremendous marches, the most frugal way of life, uninterrupted sojourn in the open air, continuous exertion—these are, in general, the universal rules of preservation and protection against the extreme vulner-

---

[1] Wagner himself calls Parsifal "the pure fool."

ability of that subtle machine, working under the highest pressure, which we call genius.

32

The immoralist speaks. Nothing offends the philosopher's taste more than man, insofar as man desires. If he sees man in action, even if he sees this most courageous, most cunning, most enduring animal lost in labyrinthian distress—how admirable man appears to him! He still likes him. But the philosopher despises the desiring man, also the "desirable" man—and altogether all desirabilities, all ideals of man. If a philosopher could be a nihilist, he would be one because he finds nothing behind all the ideals of man. Or not even nothing—but only what is abject, absurd, sick, cowardly, and weary, all kinds of dregs out of the emptied cup of his life. Man being so venerable in his reality, how is it that he deserves no respect insofar as he desires? Must he atone for being so capable in reality? Must he balance his activity, the strain on head and will in all his activity, by stretching his limbs in the realm of the imaginary and the absurd?

The history of his desirabilities has so far been the *partie honteuse* of man: one should beware of reading in it too long. What justifies man is his reality—it will eternally justify him. How much greater is the worth of the real man, compared with any merely desired, dreamed-up, foully fabricated man? with any ideal man? And it is only the ideal man who offends the philosopher's taste.

33

The natural value of egoism. Self-interest is worth as much as the person who has it: it can be worth a great deal, and it can be unworthy and contemptible.

Every individual may be scrutinized to see whether he represents the ascending or the descending line of life. Having made that decision, one has a canon for the worth of his self-interest. If he represents the ascending line, then his worth is indeed extraordinary—and for the sake of life as a whole, which takes a step farther through him, the care for his preservation and for the creation of the best conditions for him may even be extreme. The single one, the "individual," as hitherto understood by the people and the philosophers alike, is an error after all: he is nothing by himself, no atom, no "link in the chain," nothing merely inherited from former times; he is the whole single line of humanity up to himself. If he represents the descending development, decay, chronic degeneration, and sickness (sicknesses are, in general, the consequences of decay, not its causes), then he has small worth, and the minimum of decency requires that he take away as little as possible from those who have turned out well. He is merely their parasite.

34

Christian and anarchist. When the anarchist, as the mouthpiece of the declining strata of society, demands with a fine indignation what is "right," "justice," and "equal rights," he is merely under the pressure of his own uncultured state, which cannot comprehend the real reason for his suffering—what it is that he is poor in: life. A causal instinct asserts itself in him: it must be somebody's fault that he is in a bad way.

Also, the "fine indignation" itself soothes him; it is a pleasure for all wretched devils to scold: it gives a slight but intoxicating sense of power. Even plaintiveness and complaining can give life a charm for the sake of which one endures it: there is a fine dose of revenge in every complaint; one charges one's own bad situation, and under certain circumstances even one's own badness, to those who are different, as if that were an injustice, a forbidden privilege. "If I am canaille, you ought to be too"—on such logic are revolutions made.

Complaining is never any good: it stems from weakness. Whether one charges one's misfortune to others or to oneself—the socialist does the former; the Christian, for example, the latter—really makes no difference. The common and, let us add, the unworthy, thing is that it is supposed to be somebody's fault that one is suffering; in short, that the sufferer prescribes the honey of revenge for himself against his suffering. The objects of this need for revenge, as a need for pleasure, are mere occasions: everywhere the sufferer finds occasions for satisfying his little revenge. If he is a Christian—to repeat it once more—he finds them in himself. The Christian and the anarchist are both decadents. When the Christian condemns, slanders, and besmirches "the world," his instinct is the same as that which prompts the socialist worker to condemn, slander, and besmirch *society*. The "last judgment" is the sweet comfort of revenge—the revolution, which the socialist worker also awaits, but conceived as a little farther off. The "beyond"—why a beyond, if not as a means for besmirching *this* world?

35

Critique of the morality of decadence. An "altruistic" morality—a morality in which self-interest wilts away—remains a bad sign under all circumstances. This is true of individuals; it is particularly true of nations. The best is lacking when self-interest begins to be lacking. Instinctively to choose what is harmful for *oneself*, to feel attracted by "disinterested" motives, that is virtually the formula of decadence. "Not to seek one's own advantage"—that is merely the moral fig leaf for quite a different, namely, a physiological, state of affairs: "I no longer know how to *find* my own advantage." Disgregation of the instincts! Man is finished when he becomes altruistic. Instead of saying naïvely, "*I* am no longer worth anything," the moral lie in the mouth of the decadent says, "Nothing is worth anything, life is not worth anything." Such a judgment always remains very dangerous, it is contagious: throughout the morbid soil of society it soon proliferates into a tropical vegetation of concepts—now as a religion (Christianity), now as a philosophy (Schopenhauerism). Sometimes the poisonous vegetation which has grown out of such decomposition poisons life itself for millennia with its fumes.

36

Morality for physicians. The sick man is a parasite of society. In a certain state it is indecent to live longer. To go on vegetating in cowardly dependence on physicians and machinations, after the meaning of life, the right to life, has been lost, that ought to prompt a profound contempt in society. The physicians, in turn, would have to be the mediators of this contempt—not prescriptions, but every day a new dose of nausea with their patients. To create a new responsibility, that of the physician, for all cases in which the highest interest of life, of ascending life, demands the most inconsiderate pushing down and aside of degenerating life—for example, for the right of procreation, for the right to be born, for the right to live.

To die proudly when it is no longer possible to live proudly. Death freely chosen, death at the right time, brightly and cheerfully accomplished amid children and witnesses: then a real farewell is still possible, as the one who is taking leave is still there; also a real estimate of what one has achieved and what one has wished, drawing the sum of one's life—all in opposition to the wretched and revolting comedy that Christianity has made of the hour of death. One should never forget that Christianity has exploited the weakness of the dying for a rape of the conscience; and the manner of death itself, for value judgments about man and the past.

Here it is important to defy all the cowardices of prejudice and to establish, above all, the real, that is, the physiological, appreciation of so-called *natural* death—which is in the end also "unnatural," a kind of suicide. One never perishes through anybody but oneself. But usually it is death under the most contemptible conditions, an unfree death, death *not* at the right time, a coward's death. From love of *life*, one should desire a different death: free, conscious, without accident, without ambush.

Finally, some advice for our dear pessimists and other decadents. It is not in our hands to prevent our birth; but we can correct this mistake—for in some cases it is a mistake. When one does away with oneself, one does the most estimable thing possible: one almost earns the right to live. Society—what am I saying?—life itself derives more advantage from this than from any "life" of renunciation, anemia, and other virtues: one has liberated the others from one's sight; one has liberated life from an objection. Pessimism, *pur, vert,* is proved only by the self-refutation of our dear pessimists: one must advance a step further in its logic and not only negate life with "will and representation," as Schopenhauer did—one must first of all negate Schopenhauer.

Incidentally, however contagious pessimism is, it still does not increase the sickliness of an age, of a generation as a whole: it is an expression of this sickliness. One falls victim to it as one falls victim to cholera: one has to be morbid enough in one's whole predisposition. Pessimism itself does not create a single decadent more; I recall the statistics which show that the years in which cholera rages do not differ from other years in the total number of deaths.

37

Whether we have become more moral. Against my conception of "beyond good and evil"—as was to be expected—the whole ferocity of moral hebetation, mistaken for morality itself in Germany, as is well known, has gone into action: I could tell fine stories about that. Above all I was asked to consider the "undeniable superiority" of our age in moral judgment, the real *progress* we have made here: compared with *us,* a Cesare Borgia is by no means to be represented after my manner as a "higher man," a kind of overman. A Swiss editor of the *Bund* went so far that he "understood" the meaning of my work—not without expressing his respect for my courage and daring—to be a demand for the abolition of all decent feelings. Thank you! In reply, I take the liberty of raising the question whether we have really become more moral. That all the world believes this to be the case merely constitutes an objection.

We modern men, very tender, very easily hurt, and offering as well as receiving consideration a hundredfold, really have the conceit that this tender humanity which we represent, this attained unanimity in sympathetic regard, in readiness to help, in mutual trust, represents positive progress and that in this respect we are

far above the men of the Renaissance. But that is how
every age thinks, how it *must* think. What is certain is
that we may not place ourselves in Renaissance conditions, not even by an act of thought: our nerves would
not endure that reality, not to speak of our muscles. But
such incapacity does not prove progress, only another,
later constitution, one which is weaker, frailer, more
easily hurt, and which necessarily generates a morality
rich in consideration. Were we to think away our
frailty and lateness, our physiological senescence, then
our morality of "humanization" would immediately lose
its value too (in itself, no morality has any value)—it
would even arouse disdain. On the other hand, let us
not doubt that we moderns, with our thickly padded
humanity, which at all costs wants to avoid bumping
into a stone, would have provided Cesare Borgia's contemporaries with a comedy at which they could have
laughed themselves to death. Indeed, we are unwittingly
funny beyond all measure with our modern "virtues."

The decrease in instincts which are hostile and arouse
mistrust—and that is all our "progress" amounts to—
represents but one of the consequences attending the
general decrease in *vitality*: it requires a hundred times
more trouble and caution to make so conditional and
late an existence prevail. Hence each helps the other;
hence everyone is to a certain extent sick, and everyone
is a nurse for the sick. And that is called "virtue."
Among men who still knew life differently—fuller, more
squandering, more overflowing—it would have been
called by another name: "cowardice" perhaps, "wretchedness," "old ladies' morality."

Our softening of manners—that is my proposition;
that is, if you will, my innovation—is a consequence of
decline; the hardness and terribleness of morals, conversely, can be a consequence of an excess of life. For

in that case much may also be dared, much challenged, and much squandered. What was once the spice of life would be poison for us.

To be indifferent—that too is a form of strength— for that we are likewise too old, too late. Our morality of sympathy, against which I was the first to issue a warning—that which one might call *l'impressionisme morale*—is just another expression of that physiological overexcitability which is characteristic of everything decadent. That movement which tried to introduce itself scientifically with Schopenhauer's morality of pity—a very unfortunate attempt!—is the real movement of decadence in morality; as such, it is profoundly related to Christian morality. Strong ages, noble cultures, consider pity, "neighbor-love," and the lack of self and self-assurance something contemptible. Ages must be measured by their positive strength—and then that lavishly squandering and fatal age of the Renaissance appears as the last *great* age; and we moderns, with our anxious self-solicitude and neighbor-love, with our virtues of work, modesty, legality, and scientism— accumulating, economic, machinelike—appear as a *weak* age. Our virtues are conditional on, are provoked by, our weaknesses. "Equality," as a certain factual increase in similarity, which merely finds expression in the theory of "equal rights," is an essential feature of decline. The cleavage between man and man, status and status, the plurality of types, the will to be oneself, to stand out—what I call the *pathos of distance*, that is characteristic of every strong age. The strength to withstand tension, the width of the tensions between extremes, becomes ever smaller today; finally, the extremes themselves become blurred to the point of similarity.

All our political theories and constitutions—and the

"German *Reich*" is by no means an exception—are consequences, necessary consequences, of decline; the unconscious effect of decadence has assumed mastery even over the ideals of some of the sciences. My objection against the whole of sociology in England and France remains that it knows from experience only the forms of social decay, and with perfect innocence accepts its own instincts of decay as the norm of sociological value-judgments. The decline of life, the decrease in the power to organize, that is, to separate, tear open clefts, subordinate and super-ordinate—all this has been formulated as the ideal in contemporary sociology. Our socialists are decadents, but Mr. Herbert Spencer is a decadent too: he considers the triumph of altruism desirable.

38

My conception of freedom. The value of a thing sometimes does not lie in that which one attains by it, but in what one pays for it—what it costs us. I shall give an example. Liberal institutions cease to be liberal as soon as they are attained: later on, there are no worse and no more thorough injurers of freedom than liberal institutions. Their effects are known well enough: they undermine the will to power; they level mountain and valley, and call that morality; they make men small, cowardly, and hedonistic—every time it is the herd animal that triumphs with them. Liberalism: in other words, herd-animalization.

These same institutions produce quite different effects while they are still being fought for; then they really promote freedom in a powerful way. On closer inspection, it is war that produces these effects, the war *for* liberal institutions, which, as a war, permits illiberal instincts to continue. And war educates for freedom.

For what is freedom? That one has the will to assume responsibility for oneself. That one maintains the distance which separates us. That one becomes more indifferent to difficulties, hardships, privation, even to life itself. That one is prepared to sacrifice human beings for one's cause, not excluding oneself. Freedom means that the manly instincts which delight in war and victory dominate over other instincts, for example, over those of "pleasure." The human being who has *become free*—and how much more the *spirit* who has become free—spits on the contemptible type of well-being dreamed of by shopkeepers, Christians, cows, females, Englishmen, and other democrats. The free man is a *warrior*.

How is freedom measured in individuals and peoples? According to the resistance which must be overcome, according to the exertion required, to remain on top. The highest type of free men should be sought where the highest resistance is constantly overcome: five steps from tyranny, close to the threshold of the danger of servitude. This is true psychologically if by "tyrants" are meant inexorable and fearful instincts that provoke the maximum of authority and discipline against themselves; most beautiful type: Julius Caesar. This is true politically too; one need only go through history. The peoples who had some value, *attained* some value, never attained it under liberal institutions: it was great danger that made something of them that merits respect. Danger alone acquaints us with our own resources, our virtues, our armor and weapons, our *spirit*, and *forces* us to be strong. *First* principle: one must need to be strong—otherwise one will never become strong.

Those large hothouses for the strong—for the strongest kind of human being that has so far been known—the aristocratic commonwealths of the type of Rome or

Venice, understood freedom exactly in the sense in which I understand it: as something one has or does *not* have, something one *wants*, something one *conquers*.

39

Critique of modernity. Our institutions are no good any more: on that there is universal agreement. However, it is not their fault but ours. Once we have lost all the instincts out of which institutions grow, we lose institutions altogether because we are no longer good for them. Democracy has ever been the form of decline in organizing power: in *Human, All-Too-Human* (I, 472) I already characterized modern democracy, together with its hybrids such as the "German *Reich*," as the form of decline of the state. In order that there may be institutions, there must be a kind of will, instinct, or imperative, which is anti-liberal to the point of malice: the will to tradition, to authority, to responsibility for centuries to come, to the solidarity of chains of generations, forward and backward *ad infinitum*. When this will is present, something like the *imperium Romanum* is founded; or like Russia, the *only* power today which has endurance, which can wait, which can still promise something—Russia, the concept that suggests the opposite of the wretched European nervousness and system of small states, which has entered a critical phase with the founding of the German *Reich*.

The whole of the West no longer possesses the instincts out of which institutions grow, out of which a *future* grows: perhaps nothing antagonizes its "modern spirit" so much. One lives for the day, one lives very fast, one lives very irresponsibly: precisely this is called "freedom." That which makes an institution an institution is despised, hated, repudiated: one fears the danger of a new slavery the moment the word "authority" is even spoken out loud. That is how far decadence has advanced in the value-instincts of our politicians, of our political parties: *instinctively* they prefer what disintegrates, what hastens the end.

Witness *modern marriage*. All rationality has clearly vanished from modern marriage; yet that is no objection to marriage, but to modernity. The rationality of marriage—that lay in the husband's sole juridical responsibility, which gave marriage a center of gravity, while today it limps on both legs. The rationality of marriage—that lay in its indissolubility in principle, which lent it an accent that could be heard above the accident of feeling, passion, and what is merely momentary. It also lay in the family's responsibility for the choice of a spouse. With the growing indulgence of love matches, the very foundation of marriage has been eliminated, that which alone makes an institution of it. Never, absolutely never, can an institution be founded on an idiosyncrasy; one cannot, as I have said, found marriage on "love"—it can be founded on the sex drive, on the property drive (wife and child as property), on the drive to dominate, which continually organizes for itself the smallest structure of domination, the family, and which needs children and heirs to hold fast—physiologically too—to an attained measure of power, influence, and wealth, in order to prepare for long-range tasks, for a solidarity of instinct between the centuries. Marriage as an institution involves the affirmation of the largest and most enduring form of organization: when society cannot affirm itself as a whole, down to the most distant generations, then marriage has altogether no meaning. Modern marriage has lost its meaning—consequently one abolishes it.

40

The labor question. The stupidity—at bottom, the degeneration of instinct, which is today the cause of *all* stupidities—is that there is a labor question at all. Certain things one does not question: that is the first imperative of instinct. I simply cannot see what one proposes to do with the European worker now that one has made a question of him. He is far too well off not to ask for more and more, not to ask more immodestly. In the end, he has numbers on his side. The hope is gone forever that a modest and self-sufficient kind of man, a Chinese type, might here develop as a class: and there would have been reason in that, it would almost have been a necessity. But what was done? Everything to nip in the bud even the preconditions for this: the instincts by virtue of which the worker becomes possible as a class, possible in his own eyes, have been destroyed through and through with the most irresponsible thoughtlessness. The worker was qualified for military service, granted the right to organize and to vote: is it any wonder that the worker today experiences his own existence as distressing—morally speaking, as an injustice? But what is *wanted?* I ask once more. If one wants an end, one must also want the means: if one wants slaves, then one is a fool if one educates them to be masters.

41

"Freedom which I do *not* mean." In times like these, abandonment to one's instincts is one calamity more. Our instincts contradict, disturb, destroy each other; I have already defined what is *modern* as physiological self-contradiction. Rationality in education would require that under iron pressure at least one of these instinct systems be paralyzed to permit another to gain in power, to become strong, to become master. Today the individual still has to be made possible by being pruned: possible here means *whole*. The reverse is what happens: the claim for independence, for free development, for *laisser aller* is pressed most hotly by the very people for whom no reins would be too strict. This is true *in politics*, this is true in art. But that is a symptom of decadence: our modern conception of "freedom" is one more proof of the degeneration of the instincts.

42

Where faith is needed. Nothing is rarer among moralists and saints than honesty. Perhaps they say the contrary, perhaps they even *believe* it. For when a faith is more useful, more effective, and more persuasive than *conscious* hypocrisy, then hypocrisy soon turns instinctively into *innocence*: first principle for the understanding of great saints. The philosophers are merely another kind of saint, and their whole craft is such that they admit only certain truths—namely those for the sake of which their craft is accorded *public* sanction—in Kantian terms, truths of *practical* reason. They know what they must prove; in this they are practical. They recognize each other by their agreement about "the truths." "Thou shalt not lie": in other words, beware, my dear philosopher, of telling the truth.

43

Whispered to the conservatives. What was not known formerly, what is known, or might be known, today: a reversion, a return in any sense or degree is simply not possible. We physiologists know that. Yet all priests and moralists have believed the opposite—they wanted to take mankind back, to screw it back, to a former measure of virtue. Morality was always a bed of Procrustes. Even the politicians have aped the preachers of virtue at this point: today too there are still parties whose dream it is that all things might walk backwards like crabs. But no one is free to be a crab. Nothing avails: one *must* go forward—step by step further into decadence (that is *my* definition of modern "progress"). One can *check* this development and thus dam up degeneration, gather it and make it more vehement and *sudden:* one can do no more.

44

My conception of genius. Great men, like great ages, are explosives in which a tremendous force is stored up; their precondition is always, historically and physiologically, that for a long time much has been gathered, stored up, saved up, and conserved for them—that there has been no explosion for a long time. Once the tension in the mass has become too great, then the most accidental stimulus suffices to summon into the world the "genius," the "deed," the great destiny. What does the environment matter then, or the age, or the "spirit of the age," or "public opinion"!

Take the case of Napoleon. Revolutionary France, and even more, prerevolutionary France, would have brought forth the opposite type; in fact, it did. Because Napoleon was *different,* the heir of a stronger, older, more ancient civilization than the one which was then perishing in France, he became the master there, he *was* the only master. Great men are necessary, the age in which they appear is accidental; that they almost always become masters over their age is only because they are stronger, because they are older, because for a

longer time much was gathered for them. The relationship between a genius and his age is like that between
strong and weak, or between old and young: the age
is relatively always much younger, thinner, more immature, less assured, more childish.

That in France today they think quite differently on
this subject (in Germany too, but that does not matter),
that the milieu theory, which is truly a neurotic's theory,
has become sacrosanct and almost scientific and has
found adherents even among physiologists—that "smells
bad" and arouses sad reflections. It is no different in
England, but that will not grieve anybody. For the
English there are only two ways of coming to terms
with the genius and the "great man": either democrati-
cally in the manner of Buckle or religiously in the
manner of Carlyle.

The danger that lies in great men and ages is extraordinary; exhaustion of every kind, sterility, follow
in their wake. The great human being is a finale; the
great age—the Renaissance, for example—is a finale.
The genius, in work and deed, is necessarily a squanderer: that he squanders himself, that is his greatness.
The instinct of self-preservation is suspended, as it
were; the overpowering pressure of outflowing forces
forbids him any such care or caution. People call this
"self-sacrifice" and praise his "heroism," his indifference to his own well-being, his devotion to an idea, a
great cause, a fatherland: without exception, misunderstandings. He flows out, he overflows, he uses himself
up, he does not spare himself—and this is a calamitous,
involuntary fatality, no less than a river's flooding the
land. Yet, because much is owed to such explosives,
much has also been given them in return: for example,
a kind of higher morality. After all, that is the way of
human gratitude: it *misunderstands* its benefactors.

45

The criminal and what is related to him. The criminal type is the type of the strong human being under unfavorable circumstances: a strong human being made sick. He lacks the wilderness, a somehow freer and more dangerous environment and form of existence, where everything that is weapons and armor in the instinct of the strong human being has its rightful place. His *virtues* are ostracized by society; the most vivid drives with which he is endowed soon grow together with the depressing affects—with suspicion, fear, and dishonor. Yet this is almost the recipe for physiological degeneration. Whoever must do secretly, with long suspense, caution, and cunning, what he can do best and would like most to do, becomes anemic; and because he always harvests only danger, persecution, and calamity from his instincts, his attitude to these instincts is reversed too, and he comes to experience them fatalistically. It is society, our tame, mediocre, emasculated society, in which a natural human being, who comes from the mountains or from the adventures of the sea necessarily degenerates into a criminal. Or almost necessarily; for there are cases in which such a man proves stronger than society: the Corsican, Napoleon, is the most famous case.

The testimony of Dostoevski is relevant to this problem—Dostoevski, the only psychologist, incidentally, from whom I had something to learn; he ranks among the most beautiful strokes of fortune in my life, even more than my discovery of Stendhal. This *profound* human being, who was ten times right in his low estimate of the superficial Germans, lived for a long time among the convicts in Siberia—hardened criminals for whom there was no way back to society—and found them very different from what he himself had expected: they were carved out of just about the best, hardest, and most valuable wood that grows anywhere on Russian soil.

Let us generalize the case of the criminal: let us think of men so constituted that, for one reason or another, they lack public approval and know that they are not felt to be beneficent or useful—that Chandala feeling that one is not considered equal, but an outcast, unworthy, contaminating. All men so constituted have a subterranean hue to their thoughts and actions; everything about them becomes paler than in those whose existence is touched by daylight. Yet almost all forms of existence which we consider distinguished today once lived in this half tomblike atmosphere: the scientific character, the artist, the genius, the free spirit, the actor, the merchant, the great discoverer. As long as the priest was considered the supreme type, *every* valuable kind of human being was devaluated. The time will come, I promise, when the priest will be considered the lowest type, *our* Chandala, the most mendacious, the most indecent kind of human being.

I call attention to the fact that even now—under the mildest regimen of morals which has ever ruled on earth, or at least in Europe—every deviation, every long, all-too-long sojourn below, every unusual or opaque form of existence, brings one closer to that type which is perfected in the criminal. All innovators of the spirit must for a time bear the pallid and fatal mark of the Chandala on their foreheads—*not* because they are considered that way by others, but because they themselves feel the terrible cleavage which separates them from everything that is customary or reputable. Almost every genius knows, as one stage of his development, the "Catilinarian existence"—a feeling of hatred, revenge, and rebellion against everything which already *is*, which no longer *becomes*. Catiline—the form of pre-existence of *every* Caesar.

46

Here the view is free. It may be nobility of the soul when a philosopher is silent; it may be love when he contradicts himself; and he who has knowledge may be polite enough to lie. It has been said, not without delicacy: *Il est indigne des grand coeurs de répandre le trouble qu'ils ressentent.*[1] But one must add that not to be afraid of the most unworthy may also be greatness of soul. A woman who loves, sacrifices her honor; a knower who "loves" may perhaps sacrifice his humanity; a God who loved became a Jew.

47

Beauty no accident. The beauty of a race or family, their grace and graciousness in all gestures, is won by work: like genius, it is the end result of the accumulated work of generations. One must have made great sacrifices to good taste, one must have done much and omitted much for its sake—seventeenth-century France is admirable in both respects—and good taste must have furnished a principle for selecting company, place, dress, sexual satisfaction; one must have preferred beauty to advantage, habit, opinion, and inertia. Supreme rule of conduct: before oneself too, one must not "let oneself go." The good things are immeasurably costly; and the law always holds that those who *have* them are different from those who *acquire* them. All that is good is inherited: whatever is not inherited *is* imperfect, is a mere beginning.

[1] "It is unworthy of great hearts to pour out the confusion they feel."

In Athens, in the time of Cicero, who expresses his surprise about this, the men and youths were far superior in beauty to the women. But what work and exertion in the service of beauty had the male sex there imposed on itself for centuries! For one should make no mistake about the method in this case: a breeding of feelings and thoughts alone is almost nothing (this is the great misunderstanding underlying German education, which is wholly illusory); one must first persuade the *body*. Strict perseverance in significant and exquisite gestures together with the obligation to live only with people who do not "let themselves go"—that is quite enough for one to become significant and exquisite, and in two or three generations all this becomes inward. It is decisive for the lot of a people and of humanity that culture should begin in the right place —not in the "soul" (as was the fateful superstition of the priests and half-priests): the right place is the body, the gesture, the diet, physiology; the rest follows from that. Therefore the Greeks remain the first cultural event in history: they knew, they *did*, what was needed; and Christianity, which despised the body, has been the greatest misfortune of humanity so far.

48

Progress in my sense. I too speak of a "return to nature," although it is really not a going back but an *ascent*—up into the high, free, even terrible nature and naturalness where great tasks are something one plays with, one *may* play with. To put it metaphorically: Napoleon was a piece of "return to nature," as I understand the phrase (for example, *in rebus tacticis;* even more, as military men know, in matters of strategy).

But Rousseau—to what did he really want to return? Rousseau, this first modern man, idealist and rabble in

one person—one who needed moral "dignity" to be able
to stand his own sight, sick with unbridled vanity and
unbridled self-contempt. This miscarriage, couched on
the threshold of modern times, also wanted a "return
to nature"; to ask this once more, to what did Rousseau
want to return? I still hate Rousseau in the French
Revolution: it is the world-historical expression of this
duality of idealist and rabble. The bloody farce which
became an aspect of the Revolution, its "immorality,"
are of little concern to me: what I hate is its Rousseauan
morality—the so-called "truths" of the Revolution
through which it still works and attracts everything
shallow and mediocre. The doctrine of equality! There
is no more poisonous poison anywhere: for it seems to
be preached by justice itself, whereas it really is the
termination of justice. "Equal to the equal, unequal to
the unequal"—*that* would be the true slogan of justice;
and also its corollary: "Never make equal what is unequal." That this doctrine of equality was surrounded
by such gruesome and bloody events, that has given
this "modern idea" par excellence a kind of glory and
fiery aura so that the Revolution as a *spectacle* has
seduced even the noblest spirits. In the end, that is no
reason for respecting it any more. I see only one man
who experienced it as it must be experienced, with
nausea—Goethe.

49

Goethe—not a German event, but a European one:
a magnificent attempt to overcome the eighteenth century by a return to nature, by an *ascent* to the naturalness of the Renaissance—a kind of self-overcoming on
the part of that century. He bore its strongest instincts
within himself: the sensibility, the idolatry of nature,
the anti-historic, the idealistic, the unreal and revolu-

tionary (the latter being merely a form of the unreal).
He sought help from history, natural science, antiquity,
and also Spinoza, but, above all, from practical activity;
he surrounded himself with limited horizons; he did not
retire from life but put himself into the midst of it; he
was not fainthearted but took as much as possible upon
himself, over himself, into himself. What he wanted was
totality; he fought the mutual extraneousness of reason,
senses, feeling, and will (preached with the most abhorrent scholasticism by *Kant,* the antipode of Goethe);
he disciplined himself to wholeness, he *created* himself.

In the middle of an age with an unreal outlook,
Goethe was a convinced realist: he said Yes to everything that was related to him in this respect—and he
had no greater experience than that *ens realissimum*[1]
called Napoleon. Goethe conceived a human being who
would be strong, highly educated, skillful in all bodily
matters, self-controlled, reverent toward himself, and
who might dare to afford the whole range and wealth
of being natural, being strong enough for such freedom;
the man of tolerance, not from weakness but from
strength, because he knows how to use to his advantage,
even that from which the average nature would perish;
the man for whom there is no longer anything that is
forbidden—unless it be *weakness,* whether called vice
or virtue.

Such a spirit who has *become free* stands amid the
cosmos with a joyous and trusting fatalism, in the *faith*
that only the particular is loathsome, and that all is
redeemed and affirmed in the whole—*he does not
negate any more.* Such a faith, however, is the highest
of all possible faiths: I have baptized it with the name
of *Dionysus.*

[1] "Most real being."

50

One might say that in a certain sense the nineteenth century *also* strove for all that which Goethe as a person had striven for: universality in understanding and in welcoming, letting everything come close to oneself, an audacious realism, a reverence for everything factual. How is it that the over-all result is no Goethe, but chaos, a nihilistic sigh, an utter bewilderment, an instinct of weariness which in practice continually drives toward a recourse to the eighteenth century? (For example, as a romanticism of feeling, as altruism and hypersentimentality, as feminism in taste, as socialism in politics.) Is not the nineteenth century, especially at its close, merely an intensified, *brutalized* eighteenth century, that is, a century of *decadence*? So that Goethe would have been—not merely for Germany, but for all of Europe—a mere interlude, a beautiful "in vain"? But one misunderstands great human beings if one views them from the miserable perspective of some public use. That one cannot put them to any use, that in itself may belong to greatness.

51

Goethe is the last German for whom I feel any reverence: he would have felt three things which I feel— and we also understand each other about the "cross."

I am often asked why, after all, I write in German: nowhere am I read worse than in the fatherland. But who knows in the end whether I even *wish* to be read today? To create things on which time tests its teeth in vain; in form, in *substance*, to strive for a little immortality—I have never yet been modest enough to demand less of myself. The aphorism, the apothegm, in which I am the first among the Germans to be a master, are the forms of "eternity"; it is my ambition to say in ten sentences what everyone else says in a book—what everyone else does *not* say in a book.

I have given mankind the most profound book it possesses, my *Zarathustra;* shortly I shall give it the most independent.

WHAT I OWE TO THE ANCIENTS

1

In conclusion, a word about that world to which I sought approaches, to which I have perhaps found a new approach—the ancient world. My taste, which may be the opposite of a tolerant taste, is in this case too far from saying Yes indiscriminately: it does not like to say Yes; rather even No; but best of all, nothing. That applies to whole cultures, it applies to books—also to places and landscapes. At bottom it is a very small number of ancient books that counts in my life; the most famous are not among them. My sense of style, for the epigram as a style, was awakened almost instantly when I came into contact with Sallust. I have not forgotten the surprise of my honored teacher, Corssen, when he had to give his worst Latin pupil the best grade: I had finished with one stroke. Compact, severe, with as much substance as possible, a cold sarcasm against "beautiful words" and "beautiful sentiments"— here I found myself. And even in my *Zarathustra* one will recognize a very serious ambition for a *Roman* style, for the *aere perennius*[1] in style.

Nor was my experience any different in my first contact with Horace. To this day, no other poet has given me the same artistic delight that a Horatian ode gave me from the first. In certain languages that which has

[1] "More enduring than bronze."

been achieved here could not even be attempted. This mosaic of words, in which every word—as sound, as place, as concept—pours out its strength right and left and over the whole, this *minimum* in the extent and number of the signs, and the maximum thereby attained in the energy of the signs—all that is Roman and, if one will believe me, *noble* par excellence. All the rest of poetry becomes, in contrast, something too popular —a mere garrulity of feelings.

2

To the Greeks I do not by any means owe similarly strong impressions; and—to come right out with it— they *cannot* mean as much to us as the Romans. One does not *learn* from the Greeks—their manner is too foreign, and too fluid, to have an imperative, a "classical" effect. Who could ever have learned to write from a Greek? Who could ever have learned it *without* the Romans?

For heaven's sake, do not throw Plato at me. I am a complete skeptic about Plato, and I have never been able to join in the admiration for the *artist* Plato which is customary among scholars. In the end, the subtlest judges of taste among the ancients themselves are here on my side. Plato, it seems to me, throws all stylistic forms together and is thus a first-rate decadent in style: his responsibility is thus comparable to that of the Cynics, who invented the *satura Menippea*.[1] To be attracted by the Platonic dialogue, this horribly self-satisfied and childish kind of dialectic, one must never have read good French writers—Fontenelle, for example. Plato is boring. In the end, my mistrust of Plato goes deep: he represents such an aberration from all the basic instincts of the Hellene, is so moralistic, so

---

[1] Varro's satire on the model of Menippus the Cynic.

pre-existently Christian—he already takes the concept "good" for the highest concept—that for the whole phenomenon Plato I would sooner use the harsh phrase "higher swindle," or, if it sounds better, "idealism," than any other. We have paid dearly for the fact that this Athenian got his schooling from the Egyptians (or from the Jews in Egypt?). In that great calamity, Christianity, Plato represents that ambiguity and fascination, called an "ideal," which made it possible for the nobler spirits of antiquity to misunderstand themselves and to set foot on the bridge leading to the cross. And how much Plato there still is in the concept "church," in the construction, system, and practice of the church!

My recreation, my preference, my *cure* from all Platonism has always been *Thucydides*. Thucydides and, perhaps, Machiavelli's *Principe* are most closely related to myself by the unconditional will not to gull oneself and to see reason in *reality*—not in "reason," still less in "morality." For the wretched embellishment of the Greeks into an ideal, which the "classically educated" youth carries into life as a prize for his classroom drill, there is no more complete cure than Thucydides. One must follow him line by line and read no less clearly between the lines: there are few thinkers who say so much between the lines. With him the culture of the Sophists, by which I mean the culture of the realists, reaches its perfect expression—this inestimable movement amid the moralistic and idealistic swindle set loose on all sides by the Socratic schools. Greek philosophy: the decadence of the Greek instinct. Thucydides: the great sum, the last revelation of that strong, severe, hard factuality which was instinctive with the older Hellenes. In the end, it is *courage* in the face of reality that distinguishes a man like Thucydides from Plato: Plato is a coward before reality, consequently he flees into the ideal; Thucydides has control of *himself*, consequently he also maintains control of things.

3

To smell out "beautiful souls," "golden means," and other perfections in the Greeks, or to admire their calm in greatness, their ideal cast of mind, their noble simplicity—the psychologist in me protected me against such "noble simplicity," a *niaiserie allemande* anyway. I saw their strongest instinct, the will to power; I saw them tremble before the indomitable force of this drive—I saw how all their institutions grew out of preventive measures taken to protect each other against their inner explosives. This tremendous inward tension then discharged itself in terrible and ruthless hostility to the outside world: the city-states tore each other to pieces so that the citizens of each might find peace from themselves. One needed to be strong: danger was near, it lurked everywhere. The magnificent physical suppleness, the audacious realism and immoralism which distinguished the Hellene constituted a *need*, not "nature." It only resulted, it was not there from the start. And with festivals and the arts they also aimed at nothing other than to feel *on top*, to *show* themselves on top. These are means of glorifying oneself, and in certain cases, of inspiring fear of oneself.

How could one possibly judge the Greeks by their philosophers, as the Germans have done, and use the Philistine moralism of the Socratic schools as a clue to what was basically Hellenic! After all, the philosophers are the decadents of Greek culture, the counter-movement to the ancient, noble taste (to the agonistic instinct, to the *polis*, to the value of race, to the authority of descent). The Socratic virtues were preached because the Greeks had lost them: excitable, timid, fickle comedians, every one of them, they had a few reasons too many for having morals preached to them. Not that it did any good—but big words and attitudes suit decadents so well.

4

I was the first to take seriously, for the understanding of the older, the still rich and even overflowing Hellenic instinct, that wonderful phenomenon which bears the name of Dionysus: it is explicable only in terms of an *excess* of force. Whoever followed the Greeks, like that most profound student of their culture in our time, Jacob Burckhardt in Basel, knew immediately that something had been accomplished thereby; and Burckhardt added a special section on this phenomenon to his *Civilization of the Greeks.* To see the opposite, one should look at the almost amusing poverty of instinct among the German philologists when they approach the Dionysian. The famous Lobeck, above all, crawled into this world of mysterious states with all the venerable sureness of a worm dried up between books, and persuaded himself that it was scientific of him to be glib and childish to the point of nausea—and with the utmost erudition, Lobeck gave us to understand that all these curiosities really did not amount to anything. In fact, the priests could have told the participants in such orgies some not altogether worthless things; for example, that wine excites lust, that man can under certain circumstances live on fruit, that plants bloom in the spring and wilt in the fall. As regards the astonishing wealth of rites, symbols, and myths of an orgiastic origin, with which the ancient world is literally overrun, this gave Lobeck an opportunity to become still more ingenious. "The Greeks," he said (*Aglaophamus* I,

672), "when they had nothing else to do, laughed, jumped, and ran around; or, since man sometimes feels that urge too, they sat down, cried, and lamented. *Others* came later on and sought some reason for this spectacular behavior; and thus there originated, as explanations for these customs, countless traditions concerning feasts and myths. On the other hand, it was believed that this *droll ado*, which took place on the feast days after all, must also form a necessary part of the festival and therefore it was maintained as an indispensable feature of the religious service." This is contemptible prattle; a Lobeck simply cannot be taken seriously for a moment.

We have quite a different feeling when we examine the concept "Greek" which was developed by Winckelmann and Goethe, and find it incompatible with that element out of which Dionysian art grows—the orgiastic. Indeed I do not doubt that as a matter of principle Goethe excluded anything of the sort from the possibilities of the Greek soul. *Consequently Goethe did not understand the Greeks.* For it is only in the Dionysian mysteries, in the psychology of the Dionysian state, that the *basic fact* of the Hellenic instinct finds expression—its "will to life." What was it that the Hellene guaranteed himself by means of these mysteries? *Eternal* life, the eternal return of life; the future promised and hallowed in the past; the triumphant Yes to life beyond all death and change; *true* life as the over-all continuation of life through procreation, through the mysteries of sexuality. For the Greeks the *sexual* symbol was therefore the venerable symbol par excellence, the real profundity in the whole of ancient piety. Every single element in the act of procreation, of pregnancy, and of birth aroused the highest and most solemn feelings. In the doctrine of the mysteries, *pain* is pronounced holy: the pangs of the woman giving birth hallow all pain; all becoming and growing —all that guarantees a future—involves pain. That there may be the eternal joy of creating, that the will to life may eternally affirm itself, the agony of the woman giving birth *must* also be there eternally.

All this is meant by the word Dionysus: I know no higher symbolism than this *Greek* symbolism of the Dionysian festivals. Here the most profound instinct of life, that directed toward the future of life, the eternity of life, is experienced religiously—and the way to life, procreation, as the *holy* way. It was Christianity, with its *ressentiment* against life at the bottom of its heart, which first made something unclean of sexuality: it threw *filth* on the origin, on the presupposition of our life.

5

The psychology of the orgiastic as an overflowing feeling of life and strength, where even pain still has the effect of a stimulus, gave me the key to the concept of *tragic* feeling, which had been misunderstood both by Aristotle and, quite especially, by our modern pessimists. Tragedy is so far from proving anything about the pessimism of the Hellenes, in Schopenhauer's sense, that it may, on the contrary, be considered its decisive repudiation and counter-instance. Saying Yes to life even in its strangest and hardest problems, the will to life rejoicing over its own inexhaustibility even in the very sacrifice of its highest types—*that* is what I called Dionysian, *that* is what I guessed to be the bridge to the psychology of the *tragic* poet. *Not* in order to be liberated from terror and pity, not in order to purge oneself of a dangerous affect by its vehement discharge—Aristotle understood it that way—but in order to be *oneself* the eternal joy of becoming, beyond all terror and pity—that joy which included even joy in destroying.

And herewith I again touch that point from which I once went forth: *The Birth of Tragedy* was my first revaluation of all values. Herewith I again stand on the soil out of which my intention, my *ability* grows—I, the last disciple of the philosopher Dionysus—I, the teacher of the eternal recurrence.

THE HAMMER SPEAKS

"Why so hard?" the kitchen coal once said to the diamond. "After all, are we not close kin?"

Why so soft? O my brothers, thus I ask you: are you not after all my brothers?

Why so soft, so pliant and yielding? Why is there so much denial, self-denial, in your hearts? So little destiny in your eyes?

And if you do not want to be destinies and inexorable ones, how can you one day triumph with me?

And if your hardness does not wish to flash and cut and cut through, how can you one day create with me?

For all creators are hard. And it must seem blessedness to you to impress your hand on millennia as on wax,

Blessedness to write on the will of millennia as on bronze—harder than bronze, nobler than bronze. Only the noblest is altogether hard.

This new tablet, O my brothers, I place over you: become hard!

Zarathustra, III, p. 326

THE ANTICHRIST

EDITOR'S PREFACE

After completing *Twilight of the Idols*, Nietzsche abandoned his previous plans for writing a work to be called *The Will to Power*. Instead, he decided to write a four-part *Revaluation of All Values:* not a collection of notes or aphorisms, but four essays; and he succeeded in completing the preface and the first essay: *Der Antichrist.*

The title is ambiguous. It first calls to mind the apocalyptic Antichrist, and this more sensational meaning is in keeping with the author's intention to be as provocative as possible. But the title could also mean "The Anti-Christian," and this interpretation is much more in keeping with the contents of the book, and in sections 38 and 47 the word is used in a context in which this is the only possible meaning.

It is also likely that a parallel to "anti-Semite" is intended. Nietzsche's attitude toward anti-Semitism in this work is, at first glance, puzzling; it has even been suggested that his anti-Christianity might have been motivated by anti-Semitism. But he is as opposed to anti-Semitism as ever. This is plain in all the other works of 1888, including the two books he composed after *The Antichrist: Ecce Homo* and *Nietzsche contra Wagner.* The latter consists of passages from his earlier works, edited slightly; and the relatively few additions include several aimed at anti-Semitism. And in his last letters he would even like to shoot all anti-Semites. Nietzsche's sharply divergent attitudes toward the Old and the New Testaments furnish another clue. For the Old Testament was one of his great loves. "The dignity of death and a kind of *consecration* of passion have perhaps never yet been represented more beautifully . . . than by certain Jews of the Old Testament: to these even the Greek could have gone to school!" he writes in a late note; and the same theme is developed more fully, together with his dislike for the New Testament, in *Beyond Good and Evil* (aphorism 52, included in this volume) and in the last part of the *Genealogy* (aphorism 22); and still later it is condensed into a mere eight words in an addition to a passage cited in *Nietzsche contra Wagner*.[1] In *The Antichrist* itself, Nietzsche cites Luke 6:23, "for in the like manner did their fathers unto the prophets," and comments: "Impertinent rabble! They compare themselves with the prophets, no less."

The Antichrist is Part One of the *Revaluation*, and one of its main themes is the reversal of the traditional appraisal of the relationship between Christianity and Judaism—an appraisal that had reached an extreme form in the self-styled "Christian" anti-Semitism of those days. One may think of Hofprediger Stöcker, of Richard Wagner and his son-in-law Chamberlain, whose tracts made such a tremendous impression on Hitler and Rosenberg, and also of the man whom Nietzsche's sister married, Bernhard Förster. (Of Nietzsche's many bitter letters about this marriage, only one has been included in this volume, dated Christmas 1887.) In Förster's representative formulation, Christ had appeared among the Jews because "on the dark background of the most depraved of all nations, the bright figure of the Savior of the world would stand out the more impressively." Even before he knew Förster, Nietzsche had noted down: "Jesus and Saul: the two most Jewish Jews perhaps who ever lived"; and in *The Antichrist* this point is elaborated. The New Testament, far from representing any progress over the Old, confronts us with "the people at the bottom, the outcasts and 'sinners,' the chandalas within Judaism." Where—Nietzsche is saying to the Christian anti-Semites

[1] See p. 668.

of his day, whose dragon seed Hitler reaped—where do you find all the qualities which you denounce as typically Jewish if not in the New Testament? Not Moses and the prophets, but Paul and the early Christians are "little superlative Jews." This irony at the expense of Christian anti-Semitism (compare also section 55: "An anti-Semite certainly is not any more decent because he lies as a matter of principle") so delights Nietzsche that he reverts again and again to *ad hominem* arguments and digs which involve him in the adoption of his opponents' cant.

The two main types of the book, apart from the individual personalities of Jesus and Paul, are the priest and the chandala. Two sentences in section 51 are central for an understanding of the book: Christianity was "not a function of race—it turned to every kind of man who was disinherited by life, it had its allies everywhere. At the bottom of Christianity is the rancor of the sick, instinct directed *against* the healthy, *against* health itself." The motif here suggested, of Christianity as the religion of vengefulness par excellence—this complete revaluation of the accepted point of view—is the main point of the essay. In what other religion, Nietzsche asks, are the great figures so consistently and so characteristically imbued with the spirit of revenge? Nietzsche excepts Jesus, against whom he advances different objections; and he dismisses St. Francis as "neurotic, epileptic, a visionary, like Jesus" (*The Will to Power*, 221).

Stylistically, the work is, like most of Nietzsche's books, very uneven. The often clipped cadences offer a refreshing contrast to *Zarathustra;* but frequently the rhetoric gets out of hand. Nietzsche is at his best when he manages to restrain himself; for example, in sections 45 and 48. Voltaire and Shaw might well have envied him such passages.

Philosophically, his uncritical use of terms like life, nature, and decadence greatly weakens his case. Historically, he is often ignorant: the two Hebrew words he sticks in for effect do not make sense, and his conception of Jesus—to mention a more important matter—is quite unconvincing, though no more so than most such portraits. That the book is meant to be shockingly blasphemous scarcely needs saying.

Like Nietzsche's first essay, *The Birth of Tragedy*, *The Antichrist* is unscholarly and so full of faults that only a pedant could have any wish to catalogue them. But unlike most scholars, Nietzsche sees vital things and has the power to communicate them vividly. And as he himself noted at twenty-three: The errors of great men are more fruitful than the truths of little men.

PREFACE

Revaluation of All Values

This book belongs to the very few. Perhaps not one of them is even living yet. Maybe they will be the readers who understand my *Zarathustra*: how *could* I mistake myself for one of those for whom there are ears even now? Only the day after tomorrow belongs to me. Some are born posthumously.

The conditions under which I am understood, and then of *necessity*—I know them only too well. One must be honest in matters of the spirit to the point of hardness before one can even endure my seriousness and my passion. One must be skilled in living on mountains —seeing the wretched ephemeral babble of politics and national self-seeking *beneath* oneself. One must have become indifferent; one must never ask if the truth is useful or if it may prove our undoing. The predilection of strength for questions for which no one today has the courage; the courage for the *forbidden;* the predestination to the labyrinth. An experience of seven solitudes. New ears for new music. New eyes for what is most distant. A new conscience for truths that have so far remained mute. *And* the will to the economy of the great style: keeping our strength, our *enthusiasm* in harness. Reverence for oneself; love of oneself; unconditional freedom before oneself.

Well then! Such men alone are my readers, my right readers, my predestined readers: what matter the *rest?* The rest—that is merely mankind. One must be above mankind in strength, in *loftiness* of soul—in contempt.

FRIEDRICH NIETZSCHE

First Book: The Antichrist

ATTEMPT AT A CRITIQUE OF CHRISTIANITY

1

Let us face ourselves. We are Hyperboreans; we know very well how far off we live. "Neither by land nor by sea will you find the way to the Hyperboreans"— Pindar already knew this about us. Beyond the north, ice, and death—*our* life, *our* happiness. We have discovered happiness, we know the way, we have found the exit out of the labyrinth of thousands of years. Who *else* has found it? Modern man perhaps? "I have got lost; I am everything that has got lost," sighs modern man.

This modernity was our sickness: lazy peace, cowardly compromise, the whole virtuous uncleanliness of the modern Yes and No. This tolerance and *largeur* of the heart, which "forgives" all because it "understands" all, is *sirocco* for us. Rather live in the ice than among modern virtues and other south winds!

We were intrepid enough, we spared neither ourselves nor others; but for a long time we did not know where to turn with our intrepidity. We became gloomy, we were called fatalists. *Our fatum*—the abundance, the tension, the damming of strength. We thirsted for lightning and deeds and were most remote from the happiness of the weakling, "resignation." In our atmosphere was a thunderstorm; the nature we are became dark—*for we saw no way.* Formula for our happiness: a Yes, a No, a straight line, a goal.

2

What is good? Everything that heightens the feeling of power in man, the will to power, power itself.

What is bad? Everything that is born of weakness.

What is happiness? The feeling that power is *growing*, that resistance is overcome.

Not contentedness but more power; not peace but war; not virtue but fitness (Renaissance virtue, *virtù*, virtue that is moraline[1]-free).

The weak and the failures shall perish: first principle of *our* love of man. And they shall even be given every possible assistance.

What is more harmful than any vice? Active pity for all the failures and all the weak: Christianity.

3

The problem I thus pose is not what shall succeed mankind in the sequence of living beings (man is an *end*), but what type of man shall be *bred*, shall be *willed*, for being higher in value, worthier of life, more certain of a future.

Even in the past this higher type has appeared often —but as a fortunate accident, as an exception, never as something *willed*. In fact, this has been the type most dreaded—almost *the* dreadful—and from dread the op-

[1] The coinage of a man who neither smoked nor drank coffee.

posite type was willed, bred, and *attained:* the domestic
animal, the herd animal, the sick human animal—the
Christian.

4

Mankind does *not* represent a development toward
something better or stronger or higher in the sense
accepted today. "Progress" is merely a modern idea,
that is, a false idea. The European of today is vastly
inferior in value to the European of the Renaissance:
further development is altogether *not* according to any
necessity in the direction of elevation, enhancement, or
strength.

In another sense, success in individual cases is constantly encountered in the most widely different places
and cultures: here we really do find a *higher type,*
which is, in relation to mankind as a whole, a kind of
overman. Such fortunate accidents of great success have
always been possible and *will* perhaps always be possible. And even whole families, tribes, or peoples may
occasionally represent such a *bull's-eye.*

5

Christianity should not be beautified and embellished: it has waged deadly war against this higher
type of man; it has placed all the basic instincts of this
type under the ban; and out of these instincts it has
distilled evil and the Evil One: the strong man as the
typically reprehensible man, the "reprobate." Christianity has sided with all that is weak and base, with all
failures; it has made an ideal of whatever *contradicts*
the instinct of the strong life to preserve itself; it has
corrupted the reason even of those strongest in spirit
by teaching men to consider the supreme values of the
spirit as something sinful, as something that leads into

error—as temptations. The most pitiful example: the corruption of Pascal, who believed in the corruption of his reason through original sin when it had in fact been corrupted only by his Christianity.

6

It is a painful, horrible spectacle that has dawned on me: I have drawn back the curtain from the *corruption* of man. In my mouth, this word is at least free from one suspicion: that it might involve a moral accusation of man. It is meant—let me emphasize this once more—*moraline-free*. So much so that I experience this corruption most strongly precisely where men have so far aspired most deliberately to "virtue" and "godliness." I understand corruption, as you will guess, in the sense of decadence: it is my contention that all the values in which mankind now sums up its supreme desiderata are *decadence-values*.

I call an animal, a species, or an individual corrupt when it loses its instincts, when it chooses, when it prefers, what is disadvantageous for it. A history of "lofty sentiments," of the "ideals of mankind"—and it is possible that I shall have to write it—would almost explain too *why* man is so corrupt. Life itself is to my mind the instinct for growth, for durability, for an accumulation of forces, for *power:* where the will to power is lacking there is decline. It is my contention that all the supreme values of mankind *lack* this will— that the values which are symptomatic of decline, *nihilistic* values, are lording it under the holiest names.

7

Christianity is called the religion of *pity*. Pity stands opposed to the tonic emotions which heighten our vitality: it has a depressing effect. We are deprived of strength when we feel pity. That loss of strength which suffering as such inflicts on life is still further increased and multiplied by pity. Pity makes suffering contagious. Under certain circumstances, it may engender a total loss of life and vitality out of all proportion to the magnitude of the cause (as in the case of the death of the Nazarene). That is the first consideration, but there is a more important one.

Suppose we measure pity by the value of the reactions it usually produces; then its perilous nature appears in an even brighter light. Quite in general, pity crosses the law of development, which is the law of *selection*. It preserves what is ripe for destruction; it defends those who have been disinherited and condemned by life; and by the abundance of the failures of all kinds which it keeps alive, it gives life itself a gloomy and questionable aspect.

Some have dared to call pity a virtue (in every *noble* ethic it is considered a weakness); and as if this were not enough, it has been made *the* virtue, the basis and source of all virtues. To be sure—and one should always keep this in mind—this was done by a philosophy that was nihilistic and had inscribed the *negation of life* upon its shield. Schopenhauer was consistent enough: pity negates life and renders it *more deserving of negation*.

Pity is the *practice* of nihilism. To repeat: this depressive and contagious instinct crosses those instincts which aim at the preservation of life and at the enhancement of its value. It multiplies misery and conserves all that is miserable, and is thus a prime instrument of the advancement of decadence: pity persuades men to *nothingness!* Of course, one does not say "nothingness" but "beyond" or "God," or *"true* life," or Nirvana, salvation, blessedness.

This innocent rhetoric from the realm of the religious-moral idiosyncrasy appears much less innocent as soon as we realize which tendency it is that here shrouds itself in sublime words: *hostility against life*. Schopenhauer was hostile to life; therefore pity became a virtue for him.

Aristotle, as is well known, considered pity a pathological and dangerous condition, which one would be well advised to attack now and then with a purge: he understood tragedy as a purge. From the standpoint of the instinct of life, a remedy certainly seems necessary for such a pathological and dangerous accumulation of pity as is represented by the case of Schopenhauer (and unfortunately by our entire literary and artistic decadence from St. Petersburg to Paris, from Tolstoi to Wagner)—to puncture it and make it *burst*.

In our whole unhealthy modernity there is nothing more unhealthy than Christian pity. To be physicians *here*, to be inexorable *here*, to wield the scalpel *here* —that is *our* part, that is *our* love of man, that is how *we* are philosophers, we *Hyperboreans*.

8

It is necessary to say whom we consider our antithesis: it is the theologians and whatever has theologians' blood in its veins—and that includes our whole philosophy.

Whoever has seen this catastrophe at close range or, better yet, been subjected to it and almost perished of it, will no longer consider it a joking matter (the freethinking of our honorable natural scientists and physiologists is, to my mind, a joke: they lack passion in these matters, they do not suffer them as their passion and martyrdom). This poisoning is much more extensive than is generally supposed: I have found the theologians' instinctive arrogance wherever anyone today considers himself an "idealist"—wherever a right is assumed, on the basis of some higher origin, to look at reality from a superior and foreign vantage point.

The idealist, exactly like the priest, holds all the great concepts in his hand (and not only in his hand!); he plays them out with a benevolent contempt for the "understanding," the "senses," "honors," "good living," and "science"; he considers all that *beneath* him, as so many harmful and seductive forces over which "the spirit" hovers in a state of pure for-itselfness—as if humility, chastity, poverty, or, in one word, *holiness*, had not harmed life immeasurably more than any horrors or vices. The pure spirit is the pure lie.

As long as the priest is considered a *higher* type of man—this *professional* negator, slanderer, and poisoner of life—there is no answer to the question: what *is* truth? For truth has been stood on its head when the conscious advocate of nothingness and negation is accepted as the representative of "truth."

9

Against this theologians' instinct I wage war: I have found its traces everywhere. Whoever has theologians' blood in his veins, sees all things in a distorted and dishonest perspective to begin with. The pathos which develops out of this condition calls itself *faith:* closing one's eyes to oneself once and for all, lest one suffer the sight of incurable falsehood. This faulty perspective on all things is elevated into a morality, a virtue, a holiness; the good conscience is tied to faulty vision; and no *other* perspective is conceded any further value once one's own has been made sacrosanct with the names of "God," "redemption," and "eternity." I have dug up the theologians' instinct everywhere: it is the most widespread, really *subterranean,* form of falsehood found on earth.

Whatever a theologian feels to be true *must* be false: this is almost a criterion of truth. His most basic instinct of self-preservation forbids him to respect reality at any point or even to let it get a word in. Wherever the theologians' instinct extends, *value judgments* have been stood on their heads and the concepts of "true" and "false" are of necessity reversed: whatever is most harmful to life is called "true"; whatever elevates it, enhances, affirms, justifies it, and makes it triumphant, is called "false." When theologians reach out for *power* through the "conscience" of princes (*or* of peoples), we need never doubt what really happens at bottom: the will to the end, the *nihilistic* will, wants power.

10

Among Germans I am immediately understood when I say that philosophy has been corrupted by theologians' blood. The Protestant parson is the grandfather of German philosophy; Protestantism itself, its *peccatum originale.*[1] Definition of Protestantism: the partial paralysis of Christianity—*and* of reason. One need merely say "Tübingen Seminary" to understand what German philosophy is at bottom: an *insidious* theology. The Swabians are the best liars in Germany: they lie innocently.

Why was Kant's appearance greeted with jubilation among German scholars—of whom three-fourths are the sons of parsons and teachers—and whence came the German conviction, echoed even today, that a change for the *better* began with Kant? The theologians' instinct in the German scholars divined *what* had once

[1] "Original sin."

again been made possible. A path had been found on which one could sneak back to the old ideal. The conception of a *"true world,"* the conception of morality as the *essence* of the world (these two most malignant errors of all time!), were once again, thanks to a wily and shrewd skepticism, if not provable, at least no longer *refutable.* Reason, the *right* of reason, does not extend that far. Reality had been reduced to mere "appearance," and a mendaciously fabricated world, the world of being, was honored as reality. Kant's success is merely a theologians' success: like Luther, like Leibniz, Kant was one more clog for German honesty, which was none too steady in the first place.

11

One more word against Kant as a *moralist.* A virtue must be *our own* invention, *our* most necessary self-expression and self-defense: any other kind of virtue is merely a danger. Whatever is not a condition of our life *harms* it: a virtue that is prompted solely by a feeling of respect for the concept of "virtue," as Kant would have it, is harmful. "Virtue," "duty," the "good in itself," the good which is impersonal and universally valid—chimeras and expressions of decline, of the final exhaustion of life, of the Chinese phase of Königsberg. The fundamental laws of self-preservation and growth demand the opposite—that everyone invent *his own* virtue, *his own* categorical imperative. A people perishes when it confuses *its* duty with duty in general. Nothing ruins us more profoundly, more intimately, than every "impersonal" duty, every sacrifice to the Moloch of abstraction. How could one fail to feel how Kant's categorical imperative endangered life itself! The theologians' instinct alone protected it!

An action demanded by the instinct of life is proved

to be *right* by the pleasure that accompanies it; yet this nihilist with his Christian dogmatic entrails considered pleasure an *objection*. What could destroy us more quickly than working, thinking, and feeling without any inner necessity, without any deeply personal choice, without *pleasure*—as an automaton of "duty"? This is the very recipe for decadence, even for idiocy. Kant became an idiot. And this man was a contemporary of *Goethe!* This catastrophic spider was considered the *German* philosopher—he still is!

I beware of saying what I think of the Germans. Did not Kant find in the French Revolution the transition from the inorganic form of the state to the *organic?* Did he not ask himself whether there was any event which could be explained only in terms of a moral disposition of mankind, an event which would *demonstrate* once and for all the "tendency of mankind toward the good"? Kant's answer: "This is the Revolution." The instinct which errs without fail, *anti-nature* as instinct, German decadence as philosophy—*that is Kant!*

12

I except a few skeptics—the decent type in the history of philosophy: the rest are simply unaware of the most basic requirements of intellectual honesty. All these great enthusiasts and prodigies behave like our little females: they consider "beautiful sentiments" adequate arguments, regard a heaving bosom as the bellows of the deity, and conviction a *criterion* of truth. In the end, Kant tried, with "German" innocence, to give this corruption, this lack of any intellectual conscience, scientific status with his notion of "practical reason": he invented a special kind of reason for cases in which one need not bother about reason—that is, when moral-

ity, when the sublime command "thou shalt," raises its
voice.

When we consider that among almost all peoples the
philosopher is merely the next development of the
priestly type, then this legacy of the priest, this self-
deceiving counterfeit, ceases to be surprising. Having
sacred tasks, such as improving, saving, or redeeming
mankind—carrying the deity in his bosom and being the
mouthpiece of imperatives from the beyond—with such
a mission a man naturally stands outside all merely intellectual valuations: *he himself* is sanctified by such a
task, he himself is a type of a higher order! What is
science to the priest? He is above that! And until now
the priest has ruled! He determined the concepts of
"true" and "untrue"!

13

Let us not underestimate this: *we ourselves,* we free
spirits, are nothing less than a "revaluation of all
values," an *incarnate* declaration of war and triumph
over all the ancient conceptions of "true" and "untrue."
The most valuable insights are discovered last; but the
most valuable insights are the *methods.* *All* the methods, *all* the presuppositions of our current scientific outlook, were opposed for thousands of years with the most
profound contempt. For their sake, men were excluded
from the company of "decent" people and considered
"enemies of God," despisers of the truth, and "possessed." Anyone with a scientific bent was a Chandala.

We have had the whole pathos of mankind against
us—their conception of what truth *ought* to be, of
what the service of the truth *ought* to be: every "thou
shalt" has hitherto been aimed against us. Our objec-
tives, our practice, our quiet, cautious, mistrustful man-

ner—all these were considered utterly unworthy and contemptible.

In the end one might well ask whether it was not really an *aesthetic* taste that kept mankind in blindness for so long: a picturesque effect was demanded of the truth, and the lover of knowledge was expected to make a strong impression on the senses. Our *modesty* offended men's taste longest of all. How well they divined that, these turkeycocks of God!

14

We have learned differently. We have become more modest in every way. We no longer derive man from "the spirit" or "the deity"; we have placed him back among the animals. We consider him the strongest animal because he is the most cunning: his spirituality is a consequence of this. On the other hand, we oppose the vanity that would raise its head again here too— as if man had been the great hidden purpose of the evolution of the animals. Man is by no means the crown of creation: every living being stands beside him on the same level of perfection. And even this is saying too much: relatively speaking, man is the most bungled of all the animals, the sickliest, and not one has strayed more dangerously from its instincts. But for all that, he is of course the most *interesting*.

As regards the animals, Descartes was the first to have dared, with admirable boldness, to understand the animal as *machina:* the whole of our physiology endeavors to prove this claim. And we are consistent enough not to except man, as Descartes still did: our knowledge of man today goes just as far as we understand him mechanistically. Formerly man was given a "free will" as his dowry from a higher order: today we have taken his will away altogether, in the sense that we no longer admit the will as a faculty. The old word "will" now serves only to denote a resultant, a kind of individual reaction, which follows necessarily upon a number of partly contradictory, partly harmonious stimuli: the will no longer "acts" or "moves."

Formerly, the proof of man's higher origin, of his divinity, was found in his consciousness, in his "spirit." To become *perfect*, he was advised to draw in his senses, turtle fashion, to cease all intercourse with earthly things, to shed his mortal shroud: then his essence would remain, the "pure spirit." Here too we have reconsidered: the development of consciousness, the "spirit," is for us nothing less than the symptom of a relative imperfection of the organism; it means trying, groping, blundering—an exertion which uses up an unnecessary amount of nervous energy. We deny that anything can be done perfectly as long as it is still done consciously. The "pure spirit" is a pure stupidity: if we subtract the nervous system and the senses—the "mortal shroud"—*then we miscalculate*—that is all!

15

In Christianity neither morality nor religion has even a single point of contact with reality. Nothing but imaginary *causes* ("God," "soul," "ego," "spirit," "free will"—for that matter, "unfree will"), nothing but imaginary *effects* ("sin," "redemption," "grace," "punishment," "forgiveness of sins"). Intercourse between imaginary *beings* ("God," "spirits," "souls"); an imaginary *natural* science (anthropocentric; no trace of any concept of natural causes); an imaginary *psychology* (nothing but self-misunderstandings, interpretations of agreeable or disagreeable general feelings—for example, of the states of the *nervus sympathicus*—with the aid of the sign language of the religio-moral idiosyncrasy: "re-

pentance," "pangs of conscience," "temptation by the
devil," "the presence of God"); an imaginary *teleology*
("the kingdom of God," "the Last Judgment," "eternal
life").

This *world of pure fiction* is vastly inferior to the
world of dreams insofar as the latter *mirrors* reality,
whereas the former falsifies, devalues, and negates reality. Once the concept of "nature" had been invented as
the opposite of "God," "natural" had to become a syn-
onym of "reprehensible": this whole world of fiction is
rooted in *hatred* of the natural (of reality!); it is the
expression of a profound vexation at the sight of reality.

But this explains everything. Who alone has good
reason to lie his way out of reality? He who suffers
from it. But to suffer from reality is to be a piece of
reality that has come to grief. The preponderance of
feelings of displeasure over feelings of pleasure is the
cause of this fictitious morality and religion; but such
a preponderance provides the very formula for decadence.

16

A critique of the *Christian conception of God* forces
us to the same conclusion. A people that still believes
in itself retains its own god. In him it reveres the conditions which let it prevail, its virtues: it projects its
pleasure in itself, its feeling of power, into a being to
whom one may offer thanks. Whoever is rich wants to
give of his riches; a proud people needs a god: it wants
to *sacrifice*. Under such conditions, religion is a form
of thankfulness. Being thankful for himself, man needs
a god. Such a god must be able to help and to harm,
to be friend and enemy—he is admired whether good
or destructive. The *anti-natural* castration of a god, to
make him a god of the good alone, would here be con-

trary to everything desirable. The evil god is needed no
less than the good god: after all, we do not owe our
own existence to tolerance and humanitarianism.

What would be the point of a god who knew nothing
of wrath, revenge, envy, scorn, cunning, and violence?
who had perhaps never experienced the delightful
ardeurs of victory and annihilation? No one would
understand such a god: why have him then?

To be sure, when a people is perishing, when it feels
how its faith in the future and its hope of freedom are
waning irrevocably, when submission begins to appear
to it as the prime necessity and it becomes aware of
the virtues of the subjugated as the conditions of self-
preservation, then its god *has to* change too. Now he
becomes a sneak, timid and modest; he counsels "peace
of soul," hate-no-more, forbearance, even "love" of
friend and enemy. He moralizes constantly, he crawls
into the cave of every private virtue, he becomes god
for everyman, he becomes a private person,[1] a cosmopolitan.

Formerly, he represented a people, the strength of a
people, everything aggressive and power-thirsty in the
soul of a people; now he is merely the good god.

Indeed, there is no other alternative for gods: *either*
they are the will to power, and they remain a people's
gods, *or* the incapacity for power, and then they necessarily become *good*.

17

Wherever the will to power declines in any form,
there is invariably also a physiological retrogression,
decadence. The deity of decadence, gelded in his most
virile virtues and instincts, becomes of necessity the

[1] Literal translation of the Greek *idiotes*; cf. section 29,
p. 601.

god of the physiologically retrograde, of the weak. Of
course, they do not *call* themselves the weak; they call
themselves "the good."

No further hint is required to indicate the moments
in history at which the dualistic fiction of a good and an
evil god first became possible. The same instinct which
prompts the subjugated to reduce their god to the
"good-in-itself" also prompts them to eliminate all the
good qualities from the god of their conquerors; they
take revenge on their masters by turning their god into
the *devil*. The *good* god and the devil—both abortions
of decadence.

How can anyone today still submit to the simplicity
of Christian theologians to the point of insisting with
them that the development of the conception of God
from the "God of Israel," the god of a people, to the
Christian God, the quintessence of everything good,
represents *progress?* Yet even Renan does this. As if
Renan had the right to be simple-minded! After all, the
opposite stares you in the face. When the presuppositions of *ascending* life, when everything strong, brave,
masterful, and proud is eliminated from the conception
of God; when he degenerates step by step into a mere
symbol, a staff for the weary, a sheet-anchor for the
drowning; when he becomes the god of the poor, the
sinners, and the sick par excellence, and the attribute
"Savior" or "Redeemer" remains in the end as the one
essential attribute of divinity—just *what* does such a
transformation signify? what, such a *reduction* of the
divine?

To be sure, "the kingdom of God" has thus been enlarged. Formerly he had only his people, his "chosen"
people. Then he, like his people, became a wanderer
and went into foreign lands; and ever since, he has not
settled down anywhere—until he finally came to feel

at home anywhere, this great cosmopolitan—until "the great numbers" and half the earth were on his side. Nevertheless, the god of "the great numbers," the democrat among the gods, did not become a proud pagan god: he remained a Jew, he remained a god of nooks, the god of all the dark corners and places, of all the unhealthy quarters the world over!

His world-wide kingdom is, as ever, an underworld kingdom, a hospital, a *souterrain*[1] kingdom, a ghetto kingdom. And he himself: so pale, so weak, so decadent. Even the palest of the pale were able to master him: our honorable metaphysicians, those concept-albinos. They spun their webs around him until, hypnotized by their motions, he himself became a spider, another metaphysician. Now he, in turn, spun the world out of himself—*sub specie Spinozae*. Now he transfigured himself into something ever thinner and paler; he became an "ideal," he became "pure spirit," the "Absolute," the "thing-in-itself." The deterioration of a god: God became the "thing-in-itself."

18

The Christian conception of God—God as god of the sick, God as a spider, God as spirit—is one of the most corrupt conceptions of the divine ever attained on earth. It may even represent the low-water mark in the descending development of divine types. God degenerated into the *contradiction* of life, instead of being its transfiguration and eternal Yes! God as the declaration of war against life, against nature, against the will to live! God—the formula for every slander against "this world," for every lie about the "beyond"! God—the

---

[1] *L'esprit souterrain* was the title of the first volume by Dostoevski that Nietzsche picked up in 1887, in French translation.

deification of nothingness, the will to nothingness pronounced holy!

19

That the strong races of northern Europe did not reject the Christian God certainly does no credit to their religious genius—not to speak of their taste. There is no excuse whatever for their failure to dispose of such a sickly and senile product of decadence. But a curse lies upon them for this failure: they have absorbed sickness, old age, and contradiction into all their instincts— and since then they have not *created* another god. Almost two thousand years—and not a single new god! But still, as if his existence were justified, as if he represented the ultimate and the maximum of the god-creating power, of the *creator spiritus* in man, this pitiful god of Christian monotono-theism! This hybrid product of decay, this mixture of zero, concept, and contradiction, in which all the instincts of decadence, all cowardices and wearinesses of the soul, find their sanction!

20

I hope that my condemnation of Christianity has not involved me in any injustice to a related religion with an even larger number of adherents: *Buddhism*. Both belong together as nihilistic religions—they are religions of decadence—but they differ most remarkably. For being in a position now to compare them, the critic of Christianity is profoundly grateful to the students of India.

Buddhism is a hundred times more realistic than Christianity: posing problems objectively and coolly is part of its inheritance, for Buddhism comes after a philosophic movement which spanned centuries. The concept of "God" had long been disposed of when it arrived. Buddhism is the only genuinely positivistic religion in history. This applies even to its theory of knowledge (a strict phenomenalism): it no longer says "struggle against *sin*" but, duly respectful of reality, "struggle against *suffering*." Buddhism is profoundly distinguished from Christianity by the fact that the self-deception of the moral concepts lies far behind it. In my terms, it stands *beyond* good and evil.

The *two* physiological facts on which it is based and which it keeps in mind are: *first*, an excessive sensitivity, which manifests itself in a refined susceptibility to pain; and *second*, an overspiritualization, an all-too-long preoccupation with concepts and logical procedures, which has damaged the instinct of personality by subordinating it to the "impersonal" (both states which at least some of my readers, those who are "objective" like myself, will know from experience). These physiological conditions have led to a depression, and the Buddha proceeds against this with hygienic measures. Against it he recommends life in the open air, the wandering life; moderation in eating and a careful selection of foods; wariness of all intoxicants; wariness also of all emotions that activate the gall bladder or heat the blood; no *worry* either for oneself or for others. He prescribes ideas which are either soothing or cheering, and he invents means for weaning oneself from all the others. He understands goodness and graciousness as health-promoting.

Prayer is ruled out, and so is *asceticism;* there is no categorical imperative, no *compulsion* whatever, not even in the monastic societies (one may leave again). All these things would merely increase the excessive sensitivity we mentioned. For the same reason, he does not ask his followers to fight those who think otherwise: there is nothing to which his doctrine is more opposed than the feeling of revenge, antipathy, *ressentiment* ("it is not by enmity that enmity is ended"—that is the stirring refrain of all Buddhism). And all this is quite right: these emotions would indeed be utterly *unhealthy* in view of the basic hygienic purpose.

Against the spiritual exhaustion he encounters, which manifests itself in an excessive "objectivity" (that is, in the individual's loss of interest in himself, in the loss of a center of gravity, of "egoism"), he fights with a rigorous attempt to lead back even the most spiritual interests to the *person*. In the Buddha's doctrine, egoism becomes a duty: the "one thing needful," the question "how can *you* escape from suffering?" regulates and limits the whole spiritual diet. (Perhaps one may here recall that Athenian who also waged war against any pure "scientism"—Socrates, who elevated personal egoism to an ethic, even in the realm of problems.)

21

Buddhism presupposes a very mild climate, customs of great gentleness and liberality, and the absence of militarism; moreover, the movement had to originate among the higher, and even the scholarly, classes. Cheerfulness, calm, and freedom from desire are the highest goal, and the goal is *attained*. Buddhism is not a religion in which one merely aspires to perfection: perfection is the normal case.

In Christianity the instincts of the subjugated and oppressed come to the fore: here the lowest classes seek their salvation. The casuistry of sin, self-criticism, the inquisition of the conscience, are pursued as a *pastime*, as a remedy for boredom; the emotional reaction to one who has *power*, called "God," is constantly sustained (by means of prayer); and what is highest is considered unattainable, a gift, "grace." Public acts are precluded;

the hiding-place, the darkened room, is Christian. The body is despised, hygiene repudiated as sensuality; the church even opposes cleanliness (the first Christian measure after the expulsion of the Moors was the closing of the public baths, of which there were two hundred and seventy in Cordova alone). Christian too is a certain sense of cruelty against oneself and against others; hatred of all who think differently; the will to persecute. Gloomy and exciting conceptions predominate; the most highly desired states, designated with the highest names, are epileptoid; the diet is so chosen as to favor morbid phenomena and overstimulate the nerves. Christian too is mortal enmity against the lords of the earth, against the "noble"—along with a sly, secret rivalry (one leaves them the "body," one wants *only* the "soul"). Christian, finally, is the hatred of the *spirit*, of pride, courage, freedom, liberty of the spirit; Christian is the hatred of the *senses*, of joy in the senses, of joy itself.

22

When Christianity left its native soil, the lowest classes, the *underworld* of the ancient world, when it began to seek power among barbarian peoples, it was no longer confronted with *weary* men but with inwardly brutalized, cruel people—strong but bungled men. Here, dissatisfaction with oneself, suffering from oneself, are *not* due to an excessive sensitivity and susceptibility to pain, as among the Buddhists, but, on the contrary, to an overpowering desire to inflict pain and to find an outlet for inner tensions in hostile acts and ideas. Christianity needed *barbaric* concepts and values to become master over barbarians; for example, the sacrifice of the first-born, the drinking of blood in the Lord's Supper, the contempt for the spirit and for culture, torture in all its forms, both sensuous and not sensuous, and the great pomp of the cult.

Buddhism is a religion for *late* men, for gracious and gentle races who have become overspiritual and excessively susceptible to pain (Europe is far from ripe for it): it is a way of leading them back to peace and cheerfulness, to a diet for the spirit and a certain inuring of the body. Christianity would become master over *beasts of prey:* its method is to make them *sick;* enfeeblement is the Christian recipe for *taming,* for "civilizing." Buddhism is a religion for the end and the weariness of civilization; Christianity finds no civilization as yet—under certain circumstances it might lay the foundation for one.

23

Buddhism, I repeat, is a hundred times colder, more truthful, more objective. It is no longer confronted with the need to make suffering and the susceptibility to pain *respectable* by interpreting them in terms of sin— it simply says what it thinks: "I suffer." To the barbarian, however, suffering as such is not respectable: he requires an exegesis before he will admit to himself that he is suffering (his instinct would sooner direct him to deny his suffering and bear it in silence). Here the word "devil" was a blessing: man had an overpowering and terrible enemy—man need not be ashamed of suffering at the hands of such an enemy.

At the bottom of Christianity there are some subtleties that belong to the Orient. Above all, it knows that it is a matter of complete indifference whether something is true, while it is of the utmost importance whether it is believed to be true. Truth and the *faith* that something is true: two completely separate realms of interest—almost diametrically opposite realms—they are reached by utterly different paths. Having knowledge of this—that is almost the definition of the wise man in the Orient: the Brahmins understand this; Plato understands this; and so does every student of esoteric wisdom. If, for example, it makes men happy to believe that they have been redeemed from sin, it is not necessary, as a condition for this, that man is, in fact, sinful, but merely that he feels sinful. And if faith is quite generally needed above all, then reason, knowledge, and inquiry must be discredited: the way to truth becomes the *forbidden* way.

Strong *hope* is a far more powerful stimulant of life than any single realization of happiness could ever be. Those who suffer must be sustained by a hope that can never be contradicted by any reality or be disposed of by any fulfillment—a hope for the beyond. (Precisely because of its ability to keep the unfortunate in continual suspense, the Greeks considered hope the evil of evils, the truly insidious evil: it remained behind in the barrel of evils.[1])

To make *love* possible, God must be a person; to permit the lowest instincts to participate, God must be young. To excite the ardor of the females, a beautiful saint must be placed in the foreground, and to excite that of the men, a Mary—presupposing all along that Christianity wants to become master on soil where some aphrodisiac or Adonis cult has already established the general conception of a cult. The requirement of chastity strengthens the vehemence and inwardliness of the religious instinct: it makes the cult warmer, more enthusiastic, more soulful.

Love is the state in which man sees things most decidedly as they are not. The power of illusion is at its

[1] Pandora's box.

peak here, as is the power to sweeten and transfigure. In love man endures more, man bears everything. A religion had to be invented in which one could love: what is worst in life is thus overcome—it is not even seen any more.

So much for the three Christian virtues: faith, love, hope—I call them the three Christian *shrewdnesses*. Buddhism is too late, too positivistic, to be shrewd in this way.

24

Here I merely touch on the problem of the *genesis* of Christianity. The *first* principle for its solution is: Christianity can be understood only in terms of the soil out of which it grew—it is *not* a counter-movement to the Jewish instinct, it is its very consequence, one inference more in its awe-inspiring logic. In the formula of the Redeemer: "Salvation is of the Jews." The *second* principle is: the psychological type of the Galilean is still recognizable; but only in its complete degeneration (which is at the same time a mutilation and an overloading with alien features) could it serve as that for which it has been used—as the type of a redeemer of mankind.

The Jews are the strangest people in world history because, confronted with the question whether to be or not to be, they chose, with a perfectly uncanny deliberateness, to be *at any price:* this price was the radical *falsification* of all nature, all naturalness, all reality, of the whole inner world as well as the outer. They defined themselves sharply *against* all the conditions under which a people had hitherto been able to live, been *allowed* to live; out of themselves they created a counterconcept to *natural* conditions: they turned religion, cult, morality, history, psychology, one after the other, into an incurable *contradiction to their natural values*. We encounter this same phenomenon once again and in immeasurably enlarged proportions, yet merely as a copy: the Christian church cannot make the slightest claim to originality when compared with the "holy people." That precisely is why the Jews are the *most catastrophic* people of world history: by their aftereffect they have made mankind so thoroughly false that even today the Christian can feel anti-Jewish without realizing that he himself is *the ultimate Jewish consequence*.

In my *Genealogy of Morals* I offered the first psychological analysis of the counter-concepts of a *noble* morality and a morality of *ressentiment*—the latter born of the No to the former: but this is the Judaeo-Christian morality pure and simple. So that it could say No to everything on earth that represents the ascending tendency of life, to that which has turned out well, to power, to beauty, to self-affirmation, the instinct of *ressentiment*, which had here become genius, had to invent *another* world from whose point of view this affirmation of life appeared as evil, as the reprehensible as such.

Psychologically considered, the Jewish people are a people endowed with the toughest vital energy, who, placed in impossible circumstances, voluntarily and out of the most profound prudence of self-preservation, take sides with all the instincts of decadence—*not* as mastered by them, but because they divined a power in these instincts with which one could prevail against "the world." The Jews are the antithesis of all decadents: they have had to *represent* decadents to the point of illusion; with a *non plus ultra* of histrionic genius they have known how to place themselves at the head of all movements of decadence (as the Christianity of *Paul*), in order to create something out of them which is stronger than any *Yes-saying* party of life. Decadence is only a *means* for the type of man who demands power in Judaism and Christianity, the *priestly* type: this type of man has a life interest in making mankind *sick* and in so twisting the concepts of good and evil, true and false, as to imperil life and slander the world.

25

The history of Israel is invaluable as the typical history of all *denaturing* of natural values. I indicate five points.

Originally, especially at the time of the kings, Israel also stood in the right, that is, the natural, relationship to all things. Its Yahweh was the expression of a consciousness of power, of joy in oneself, of hope for oneself: through him victory and welfare were expected; through him nature was trusted to give what the people needed—above all, rain. Yahweh is the god of Israel and therefore the god of justice: the logic of every people that is in power and has a good conscience. In the festival cult these two sides of the self-affirmation of a people find expression: they are grateful for the great destinies which raised them to the top; they are grateful in relation to the annual cycle of the seasons and to all good fortune in stock farming and agriculture.

This state of affairs long remained the ideal, even after it had been done away with in melancholy fashion: anarchy within, the Assyrian without. The people, however, clung to the vision, as the highest desirability, of a king who is a good soldier and severe judge: above all, that typical prophet (that is, critic and satirist of the moment), Isaiah.

But all hopes remained unfulfilled. The old god was no longer able to do what he once could do. They should have let him go. What happened? They changed his concept—they denatured his concept: at this price they held on to him. Yahweh the god of "justice"—no longer one with Israel, an expression of the self-confidence of the people: now a god only under certain conditions.

The concept of God becomes a tool in the hands of priestly agitators, who now interpret all happiness as a reward, all unhappiness as punishment for disobeying God, as "sin": that most mendacious device of interpretation, the alleged "moral world order," with which the natural concepts of cause and effect are turned upside down once and for all. When, through reward and punishment, one has done away with natural causality, an *anti-natural* causality is required: now everything else that is unnatural follows. A god who *demands*—in place of a god who helps, who devises means, who is at bottom the word for every happy inspiration of courage and self-confidence.

Morality—no longer the expression of the conditions for the life and growth of a people, no longer its most basic instinct of life, but become abstract, become the antithesis of life—morality as the systematic degradation of the imagination, as the "evil eye" for all things. What is Jewish, what is Christian, morality? Chance done out of its innocence; misfortune besmirched with the concept of "sin"; well-being as a danger, a "temptation"; physiological indisposition poisoned with the worm of conscience.

26

The concept of God falsified, the concept of morality falsified: the Jewish priesthood did not stop there. The whole of the *history* of Israel could not be used: away with it! These priests accomplished a miracle of falsification, and a good part of the Bible now lies before us as documentary proof. With matchless scorn for every tradition, for every historical reality, they translated the past of their own people into religious terms, that is, they turned it into a stupid salvation mechanism of guilt before Yahweh, and punishment; of piety before Yahweh, and reward. We would experience this most disgraceful act of historical falsification as something much more painful if the *ecclesiastical* interpretation of history had not all but deafened us in the course of thousands of years to the demands of integrity *in historicis*. And the church was seconded by the philosophers: the *lie* of the "moral world order" runs through the whole development of modern philosophy. What does "moral world order" mean? That there is a will of God, once and for all, as to what man is to do and what he is not to do; that the value of a people, of an individual, is to be measured according to how much or how little the will of God is obeyed; that the will of God manifests itself in the destinies of a people, of an individual, as the ruling factor, that is to say, as punishing and rewarding according to the degree of obedience.

The reality in place of this pitiful lie is this: a parasitical type of man, thriving only at the expense of all healthy forms of life, the priest, uses the name of God in vain: he calls a state of affairs in which the priest determines the value of things "the kingdom of God"; he calls the means by which such a state is attained or maintained "the will of God"; with cold-blooded cynicism he measures peoples, ages, individuals, according to whether they profited or resisted the overlordship of the priests. One should see them at work: in the hands of the Jewish priests the great age in the history of Israel became an age of decay; the Exile, the long misfortune, was transformed into an eternal punishment for the great age—an age in which the priest was still a nobody. Depending on their own requirements, they made either wretchedly meek and sleek prigs or "godless ones" out of the powerful, often very bold, figures in the history of Israel; they simplified the psychology of every great event by reducing it to the idiotic formula, "obedience *or* disobedience to God."

One step further: the "will of God" (that is, the conditions for the preservation of priestly power) must be *known:* to this end a "revelation" is required. In plain language: a great literary forgery becomes necessary, a "holy scripture" is discovered; it is made public with full hieratic pomp, with days of repentance and cries of lamentation over the long "sin." The "will of God" had long been fixed: all misfortune rests on one's having become estranged from the "holy scripture." The "will of God" had already been revealed to Moses. What happened? With severity and pedantry, the priest formulated once and for all, down to the large and small taxes he was to be paid (not to forget the tastiest pieces of meat, for the priest is a steak eater), what he wants to have, "what the will of God is." From now on all things in life are so ordered that the priest is indispensable everywhere; at all natural occurrences in life, at birth, marriage, sickness, death, not to speak of "sacrifices" (meals), the holy parasite appears in order to denature them—in his language: to "consecrate."

For one must understand this: every natural custom, every natural institution (state, judicial order, marriage, care of the sick and the poor), every demand inspired by the instinct of life—in short, everything that contains its value *in itself* is made altogether valueless, *anti-*valuable by the parasitism of the priest (or the "moral world order"): now it requires a sanction after the event—a *value-conferring* power is needed to negate what is natural in it and to *create* a value by so doing. The priest devalues, *desecrates* nature: this is the price of his existence. Disobedience of God, that is, of the priest, of "the Law," is now called "sin"; the means for "reconciliation with God" are, as is meet, means that merely guarantee still more thorough submission to the priest: the priest alone "redeems."

Psychologically considered, "sins" become indispensable in any society organized by priests: they are the real handles of power. The priest *lives* on sins, it is essential for him that people "sin." Supreme principle: "God forgives those who repent"—in plain language: those who submit to the priest.

27

On such utterly *false* soil, where everything natural, every natural value, every *reality* was opposed by the most profound instincts of the ruling class, *Christianity* grew up—a form of mortal enmity against reality that has never yet been surpassed. The "holy people," who had retained only priestly values, only priestly words for all things and who, with awe-inspiring consistency, had distinguished all other powers on earth from themselves as "unholy," as "world," as "sin"—this people produced an ultimate formula for its instinct that was logical to the point of self-negation: as *Christianity*, it negated even the last form of reality, the "holy people," the "chosen people," the Jewish reality itself. This case is of the first rank: the little rebellious movement which is baptized with the name of Jesus of Nazareth represents the Jewish instinct *once more*—in other words, the priestly instinct which can no longer stand the priest as a reality: the invention of a still more abstract form of existence, of a still more unreal vision of the world than is involved in the organization of a church. Christianity *negates* the church.

Jesus has been understood, or *misunderstood* as the cause of a rebellion; and I fail to see against what this

rebellion was directed, if it was not the Jewish church—
"church" exactly in the sense in which we use the word
today. It was a rebellion against "the good and the just,"
against "the saints of Israel," against the hierarchy of
society—*not* against its corruption, but against caste,
privilege, order, and formula; it was the *disbelief* in the
"higher man," the No to all that was priest or theologian.
But the hierarchy which was thus questioned, even
though for just a moment, was the lake-dwelling on
which alone the Jewish people could continue to exist
amid the "water"—the hard-won *last* chance of survival,
the residue of its independent political existence. An
attack on this was an attack on the deepest instinct of
a people, on the toughest life-will which has ever existed
in any people on earth. That holy anarchist who sum-
moned the people at the bottom, the outcasts and "sinners," the chandalas within Judaism, to opposition
against the dominant order—using language, if the
Gospels were to be trusted, which would lead to Siberia
today too—was a political criminal insofar as political
criminals were possible at all in an absurdly unpolitical
community. This brought him to the cross: the proof for
this is the inscription on the cross. He died for *his* guilt.
All evidence is lacking, however often it has been
claimed, that he died for the guilt of others.

28

It is a completely different question whether any such
opposition ever entered his consciousness—whether he
was not merely experienced by others as representing
this opposition. And it is only at this point that I touch
on the problem of the *psychology of the Redeemer.*

I confess that I read few books with as many difficulties as the Gospels. These difficulties are different
from those whose demonstration has provided the schol-

arly curiosity of the German spirit with one of its most unforgettable triumphs. The time is long past when I too, like every young scholar, slowly drew out the savor of the work of the incomparable Strauss, with the shrewdness of a refined philologist. I was twenty years old then: now I am too serious for that. What do I care about the contradictions in the "tradition"? How can one call saints' legends "tradition" in the first place? The biographies of saints are the most ambiguous kind of literature there is: to apply scientific methods to them, *in the absence of any other documents*, strikes me as doomed to failure from the start—mere scholarly idleness.

29

What concerns *me* is the psychological type of the Redeemer. After all, this could be contained in the Gospels despite the Gospels, however mutilated or overloaded with alien features: as Francis of Assisi is preserved in his legends, despite his legends. *Not* the truth concerning what he did, what he said, how he really died; but the question *whether* his type can still be exhibited at all, whether it has been "transmitted."

The attempts I know to read the *history* of a "soul" out of the Gospels seem to me proof of a contemptible psychological frivolity. M. Renan, that buffoon *in psychologicis*, has introduced the two most inappropriate concepts possible into his explanation of the Jesus type: the concept of *genius* and the concept of the *hero* (*"héros"*). But if anything is unevangelical it is the concept of the hero. Just the opposite of all wrestling, of all feeling-oneself-in-a-struggle, has here become instinct: the incapacity for resistance becomes morality here ("resist not evil"—the most profound word of the Gospels, their key in a certain sense), blessedness in peace, in gentleness, in not *being able* to be an enemy. What are the "glad tidings"? True life, eternal life, has been found—it is not promised, it is here, it is *in you:* as a living in love, in love without subtraction and exclusion, without regard for station. Everyone is the child of God—Jesus definitely presumes nothing for himself alone—and as a child of God everyone is equal to everyone. To make a *hero* of Jesus! And even more, what a misunderstanding is the word "genius"! Our whole concept, our cultural concept, of "spirit" has no meaning whatever in the world in which Jesus lives. Spoken with the precision of a physiologist, even an entirely different word would still be more nearly fitting here—the word *idiot.*[1]

We know a state in which the *sense of touch* is pathologically excitable and shrinks from any contact, from grasping a solid object. One should translate such a physiological *habitus* into its ultimate consequence—an instinctive hatred of every reality, a flight into "what cannot be grasped," "the incomprehensible," an aversion to every formula, to every concept of time and space,

[1] The last three words were suppressed by Nietzsche's sister when she first published *The Antichrist* in 1895, in Volume VIII of the Collected Works. They were first made public by Hofmiller in 1931, to prove that Nietzsche must have been insane when he wrote the book. But he was, of course, thinking of Dostoevski's *The Idiot.* The references to Dostoevski in section 31 below and in section 45 of *Twilight of the Idols* should also be noted. The word "idiot" assumes a sudden significance in Nietzsche's work after his discovery of Dostoevski: see section 5 of *The Wagner Case;* section 7 in Chapter 2 of *Twilight of the Idols;* sections 11, 26, 31, 42, 51-53 of *The Antichrist;* section 2 of "The Wagner Case" in *Ecce Homo;* sections 2 and 3 of *Nietzsche contra Wagner;* the letters to Brandes and Strindberg, dated October 20 and December 7, 1888; and note 734 in *The Will to Power.*

to all that is solid, custom, institution, church; a being at home in a world which is no longer in contact with any kind of reality, a merely "inner" world, a "true" world, an "eternal" world. "The kingdom of God is *in you.*"

30

The instinctive hatred of reality: a consequence of an extreme capacity for suffering and excitement which no longer wants any contact at all because it feels every contact too deeply.

The instinctive exclusion of any antipathy, any hostility, any boundaries or divisions in man's feelings: the consequence of an extreme capacity for suffering and excitement which experiences any resistance, even any compulsion to resist, as unendurable *displeasure* (that is, as *harmful,* as something against which the instinct of self-preservation *warns* us); and finds blessedness (pleasure) only in no longer offering any resistance to anybody, neither to evil nor to him who is evil—love as the only, as the *last* possible, way of life.

These are the two *physiological realities* on which, out of which, the doctrine of redemption grew. I call this a sublime further development of hedonism on a thoroughly morbid basis. Most closely related to it, although with a generous admixture of Greek vitality and nervous energy, is Epicureanism, the pagan doctrine of redemption. Epicurus, a *typical decadent*—first recognized as such by me. The fear of pain, even of infinitely minute pain—that can end in no other way than in a *religion of love.*

31

I have already given my answer to the problem. Its presupposition is that the Redeemer type is preserved for us only in extensive distortion. This distortion is very probable in any case; for several reasons, such a type could not remain pure, whole, free from accretions. He must show traces of the milieu in which he moved as a foreign figure; and even more of the history, the *fate* of the first Christian community, from which the type was enriched, retroactively, with features which are comprehensible only in terms of later polemics and propaganda purposes.

That queer and sick world into which the Gospels introduce us—as in a Russian novel, a world in which the scum of society, nervous disorders, and "childlike" idiocy seem to be having a rendezvous—must at all events have *coarsened* the type: in order to be able to understand anything of it, the first disciples, in particular, first translated into their own crudity an existence which was wholly embedded in symbols and incomprehensibilities—for them the type did not *exist* until it had been reshaped in better-known forms. The prophet, the Messiah, the future judge, the moral teacher, the miracle man, John the Baptist—each another chance to misconstrue the type.

Finally, let us not underestimate the *proprium* of all great, and especially sectarian, veneration: it blots out the original, often painfully strange features and idiosyncrasies of the venerated being—*it does not even see them*. It is regrettable that a Dostoevski did not live near this most interesting of all decadents—I mean someone who would have known how to sense the very stirring charm of such a mixture of the sublime, the sickly, and the childlike.

A final consideration: as a type of decadence, the type *might* actually have been peculiarly manifold and contradictory. Such a possibility cannot be excluded altogether. Nevertheless, everything speaks against this:

precisely the tradition would have to be curiously faithful and objective in this case—and we have reasons for
supposing the opposite. Meanwhile there is a gaping
contradiction between the sermonizer on the mount, lake,
and meadow, whose appearance seems like that of a Buddha on soil that is not at all Indian, and that fanatic of
aggression, that mortal enemy of theologians and priests,
whom Renan's malice has glorified as *le grand maître en
ironie.* I myself have no doubt that the generous dose of
gall (and even of *esprit*) first flowed into the type of
the Master from the excited state of Christian propaganda; after all, the unscrupulousness of all sectarians,
when it comes to constructing their own *apology* out of
their master, is only too well known. When the first community needed a judging, quarreling, angry, malignantly
sophistical theologian, *against* theologians, it *created* its
"God" according to its needs—just as it put into his
mouth, without any hesitation, those wholly unevangelical concepts which now it cannot do without: "the
return," the "Last Judgment," every kind of temporal
expectation and promise.

32

To repeat, I am against any attempt to introduce the
fanatic into the Redeemer type: the word *impérieux,*
which Renan uses, is alone enough to annul the type.
The "glad tidings" are precisely that there are no longer
any opposites; the kingdom of heaven belongs to the
children; the faith which finds expression here is not a
faith attained through struggle—it is there, it has been
there from the beginning; it is, as it were, an infantilism
that has receded into the spiritual. The case of puberty
being retarded and not developing in the organism, as a
consequence of degeneration, is well known, at least to
physiologists. Such a faith is not angry, does not re-

proach, does not resist: it does not bring "the sword"—
it simply does not foresee how it might one day separate. It does not prove itself either by miracle or by
reward and promise, least of all "by scripture": at every
moment it is its own miracle, its own reward, its own
proof, its own "kingdom of God." Nor does this faith
formulate itself: it *lives*, it resists all formulas. Of course,
the accidents of environment, of language, of background
determine a certain sphere of concepts: the earliest Christianity uses only Jewish-Semitic concepts (the eating
and drinking at the Last Supper belong here, that concept which, like everything Jewish, has been misused so
badly by the church). But one should beware of finding
more than a sign language in this, a semeiology, an occasion for parables. For this anti-realist, that not a word
is taken literally is precisely the presupposition of being
able to speak at all. Among Indians he would have
availed himself of Sankhya concepts; among the Chinese, of those of Lao-tse—without having felt any difference. Using the expression somewhat tolerantly, one
could call Jesus a "free spirit"—he does not care for
anything solid: the word kills, all that is solid kills. The
concept, the *experience* of "life" in the only way he
knows it, resists any kind of word, formula, law, faith,
dogma. He speaks only of the innermost: "life" or
"truth" or "light" is his word for the innermost—all the
rest, the whole of reality, the whole of nature, language
itself, has for him only the value of a sign, a simile.

Make no mistake at this point, however seductive the
Christian, in other words, the *ecclesiastical*, prejudice
may be: such a symbolist par excellence stands outside
all religion, all cult concepts, all history, all natural science, all experience of the world, all knowledge, all
politics, all psychology, all books, all art—his "knowledge" is *pure foolishness* precisely concerning the fact

that such things exist. *Culture* is not known to him even by hearsay, he does not need to fight it—he does not negate it. The same applies to the state, to the whole civic order and society, to work, to war—he never had any reason to negate "the world"; the ecclesiastical concept of "world" never occurred to him. To negate is the very thing that is impossible for him. Dialectic is equally lacking; the very idea is lacking that a faith, a "truth," might be proved by reasons (his proofs are inner "lights," inner feelings of pleasure and self-affirmations, all of them "proofs of strength"). Such a doctrine is also incapable of contradicting: it does not even comprehend that there are, that there *can* be, other doctrines; it cannot even imagine a contradictory judgment. Where it encounters one, from innermost sympathy it will mourn over "blindness"—for it sees the "light"—but it will offer no objection.

33

In the whole psychology of the "evangel" the concept of guilt and punishment is lacking; also the concept of reward. "Sin"—any distance separating God and man— is abolished: *precisely this is the "glad tidings."* Blessedness is not promised, it is not tied to conditions: it is the only reality—the rest is a sign with which to speak of it.

The consequence of such a state projects itself into a new practice, the genuine evangelical practice. It is not a "faith" that distinguishes the Christian: the Christian *acts,* he is distinguished by acting *differently:* by not resisting, either in words or in his heart, those who treat him ill; by making no distinction between foreigner and native, between Jew and not-Jew ("the neighbor" —really the coreligionist, the Jew); by not growing angry with anybody, by not despising anybody; by not permitting himself to be seen or involved at courts of law ("not swearing"); by not divorcing his wife under any circumstances, not even if his wife has been proved unfaithful. All of this, at bottom one principle; all of this, consequences of one instinct.

The life of the Redeemer was nothing other than *this* practice—nor was his death anything else. He no longer required any formulas, any rites for his intercourse with God—not even prayer. He broke with the whole Jewish doctrine of repentance and reconciliation; he knows that it is only in the *practice* of life that one feels "divine," "blessed," "evangelical," at all times a "child of God." Not "repentance," not "prayer for forgiveness," are the ways to God: *only the evangelical practice* leads to God, indeed, it *is* "God"! What was disposed of with the evangel was the Judaism of the concepts of "sin," "forgiveness of sin," "faith," "redemption through faith"— the whole Jewish *ecclesiastical* doctrine was negated in the "glad tidings."

The deep instinct for how one must *live,* in order to feel oneself "in heaven," to feel "eternal," while in all other behavior one decidedly does *not* feel oneself "in heaven"—this alone is the psychological reality of "redemption." A new way of life, *not* a new faith.

34

If I understand anything about this great symbolist, it is that he accepted only *inner* realities as realities, as "truths"—that he understood the rest, everything natural, temporal, spatial, historical, only as signs, as occasions for parables. The concept of "the son of man" is not a concrete person who belongs in history, something individual and unique, but an "eternal" factuality, a psychological symbol redeemed from the concept of time. The same applies once again, and in the highest sense, to the *God* of this typical symbolist, to the "king-

dom of God," to the "kingdom of heaven," to the "filia-
tion of God." Nothing is more unchristian than the
ecclesiastical crudities of a god as person, of a "kingdom of God" which is to come, of a "kingdom of heaven"
beyond, of a "son of God" as the second person in the
Trinity. All this is—forgive the expression—like a fist
in the eye—oh, in what an eye!—of the evangel—a
world-historical cynicism in the derision of symbols. But
what the signs "father" and "son" refer to is obvious—
not to everyone, I admit: the word "son" expresses the
entry into the over-all feeling of the transfiguration of
all things (blessedness); the word "father" expresses
this feeling itself, the feeling of eternity, the feeling of
perfection. I am ashamed to recall what the church has
made of this symbolism: Has it not placed an Amphi-
tryon story at the threshold of the Christian "faith"?
And a dogma of "immaculate conception" on top of
that? *But with that it has maculated conception.*

The "kingdom of heaven" is a state of the heart—not
something that is to come "above the earth" or "after
death." The whole concept of natural death is lacking
in the evangel: death is no bridge, no transition; it is
lacking because it belongs to a wholly different, merely
apparent world, useful only insofar as it furnishes signs.
The "hour of death" is *no* Christian concept—an "hour,"
time, physical life and its crises do not even exist for
the teacher of the "glad tidings." The "kingdom of God"
is nothing that one expects; it has no yesterday and no
day after tomorrow, it will not come in "a thousand
years"—it is an experience of the heart; it is everywhere, it is nowhere.

35

This "bringer of glad tidings" died as he had lived,
as he had taught—*not* to "redeem men" but to show

how one must live. This practice is his legacy to mankind: his behavior before the judges, before the catchpoles, before the accusers and all kinds of slander and scorn—his behavior on the *cross*. He does not resist, he does not defend his right, he takes no step which might ward off the worst; on the contrary, he *provokes* it. And he begs, he suffers, he loves *with* those, *in* those, who do him evil. *Not* to resist, *not* to be angry, *not* to hold responsible—but to resist not even the evil one—to *love* him.

36

Only we, we spirits who have *become free*, have the presuppositions for understanding something that nineteen centuries have misunderstood: that integrity which, having become instinct and passion, wages war against the "holy lie" even more than against any other lie. Previous readers were immeasurably far removed from our loving and cautious neutrality, from that discipline of the spirit which alone makes possible the unriddling of such foreign, such tender things: with impudent selfishness they always wanted only their own advantage; out of the opposite of the evangel the church was constructed.

If one were to look for signs that an ironical divinity has its fingers in the great play of the world, one would find no small support in the *tremendous question mark* called Christianity. Mankind lies on its knees before the opposite of that which was the origin, the meaning, the *right* of the evangel; in the concept of "church" it has pronounced holy precisely what the "bringer of the glad tidings" felt to be *beneath* and *behind* himself—one would look in vain for a greater example of *world-historical irony*.

37

Our age is proud of its historical sense: How could it ever make itself believe the nonsense that at the beginning of Christianity there stands the *crude fable of the miracle worker and Redeemer*—and that everything spiritual and symbolical represents only a later development? On the contrary: the history of Christianity, beginning with the death on the cross, is the history of the misunderstanding, growing cruder with every step, of an *original* symbolism. With every diffusion of Christianity to still broader, still cruder masses of people, more and more lacking in the presuppositions to which it owed its birth, it became more necessary to *vulgarize*, to *barbarize* Christianity: it has swallowed doctrines and rites of all the *subterranean* cults of the *imperium Romanum* as well as the nonsense of all kinds of diseased reason. The destiny of Christianity lies in the necessity that its faith had to become as diseased, as base and vulgar, as the needs it was meant to satisfy were diseased, base, and vulgar. In the church, finally, *diseased barbarism* itself gains power—the church, this embodiment of mortal hostility against all integrity, against all *elevation* of the soul, against all discipline of the spirit, against all frank and gracious humanity. *Christian* values—*noble* values: only we, we spirits who have *become free,* have restored this contrast of values, the greatest that there is!

38

At this point I do not suppress a sigh. There are days when I am afflicted with a feeling blacker than the blackest melancholy—*contempt of man.* And to leave no doubt concerning what I despise, whom I despise: it is the man of today, the man with whom I am fatefully contemporaneous. The man of today—I suffocate from his unclean breath. My attitude to the past, like that of all lovers of knowledge, is one of great tolerance, that is, *magnanimous* self-mastery: with gloomy caution I go through the madhouse world of whole millennia, whether it be called "Christianity," "Christian faith," or "Christian church"—I am careful not to hold mankind responsible for its mental disorders. But my feeling changes, breaks out, as soon as I enter modern times, *our* time. Our time *knows better.*

What was formerly just sick is today indecent—it is indecent to be a Christian today. *And here begins my nausea.* I look around: not one word has remained of what was formerly called "truth"; we can no longer stand it if a priest as much as uses the word "truth." If we have even the smallest claim to integrity, we must know today that a theologian, a priest, a pope, not merely is wrong in every sentence he speaks, but *lies*—that he is no longer at liberty to lie from "innocence" or "ignorance." The priest too knows as well as anybody else that there is no longer any "God," any "sinner," any "Redeemer"—that "free will" and "moral world order" are *lies:* seriousness, the profound self-overcoming of the spirit, no longer permits anybody *not* to know about this.

All the concepts of the church have been recognized for what they are, the most malignant counterfeits that exist, the aim of which is to devalue nature and natural values; the priest himself has been recognized for what he is, the most dangerous kind of parasite, the real poison-spider of life. We know, today our *conscience* knows, what these uncanny inventions of the priests and the church are really worth, *what ends they served* in reducing mankind to such a state of self-violation that its sight can arouse nausea: the concepts "beyond,"

"Last Judgment," "immortality of the soul," and "soul" itself are instruments of torture, systems of cruelties by virtue of which the priest became master, remained master.

Everybody knows this, *and yet everything continues as before*. Where has the last feeling of decency and self-respect gone when even our statesmen, an otherwise quite unembarrassed type of man, anti-Christians through and through in their deeds, still call themselves Christians today and attend communion? A young prince at the head of his regiments, magnificent as an expression of the selfishness and conceit of his people—but, *without* any shame, confessing himself a Christian! *Whom* then does Christianity negate? *What* does it call "world"? That one is a soldier, that one is a judge, that one is a patriot; that one resists; that one sees to one's honor; that one seeks one's advantage; that one is proud. Every practice of every moment, every instinct, every valuation that is translated into *action* is today anti-Christian: what a *miscarriage of falseness* must modern man be, that he is *not ashamed* to be called a Christian in spite of all this!

39

I go back, I tell the *genuine* history of Christianity. The very word "Christianity" is a misunderstanding: in truth, there was only *one* Christian, and he died on the cross. The "evangel" *died* on the cross. What has been called "evangel" from that moment was actually the opposite of that which *he* had lived: "*ill* tidings," a *dysangel*. It is false to the point of nonsense to find the mark of the Christian in a "faith," for instance, in the faith in redemption through Christ: only Christian *practice*, a life such as he *lived* who died on the cross, is Christian.

Such a life is still possible today, for certain people even necessary: genuine, original Christianity will be possible at all times.

Not a faith, but a doing; above all, a *not* doing of many things, another state of *being*. States of consciousness, any faith, considering something true, for example —every psychologist knows this—are fifth-rank matters of complete indifference compared to the value of the instincts: speaking more strictly, the whole concept of spiritual causality is false. To reduce being a Christian, Christianism, to a matter of considering something true, to a mere phenomenon of consciousness, is to negate Christianism. *In fact, there have been no Christians at all.* The "Christian," that which for the last two thousand years has been called a Christian, is merely a psychological self-misunderstanding. If one looks more closely, it was, in spite of all "faith," only the instincts that ruled in him—and *what instincts!*

"Faith" was at all times, for example, in Luther, only a cloak, a pretext, a *screen* behind which the instincts played their game—a shrewd *blindness* about the dominance of *certain* instincts. "Faith"—I have already called it the characteristic Christian *shrewdness*—one always *spoke* of faith, but one always *acted* from instinct alone.

In the Christian world of ideas there is nothing that has the least contact with reality—and it is in the instinctive hatred of reality that we have recognized the only motivating force at the root of Christianity. What follows from this? That *in psychologicis* too, the error here is radical, that it is that which determines the very essence, that it is the *substance*. One concept less, one single reality in its place—and the whole of Christianity hurtles down into nothing.

Viewed from high above, this strangest of all facts—

a religion which is not only dependent on errors but which has its inventiveness and even its genius *only* in harmful errors, *only* in errors which poison life and the heart—is really a *spectacle for gods*, for those gods who are at the same time philosophers and whom I have encountered, for example, at those famous dialogues on Naxos. The moment *nausea* leaves them (*and* us!), they become grateful for the spectacle of the Christian: perhaps the miserable little star that is called earth deserves a divine glance, a divine sympathy, just because of *this* curious case. For let us not underestimate the Christian: the Christian, false *to the point of innocence*, is far above the ape—regarding Christians, a well-known theory of descent becomes a mere compliment.

40

The catastrophe of the evangel was decided with the death—it was attached to the "cross." Only the death, this unexpected, disgraceful death, only the cross which was generally reserved for the rabble—only this horrible paradox confronted the disciples with the real riddle: "*Who was this? What was this?*" Their profoundly upset and insulted feelings, and their suspicion that such a death might represent the *refutation* of their cause, the terrible question mark, "Why in this manner?"—this state is only too easy to understand. Here everything *had* to be necessary, had to have meaning, reason, the highest reason; a disciple's love knows no accident. Only now the cleft opened up: "*Who* killed him? *Who* was his natural enemy?" This question leaped forth like lightning. Answer: *ruling* Jewry, its highest class. From this moment one felt oneself in rebellion against the existing order, and in retrospect one understood Jesus to have been *in rebellion against the existing order*. Until then this warlike, this No-saying, No-doing trait had been *lacking* in his image; even more, he had been its opposite.

Evidently the small community did *not* understand the main point, the exemplary character of this kind of death, the freedom, the superiority over any feeling of *ressentiment:* a token of how little they understood him altogether! After all, Jesus could not intend anything with his death except to give publicly the strongest exhibition, the *proof* of his doctrine. But his disciples were far from *forgiving* this death—which would have been evangelic in the highest sense—or even from offering themselves for a like death in gentle and lovely repose of the heart. Precisely the most unevangelical feeling, *revenge,* came to the fore again. The matter could not possibly be finished with this death: "retribution" was needed, "judgment" (and yet, what could possibly be more unevangelical than "retribution," "punishment," "sitting in judgment"!). Once more the popular expectation of a Messiah came to the foreground; a historic moment was envisaged: the "kingdom of God" comes as a judgment over his enemies.

But in this way everything is misunderstood: the "kingdom of God" as the last act, as a promise! After all, the evangel had been precisely the presence, the fulfillment, the *reality* of this "kingdom." Just such a death was this very "kingdom of God." Now for the first time all the contempt and bitterness against the Pharisees and theologians were carried into the type of the Master— and in this way he himself was made into a Pharisee and theologian! On the other hand, the frenzied veneration of these totally unhinged souls no longer endured the evangelic conception of everybody's equal right to be a child of God, as Jesus had taught: it was their revenge to *elevate* Jesus extravagantly, to sever him from themselves—precisely as the Jews had formerly, out of revenge against their enemies, severed their God from themselves and elevated him. The one God and the one Son of God—both products of *ressentiment.*

41

And from now on an absurd problem emerged: "How *could* God permit this?" To this the deranged reason of the small community found an altogether horribly absurd answer: God gave his son for the remission of sins, as a *sacrifice.* In one stroke, it was all over with the evangel! The *trespass sacrifice*—in its most revolting, most barbarous form at that, the sacrifice of the *guiltless* for the sins of the guilty! What gruesome paganism!

Jesus had abolished the very concept of "guilt"—he had denied any cleavage between God and man; he *lived* this unity of God and man as his "glad tidings." And *not* as a prerogative! From now on there enters into the type of the Redeemer, step by step, the doctrine of judgment and return, the doctrine of death as a sacrificial death, the doctrine of the *resurrection* with which the whole concept of "blessedness," the whole and only actuality of the evangel, is conjured away—in favor of a state after death.

Paul, with that rabbinical impudence which distinguishes him in all things, logicalized this conception, this *obscenity* of a conception, in this way: "*If* Christ was not resurrected from the dead, then our faith is vain." And all at once the evangel became the most contemptible of all unfulfillable promises, the *impertinent* doctrine of personal immortality. Paul himself still taught it as a *reward.*

42

It is plain *what* was finished with the death on the cross: a new, an entirely original basis for a Buddhistic peace movement, for an actual, *not* merely promised, *happiness on earth*. For this, as I have already emphasized, remains the fundamental difference between the two religions of decadence: Buddhism does not promise but fulfills; Christianity promises everything but fulfills nothing. On the heels of the "glad tidings" came the *very worst*: those of Paul. In Paul was embodied the opposite type to that of the "bringer of glad tidings": the genius in hatred, in the vision of hatred, in the inexorable logic of hatred. *How much* this dysangelist [1] sacrificed to hatred! Above all, the Redeemer: he nailed him to *his own* cross. The life, the example, the doctrine, the death, the meaning and the right of the entire evangel—nothing remained once this hate-inspired counterfeiter realized what alone he could use. *Not* the reality, *not* the historical truth! And once more the priestly instinct of the Jew committed the same great crime against history—he simply crossed out the yesterday of Christianity and its day before yesterday; he *invented his own history of earliest Christianity*. Still *further*: he falsified the history of Israel once more so that it might appear as the prehistory of *his* deed: all the prophets spoke of *his* "Redeemer." Later the church even falsified the history of mankind into the prehistory of Christianity.

The Redeemer type, the doctrine, the practice, the death, the meaning of the death, even what came after the death—nothing remained untouched, nothing remained even similar to the reality. Paul simply transposed the center of gravity of that whole existence *after* this existence—in the *lie* of the "resurrected" Jesus. At bottom, he had no use at all for the life of the Redeemer—he needed the death on the cross *and* a little more.

[1] "Bringer of ill tidings" (see section 39).

To consider a Paul, whose home was in the main seat of Stoic enlightenment, honest when he dresses up a hallucination as *proof* that the Redeemer still lives, or even to believe his story that he had this hallucination, would be a true *niaiserie* for a psychologist: Paul wanted the end, *consequently* he also wanted the means. What he himself did not believe, the idiots among whom he threw his doctrine believed. His need was for power; in Paul the priest wanted power once again—he could use only concepts, doctrines, symbols with which one tyrannizes masses and forms herds. What was the one thing that Mohammed later borrowed from Christianity? Paul's invention, his means to priestly tyranny, to herd formation: the faith in immortality—*that is, the doctrine of the "judgment."*

43

When one places life's center of gravity not in life but in the "beyond"—*in nothingness*—one deprives life of its center of gravity altogether. The great lie of personal immortality destroys all reason, everything natural in the instincts—whatever in the instincts is beneficent and life-promoting or guarantees a future now arouses mistrust. To live so, that there is no longer any *sense* in living, *that* now becomes the "sense" of life. Why communal sense, why any further gratitude for descent and ancestors, why cooperate, trust, promote, and envisage any common welfare? Just as many "temptations," just as many distractions from the "right path" —*"one* thing is needful."

That everyone as an "immortal soul" has equal rank with everyone else, that in the totality of living beings the "salvation" of *every* single individual may claim eternal significance, that little prigs and three-quarter-madmen may have the conceit that the laws of nature are constantly broken for their sakes—such an intensification of every kind of selfishness into the infinite, into the *impertinent*, cannot be branded with too much contempt. And yet Christianity owes its triumph to this miserable flattery of personal vanity: it was precisely all the failures, all the rebellious-minded, all the less favored, the whole scum and refuse of humanity who were thus won over to it. The "salvation of the soul"— in plain language: "the world revolves around *me*."

The poison of the doctrine of "equal rights for all"— it was Christianity that spread it most fundamentally. Out of the most secret nooks of bad instincts, Christianity has waged war unto death against all sense of respect and feeling of distance between man and man, that is to say, against the *presupposition* of every elevation, of every growth of culture; out of the *ressentiment* of the masses it forged its chief weapon against *us*, against all that is noble, gay, high-minded on earth, against our happiness on earth. "Immortality" conceded to every Peter and Paul has so far been the greatest, the most malignant, attempt to assassinate *noble* humanity.

And let us not underestimate the calamity which crept out of Christianity into politics. Today nobody has the courage any longer for privileges, for masters' rights, for a sense of respect for oneself and one's peers —for a *pathos of distance*. Our politics is sick from this lack of courage.

The aristocratic outlook was undermined from the deepest underworld through the lie of the equality of souls; and if faith in the "prerogative of the majority" makes and *will make* revolutions—it is Christianity, beyond a doubt, it is *Christian* value judgments, that every revolution simply translates into blood and crime.

Christianity is a rebellion of everything that crawls on the ground against that which has *height*: the evangel of the "lowly" *makes* low.

44

The Gospels are valuable as testimony to the irresistible corruption *within* the first community. What Paul later carried to its conclusion, with the logician's cynicism of a rabbi, was nevertheless nothing other than that process of decay which had begun with the death of the Redeemer.

One cannot read these Gospels cautiously enough; every word poses difficulties. I confess—one will pardon me—that precisely on this account they are a first-rate delight for a psychologist—as the *opposite* of all naïve corruption, as subtlety par excellence, as artistry in psychological corruption. The Gospels stand apart. The Bible in general suffers no comparison. One is among Jews: *first* consideration to keep from losing the thread completely. The simulation of "holiness" which has really become genius here, never even approximated elsewhere in books or among men, this counterfeit of words and gestures as an *art*, is not the accident of some individual talent or other or of some exceptional character. This requires *race*. In Christianity all of Judaism, a several-century-old Jewish preparatory training and technique of the most serious kind, attains its ultimate mastery as the art of lying in a holy manner. The Christian, this *ultima ratio* of the lie, is the Jew once more—even *three* times more.

To be determined, as a matter of principle, to apply only concepts, symbols, attitudes which have been proved by the practice of the priest; instinctively to reject every other practice, every other perspective of value and usefulness—that is not merely tradition, that

is *heritage:* only as heritage does it seem like nature itself. The whole of mankind, even the best heads of the
best ages (except one, who is perhaps merely inhuman),
have permitted themselves to be deceived. The Gospel
has been read as a *book of innocence*—no small indication of the mastery here attained in histrionics. Of
course, if we *saw* them, even if only in passing, all these
queer prigs and synthetic saints, that would be the end
—and precisely because *I* do not read words *without*
seeing gestures, *I make an end of them.* I cannot stand
a certain manner they have of turning up their eyes.
Fortunately, for the great majority books are mere *literature.*

One must not let oneself be led astray: "judge not,"
they say, but they consign to hell everything that
stands in their way. By letting God judge, they themselves judge; by glorifying God, they glorify themselves;
by *demanding* the virtues of which they happen to be
capable—even more, which they require in order to
stay on top at all—they give themselves the magnificent
appearance of a struggle for virtue, of a fight for the
domination of virtue. "We live, we die, we sacrifice ourselves *for the good*" ("truth," "light," the "kingdom of
God"): in truth, they do what they cannot help doing.
Slinking around like typical sneaks, sitting in the corner,
leading a shadowy existence in the shadow, they make
a *duty* of all this: their life of humility appears as a
duty; as humility it is one more proof of piety. Oh, this
humble, chaste, merciful variety of mendaciousness!
"Virtue itself shall bear witness for us." One should
read the Gospels as books of seduction by means of
morality: these petty people reserve morality for themselves—they know all about morality! With morality it
is easiest to lead mankind *by the nose!*

What really happens here is that the most conscious

conceit of being chosen plays modesty: once and for all one has placed *oneself*, the "community," the "good and the just," on one side, on the side of "truth"—and the rest, "the world," on the other. This was the most disastrous kind of megalomania that has yet existed on earth: little miscarriages of prigs and liars began to claim for themselves the concepts of God, truth, light, spirit, love, wisdom, life—as synonyms for themselves, as it were, in order to define themselves against "the world": little superlative Jews, ripe for every kind of madhouse, turned all values around in their own image, just as if "the Christian" alone were the meaning, the salt, the measure, also the *Last Judgment*, of all the rest. The whole calamity became possible only because a related, racially related, kind of megalomania already existed in this world: the *Jewish* one. As soon as the cleft between the Jews and the Jewish Christians opened, no choice whatever remained to the latter but to apply *against* the Jews themselves the same procedures of self-preservation that the Jewish instinct recommended, whereas hitherto the Jews had applied them only against everything *non*-Jewish. The Christian is merely a Jew of "more liberal" persuasion.

45

I give some examples of what these little people put into their heads, what they *put into the mouth* of their master: without exception, confessions of "beautiful souls":

"And whosoever shall not receive you, nor hear you, when ye depart thence, shake off the dust under your feet for a testimony against them. Verily I say unto you, It shall be more tolerable for Sodom and Gomorrah in the day of judgment, than for that city" (Mark 6:11). How *evangelical!*

"And whosoever shall offend one of these little ones that believe in me, it is better for him that a millstone were hanged about his neck, and he were cast into the sea" (Mark 9:42). How *evangelical!*

"And if thine eye offend thee, pluck it out: it is better for thee to enter into the kingdom of God with one eye, than having two eyes to be cast into hell fire: Where their worm dieth not, and the fire is not quenched" (Mark 9:47 *f.*). It is not exactly the eye which is meant.

"Verily I say unto you, That there be some of them that stand here, which shall not taste of death, till they have seen the kingdom of God come with power" (Mark 9:1). Well *lied,* lion!

"Whosoever will come after me, let him deny himself, and take up his cross, and follow me. *For—*" (*Note of a psychologist.* Christian morality is refuted by its *For's:* its "reasons" refute—thus is it Christian.) Mark 8:34.

"Judge not, that ye be not judged. . . . With what measure ye mete, it shall be measured to you again" (Matt. 7:1 *f.*). What a conception of justice and of a "just" judge!

"For if ye love them which love you, what reward have ye? do not even the publicans the same? And if ye salute your brethren only, what do ye more *than others?* do not even the publicans so?" (Matt. 5:46 *f.*). The principle of "Christian love": in the end it wants to be *paid* well.

"But if ye forgive not men their trespasses, neither will your Father forgive your trespasses" (Matt. 6:15). Very compromising for said "Father."

"But seek ye first the kingdom of God, and his righteousness; and all these things shall be added unto you" (Matt. 6:33). All these things: namely, food, clothing, all the necessities of life. An *error,* to put it modestly. Shortly before this, God appears as a tailor, at least in certain cases.

"Rejoice ye in that day, and leap for joy: for, behold, your reward is great in heaven: for in the like manner did their fathers unto the prophets" (Luke 6:23). *Impertinent* rabble! They compare themselves with the prophets, no less.

"Know ye not that ye are the temple of God, and that the Spirit of God dwelleth in you? If any man defile the temple of God, him shall God destroy; for the temple of God is holy, which temple ye are" (Paul, I Cor. 3:16 *f.*). This sort of thing one cannot despise enough.

"Do ye not know that the saints shall judge the world? and if the world shall be judged by you, are ye unworthy to judge the smallest matters?" (Paul, I Cor. 6:2). Unfortunately not merely the talk of a lunatic. This *frightful swindler* continues literally: "Know ye not that we shall judge angels? how much more things that pertain to this life!"

"Hath not God made foolish the wisdom of this world? For after that the world by its wisdom knew not God in his wisdom, it pleased God by foolish preaching to make blessed them that believe in it. . . . Not many wise men after the flesh, not many mighty, not many noble, are called. But God hath chosen the foolish things of the world to ruin the wise; and God hath chosen the weak things of the world to ruin what is strong; And base things of the world, and things which are despised, hath God chosen, yea, and what is nothing, to bring to nought what is something: That no flesh should glory in his presence" (Paul, I Cor. 1:20 *ff.*).[1] To understand this passage, a first-rate docu-

[1] Nietzsche quotes Luther's translation, and some departures from the King James Bible were found necessary

ment for the psychology of every chandala morality,
one should read the first inquiry in my *Genealogy of
Morals*: there the contrast between a *noble* morality
and a chandala morality, born of *ressentiment* and
impotent vengefulness, was brought to light for the first
time. Paul was the greatest of all apostles cf vengeance.

46

What follows from this? That one does well to put
on gloves when reading the New Testament. The proximity of so much uncleanliness almost forces one to do
this. We would no more choose the "first Christians"
to associate with than Polish Jews—not that one even
required any objection to them: they both do not smell
good.

I have looked in vain through the New Testament to
descry even a single sympathetic feature: there is nothing in it that is free, gracious, candid, honest. Humaneness did not even make its first beginnings here—the
instincts of *cleanliness* are lacking. There are only *bad*
instincts in the New Testament, and not even the
courage to have these bad instincts. Everything in it is
cowardice, everything is shutting-one's-eyes and self-
deception. Every book becomes clean just after one has
read the New Testament: to give an example, it was
with utter delight that, right after Paul, I read that
most graceful, most prankish mocker Petronius, of
whom one might say what Domenico Boccaccio wrote
to the Duke of Parma about Cesare Borgia: *è tutto
festo*—immortally healthy, immortally cheerful and well
turned out.

For these little prigs miscalculate precisely where it
matters most. They attack, but everything they attack

in this quotation because some of its phrases are echoed in
subsequent sections.

is *distinguished* thereby. To be attacked by a "first Christian" is *not* to be soiled. On the contrary: it is an honor to be opposed by "first Christians." One does not read the New Testament without a predilection for that which is maltreated in it—not to speak of "the wisdom of this world," which an impudent windmaker tries in vain to ruin with "foolish preaching."

But even the Pharisees and scribes derive an advantage from such opposition: they must have been worth something to have been hated in so indecent a manner. Hypocrisy—what a reproach in the mouths of "first Christians"! In the end, they were men of *privilege:* that is enough—chandala hatred requires no further grounds. The "first Christian"—I am afraid, the "last Christian" too, *and I may yet live to see him*—is, from his lowest instincts, a rebel against everything privileged: he lives, he fights always for *"equal rights."* Examined more closely, he has no choice. If one wants to be "chosen by God"—or a "temple of God" or a "judge of the angels"—then any other principle of selection—for example, according to integrity, spirit, virility and pride, beauty and freedom of the heart—is merely "world," *evil in itself.* Moral: every word in the mouth of a "first Christian" is a lie; every act he performs a falseness of instinct—all his values, all his goals are harmful; but *whomever he hates, whatever he hates, that has value.* The Christian, the priestly Christian in particular, is a *criterion of value.*

Need I add that in the whole New Testament there is only a *single* figure who commands respect? Pilate, the Roman governor. To take a Jewish affair *seriously* —he does not persuade himself to do that. One Jew more or less—what does it matter? The noble scorn of a Roman, confronted with an impudent abuse of the word "truth," has enriched the New Testament with the only saying *that has value*—one which is its criticism, even its *annihilation:* "What is truth?"

47

That we find no God—either in history or in nature or behind nature—is not what differentiates *us,* but that we experience what has been revered as God, not as "godlike" but as miserable, as absurd, as harmful, not merely as an error but as a *crime against life.* We deny God as God. If one were to *prove* this God of the Christians to us, we should be even less able to believe in him. In a formula: *deus, qualem Paulus creavit, dei negatio.*[1]

A religion like Christianity, which does not have contact with reality at any point, which crumbles as soon as reality is conceded its rights at even a single point, must naturally be mortally hostile against the "wisdom of this world," which means *science.* It will applaud all means with which the discipline of the spirit, purity and severity in the spirit's matters of conscience, the noble coolness and freedom of the spirit, can be poisoned, slandered, brought into disrepute. "Faith" as an imperative is the *veto* against science—in practice, the lie at any price.

Paul comprehended that the lie—that "faith"—was needed; later the church in turn comprehended Paul. The "God" whom Paul invented, a god who "ruins the wisdom of the world" (in particular, philology and medicine, the two great adversaries of all superstition), is in truth merely Paul's own resolute *determination* to do this: to give the name of "God" to one's own will, *torah,* that is thoroughly Jewish. Paul *wants* to ruin the "wisdom of the world": his enemies are the good philologists and physicians with Alexandrian training—it is

[1] "God, as Paul created him, is the negation of God."

they against whom he wages war. Indeed, one cannot be a philologist or physician without at the same time being an *anti-Christian*. For as a philologist one sees *behind* the "holy books"; as a physician, *behind* the physiological depravity of the typical Christian. The physician says "incurable"; the philologist, "swindle."

48

Has the famous story that stands at the beginning of the Bible really been understood? the story of God's hellish fear of *science*? It has not been understood. This priestly book par excellence begins, as is fitting, with the great inner difficulty of the priest: he knows only one great danger, consequently "God" knows only one great danger.

The old God, all "spirit," all high priest, all perfection, takes a stroll in his garden; but he is bored. Against boredom even gods struggle in vain. What does he do? He invents man—man is entertaining. But lo and behold! Man too is bored. God's compassion with the sole distress that distinguishes all paradises knows no limits: soon he creates other animals as well. God's *first* mistake: man did not find the animals entertaining; he ruled over them, he did not even want to be "animal." Consequently God created woman. And indeed, that was the end of boredom—but of other things too! Woman was God's *second* mistake. "Woman is by nature a snake, Heve" [1]—every priest knows that; "from woman comes all calamity in the world"—every priest knows that, too. "Consequently, it is from her too that

[1] Although Nietzsche seems to have in mind a well-known etymology of the Hebrew "Havvah" ("Eva" in German), not one of the Hebrew words for snake resembles this name. Genesis 3:20 links the name with life, and the only other verse in which it figures is Genesis 4:1.

science comes." Only from woman did man learn to taste of the tree of knowledge.

What had happened? The old God was seized with hellish fear. Man himself had turned out to be his *greatest* mistake; he had created a rival for himself; science makes godlike—it is all over with priests and gods when man becomes scientific. Moral: science is the forbidden as such—it alone is forbidden. Science is the *first* sin, the seed of all sin, the *original* sin. *This alone is morality.* "Thou shalt not know"—the rest follows.

God's hellish fear did not prevent him from being clever. How does one resist science? This became his main problem for a long time. Answer: out of paradise with man! Happiness, idleness, give rise to ideas—all ideas are bad ideas. Man *shall* not think. And the "priest-as-such" invents distress, death, the mortal danger of pregnancy, every kind of misery, old age, trouble, and, above all, *sickness*—all means in the fight against science. Distress does not permit man to think. And yet—horrible!—the edifice of knowledge begins to tower, heaven-storming, suggesting twilight to the gods. What is to be done? The old God invents *war,* he divides the peoples, he fixes it so men will annihilate each other (priests have always required wars). War —among other things a great disrupter of science! Incredible! Knowledge, the *emancipation from the priest,* continues to grow in spite of wars. And the old God makes a final decision: "Man has become scientific— *there is no other way, he has to be drowned.*"

49

I have been understood. The beginning of the Bible contains the *whole* psychology of the priest. The priest knows only one great danger: that is science, the sound conception of cause and effect. But on the whole science prospers only under happy circumstances—there must be a *surplus* of time, of spirit, to make "knowledge" possible. "Consequently, man must be made unhappy" —this was the logic of the priest in every age.

It will now be clear what was introduced into the world for the first time, in accordance with this logic: *"sin."* The concept of guilt and punishment, the whole "moral world order," was invented *against* science, *against* the emancipation of man from the priest. Man *shall not* look outside, he shall look into himself; he *shall not* look into things cleverly and cautiously, like a learner, he shall not look at all—he shall *suffer*. And he shall suffer in such a way that he has need of the priest at all times. Away with physicians! *A Savior is needed.* The concept of guilt and punishment, including the doctrine of "grace," of "redemption," of "forgiveness"—*lies* through and through, and without any psychological reality—were invented to destroy man's *causal sense:* they are an attempt to assassinate cause and effect. And not an attempt to assassinate with the fist, with the knife, with honesty in hatred and love! But born of the most cowardly, most cunning, lowest instincts. A *priestly* attempt! A *parasite's* attempt! A vampirism of pale, subterranean bloodsuckers!

When the natural consequences of a deed are no longer "natural," but thought of as caused by the conceptual specters of superstition, by "God," by "spirits," by "souls," as if they were merely "moral" consequences, as reward, punishment, hint, means of education, then the presupposition of knowledge has been destroyed— *then the greatest crime against humanity has been committed.* Sin, to repeat it once more, this form of man's self-violation par excellence, was invented to make science, culture, every elevation and nobility of man, impossible; the priest rules through the invention of sin.

50

At this point I do not let myself off without a psychology of "faith," of "believers"—precisely for the benefit of "believers," as is fitting. If today there is no lack of people who do not know in what way it is *indecent* to "believe"—*or* a sign of decadence, of broken will to life—tomorrow they will already know it. My voice reaches even the hard of hearing.

Unless I have heard wrong, it seems that among Christians there is a kind of criterion of truth that is called the "proof of strength." "Faith makes blessed: *hence* it is true." Here one might object first that it is precisely the making blessed which is not proved but merely *promised:* blessedness tied to the condition of "faith"—one *shall* become blessed *because* one believes. But whether what the priest promises the believer in fact occurs in a "beyond" which is not subject to any test—how is that proved? The alleged "proof of strength" is thus at bottom merely another faith, namely, that the effect one expects from faith will not fail to appear. In a formula: "I believe that faith makes blessed; consequently it is true." But with this we are already at the end. This "consequently" would be absurdity itself as the criterion of truth.

But let us suppose, with some leniency, that it was proved that faith makes blessed (not merely desired, not merely promised by the somewhat suspicious mouth of a priest): would blessedness—or more technically speaking, *pleasure*—ever be a proof of truth? This is so far from the case that it almost furnishes a counterproof; in any event, the greatest suspicion of a "truth" should arise when feelings of pleasure enter the discussion of the question "What is true?" The proof of "pleasure" is a proof of "pleasure"—nothing else: how in all the world could it be established that true judgments should give greater delight than false ones and, according to a pre-established harmony, should necessarily be followed by agreeable feelings?

The experience of all severe, of all profoundly inclined, spirits teaches the *opposite*. At every step one has to wrestle for truth; one has had to surrender for it almost everything to which the heart, to which our love, our trust in life, cling otherwise. That requires greatness of soul: the service of truth is the hardest service. What does it mean, after all, to have *integrity* in matters of the spirit? That one is severe against one's heart, that one despises "beautiful sentiments," that one makes of every Yes and No a matter of conscience. Faith makes blessed: consequently it lies.

51

That faith makes blessed under certain circumstances, that blessedness does not make of a fixed idea a *true* idea, that faith moves no mountains but *puts* mountains where there are none—a quick walk through a madhouse enlightens one sufficiently about this. *Not,* to be sure, a priest: for he denies instinctively that sickness is sickness, that madhouse is madhouse. Christianity *needs* sickness just as Greek culture needs a superabundance of health—to *make* sick is the true, secret purpose of the whole system of redemptive procedures constructed by the church. And the church itself—is it not the catholic madhouse as the ultimate ideal? The earth altogether as a madhouse?

The religious man, as the church wants him, is a typical decadent; the moment when a religious crisis overcomes a people is invariably marked by epidemics of the nerves; the "inner world" of the religious man looks exactly like the "inner world" of the overexcited and the exhausted; the "highest" states that Christianity has hung over mankind as the value of all values are epileptoid forms—only madmen or great impostors have been pronounced holy by the church *in maiorem dei honorem*. I once permitted myself to designate the whole Christian repentance and redemption training (which today is best studied in England) as a methodically produced *folie circulaire*, as is proper, on soil prepared for it, that is to say, thoroughly morbid soil. Nobody is free to become a Christian: one is not "converted" to Christianity—one has to be sick enough for it.

We others who have the *courage* to be healthy and also to despise—how may we despise a religion which taught men to misunderstand the body! which does not want to get rid of superstitious belief in souls! which turns insufficient nourishment into something "meritorious"! which fights health as a kind of enemy, devil, temptation! which fancies that one can carry around a "perfect soul" in a cadaver of a body, and which therefore found it necessary to concoct a new conception of "perfection"—a pale, sickly, idiotic-enthusiastic character, so-called "holiness." Holiness—merely a series of symptoms of an impoverished, unnerved, incurably corrupted body.

The Christian movement, as a European movement, has been from the start a collective movement of the dross and refuse elements of every kind (these want to get power through Christianity). It does *not* express the decline of a race, it is an aggregate of forms of decadence flocking together and seeking each other out from everywhere. It is *not*, as is supposed, the corruption of antiquity itself, of *noble* antiquity, that made

Christianity possible. The scholarly idiocy which upholds such ideas even today cannot be contradicted harshly enough. At the very time when the sick, corrupt chandala strata in the whole *imperium* adopted Christianity, the *opposite type,* nobility, was present in its most beautiful and most mature form. The great number became master; the democratism of the Christian instincts *triumphed.* Christianity was not "national," not a function of a race—it turned to every kind of man who was disinherited by life, it had its allies everywhere. At the bottom of Christianity is the rancor of the sick, instinct directed *against* the healthy, *against* health itself. Everything that has turned out well, everything that is proud and prankish, beauty above all, hurts its ears and eyes. Once more I recall the inestimable words of Paul: "The *weak* things of the world, the *foolish* things of the world, the *base* and *despised* things of the world hath God chosen." [1] This was the formula; *in hoc signo* decadence triumphed.

God on the cross—are the horrible secret thoughts behind this symbol not understood yet? All that suffers, all that is nailed to the cross, is *divine.* All of us are nailed to the cross, consequently *we* are divine. We alone are divine. Christianity was a victory, a nobler outlook perished of it—Christianity has been the greatest misfortune of mankind so far.

52

Christianity also stands opposed to every *spirit* that has turned out well; it can use only sick reason as Christian reason, it sides with everything idiotic, it utters a curse against the spirit, against the *superbia* of the healthy spirit. Because sickness is of the essence of Christianity, the typical Christian state, "faith," must

[1] See the last quotation in section 45.

also be a form of sickness, and all straight, honest, scientific paths to knowledge must be rejected by the church as forbidden paths. Even doubt is a sin.

The complete lack of psychological cleanliness in the priest—betrayed by his eyes—is a consequence of decadence: one should observe hysterical females and children with a tendency to rickets to see how regularly instinctive falseness, the inclination to lie in order to lie, and the incapacity for straight glances and steps are the expression of decadence. "Faith" means not *wanting* to know what is true.

The pietist, the priest of both sexes, is false because he is sick: his instinct demands that truth not be conceded its right at any point. "Whatever makes sick is *good;* whatever comes out of fullness, out of superabundance, out of power, is *evil"*—thus feels the believer. *Having no choice but to lie*—from that I can see at a glance if a man is a predestined theologian. Another sign of the theologian is his *incapacity for philology.* What is here meant by philology is, in a very broad sense, the art of reading well—of reading facts without falsifying them by interpretation, without losing caution, patience, delicacy, in the desire to understand. Philology as *ephexis* in interpretation—whether it is a matter of books, the news in a paper, destinies, or weather conditions, not to speak of the "salvation of the soul." The manner in which a theologian, in Berlin as in Rome, interprets a "verse of Scripture" or an event—for example, a victory of the armies of the fatherland, in the higher light of the Psalms of David—is always so audacious that a philologist can only tear his hair. And what is he to do when pietists and other cows from Swabia, with the aid of the "finger of God," transform the wretched everyday and the parlor smoke of their existence into a miracle of "grace,"

of "providence," of "experiences of salvation"? Even
the most modest expenditure of spirit, not to speak of
decency, would suffice to bring these interpreters to the
point of convincing themselves of the utter childishness
and unworthiness of such an abuse of the dexterity of
the divine fingers. Possessing even the tiniest bit of
piety in the body, we should find a god who cures a
cold at the right time or who bids us enter a coach
at the very moment when a violent rainstorm begins,
such an absurd god that we should have to abolish him
if he existed. A god as servant, as mailman, as calendar
man—at bottom, a word for the most stupid of all accidents. "Divine providence" of the kind in which ap-
proximately every third person in "educated Germany"
still believes would be an objection to God so strong
that one simply could not imagine a stronger one. And
in any case, it is an objection to the Germans!

53

That *martyrs* prove anything about the truth of a
matter is so far from true that I would deny that any
martyr ever had anything whatsoever to do with truth.
The tone with which a martyr throws his considering-
something-true into the face of the world expresses such
a low degree of intellectual integrity, such an *obtuse-
ness* for the question of truth, that one never needs to
refute a martyr. Truth is not something which one person might have and another not have: only peasants and
peasant apostles like Luther can think that way about
truth. One may be sure that modesty, *moderation* in this
matter, becomes greater in proportion to the degree of
conscientiousness in matters of the spirit. To have
knowledge of five matters, and to refuse with a gentle
hand to have *other* knowledge.

"Truth," as the word is understood by every prophet,

every sectarian, every free spirit, every socialist, every churchman, is a perfect proof that not even a beginning has been made with that discipline of the spirit, that self-overcoming which is needed if any small, however small, truth is to be found.

The deaths of the martyrs, incidentally, have been a great misfortune in history: they *seduced*. The inference of all idiots, woman and the people included, that there must be something to a cause for which someone goes to his death (or which even, like early Christianity, generates death-seeking epidemics)—this inference has immeasurably thwarted examination, the spirit of examination, and caution. The martyrs have *harmed* truth.

Even today it takes only the crudity of a persecution to give an otherwise completely indifferent sectarianism an honorable name. How? Does it change the value of a thing if someone gives his life for it? An error that becomes honorable is an error which is that much more seductive. Do you believe, my dear theologians, that we would give you an occasion to become martyrs for your lie? One refutes a matter by laying it respectfully on ice—that is how one also refutes theologians. This precisely was the world-historical stupidity of all persecutors, that they gave the opposing cause the appearance of being honorable—that they gave it the fascination of martyrdom as a gift. Even today woman lies on her knees before an error because she has been told that somebody died on the cross for it. *Is the cross an argument?* But about all these things, only one man has said the word which was needed for thousands of years—*Zarathustra:*

They wrote signs of blood on the way they walked, and their folly taught that with blood one proved truth. But blood is the worst witness of truth; blood poisons even the purest doctrine and turns it into delusion and hatred of the heart. And if a man goes through fire for his doctrine—what does that prove? Verily, it is more if your own doctrine comes out of your own fire.[1]

54

One should not be deceived: great spirits are skeptics. Zarathustra is a skeptic. Strength, *freedom* which is born of the strength and overstrength of the spirit, proves itself by skepticism. Men of conviction are not worthy of the least consideration in fundamental questions of value and disvalue. Convictions are prisons. Such men do not look far enough, they do not look *beneath* themselves: but to be permitted to join in the discussion of value and disvalue, one must see five hundred convictions *beneath* oneself—*behind* oneself.

A spirit who wants great things, who also wants the means to them, is necessarily a skeptic. Freedom from all kinds of convictions, to be able to see freely, is part of strength. Great passion, the ground and the power of his existence, even more enlightened, even more despotic than he is himself, employs his whole intellect; it makes him unhesitating; it gives him courage even for unholy means; under certain circumstances it does not begrudge him convictions. Conviction as a *means*: many things are attained only by means of a conviction. Great passion uses and uses up convictions, it does not succumb to them—it knows itself sovereign.

Conversely: the need for faith, for some kind of unconditional Yes and No, this Carlylism, if one will forgive me this word, is a need born of *weakness*. The man of faith, the "believer" of every kind, is necessarily a dependent man—one who cannot posit *himself* as an end, one who cannot posit any end at all by himself. The "believer" does not belong to *himself*, he can only

[1] See pp. 204-205.

be a means, he must be *used up*, he requires somebody to use him up. His instinct gives the highest honor to a morality of self-abnegation; everything persuades him in this direction: his prudence, his experience, his vanity. Every kind of faith is itself an expression of self-abnegation, of self-alienation.

If one considers how necessary most people find something regulatory, which will bind them from without and tie them down; how compulsion, *slavery* in a higher sense, is the sole and ultimate condition under which the more weak-willed human being, woman in particular, can prosper—then one will also understand conviction, "faith." The man of conviction has his backbone in it. *Not* to see many things, to be impartial at no point, to be party through and through, to have a strict and necessary perspective in all questions of value—this alone makes it possible for this kind of human being to exist at all. But with this they are the opposite, the antagonists, of what is truthful—of truth.

The believer is not free to have any conscience at all for questions of "true" and "untrue": to have integrity on *this* point would at once destroy him. The pathological condition of his perspective turns the convinced into fanatics—Savonarola, Luther, Rousseau, Robespierre, Saint-Simon: the opposition-type of the strong spirit who has *become* free. Yet the grand pose of these *sick* spirits, these epileptics of the concept, makes an impression on the great mass: the fanatics are picturesque; mankind prefers to see gestures rather than to hear *reasons*.

55

One step further in the psychology of conviction, of "faith." Long ago I posed the problem whether convictions are not more dangerous than lies as enemies of truth (*Human, All-Too-Human* I, aphorisms 54 and 483). Now I should like to ask the decisive question: Is there any contrast at all between a lie and a conviction? All the world believes there is; but what does all the world *not* believe!

Every conviction has its history, its preliminary forms, its trials and errors: it *becomes* a conviction after *not* having been one for a long time, and after *scarcely* having been one for an even longer time. How? Could not the lie be among these embryonic forms of conviction? Sometimes a mere change of person suffices: in the son that becomes conviction which in the father still was a lie.

By lie I mean: wishing *not* to see something that one does see; wishing not to see something *as* one sees it. Whether the lie takes place before witnesses or without witnesses does not matter. The most common lie is that with which one lies to oneself; lying to others is, relatively, an exception.

Now this wishing-*not*-to-see what one does see, this wishing-not-to-see *as* one sees, is almost the first condition for all who are *party* in any sense: of necessity, the party man becomes a liar. German historiography, for example, is convinced that Rome represented despotism and that the Germanic tribes brought the spirit of freedom into the world. What is the difference between this conviction and a lie? May one still be surprised when all parties, as well as the German historians, instinctively employ the big words of morality, that morality almost continues to exist because the party man of every description needs it at every moment?

"This is *our* conviction: we confess it before all the world, we live and die for it. Respect for all who have convictions!" I have heard that sort of thing even out of the mouths of anti-Semites. On the contrary, gentlemen! An anti-Semite certainly is not any more decent because he lies as a matter of principle.

The priests are much more delicate in such matters and they understand very well the objection which lies in the concept of a conviction, namely, a mendaciousness which is a matter of principle because it serves an end; so they have accepted the clever procedure of the Jews to introduce at this point the concept of "God," "will of God," "revelation of God." Kant too, with his categorical imperative, was on the same path: in this respect, his reason became *practical*. There are questions in which man is not entitled to a decision about truth and untruth; all the highest questions, all the highest value problems, lie beyond human reason. To comprehend the limits of reason—that alone is truly philosophy. What did God give man revelation for? Would God have done something superfluous? Man is not capable of knowing by himself what is good and evil, therefore God taught him his will. Moral: the priest does *not* lie; the question of "true" and "untrue" does not *exist* in the matters about which priests speak; these matters do not allow one to lie at all. For, to be able to lie, one would have to be capable of deciding *what* is true here. But of this man is not capable; thus the priest is merely the mouthpiece of God.

Such a priestly syllogism is by no means merely Jewish and Christian; the right to lie and the shrewdness of "revelation" belong to the priestly type, to the decadent priests as well as to the priests of paganism (pagans are all those who say Yes to life, for whom "god" is the word for the great Yes to all things). The "law," the "will of God," the "holy book," "inspiration" —all mere words for the conditions *under* which the priest attains power, *with* which the priest preserves his power; these concepts are found at the basis of all priestly organizations, of all forms of priestly or philo-sophic-priestly rule. The "holy lie"—common to Con-fucius, the law of Manu, Mohammed, the Christian church—is not absent in Plato. "Truth is there": this means, wherever it is announced, *the priest lies*.

56

Ultimately, it is a matter of the end to which one lies. That "holy" ends are lacking in Christianity is *my* objection to its means. Only *bad* ends: poisoning, slan-der, negation of life, contempt for the body, the deg-radation and self-violation of man through the con-cept of sin—consequently its means too are bad. It is with an opposite feeling that I read the law of Manu, an incomparably spiritual and superior work: even to mention it in the same breath with the Bible would be a sin against the spirit. One guesses immediately: there is a real philosophy behind it, in it, not merely an ill-smelling Judaine[1] of rabbinism and superstition; it offers even the most spoiled psychologist something to chew on. Not to forget the main point, the basic difference from every kind of Bible: here the *noble* classes, the philosophers and the warriors, stand above the mass; noble values everywhere, a feeling of perfection, an affirmation of life, a triumphant delight in oneself and in life—the *sun* shines on the whole book. All the things on which Christianity vents its unfathomable meanness—procreation, for example, woman, marriage —are here treated seriously, with respect, with love and trust.

Really, how can one put a book in the hands of chil-dren and women which contains that vile dictum: "to avoid fornication, let every man have his own wife, and let every woman have her own husband. . . . It is

[1] Judaism conceived as a poison. See note, p. 570.

better to marry than to burn"?[1] And how can one be a Christian as long as the notion of the *immaculata conceptio* christianizes, that is, *dirties*, the origin of man?

I know no other book in which so many tender and gracious things are said to woman as in the law of Manu; those old greybeards and saints have a way of being courteous to women which has perhaps never been surpassed. "The mouth of a woman"—it is written in one place—"the bosom of a girl, the prayer of a child, the smoke of the sacrifice, are always pure." Another passage: "There is nothing purer than the light of the sun, the shadow of a cow, the air, water, fire, and the breath of a girl." A final passage—perhaps also a holy lie: "All apertures of the body above the navel are pure, all below are impure. Only in the girl is the whole body pure."

57

One catches the *unholiness* of the Christian means *in flagranti* if one once measures the *Christian end* against the end of the law of Manu—if one throws a strong light on this greatest contrast of ends. The critic of Christianity cannot be spared the task of making Christianity look *contemptible*.

Such a law as that of Manu originates like every good code of laws: it sums up the experience, prudence, and experimental morality of many centuries; it concludes: it creates nothing further. The presupposition for a codification of this sort is the insight that the means of ensuring authority for a *truth*, which has been won slowly and at considerable expense, are utterly different from the means needed to prove it. A code of laws never relates the advantage, the reasons, the casuistry, in the

[1] I Cor. 7:2,9

prehistory of a law: if it did, it would lose the imperative tone, the "thou shalt," the presupposition for being obeyed. This is precisely where the problem lies.

At a certain point in the development of a people, the most circumspect stratum, that is, the one which sees farthest back and ahead, declares the experience according to which one should live—that is, *can* live—to be concluded. Their aim is to bring home as rich and complete a harvest as possible from the times of experiment and *bad* experience. Consequently, what must now be prevented above all is further experimentation, a continuation of the fluid state of values, testing, choosing, criticizing values *in infinitum*. Against this a double wall is put up: one, *revelation*, the claim that the reason in these laws is not of human origin, not sought and found slowly and after many errors, but of divine origin, and hence whole, perfect, without history, a gift, a miracle, merely communicated. Then, *tradition*, the claim that the law has existed since time immemorial and that it would be irreverent, a crime against one's forefathers, to raise any doubt against it. The authority of the law is founded on the theses: God *gave* it, the forefathers *lived* it. The higher reason in such a procedure lies in the aim, step by step to push consciousness back from what had been recognized as the right life (that is, *proved* right by a tremendous and rigorously filtered experience), so as to attain the perfect automatism of instinct—that presupposition of all mastery, of every kind of perfection in the art of life. To set up a code of laws after the manner of Manu means to give a people the chance henceforth to become master, to become perfect—to aspire to the highest art of life. *To that end, it must be made unconscious:* this is the aim of every holy lie.

The *order of castes,* the supreme, the dominant law,

is merely the sanction of a *natural order*, a natural law-fulness of the first rank, over which no arbitrariness, no "modern idea" has any power. In every healthy society there are three types which condition each other and gravitate differently physiologically; each has its own hygiene, its own field of work, its own sense of perfection and mastery. Nature, not Manu, distinguishes the pre-eminently spiritual ones, those who are pre-eminently strong in muscle and temperament, and those, the third type, who excel neither in one respect nor in the other, the mediocre ones—the last as the great majority, the first as the elite.

The highest caste—I call them *the fewest*—being perfect, also has the privileges of the fewest: among them, to represent happiness, beauty, and graciousness on earth. Only to the most spiritual human beings is beauty permitted: among them alone is graciousness not weakness. *Pulchrum est paucorum hominum:* the good is a privilege. On the other hand, there is nothing that they may be conceded less than ugly manners or a pessimistic glance, an eye that makes ugly—or indignation at the total aspect of things. Indignation is the privilege of the chandalas; pessimism too.

"*The world is perfect*"—thus says the instinct of the most spiritual, the Yes-saying instinct; "imperfection, whatever is beneath us, distance, the pathos of distance—even the chandala still belongs to this perfection." The most spiritual men, as the *strongest,* find their happiness where others would find their destruction: in the labyrinth, in hardness against themselves and others, in experiments; their joy is self-conquest; asceticism becomes in them nature, need, and instinct. Difficult tasks are a privilege to them; to play with burdens which crush others, a recreation. Knowledge—a form of asceticism. They are the most venerable kind of man;

that does not preclude their being the most cheerful and the kindliest. They rule not because they want to but because they *are;* they are not free to be second.

The *second:* they are the guardians of the law, those who see to order and security, the noble warriors, and above all the king as the highest formula of warrior, judge, and upholder of the law. The second are the executive arm of the most spiritual, that which is closest to them and belongs to them, that which does everything gross in the work of ruling for them—their retinue, their right hand, their best pupils.

In all this, to repeat, there is nothing arbitrary, nothing contrived; whatever is *different* is contrived—contrived for the ruin of nature. The order of castes, the *order of rank,* merely formulates the highest law of life; the separation of the three types is necessary for the preservation of society, to make possible the higher and the highest types. The *inequality* of rights is the first condition for the existence of any rights at all.

A right is a privilege. A man's state of being is his privilege. Let us not underestimate the privileges of the *mediocre.* As one climbs *higher,* life becomes ever harder; the coldness increases, responsibility increases.

A high culture is a pyramid: it can stand only on a broad base; its first presupposition is a strong and soundly consolidated mediocrity. Handicraft, trade, agriculture, *science,* the greatest part of art, the whole quintessence of *professional* activity, to sum it up, is compatible only with a mediocre amount of ability and ambition; that sort of thing would be out of place among exceptions; the instinct here required would contradict both aristocratism and anarchism. To be a public utility, a wheel, a function, for that one must be destined by nature: it is *not* society, it is the only kind of *happiness* of which the great majority are capable that makes intelligent machines of them. For the mediocre, to be mediocre is their happiness; mastery of one thing, specialization—a natural instinct.

It would be completely unworthy of a more profound spirit to consider mediocrity as such an objection. In fact, it is the very *first* necessity if there are to be exceptions: a high culture depends on it. When the exceptional human being treats the mediocre more tenderly than himself and his peers, this is not mere politeness of the heart—it is simply his *duty*.

Whom do I hate most among the rabble of today? The socialist rabble, the chandala apostles, who undermine the instinct, the pleasure, the worker's sense of satisfaction with his small existence—who make him envious, who teach him revenge. The source of wrong is never unequal rights but the claim of "equal" rights.

What is *bad*? But I have said this already: all that is born of weakness, of envy, of *revenge*. The anarchist and the Christian have the same origin.

58

Indeed, it makes a difference to what end one lies: whether one preserves or *destroys*. One may posit a perfect equation between *Christian* and *anarchist*: their aim, their instinct, are directed only toward destruction. The proof of this proposition can easily be read in history: it is written there in awful clarity. If we have just become acquainted with a religious legislation whose aim it was to "eternalize" the highest condition of life's *prospering*, a great organization of society—Christianity found its mission in putting an end to precisely such an organization *because life prospered in it*. There the gains of reason, after a long period of experiments and uncertainty, were to be invested for the greatest long-term advantage and the harvest to be brought home as great, as ample, as complete as possible; here, conversely, the harvest was *poisoned* overnight. That which stood there *aere perennius,* the *imperium Romanum,* the most magnificent form of organization under difficult circumstances which has yet been achieved, in comparison with which all before and all afterward are mere botch, patchwork, and dilettantism—these holy anarchists made it a matter of "piety" for themselves to destroy "the world," *that is,* the *imperium Romanum,* until not one stone remained on the other, until even Teutons and other louts could become masters over it.

The Christian and the anarchist: both decadents, both incapable of having any effect other than disintegrating, poisoning, withering, bloodsucking; both the instinct of mortal hatred against everything that stands, that stands in greatness, that has duration, that promises life a future. Christianity was the vampire of the *imperium Romanum:* overnight it undid the tremendous deed of the Romans—who had won the ground for a great culture *that would have time.*

Is it not understood yet? The *imperium Romanum* which we know, which the history of the Roman provinces teaches us to know better and better, this most admirable work of art in the grand style was a beginning; its construction was designed to prove itself through thousands of years: until today nobody has built again like this, nobody has even dreamed of building in such proportions *sub specie aeterni.* This organization was firm enough to withstand bad emperors: the accident of persons may not have anything to do with such matters —*first* principle of all grand architecture. But it was not firm enough against the *most corrupt* kind of corruption, against the *Christians.*

This stealthy vermin which sneaked up to every single one in the night, in fog and ambiguity, and sucked

out of each single one the seriousness for *true* things
and any instinct for *realities*—this cowardly, effeminate,
and saccharine pack alienated "souls" step by step from
that tremendous structure—those valuable, those virile,
noble natures who found their own cause, their own
seriousness, their own pride in the cause of Rome. The
sneakiness of prigs, the conventicle secrecy, gloomy concepts like hell, like sacrifice of the guiltless, like *unio
mystica* in drinking blood; above all, the slowly fanned
fire of revenge, of chandala revenge—all that is what
became master over Rome, the same kind of religion
against which, in its pre-existent form, Epicurus already
had waged war. One should read Lucretius to comprehend *what* Epicurus fought: *not* paganism but "Christianity," by which I mean the corruption of souls by the
concepts of guilt, punishment, and immortality. He
fought the *subterranean* cults which were exactly like
a latent form of Christianity: to deny immortality was
then nothing less than a real *salvation*.

And Epicurus would have won; every respectable
spirit in the Roman Empire was an Epicurean. Then
Paul appeared—Paul, the chandala hatred against
Rome, against "the world," become flesh, become genius,
the Jew, the *eternal* Wandering Jew par excellence.
What he guessed was how one could use the little
sectarian Christian movement apart from Judaism to
kindle a "world fire"; how with the symbol of "God on
the cross" one could unite all who lay at the bottom, all
who were secretly rebellious, the whole inheritance of
anarchistic agitation in the Empire, into a tremendous
power. "Salvation is of the Jews." Christianity as a
formula with which to outbid the subterranean cults of
all kinds, those of Osiris, of the Great Mother, of Mithras, for example—*and* to unite them: in this insight lies
the genius of Paul. His instinct was so sure in this that

he took the ideas with which these chandala religions fascinated, and, with ruthless violence, he put them into the mouth of the "Savior" whom he had invented, and not only into his mouth—he *made* something out of him that a priest of Mithras too could understand.

This was his moment at Damascus: he comprehended that he *needed* the belief in immortality to deprive "the world" of value, that the concept of "hell" would become master even over Rome—that with the "beyond" one *kills life*. Nihilism and Christianity: that rhymes, that does not only rhyme.

59

The whole labor of the ancient world *in vain:* I have no word to express my feelings about something so tremendous. And considering that its labor was a preliminary labor, that only the foundation for the labors of thousands of years had just then been laid with granite self-confidence—the whole *meaning* of the ancient world in vain! Wherefore Greeks? Wherefore Romans?

All the presuppositions for a scholarly culture, all scientific *methods,* were already there; the great, the incomparable art of reading well had already been established—that presupposition for the tradition of culture, for the unity of science; natural science, allied with mathematics and mechanics, was well along on the best way—the *sense for facts,* the last and most valuable of all the senses, had its schools and its tradition of centuries. Is this understood? Everything *essential* had been found, so that the work could be begun: the methods, one must say it ten times, *are* what is essential, also what is most difficult, also what is for the longest time opposed by habits and laziness. What we today have again conquered with immeasurable self-mastery

—for each of us still has the bad instincts, the Christian ones, in his system—the free eye before reality, the cautious hand, patience and seriousness in the smallest matters, the whole *integrity* in knowledge—that had already been there once before! More than two thousand years ago! *And,* in addition, the good, the delicate sense of tact and taste. *Not* as brain drill! *Not* as "German" education with loutish manners! But as body, as gesture, as instinct—as reality, in short. *All in vain!* Overnight nothing but a memory!

Greeks! Romans! The nobility of instinct, the taste, the methodical research, the genius of organization and administration, the faith in, the *will* to, man's future, the great Yes to all things, become visible in the *imperium Romanum*, visible for all the senses, the grand style no longer mere art but become reality, truth, *life*. And not buried overnight by a natural catastrophe, not trampled down by Teutons and other buffaloes, but ruined by cunning, stealthy, invisible, anemic vampires. Not vanquished—merely drained. Hidden vengefulness, petty envy become master. Everything miserable that suffers from itself, that is afflicted with bad feelings, the whole ghetto-world of the soul *on top* all at once.

One need only read any Christian agitator, St. Augustine, for example, to comprehend, to *smell,* what an unclean lot had thus come to the top. One would deceive oneself utterly if one presupposed any lack of intelligence among the leaders of the Christian movement: oh, they are clever, clever to the point of holiness, these good church fathers! What they lack is something quite different. Nature has neglected them—she forgot to give them a modest dowry of respectable, of decent, of *clean* instincts. Among ourselves, they are not even men. Islam is a thousand times right in despising Christianity: Islam presupposes *men.*

60

Christianity has cheated us out of the harvest of ancient culture; later it cheated us again, out of the harvest of the culture of *Islam*. The wonderful world of the Moorish culture of Spain, really more closely related to *us*, more congenial to our senses and tastes than Rome and Greece, was *trampled down* (I do not say by what kind of feet). Why? Because it owed its origin to noble, to *male* instincts, because it said Yes to life even with the rare and refined luxuries of Moorish life.

Later the crusaders fought something before which they might more properly have prostrated themselves in the dust—a culture compared to which even our nineteenth century might well feel very poor, very "late." To be sure, they wanted loot; the Orient was rich. One should not be so prejudiced. Crusades—higher piracy, nothing else! The German nobility, Viking nobility at bottom, was in its proper element here: the church knew only too well what it takes to *get* the German nobility. The German nobility, always the "Swiss Guards" of the church, always in the service of all the bad instincts of the church—but *well paid*. That the church should have used German swords, German blood and courage, to wage its war unto death against everything noble on earth! There are many painful questions at this point. The German nobility is almost *missing* in the history of higher culture: one guesses the reason—Christianity, alcohol, the two *great* means of corruption.

Really there should not be any choice between Islam and Christianity, any more than between an Arab and a Jew. The decision is given; nobody is free to make any further choice. Either one *is* a chandala, or one *is not.* "War to the knife against Rome! Peace and friendship with Islam"—thus felt, thus *acted*, that great free spirit, the genius among German emperors, Frederick II. How? Must a German first be a genius, a free spirit, to have *decent* feelings? I do not understand how a German could ever have *Christian* feelings.

61

Here it becomes necessary to touch on a memory which is even a hundred times more painful for Germans. The Germans have cheated Europe out of the last great cultural harvest which Europe could still have brought home—that of the *Renaissance*. Does one understand at last, does one *want* to understand, what the Renaissance was? The *revaluation of Christian values*, the attempt, undertaken with every means, with every instinct, with all genius, to bring the *counter*values, the *noble* values to victory.

So far there has been only this one great war, so far there has been no more decisive question than that of the Renaissance—*my* question is its question—nor has there ever been a more fundamental, a straighter form of *attack* in which the whole front was led more strictly against the center. Attacking in the decisive place, in the very seat of Christianity, placing the *noble* values on the throne *here*, I mean, bringing them right into the instincts, into the lowest needs and desires of those who sat there!

I envisage a *possibility* of a perfectly supraterrestrial magic and fascination of color: it seems to me that it glistens in all the tremors of subtle beauty, that an art is at work in it, so divine, so devilishly divine that one searches millennia in vain for a second such possibility; I envisage a spectacle so ingenious, so wonderfully paradoxical at the same time, that all the deities on Olympus would have had occasion for immortal laughter: *Cesare Borgia as pope*. Am I understood? Well then, that would have been the victory which alone I crave today: with that, Christianity would have been *abolished*.

What happened? A German monk, Luther, came to Rome. This monk, with all the vengeful instincts of a shipwrecked priest in his system, was outraged in Rome —*against* the Renaissance. Instead of understanding, with the most profound gratitude, the tremendous event that had happened here, the overcoming of Christianity in its very seat, his hatred understood only how to derive its own nourishment from this spectacle. A religious person thinks only of himself.

Luther saw the *corruption* of the papacy when precisely the opposite was more than obvious: the old corruption, the *peccatum originale*, Christianity no longer sat on the papal throne. But life! But the triumph of life! But the great Yes to all high, beautiful, audacious things! And Luther *restored the church:* he attacked it.

The Renaissance—an event without meaning, a great *in vain*. Oh, these Germans, what they have cost us already! In vain—that has always been the doing of the Germans. The Reformation, Leibniz, Kant and so-called German philosophy, the Wars of "Liberation," the *Reich* —each time an in vain for something that had already been attained, for something irrevocable.

They are my enemies, I confess it, these Germans: I despise in them every kind of conceptual and valuational uncleanliness, of *cowardice* before every honest Yes and No. For almost a thousand years they have messed up and confused everything they touched with their fingers; they have on their conscience everything half-hearted—three-eighths-hearted!—of which Europe is sick; they also have on their conscience the most unclean kind of Christianity that there is, the most incurable, the most irrefutable: Protestantism. If we do not get rid of Christianity, it will be the fault of the *Germans*.

62

With this I am at the end and I pronounce my judgment. I *condemn* Christianity. I raise against the Christian church the most terrible of all accusations that any accuser ever uttered. It is to me the highest of all conceivable corruptions. It has had the will to the last corruption that is even possible. The Christian church has left nothing untouched by its corruption; it has turned every value into an un-value, every truth into a lie, every integrity into a vileness of the soul. Let anyone dare to speak to me of its "humanitarian" blessings! To *abolish* any distress ran counter to its deepest advantages: it lived on distress, it *created* distress to eternalize *itself*.

The worm of sin, for example: with this distress the church first enriched mankind. The "equality of souls before God," this falsehood, this *pretext* for the rancor of all the base-minded, this explosive of a concept which eventually became revolution, modern idea, and the principle of decline of the whole order of society— is *Christian* dynamite. "Humanitarian" blessings of Christianity! To breed out of *humanitas* a self-contradiction, an art of self-violation, a will to lie at any price, a repugnance, a contempt for all good and honest instincts! Those are some of the blessings of Christianity!

Parasitism as the *only* practice of the church; with its ideal of anemia, of "holiness," draining all blood, all love, all hope for life; the beyond as the will to negate every reality; the cross as the mark of recognition for the most subterranean conspiracy that ever existed—

against health, beauty, whatever has turned out well, courage, spirit, *graciousness* of the soul, *against life itself*.

This eternal indictment of Christianity I will write on all walls, wherever there are walls—I have letters to make even the blind see.

I call Christianity the one great curse, the one great innermost corruption, the one great instinct of revenge, for which no means is poisonous, stealthy, subterranean, *small* enough—I call it the one immortal blemish of mankind.

And time is reckoned from the *dies nefastus* with which this calamity began—after the *first* day of Christianity! *Why not rather after its last day? After today?* Revaluation of all values!

FROM
Ecce Homo

HOW ONE BECOMES WHAT ONE IS

EDITOR'S NOTE

No sooner had Nietzsche finished *The Antichrist* than he
wrote the preface to *Twilight of the Idols*—in fact, on the
same day. Then, instead of going to work on the second
book of the *Revaluation*, tentatively entitled "The Free
Spirit: A Critique of Philosophy as a Nihilistic Movement,"
he wrote *Ecce Homo*, an incomparably sarcastic review of
his life and works, including sections on all of his books,
except *The Antichrist*, which he now thought of holding
back until *Ecce Homo* had prepared the public for it.

  Ecce Homo consists of four chapters: "Why I Am So
Wise," "Why I Am So Clever," "Why I Write Such Good
Books," and "Why I Am a Destiny." Of the following
selections, the first three are from sections 1, 5, and 7, respectively, of the first chapter; the bit on Heine is from
section 4 of the second chapter; and the epigram on immortality is from the discussion of *Zarathustra* in the third
chapter. The final sentence is from the third section of the
last chapter.

※※※

The perfect lightness and levity, even exuberance of
the spirit, which *The Dawn* reflects, are quite compatible in my case not only with the deepest physiological weakness, but even with excessive pain. Amid
the tortures that go with an uninterrupted three-day
migraine and agonizing phlegm-wretching, I possessed
a dialectician's clarity par excellence, and very cold-
bloodedly thought through matters for which, in health-

ier states, I am not enough of a climber, not subtle, not *cold* enough. Perhaps my readers know in what way I consider dialectics a symptom of decadence; for example, in the most famous case of all: in the case of Socrates.

All sickly disturbances of the intellect, even that half-dazed state which follows a fever, are to this day complete strangers to me, and to instruct myself concerning their nature and frequency I have had to turn to scholars. My blood circulates slowly. Nobody has ever found me feverish. A physician who treated me as a nervous case for a while said in the end, "No! It is not a matter of your nerves; it is I who am nervous." Any local degeneration is altogether indemonstrable; nor is there any organic disease of the stomach, though, as a consequence of over-all exhaustion, the gastric system is as weak as possible. My eye trouble too, which at times comes dangerously close to blindness, is only a consequence, not a cause; thus my vision has always improved again with every gain in vitality.

A long, all-too-long series of years signifies my convalescence; unfortunately, it also signifies relapse, ruin, and the periodic rhythm of a kind of decadence. Need I say after all this that I am *experienced* in questions of decadence? I have spelled them forward and backward. Even that filigree art of clasping and grasping in general, those fingers for nuances, that psychology which knows how to look around corners, and whatever else is characteristic of me, were learned only then, are the real gift of that time in which everything in me became more delicate: observation itself as well as all the organs of observation. To see *healthier* concepts and values in the perspective of the sick, and conversely, to look down out of the abundance and self-assurance of a *rich* life to behold the secret doings of the instinct of decadence

—in this I have had the longest training, my most characteristic experience: here, if anywhere, I became a master. Now this gift is mine, now I have the gift of *reversing perspectives:* the first reason why it is perhaps for me alone that a "revaluation of values" is at all possible today.

※※※

It seems to me that even the bluntest word, the bluntest letter is still more good-natured, still more honest, than silence. Those who remain silent are almost always lacking in delicacy and politeness of the heart. Silence is an objection, and swallowing things down necessarily makes for a bad character—it even upsets the digestion. All who remain silent are dyspeptic. Clearly, I would not have bluntness underestimated: it is by far the *most humane* form of contradiction and, amid modern pampering, one of our foremost virtues. When one is rich enough for this, it is even good fortune to be wrong. Were a god to come down upon earth, he should do nothing but wrong: to take upon oneself *guilt* and not punishment, that alone would be godlike.

※※※

My practice of war may be summarized in four propositions. First: I attack only causes which are victorious—and at times I wait until they are victorious. Second: I attack only causes against which I cannot expect to find allies, against which I shall stand alone —against which I shall compromise myself alone. I have never taken a step in public which was not compromising: that is *my* criterion of doing what is right. Third: I never attack persons; I only avail myself of the person as of a strong magnifying glass with which one can render visible a general but creeping calamity which it is otherwise hard to get hold of. Thus I attacked David Strauss—or more precisely, the *success* of a decrepit book among German "educated people"— here I caught these educated people in the act. Thus I attacked Wagner—or, more precisely, the falsity, the half-wittedness of instinct in our "culture," which mistakes the subtle for the abundant, and the latecomers for the great. Fourth: I attack only causes in which any personal difference is out of the question, and in which any background of unwholesome experiences is lacking. On the contrary, to attack is with me a proof of good will, and sometimes of gratitude.

***

Heinrich Heine gave me the highest conception of the lyric poet. I seek in vain in all the realms of thousands of years for an equally sweet and passionate music. He possessed that divine sarcasm without which I cannot conceive the perfect. I estimate the value of human beings, of races, according to the necessity with which they cannot understand the god apart from the satyr. And how Heine handles the German language! It will be said one day that he and I have been by far the first artists of the German language—at an incalculable distance from everything that mere Germans have done with it.

***

One must pay dearly for immortality: one has to die several times while still alive.

***

The whole of history is the refutation by experiment of the principle of the so-called "moral world order."

NIETZSCHE
CONTRA WAGNER
OUT OF THE FILES
OF A PSYCHOLOGIST

CONTENTS

The locations of the original versions of the various sections of *Nietzsche contra Wagner* are given in parentheses.

1 (*Gay Science*, Preface, 3)
2 (*Gay Science*, Preface, 4)

PREFACE

All of the following chapters have been selected, not
without caution, from my older writings—some go back
all the way to 1877—perhaps clarified here and there,
above all, shortened. Read one after another, they will
leave no doubt either about Richard Wagner or about
myself: we are antipodes. Other things too will become
clear; for example, that this is an essay for psychologists,
but *not* for Germans. I have my readers everywhere, in
Vienna, in St. Petersburg, in Copenhagen and Stock-
holm, in Paris, in New York—I do *not* have them in
Europe's shallows, Germany.

And perhaps I could whisper something to my good
Italians whom I *love* as much as I—.[1] *Quousque tandem,
Crispi?* [2] Triple alliance: with the *Reich* an intelligent
people can enter only a *mésalliance*.

FRIEDRICH NIETZSCHE

Turin, Christmas 1888

WHERE I ADMIRE

I believe that artists often do not know what they can
do best: they are too vain. They are intent on something
prouder than these small plants seem to be which grow
on their soil, new, strange and beautiful, in real perfection. What is ultimately good in their own garden and

[1] Nietzsche refrains from completing the sentence, having
left no doubt about his meaning: "hate the Germans."

[2] "How far, for heaven's sake?" Crispi was Italian prime
minister.

vineyard they esteem lightly, and their love and insight are not equal. There is a musician who, more than any other musician, is a master at finding the tones in the realm of suffering, depressed, and tortured souls, at giving language even to mute misery. None can equal him in the colors of late fall, in the indescribably moving happiness of the last, truly last, truly shortest joy; he knows a sound for those quiet, disquieting midnights of the soul, where cause and effect seem to be out of joint and where at any moment something might originate "out of nothing." He draws most happily of all out of the profoundest depth of human happiness, and, as it were, out of its drained goblet, where the bitterest and most repulsive drops have finally and evilly run together with the sweetest. He knows that weariness of the soul which drags itself, unable to leap or fly any more, even to walk; he masters the shy glance of concealed pain, of understanding without comfort, of the farewell without confession—indeed, as the Orpheus of all secret misery he is greater than any; and some things have been added to the realm of art by him alone, things that had hitherto seemed inexpressible and even unworthy of art —the cynical rebellion, for example, of which only those are capable who suffer most bitterly; also some very minute and microscopic aspects of the soul, as it were the scales of its amphibian nature: indeed, he is the master of the very minute. But he does not *want* to be that! His character prefers large walls and audacious frescoes.

It escapes him that his spirit has a different taste and inclination—the opposite *perspective*—and prefers to sit quietly in the nooks of collapsed houses: there, hidden, hidden from himself, he paints his real masterpieces, all of which are very short, often only one beat long—only then does he become wholly good, great, and perfect, perhaps there alone. Wagner is one who has suffered deeply—that is his *distinction* above other musicians. I admire Wagner wherever he puts himself into music.

WHERE I OFFER OBJECTIONS

This does not mean that I consider this music healthy —least of all precisely where it speaks of Wagner. My objections to the music of Wagner are physiological objections: why should I trouble to dress them up in aesthetic formulas? After all, aesthetics is nothing but a kind of applied physiology.

My "fact," my *petit fait vrai*, is that I no longer breathe easily when this music begins to affect me; that my foot soon resents it and rebels: my foot feels the need for rhythm, dance, march—to Wagner's "Kaisermarsch" not even the young German Kaiser could march —it demands of music first of all those delights which are found in *good* walking, striding, dancing. But does not my stomach protest too? my heart? my circulation? Are not my entrails saddened? Do I not suddenly become hoarse? To listen to Wagner I need pastilles Gérandel.

And so I ask myself: What is it that my whole body really expects of music? For there is no soul. I believe, its own *ease*: as if all animal functions should be quickened by easy, bold, exuberant, self-assured rhythms; as if iron, leaden life should lose its gravity through golden, tender, oil-smooth melodies. My melancholy wants to rest in the hiding-places and abysses of *perfection:* that is why I need music. But Wagner makes sick.

What is the theater to me? What, the convulsions of his "moral" ecstasies which give the people—and who is not "people"?—satisfaction? What, the whole gesture hocus-pocus of the actor? It is plain that I am essentially anti-theatrical: confronted with the theater, this mass art par excellence, I feel that profound scorn at the bottom of my soul which every artist today feels. *Success* in the theater—with that one drops in my respect forever; *failure*—I prick up my ears and begin to respect.

But Wagner was the other way around; besides the Wagner who made the loneliest music in existence, he was essentially also a man of the theater and an actor, the most enthusiastic mimomaniac, perhaps, who ever existed, *even as a musician*. And, incidentally, if it was Wagner's theory that "the drama is the end, the music is always a mere means," his *practice* was always, from beginning to end, "the pose is the end; the drama, also the music, is always merely its means." Music as a means to clarify, strengthen, and lend inward dimension to the dramatic gesture and the actor's appeal to the senses— and the Wagnerian drama, a mere occasion for many interesting poses! Besides all other instincts, he had the commanding instincts of a great actor in absolutely everything—and, as already mentioned, also as a musician.

Once there was a Wagnerian *pur sang* to whom I made this clear, not without trouble—clarity and Wagnerian! Not another word is needed. There were reasons then for adding: "Do be a little more honest with yourself! After all, we are not in Bayreuth. In Bayreuth one is honest only in the mass; as an individual one lies, one lies to oneself. One leaves oneself at home when one goes to Bayreuth; one renounces the right to one's own tongue and choice, to one's taste, even to one's courage as one has it and exercises it between one's own four walls against both God and world. No one brings along the finest senses of his art to the theater, least of all the artist who works for the theater—solitude is lacking; whatever is perfect suffers no witnesses. In the theater one becomes people, herd female, pharisee, voting cattle, patron, idiot—*Wagnerian:* even the most personal conscience is vanquished by the leveling magic of the great number; the neighbor reigns, one becomes a mere neighbor."

WAGNER AS A DANGER

1

The intention pursued by recent music with what is now vigorously, but not at all clearly, called "infinite melody," can be clarified by an illustration. One walks into the sea, gradually loses one's secure footing, and finally surrenders oneself to the elements without reservation: one must *swim*. In older music, what one had to do in the dainty, or solemn, or fiery back and forth, quicker and slower, was something quite different, namely, to *dance*. The measure required for this, the maintenance of certain equally balanced units of time and force, demanded continual *wariness* of the listener's soul—and on the counterplay of this cooler breeze that came from wariness and the warm breath of enthusiasm rested the magic of all *good* music. Richard Wagner wanted a different kind of movement; he overthrew the physiological presupposition of previous music. Swimming, floating—no longer walking and dancing.

Perhaps the decisive point has now been stated. The "infinite melody" seeks deliberately to break all evenness of time and force and even scorns it occasionally; the wealth of its invention lies precisely in that which to an older ear sounds like a rhythmic paradox and blasphemy. The imitation or domination of such a taste would result in a danger to music which cannot be exaggerated: the complete degeneration of rhythmic feeling, *chaos* in place of rhythm. This danger reaches its climax when such music leans more and more heavily on a wholly naturalistic style of acting and gestures, which is no longer dominated by any law of plasticity and wants *effect*, nothing more. *Espressivo* at any price, and music in the service, the slavery, of poses—*that is the end.*

2

What? Should it really be the supreme virtue of a performance, as the virtuosos of musical performance now seem to believe, that one must under all circumstances achieve an *hautrelief* which is simply unsurpassable? Is not this, when applied to Mozart, for example, the true sin against the spirit of Mozart—the cheerful, enthusiastic, tender, enamored spirit of Mozart, who was happily no German and whose seriousness is a gracious, a golden, seriousness and *not* the seriousness of a German Philistine? Not to speak of the seriousness of the "Stone Guest." [1] But apparently you think *all* music is like the music of the "Stone Guest"—*all* music must leap out of the wall and shake the listener to his very intestines. Only then you consider music "effective." But on *whom* are such effects achieved? On those whom a *noble* artist should never impress: on the mass, on the immature, on the blasé, on the sick, on the idiots, on *Wagnerians!*

A MUSIC WITHOUT A FUTURE

Music makes its appearance as the last plant among all the arts which grow on the soil of a particular culture—perhaps because it is the most inward and hence arrives last, in the fall, when the culture which belongs to it is fading. Only in the art of the Dutch masters did the soul of the Christian Middle Ages attain its last

[1] In *Don Giovanni.*

vibrations: their tone architecture is the posthumous, but legitmate and equal sister of the Gothic. Only in Handel's music did there resound what was best in the souls of Luther and those related to him, the Jewish-heroic trait that gave the Reformation a trait of greatness—the Old Testament become music, *not* the New. Only Mozart transformed the age of Louis XIV and the art of Racine and Claude Lorrain into ringing gold; only in the music of Beethoven and Rossini did the eighteenth century sing itself out—the century of enthusiasm, of broken ideals, and of evanescent happiness. All true, all original music, is a swan song.

Perhaps our latest music too, however dominant and domineering it is, has but a short span of time ahead of it: for it developed out of a culture whose soil is rapidly sinking—a culture which will soon have sunk out of sight. A certain catholicism of feeling and a delight in some old indigenous, so-called "national" sense and nonsense are its presuppositions. Wagner's appropriation of old sagas and songs, which scholarly prejudice had held up as something Teutonic par excellence—today we laugh at that—his reanimation of those Scandinavian monsters with a thirst for ecstatic sensuality and de-sensualization—this whole give-and-take of Wagner concerning materials, figures, passions, and nerves clearly expresses the *spirit of his music* too, supposing that this, like any music, could not speak of itself except ambiguously: for music is a *woman*.

We must not allow ourselves to be deceived about this state of affairs simply because at the moment we happen to live in a period of reaction *within* reaction. The age of national wars, of ultramontane martyrdom, this whole *entr'acte* character of the current situation in Europe may indeed help such an art as Wagner's to a sudden glory, without thereby guaranteeing it a future. The Germans themselves have no future.

WE ANTIPODES

It may perhaps be recalled, at least among my friends, that at first I approached the modern world with a few errors and overestimations, in any case, full of *hopes*. I understood—who knows on the basis of what personal experiences?—the philosophic pessimism of the nineteenth century as a symptom of a greater strength of thought, of a more triumphant fullness of life, than had found expression in the philosophy of Hume, Kant, and Hegel: I took *tragic* insight for the most beautiful luxury of our culture, for its most precious, noblest, most dangerous kind of squandering—but nevertheless, in view of its excessive wealth, as a *permissible* luxury. Similarly, I interpreted Wagner's music as an expression of a Dionysian power of the soul; I believed I heard in it the earthquake with which a primordial force of life, dammed up from time immemorial, finally vents itself, indifferent to the possibility that everything that calls itself culture today might start tottering. It is plain what I misunderstood in, equally plain what I read into, Wagner and Schopenhauer—myself.

Every art, every philosophy, may be considered a remedy and aid in the service of either growing or declining life: it always presupposes suffering and sufferers. But there are two kinds of sufferers: first, those who suffer from the *overfullness* of life and want a Dionysian art as well as a tragic insight and outlook on life—and then those who suffer from the *impoverishment* of life and demand of art and philosophy, calm, stillness, smooth seas, or, on the other hand, frenzy, convulsion, and anesthesia. Revenge against life itself—the most voluptuous kind of frenzy for those so impoverished!

Wagner responds to this dual need of the latter no less than Schopenhauer: they negate life, they slander it, hence they are my antipodes. He that is richest in the fullness of life, the Dionysian god and man, can afford not only the *sight* of the terrible and the questionable, but even the terrible deed and any luxury of destruction, decomposition, and negation: in his case, what is evil, senseless, and ugly seems, as it were, permissible, as it seems permissible in nature, because of an excess of procreating, restoring powers which can yet turn every desert into luxurious farm land. Conversely, those who suffer most and are poorest in life would need mildness, peacefulness, and goodness most—what is today called humaneness—in thought as well as in deed, and, if possible, a god who would be truly a god for the sick, a healer and "savior"; also logic, the conceptual understandability of existence even for idiots—the typical "free spirits," like the "idealists" and "beautiful souls," are all decadents—in short, a certain warm, fear-repulsing narrowness and enclosure within optimistic horizons which permit *hebetation*.

Thus I gradually learned to understand Epicurus, the opposite of a Dionysian Greek; also the Christian, who is, in fact, only a kind of Epicurean, and, with his "faith makes blessed," follows the principle of hedonism as far as possible—far beyond any intellectual integrity. If there is anything in which I am ahead of all psychologists, it is that my eye is sharper for that most difficult and captious kind of *backward inference* in which the most mistakes are made: the backward inference from the work to the maker, from the deed to the doer, from the ideal to him who *needs* it, from every way of thinking and valuing to the *want* behind it that prompts it.

Regarding artists of all kinds, I now avail myself of this main distinction: is it the *hatred* against life or the *excess* of life which has here become creative? In Goethe, for example, the excess became creative; in Flaubert, hatred: Flaubert—a new edition of Pascal, but as an artist, with the instinctive judgment deep down: *"Flaubert est toujours haïssable, l'homme n'est rien, l'oeuvre est tout."* [1] He tortured himself when he wrote, just as Pascal tortured himself when he thought; they were both unegoistic. "Selflessness"—the principle of decadence, the will to the end, in art as well as in morals.

WHERE WAGNER BELONGS

Even now France is still the seat of the most spiritual and refined culture in Europe and the foremost school of taste: but one must know where to find this "France of taste." The *Norddeutsche Zeitung*, for example, or whoever uses this newspaper as a mouthpiece, considers the French "barbarians"; I, for my own part, look for the Dark Continent, where the "slaves" ought to be freed, in the vicinity of the North Germans.

Whoever belongs to *that* France keeps himself well concealed: it may be a small number in whom it lives and continues, and at that, perhaps human beings who are not among the sturdiest: partly fatalists, somber and sick, partly pampered and artificial, such as have the *ambition* to be artificial—but they possess everything high and delicate that is still left in this world. In this France of the spirit, which is also the France of pessimism, Schopenhauer is even now more at home than he has ever been in Germany; his main work has already

[1] "Flaubert is always hateful; the man is nothing, the work is all."

been translated twice, the second time excellently, so that I now prefer to read Schopenhauer in French (he was an accident among Germans, as I am such an accident; the Germans have no fingers for us, they have no fingers altogether, they have only paws). Not to speak of Heinrich Heine—*l'adorable Heine,* they say in Paris —who has long become part of the very flesh and blood of the more profound and soulful lyrical poets in France. How could German oxen be anything but dumfounded by the *délicatesses* of such a nature!

As regards Richard Wagner, finally, it is so plain that one could grasp it with the hands, though perhaps not with fists, that Paris is the real soil for Wagner: the more French music develops according to the needs of the *âme moderne,* the more it will Wagnerize—in fact, that is what it is doing even now. We must not let ourselves be led astray about this by Wagner himself: it was real badness in Wagner to mock Paris in its agony in 1871. In Germany, Wagner is nevertheless merely a misunderstanding: who could be more incapable of understanding Wagner than, for example, the young Kaiser? It remains a certain fact for anyone familiar with European cultural movements that French romanticism and Richard Wagner belong together most closely. All dominated by literature right into their eyes and ears—the first artists in Europe to have an education in *world literature*—in most cases, themselves writers, poets, mediators, and mixers of the senses and the arts; all fanatics of *expression,* great discoverers in the realm of the sublime, also of the ugly and the horrible, still greater discoverers in the sphere of effects and spectacular displays, in the art of display windows; all talents far beyond their genius—*virtuosos* through and through, with uncanny access to everything that seduces, lures, forces, overthrows, born enemies of logic and of the straight line, covetous of the strange, the exotic, the tremendous, and all opiates of the senses and the understanding. On the whole, an audaciously daring, magnificently violent, high-soaring, and high-sweeping type of artist, they alone have taught *their* century—it is the century of the *mass*—the concept of the "artist." But *sick*.

WAGNER AS THE APOSTLE OF CHASTITY

1

Is this still German?
Out of a German heart, this torrid screeching?
a German body, this self-laceration?
German, this priestly affectation,
this incense-smelling lurid preaching?
German, this plunging, halting, reeling,
this sugar-sweetish bim-bam pealing?
this nunnish ogling, *Ave* leavening,
this whole falsely ecstatic heaven over-heavening?

Is this still German?
Consider! Stay! You are perplexed?
That which you hear is Rome—*Rome's faith without the text.*

2

There is no necessary opposition between sensuality and chastity; every good marriage, every love affair, that comes from the heart is beyond this opposition. But in a case in which this opposition really exists, fortunately it need by no means be a tragic opposition. This would seem to hold at least for all the better turned out, more cheerful mortals, who are far from counting their labile balance between angel and *petite bête* as necessarily among the objections to existence: the finest, the brightest, like Hafiz, like Goethe, have even considered this one attraction more. Such contradictions actually seduce to existence. On the other hand, it is only too easy to understand that, should those whom misfortune has changed into the animals of Circe ever be brought to the point of adoring chastity, they will see only their own opposite in it and will *adore* it—oh, with what tragic grunting and fervor one can imagine. And at the end of his life Richard Wagner undeniably wanted to set this embarrassing and perfectly superfluous opposition to music and produce it on the stage. *Why?* we are entitled to ask.

3

At this point, of course, we cannot escape another question: What could that male (yet so unmasculine) "innocence from the country" really be to him, that poor devil and child of nature, Parsifal, whom Wagner finally makes a Catholic by such captious means? How now? Was this Parsifal meant at all *seriously?* For, that he has been laughed at, I would certainly be in no position to dispute—nor would Gottfried Keller.[1]

I should really wish that the Wagnerian *Parsifal* were intended as a prank—as the epilogue and satyr play, as it were, with which the tragedian Wagner wanted to say farewell in a fitting manner worthy of himself—to us, to himself, and above all *to tragedy,* with an excessive, sublimely wanton parody on the tragic itself, on all the former horrid earthly seriousness and earthly misery, on the *most stupid* form, overcome at long last, of the anti-nature of the ascetic ideal. After all, Parsifal is operetta material par excellence. Is Wagner's *Parsifal* his secretly superior laughter at himself, the triumph of his ultimate

[1] The famous Swiss writer (1819-1890) whom Nietzsche admired.

artistic freedom, his artistic *non plus ultra*—Wagner able to *laugh* at himself?

Clearly, one should wish that; for what would *Parsifal* amount to if intended as a *serious* piece? Must we really see in it (as somebody has expressed it against me) "the abortion gone mad of a hatred of knowledge, spirit, and sensuality"? A curse on the senses and the spirit in a single hatred and breath? An apostasy and reversion to sickly Christian and obscurantist ideals? And in the end even a self-abnegation, a self-crossing-out on the part of an artist who had previously aimed at the very opposite of this, striving with all the power of his will to achieve the highest spiritualization and sensualization in his art? And not only in his art, but also in his life.

We should remember how enthusiastically Wagner once followed in the footsteps of the philosopher Feuerbach. In the thirties and forties, Feuerbach's slogan of "healthy sensuality" sounded to Wagner, as to many other Germans—they called themselves the *young* Germans—like the words of redemption. Had he learned differently in the end? For it seems, at least, that he finally had the will to *teach* differently. Did the *hatred against life* become dominant in him, as in Flaubert? For *Parsifal* is a work of perfidy, of vindictiveness, of a secret attempt to poison the presuppositions of life— a *bad* work. The preaching of chastity remains an incitement to anti-nature: I despise everyone who does not experience *Parsifal* as an attempted assassination of basic ethics.

HOW I BROKE AWAY FROM WAGNER

1

By the summer of 1876, during the time of the first *Festspiele,* I said farewell to Wagner in my heart. I suffer no ambiguity; and since Wagner had moved to Germany, he had condescended step by step to everything I despise—even to anti-Semitism.

It was indeed high time to say farewell: soon after, I received the proof. Richard Wagner, apparently most triumphant, but in truth a decaying and despairing decadent, suddenly sank down, helpless and broken, before the Christian cross. Did no German have eyes in his head or pity in his conscience for this horrid spectacle? Was I the only one whom it *pained?* Enough; this unexpected event struck me like lightning and gave me clarity about the place I had left—and also that shudder which everybody feels after he has unconsciously passed through a tremendous danger. As I proceeded alone I trembled; not long after, I was sick, more than sick, namely, *weary*—weary from the inevitable disappointment about everything that is left to us modern men for enthusiasm, about the universally *wasted* energy, work, hope, youth, love—weary from nausea at the whole idealistic lie and pampering of the conscience, which had here triumphed once again over one of the bravest —weary, finally and not least of all, from the grief aroused by an inexorable suspicion that I was henceforth sentenced to mistrust more profoundly, to despise more profoundly, to be more profoundly *alone* than ever before. For I had had nobody except Richard Wagner. I have always been *sentenced* to Germans.

2

Lonely henceforth and badly mistrustful of myself, I then took sides, not without indignation, *against* myself and *for* everything that hurt and was hard just for me: thus I found the way again to that courageous pessimism which is the opposite of all idealistic mendaciousness, and also, it seems to me, the way to *myself*, to *my*

task. That hidden and masterful something for which we long do not have a name, until finally it proves itself to be our task—this tyrant in us wreaks horrible revenge for every attempt we make to dodge or escape it, for every premature resignation, for every acceptance of equality with those among whom we do not belong, for every activity, however respectable, which distracts us from our main cause—indeed, for every virtue which would protect us from the hardness of our inmost responsibility. Every time, sickness is the response when we want to doubt our right to *our* task, when we begin to make things easier for ourselves in any way. Strange and at the same time terrible! It is the *easing* of our burden which we must atone most harshly. And if we want to return to health afterward, we have no choice: we must assume a *heavier* burden than we ever carried before.

THE PSYCHOLOGIST SPEAKS UP

1

The more a psychologist—a born and inevitable psychologist and unriddler of souls—applies himself to the more exquisite cases and human beings, the greater becomes the danger that he might suffocate of pity. He *needs* hardness and cheerfulness more than anyone else. For the corruption, the destruction, of the higher men is the rule: it is terrible constantly to have such a rule before one's eyes. The manifold torture of the psychologist who has discovered this corruption, who discovers this whole inner haplessness of the higher man, this eternal "too late" in every sense, first in one case and then *almost* always again through the whole of history—one day this may perhaps bring about his own corruption.

In almost every psychologist one will perceive a tell-

tale preference for association with everyday, well-ordered people: this reveals that he always requires a cure, that he needs a kind of escape and forgetting, away from all that with which his insights, his incisions, his *craft*, burden his conscience. He is characterized by fear of his memory. He is easily silenced by the judgments of others; he listens with an immobile face as they venerate, admire, love, and transfigure where he has *seen*—or he even conceals his silence by explicitly agreeing with some foreground opinion. Perhaps the paradox of his situation is so horrible that the "educated," on their part, learn the greatest veneration precisely where he has learned the greatest pity coupled with the greatest contempt.

And who knows whether what happened in all great cases was not simply this—that one adored a god, and that the god was merely a poor sacrificial animal. *Success* has always been the greatest liar—and the *work*, the *deed* too, is a success. The great statesman, the conqueror, the discoverer is disguised by his creations, concealed beyond recognition; it is the work, of the artist as of the philosophers, that invents the man who has created it, who is *supposed* to have created it. "Great men," as they are venerated, are subsequent pieces of wretched minor fiction: in the world of historical values, counterfeit *rules*.

2

Those great poets, for example, men like Byron, Musset, Poe, Leopardi, Kleist, Gogol—I do not dare mention far greater names, but I mean them—are and must be men of the moment, sensual, absurd, fivefold, irresponsible, and sudden in mistrust and trust; with souls in which they must usually conceal some fracture; often taking revenge with their works for some inner

contamination, often seeking with their high flights to escape into forgetfulness from an all-too-faithful memory; idealists from the vicinity of *swamps*—what torture are these great artists and all the so-called higher men for him who has guessed their true nature! We are all advocates of the mediocre. It is easy to understand that it is woman—clairvoyant in the world of suffering, and, unfortunately, also desirous far beyond her strength to help and to save—who so readily accords these men those outbreaks of infinite pity on which the mass, particularly the venerating mass, then lavish inquisitive and self-satisfied interpretations. This pity regularly deceives itself about its own strength: woman would like to believe that love can achieve *everything*—it is her characteristic superstition. Alas, whoever knows the heart will guess how poor, helpless, arrogant, and mistaken is even the best, the profoundest love—how it even destroys rather than saves.

3

The spiritual nausea and haughtiness of every human being who has suffered deeply—how deeply one can suffer almost determines the order of rank—his shuddering certainty, which permeates and colors him through and through, that by virtue of his suffering he *knows more t*han the cleverest and wisest could possibly know, and that he knows his way and has once been at home in many distant, terrifying worlds of which "*you* know nothing"—this spiritual and silent haughtiness, this pride of the elect of cognition, of the "initiated," of the almost sacrificed, finds all kinds of disguise necessary to protect itself against contact with officious and pitying hands, and against everything that is not a peer in suffering. Deep suffering makes noble; it separates.

One of the finest disguises is Epicureanism, and a

certain ostentatious courage of taste which takes suffering glibly and wards off everything sad and deep. There are "cheerful people" who employ cheerfulness in order to be misunderstood—they *want* to be misunderstood. There are "scientific spirits" who employ science because it gives a cheerful appearance, and because scientism suggests that a man is superficial—they *want* to seduce others to such a false inference. There are free, impudent spirits who would like to conceal and deny that at bottom they are broken, incurable hearts—the case of Hamlet: and then even foolishness can be the mask for an unblessed all-too-certain certainty.

EPILOGUE

1

I have often asked myself whether I am not more heavily obligated to the hardest years of my life than to any others. As my inmost nature teaches me, whatever is necessary—as seen from the heights and in the sense of a *great* economy—is also the useful par excellence: one should not only bear it, one should *love* it. *Amor fati:* that is my inmost nature. And as for my long sickness, do I not owe it indescribably more than I owe to my health? I owe it a *higher* health—one which is made stronger by whatever does not kill it. *I also owe my philosophy to it.* Only great pain is the ultimate liberator of the spirit, as the teacher of great suspicion which turns every U into an X, a real, genuine X, that is, the letter before the *penultimate* one. Only great pain, that long, slow pain in which we are burned with green wood, as it were—pain which takes its time—only this forces us philosophers to descend into our ultimate depths and to put away all trust, all good-naturedness, all that would veil, all mildness, all that is medium—

things in which formerly we may have found our humanity. I doubt that such a pain makes us "better," but I know that it makes us more *profound*.

Whether we learn to pit our pride, our scorn, our will power against it, equaling the American Indian who, however tortured, evens the score with his torturer by the malice of his tongue; or whether we withdraw from pain into that Nothing, into mute, rigid, deaf resignation, self-forgetting, self-extinction: out of such long and dangerous exercises of self-mastery one emerges as a different person, with a few *more* question marks—above all, with the will to question more persistently, more deeply, severely, harshly, evilly, and quietly than has ever been questioned on this earth before. The trust in life is gone; life itself has become a problem. Yet one should not jump to the conclusion that with all this a man has necessarily become dusky, a barn owl. Even the love of life is still possible—only, one loves differently. It is the love for a woman who raises doubts in us.

2

What is strangest is this: afterward one has a different taste—a *second* taste. Out of such abysses, also out of the abyss of great suspicion, one returns newborn, having shed one's skin, more ticklish and sarcastic, with a more delicate taste for joy, with a more tender tongue for all good things, with gayer senses, with a second dangerous innocence in joy, more childlike and yet a hundred times more subtle than one has ever been before.

How repulsive pleasure is now, that crude, musty, brown pleasure as it is understood by those who like pleasure, our "educated" people, our rich people, and our rulers! How sarcastically we listen now to the big county-fair boom-boom with which the "educated" person and city dweller today permits art, books, and music to rape him and provide "spiritual pleasures"—with the aid of spirituous liquors! How the theatrical scream of passion now hurts our ears, how strange to our taste the whole romantic uproar and tumult of the senses have become, which the educated rabble loves, and all its aspirations after the elevated, inflated, and exaggerated! No, if we who have recovered still need art, it is another kind of art—a mocking, light, fleeting, divinely untroubled, divinely artificial art, which, like a pure flame, licks into unclouded skies. Above all, an art for artists, *for artists only!* We know better afterward what above all is needed for this: cheerfulness, *any* cheerfulness, my friends. There are a few things we now know too well, we knowing ones: oh, how we learn now to forget well, and to be good at *not* knowing, as artists!

And as for our future, one will hardly find us again on the paths of those Egyptian youths who endanger temples by night, embrace statues, and want by all means to unveil, uncover, and put into a bright light whatever is kept concealed for good reasons.[1] No, this bad taste, this will to truth, to "truth at any price," this youthful madness in the love of truth, have lost their charm for us: for that we are too experienced, too serious, too gay, too burned, too *deep*. We no longer believe that truth remains truth when the veils are withdrawn— we have lived enough not to believe this. Today we consider it a matter of decency not to wish to see everything naked, or to be present at everything, or to understand and "know" everything. *Tout comprendre—c'est tout mépriser.*[2]

"Is it true that God is present *everywhere?*" a little

[1] Allusion to a Schiller ballad.
[2] "To understand all is to despise all."

girl asked her mother; "I think that's indecent"—a hint for philosophers! One should have more respect for the bashfulness with which nature has hidden behind riddles and iridescent uncertainties. Perhaps truth is a woman who has reasons for not letting us see her reasons? Perhaps her name is—to speak Greek—*Baubo?*

Oh, those Greeks! They knew how to live. What is required for that is to stop courageously at the surface, the fold, the skin, to adore appearance, to believe in forms, tones, words, in the whole Olympus of appearance. Those Greeks were superficial—*out of profundity.* And is not this precisely what we are again coming back to, we daredevils of the spirit who have climbed the highest and most dangerous peak of present thought and looked around from up there—we who have looked *down* from there? Are we not, precisely in this respect, Greeks? Adorers of forms, of tones, of words? And therefore—*artists?*

LETTERS (1889)

EDITOR'S NOTE

Early in January 1889 Nietzsche, then in Turin, saw a coachman flog a horse, rushed toward the horse, and collapsed with his arms around it. He was carried home, and, after recovering consciousness, wrote and mailed a number of letters which mirror the sudden outbreak of his madness. They are the last meaningful things he wrote.

The men referred to in the letter to Burckhardt had been in the news recently. Prado and Chambige had been tried for murder in November 1888, in Paris and Algeria, respectively; and in a letter to Strindberg, Nietzsche had written on December 7: "Prado was superior to his judges and even to his lawyers in his self-control, *esprit*, and prankishness." Lesseps, of course, is the man who had built the Suez Canal. Alphonse Daudet had recently published *L'Immortel*, a satirical attack on Les Quarante (that is, the French Academy). The hero of this work is called Astier, and this may help to account for the word "Astu" in the letter. In a letter to Overbeck, on November 13, Nietzsche had mentioned the funeral of Conte Robilant, "the most venerable type of the Piedmontese nobility and incidentally, as is known, a son of King Carlo Alberto." Antonelli, finally, was papal Secretary of State under Pius IX.[1]

Burckhardt took this letter to Overbeck, who went to Turin to bring his friend home. After a short spell in an asylum he was released in care of his mother; and after her death, his sister moved him to Weimar—the city of Goethe and Schiller—as part of her attempt to start a Nietzsche cult. He died on August 25, 1900.

[1] Cf. C. A. Bernoulli's *Franz Overbeck und Friedrich Nietzsche* (1908), which also contains brief accounts of the Prado and Chambige trials, and E. F. Podach's *Nietzsches Zusammenbruch* (1930), which features a facsimile of the letter.

TO GAST

Turin, January 4, 1889

To my maëstro Pietro.

Sing me a new song: the world is transfigured and all
the heavens are full of joy.

The Crucified

TO JACOB BURCKHARDT

January 6, 1889 [1]

Dear Professor,

In the end I would much rather be a Basel professor
than God; but I have not dared push my private egoism
so far as to desist for its sake from the creation of the
world. You see, one must make sacrifices however and
wherever one lives.

But I have reserved myself a small student's room,
situated opposite the Palazzo Carignano (in which I was
born as Vittorio Emanuele), which also permits me to
hear from the desk the magnificent music below, in the
Galleria Subalpina. I pay twenty-five francs, including
service, buy my tea, and do all my shopping myself,
suffer from torn shoes, and thank heaven every moment
for the old world for which men have not been simple
and quiet enough.

Since I am sentenced to while away the next eternity
with bad jokes, I have my writing here, which really
does not leave anything to be desired—very nice and
not at all exhausting. The post office is five steps from
here, so I mail my letters myself to play the great

[1] But postmarked Turin, January 5.

feuilletonist of the *grande monde*. Of course, I maintain close relations with *Figaro*; and in order to get an
idea how harmless I can be, listen to my first two bad
jokes.

Do not take the Prado case too hard. I am Prado; I
am also father Prado; I dare say that I am Lesseps too.
I wanted to give my Parisians, whom I love, a new
notion: that of a decent criminal. I am also Chambige—
also a decent criminal. *Second joke:* I salute the immortal one; Monsieur Daudet belongs to the *quarante*.
Astu.

What is disagreeable and offends my modesty is that
at bottom I am every name in history. With the children
I have put into the world too, I consider with some mistrust whether it is not the case that all who come *into*
the kingdom of God also come *out* of God. This fall I
was blinded as little as possible when I twice witnessed
my funeral, first as Conte Robilant (no, that is my son,
insofar as I am Carlo Alberto, unfaithful to my nature);
but Antonelli I was myself. Dear Professor, this edifice
you should see: since I am utterly inexperienced in the
things which I create, you are entitled to any criticism;
I am grateful without being able to promise that I shall
profit. We artists are incorrigible.

Today I saw an operetta, Quirinal-Moorish, and on
this occasion also noted with delight that Moscow as
well as Rome are now grandiose affairs. You see, I am
not denied considerable talent for landscapes too.

Consider, now we have beautiful, beautiful chats;
Turin is not far; very serious professional obligations are
lacking just now; a glass of Veltliner could be obtained.
Négligé of dress, a condition of being decent.

With affectionate love, your

Nietzsche

[On the margins of this letter are four postscripts.]

You may make any use of this letter which will not degrade me in the eyes of those at Basel.

I have had Caiphas put in fetters. Also, last year I was crucified by the German doctors in a very drawn-out manner. Wilhelm, Bismarck, and all anti-Semites abolished.

I go everywhere in my student's coat, and here and there slap somebody on the shoulder and say, *Siamo contenti? Son dio ho fatto questa caricatura.*[1]

Tomorrow my son Umberto will come with the lovely Margharita, whom, however, I shall also receive here only in shirtsleeves. The rest for Frau Cosima—Ariadne —from time to time there is magic.

TO OVERBECK

January 6, 1889

To friend Overbeck and wife. Although you have so far demonstrated little faith in my ability to pay, I yet hope to demonstrate that I am somebody who pays his debts —for example, to you. I am just having all anti-Semites shot.

Dionysus

---

[1] "Are we content? I am the god who has made this caricature."

Editions of Nietzsche

For a much more comprehensive bibliography, see the 3rd rev. ed. of Kaufmann's *Nietzsche* (Princeton: Princeton University Press, and New York: Random House, Vintage Books, 1968). *The International Nietzsche Bibliography*, described on p. 24, above, does not include writings *by* Nietzsche.

A. German Editions of His Works

There are a great many collected editions. For scholars, the two most important are:

1. *Werke, Grossoktavausgabe,* 2nd ed. 20 vols. Leipzig: Kröner, 1901–1913 and 1926 (vol. XX, containing indices for vols. I–XVI). Vols. I–VIII, works; vols. IX–XVI, *Nachlass* (i.e., notes, fragments, and other manuscript material not published by Nietzsche himself and for the most part not intended for publication); vols. XVII–XIX, *Philologica* (i.e., lecture notes and related materials belonging to the period when Nietzsche was a classical philologist).

2. *Gesammelte Werke, Musarionausgabe.* 23 vols. Munich: Musarion Verlag, 1920–1929. Books, *Nachlass,* and *Philologica* are arranged in a single chronological sequence; vol. I contains previously unpublished *juvenilia;* half of vol. XXI contains an index of names, which, like the index of subjects (all of vols. XXII–XXIII), covers the *Philologica* too. In most ways this edition is obviously preferable to the *Grossoktavausgabe;* but the earlier edition contains an appendix of interesting editorial notes on *The Will to Power* (vol. XVI) which is not to be found anywhere else.

Four other editions deserve mention here:

3. *Werke und Briefe: Historisch-Kritische Gesamtausgabe.* 9 vols. Munich: Beck, 1933–1942. Discontinued after 5 vols. of *Werke* and 4 vols. of *Briefe* had appeared. The

arrangement is chronological, and the "works" do not include any of Nietzsche's books but cover only the period from 1854, when Nietzsche was ten, to 1869. But H. J. Mette's discussion of the MSS in *Werke*, I, xxxi-cxxvi, includes the MSS of Nietzsche's later works.

4. *Werke in drei Bänden.* Ed. Karl Schlechta. 3 vols. Munich: Carl Hanser, 1954–1956. Vols. I–II contain all Nietzsche's books as well as some of his late poems; vol. III contains a selection from the *Nachlass*, 278 letters, a chronology (pp. 1359–82), and a long Philological Post-script (pp. 1383–1432). In 1965 a 4th vol. was added: *Nietzsche-Index.* Some minor errors mar vols. I–II; vol. III is most open to objections. On the positive side, it contains a few previously unpublished letters, and the Philological Postscript details the forgeries perpetrated by Nietzsche's sister, but these forgeries concern letters only and are of no philosophical interest. On the negative side, the selections from the *Nachlass* of the 1880s are confined exclusively to the notes previously known as *The Will to Power;* these notes have been edited very badly, and all late notes that the editors of the more comprehensive editions had not included in *The Will to Power* have been omitted, though in entries 1 and 2 above they fill many volumes. The editorial arrangement is neither systematic nor, as claimed by the editor, faithful to the manuscripts; the text departs from the manuscripts wherever entries 1 and 2 do and disregards the interesting notes in vol. XVI of 1 which indicate departures from the manuscripts. For more detailed discussion, see the Kaufmann translations (C. II below).

5. *Kröners Taschenausgabe.* Vols. 70–77 contain Nietzsche's books as well as selections from the *Nachlass* of his Basel period; 78 contains *The Will to Power;* 82–83 a selection from the late *Nachlass* material; 170 an index for all these volumes. These handy volumes can be bought separately. The postscripts by Alfred Bäumler, who was a Nazi, are objectionable, and volumes 82–83 are inadequate; but vols. 70–78 are adequate for most purposes.

6. *Werke: Kritische Ausgabe sämtlicher Schriften und nach-gelassenen Fragmente.* Ed. Giorgio Colli. 30 vols. Berlin: de Gruyter, 1967ff. Instead of continuing edition 3, above, plans have been made for yet another monumental collected edition.

B. German Editions of His Letters

1. *Friedrich Nietzsches Gesammelte Briefe.* 5 vols. Berlin und Leipzig: Schuster & Loeffler (later, Insel-Verlag), 1900ff. Some of Nietzsche's letters to his sister in vol. V (actually two volumes with consecutive pagination) are not authentic (see A.4, above). Still, this edition has never been replaced, though it has been importantly supplemented by the following collections.

2. *Nietzsches Briefwechsel mit Franz Overbeck.* Leipzig: Insel, 1916. Overbeck was Nietzsche's colleague at Basel and remained a loyal friend to the end. These important letters are not included in B.1.

3. Elisabeth Förster-Nietzsche. *Wagner und Nietzsche zur Zeit ihrer Freundschaft.* Munich: Müller, 1915; tr. by C. V. Kerr, introduction by H. L. Mencken, as *The Nietzsche-Wagner Correspondence.* London: Duckworth, 1922.

4. *Werke und Briefe* (A.3, above) includes 4 vols. of letters (Munich: Beck, 1938–1942), which span the period from 1850 to 1877. *Briefe,* vol. I, pp. xii–lviii, offer a detailed and valuable survey of the whereabouts of all Nietzsche letters of which the Nietzsche Archive had any knowledge at that time. This survey also lists letters published in periodicals and in biographical works. Many letters are privately owned and as yet unpublished.

5. See A.4, above.

C. Nietzsche in English
I. The Oscar Levy Translations

1. *The Complete Works of Friedrich Nietzsche.* 18 vols. Ed. Oscar Levy. New York: Macmillan, 1909–1911, reissue, New York: Russell & Russell, 1964.

2. *Selected Letters of Friedrich Nietzsche.* Ed. Oscar Levy. Tr. A. M. Ludovici. New York and Toronto: Doubleday, Page & Co., 1921.

These translations, none of them by Dr. Levy himself, represent an immense labor of love but are thoroughly unreliable. In his preface to the collected edition, Dr. Levy called Ludovici "the most gifted and conscientious of my collaborators." But in the latest edition Ludovici still has "cosmopolitan" where Nietzsche has "cosmological"; and where Nietzsche says, "Ibsen has become very clear to me," Ludovici still says, "Ibsen has become very German." Similar mistakes abound.

II. The Walter Kaufmann Translations

Nietzsche's most important writings are available in three volumes. The translations of *On the Genealogy of Morals* and *The Will to Power* are by Kaufmann and R. J. Hollingdale jointly; all the others, as well as all the introductions and commentaries, are by Kaufmann alone.

1. *The Portable Nietzsche.* New York: The Viking Press, 1954. Contains complete new translations of *Thus Spoke Zarathustra, Twilight of the Idols, The Antichrist,* and *Nietzsche contra Wagner,* and of more than 100 pages of additional selections.

2. *Basic Writings of Nietzsche.* New York: Random House, Modern Library Giant, 1968. Contains complete new translations, with footnote commentaries, of *The Birth of Tragedy, Beyond Good and Evil, On the Genealogy of Morals, The Case of Wagner,* and *Ecce Homo,* as well as 75 aphorisms from *Human, All-too-Human; Dawn;* and *The Gay Science.*

3. *The Will to Power,* with commentary and facsimiles of the original manuscript. New York: Random House, 1967.

4. *Twenty German Poets: A Bilingual Collection.* New York: Random House, 1962; reprinted in the Modern Library, 1963. Includes eleven poems by and three about Nietzsche.

Many of these translations are also available separately, in paperback editions, as follows:

Thus Spoke Zarathustra. New York: The Viking Press, Compass Viking Edition, 1966.

Beyond Good and Evil, 1966; *The Birth of Tragedy* and *The Case of Wagner,* 1967; *On the Genealogy of Morals* and *Ecce Homo,* with 75 aphorisms, 1967; *The Will to Power,* 1968: all New York: Random House, Vintage Books.

III. Other Translations

There are other translations of single works, but no one else has translated more than two or three, and none of the major works has been rendered into English by another philosopher. In Francis Golffing's versions of *The Birth of Tragedy* and *The Genealogy of Morals* (Garden City, N.Y.: Doubleday Anchor Books, 1956), the accent is on freedom, and there are striking omissions.

The works not included in the Kaufmann translations need redoing. Of the *Untimely Meditations; Human, All-too-Human; The Dawn;* and *The Gay Science,* only the third *Meditation* has been done in recent years: *Schopenhauer as Educator,* tr. J. W. Hillesheim and Malcolm R. Simpson (Chicago: Henry Regnery, Gateway Editions, 1965).

Different selections from the three aphoristic books are included in II.1 and II.2, above.

Nietzsche: Unpublished Letters. Tr. and ed. by Kurt F. Leidecker. New York: Philosophical Library, 1959. Offers a selection of 75 items from Schlechta's selection of 278 letters. The translations and the preface contain many errors; the title of the book is grossly misleading, and some of these letters were actually included in the present volume in 1954.

IV. Forgery

My Sister and I, published over Nietzsche's name in 1951, in English only, is an insipid forgery. See Kaufmann's exposés, listed on p. 26, above.

AVAILABLE FROM PENGUIN CLASSICS

The Portable Abraham Lincoln
Edited with an Introduction
by Andrew Delbanco

The Portable Arthur Miller
Edited by Christopher Bigsby
with an Introduction
by Harold Clurman

The Portable Beat Reader
Edited with an Introduction
by Ann Charters

*The Portable
Benjamin Franklin*
Edited with an Introduction
by Larzer Ziff

*The Portable
Charles W. Chesnutt*
Edited with an Introduction by
William L. Andrews
General Editor: Henry Louis
Gates, Jr.

The Portable Conrad
Edited with an Introduction
by Michael Gorra

The Portable Dante
Translated and Edited with an
Introduction by Mark Musa

The Portable Edgar Allan Poe
Edited by J. Gerald Kennedy

The Portable Emerson
Edited with an Introduction
by Jeffrey S. Cramer

The Portable Faulkner
Edited with an Introduction
by Malcolm Cowley

The Portable Frederick Douglass
Edited with an Introduction
by John Stauffer
General Editor: Henry Louis
Gates, Jr.

The Portable Graham Greene
Edited with an Introduction
by Philip Stratford

The Portable Hannah Arendt
Edited with an Introduction
by Peter Baehr

**PENGUIN
CLASSICS**

AVAILABLE FROM PENGUIN CLASSICS

The Portable Hawthorne
Edited with an Introduction
by William C. Spengemann

The Portable Henry James
Edited by John Auchard

The Portable Jack Kerouac
Edited with an Introduction
by Ann Charters

The Portable John Adams
Edited with an Introduction
by Jack Diggins

The Portable Malcolm X Reader
Edited by Manning Marable
and Garrett Felber

The Portable Mark Twain
Edited with an Introduction
by Tom Quirk

The Portable Shakespeare
Edited by Stephen Orgel

The Portable Sixties Reader
Edited with an Introduction
by Ann Charters

The Portable Steinbeck
Edited by Pascal Covici, Jr.
with an Introduction
by Susan Shillinglaw

The Portable Thoreau
Edited with an Introduction
by Jeffrey S. Cramer

The Portable Walt Whitman
Edited with an Introduction
by Michael Warner

The Portable Twentieth-Century Russian Reader
Edited with an Introduction
by Clarence Brown

**PENGUIN
CLASSICS**